SPATIAL FORMATIONS

Theory, Culture & Society

Theory, Culture & Society caters for the resurgence of interest in culture within contemporary social science and the humanities. Building on the heritage of classical social theory, the book series examines ways in which this tradition has been reshaped by a new generation of theorists. It will also publish theoretically informed analyses of everyday life, popular culture, and new intellectual movements.

Recent volumes include:

The Cinematic Society
The Voyeur's Gaze
Norman K. Denzin

Decentring Leisure
Rethinking Leisure Theory
Chris Rojek

Global Modernities
Mike Featherstone, Scott Lash and Roland Robertson

The Masque of Femininity
The Presentation of Woman in Everyday Life
Efrat Tseëlon

The Arena of Racism
Michel Wieviorka

Undoing Culture
Globalization, Postmodernism and Identity
Mike Featherstone

The Time of the Tribes
The Decline of Individualism in Mass Society
Michel Maffesoli

Risk, Environment and Modernity
Towards a New Ecology
edited by Scott Lash, Bronislaw Szerszynski and Brian Wynne

For Weber
Essays on the Sociology of Fate
Bryan S. Turner

Cyberspace/Cyberbodies/Cyberpunk
Cultures of Technological Embodiment
edited by Mike Featherstone and Roger Burrows

SPATIAL FORMATIONS

Nigel Thrift

SAGE Publications
London • Thousand Oaks • New Delhi

First published 1996

Published in association with *Theory, Culture & Society*,
School of Human Studies, University of Teesside.

 SAGE Publications Ltd
6 Bonhill Street
London EC2A 4PU

SAGE Publications Inc
2455 Teller Road
Thousand Oaks, California 91320

SAGE Publications India Pvt Ltd
32, M-Block Market
Greater Kailash – I
New Delhi 110 048

British Library Cataloguing in Publication data

A catalogue record for this book is
available from the British Library

ISBN 0 8039 8545 2
ISBN 0 8039 8546 0 (pbk)

Library of Congress catalog record available

Typeset by Mayhew Typesetting, Rhayader, Powys
Printed in Great Britain by The Cromwell Press Ltd,
Broughton Gifford, Melksham, Wiltshire

For my parents

Everything in the universe is encounters, happy or unhappy encounters

Gilles Deleuze

The essence of being radical is physical

Michel Foucault

Subjects cannot exist outside a world, nor in any conceivable world. The meaning of the term 'objective' is here: the possibility supplied to subjects as beings for-themselves by what there is to exist in a world and to organise, each time in another way, what there is.

Cornelius Castoriadis

Perceiving is . . . not an appearance in the theatre of (the individual's) consciousness. It is a keeping-in-touch with the world, an experience of things, rather than a having of experiences. It involves awareness-of instead of just awareness. It may be an awareness of something in the environment or something in the observer or both at once, but there is no content of awareness independent of that of which one is aware.

James Gibson

Social events and not social systems should be our concern in any examination of the human world. Such events are always situated in and brought forth by human actions within a human domain or space; they are never stable because they constantly generate responsive actions that differ from the events that elicited them. This background of human practices (linguistic and nonlinguistic) is what corresponds in the human sciences to the structural coupling in the natural world.

Francisco Varela

The difficulty – I might say – is not that of finding a solution but rather of recognising as the solution something that looks as if it were only a preliminary to it. . . . This is connected, I believe, with wrongly expecting an explanation, whereas the solution of the difficulty is description, if we give it the right place in our considerations.

Ludwig Wittgenstein

One of the most harmful habits in contemporary thought is the analysis of the present as being, precisely, in history, a present of rupture, or of high point, or of completion or a returning dawn. The solemnity with which everyone engaged in philosophical discourse reflects on his own time strikes me as a flaw. I think we should have the modesty to say to ourselves that, on the one hand, the time we live in is not the unique or fundamental or irruptive point in history where everything is completed and begun again. We must have the modesty to say, on the other hand, that – even without this solemnity – the time we live in is very interesting.

Michel Foucault

Contents

List of Tables and Figures

Tables

Figures

Preface

The bulk of this book consists of a set of seven extended essays. The first essay was written especially for this book. It is followed by three 'earlier' essays, originally published in 1983, 1985 and 1986, which are reproduced here in their original form. Three 'later' essays, one published in 1988, the other two in 1994, have been extended and updated for this volume.

Each of these different essays has one thing in common. Hovering, like a buzzing fly, in the background of all of them is a commitment to developing a historical geography of thought, defined as the study of 'the problematizations through which being offers itself to be, necessarily, thought – and the practices on the basis of which these problematizations are formed' (Foucault, 1985, p. 11). This is a project with a particular ontological-cum-epistemological stance which includes, at the very least, a commitment to a historicism, but of a limited rather than a full-blown kind, to situated knowledges, and to a light theoretical touch. In turn, this stance has four consequences.

First, it has led me towards *'flatter' theories of society*, theories which see society as neither an underlying code nor an inscribed surface but rather as more or less spatially and temporally extensive networks of practices which point not only to the absences in every presence, a common poststructuralist mantra, but also to the presences in every absence. In other words, practices are inherently dialogical, affectively charged and oriented towards mutual re-cognition (J. Benjamin, 1988). Second, it has meant *thinking of 'objects' as active presences* in these networks of practices. In this book, timekeeping devices, money and machines, for example, all both lean on and are attached to these networks but, in turn, they also take on a kind of life of their own (Theweleit, 1994). Third, it has forced me to express considerable *scepticism about 'representation'*, understood as singularised images standing for something else. Representational habits of thinking still doggedly persist in the social sciences and humanities. In contrast, this book is more concerned with 'presentations', with showings and manifestations, that characterise social knowledge in use (Curt, 1994). In turn, that means being able to escape a set of tyrannies:

> accounts of a 'real' world do not, then, depend on a logic of 'discovery', but on a power-charged social relation of 'conversation'. The world neither speaks itself nor disappears in favour of a master decoder. The codes of the world are not still, waiting only to be read . . . no particular doctrine or representation or decoding or discovery guarantees anything. (Haraway, 1991a, pp. 198–9)

Fourth, and relatedly, it has guided me towards *a modest view of the accomplishments of 'theory'*. Theory is situated and recast as a set of narrative sketches, as 'fictions' in Foucault's sense of the term, arising out of 'a deficiency in our having-to-do with the world concertfully' (Heidegger, 1962, p. 88). And the knowledge produced and regulated by that 'theory' is 'radial':

> knowledge, like truth, is relative to understanding. Our folk view of knowledge as being absolute comes from the same source as our folk view that truth is absolute, which is the folk theory that there is only one way to understand a situation. When that folk theory fails, and we have multiple ways of understanding, or 'framing' a situation, then knowledge, like truth, becomes relative to that understanding. (Lakoff, 1987, p. 300)

In other words, I want to achieve a contingent foundationalism. 'This is not to say no foundations exist but rather, that wherever there is one, there will also be a foundering, a contestation. . . . Foundations exist only to be put into question' (Butler, 1992, p. 16). Put another way, I have been concerned to provide narrative sketches of the world which always leave open the possibility of creative play and I have told these stories from within a number of different arenas, from the landscapes of war (*1983b, 1985c, 1986a*) to the search for democratic economic practices (*1994a, 1994m, 1995k*)[1] and, as the six chapters that follow the introductory chapter show, from medieval time consciousness to modern international finance.

These six chapters are also bound together by other concerns. First, I make claims about orderings and not about orders. It follows that I am not particularly interested in producing a finished, systematic theory of modernity or postmodernity in these chapters, in part because I do not believe that such a feat is possible (or necessary) and, in part, because too many attempts to do so have been laced with all kinds of customs and traditions (many of them inherited from the patrician élite of Ancient Greece) which are actually to do with forming a specular watchtower. However, it also follows that I am also not particularly interested in going to the opposite extreme, which, in fact, only holds up a mirror to these customs and practices, by adding to the multiplying kinds of self-conscious commentaries on academic texts which now seem to be in vogue. Like Latour (1988) and Bourdieu (1990a; Bourdieu and Wacquant, 1992), I believe that too many of these exercises in 'reflexivity' are simply a means of retreating from the one special responsibility that I do think academics have, which is to multiply the communicative resources that people have available to them. In other words, these reflexive exercises too often end up simply patronising readers, both through making the absurd assumption that readers naïvely believe that texts are in some way related to a referent out there and through making the assumption that a text about the way a text is produced is somehow more reflexive than a text with an actual object. Instead, I am in favour of what Latour (1988) calls 'infra-reflexivity', which includes in its credo: the deflation of methodology and its replacement by style; self-exemplification rather than self-reference; being on the side of the known rather than on the side of knowing; not being ashamed of weak explanations; working for equal relations between the represented and the representational; and automatically assuming transdisciplinarity. Whether this means that my stories are 'theories', I am not sure (M. Hannah, 1992).

Second, these six chapters constantly cross the boundaries between categories like the economic, the social and the cultural. I want to see these categories, which are in any case increasingly redundant, fail. Why? Because, too often, they signal a kind of self-censorship on the part of authors about what it is appropriate for them to study (M. Morris, 1992b), or, even worse, a kind of intellectual snobbery.

Third, I use large amounts of historically and geographically specific material. I do this because, on the whole, I am wary of purely theoretical excursions. Their lack of contextual detail (which usually means that they have a very specific but uncharted context) often makes these exercises obscure, even as claims to the contrary are being registered (Bordo and Moussa, 1993).

Fourth, and finally, I have striven for a particular, tentative written style, which at one time might have been called 'meat and potatoes' but nowadays is probably best described as 'simple side salad'. One of the most important insights of poststructuralism is that 'what we can communicate . . . can be overcome by a change of style' (Wood, 1990, p. 116), but, in practice, this has often meant that writing has become elliptical rather than multidirectional and therefore reliant on petrified exegetical and interpretational habits (including many of the manifestations of deconstruction). In particular, I have tried to write in a way which mirrors my concern with undermining the 'representation' of intention or meaning which can so easily turn into the compulsion 'to see meanings, and particularly hidden ones, everywhere' (Pfeiffer, 1994, p. 7).

It has to be said that this book has been a long time coming. In part, this tardiness is the result of my aforementioned suspicions about the powers of what is conventionally regarded as theory. In part, it is because I have tried to forge a particular form of theory, one that is always situated, and, in consequence, I have tried to move away from the kind of abstract theory which washes away content by ignoring context, leaving only empty panoptic visions. In part, it is because, except for a brief period when structuration theory was 'in', I have pursued these thoughts outside the theoretical and empirical mainstream of geography, a subject within which I have been glad to live my life but which seems to me to have a disturbing tendency to sort itself into cosy intellectual–interactional coteries too quickly and too finally. Then last, it is also because, in part, I have some doubts about the ethics of sitting comfortably theorising in a study when the world is clearly in such a dreadful state: I have always wanted to produce 'theoretical' excursions in parallel with more 'applied' work which can have some immediate impacts, however humble these might be.

What is certain is that this book could not have been produced at all without being able to translate the affirmative energies of many people. It is difficult to know where to start – or stop – in making due acknowledgement to them.

Any book is, first of all, the product of convivial contexts. I want to single out three of these. At the Australian National University, I want to thank Dean Forbes, Mike Taylor and Peter Williams. At Saint David's University College, Lampeter, I want to acknowledge the sturdy companionship of Paul Cloke and David Kay. At the University of Bristol I have received the support of many, many people but especially Malcolm Anderson, Keith Bassett, Allan Frey, Paul Glennie, Peter Haggett, Les Hepple, Tony Hoare, Paul Routledge, John Thornes and Sarah Whatmore.

Second, I want to single out some of my co-authors over the years. I often work with others (as the list of Selected Writings makes clear). I would only add that this has been a matter of principle as well as a source of pleasure since it seems to me that if, as I believe, authorship, like subjectivity, exists between people, then we can either acknowledge this overtly or covertly, and I prefer the former option. Those who have shared a third space over the years have included Ash Amin, Jonathan Beaverstock, Tommy Carlstein, Paul Cloke, Stuart Corbridge, Peter Daniels, Michael Dear, Peter Dicken, Paul Glennie, Peter Jackson, Ron Johnston, Andrew Leyshon, John Lovering, Don Parkes, Richard Peet, Steve Pile, Allan Pred, Mike Taylor and Peter Williams.

Third, I want to thank the postgraduate students who I have been involved in supervising or co-supervising over the years. They have produced inspiration (and references) when I most needed them: Jonathan Beaverstock, Nick Bingham, James Boardwell, Catherine Brace, Paul Chatterton, Rebecca Chiu, Ian Clarke, Ian Cook, Mike Crang, Neil Cuthbertson, Marcus Doel, Rowan Douglas, Shaun French, Emily Gilbert, Darren Hall, Billy Harris, Rob Harris, Bon Holloway, Sonia Juvik, Birgit Kehrer, Alan Latham, Phil McManus, Kris Olds, Doug Porter, Martin Roche, Paul Sheard and Richard Smith.

Fourth, I want to make mention of my journal compatriots over many years: Michael Dear, Derek Gregory, Peter Jackson, Gerry Pratt and Allen Scott at *Society and Space*, and John Ashby, Trevor Barnes, Bill Clark, Ron Johnston, Paul Knox, Jan Schubert, Sarah Whatmore, Ros Whitehead and Alan Wilson at *Environment and Planning A*.

Fifth, I want to note all the people who specifically commented on one or more of the seven essays in this book: Barbara Adam, John Allen, David Austin, Etienne Balibar, Jack Barbalet, Deirdre Boden, Robert Brenner, Phil Cooke, Denis Cosgrove, Mike Crang, Mike Davis, Dipesh Chakrabarty, Nigel Dodds, Gary Dymski, Neil Fligstein, Anthony Giddens, Derek Gregory, Chris Hamnett, Ray Hudson, Geoffrey Ingham, Bob Jessop, Marina Jirotka, Ron Johnston, Kenichi Kawasaki, Andrew Leyshon, John Lovering, Tim Luke, Doreen Massey, Danny Miller, Gunnar Olsson, Chris Paris, Steve Pile, Allan Pred, Ulker Seymen, John Shotter, Ed Soja, Malcolm Smith, Judith Squires, Richard Swedberg,

Peter Taylor, John Urry, Richard Walker, Ed Weissmann, Sarah Whatmore, Peter Williams and Anna Wynne. Andrew Sayer gave the complete manuscript of the book a close and careful reading and his constructive challenges have often forced me to rethink or rephrase, always for the better.

Sixth, I cannot help but acknowledge the particular help and comradeship of Ash Amin, Trevor Barnes, Gordon Clark, Paul Cloke, Paul Glennie, Derek Gregory, Chris Hamnett, Andrew Leyshon, Allan Pred, Mike Taylor, John Urry (who suggested the book's title) and Sarah Whatmore.

Last, but certainly not least, my love and apologies go to Lynda, Victoria and Jessica. They chiefly experienced this book as a series of bad moods.

Note

1. Italicised date references relate to entries in the list of Selected Writings.

Acknowledgements

The author and publisher wish to thank the following publishers, journals and editors for kind permission to reprint these papers: to Edward Arnold for 'The arts of the living and the beauty of the dead: anxieties of being in the work of Anthony Giddens', *Progress in Human Geography* (1993), 17, 111–21; Pion Ltd for 'On the determination of social action in space and time', *Environment and Planning D. Society and Space* (1983), 1, 23–57; Macmillan for 'Flies and germs: a geography of knowledge', in D. Gregory and J. Urry (eds) *Social Relations and Spatial Structures* (1985), pp. 330–73; Croom Helm for 'Little games and big stories: accounting for the practices of personality and politics in the 1945 General Election', in K. Hoggart and E. Kofman (eds) *Politics, Geography and Social Stratification* (1986), pp. 90–155; Routledge for "*Vivos voco*: ringing the changes in the historical geography of time consciousness', in T. Schuller and M. Young (eds) *The Rhythms of Society* (1988), pp. 53–94; Butterworth-Heinemann for (with A. Leyshon) 'A phantom state? The detraditionalisation of money, the international financial system and international financial centres', *Political Geography* (1994), 13, 299–327; Paul Chapman for 'Inhuman geographies: landscapes of speed, light and power', in P.J. Cloke, M. Doel, D. Matless, M. Phillips and N.J. Thrift *Writing the Rural. Five Cultural Geographies* (1994), pp. 191–248.

1

'Strange Country': Meaning, Use and Style in Non-Representational Theories

> Someone coming into a strange country will sometimes learn the language of the inhabitants from ostensive definitions that they give him [*sic*], and he will often have to *guess* the meaning of these definitions, and will guess sometimes right, sometimes wrong.
>
> (Wittgenstein, 1958, part I, no. 32)

Introduction

The six chapters that follow on from this one are informed by a developing theoretical framework, one which has been laid down gradually over a number of years. In the chapters that follow, that framework is often implicit: in this introductory chapter I want to make it explicit.

Authors are often accused of simply wanting to share their obsessions with the reader. I am afraid that I am no different. From an early point in my academic career, my obsessions have been fourfold. The first obsession has been with *time-space*. The first two working papers I produced, as a postgraduate student, in 1973 and 1974, were both on time-space and they have subsequently been followed by a stream of books and papers on theoretical accounts of time and space, from Althusser and Gurvitch to Moore and Žižek, on time-space entrainment, on time-space convergence (now, for some odd reason, known as time-space compression), on time-space budgets, and on the historical geography of time consciousness. Each of these works, from the earliest one on, were informed by one simple principle, that it is neither time nor space that is central to the study of human interactional orders, but time-space. Whilst I might now quibble with the details of my conclusion to two linked papers published in 1977 (*1977b*, *1977c*),[1] the sentiments expressed therein still ring true:

> The essential unit of geography is not spatial, it lies in regions of time-space and in the relation of such units to the larger spatio-temporal configurations. Geography is the study of these configurations. Marx once said, 'one must force the frozen circumstances to dance by singing to them their own melody'. The frozen circumstances of space only come alive when the melody of time is played. (*1977b*, p. 448)

The second obsession is with the sensuousness of *practice*. My focus on practice was initially the result of reading Marx but some of the limitations of his account of how social being determines consciousness became clear in the attempts of E.P. Thompson and Raymond Williams to forge a 'cultural' Marxism based on ways of life (for a review, see *1983b*). For me, these attempts contained some fundamental flaws.[2] But they also made me think more openly about practice. Indeed, it was the work of E.P. Thompson which pointed me to the importance of both Pierre Bourdieu (in E.P. Thompson, 1967, 1978) and Cornelius Castoriadis (as Castoriadis and as 'Paul Cardan', in E.P. Thompson, 1978, fn. 167) (*1979f*). In turn, it was Bourdieu's work which directed me to the triptych of Heidegger, Wittgenstein and Merleau-Ponty, and to the importance of properly theorising time, ways of life and embodiment. At the same time, Castoriadis made me aware of the dynamics of the imaginary and, incidentally, in *The Imaginary Institution of Society* (1987), provided what is still the seminal critique of certain kinds of Marxism.

I have also always been obsessed by the *subject*. My idea of the subject started out by being synonymous with human individuals, fuelled by work on 'time-geography', life histories and biography more generally, and by Williams's and Thompson's more open versions of Marxism which opened up a space for the person, both theoretically and historically. But it rapidly became clear that I was interpreting these accounts in ways that came perilously close to a Cartesian view of the subject. As a result, I underestimated the importance of the between-ness of joint action, and in general drew the bounds of the subject too tightly so that I was excluding many crucial relations between subjects and objects (and, indeed, misunderstanding the very nature of the subject–object relationship). In later work, I have attempted to correct these kinds of problems by paying more attention to processes of subjectification, by attempting to reconfigure what Merleau-Ponty (1962) called 'self–other-things', and by trying to imagine and image new figurations of the subject.

Finally, I have an obsession with *agency*, understood as both the production of action and of what counts as action (and of actors and of what counts as actors). In the first case, that has meant being mainly concerned with the 'wellsprings' of active participation in new beginnings and how these have varied historically and geographically, and most especially, in my case, in the growth of texts and their investment with productive potential and affect. In the second case, that has meant a concern with a new 'classification of things' (Latour, 1993) in which the bounds between subject and object become less easily drawn, both because the inside and the outside of the subject are seen as folded into each other and because the things we have conventionally depicted as objects, for example machines, are allowed into the realm of action and the actor. Many of these thoughts on agency were initially stimulated by the work of Anthony Giddens. Although the mention of Giddens's name nowadays hearkens back to debates over structure and agency which have become passé, I believe that the task he set of describing agency remains a significant one. Whilst it would not be true to say that the importance of agency has been forgotten in the social sciences and humanities (feminist work on new figurations of the subject is a shining case in point), I do not believe it would be unfair to say that it still receives less attention than it deserves and, to revert to the terms of the old debates, I do not apologise for the fact that this book is weighted towards the consideration of agency rather than structure.

These four obsessions are coded in nearly all of my work as a concern for the *context* of the situation (or the complexification or mediation or spacing of the event). By 'context' I most decidedly do not mean an impassive backdrop to situated human activity. Rather, I take context to be a necessary constitutive element of interaction, something active, differentially extensive and able to problematise and work on the bounds of subjectivity. Context operates on three levels in my work. On one level, it simply reflects an ambition to move away from doing theory by conducting abstract thought experiments towards a style of work which attends to the knowledge we already have, and does not assume a common background when this is precisely what is at stake (Wilkes, 1988). On another level, it is an empirical pointer to the ways in which the constitution of practices varies with context. Take, just as one example, the case of language. The consideration of context automatically challenges correspondence theories of meaning. A contextual approach challenges the ability of any semantic approach to offer an exact characterisation of words since the meaning of utterances is rooted in action-in-context. Then on one more level, it is a theoretically loaded term. Take the example of language again. Here,

> contextual variations exacerbate the problematic nature of the featural characterisation. Not only can a definition not account for all possible cases, but the definition of each case may itself be subject to contextual variations . . . a given characteristic may hold in one context but not in another. (Shanon, 1993, pp. 29–30)

Shanon goes on to point to a whole series of features of language which critically depend on context: polysemy, novel uses of words, misusages, phrasal composition, translation, labelling, even prototypes. Such linguistic considerations of context hardly exhaust the ramifications of the term but they start to hint at its richness and importance in the kind of non-representational framework I am at pains to develop through the rest of this book. In the matter of context, in other words, the four obsessions I have listed gather together and become one.

These kinds of obsessions could not be easily handled in a number of the intellectual frameworks which existed when I first began to be gripped by them. These frameworks tended to privilege time over space, clung to a specular and implicitly male model of the subject–object relation, tended to the neo-Kantian (in that they gave precedence to an *a priori* system of categorisation, whether the unconscious or the symbolic, discursive or ideological order, which defined the mode of being in which objects appear

and can be recognised, and in which the subjectivity of persons is constructed) and insufficiently problematised representation. Such frameworks
are less common now but it can hardly be said that all their sins have been
excised. The privileging of time often seems to have been substituted for by
the privileging of space (for example, Soja, 1989). The specular model of
the subject–object relation still has its effects on theory (for example, D.W.
Harvey, 1989). Neo-Kantianism can still be seen at work in a number of
interpretations of Marx, Derrida and Foucault and others which too
quickly connect the things of logic to the logic of things. A hardly
problematised sphere of representation is allowed to take precedence over
lived experience and materiality, usually as a series of images or texts which
a theorist contemplatively deconstructs, thus implicitly degrading practices.[3]
In other words, the kind of hesitant, partial and situated thinking I have
striven for in the chapters that follow is still relatively unfamiliar in the
social sciences and humanities, most especially in human geography, which
still registers only a very small number of theoretical traditions.[4] The result
is that problems of misrecognition abound, of which I will point, very
briefly, to just a few.

First, there is the problem of what Merleau-Ponty called the 'retro-
spective illusion': theorists produce a logocentric presence which then
becomes the precondition of research, a towering structure of categories
lowering over the ant-like actions of humans and others which constitutes
the 'empirical' raw material. Such an illusion still exists in some parts of the
social sciences and humanities. Even in cultural studies, which has invested
most in a critique of this tendency, there is a tendency to fall back on
phrases which smuggle an absent presence into the centre of what are
meant to be decentred accounts, a villain called 'capitalism', or 'patriarchy',
which can be hissed off stage at convenient moments.

Second, and related, the production of such a presence is often associated
with what Bernstein (M.A. Bernstein, 1994) has called 'foreshadowing',
that is, an apocalyptic history of inevitable moments leading inevitably
towards a predefined goal or fate which commentators already know, a
goal or fate in which everything becomes faster, more compressed in space
and time, more commodified, and so on. This logic of historical inevit-
ability depends upon the dubious idea that history has a coherence other
than what we impress upon it. It is rather like someone running through
the town after the Pruitt-Igoe Flats were dynamited in 1972 shouting
'postmodern capitalism has began'. In its most pernicious variant, foreshadowing leads to what Bernstein (M.A. Bernstein, 1994, p. 16) calls
'backshadowing', in which 'the shared knowledges of the outcome of a
series of events by narrator and listener is used to judge the participants in
those events, as though they too should have known what was to come'.
Found most commonly in retroactive accounts of the Shoah, this practice is
also common in accounts of the onset of new technologies.

A third, seemingly eternal problem is making the micro–macro distinction. This distinction is still remarkably common in the social sciences

and humanities, even though it is neither empirically observable nor theoretically sensible (Giddens, 1984; Boden, 1994); only the latest variant is the 'local' and the 'global'. Yet, as Latour (1993, p. 122) puts it, the words 'local' and 'global' 'offer points of view on networks that are by nature neither local nor global but are more or less long and more or less connected'.

A fourth problem is often, although not always, linked to this distinction. It is the problem of misrecognising the flow of everyday life as, well, everyday. But what Pollner (1987, p. xvii) calls 'the extraordinary organis- ation of the ordinary' has to be seen in a different way. 'It is not a predicate, or an entity, nor is it self-evident' (Dreyfus, 1991, pp. 10–11). It cannot, therefore, be seen as just a frill or a frame (Vattimo, 1988) around social structures, a side-show to the 'real' business of existence. It cannot be seen, either, as a separate and somehow more authentic sphere of 'everyday life', a 'lifeworld' which, in different formulations, can be found in authors as diverse as Habermas and Lefebvre. And it is not just a call to bring people 'back in', as though one was a humanist trying to balance up anti- humanist scales.

A fifth, widespread, problem is the assumption that there has been a general erosion of the social and that we are inevitably moving towards a more abstract, decontextualised, dehumanised and generally disenchanted world, one in which the lifeworld is taken over by the system, 'authentic' spaces by programmed consumer spaces, tactics by strategies, and so on. But this argument is more often assumed than demonstrated; many authors are now beginning to believe that our world may not be so very different from the worlds that have gone before it and that such a view rests on a series of false oppositions (Latour, 1993; Knorr-Cetina, 1994; Ingold, 1995).

> The thesis of the disenchantment of the world fails in several ways. First, it rests on the equation of the content of particular belief systems or modes of operation – which have changed – with 'substance', 'meaning', the 'life-world', etc. in general. If the proposition of the loss of meaning in modern and postmodern life is stripped of this equation, it amounts to a historically plausible but trivial assertion about the changing nature of meaning structures. Second, the assump- tion of the increase in formal, technical and abstract systems ignores the phenomenon that these systems are never abstract when they are enacted. Presumably, the meaning of abstract elements lies not in their formal definition but in their use. Third, the thesis fails in that it has not been systematically demonstrated empirically. In fact, assessments like that of a trend towards the elimination of the life world are ironic in the face of . . . microsociological studies in the last twenty years which demonstrate the procedures and forms of this life- world. (Knorr-Cetina, 1994, p. 6)

Finally, then, what we see over and over again is the problem of theor- etical purification of practical orders. Commentators conjure up a purified system which is able to move inevitably on its way, an unstoppable glacier, transforming all before it and stamping out everything behind it, a system which is inured to the idea that 'nothing is settled; everything can still be altered. What was done, but turned out wrong, can be done again' (Lévi-Strauss, 1973, p. 393), and which therefore continually elevates uncertain forces into certain gods.

> Take some small business-owner hesitatingly going after a few market shares, some conqueror trembling with fever, some poor scientist tinkering in his lab, a lowly engineer piecing together a few more or less favourable relationships of force, some stuttering and fearful politicians; turn the critics loose on them, and what do you get? Capitalism, imperialism, science, technology, domination – all equally absolute, systematic, totalising. In the first scenario, the actors were trembling; in the second they were not. The actors in the first scenario could be defeated; in the second they no longer can. In the first scenario, the actors were still quite close to the modest work of fragile and modifiable mediations, now they are purified and they are all equally formidable. (Latour, 1993, p. 126)

This chapter tries to elaborate on some of these preliminary thoughts in two sections. The first section constitutes a kind of intellectual accounting in that it sets out some of the main strands of thought that have influenced my thinking on time-space, practice, subject and context. The second section moves on from this process of accounting to the bottom line; an exposition of the principles that – in one way or another and in more or less developed form – motivate the chapters in this book.

Theories of Practice

This first and longest section of the introductory chapter lays out some of the main tenets of non-representational thinking which, in turn, have had a major influence on my own work. These schools of thought all deny the efficacy of representational models of the world, whose main focus is the 'internal', and whose basic terms or objects are symbolic representations, and are instead committed to non-representational models of the world, in which the focus is 'external', and in which basic terms and objects are forged in a manifold of actions and interactions. I will not be giving a complete review of all such non-representational models: this is a task which is well beyond the scope of an introduction. In particular I will be referring to, but not producing a more extensive account of: the work of the Russian school of activity theory, consisting of writers like Vygotsky, Leonti'ev and Luria (for example, Wertsch, 1985a, 1985b), the ecological psychology of Gibson (for example, Gibson, 1979), the Latin American 'autopoietic' school of Maturana and Varela (1980, 1987; Varela, 1989; Varela et al., 1991; Varela and Anspach, 1994), the work of Taussig on mimesis (for example, Taussig, 1993), or Bakhtin's (1984, 1986) dialogical philosophy of language (for example, Clark and Holquist, 1984; Folch-Serra, 1990).

But what it does seem worthwhile providing at this juncture is a summary of some of the main tenets of these non-representational models. Of course, non-representational thinking is a broad church and not all these tenets are shared equally (or equally well) by all its members. An act of

survey therefore always runs the risk of producing a non-existent average.
However, with such a caution borne in mind, it is possible to identify at
least six of these tenets.

First, and most trivially, non-representational thinking throws a critical
light on theories that claim to re-present some naturally present reality, or,
in Foucault's (1972, p. 26) telling phrase, 'the pure gold of things themselves'. Instead, it argues that practices constitute our sense of the real.
Second, and accordingly, it valorises practical expertise. That is, it is concerned with thought-in-action, with presentation rather than representation.

> The traditional emphasis on the cognitive, the attempt to explain all human
> behaviour in terms of what we believe and how we consciously represent things
> to ourselves cannot account for the implicit familiarity and competence that
> are the hallmarks of everyday practical activity. Explicit representations of things
> in the practical world and conscious beliefs we form within practical contexts
> always presuppose this non-represented and . . . non-representable background of
> familiarity and expertise. (H. Hall, 1993, p. 131)

Third, this valorisation of thought-in-action emphasises the particular
moment, in that it suggests that representation is always a part of presentation, laid out in a specific context which invites only particular kinds of
presencing practices. But it does not do this naïvely, by producing
'presentist' accounts which isolate each moment from the one preceding
and the one following it (Carr, 1986; Copjec, 1994b).

Fourth, it is concerned with thinking with the entire body. In turn, this
means that non-representational models valorise all the senses, and not just
the visual, and their procedures are not modelled solely on the act of
looking. It also means that affect is seen as of primary importance, because
'thought . . . is not born of other thoughts. Thought has its origin in the
motivating sphere of consciousness, a sphere that includes our inclinations
and needs, our interests and impulses, and our affect and emotions. The
affective and volitional tendency stands behind thought' (Vygotsky, 1987,
p. 282).

Fifth, and relatedly, it invites a degree of scepticism about the 'linguistic
turn' in the social sciences and humanities, suggesting that this turn has too
often cut us off from much that is most interesting about human practices,
most especially their embodied and situated nature, by stressing certain
aspects of the verbal-cum-visual as 'the only home of social knowledge'
(Curt, 1994, p. 139) at the expense of the haptic, the acoustic, the
kinesthetic and the iconic (Claasen, 1993; Serres, 1986).

Then, sixth and finally, it is concerned with a rather different notion of
'explanation' which is probably best likened to understanding a person, a
phenomenalism of character which involves, more than other approaches,
empathic and ethical components: 'one reads the story of the life of a
person. One follows the story, one travels for awhile together with that
individual and eventually one gains understanding of him or her. When
understanding has been achieved one discovers that one can tell a story'
(Shanon, 1993, p. 362). Or, put another way, 'how does one determine that

a painting is well composed, that it sits well? By dancing it' (Shanon, 1993, p. 353).[5] Ultimately, in other (than) words, one depends – one has to depend – on non-cognitive 'facts':

> The body knows whether things are balanced or not, whether they are in equilibrium, or not, whether they fit or not. Agents moving about in the world know how to find their way in it. Social agents appreciate whether the other is kind, honest, or boring, or attractive. Likewise, affectively one knows that things are good or bad (for the given agent), pleasant or not so. And ethically, one appreciates that things are right or wrong, fair or despicable. In all these cases what is being determined is whether or not things fit, click, or feel right. (Shanon, 1993, p. 353)

Understanding is not so much, then, about unearthing something of which we might previously have been ignorant, delving for deep principles or digging for rock-bottom, ultimate causes (Diamond, 1991) as it is about discovering the options people have as to how to live. Not empiricism, then, yet a kind of realism (Wittgenstein, 1956), since 'what I do with examples, what I do in explaining, may be essential in making manifest what I mean, but the explanation of what I mean cannot be given by examples, because they cannot adequately represent my relation to what is possible' (Diamond, 1991, p. 69).

Of course, none of the aforegoing is to deny processes of cognition, or the reality of representations. There are a whole stock of imagined understandings, which are shared and drawn upon in any culture (Castoriadis, 1987). It is, rather, to situate these imagined understandings as only a part of a broader process of knowledging. In other words, representational *effort* is always firmly embedded in a contextually specific process of social negotiation (Curt, 1994).

Take 1: 'But ask yourself: in what sort of case, in what kind of circumstances, do we say, "Now I know how to go on"?'[6]

The body is in constant motion. Even at rest, the body is never still. As bodies move they trace out a path from one location to another. These paths constantly intersect with those of others in a complex web of biographies. These others are not just human bodies but also all other objects that can be described as trajectories in time-space: animals, machines, trees, dwellings, and so on.

In embryo, this is a description of the time-space demography (or time-geography, as it is more commonly known) of Torsten Hägerstrand, the Swedish geographer (Hägerstrand, 1970, 1973, 1982; *1977a, 1977c, 1978a, 1980a*). Yet, as a written description, it precisely misses Hägerstrand's main aim, which was to find a geographical vocabulary that could describe these pre-linguistic movements pre-linguistically. That was the purpose of his now famous time-space diagrams. He often compared these diagrams to a musical score, which is a similar set of marks of movement, producing similarly complex existential effects. More than this, Hägerstrand took pains to point out that these diagrams, like a musical score, could stand for a different kind of (non-intellectual) intelligibility.[7]

One more point needs to be made concerning Hägerstrand's work. That is that it is inherently dialogical. In opposition to a number of critics in geography (for example, G. Rose, 1993) who have seen it as a robustly individualistic approach, Hägerstrand clearly saw time-geography in precisely the opposite terms. His stress was constantly on the congruences and disparities of *meeting* and *encountering*, that is, on the *situated interdependence* of life. His intent was, in other words, to capture the pragmatic sense of possibility inherent in practical situations of 'going-on'. In consequence,

> rather than implying an idealist framework of intentional action shaping the resulting totality, it should be evident that Hägerstrand pointed to competitive allocation and displacement effects which made the total outcome anything but the sum total of intentions at the level of actors (be they organisms, human individuals, groups, organisations, or even states). (Carlstein, 1982, p. 61)

Hägerstrand's maps of everyday coping can best be placed, therefore, in a line of thinking which stretches from the early Heidegger and the later Wittgenstein, through Merleau-Ponty, to, most recently, Bourdieu, de Certeau and Shotter, who have tried to conjure up the situated, pre-linguistic, embodied, states that give intelligibility (but, not necessarily meaning) to human action – what Heidegger called the primordial or pre-ontological understanding of the common world, our ability to make sense of things, what Wittgenstein knew as the background, what Merleau-Ponty conceived of as the space of the lived body, or, later, 'the flesh', and what Bourdieu means by the habitus. Each of these authors is concerned, in other words, to get away from Cartesian intellectualism, with its understanding of being as a belief system implicit in the minds of individual subjects, and return to an understanding of being as 'the social with which we are in contact by the mere fact of existing and which we carry with us inseparably before any objectifications' (Merleau-Ponty, 1962, p. 362). In this 'view', being is not an entity but a way of being which constitutes a shared agreement in our practices about what entities can show up, and, likewise, 'humans are not entities but the clearing in which entities appear' (Zimmerman, 1993, p. 242).

In each case, what these authors have in common is that they see the subject as primarily derived *in practice*:

> In the mainstream epistemological view, what distinguishes the agent from the inanimate entities which can also effect their surroundings is the former's capacity for inner representation, whether these are placed in the 'mind' or in the brain understood as a computer. What we have which inanimate beings don't have – representations – is identified with representations and the operations we effect on them. To situate our understandings in practices is to see it as implicit in our activity, and hence as going well beyond what we manage to frame representations of. We do frame representations: we explicitly formulate what our world

is like, what we aim at, what we are doing. But much of our intelligent action, sensitive as it usually is to our situation and goals, is usually carried on unformulated. It flows from an understanding which is largely inarticulate. (Taylor, 1993a, pp. 49–50)

Thus understanding of the subject in practice is fundamental in two ways. First, this kind of subjectivity is always present. Sometimes we frame representations. Sometimes we do not. But the practical intelligibility is always there. More to the point, and second, the kind of representations we make are only comprehensible against the *background* provided by this inarticulate understanding. 'Rather than representations being the primary focus of understanding, they are islands in the sea of our unformulated practical grasp of the world' (Taylor, 1993a, p. 50). Yet the articulation of something that is at heart inarticulate remains a constant problem:

> There is a real difficulty in finding ordinary language terms to describe the Background: one speaks vaguely of 'practices', 'capacities', or 'stances' or one speaks suggestively but misleading of 'assumptions' and 'predispositions'. These latter terms must be literally wrong, because they imply the apparatus of representation. . . . The fact that we have no natural vocabulary for discussing the phenomenon in question and the fact that we tend to lapse into an intentionalistic vocabulary ought to arouse our interest. . . . There simply is no first-order vocabulary for the Background, because the Background is as invisible to intentionality as the eye which sees is invisible to itself. (Searle, 1983, pp. 156–7)

Heidegger was one of the first philosophers to take an anti-representationalist view of being and subjectivity as paramount and he has, of course, been highly influential (Dreyfus, 1991; Dreyfus and Hall, 1992; Guignon, 1993). Dreyfus and Hall (1992) list several generations of thinkers who have acknowledged a major debt to his work, including Sartre, Merleau-Ponty, Gadamer, Arendt, Foucault, Bourdieu, Derrida, Taylor, Rorty and even Habermas. Heidegger's wide influence can be traced to the fact that Heidegger 'does not ground his thinking in everyday *concepts*, but in average everyday *practice*; in what people do, not what they say they do' (Dreyfus and Hall, 1992, p. 2). Such a view of an 'engaged agency' (Taylor, 1993b) leads Heidegger to jettison the Cartesian way of thinking of human beings, as isolated and disengaged subjects who represent objects to themselves, and to settle instead for the world-disclosing function of practices which always assumes a background of implicit familiarity, competence and concern or involvement. Thus,

> Rather than thinking of action as based on beliefs and desires, Heidegger describes what actually goes on in our everyday skilful coping with things and people and how we are socialised into a shared world. He describes simple skills – hammering, walking into a room, using turn signals, etc. – and shows how these everyday coping skills contain a familiarity with the world that enables us to make sense of things and 'to find [our] way about in [our] public environment'. Thus, like Ludwig Wittgenstein, Heidegger finds that the only ground for the intelligibility of thought and action we have or need is in the everyday practices themselves, not in some hidden process of thinking or of history. (Dreyfus and Hall, 1992, p. 2)

The skills involved in these practices are, in their way, remarkable. For example, Searle (1983, p. 143) writes:

> Think of what is necessary to go to the refrigerator and get a bottle of cold beer to drink. The biological and cultural resources that I must bring to bear on this task, even to form the intention to perform the task are (considered in a certain light) truly staggering. But without these resources I could not form the intention at all: standing, walking, opening and closing doors, manipulating bottles, glass, refrigerators, queuing, partying and drinking.

What Heidegger is suggesting is that being-in the-world does not consist of an organism or an ego containing a stream of experiences but is rather an average *mode of comportment*, a skilful coping which consists of a shared readiness to deal 'appropriately' with people and things, 'a way of being that is concerned about its own being, and yet must get its meaning by assigning itself to the occupations (including roles and equipment) provided by the one' (Dreyfus, 1991, p. 159), where the one is a set of cultural norms that do not depend on the existence of any particular human being but rather produce particular human beings. Clearly, the one is hard to grasp, but Heidegger makes it clear that it cannot be appropriated as something like a pre-existent Hegelian spirit that expresses itself in the world, nor as the conscious meaning-giving activity of an individual human subject; in other words,

> on the one hand, cultural norms are not given in such a way that their intelligibility can be traced back to lucid absolute consciousness. 'The one is not something like a "universal subject" which a plurality of subjects have hovering above them.' On the other hand, once a human being is socialised by other human beings – trained to comply with norms that are not fully available to consciousness – the result is misdescribed if we call it inter-subjectivity. (Dreyfus, 1991, p. 162)

Such a view tends to lead to the deduction that social change will usually be slow-moving since, as Heidegger (1985, p. 265) puts it,[8]

> this polished averageness of the everyday determination of Dasein, of the assessment of the world and the similar averageness of customs and manner, watches over every exception which thrusts itself to the fore. Every exception is short-lived and quietly suppressed.

But this need not mean social fixity either:

> New technological and social developments are constantly changing ways for Dasein to be. Nor does it mean there is no room for an individual or political group to develop new possibilities, which could then be available to the society. But it does mean that such 'creativity' always takes place on a background of what *one* does – of accepted-for-the-sake-of-whichs that cannot all be called into question at once because they are not presuppositions and in any case must remain in the background to lend intelligibility to criticism and change. (Dreyfus, 1991, p. 161)

However, Heidegger was not interested in how his understanding of being was instantiated or in how it was passed from one generation to another. Following the 'ontic trail' from ontology into the realm of social

and historical structures requires us to move on, specifically to the work of
the later Wittgenstein and to Merleau-Ponty. Wittgenstein agreed with
Heidegger insofar as he stressed that the source of the intelligence of the
world is average public practices:

> 'So you are saying that human agreement decides what is true and what is false?'
> – It is what human beings *say* that is true and false; and they agree in the
> *language* they use. That is not agreement in opinions [intentional states] but in
> form of life (background practices). (Wittgenstein, 1958, no. 241)

But Wittgenstein differed from Heidegger in that he did not believe that the
practices that make up a human form of life could be described by an
existential analytic of the kind Heidegger devoted much of his life to. For
him, practices form an impenetrable thicket which cannot be systematised:

> How could human behaviour be described? Surely only by showing the actions of
> a variety of humans, as they are all mixed up together. Not what *one* man [*sic*] is
> doing *now*, but the whole hurly-burly, is the background against which we see an
> action, and it determines our judgement, our concepts, and our reactions.
> (Wittgenstein, 1980, p. 97, no. 509)

However, Wittgenstein produces another orientation to theories of practice
in his concentration on the *ways of life* of different social groups, on the
way that these different groups produce different 'pictures', via the 'finitist'
doctrine that proper usage is developed step-by-step, in processes involving
successions of on-the-spot judgements. 'Every instance of use, or of proper
use, of a concept must in the last analysis be accounted for separately by
reference to specific, local contingent determinants' (Barnes, 1982, p. 30).
What in Heidegger is thinking about practices in Wittgenstein becomes
thinking about the 'rough ground' of social practices conceived as forms or
patterns of collective life (Wittgenstein, 1958, 1964; Kripke, 1982;
Diamond, 1991). Through now famous notions like the language-game
Wittgenstein battled against the 'discourse of thinking' which directly
relates meanings to words. Wittgenstein insisted that thought is fully
centred in thready, knotty social interactions (Rubinstein, 1981):

> Giving ground . . . comes to an end; but the end is not certain presuppositions
> striking us immediately as true, i.e. it is not a kind of *seeing* on our part; it is our
> *acting* which lies at the bottom of the language-game. (Bloor, 1983, p. 183)

Merleau-Ponty can also help on this journey from the ontological to the
ontic, and especially the later Merleau-Ponty of *The Visible and the
Invisible* (1968). In the earlier Merleau-Ponty, practices are embodied skills
that have a common style and can be transposed to various domains. In
this point of view, 'existential understanding' (Crossley, 1994) can be
found, through the development of a sensuous phenomenology of *lived
experience*, as constructed, as synthetic, as simultaneously active and
passive, and as located at the 'mid-point' between mind and body (here
Merleau-Ponty prefigures notions of a third space of joint action). Most
importantly of all, lived experience is necessarily, ineliminably and ineffably
embodied, 'corporeally constituted, located in and as the subject's

incarnation' (Grosz, 1993, p. 41). This means, first of all, that the human body is unique in playing a dual role as both the vehicle of perception and the object perceived, as the body-in-the-world which 'knows' itself by virtue of its active relation to its world.

Second, the body is always active. 'The body . . . does not tend to a state of rest; it maintains levels of tension available for efficacious operations' (Lingis, 1994, p. 9). In other words, body sensing is active from the start; it takes a 'hold' of the world; 'the concept is Heideggerian; Merleau-Ponty envisions looking – participating with the eyes – tasting, smelling, and even hearing as variants of handling' (Lingis, 1994, p. 7). Then, third, the body is always located in time and space, which are conceived through the body. Thus,

> Our body is not a space like things; it inhabits or haunts space. It applies itself to space like a hand to an instrument, and when we wish to move about we do not move the body, as we move an object. We transport it without instruments . . . since it is us and because, through it, we have access to space. (Merleau-Ponty, 1962, p. 5)

Further,

> By considering the body in movement, we can see better how it inhabits space (and possibly time) because movement is not limited to submitting passively to space and time, it actually measures them, it takes them up in their basic significance which is obscured in the commonplace of established situations. (Merleau-Ponty, 1962, pp. 100–2)

Fourth, and finally, bodies and things are not easily separated terms, precisely because of this locatedness:

> For example, it is not by means of access to a Cartesian abstract or geometrical space that one knows where to scratch in order to satisfy an itch on one's back. This is true, even if I use an instrument like a stick. From this point, Merleau-Ponty claims, the stick is no longer an object for me but has been absorbed or incorporated into my perceptual faculties or body parts. (Grosz, 1994b, p. 91)

But in his last text, *The Visible and the Invisible* (which might well have been retitled *The Sensible and the Intelligible*), Merleau-Ponty (1968) goes farther in his introduction of the concept of 'la chair', *flesh*. Here, he moves close to a Heideggerian pre-reflective predicate, a single fabric which refers to both the flesh of the body and the flesh of the world:

> Flesh is neither matter nor spirit nor substance, says Merleau-Ponty. The best analogy is with the old concept of 'elements' as applied to earth, air, fire and water. In something like that sense 'la chair' is an element of being in general. It is that which makes facts to be facts. It is as if in seeing something, I experience it as if I myself were visible to it. (Harré, 1991, p. 96)

To expand, Merleau-Ponty wants to 'return' to pre-discursive experience, a 'wild being', that is unarticulated but not unintelligible:

> In returning to a pre-reflective sensible, however, he is not seeking a pure domain uninfluenced by the social: instead his goal is to find precisely the preconditions within sensibility itself, within the subject (as well as the world) that make the

> subject open up to be completed by the world, things, others, objects, qualities, interrelations. Neither subject nor object can be conceived as cores, atoms, little nuggets of being, pure presence: not bounded unified entities, they interpretrate, they have a fundamental openness to each other. (Grosz, 1993, p. 43)

Thus the inside and the outside fold back into each other; to see is also the possibility of being seen, to touch is always to be touched, and so on. But

> Merleau-Ponty's claim is stronger than that everyone who sees is capable of being seen (by someone else). His point is ontological: the painter sees trees but the tree also, in some sense, sees the painter. This attribution of visibility to the visible as well as the seen is not an anthropomorphism, but rather a claim about the flesh, about a (non-identical, non-substantive) 'materiality' shared by the subjects and objects of perception. . . . The subject and object are inherently open to each other for they are constituted in the one stroke dividing the flesh into its various modalities. They are interlaced one with the other not externally but through their reversibility and exchangeability, their similarity-in-difference and their difference-in-similarity. Things solicit the flesh just as the flesh beckons to and as an object for things. Perception is the flesh's reversibility, the flesh touching, seeing, perceiving, itself, one fold (provisionally) catching the other in its self-embrace. (Grosz, 1993, pp. 45–6)

More recent writings make it possible to edge a little further towards social, historical and geographical specificity. The writings I am most concerned to engage with are those of Bourdieu and de Certeau, who both cite Heidegger, Wittgenstein[9] and Merleau-Ponty as major influences 'for a non-intellectualist, non-relativistic analysis of the relation between the agent and the world' (Bourdieu, 1990a, p. 10). Bourdieu's notions of field and habitus are crucial to the 'historicist ontology' (Bourdieu, 1993, p. 273) that he offers.[10] In modern societies, the social cosmos is made up of a number of 'relatively autonomous social microcosms [which are] specific and irreducible' (Bourdieu and Wacquant, 1992, p. 97). Each of these microcosms is a network of objective relations between positions based in certain forms of power whose possession commands access to the specific advantages that are at stake in that field (which are defined historically). The field is usually in a state of dynamic tension since the relations between positions, what counts as advantage and even where the borders of the field are drawn are constantly being redefined in struggle by the agents who are situated in it by virtue of a configuration of properties which define their eligibility and therefore their ability to participate.[11]

The correlate of the field of objective positions is the structured system of practices and expressions of agents, the 'symbolic stances' that make up what Bourdieu calls the *'habitus'*. Whereas the field is the objectified state of historical process, the habitus is the embodied state. They are what Bourdieu, citing Spinoza, calls 'two translations of the same sentence'. Together they are the means by which 'the dead seizes the living' (Bourdieu, 1993).

More specifically;

> The concept of habitus refers to an ensemble of schemata of perception, thinking, feeling, evaluating, speaking, and acting – that structures all the expressive,

verbal and practical manifestations and utterances of a person. Habitus has to be thought of as 'a generative principle of regulated improvisations' (Bourdieu, 1977, p. 78) (which are called practice), an incorporated structure formed by the objective conditions of its genesis. It is 'embodied history, internalised as a second nature', as Bourdieu says, 'the active presence of the whole past of which it is the product' [1990a, p. 56]. By contrast with the familiar sociological concept of role, habitus refers to something *incorporated*, *not* to a set of norms or expectations existing independently of and externally to the agent. Likewise, as it is thought to be part of the living organism, thus functioning in the way of living systems, habitus refers to a *generative* principle, *not* to a set of fixed and finite rules. (Krais, 1993, pp. 169–70)

In other words, the habitus is a kind of 'embodied unconscious' which

makes it possible to inhabit institutions, to appropriate them practically, and so to keep them in activity, continuously pulling them from the state of dead letters, reviving the sense deposited in them, but at the same time imposing the revisions and transformations that realisation entails. (Bourdieu, 1990a, p. 57)

Habitus and field are obviously intimately related to one another:

habitus reacts to the solicitations of the field in a roughly coherent and systematic manner. As the collective individuated through embodiment or the biological individual 'collectivised' by socialisation, habitus is action to the intention in action of Searle or to the 'deep structure' of Chomsky except that, instead of being an anthropological invariant, this deep structure is a historically con- stituted, intrinsically grounded, and thus socially variable generative matrix. It is an operator of rationality, but of a practical rationality, immanent in an historical system of social relations and therefore transcendent to the individual. The strategies it 'manages' are systematic, yet ad hoc because they are 'triggered' by the encounter with a particular field. Habitus is creative, inventive, but within the limits of its structures, which are the embodied sedimentation of the social structures which produced it. (Bourdieu and Wacquant, 1992, pp. 18–19)

In other words, there is 'an ontological complicity between habitus and the social field' (Bourdieu, 1990a, p. 194). Or, as Dreyfus and Rabinow (1993, p. 38) put it even more succinctly, 'our socially inculcated dispositions to act make the world solicit action, and our actions are a response to this solicitation'.

Bourdieu is clearly interested in framing the encounter between practices and history. It is left to de Certeau (1984, 1986) to frame the encounter between practices and geography. It is too rarely noted that de Certeau wrote critically on Bourdieu, and the terms of his critique were explicitly spatial. Thus, de Certeau praised Bourdieu's ethnological work on the everyday tactical practices of the Kabyle and the Béarnais but he was unable to find the same kind of subtlety in Bourdieu's work closer to home on the French educational system. As both Lave and Wenger (1991) and Reed-Danahy (1985) also point out, in this work, the subtle energies of habitus are absorbed in a complex but still recognisable regulation model which confuses 'the ideology of his own milieu with its practices' (Herzfeld, 1987, p. 83). For de Certeau (1984, p. 59), Bourdieu extinguishes tactics' fire 'by certifying their amenability to socio-economic rationality . . . as if to mourn their death by declaring them unconscious'. Perhaps this is because of Bourdieu's need for an

> *other* (Kabylian or Béarnian) which furnishes the element that the theory needs to work and 'to explain everything'. This remote foreign element has all the characteristics that define the habitus: coherence, stability, unconsciousness, territoriality. . . . It is represented by the habitus where, as in the Kabylian dwelling, the structures are inverted as they are interiorised, and where the writing flips over again in exteriorising itself in the form of practices that have the deceptive appearance of being free improvisations. (de Certeau, 1984, p. 58)

De Certeau's answer to this occidentalist dilemma is interesting. It is to concentrate on the importance of tactics by exploring the importance of *space*. De Certeau tries to surmount the problem of Bourdieu's implicit denigration of the tactical properties of practices by exploring how space intervenes both in constituting tactics and in forming the other. Thus, 'a tactic insinuates into the other's place, fragmentarily, without taking it over in its entirety, without being able to keep it at a distance' (de Certeau, 1984, p. xix). For de Certeau practices are always spatial-symbolic practices which can be discovered via spatial-symbolic metaphors like walking, pathways and the city. Through the movements of the body and the powers of speech the subject (now a walker) can jointly produce the possibility of converting one spatial signifier into another. New places and meanings, 'acts and footsteps', 'meanings and directions' are produced and they produce;

> liberated spaces that can be occupied. A rich indetermination gives them . . . the function of articulating a second poetic geography on top of the geography of the literal, forbidden or permitted meaning. They insinuate other routes into the functionalist and historical order of movement. (de Certeau, 1984, p. 105)

Space intervenes in another way too, in the production of narrativities. For de Certeau:

> Narrative structures have the status of spatial syntaxes. By means of a whole panoply of codes, ordered ways of proceeding and constraints, they regulate changes in space (or moves from one place to another) made by stories in the form of places put in linear or interrelated series. . . . More than that, when they are represented in descriptions or acted out by actors (a foreigner, or city dweller, a ghost) these places are linked together more or less tightly or easily by 'modalities' that specify the kind of passage leading from the one to the other. . . .
> Every story is a travel story – a spatial practice. For this reason, spatial practices concern everyday tactics, are part of them, from the alphabet of spatial indication ('its to the right', 'take a left'), the beginning of a story the rest of which is written by footsteps, to the daily news ('guess who I met at the bakery'), television news reports (Teheran: Khomeni: is becoming increasingly isolated), legends (Cinderellas living in hovels) and stories that are told (memories and functions of foreign lands or more or less distant times in the past). These narrated adventures simultaneously producing geographies of actions and drifting into the commonplaces of an order, do not merely constitute a 'supplement' to pedestrian enunciations and rhetorics. They are not satisfied with displacing the latter and transposing them into the field of language. In reality, they organise

walks. They make the journey before or during the time the feet perform it. (de Certeau, 1984, pp. 115–16)

In the latter parts of his career, de Certeau explained these spatial stories as a vital constituent of the other, specifically through the construction of practices of Empire and colonisation (de Certeau, 1991).

Take 2: Further Down the Ontic Trail

This brief exposition of the work of Heidegger, Wittgenstein, Merleau-Ponty, Bourdieu and de Certeau has allowed me to consider the main theorists of practices. It has also allowed me to travel some way down the ontic trail towards social, historical and geographical particularity. Now I want to both fill in some more of the details in theories of practice and, at the same time, travel still further down the ontic trail, through an appeal to three different sets of literatures concerned with, respectively, the conversational nature of practices, the conundrum of subjectivity and the deployment of power. In so doing, I also want to face up to the kind of criticism made by Copjec (1994b) and like-minded authors, that a framework built on the principles of Heidegger and the four other theorists we have encountered so far is incapable of 'supposing' a subject, by actively showing how their work can be extended in precisely this direction without damaging its most important insights.

The first of these literatures is concerned with the nature of practices themselves. Each of the exponents of theories of practice so far addressed, for different reasons, tends to leave the exact ways in which practices are reproduced/revised in abeyance.[12] For example, the fast and often unpredictable interactional to and fro of everyday life is missing, concepts of the self and personality tend to lie dormant, certain issues concerning language are passed over, and processes of socialisation of the child get short shrift. These omissions can at least start to be redressed through an appeal to the North American pragmatic tradition, which begins with the work of Dewey and Mead. No one who is interested in theories of practice can readily ignore this tradition. Mead was, of course, a remarkably prescient thinker who, from the start, was intent on avoiding the demarcation of social and personal regions. Thus, in his account of language and the social self, thought and self-awareness arose from interpersonal processes. Initially this means communication by gesture.[13] Later, other forms of language emerge. The inner conversation which we denote as 'thinking' takes on an impersonal form, because the conversation in our minds is no longer with actual persons but with a 'generalised other'; the values and morals of the social group which are embodied in discourse. In other words, the 'inner' organisation of the self 'rests on the dialectical interchange with everything outside that is outside it: that is to say: its natural environment as it is mediated through social activity and communication' (Burkitt, 1991, p. 48):

from this standpoint, perfect individuality or a fully developed personality, instead of being something given and simply to be recognised, is the result of deep and profound consciousness of the actual social relations. Furthermore, as a prerequisite of this consciousness, we imply the formation of the most extensive and essential social relationships whose control must lie within themselves and in their interaction upon each other, rather than in any internal judgement. From this standpoint personality is an *achievement* rather than a given fact. (Mead, cited in Burkitt, 1991, p. 48)

It is also clear from the quotation that, for Mead, 'extensive and essential social relationships' refer to pre-conscious patterns of conduct which are necessary to the entire economy of conduct, and 'this is similar to Heidegger's notion of being-in-the-world, where the future of objects is constructed by habitual everyday activity in the material world, and the meaning that objects have for us is the part that they play in that habitual activity' (Burkitt, 1991, p. 49).

Mead's work was chiefly taken up in sociology, where it became incorporated into the symbolic interactionism of Blumer and others (for accounts, see Alexander, 1989; Denzin, 1992) as a 'down-to-earth' approach to the study of human group life and human conduct resting on three main assumptions: first, that 'human beings act towards things on the basis of the meanings that the things have for them' (Blumer, 1969, p. 2); second, that meanings arise out of the process of social interaction; and, third, that meanings are modelled through an interpretive process which involves self-reflective individuals who symbolically interact with each other. In appealing to these assumptions, symbolic interactionism clearly tended towards an individualist and representationalist view. However, the work of many of its scions is still instructive for theories of practice, and can be recast in their terms. In particular, there is the work of Garfinkel and Goffman. Garfinkel's 'ethnomethodology' (Heritage, 1984) is an approach which shows the stuff of social order as people's familiar, everyday actions, arising out of the 'local logics' connected with concrete social situations. But these actions are achieved in ways which are artful as well as taken-for-granted. To accomplish them people must constantly utilise well-known and well-used procedures or codes *creatively*, or, as it is often and famously phrased, 'for another first time'.[14] These procedures are the folk – or 'ethno' – methods which we must try to understand if we are to make everyday actions intelligible. In other words, Garfinkel was concerned to produce an analysis of social phenomena which recognised them as

the managed accomplishment of organised settings of practical actions, and that particular determinations in members' practices of consistency, thankfulness, relevance, or reproducibility of their practices and results – from witchcraft to topology – are accompanied and assured only through particular, located organisations of artful practices. (Garfinkel, 1967, p. 32)

By the same token, Garfinkel goes on:

it is not satisfactory to describe how actual investigative practices, as constitutive features of members' ordering and organised affairs, are accomplished by members as recognisably rational actions in actual occasions of organisational instances by saying that members invoke some rule with which to define the coherent, or consistent or planful, i.e. rational, character of their actual activities. (Garfinkel, 1967, p. 32)

Thus, it follows that:

a leading policy is to refuse serious consideration to the prevailing proposal that efficiency, efficacy, effectiveness, intelligibility, consistency, planfulness, typicality, uniformity, replicability of activities – i.e. that rational properties of practical activities – be assessed, recognised, categorised, described by using a rule or standard obtained outside actual settings within which such properties are recognised, used, produced and talked about by settings' members. (Garfinkel, 1967, pp. 32–3)

Most particularly, Garfinkel attached importance to the *accountable* character of social action as a reflexive, inferential and inevitably ethical (since it must involve moral intuition) product of the interpretation of shared procedures: 'by his [*sic*] accounting practices the member makes familiar commonplace activities of everyday life recognisable *as* familiar, commonplace activities' (Garfinkel, 1967, p. 9). In other words, social actors are, through their own actions, unavoidably engaged in producing and reproducing the intelligible character of their own circumstances by constituting practically adequate situations (in contrast to the standard sociological view of situations as stable objects of consensual identification). Thus,

Garfinkel's interest is in descriptive accounts and accountings as data which are to be examined to see how they organise, and are organised by, the empirical circumstances in which they occur. Far from being treated as external to social activity, accounts are to be treated as subject to the same range of circumstantial and interpretative categories as the actions and instances they describe. In this context, Garfinkel begins his description of accounts by noting that their 'fit' to the instances they describe is 'loose' and subject to adjustment by *ad hoc* devices: that accounts, like actions, are understood by reference to a mass of unstated assumptions and that the sense of an account is heavily dependent on the context of its production. Descriptive accounts, in short, are indexical. (Burkitt, 1991, p. 56)

The same emphasis on social action as being designed with reference to how it will be recognised and described, and on language as *language-in-use*, can also be found in the work of Goffman. Here I do not want to concentrate on Goffman's dramaturgical models of impression management but on his later work on micro-social interaction, where, as he put it, 'most of the work gets done'. Most particularly, in this later work, Goffman was interested in recognising the *rhetorical* character of *talk*. For Goffman, 'talking is not experiencing or perceiving, the objects and happenings around us, but doing. Talk is performance, a form of acting on and interacting with what is, and with what is going on around us' (Burns, 1992, p. 301). But talk is not just performance:

While it is true that utterances are performative and convey commitment to action, or promises, or assent, dissent, caution and much else, a good deal of the talk in which performative utterances are conveyed is only indirectly connected with the performative content; indeed, this may be a minor feature. (Burns, 1992, p. 303)

Thus,

What the individual spends most of his [*sic*] time doing is providing evidence for the fairness or unfairness of his current situation and other grounds for sympathy, approval, exoneration, understanding, or amusement. And what his listeners are obliged to do is to show some kind of audience appreciation. (Goffman, 1974, p. 503)

These kinds of concerns with accounts and the rhetorical properties of talk have been taken up again more recently in the *conversational* models of human conduct pursued by Harré and Shotter. For both Harré and Shotter reality is 'conversational':

The fundamental human reality is a conversation, effectively without beginning or end, to which, from time to time, individuals may make contributions. All that is personal in our mental and emotional lives is individually appropriated from the conversation going on around us and perhaps idiosyncratically transformed. The state of our thinking and feeling will reflect, in various ways, the form and content of that conversation. (Harré, 1983, p. 20)

It is possible to argue with Harré's approach to the conversational reality with its rather odd distinction between a practical and expressive order, and its tendency to neo-Kantianism. Therefore, I will concentrate on the work of Shotter (1984, 1985a, 1985b, 1993a, 1993b; see also Shotter and Gergen, 1994), which mixes Harré with Vico, Wittgenstein, Vygotsky and Bakhtin to produce an intriguing conversational version of social constructionism which fits with the main tenets of theories of practice in its attempt to move 'beyond representationalism'. Shotter's work on conversation (understood as everyday practical talk) depends on four main principles. First, and most importantly, it concentrates on the third space 'between' the individual psyche and the abstract systems or principles which supposedly characterise the external world.[15] This is the space of everyday social life, a flow of responsive and relational activities that are joint, practical-moral and situated in character and constitute a new understanding 'of the third kind'. This is the space of 'joint action' in which 'all the other socially significant dimensions of interpersonal interaction, with their associated modes of subjective or objective being, originate and are formed' (Shotter, 1993b, p. 7). It is, in effect, Wittgenstein's background foregrounded.

Second, Shotter's work assigns a crucial role to the use of language, not as a communicative device for transmitting messages from the psyche or social structure, but as a rhetorical-responsive means of moving people or changing their perceptions. Thus in this rhetorical-responsive version of social constructionism the account of language that is offered is 'sensuous' – language is a communicational, conversational, dialogical and persuasive means of responding to others (and 'ourselves'):

all of what we might call the person–world, referential–representational, dimensions of interaction at the moment available to us as individuals – all the familiar ways we have of talking about ourselves, about our world(s), and about their possible relationships which in the past we have taken as in some way primary – we now claim must be seen as secondary and derived, as emerging out of the everyday, conversational background to our lives. (Shotter, 1993b, p. 8)

Thus, and third, Shotter is clearly committed to a highly *situated* view of human life and language use. Situations 'exist as third entities, between us and the others around us' (Shotter, 1993b, p. 9).

In turn, such a view of situations produces an orientation to the other, which is necessarily ethical:

To us as individuals, . . . situations may seem like one or another kind of 'external' world. . . . However, such situations are not external to 'us' as a social group. As neither 'mine' nor 'yours', they constitute an Otherness. And it is from within this Otherness that we must distinguish, slowly and gradually, between that which is due to our relations to each other, and that which is not – the task of distinguishing what is dependent upon factors of our talk from what is independent of it. This will be a difficult and politically contested task; but it is clear that until now, it is a task that has been ignored. (Shotter, 1993b, p. 9)

Therefore, fourth and finally, in Shotter's rhetorical-responsive account a careful emphasis is placed on self–other relationships:

Social constructionists are concerned with how, without a conscious grasp of the processes involved in doing so, in living out different, particular forms of self–other relationships, we unthinkingly construct different, particular forms of . . . person–world relationships: the special ways in which, as scientists, say, we interact with the different worlds of only theoretically defined entities, the routine ways in which as ordinary persons we function in the different realities we occupy in our everyday social lives; as well as the extraordinary ways in which we act, say, when in 'love'. (Shotter, 1993a, p. 12)

The second literature I want to appeal to is concerned with filling out the notion of subjectivity. What I have outlined so far suggests something not so far from the classical poststructuralist decentred subject; this is as I believe it should be (*1991b*). But I also believe that the subject *is* psychically 'anchored' in various ways: by narrative surely, as Freud and de Certeau make clear; by the recording of early pre-discursive experiences of the object certainly (Winnicott, 1974, 1975; Bollas, 1987; Rustin, 1991); by the word even – I have not entirely given up on Lacan! But most importantly of all, there is the *primary unconscious imaginary*, defined as 'the key psychical mechanism through which human beings establish an imaginary relation with the self, others, received social meanings, and society' (Elliott, 1992, p. 4). Here I want to draw on the work of Castoriadis (1984, 1987, 1991a, 1991b). Castoriadis's work is, without doubt, exceptional: as Lecercle (1993, p. 58) puts it, 'he was so obviously right forty years before everybody else. More importantly, he is the only living incarnation of two figures who ought to be close to our hearts: the philosopher-cum-psycho-analyst who manages to articulate Freud and Marx.' But this may still seem a rather odd choice. After all, Castoriadis is known for his commitment to a human psyche which produces representation; and to an actual faculty of signification:

> the imaginary ultimately stems from the ongoing positioning or presenting oneself with things and relations which do not exist, in the form of representations (things and relations that are not or have never been given in perception). We shall speak of a final or radical imaginary as the common root of the actual imaginary and of the symbolic. This is, finally, the elementary and irreducible capacity of evolving images. (Castoriadis, 1987, p. 127)

But what Castoriadis means by 'representation' is actually quite specific; and has very little to do with most definitions of representation; especially those definitions that are based on notions of the reflection of a 'real world':

> Those who speak of 'imaginary' understanding by this the specular, the reflection of the 'fictive', do no more than repeat, usually without realising it, the affirmation which has for all time chained them to the underground of the famous cave: it is necessary that this would be an image of something. The imaging of which I am speaking is not an image *of*. It is the unceasing and essentially undetermined (social historical and psychical) creation of figures/forms/images, on the basis of which alone there can ever be a question *of* something. What we call 'reality' and 'rationality' are its works. (Castoriadis, 1987, p. 3)

It clearly follows that:

> The term 'representation', as used by Castoriadis, does not denote some organic bond between images and things, ideas and the object world. Rather, the nature of representation for Castoriadis is anchored firmly in bodily reality, lit by the moment of creation *ex nihilo* between the thrust of the drive and the individual's unique mode of being. 'The individual' writes Castoriadis 'is not just a first concentration of representations – or better, a first "total representation" – he [*sic*] is also, above all, a ceaseless emergence of representations and the unique mode in which this representation/flux exists.' Unconscious representation, then, is a finite–infinite 'flux': it is indefinite in form, and is indifferent to the rules of ordinary logic. (Elliott, 1992, p. 28)

For Castoriadis, then, representation is a creative and constitutive feature of social experience, intention and affect. In the guise of the (primary and unconscious) imaginary, it is the endless emergence of these representations, drives and affects (originary investments), 'understood as an imaginary dimension of subjectivity, the dimension through which human beings create themselves anew and the political shape of their society' (Elliott, 1992, p. 4), by 'opening out' to

> self-identity, others, reason, society, and political engagement. Thus, the decisive grip the imaginary holds on the symbolic can be understood on the basis of the following consideration: symbolism assumes the capacity of positioning a permanent connection between two themes in such a way that one 'represents' the other. It is only at very advanced stages in lucid rational thinking that these three elements (the signifier, the signified and their *sui generis* tie) are maintained as simultaneously united and disjoint in a relation that is at once firm and flexible. (Castoriadis, 1987, p. 127)

The third literature to which I want to make an appeal is concerned with the issue of how *power* is constructed, enacted and exerted. Theories of practice have undoubtedly tended to avoid this issue; in a world of violence, oppression and cruelty they too often tend to the anaemic. The work of Bourdieu on the social field and habitus and on what he calls 'symbolic violence' and the writings of de Certeau on the interplay between the strategies of the powerful and the tactics of the weak have clearly begun to address the issue of agonistically constructed power more forcefully, but I am going to consider power instead through the body of work known as actor-network theory,[16] or sometimes the sociology of 'translation', where translation is defined as 'the mechanism by which the social and natural worlds progressively take form' (Callon, 1986, p. 224; 1991; Latour, 1986, 1988, 1991, 1993; Law, 1991, 1994).

Actor-network theory is not, of course, only concerned with how power is constructed. It also, and rather usefully, fills in other lacunae in theories of practices; of which five are particularly noteworthy. First, it provides a means of understanding how everyday practices are transmitted into wider processes of *social* formation, but without falling back on either an all-encompassing theoretical order of the kind that is so deeply suspect or a (sophisticated) restatement of the problem, as in Giddens's notions of time-space distanciation, and social and system integration. Second, it points to the way in which social *agency* is constructed *in* these social processes, rather than being assumed to be a property of them. Third, it identifies the process of construction as one that requires constant *effort*, and is always halting. (Thus, for example, actor-network theory recognises the importance of the work of maintenance of networks: constant, unrelenting work that has to be invested simply to keep networks together – as any glance at the Yellow Pages, with its vast lists of repairers, shows. Actor-network theory also recognises the importance of mistakes, and as creative as well as negative moments.) Fourth, it problematises *subject–object* relations because of its catholic view of what can count as actors. Then, fifth and finally, it demonstrates how *reality* is constructed through processes of translation, association and alliance which strengthen particular positions/accounts of practices at the expense of others. In other words 'building reality and truth, like building a freeway or a super-computer, must be recognised as intricately organised socio-political processes' (Ward, 1994, p. 89). Let me now expand on these points.

Actor-network theory uses the 'topological presupposition' (Mol and Law, 1994) of the network to consider how social agency is constructed. The bloodline of actor-network theory is poststructuralism (and especially Foucault), by symbolic interactionism out of network philosophies of science. As Law (1994, p. 18) has it:

The provenance of actor-network theory lies in poststructuralism: the vision is of many semiotic systems, many orderings, jostling together to generate the social. On the other hand, actor-network theory is more concerned with changing recursive *processes* than is usual in writing influenced by structuralism. It tends to tell *stories*, stories that have to do with the processes of ordering that generate effects such as technologies, stories about how actor-networks elaborate themselves, and stories which erode the analytical status of the distinction between the macro- and micro-social.

Actor-network theory has three main characteristics. First, agents – which can vary in size from individual human subjects to the largest organisations – are treated as relational effects. Second, however, agents are not unified effects. They are contingent achievements. Many of the stories of actor-network theorists recount 'how it is that agents more or less, and for a period only, manage to constitute themselves. Agency, if it is anything, is a precarious achievement' (Law, 1994, p. 101). Third, the social world is conceived of as fragmentary. It is a set of more or less related bits and pieces which are the result of endless attempts at producing networks, some of which are currently relatively successful, some of which are currently the social equivalent of the faded silk flowers in the attic. The 'social' is the outcome of this 'recursive but incomplete performance of an unflavourable number of intertwined orderings' (Law, 1994, p. 101). Thus in actor-network theory 'modes of production', 'structures', 'classes', 'interests', and the like, are not treated as the carriers of events but rather as a set of *effects* arising from a whole complex of network relations: 'translation is a process before it is a result' (Callon, 1986, p. 224).

It is often written that actor-network theory is an attempt to combine the insight of economics, that it is *things* that draw actors in relationships, with the insight of sociology, that actors come to define themselves, and others, through *interactions*. Thus, 'actors define one another in interaction – in the intermediaries that they put into circulation' (Callon, 1991, p. 135). These intermediaries – usually considered to be texts, technical artefacts, human beings and money – allow networks to come into being by giving social links shape and consistency and therefore some degree of longevity and size. But they are not passive tools. For example, texts and technical artefacts can clearly define the role played by others in the network – both humans and non-humans. In other words, the 'material' and the 'social' intertwine and interact in all manner of promiscuous combinations.

A network is, therefore, defined by the actors and by the circulation of intermediaries in interaction. But that still leaves open the question of how networks are established and stabilised. Murdoch (1995, pp. 747–8) provides the best explanation of this process:

In order for an actor to successfully enrol entities (human and non-human) within a network their behaviour must be standardised and channelled in the directions desired by the enrolling actor. This will entail redefining the roles of the actors and entities as they come into alignment, such that they come to gain new identities or attributes within the network. It is the intermediaries which act to bind actors together, 'cementing' the links. When there is a perfect translation, or redefinition, of actors' identities and behaviours, then these are stabilised within the network. The stronger the network, the more tightly the various entities (human and non-human) are tied in. Despite their heterogeneity they work in unison. Each actor is able to 'speak for all, and to mobilise all the skills and alliances within the network' (Callon, 1991, p. 151). The more stable the network, the more irreversible the translations. The links and relationships would be predictable, standardised; the network would be 'heavy with norms' (Callon, 1991, p. 151). However the 'power' of the intermediaries may be curtailed by actors modifying or appropriating them in accordance with their own projects. When the translation process has been weakly executed, the enrolling actors find their states continually in question and find it hard to mobilise other parts of the network. Thus successful or strong networks might be considered to be those where the processes of translation have been effectively executed, allowing the enrolling actor to consolidate the network on its own terms.

These successful, strong networks will clearly often involve action at a distance and this kind of action is in itself an achievement, one that can often only be guaranteed by socio-technical innovations which circulate intermediaries – from postal systems to long-distance navigation to modern computerised telecommunications. In other words, in actor-network theory, scale is an ongoing and transient achievement and the world is one in which 'actors have only relative size and are fighting hard to vary the size of everyone else' (Latour, 1988, p. 174).

Such an account of the struggle to achieve scale leads easily on to the question of power (Law, 1991). In actor-network theory, power is conceived of as the continuous outcome of the strength of the associations between actors and 'understanding what sociologists generally call power relationships means describing the way in which actors are defined, associated and simultaneously obliged to remain faithful to their alliances' (Callon, 1986, p. 224). As Murdoch (1995, p. 748) again puts it

> The stronger the network the more powerful the translating actor. Thus, those who are powerful are not those who 'hold' power but are those able to enrol, convince and enlist others into networks on terms which allow the initial actors to 'represent' these others. Powerful actors 'speak for' all the enrolled entities and actors and control the means of representation (they 'speak for the others that have been deprived of a voice, that have been transformed from objects that spoke for themselves into new shadows of their former selves' (Law and Whittaker, 1988, p. 79)). The controlling actor grows by borrowing the force of others; it can inflate to a larger size. . . . Power is, therefore, the composition of the network: if it lies anywhere it is in the resources used to strengthen the bonds.

Thus actor-network theory, as a sociology of *ordering* rather than order, is, at least in its later forms, 'all about distribution, unfairness and pain' (Law, 1994, p. 134). But, most importantly of all, it is about how these are *done in practice*. So,

> When the sociology of order complains that inequality is absent what I now hear is a different kind of complaint: an objection to the fact that the sociologies of ordering (like actor-network theory) do not buy into a reductionist commitment to some final version of order; that they are not, for instance, committed to a particular theory of class or gender exploitation; that they refuse to adopt what some feminists call a 'standpoint epistemology'; that their materialism is relational rather than dualist; that there is no *a priori* distinction between the macro-social and the micro-social. These complaints are right but I don't believe that they are justified. For ordering sociologies, whether legislative or interpretative, prefer to explore *how* hierarchies come to be told, embodied, performed

and resisted. But to choose to look at hierarchy in this way is neither to ignore it, nor to deny it. Rather it is to tell stories about its mechanics, about its instances, about how we all do it, day by day. (Law, 1994, p. 134)

Clearly, activating networks of actors, and therefore agency, requires mobilisation of all manner of things and this is probably where actor-network theory makes its most original contributions (*1994g*). In actor-network theory things other than human agency are given their due, with two main results. First, and as a matter of principle, actor-network theory recognises networks as collectivities of all manner of objects which all contribute in their way to the achievement (and attribution) of agency. In other words, actor-network theorists argue for a 'symmetrical anthropology'[17] which is more likely to recognise (and value) the contribution of the non-human by shifting our cultural classification of entities. Latour (1993, p. 67) goes so far as to argue for the necessity of a new constitution which will complete 'the impossible project undertaken by Heidegger', both by correcting Heidegger's archaic bias, and also by restoring the part of the 'anthropological matrix' which has been lost. Thus, says Latour (1993, p. 107),

> All collectives are different from one another in the way they divide up beings, in the properties they attribute to them, in the mobilisation they consider acceptable. These differences constitute countless small divides, and there is no longer a great divide to tell them apart from all the others. Among these small, small divides, there is one that we are now capable of recognising as such, one that has distinguished the official version of certain segments of certain collectivities for three centuries. This is our Constitution, which attributes the role of non-humans to one set of entities, the role of citizens to another, the function of an arbitrary and powerless God to a third, and cuts off the work of mediation from that of purification.

It is this constitution that Latour wants to say farewell to. He wants a new constitution that recognises hybrid, or variable, geometry entities, which restores 'the shape of things', and which redefines the human as 'mediator' or 'weaver'. Second, and following on from the latter point, because things are so intimately bound up in the production of networks that will last and spread, actor-network theory conjures up the idea of a world where 'the human' must be redefined as highly decentred (or as reaching farther) and as unable to be placed in opposition to the non-human: 'The human is not a constitutional pole to be opposed to that of the non-human' (Latour, 1993, p. 137). Thus some of our most cherished dualities – like nature and society – fall away to be replaced by new hybrid representations and new ethical considerations:

> the human is in the delegation itself, in the pass, in the sending, in the continuous exchange of forms. Of course, it is not a thing, but things are not things either. Of course it is not a merchandise, but merchandise is not merchandise either. Of course, it is not a machine, but anyone who has seen machines knows they are scarcely mechanical. Of course, it is not in God, but what relation is there between the God above and the God below. . . . Human nature is the set of its

delegates and its representatives, its figures and its messengers. (Latour, 1993, p. 138)

Finally, the mention of the influence of poststructuralism on actor-network theory allows me to comment briefly on this area of theoretical work in relation to theories of practice. In part, I do this because theories of practice share some of the same theoretical forebears – Heidegger being perhaps the most obvious (though read in a different way). In part, I do it because it allows me to make clear where theories of practice differ not only from conventional sociologies of order but also from certain post-structuralist readings. And, in part, I do it because I also want to identify certain forms of poststructuralist work which are, I believe, quite close to the theories of practice I have been expounding, and can add significantly to them.

It is possible to identify two different schools at work in poststructuralist thinking (Shotter, 1993a). One of these we might call the 'representational–referential' strand. Primarily influenced by the work of Saussure, it consists of the works of writers like Derrida and Lyotard who look on language as 'working in terms of already existing, decontextualised systems of conventionalised meanings of usages, characterised either by systems of differences, or in terms of rule-governed language games' (Shotter, 1993b, p. 13). In other words they focus on 'already spoken words'. Shotter (1993a) claims that this strand of work is still tainted by the 'systematic spirit' of the Enlightenment. I think that it is hard to disagree with this judgement. In particular, Shotter and others have pointed to the warning signs in this work; a certain inherent representationalism, a certain idea of a theoretical account that can speak ahead of time, the over-valuing of the lexical and the systematic linguistic form, the retention of a privileged centre for the intellectual but now as the interpreter of analytical language games, as signalled by, for example, 'Derrida's continued allegiance to classical values of theory, rigor, system, precision and control' (Wood, 1987, p. 287), and so on. One cannot help but suspect that the continuing commitment of writers like Derrida and Lyotard to the register of theory stems from their social investments in a very specific practical world;

Since the Second World War there has been a vast proliferation of academic activity, such that the academic realm has become far larger than any individual can grasp in their lifetime; thus, for all practical purposes, academia has become an infinite semantic universe. Growth has altered the people within this universe; whereas Wittgenstein never read other philosophers as they said nothing to him, Derrida writes only by commenting on other people's writings. Derrida works in a textual arena composed of philosophy, literature and the arts, and is not often called upon to think about how words and things relate. (Gosden, 1994, p. 60)

As I hope I have made clear, this first strand of thought is a long, long way from the kind of modest account I want to offer of a world of inherently dialogical joint action, a 'spontaneous, unself-conscious, unknowing (although not unknowledgeable) kind of activity' (Shotter, 1993a, p. 47).

But there is a second non-representational–practical strand of post-structuralist work, represented by writers like Foucault and Deleuze and Guattari. I do not want to take up Foucault's banner: enough has been written about his work already and, in fact, I have severe problems with some of it (including the incompatibility of his conceptions of individuality and subjectivity, his over-emphasis on the discursive production of humans by language at the expense of the practical production of language by humans, the outdatedness of his analysis of biopolitics,[18] the implicit Eurocentrism, identified by Bhabha [1994] and others, and so on). Instead I want to concentrate on the work of that dissident poststructuralist Gilles Deleuze (and Felix Guattari). In part, I want to do this because the kind of vivid, moving, contingent and open-ended thaumaturgy that Deleuze conjures up others seems to be not so very far from the vision offered by some other theorists of practice. For example, the echoes of Latour can be clearly heard here:[19]

> the Deleuzian framework insists on the flattening out of relations between the social and psychical so that there is neither a relation of causation (one- or two-way) nor hierarchies, levels, grounds, or foundations. The social is not privileged over the psychical (as crude Marxism entails); nor is the psychical privileged at the expense of the social (common charges directed against psycho-analytic theory). They are not parallel dimensions or orders; rather, they run into, as, and through each other. This means that individuals, subjects, microintensities, blend with, connect to, neighborhood, local, regional, social, cultural, aesthetic, and economic relations directly, not through mediation of systems of ideology or representation, not through the central organisation of an apparatus like the state or the economic order, but directly, in the formation of desiring-machines, war-machines, etc. Questions related to subjectivity, interiority, female sexual specificity, are thus not symptoms of a patriarchal culture, not simply products or effects of it, but are forces, intensities, requiring codifications or territorialisations and in turn exerting their own deterritorialising and decodifying force, systems of compliance and resistance. (Grosz, 1994b, p. 180)

Then, in part, I want to concentrate on Deleuze, because he provides what Grosz (1994b) has called the element of 'voluptuous passion', which some theorists of practice tend to miss, or underplay, and which allows me to incorporate into my account of theories of practice an erotics of thinking, sexuality and a sort of promiscuity that unites the two.[20] And finally, in part, I want to concentrate on Deleuze because of his writing strategy, with its attention to a poetics of folding and unfolding, deterritorialisation and reterritorialisation, and, in general a constancy marked only by its inconstancy.

Deleuze wishes to write a baroque 'theory' of practice, one which, like his almost ecological notions of subjectivity, is full of swirls and whorls, pleats and folds, 'not an essence, but rather . . . an operative function' (Deleuze, 1993, p. 3). In other words, Deleuze is pointing to ways of writing the world that are continuous, that do not flatten into a concept or world picture and which allow the maximum of 'tactical resourcefulness' (Conley, 1993).

Deleuze offers a number of insights for theories of practice. First, he produces a theory of practice out of an almost entirely different theoretical bloodline (Bogue, 1989; Broadhurst, 1992; Boundas, 1993; Hardt, 1993; Boundas and Olkowski, 1994). His mentors include a recast Bergson (who enables Deleuze to displace consciousness, with its function of casting light upon things, by a new field of 'nomadic' singularities, intensive magnitudes which are pre-individual and pre-personal), a reworked Spinoza (who provides an ethology of striving passions that can energise this field), a refitted Nietzsche and Foucault (who enable Deleuze to reflect on how subjectivity is constructed from the internalisation of 'outside' forces *without* reproducing a philosophy of interiority) and, latterly, a renovated Leibniz (who provides an account of the constitution of the 'individual').

Second, Deleuze concentrates, most especially via Spinoza and Nietzsche, on qualities of force and affect that have sometimes been neglected in other theories of practice that we might call, after Brennan (1993), the 'energetics' of 'activity, joy, affirmation and dynamic becoming' (Braidotti, 1994, p. 164). Most particularly, that means that life is refigured as a slip-sliding flux of intensity and impersonal forces. This allows Deleuze to rework ideas of the body, thinking and the self. Thus the body becomes a 'complex interplay of highly constructed social and symbolic forces. The body is not an essence, let alone a biological substance. It is a play of forces, a surface of intensities: pure simulacra without originals' (Braidotti, 1994, p. 163). Thinking itself becomes an interplay of forces. Deleuze brings to the fore

> the affective foundations of the thinking process. It is as if beyond/behind the propositional content of an idea there lay another category – the affective force, level of intensity, desire and affinity – that conveys the idea and ultimately governs its truth value. Thinking, in other words, is to a very large extent unconscious, in that it expresses the desire to know, and this desire is that which cannot be adequately expressed in language, simply because it is that which sustains language. (Braidotti, 1994, p. 165)

And the self becomes both disjunctive and nomadic, a highly variable speaking stance attuned to Deleuze's basic message that 'everything in the universe is encounters, happy or unhappy encounters' (Deleuze and Parnet, 1987, p. 79).

Third, Deleuze produces a radically different idea of subjectivity,[21] one which privileges intensity, multiplicity, productivity and discontinuity, one which is pitted against Lacan's negative vision of desire as lack, and one which hunts down all notions of interiority 'in search of an inside that lies deeper than any internal world' (Deleuze, 1993, p. 163). One might argue that what is left is simply the classical poststructuralist subject without much subject, but this would be unfair. It would be more accurate to write that, just like Latour, Deleuze wants to redefine 'human' around a new 'ethical' constitution:

> In the wake of Spinoza's understanding of ethics, ethics is conceived of as the capacity for action and passion, activity and passivity; good and bad refer to the ability to increase and decrease one's capacities and strengths and abilities. Given

the vast and necessary interrelation and mutual affectivity of all beings on all others (a notion, incidentally, still very far opposed to the rampant moralism underlying ecological and environmental politics, which also stress interrelatedness but do so in a necessarily prescriptive and judgemental fashion, presuming notions of unity and wholeness, integration and cooperation rather than, as do Deleuze and Guattari, simply describing interrelations and connections without subsuming them to an overarching, wider system or totality), the question of ethics is raised wherever the question of a being's, or an assemblage's capacities and abilities are raised. Unlike Lévinasian ethics, which is still modelled on a subject-to-subject, self-to-other, relation, the relation of a being respected in its autonomy from the other as a necessarily independent autonomous being – the culmination and final flowering of a phenomenological notion of the subject – Deleuze and Guattari in no way privilege the human, autonomous, sovereign subject: the independent other; or the bonds of communication and representation between them. They are concerned more with what psychoanalysis calls 'partial objects': organs, processes, and flows, which show no respect for the authoring of the subject. Ethics is the sphere of judgement regarding the possibility and actuality of connections, arrangements, lineages, machines. (Grosz, 1994a, p. 197)

Modest Theory

I have now outlined a background. In this section I want to propose a theoretical synthesis. But it is important to note that I am not trying to offer a fully finished theoretical programme. What I want to provide here is theory with a lighter touch. In part, this is because I do not want to participate in 'fantasies of an unimpeachable method, of adequate representations of reality, [or] of an intellectual "turn" that will enable the critics to write the world newly, free of the prejudice of the past' (Bordo and Moussa, 1993, p. 122). In part, it is also because I want to avoid a theory-centred style which continually avoids the taint of particularity.[22] Such a style seems to me to perpetuate the kind of critical imperialism that so many writers have been at such pains to banish. And in part, it is because I want to point up the importance of practices as valid in themselves, existing without need of validation by some fully settled, monochromatic theory. In stressing the importance of practices I also hope to make a clearing for voices that speak from outside the authorised scholarly discourse whilst simultaneously recognising that this ambition is only necessary to an extent, since the scholarly discourse-network is but one of many forms of practice. In other words, I want to point to the perpetually inadequate (but not thereby unnecessary) powers of theory. In 1987, I wrote that my vision of theory was closer to a hand torch than a floodlight (*1987p*). I would not make this analogy, with its emphasis on a single-sourced vision, in quite the same way now, but the sentiments still hold.

Thus, in what follows, I want to provide some nearly aphoristic guidelines, most of which are prefigured in the earlier section of this chapter, which are intended to summarise a particular *style* of thought (Wood, 1990), which, like certain kinds of poststructuralist thought, stresses radical incompleteness and contextuality (*1992a*), but which, unlike these same forms of thought,[23] also stresses the limits and boundaries to that kind of thought.

(1) *Ontology*. The ontology I want to offer is best described as a 'weak ontology' (but not in Vattimo's [1988] sense), based upon the existence of an inherent order of connection, a non-subjective logic of encounters, a 'mindful connected physicalism' consisting of 'multitudinous paths which intersect, which works through things rather than imposes itself upon them from outside and above'[24] (Brennan, 1993, p. 86). Brennan claims that this kind of 'energetic ontology' is already recognised in Spinoza's philosophy of a basic physical logic of presences and absences but has subsequently been obscured by the too easy equation of any order of connection with constraint, rather than with positive creation:

> Because Spinoza sees logic as existing independently and prior to the human subject, because he does not split thought and matter, Spinoza's philosophy is in fact not guilty of most of the charges levelled against the 'metaphysical systems of the transcendental subject of reason' (supply your favourite reference). He expressly dispossesses the subject of exclusive claims to the logos, in a magnificent dispossession. (Brennan, 1993, p. 88)

It follows that this kind of energetic ontology is based on a commitment to activity, affirmation and dynamic becoming. Following Deleuze, I want to get away from the guilt-ridden and life-denying tone of much western thought. However, this does not have to mean too enthusiastically embracing a kinetic vision of nomadism, for three reasons. First, although an energetic analysis is necessarily future-oriented, this does not have to mean a denigration of the present (a sin of which Andrew Benjamin [1993] accuses Heidegger). It is only to suggest that activity is future-oriented because performative. Second, although an energetic ontology is oriented to movement, this does not mean that *it* has to ignore spatial fixity or the matter of boundaries. Space is striated, which is both a negative *and* a positive condition of existence. Third, an energetic ontology is committed to multiplicity but the process of multiplication is not unconstrained or infinite. In particular, recognition has to be given to the importance of physical presences and absences (as well as linguistic presences and absences) in producing breaks, lacunae and emissions which interrupt and transmute encountering.

Traces of this kind of energetic ontology can be found in a number of quite diverse authors. For example, it is there in Deleuze (although it is, perhaps, too quickly transferred into pulsing flows). It can be found in Giddens (for example, Giddens, 1984) as interaction in contexts of co-presence. It can also be found in Bhaskar's (1993) most recent exposition of the dialectic. For Bhaskar (1993, p. 53) 'all changes are spatio-temporal, and space-time is a relational property of the meshwork of material beings', and he is sure that this in turn means that as much attention needs to be paid to absence as presence. For example, practices involve observing from situations as much as they involve being present within them.

(2) *Epistemology*. This weak ontology is shadowed by a weak epistemology. It has become increasingly clear that there are very strong limits on
what can be known and how we can know it because of the way human
subjects are embodied as beings in time-space, because of our positioning in
social relations, and because there are numerous perspectives on, and
metaphors of, what even counts as knowledge or, more precisely,
knowledges. This does not mean that it is necessary to opt for an
unabashed nihilism or relativism, but it does mean that we cannot do much
better than Haraway in arguing for

> politics and epistemologies of location, positioning and situating, where partiality
> and not universality is the condition of being heard to make rational knowledge
> claims. These are claims on people's lives; the view from a body, always a
> complex, contradictory, structuring and structured body, versus the view from
> above, from nowhere, from simplicity. (Haraway, 1991a, p. 195)

Haraway's idea of 'situated knowledges' argues for the existence of an
archipelago of radically contingent knowledges (Serres, 1982) but she still
believes that a kind of objectivity can be attained through acknowledging
embodiment and by framing 'the object of knowledge as an actor and
agent, not a screen or a ground or a resource, never finally as slave to the
master that closes off the dialectic in his unique agency and authorship of
"objective" knowledge' (Haraway, 1991a, p. 198). In practice, such a stance
(and I mean to indicate the resonance with theories of practice with this
term) must mean a number of things. First of all, it requires an attitude of
suspicion towards totalising accounts (*1987p*). As Meaghan Morris (1992a)
has put it, in her critique of David Harvey's Enlightenment cravings in *The
Condition of Postmodernity* (1989), the 'remedy of wholeness' is not a
remedy but a disease and, in any case, it is usually a sign of an author
intent on constructing an other.

Second, it follows that concepts should be seen in a different way. Most
particularly, they need to be seen as 'open' or indefinite (Bourdieu and
Wacquant, 1992). As Wittgenstein (1980, p. 653) put it, 'if a concept
depends on a pattern of life, then there must be some indefiniteness to it.' In
practice, this means that concepts must be 'polymorphic, supple and
adaptable, rather than defined, calibrated and used rigidly' (Bourdieu and
Wacquant, 1992, p. 23). Further, they must remain relatively general and
circuitous:[25] spinning out 'middle-range' theories is likely to be unproduc-
tive because it produces both an illusion of decideability and a tendency to
calcification; too much rigour produces rigor mortis (Lakoff, 1987). (We
might even go farther still and write concepts as Deleuze and Guattari
[1983, 1994] do, as image-concepts – fragmentary wholes whose main
purpose is to resonate, intensities whose main purpose is to set up new
events; 'hitherto unsuspected possibilities of life and action' [Braidotti, 1994,
p. 165]. For Deleuze and Guattari thinking is about finding these new
passions and letting them rip.) But equally, as Haraway makes clear, this
does not mean that it is necessary to drop all pretensions to evidentialisation

of concepts. One of the blights of the recent rise of cultural studies has been the paper which is founded on the principle of 'if you can say it, it's so' (Saunders, 1995, p. 396), a principle to which Haraway would undoubtedly be opposed.

Third, because what we know and how we know it is situated, it follows that a practical or situated way of knowing is contextual, and rooted especially in embodiment (*1995c*). In particular, this can mean a new role for bodily image-concepts like experience and self as critical *practices*, as ably mapped out by authors like Game (1991) and Probyn (1992). It also means the working up of new figurations of the subject, hybrid figurations like Haraway's 'cyborg', which can articulate new relations of experience and self. Further, this line of argument suggests a much greater decentring of academic accounts than has heretofore been accepted. If we live in joint action with others, then it is clear that our discourses cannot be privileged. We might go farther and consider the ways in which academic accounts have not only downgraded the importance of practical activity by trying to represent it as representations (M. Morris, 1988), but may also have understated its power: the historical trace of practical intelligibility still remains in our gestures and in our stances.

Fourth, and relatedly, I take it that any situated epistemology must be reflexive; but at the same time I do not believe that this has to mean the author's 'subjective' experience has to be inexorably written into accounts, as is the vogue in certain of the current crop of autoethnographies: 'this merely reinscribes, not only the privileged place of experience, but the privileged place of the author's experience' (Grossberg, 1988, p. 67).

To summarise, a situated epistemology would renounce systematic theory in favour of a stance much more like Shotter's (1993a, p. 15) 'practical theory':

> the equipping of an image 'tool-kit' [which] respects the unfinalisable nature of dialogue, and even the fact that dialogic forms of talk occur within 'a plurality of unmerged consciousnesses' (Bakhtin, 1984 [1968], p. 9). For although these may draw upon resources (to an extent) held in common, every voice, every way of speaking, embodies a different evaluative stance, a different way of being or position in the world, with a differential access to such resources. It is this that keeps everyone in permanent dialogue with everyone else, which gives all the processes of interest to us their intrinsic dynamic. And by studying the different ways in which different people, and different times in different contexts, resolve the dilemmas they face *in practice*, we can both characterise the resources available to them in these contexts at those times and 'plot', so to speak, their political economy, that is, the fact that they are very much more scarce in some regions and moments of our social ecology than others.

The ontological and epistemological stance I have outlined might be termed a kind of historicism, in that it stresses the historical and geographical variability of systems of social practices. Certainly, I agree with Castoriadis (1987, p. 3) that:

> There exists no place, no point of view outside of history and society, or 'logically prior' to them, where one could be placed in order to construct a theory of them

– a place from which to inspect them, contemplate them, affirm the determined necessity of their being – thus, constitute them, reflect upon them or reflect them in their totality. Every thought of society and of history itself belongs to society and to history. Every thought, whatever it may be and whatever may be its 'object', is but a mode and a form of social-historical *doing*.

However, if this is a historicist stance, it is a pretty weak version of it, since, rather like the work of the new historicists (Veesev, 1989), its aim is a stance which rejects some of the fundamental tenets of historicism. First, I reject strong historicist programmes which construct grand schemes of historical development and progress, and protean temporalities. Then, second, I make no claim to an absolute historical transcendence in the sense that there is always something that escapes. There is always something that lies outside knowledge. There is always something that cannot be described. In other words, the claim to an absolute historical transcendence has to be rejected, and for two reasons. One is, quite simply, that social space cannot be reduced to the relations that fill it. The other is that, as Copjec (1994b, p. 3) puts it,

> What's common to both the Lacanian and Foucauldian [view] is a distinction between two sets of existence, one implied by the verb *exister* and the other by the phrase *il y a*. The existence implied by the first is subject to a predicative judgement as well as to a judgement of existence; that is, it is an existence whose character or quality can be described. The existence implied by the second is subject *only* to a judgement of existence; we can say only that it does or does not exist, without being able to say what it is, to describe it in any way.

The point about transcendence deserves further expansion. For if it is clear that the reasoning outlined above implies 'the whole of something will never reveal itself in an analytical moment; no diagram will ever be able to display it fully, once and for all' (Copjec, 1994b, p. 8), then, as Copjec goes on to write, the consequences of such a statement are not. For example, such an acknowledgement does not compel us

> to imagine a society that never quite forms, where – as the deconstructionists would have it – events never quite take place, a society about which we can say nothing and do so in an endless succession of statements that forever fail to come around to the same relevant point. To say that there is no metalanguage is to say, rather, that society never *stops realising itself*, that it *continues* to be formed over time. (Copjec, 1994b, pp. 8–9)

Copjec's answer to the innate temporality of the institution of the social is Lacanian, involving the diagramming of society's generative principle as located in the order of the real, outside everyday reality. But I want to travel another road, one that starts with Husserl's phenomenology, which was, of course, introduced primarily as a means of escaping historicism. Husserl wanted to lead philosophy back to the pursuit of incontrovertible truths by means of the description of the things presented to our experience and the description of our experience of them: 'back to the things themselves!', as Husserl puts it. Because Husserl's phenomenology 'bracketed' or suspended belief in all metaphysical constructs in order to focus solely on what shows up as it presents itself in our experience, its findings were supposed to be apodictic. The standard story has it that this enterprise gradually runs into the sand:

> the early Heidegger came along and raised questions about the viability of Husserlian phenomenology by taking an 'interpretative' turn. What is most important about Heidegger's hermeneutic ontology, so the story goes, is his recognition of the significance of the finitude, worldliness, and historicity of our human predicament – the recognition that our access to things is always coloured and preshaped by the sense of things circulating in our historical culture. The story then concludes with poststructuralist and various postmodern thinkers detecting a nostalgia for metaphysics even in such Heideggerian concepts as worldliness, finitude, and history. Jacques Derrida, especially, points out that Heidegger still seems to be trapped in essentialism and totalisation, twin sins of the very 'metaphysics of presence' that his hermeneutic approach was supposed to displace. (Dostal, 1993, p. 141)

But what I hope I have shown in the preceding section of this chapter is that the story is not that simple (see also Dreyfus, 1991; Game, 1991; Dostal, 1993; Shotter, 1993a, 1993b). Another story can be told which can both presuppose the phenomenology of Heidegger and Merleau-Ponty and also move beyond it. This is a story which is based on seeing the agent as 'shaped' by her or his form of life, history (or culture) or bodily existence, but the notion of shaping employed here is one that implies a quite different notion of relation to the world from the ordinary casual link that it sometimes gets confused with. Shotter's and Taylor's (1993b) use of Heideggerian-Wittgensteinian notions like engaged agency and background perhaps come closest to describing this relation; their concern is with 'witnessing' the *conditions of intelligibility* of certain terms of experience, and 'how the terms in which this experience is described are thus given their sense only in relation to this form of embodiment' (Taylor, 1993b, p. 319). This 'evaluative sensibility', what Castoriadis (1987) calls the work of 'elucidation', is what I am trying to cultivate, but it is not a sensibility which should be confused with the standard philosophical quest for elucidation, which relies on the notion of a fixed semantic space, chosen freely from all the possible combinations, which I can then mean. Or, to put it more succinctly still:

> The demands we make for philosophical explanations come, seem to come, from a position in which we are, as it were, looking down onto the relation between ourselves and some reality, some kind of fact or real possibility. We think that we mean something by our questions about it. Our questions are formed from notions of ordinary life, but the ways we usually ask and answer questions, our practices, our interests, the forms our reasoning and inquiries take, look from such a position to be the 'rags'. Our own linguistic constructions, cut free from the constraints of their ordinary functioning, take us in: the characteristic form of the illusion is precisely of philosophy as an area of inquiry, in the sense in which we are familiar with it. (Diamond, 1991, pp. 69–70)

(3) *Ethics.* This ontological-epistemological stance also implies a certain notion of ethics. It should be clear by now that I have an antipathy for

grand theories which abstract and decontextualise by extracting and then reapplying a set of principles from one set of practices to another (Butler, 1994), and this antipathy extends to theories of comprehensive social ideals.

> It seems to me that ideal theories – theories of the principles that perfectly just societies would implement – often distract attention from pressing social problems and that, when these problems are addressed through ideal theories, the ideas they commend are too stringent to be helpful for purposes of devising feasible solutions in a profoundly nonideal world. Abstracting from the realities of pervasive and persistent injustice and historical animosity between social groups, ideal theory overlooks the problems of entrenched domination and oppression, offers (at best) vague guidelines for eliminating these evils, and even obstructs social change by locking in place ostensibly neutral standards that in fact disadvantage some social groups. (Meyers, 1994, p. 1)

It is no surprise, then, that the account that I would want to offer of moral reflection emphasises the body, affect and expressiveness, emotion and rhetoric. Most particularly, I look toward three sets of writings. First, there are the psychoanalytic feminists like Jessica Benjamin who object to moral philosophy's conception of people as monastic subjects who are essentially rational and homogeneous bearers of duties and seekers after rights and who stress 'the role of culturally transmitted imagery in shaping people's moral perception, the contribution of empathy to moral reflection, and the potential of a complex moral identity to enhance moral insight' (Meyers, 1994, p. 3). For these writers, moral reflection demands mutual recognition, to use Benjamin's (1988) phrase, an empathy with others which, in turn, requires: counter-figurational strategies which symbolise the practices of disadvantaged groups in productive ways; notions of the responsible act as heterogeneous; and concepts of moral identity as able to take into account capacities and limitations. Thus,

> instead of seeing moral reflection as the application of an overriding philosophically approved criterion of right and wrong to a set of available options, the latter view sees moral judgement as a process of interpreting the moral signficance of various cases of conduct that one might undertake both in light of one's own values and capabilities and also in light of one's understanding of others' needs and circumstances. (Meyers, 1994, p. 17)

Second, there are 'materialist feminists' like Noddings (1984) and Ruddick (1990) who, drawing on the work of Gilligan (1982) amongst others, lay emphasis on an 'ethics of care', derived from the example of mothering, which stresses receptiveness to others, pragmatism as a distinctive way of dealing with real life rather than theoretical situations, and nonviolence (Lovibond, 1994a). This approach, which has much to commend it, also has serious flaws (Lovibond, 1994b). But these flaws can be overcome by a turn to the third set of writings: intuitionist or neo-Aristotelian ethics (Platts, 1979; Anscombe, 1981; Hurley, 1985; R. Williams, 1985; Nussbaum, 1990; Wiggins, 1991; Dancy, 1993). This is an active and practical form of ethics founded in an evaluative sensibility arising from the concrete experience of specific situations (what Dancy

[1993] calls the 'authority of the present case'), which is not, however, the same as a total particularism:

> Since intuition (from the Latin *intueri*, 'to look at, to observe') means a way of acquiring knowledge not by inference but directly, 'by looking and seeing', the central epistemological notion within such a theory would be that of *sensitivity to the particular moral fact* – for example, the fact that to make a certain remark would be insensitive or presumptuous or sycophantic, or that to act in a certain way would be to sacrifice friendship to personal ambitions. However in order to gain acceptance for this notion, its proponents must say something to disarm the objection that the very idea of a 'moral fact' is incoherent, an objection likely to be made by anyone under the sway of the expansionist view of facts as (by definition) evaluatively neutral. To this end, the new intuitionism reintroduces certain themes from the moral philosophy of Aristotle. . . . First, there is the idea of the individual's *initiation* into a particular set of prevailing social forms, a process seen as issuing in a certain range of sensibilities that dictate appropriate emotional and practical responses to particular situations. Second, and building on this presumed basis of specialised evaluative sensibilities, there is the idea of *phronesis*, or 'practical wisdom'. This is the capacity for correct judgements, often without the support of any explicit theory, as to which value considerations have the strongest practical claim on us in any given deliberate situation: for example, whether or not the given situation is one in which truthfulness matters more than the avoidance of causing distress. (Lovibond, 1994a, p. 794)

(4) *The human subject.* These brief thoughts on ontology, epistemology and ethics make it easier to consider the subject and the subject's understanding of the world. What I am looking for here is a conception of the subject which is multiple and dynamic but only partially decentred: a trace which is not just a cipher, a figuration that still configures a 'life-enhancing fiction' (Bordo and Moussa, 1993). In other words, I am looking for a relation between outside and inside which is lisible and problematic but which still allows each human subject to become 'a master [*sic*] of one's speed and, relatively speaking, a master of one's molecules and particular features, in [the] zone of subjectivation: the boat as interior of the exterior' (Deleuze, 1988, p. 123). I wish to make five points only.

First, I take it that the subject's understanding of the world comes from the ceaseless flow of conduct, conduct which is always future-oriented. In theories of practice, understanding does not come from individual subjects moving deliberately and intentionally through spaces in a serial time. That would be to revive the subject–object relation. Rather, subjects display 'absorbed coping', 'engaged agency' or, to use a Heideggerian term, 'comportment'. Comportment differs in at least five ways from an action-directed view of understanding (Dreyfus, 1991). First, it is an open mode of awareness which 'is not mental, inner, first person, private, subjective experience . . . separate from and directed towards normal life objects' (Dreyfus, 1991, p. 68). Second, it is adaptable. Comportment manifests dispositions shaped by a vast array of previous dealings, but does so in a flexible way. Third, comportment is understanding as 'aspect-dawning' (Wittgenstein, 1980). That is, it depends upon the orientation, what Heidegger calls the 'towards-which', and is typified by instant recognition/

description. Fourth, if something goes wrong with comportment, it produces a startled response because future-directed certainty is being interrupted. Fifth, and related, if something goes awry, conduct becomes deliberate and acquires a sense of effort.

A second characteristic of the subject's understanding of the world is that it is intrinsically corporeal. Following Merleau-Ponty, the socialised body is not an inscribed but an inscribing object, the generative, creative capacity to understand, 'kinetic knowledge' (see I.M. Young, 1990; Grosz, 1993), which is founded in the prevailing 'sensory order' (Claasen, 1993), which places more emphasis on some senses than others (it hardly needs to be said that many of the current problems of western styles of thought are connected with its 'ocularcentric' (Jay, 1993) bias,[26] and in the particular contextualities of action (Giddens, 1984). How can this be?

> Adapting a phrase of Proust's, one might say that arms and legs are full of dumb imperatives. One could endlessly enumerate the values given body, *made* body, by the hidden persuasion of an implicit pedagogy which can instil a whole cosmology, through injunctions as insignificant as 'sit up straight' or 'don't hold your knife in your left hand', and inscribe the most fundamental principles of the arbitrary content of a culture in seemingly innocuous details of bearing and physical manner, so putting them beyond the reach of consciousness and explicit statement. (Bourdieu, 1990b, p. 63)

Further, embodiment also produces spatiality and temporality (Giddens, 1984). As Merleau-Ponty (1962, pp. 239–40) wrote, 'In every focussing moment, my body unites present, past and future. . . . My body takes possession of time; it brings into existence a past and a future for a present, it is not a thing but creates time instead of submitting to it.'

But, as Merleau-Ponty (1962, p. 416) also points out, the temporality that the body creates tends to be future-oriented because 'ahead of what I can see and perceive there is, it is true, nothing more actually visible, but my world is carried forward by lines of intention which trace out in advance at least the style of what is to come.'

A third characteristic of the subject's understanding of the world is that it is worked out in *joint action* and is therefore *inherently dialogical*. Many actions require co-operation to complete. In other words, the flow of dialogical action is a fundamental determinant of the intelligibility of social life: understanding comes from the between of 'we', not the solitary 'I'. But this understanding has to be continually worked at, argumentatively, on the basis of differentially distributed communicative resources. Thus, firstly,

> we must note that all our behaviour, even our own thought about ourselves, is conducted in an ongoing argumentative context of criticism and justification, where every argumentative move is formulated in a response to previous moves. This accords, secondly, with a familiar aspect of rhetoric, to do with its *persuasive* function, its ability to materially affect people, to move them to action, or affect their perceptions in some way. Thirdly, we must also note that . . . what we have in common with each other in our society's traditions is not a set of agreements about meanings, beliefs or values but a set of intrinsically two-sided topics . . . or deterministic theories or commonplaces for use by us as *resources*, from which we

can draw the two or more sides of an argument. Finally, we most note another, more unfamiliar aspect of rhetoric related to those aspects of languages to do with 'giving' or 'lending' a *first form* to what otherwise are in fact only vaguely or partially ordered feelings and activities to do with the study of how common understandings are established *before* one turns to their criticism. It is this fact – that we 'see' just as much 'through' our words as through our eyes that is, for us here, rhetoric's most important characteristic. For even in the face of the vague, undescribable, open, fluid, and ever changing nature, appropriate forms of talk can work to 'make it appear as if' our everyday lives are well ordered and structured. (Shotter, 1993a, p. 14)

Further, and crucially, the dialogical flow of action presupposes the making of *moral* judgements:

we can see that in ordering the two-way flow of activity between them, people create, without a conscious realisation of the fact, a changing sea of moral enablements and contrasts, of privileges and entitlements, and obligations and sanctions – in short, an ethos. And the changing settings created are practical-moral settings because the different 'places' or 'positions' they make available have to do, not so much with people's 'rights' and 'duties' (for we might formulate its ethical nature in different ways, at different times) as with the nurturance or injury to the basic being of a person. For individual members of a people can have a sense of 'belonging' in that people's reality only if the others around them are prepared to respond to 'reality', only if the others around them are prepared to respond to what they do and say *seriously*. (Shotter, 1993b, p. 39)

Thus, often language's function is simply to set up the intersubjective spaces of common actions, rather than represent them as such. And, through language's fluid and ever-changing nature, appropriate forms of talk can work to 'make it appear as if' our everyday lives are well ordered and structured (Shotter, 1993a, p. 14).

A fourth characteristic of the human subject's understanding of the world is its situatedness. The subject can only 'know from'. Therefore abstracting human subjectivity from time and space is always an impossibility. Temporally, practices are always open and uncertain, dependent to some degree upon the immediate resources available at the moment they show up in time and space. Thus, each action is lived in time and space, and part of what each action is is a judgement on its appropriateness in time and space. Further, following any kind of social 'rule' about practice always involves some measure of openness and uncertainty associated with each moment. As Taylor (1993a, p. 57) puts it in classic finitist terms:

A rule doesn't apply itself; it has to be applied, and this may involve difficult, finely timed judgements. This was the point made by Aristotle and underlay his understanding of the virtue of *phronesis*. However situations arise in infinite varieties. Determining what a norm actually amounts to in any situation can take a high degree of insightful understanding. Just being able to formulate rules will not be enough. The person of real practical wisdom is marked out less by the ability to formulate rules than by knowing how to act in each particular situation. . . . In its operation, the rule exists in the practice it 'guides'. But we have seen that the practice not only fulfils the rule, but it also gives it concrete shape in particular situations.

Spatially, the human subject must be thought of as both inside and outside. Thus writers like de Certeau and Deleuze clearly view real, external space as a precipitate of the division between the inside and the outside of a subject strung out in time-space. Defining inner and outer space and the relation between them through notions like 'the fold' allows these writers to ponder the mismatch between 'inside' and 'outside' and 'desire' and 'reality'.

Fifth, and finally, the subject's understanding of the world depends on a sense of self which we can, most generally, define as 'not an objective thing as such, but a mobile region of continually self-reproducing activity' (Shotter, 1989b, p. 139). A number of consequences stem from this definition. It becomes possible to turn away from current characteristics of the person as possessing a psychic unity, which we call 'self', and from the whole 'inner' vocabulary that supports it (see Taylor, 1988). It also becomes possible to cease talking primarily in terms of motives:

> many of our motives are the products of our activities, not the other way around
> . . . in this view just as we talk of Godot because we wait, not of waiting because
> of Godot, so (for instance) we talk of motives because we act, not of acting
> because we have motives – crazy though it may sound to say it. While our talk of
> motives may act back upon the disorderly activities of our social lives to 'lend'
> them some order, the search for motives as such is illusory. It is an attempt to
> explain our self-formative activities in terms of a product of these self-same
> activities. (Shotter, 1989a, pp. 95–6)

It becomes possible, too, to turn towards a more pluralistic, multiplex conception of the self, 'to a view which recognises that "I"s in being "me"s must inevitably be intermingled with the "you"s of many "others"' (Shotter, 1989a, p. 96). And it becomes possible to recognise context as formative in the formation of self, as the sign of how we construct along with others.

(5) *Things*. These thoughts on ontology and epistemology also make it possible to dwell on (and in) things. In too much theory there is an implicit separation of human subjects from objects. As I hope has already been made clear, I believe that there is a need for a new 'constitution' (Latour, 1993) which recognises the power of objects as 'semiophores, or carriers of meaning (bearing witness) to a positive and instrumental materialism, (not just as) the passive drugs feeding our habit of consumption, but as cherished possessions' (Stafford, 1994, p. 3). Certainly, but as more than this also. The new constitution is therefore a progressive re-cognition. First, it makes the simple acknowledgement of the extent to which the object world is intertwined with the subject: 'Latour (1988) reminds us that even pure mathematicians . . . work with the tools of their trade. Everything we do, from epistemology to digging the garden, is a trade with its own tools' (Law, 1994, p. 142). In a sense, then, we only know the world through/with tools, and this situation has became more rather than less the case as the human body has been significantly augmented in ways that directly impact on subjectivity.[27] On one level, there is the physical extension of bodily

capacities made possible through the various media of telecommunications. The body is able, as a result, to act at a distance. At another level, the body now has much greater opportunities for peripatetic movement through the development of new modes of transportation (Figure 1.1). Then, finally, the body can be physically constructed in ways that were not available before. 'Medical' developments like IVF and plastic surgery mean that the body can be augmented and even re-presented (Stafford, 1991, 1994).

Second, there is a need to recognise the degree to which objects become a crucial part of the performance of subjects, the kind of principle embedded in actor-network theory. Thus,

> Andrew's rank is strategically performed in a series of materials. No I don't want to say that it is reducible to the materials. . . . This is the trouble with socio-logical myth-making: it tends to want to reduce too soon, to ask why someone is the boss or why there is no boss at all, rather than asking how bossing is performed. Thus if Andrew's office were gutted by fire and he were obliged to set up in the user's coffee room I guess that he'd still be performed as Director. But what could happen if they took away his phone? And his secretary? And the stream of papers that crosses his desk? And what would happen if he were no longer able to travel south to London or to Head Office at Swindon? Or receive visitors? Would he still be Director then? And what would it mean if he were? (Law, 1994, p. 142)

But, third, there is more to the act of recognition than this. This act also involves giving to objects a 'life' of their own. This is the kind of balancing act which Latour, and those who work on the 'ecological self' (Mathew, 1991), have been trying to perform:

> life in active dialogue with earth others is exhilarating and many dimensional. Many of the issues and difficulties of relationship and interplay which are familiar from the ethics and politics of the personal appear here also. We must interact, but how far am I entitled to assert myself against or impose myself on the other? We must adapt to one another, but is one party always to be the one who adapts and the other to be adapted to? How much must we leave for the other? How much can we expect to share? Here there is not just *one* play of exchange between self and other, but multiple and contextual ones. We cannot, any more than in the human case, stereotype the relationship as one of love and harmony, excluding all disharmony and conflict. Although we may aim for a relationship of mutual enrichment, cooperation and friendship, we may often have to settle for that of respectable but wondering strangers (not necessarily second best). (Plumwood, 1993, p. 139)

(6) *Context.* I want to finish this chapter by turning again to the notion of context. As I hope I have made clear, the approach I am taking to problems of ontology, epistemology, the subject and subject–object relations is radically contextual. However, as I also hope I have made clear, I do not mean to imply by this that context is necessarily 'local'. Rather I take context to be a performative social situation, a plural event which is more or less spatially extensive and more or less temporally specific. It is, in other words, a parcel of socially constructed time-space which is more or less 'elongated' (and in which socially constructed 'notions' of time-space must play their part; 'rather than living "in" space

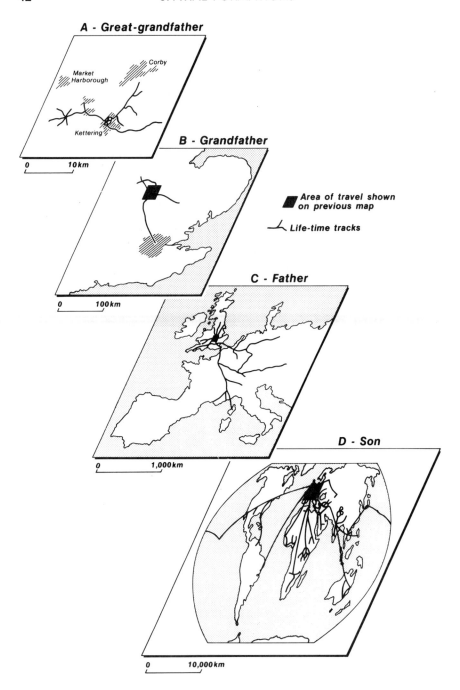

Figure 1.1   *The expansion of subjective experience: increasing travel over four generations of the same family (Bradley, 1988, Figures 1–4, pp. 2–3)*

and time, we account for time and space practically, relative to our form of living' [Shotter, 1985b, p. 449]). In each of these parcels of time-space 'subjects' and 'objects' are aligned in particular ways which provide particular orientations to action, what in ecological psychology are called 'affordances' (Gibson, 1979) (properties of complings of the agent and the environment like 'edibility', 'transversability', 'flyability', 'sittability'), and particular resources for action (which will be more open to some subjects than others). In other words, contexts are not passive; they are productive time-spaces which have to be produced. The nearest analogy I can think of to the vision of context I hold comes from work in the sociology of science using the idea of a 'productive locale'.

Much of this work has centred on the invention of the experimental laboratory, a structured site of specific forms of social interaction with cultural and physical barriers to entry which in turn functions as a site for the production/validation of new empirical knowledges:

> The physical and symbolic siting of experimental work was a way of bonding and disciplining the community of practitioners, it was a way of policing experimental discourse, and it was a way of publicly warranting that the knowledge produced in such places was reliable and authentic. That is to say, the place of experiment counted as a practical answer to the fundamental question, why ought one to give one's assent to experimental knowledge claims? (Shapin, 1988, p. 344)

In turn, Shapin (1988, 1994; Shapin and Schaffer, 1985) shows how the laboratory was tied to another new rhetorical context, the public lecture theatre, with its own socio-spatial arrangements, which was meant to faultlessly demonstrate what had hitherto been tried out in the laboratory (those same contexts still exist in different forms nowadays, as the work of Bourdieu [1990a] and Law [1994] shows only too well).

It is clear that I see human subjects as highly contextual beings but it is also clear that human subjects transpose across contexts in various ways which add up to a person's 'intentional style' (or personality). These ways are numerous. They include language, narrative, imagined relations with objects, and memory. However, equally, context has strong effects on each and every one of these transpositions. So far as language is concerned, many commentators have pointed to the heteroglossic importance of contexuality, especially when language is conceived as language-in-use. As Bakhtin (in Todorov, 1994, p. 91) puts it, 'in no instance is the extra-verbal situation only an external cause of the utterance; it does not work like a mechanical force. On the contrary, the situation enters into the utterance as a necessary constitutive element of its semantic structure.' So far as narrative is concerned, it is clear that it is also strongly contextualised. One of the points of de Certeau's notion of spatial stories and of his problematisation of writing and reading as practices is to make clear the double movement of these practices both out of and back into context.

Imagined relations between subjects and objects are also contextual. Indeed, one of the insights of the British object-relations school of

psychoanalysis has been precisely to point to the way in which early
contexts are crucial in the development of the human subject. The subject's
early prediscursive memory of the object of the 'unthought known' casts a
shadow over her or his subsequent development, in that it culturally affects
her or his style of being and relating.

> The reader of *Wind in the Willows* discovers in fact Rat and Mole are
> experiencing the sun rise, but they cannot see the sun, they only experience its
> effect on their environment. The object casts its shadow on the subject. In much
> the same way an infant experiences the mother as a process that transforms his
> [*sic*] internal and external environment, but he does not know that such
> transformation is partly sponsored by the mother. The experience of the object
> precedes the knowing of the object. The infant has a prolonged sense of the
> uncanny, as he dwells with a spirit of place the creation of which is not
> identifiable. (Bollas, 1987, p. 39)

Then, memory is also strongly contextual. For example,

> the retrieval of information from memory is sensitive to the particular categories
> of context in which the information was first acquired. When these are changed,
> memory is significantly hampered. Experiments demonstrated that the more
> similar the context of testing is to the context in which the tested information was
> acquired, the higher is subjects' level of recall. What is suggested here is that not
> only is information sensitive to context, its very definition is dependent on it.
> (Shanon, 1993, p. 45)

All of the aforegoing might be seen as a neglect of three challenges to
this contextual approach. In what follows, I want to name these challenges
and sketch the beginnings of a reply. The first challenge comes from the
psychological literature. It is that the developmental process of the individual human subject is commonly thought of as the ability to think across
(not outside) contexts by developing 'inner speech' (and therefore a self).[28]
This kind of insight is probably strongest in the Vygotskian tradition. For
Vygotsky thinking is initially a bodily process, which is limited in both
spatial and temporal terms, closely attached to practical activity and socio-
emotional attachments to carers, and bound up with 'desires and thoughts,
. . . interests and emotions. Behind every thought there is an affective
volitional tendency, which holds the answer to the lost "why" in the
analysis of thinking' (Vygotsky, 1962, p. 150). Emotion and desire remain
the motivating forces behind thought but language presents a new realm for
formulating them *and* a new, more open structure: 'speech does not merely
serve as the expression of developed thought. Thought is restructured as it
is transformed into speech. It is not expressed but completed in the word'
(Vygotsky, 1987, p. 251). But later work in this and other traditions suggest
that whilst Vygotsky was correct in suggesting that the ability to think
across contexts is an important mark of the development of the child, its
importance may have been overstated, as indexed by the way in which
children learn practical activity as patterns of behaviour appropriate to
particular situations, and expectations about the outcome of that activity in
these situations, through a process of mutual adjustment between child and

carer formed out of gesture and emotive signals like crying, by the way in
which the use of objects prefigures the use of language, by the ability of
children to construct a personality before they have acquired linguistic
competence, and, finally, by the way in which non-verbal forms of communication are not displaced by verbal forms:

> rather, words are integrated into a sequence of looks and gestures which form the
> pattern of an overall communicative setting. Social meanings therefore pattern
> the child's communicative actions and structure their intentions before they have
> mastered language. (Burkitt, 1991, p. 153)

It is also worth pointing out that contextual sensitivity seems to differ
cross-culturally, with many western cultures being less sensitive to context
(and therefore more likely to Eurocentrically recognise contextual
sensitivity as the early point in a developmental path). For example, in
Japan sense of self seems to be dependent to a far greater extent on making
appropriate adjustments to context (Rosenberger, 1992), a dependence
which may be the result of a more collective culture (although recent
writings have suggested that this emphasis on the collective self may in part
be a conscious construct resulting from Japanese writers' attempts to
distance themselves from western culture).

The second challenge to the contextual approach comes from the
geographical and sociological literatures in the shape of concepts like time-
space distanciation, time-space compression and globalisation, which, in
principle at least, might seem to herald a new, decontextualised era in
which the indirect triumphs over the direct. I do not want to deny the
historical and geographical efficacy of these processes – there are good
reasons to believe, for example, that more elements of contexts are now
found in common across the world as a result of modern telecommunications and transportation innovations (see, for example, Clifford, 1988,
1992).[29] But, *in practice*, I am not so sure, for two reasons (*1994k*). To
begin with, these concepts conjure up a world of over-arching, almost God-
like 'global' organisations 'adrift in a mythical sea' (Boden, 1994, p. 35).
But these organisations are 'not supralunar organisations made of a
different matter from our poor sublunar relations'; they are 'networks of
practices and instruments, of documents and translations' powered by
everyday talk (Boden, 1994);[30] 'the only difference stems from the fact they
are made up of hybrids and have to mobilise a greater number of objects
for their description' (Latour, 1993, p. 121). Thus, for example,

> The capitalism of Karl Marx or Fernand Braudel is not the total capitalism of
> the Marxists. It is a skein of somewhat longer networks that rather inadequately
> embrace a world on the basis of points that become centres of profit and
> calculation. In following it step by step, one never crosses the mysterious lines
> that divide the local from the global. (Latour, 1993, p. 121)

Then again, these concepts often rely, either implicitly or explicitly on a
cultural-psychological correlate which is summarised in this passage from
Nietzsche:

Our age is an agitated one, and precisely for that reason, not an age of passion, it heats itself up continuously, because it feels that it is not warm – basically it is freezing. . . In our time, it is merely by means of an echo that events acquire their 'greatness' – the echo of the newspaper. (1882, cited in Dreyfus, 1992, p. 290)

In other words, time-space compression leads to disorientation, distraction and the death of the authentic; as the world spins faster so the subject spins away. Such a correlate has a long history (Porter, 1993), typified by masculinist fears of loss of control and implicit technological determinisms. Most of all, it is a history which forgets that everyday practices are a part of time-space compression, not something set apart which is there only to react to a larger process. The socio-technical networks that have produced time-space compression are themselves made up of practices which have been sedimented over many, many years and which contain all manner of pre-discursive and discursive responses to and understandings of the spatial and temporal extension of the networks of the social. Similarly the erstwhile consumers of the emblems of time-space compression like the newspaper and now the cinema and television are involved in practices that, again, have evolved over many years and which are not simply reactive (Hermes, 1993; Silverstone, 1994). In other words,

The linking of subjective disorientation and time-space compression is circumstantial. As in the case of the actual postmodern, Jameson or Harvey cannot guarantee that time-space compression will lead to disorientation. It is possible, for example, that the changes in the relation of time and space will lead to novel forms of subjective identity based on new perceptions of time and space. This type of transformation has already taken place in the use of motorised transport and telecommunications where the subject took on board new possibilities and became modern, that is, aware of a range of choices in terms of where to live, where to work, who to live with, etc. . . . There is no reason to believe in the impossibility of such a transformation now. Jameson and Harvey can always bemoan the passing of some 'authentic' identity, they cannot predict the passing of identity in general. (J. Williams, 1992, p. 59)

None of this, of course, is to say that processes like time-space compression do not have detrimental effects and do not contain fundamental asymmetries of power. It is to say that we need to locate these processes on a different ontological and epistemological level, and, in doing so, to refine our notions of what is local, authentic, and so on. In other words, we need new 'chronotopes' (Bakhtin, 1984, 1986), generalised bundles of spatio-temporal practices and concepts (the two cannot, of course, be divorced) which are part-practical and part-representational, like those that Gilroy uses in *The Black Atlantic* (1993a) (these are further explored in Chapter 7).

The third and related challenge to the contextual approach comes from the social theory literature, from those who want to produce two kinds of space of being. Such attempts include those of de Certeau, who makes a distinction between a geometrical order of place, in which two things cannot co-exist, and a practised order of space, in which they can, and also

Deleuze and Guattari, with their distinction between a sedentary, geometric 'striated space' and a nomadic, localised smooth space. Such attempts have a useful symbolic resonance. They also point concretely to the generation of particular bounded spaces of 'exclusion', to deploy a Foucauldian term. But unless they are used with great care they can also come dangerously close to reifying power by allotting to it its own abstract spaces. In practice, all space is anthropological, all space is practised, all space is place. As Casey (1993) puts it, all being is 'im-placed', or, as I would put it, contextualised. It may be implaced in different ways and to different degrees. It may be implaced more or less securely. But being is never out of place.

Each of the six succeeding chapters in this book attempts to make this case. They have all been marinaded in space and the result, I hope, is that they convey certain priorities, priorities like care for contingency and a consequent awareness of the importance of the multiple alternatives that exist in each moment (Bernstein, 1994), devotion to a situated multiplicity of perspectives, allegiance to numerous different and intersecting spatialities (Serres, 1980, 1982, 1987), and attention to detail. In other words, I have wanted, above all, to communicate the brightness of the event.

Notes

1. Parts of this chapter follow *1995e*.

2. Although I have always found the idea of a 'structure of feeling' an extraordinarily useful one (see *1981c*, *1983c*, Chapter 7).

3. For example, recent studies of the landscape as text in cultural geography do not even seem to recognise that there is a problem, yet alone address it.

4. There is an interesting sociology of human geography to be written to account for this paucity of theoretical traditions. Urry (1989) notes that this comparatively small community has been much more heavily policed than many others, a tendency which still periodically manifests itself in sad and bad-tempered debates which pose as substantive but are chiefly, I suspect, about who controls this policing function.

5. Or, put another way, 'Understanding a sentence is much more akin to understanding a theme in music than one may think. What I mean is that understanding a theme in music lies nearer than one thinks to what is ordinarily called understanding a musical theme. Why is just *this* pattern of variation in loudness and tempo. One would like to say "Because I know what it's all about". But what is it all about? I shall not be able to say. In order to "explain", I could only compare it with something else which has the same rhythm (I mean the same pattern)' (Wittgenstein, 1958, part 1, no. 527).

6. Wittgenstein (1958, p. 154).

7. The nearest equivalent I can think of, apart from a musical score, is sign, a set of languages that fold time and space in remarkable ways (see Sacks, 1989). It is interesting that Hägerstrand's work is now becoming better known outside geography than in (see, for example, Gell, 1992).

8. One of Heidegger's grossest errors was, of course, his confusion of conformity with conformism (Dreyfus, 1991). This account avoids this trap, which is not a necessary corollary of Heidegger's work (but see Wolin, 1990, 1993).

9. Remarkably little has ever been made of de Certeau's comments on Wittgenstein.

10. Bourdieu also makes much of different kinds of capital, and although he denies (1993, p. 274) that this schema is a way of saying that 'everything that people do or say is aimed at

measuring their social profit', I am not so sure. In any case, I believe that this side of Bourdieu's work can be dispensed with without causing undue harm to concepts like habitus (see Dreyfus and Rabinow, 1993).

11. However, as Bourdieu notes, at what we might call the Foucauldian limit, the field may start to function as an apparatus 'when the dominant manage to crush and annul the resistance and the reactions of the dominated, when all movements go exclusively from the top down, [and] the effects of domination are such that the struggle and the dialectic that are constructive of the field cease' (Bourdieu and Wacquant, 1992, p. 62).

12. These reasons mean that these authors are left open to the kind of charges that Turner (1994) makes in his (flawed) critique of the social theory of practices. See also *History of the Human Sciences* (1994).

13. I do not note here or elsewhere the vast literature which is now available on non-verbal communication, which now includes an interesting historical edge (see Bremmer and Rodenberg, 1991). As we will see later, in criticisms of Vygotsky's ideas, the notion that gesture is somehow more primitive than, or antecedent to, language has been challenged.

14. This can, of course, be interpreted as a variant on Wittgenstein's points about rule-following.

15. In this section, I hope it becomes apparent that I want to separate out the discursive psychology of writers like Shotter from more general textual turns (for example, Curt, 1994). Whilst quite clearly the body, the subject etc. can be constructed as text, this hardly exhausts all of the possibilities, as Curt (1994) in fact recognises.

16. I am well aware of some of the problems connected with actor-network theory, such as, for example, the practical difficulty of drawing boundaries around each actor-network, and the theoretical accusation that actor-network theory simply avoids the problem of systematic effects. However, there seem to me to be few viable alternatives.

17. The same kind of argument is effectively made by Taussig (1993) in his discussion of mimesis and alterity.

18. In particular, I am concerned that Foucault's history of the subject can be so easily collapsed into a general history of containment, which I think is quite incorrect.

19. Or, again, there are the similarities with Shotter: 'There are several subjects because there is the other person, not the reverse' (Deleuze and Guattari, 1994, p. 16).

20. Quite clearly, it is important to note here the criticisms made by feminist theorists of theories of practice, that these theories are gender-blind or, worse still, call only to male bodies. Like Grosz (1994a, 1994b, 1994c), in her discussions of Merleau-Ponty, I am not convinced that this is exactly the case, but that there *is* a case to answer seems undeniable (I.M. Young, 1990). That case is clearest in the case of sex, sexuality and sexual identity. Here I would want to follow Butler, against writers like Foucault, in arguing that sex, sexuality and sexual identity are marked, live and function quite differently according to whether it is a male or female body that is at issue: thus 'sex is no longer the label of both sexes in their difference as in Foucault's writings, a generic term indicating sexed as opposed to inanimate existence; it is now the label and terrain of the production and enactment of sexual difference' (Grosz, 1994c, p. 140). But, against Butler, I am concerned that too often she equates bodies with practices, rather than reading practices as embodied. (Thus, for example, she tends to omit conversational orders, or subsumes them under a too general concept of performativity.) Like Grosz (1994c, p. 152), I too am attracted to the work of Deleuze, in part because of the ability of his work to produce simulations of passion which are both legible and liquid:

> what one does, or how one does it, with whom and with what effects, are ontologically open questions, . . . sexuality in and for all of us is fundamentally provisional, tenuous, mobile, even volatile, igniting in unpredictable contexts with often unsettling effects: its power, attraction and danger, the fundamental fluidity and transformability of sexuality and its enactment in sexed bodies.

21. In fact, I often feel that Deleuze has produced a wonderful account of the subjectivity of babies, but that his account needs to go much further to take in other forms of subjectivity.

22. In particular, I want to make it clear that the particular does not have to be seen as the

empirical; an equation that Bhabha (1994, p. 188), amongst others, comes close to making. Context acts as a means of theorising the particular.

23. In a sense, Derrida is the most radically contextual of all writers. After all, he holds to two key principles that I would want to support: 'that meaning is always contextual and that no context is ever saturated, completely determinate' (Wood, 1990, p. 56). However, there the similarities end. I believe that Derrida does privilege textual (and other literary) context, albeit in a general structure of 'writing' that includes both speech and writing. I want to privilege everyday conversational contexts, and, ultimately, forms of life. Derrida argues, surely with some force, that each utterance has obtained its meaning in innumerable other contexts. I would want to agree but add an important supplement: that utterance still has to be deployed dialogically in use in a particular situation which restricts its meaning and its promise as a resource. Derrida would probably argue (see Wood, 1990, p. 57) that a practical approach excludes the realms of imagination, fantasy, dream, etc. I would argue that there is no reason why this should be the case (and my appeal to Castoriadis and Deleuze is, in part, a recognition of the need to incorporate these elements). Derrida would want to think about 'play'. I would want to talk about languages, which necessarily make a lot of free play because they are the result of many different creatively managed context-interactions, but which are not thereby unconstrained. Derrida wants to argue for the development of contexts of significance which have a degree of autonomy from everyday discourse, like 'fictional truth' or 'mathematical calculation'. I would argue that such a process has taken place but only to an extent, and that this extent has to be empirically investigated (see the chapters in this book). More generally, I would argue that Derrida too often gets close to a kind of scholasticism, ignores social science research (see Bernstein, 1992) and does not sufficiently frame reading and writing as *practices* (see Chartier, 1989, 1994).

24. I think that time-geography was, in part, an attempt to articulate this kind of ontology.

25. 'In the late twentieth century, we continue to find it difficult to esteem the wild, the atypical, the anomalous, the ungeometrical, the unclear, and the indistinct' (Stafford, 1991, p. 44).

26. It is clear that senses other than sight need to be strongly incorporated into our styles of thought, as writers from Heidegger through to Irigaray have all argued (see Jay, 1993).

27. 'Man [sic], instead of growing better eyes and ears, grows spectacles, microscopes, telephones, and hearing aids. And instead of growing swifter legs, he grows swifter motor cars. . . . Instead of growing better memories and brains, he grows paper, pens, pencils, typewriters, dictaphones, the printing press, and libraries' (Popper, 1972, pp. 238–9).

28. Clearly, the development of writing and texts has had an important effect on our ability to think across contexts, something I address in detail in Chapter 3. The extensive historical and anthropological work on oral cultures and the spread of literacy and the literature on the interface between the reader and the writer paints a very different picture from that of Derrida, Foucault and others. It shows this work to be flawed because the process by which works take on meaning is something of a simplification (if that is possible) 'of the process by which works take on meaning' (Chartier, 1989, p. 161), as a result of not producing sufficient emphasis on the symbolic work of reading, and not giving enough attention to the productions of texts, and not paying enough attention to 'the text itself, the object that conveys the text, and the act that grasps it' (Chartier, 1989, p. 161). This body of work also emphasises the fluidity and complexity of meaning, but it does so in a way which is historically *and* geographically situated. Texts are not everywhere in all times, rhizomatically reproducing themselves. Instead,

we have a choice between two models for making sense of texts, books and their readers. The first contrasts discipline and invention, presenting these categories not as antagonistic but as an interrelated pair. Every textual or typographical moment that aims to create, control and constrain always secretes tactics that tame or subvert it; conversely there is no production or cultural practice that does not rely on materials imposed by tradition, authority, or the market and that is not subjected to surveillance and censures from those who have power over words or gestures. . . .

Discipline and invention must be considered, but so must distinction and divulgation. This second pair of interdependent ideas enables us to posit an understanding of objects and

cultural models that is not reductive to a simple process of diffusion, one generally thought
to descend along the social ladder. The processes of imitation or vulgarisation are more
complex and more dynamic and must be considered, above all, as struggles of competition.
In these struggles every divulgation, conceded or won, produces simultaneously the search
for a new distinction. (Chartier, 1989, pp. 173–4)

29. But, although these elements may be the same, they are, of course, still *practised* very
differently, as numerous reception studies in television have shown. Thus new 'hybrid' practices
come into being, of the kind which are now frequently pointed to in cultural studies and
elsewhere (see, for example, S. Hall, 1991a, 1991b; Gilroy, 1993a, 1993b; I. Chambers, 1994).

30. One particularly important point is that, too often, academics like to fantasise that talk
in business organisations is somehow 'instrumental' whereas their own talk is authentic. How
ridiculous. As Boden (1994, p. 51) points out, 'In most organisations, most of the time, people
mix work tasks with sociable interaction and they do so largely through talk.'

Earlier . . .

Earlier . . .

Looking back on these three earlier chapters, I can now see all manner of unsolved or unseen problems. If I had (foolishly) tried to rewrite them: I would, no doubt have wanted to situate them historically (for example, the emphasis on Marxism in Chapter 2 is, in part, the result of the almost total intellectual hegemony which Marxism held in geography at that time); I would, without a doubt, have wanted to give more space to intellectual currents like feminist thinking; I would certainly have wanted to point to the ways in which these chapters prefigure later work (for example, by connecting Chapter 3 to Haraway's work on 'situated knowledges'); I would have wanted to plot the way in which my thinking changed over the course of writing them (for example, the increasing attention given to social constructionist psychology over the course of the three chapters was, in part, prompted by a critique of Chapter 2 by Shotter [1985b]); and I would want to point to various misappropriations and misconceptions.[1]

I do not want to get involved in retelling history in this way. However, I do not feel that I can pass up the opportunity to give some attention to the matter of Giddens's structuration theory, which, along with the work of Bourdieu, Castoriadis and Shotter, was a strong influence on these three earlier chapters. Initially, I was strongly attracted to structuration theory but, as I become more and more involved in reading other (and especially poststructuralist) writings, this enthusiasm waned. Yet, that said, I still want to keep faith with certain elements of Giddens's ontological framework (which is, of course, only a small part of his copious corpus), and for two reasons.[2]

First, Giddens quite clearly wants to make an ontological turn in social theory comparable with, and to a considerable extent built upon, those two great peripheral theorists of the twentieth century, Heidegger and Wittgenstein. He wants, in other words, to evolve an ontology of everyday social practices.[3] In the most exacting sense, he wants to follow Kierkegaard by reversing Descartes's 'famous starting point': 'I am, therefore I think.'

Second, Giddens, through these attempts to evolve such an ontology, has had to negotiate with many of the themes which have nowadays become associated with poststructuralism. Although I will want to agree with some of his critics that Giddens never fully engages with poststructuralism, it would be foolish to say that he has not negotiated with it at all (as the extensive discussions of Derrida, Kristeva, Lacan and others in Giddens [1979a] or Giddens [1987] all make clear),[4] and by counterposing Giddens's ontology to poststructuralist thought, I hope to provide some fresh insights on both. I want to begin by considering four lacunae in Giddens's ontology, these being recursivity, presence, the unconscious and culture.

In the structuration theory model a large amount of emphasis is placed on recursivity, on the continual, routinised reproduction of practices in varying time-space contexts, a theme drawn in part from time-geography. Recursivity is a means of regularising and stabilising time and space. In small-scale oral cultures, and in what Giddens calls class-divided societies, tradition exerts an iron grip on routine:

> Tradition should be understood as a mode of routinisation by means of which practices are ordered across time and space. Although always open to re-interpretation, tradition is marked by the highest degree of stability when it is not understood by its practitioners to be tradition but is simply 'how things are always done'. With the advent of agrarian civilisations, and the influence of writing, 'tradition' becomes understood as one possible form of regularising time and space. At this point, the traditional becomes open to contestation and active reinterpretation, generating social struggles and clashes. (Giddens, 1989, p. 277)

I find this emphasis on recursivity as unconvincing as do a number of other writers (for example, Gregory, 1989). It seems to me that one of the lessons of the work of writers like Garfinkel, Goffman, Harré and Shotter is that human practices must be seen as far more occasional and inventive than Giddens often seems willing to give them credit for. I would therefore turn away from Giddens's vision of recursive spatially situated social practices to other visions. Most particularly, I am drawn to the model(s) of daily life provided by writers like de Certeau (1984, 1986), discussed in Chapter 1. Thus de Certeau, for example, provides a picture of micro-cultural change, of a 'make it-up-as-you-go-along' world of pliable, opaque and stubborn spaces within which ruses, camouflage and tricks subvert the appearance of routine, and make the determinate indeterminate. As de Certeau (1984, p. 203) notes:

> to eliminate the unforeseen or expel it from calculation as an illegitimate accident and an obstacle to rationality is to interdict the possibility of a living and 'mythical' practice of the city. It is to leave its inhabitants only the scraps of a programming produced by the power of the other and altered by the event.

In more ways than one, this criticism relates to a second and subsequent ones. That is, Giddens's over-emphasis on *presence*. Giddens would, I am sure, deny this criticism, insisting that his emphasis on time-space distanci-ation does the job of both stretching presence and absencing it. But I do not think that Giddens goes far enough here; I am struck by a parallel critique made by Kilminster (1991) and Bauman (1989), which is that Giddens's ontology consists of 'interacting individuals and types of indi-viduals, rather than the plurality of people in webs of interdependencies' (Kilminster, 1991, p. 98). In other words, Giddens over-emphasises action as individual and never fully considers the ghost of networked others that continually informs that action: as does, for example, Shotter with his notion of joint action. In Giddens, too often,

> individuals are seen . . . only in the first person, as positions. There is no conceptual grasp of the perspective from which they themselves are regarded by others in the social web, nor of their combined relatedness . . . people's . . .

actions may have unplanned consequences, which they did not anticipate and cannot control, brought about by the representations of others whom they do not know but with whom they are interdependent. And this process works the other way, not as an interaction or simple reciprocity, but as a functional nexus. Giddens's theorem of individuals 'making a difference' has to be rethought and cleansed of its rationalistic and volutaristic character. (Kilminster, 1991, p. 99)

A third criticism relates to the absence of absence in Giddens's presence. That is, Giddens's impoverished notion of the unconscious. It is, in fact, quite difficult to work out whether Giddens has a theory of the unconscious or whether it is simply a supplement which enables him to privilege practical consciousness and knowledge.[5] At points, he seems to regard it as a basic security system, at other points as a ground of motivation. Boyne (1991) writes, rather too emphatically, of Giddens's 'blatant Cartesianism', but, at least, in this regard, it is hard to dissent from this judgement (see Livesay, 1989).

Fourth, and finally, Giddens has little sense of culture. This may seem an outrageous judgement. After all, Giddens refers constantly to symbolic resources, texts, selves and the like which are the very stuff of culture. He even draws on a constellation of theorists of culture, from Barthes to Bourdieu and from Foucault to Geertz, and yet it seems to me that Giddens's idea of culture is curiously anaemic, precisely because the ties that bind cultures together are constantly created, only partly present and often non-conscious (if they were conscious they could be represented). I do not believe that, for all Giddens's genuflections to Heidegger and Wittgenstein, made explicit in his discussions of practical knowledge, he has ever really developed a *non-reductive* notion that parallels Heidegger's (and, indeed, Wittgenstein's) being-in-the-worldness, which is so clearly brought out in the work of Bourdieu on 'habitus', and other modern writers, like de Certeau. Perhaps this also begins to explain Giddens's relative neglect of issues of gender and ethnicity, which he has recognised (for example, in Giddens, 1989) but only quite recently started to operationalise (see Giddens, 1990, 1991, 1992).

There are clear impacts here for Giddens's whole project of constructing a social ontology, but I think all of these lacunae can be traced, in one way or another, to his limited encounter with poststructuralism (see, inter alia, Giddens, 1987). One of the most important things about Giddens's work is that it takes modern German and North American traditions of theory very seriously (a point made particularly clear in Joas, 1990, and Sica, 1991). This is all to the good. But Giddens often seems to me to take French poststructuralist theory less seriously (even though one might claim that threading through his works can be found more than a trace of Heidegger, a key source for Giddens). Certainly, as I have pointed out, Giddens appropriates many of poststructuralist theory's themes and motifs (the decentring of the subject and power–knowledge relations, for example). But often this appropriation seems to take place without paying sufficient attention to the underlying implications, or, as Boyne (1991, p. 61) puts it,

Giddens too often displays 'a powerful exegetical competence, to the exclusion of serious reflexive application'. Hekman (1990) makes much the same point.[6] Thus, Giddens's idea of the decentring of the subject is a long way from those poststructuralists who 'reject the philosophy of the subject as a version of the origin and recast the subject as a supplement, something both adding to and replacing the absent origin' (Boyne, 1991, p. 68). Even more seriously, Giddens sometimes seems loath to grasp the point of poststructuralism, which is the dismissal of appeals to the referent and the simultaneous contextualisation of normative appeals. The net result is that one cannot fill out all of a society in the way Giddens sometimes, and only sometimes, seems intent on doing. There are limits.

These are all serious, and I think supportable, charges. But care needs to be taken. If nothing else, Giddens's social ontology highlights problems that cannot just be legislated into (and therefore also out of) existence, and, in doing so, his work mounts a set of important challenges to poststructuralism.[7] First of all, Giddens points to a problem with poststructuralist theories that cannot simply be ignored. His work allows us to ask whether the subject does constantly divide, fragment, go astray, whether identity is really just the spacing of a self-address (as Derrida [1988, p. 26] puts it, 'who will prove the sender is the same man or woman?'). People do have boundaries of a kind, as an extensive literature in social psychology makes clear, and these boundaries are defined by constantly evolving inner stories, by processes of recognition (hailing) which include bodily inscription, and by disagreement. There is an excluded middle here, where subjects can still quietly and faintly function as objects, and the possibility, at least, of 'theories' of this middle. Perhaps we do not need to make quite such a stark choice between Giddens's project of forging a post-Cartesian subject and an evangelical poststructuralism (represented, if I can use such a word, by Boyne, 1991) in which the subject is *only* a collective representation, a mytheme generated by the social unconscious.

Second, neither Giddens nor the poststructuralists have had the last word on the unconscious, but Giddens does at least point to other ways of framing the unconscious than those offered by Freud, and Lacan's readings of Freud, which in turn have fostered an increasingly insular and aestheticised literature of claim and counter-claim. Thus, as Macey (1991, p. 333) points out, over the last decade 'innovative work in psychoanalysis has . . . been marked by a turn away from Lacan and by a growing interest in the work of British authors like Winnicott . . . the irony is that these authors are *persona non grata* on the Anglo-American interface between psychoanalysis and feminism.' At least they are not *persona non grata* in Giddens.

Third, poststructuralists have a notion of culture which is, I think, attenuated because it glosses over shared practices situated in time-space. If there is a charge that Giddens cannot be accused of then this is surely it. Thus, Giddens has a sense of a world where textual structures of signification (and note I do not say texts) are a part of shared practices, not the whole of them, and of time-space as quite central to shared practices. So far as time-space is concerned, Giddens has repeatedly stated his suspicion of a notion of society (although he still half-heartedly uses it) and has insisted on a notion of interconnecting social systems that, as in actor-network theories, are constantly realised spatial and temporal orders. This vision is important for poststructuralist work because, contrary to the work of some geographers who have played up the 'spatial bits' of post-structuralist texts, I doubt that time-space has ever been, with the possible exception of the work of Deleuze and Guattari, a major poststructuralist preoccupation. Derrida, for example, is a radical contextualist but his work is curiously lacking in context (except, perhaps, in his work on the postal principle with its geography of chance events). Perhaps this neglect (which in some sense is an odd one given the Heideggerian ancestry of much poststructuralist work) is because poststructuralist authors confuse fixity with stasis. As Bryant and Jary (1991, p. 13) put it, 'in Derrida and others, "mentalism" and "formalism" may give way to notions that admit the importance of time and location in the analysis of both language and society, but the outcome is a view which sees *only* movement.' So far as shared practices are concerned, Giddens has made it clear that he regards language and textuality as an important part of shared practices, but not as the whole of these practices. Thus, his notions, for all the flaws and lacunae noted above, still seem to me to provide much more of a sense of being-in-the-worldness, with its emphasis on orientation, encounter, embodied pedagogy and sheer physicality, than many poststructuralists who (again, ironically, given their Heideggerian roots) often only seem to glimpse, or play off, these issues.

I want to illustrate these points further by referring to one of Giddens's most important books, *Modernity and Self-Identity* (1991). Now I should say straightaway that I have considerable problems with the notion of modernity (as I do with the concept of postmodernity, and for the same reasons). It contains too many echoes of what D. Sayer (1991) calls that old 'Victorian hubris', the modern world's self-image of its own historical distinctiveness which seems to me to constitute a kind of orientalism over history.

That said, I will begin by briefly outlining some of the main themes of the book. As is by now well known, Giddens believes that the western world is currently in a condition of 'high modernity'. In it, we live in a world of tensions: on the one hand, there is a strong globalising influence arising from the emptying of social space and its filling up by large bureaucratic organisations, based on systems of concentrated reflexive monitoring, like multinational corporations, state apparatus, financial systems, and the like; on the other hand, selves are coalescing around projects of identity in a way apparently not found before in history, the result of far greater reflexivity about the form the self can take, which in some part comes from the multiple techniques for constructing and monitoring identities that large bureaucratic organisations have developed.

In this world of high modernity the sum total expertise about the world has accumulated massively but it has also become, partly because of this expansion of expertise, increasingly contingent and overlapping, 'the result of a puzzling diversity of options and possibilities' (Giddens, 1991, p. 3) from which choices can be made. Thus, doubt is an all-pervasive phenomenon of high modernity. But this condition of soaring doubt can be damped down and this is achieved via a combination of systems of trust and constant assessments of risk which are aspects both of personality and of institutions. Giddens makes much of the importance of risk in high modernity, both because certain endemic risks (such as certain forms of environmental pollution) are the direct result of processes of globalisation and because the consequences of incorrect assessments of risk become rapidly clear to all through what J.B. Thompson (1990) has called 'quasi-mediated electronic interaction' (or telephones and television!). In this sense, we live in the world as never before. (Quasi-mediated electronic interaction has other important effects as well, for example through its impacts on projects of self-formation and through the new forms of narrativity it engenders.)

For Giddens the high modern has a more open social texture than previous eras because of the multiplication of contexts in which action can take place and the numerous different 'authorities' that can be drawn on. The result is that active choice of lifestyle has become increasingly important in the constitution of self and daily activity. One aspect of this choice is the growing construction and importance of ideas of 'pure relationship' between people. These relationships exist for themselves through mutual disclosures and often draw on new forms of expertise which are also becoming increasingly systematised.

The increasingly reflexivity of the self and (the increasingly calculated) choice of lifestyle have other impacts too. In particular, the body is mobilised; increasingly the body is a manifestation of lifestyle choices and options. Again, experience becomes cloistered, with people living in settings set apart from others which mean that they only rarely make contact with major existential dilemmas. In other words, and to summarise, what we see here is an actualisation of the Sartrian project of the self, but this actualisation is divorced from the moral meaning which was meant to be its motivation.

The last part of *Modernity and Self-Identity* looks at ways in which moral meanings are being injected back into high modernity through new forms of what Giddens call 'life politics' based around substantial moral issues: ethics makes a determined come-back. Giddens's conclusion (1991, pp. 223–4) is worth quoting at some length:

> life politics brings back to prominence those moral and existential questions represented by the core institutions of modernity. Here we see the limitations of accounts of 'postmodernity' developed under the analysis of poststructuralism. According to such views, moral questions become completely denuded of meaning or relevance in current social circumstances. But while this perspective

accurately reflects aspects of the internally referential systems of modernity, it cannot explain why moral issues return to the centre of the agenda of life politics. Life-political issues cannot be debated outside the scope of abstract systems: information drawn from various kinds of expertise is central to their definition. Yet because they centre on questions of how we should live or lives in emancipated ways they cannot but bring to the fore problems and questions of a moral and existential type. Life-political issues supply the agenda for the return of the institutionally repressed.

Some of Giddens's theses are quite close to those of other authors. For example, some of them come close to Habermas's work on the colonisation of the lifeworld. Others are near to Ulrich Beck's (1992) already seminal work on risk societies (see Beck et al., 1994). There are little bits of Laing, Winnicott, Elias and many others as well. But where Giddens scores is in the power of the overall synthesis he offers, and this is, I think, always suggestive precisely because of the connections that he makes between the many, diverse literatures he draws on.

At the same time, and more importantly, I think that *Modernity and Self-Identity*, and the books that have followed it, *The Transformation of Intimacy* (1992) and *Beyond Left and Right* (1994), indicate quite important incremental shifts in the nature of Giddens's social ontology of everyday practices from his earlier work. I will point to just three of these shifts out of many, because I think they start to answer some of the criticisms of Giddens I laid out above. First, by taking on the work of Winnicott on early childhood, for example, Giddens is able to fashion a more convincing account of the relationship between the importance of creativity, the creation of the other, time-space absences and a generalised condition of anxiety[8] (or, rather, 'anxious readiness'). Thus, the infant is a 'going-on being' which has to be hailed by the time-space environment which the parent carer provides. The infant goes through frenzied periods of 'creative madness' which provides her or him with an early, unconscious sense of 'not-me' (this socio-spatial separation is, of course, important in the Freudian model too; for example, as Macey [1991, p. 335] points out, 'the famous fort–da game is not merely a play of signifiers but a spatial play of gestures which are gender-differentiated and which may induct boy and girl into different symbolic spaces'). Second, Giddens pays more attention to embodiment than before. Of course, in previous work Giddens (1984) has always noted the importance of the body, especially by reference to Foucault and Goffman, but what is interesting is the concreteness of what Giddens now proposes. Finally, Giddens continues to develop his links to the later Wittgenstein, as the fount of his ontology. By continually going back to Wittgenstein, as he has done since at least *New Rules of Sociological Method* (Giddens, 1976), Giddens is able to stress the importance of 'what cannot be put into words' in a period when a number of word idealisms still seem to be on the loose. As Giddens (1991, p. 205) puts it:

Post-structuralist thought is now beginning to exert a strong influence in English-speaking sociology, particularly as filtered through debate about modernity and post-modernity. But I believe Wittgenstein's work to be of more enduring importance. Wittgenstein's specification of 'differences' as mediated in the praxis of language games, seems to me superior to that filtered through signifiers or 'discourse' as understood in post-structuralism.

Giddens's connection to the later Wittgenstein forms a vital aspect of his work and yet, extraordinarily, it is hardly taken up in most critiques of his work. The point is that Wittgenstein's formulation of the arts of living does provide, at the very least, a supplement to poststructuralist approaches, and quite possibly a complete alternative. In this context, Giddens's reworking of some of Wittgenstein's themes and especially his sustained emphasis on the practical organisation of everyday social life as the ground of what can (and cannot) be said seem to me to be absolutely vital.

Yet there is one way in which I think Giddens still needs to develop his ontology and, ironically perhaps, it is in the matter of the practices of everyday life. I will try to develop this final point by returning to Heidegger and Wittgenstein. For Heidegger the spaces of everyday life have an elaborate structure which it is the job of his existential analytic to sort out, but not explain. His specialised vocabulary, like the time-geography of Hägerstrand (which was partly based on Heidegger), and a number of the conceptions of Giddens (some of which are based on Heidegger and time-geography), are all attempts to find terms that can describe the thisness and presupposedness, the continual hum of what Wittgenstein, Searle, Taylor and others have called, without detriment, the background.[9]

Now Heidegger and Wittgenstein agree on many things. Both are trying to dispose of a certain picture of the self as a centred stream of experiences that are its essential content, both would agree that we are chiefly involved in a creative coping with others that occupies most of the day, and so on. But, as I have pointed out, they *do* differ on certain issues, and the portrayal of everyday social practices is one. In particular, Wittgenstein is clear that the practices that make up the spaces of everyday life are not reducible; they simply have to be accepted. Wittgenstein surely goes too far here, but it seems to me that it is this Wittgensteinian sense of non-reducibility, indefiniteness and the limits to clarity which is too often missing from Giddens's account of everyday socio-spatial practices. In a way, perhaps, Giddens is too close to Heidegger (although in the moments when he seems to be attempting to smuggle in consciousness he is never further away) and too far from Wittgenstein. Perhaps, like the later Heidegger, he still yearns for something behind the spaces of everyday life, if not a ground then at least a storm anchor.

To conclude, I have made a number of criticisms of Giddens, but as is also clear, I believe that he still offers some important insights into the nature of practices which other authors have prematurely rejected. To summarise, I will point to two of these.

First, Giddens does offer at least a partial way out of what increasingly seems to have become, at least by implication, an opposition between grand theories and knowledges and the local, situated theories and knowledges that are now so much in vogue, precisely by suggesting the need to take geography seriously. For, as the world has globalised, so the technologies of *self* and *cognition* have also become more global: we can know others in ways that would not have been open to us before. Self and cognition have become everywhere mediated. This is not to say that local theory is not in some sense possible; it is to say that what we can regard as 'local' has changed, probably forever, and so have the conditions of theory and knowledge generation (Birmingham, 1989; Probyn, 1990; Haraway, 1991).

Second, Giddens asserts the importance of still doing social theory in a particular way. To read some writers nowadays, social theory is essentially a modernist, masculinist project, continually filling out the social world and thereby repressing otherness and difference. Now, I am not saying that such social theory doesn't exist – it does – but I would still defend Giddens's work against such a charge. Giddens's notion of social theory is in the altogether more modest Wittgensteinian mode of *seeing connections through illuminating comparisons* (Monk, 1990); theory is quite simply a way of clarifying one's ideas for emancipatory purposes. In other words, theory is limited, but it is still important.

Notes

1. For example, in Chapter 2, I misappropriated the idea of alterity. I misconceived Bourdieu as a 'structuration theorist', something that he has subsequently denied frequently; although I think he protests too much (see Bourdieu and Wacquant, 1992). I came too close to trying to provide a representation of practical activity (see Shotter, 1985b; although I think that Shotter misunderstood part of my argument). And so on.

2. This section is taken from a review essay in *Progress in Human Geography* (*1993b*).

3. One might, of course, argue about whether these ontological moves aren't actually epistemological moves brought in by the back door, so to speak, but that is another matter.

4. Giddens's extensive discussions, and limited incorporation, of poststructuralism are conveniently ignored by many commentators: they do not fit the prevailing idea of Giddens as a kind of latter-day Sorokin.

5. One has, however, to be careful in a critique of Giddens's ideas of practical consciousness/knowledge. Some commentators seem to regard them simply as a way of smuggling an individualistic behaviourism back in, and of setting up a set of oppositions (subject/object, individual/society, conscious/unconscious, etc.) in an age of non-oppositional thinking. Giddens's position, born out of Heidegger and Wittgenstein, is much more subtle than this and simply shows up the ignorance of these commentators.

6. However, Hekman's (1990) criticism that Giddens does not offer a viable epistemology for his social theory completely misses the point of Giddens's Heideggerian and Wittgensteinian roots.

7. Although this draws back from what I think is the most telling charge against much poststructuralism, namely that it constitutes an anthropomorphic ontology. As Bhaskar (1991, p. vii), in rare Wittgensteinian mode, puts it:

A picture has indeed held philosophy captive. It is a picture of ourselves or our insignia in any picture – the picture as invariably containing our mirror-image or mark. Philosophical post-narcissism will be evinced in the exercise of our capacity to draw non-anthropomorphic pictures of being.

Another charge that can, I think, be rather easily put is that poststructuralism too often leans towards the merely clever, without any deeper sense of consecration (which is why I prefer Kierkegaard and Wittgenstein). However, on this point, see the moving defences by Wood (1987) and Derrida (1987). Arguably, there is an exception to this argument, in the form of Foucault, but I think it should also be noted that geographers have constructed a geographer's Foucault which only ever partially existed and which cannot, I think, be made to exist.

8. Shades of Kierkegaard and Heidegger intervene here.

9. It seems to me that the early attempts of Lefebvre to investigate what he called 'everyday life' (before he began to equate the spaces of everyday life only with programmed consumption) offer something of the same spirit of inquiry (although from a very different perspective):

> But we are unable to seize the human facts. We fail to see them where they are, namely in humble familiar objects; the slope of fields, of ploughs. Our search for the human takes us too far, too deep, we seek it in the clouds or in mysteries, whereas it is waiting for us, besieging us on all sides. (cited in Trebitsch, 1991, p. xxiv)

2

On the Determination of Social Action in Space and Time

> If social relations are not understood as the *real essence of man* [*sic*] (in other words, as the fundamental explanatory basis of everything which concerns man) then men, conversely, will not be understood on the basis of the social relations as their essence, and in one way or another, one will fall back into an idealist conception of man.
>
> (Sève, 1978, p. 426)

Introduction: The Problem of Translation[1]

In the last few years, human geographers have become more and more involved with social theory. This involvement has ranged from the extreme determinism of some structural Marxist approaches, which hope to read off the specifics of places through the general laws or tendencies of capitalism, through to the extreme voluntarism of most 'humanistic' geography,[2] which hopes to capture the general features of place through the specifics of human interaction. But I think it is true to say that, because of the nature of human-geographical subject matter, extant social theory has proved very difficult for human geographers to handle. The reason for this is quite simple. It is very difficult to relate what are usually very abstract generalisations about social phenomena to the features of a particular place at a particular time and to the actions of 'individuals' (as discussed later, this is a difficult and problematic term to use) within that place. Of course, this is not a problem peculiar to human geography. Social historians have been having something of the same problem as the focus of their subject has moved from 'the circumstances surrounding man [*sic*] to man in circumstances' (L. Stone, 1979, p. 23); in particular, as this subject has moved to the use of selective examples of 'individuals' to illustrate the 'thinking in–acting out' of *mentalité*.

How is this problem of *translation* to be overcome; indeed, can it be overcome? Conventionally, the problem is now represented in human geography as a polarisation between social structure and human agency, a polarisation that is also known in the guise of the debates on the relative importance to be given to economy and culture or to determinism and free will. Certainly, at present, words like 'agency' and 'experience' are virtual talismans in human geography. Their mention provokes knowing nods around the seminar room, perhaps because these terms seem to suggest an almost self-explanatory criticism of social theory as presently constituted. But, in fact, there are at least four major strands to this outwardly homogeneous reaction to the problem of the relation of structure to agency. At the limit, the implication is that altogether too much ground has been ceded to structural social theory.[3] This is a proposition that appeals, naturally enough, to empiricists, who deal only in the given as it gives itself and who continually mistake a minute description of some regularity for theory. But it also finds allies amongst humanists, who pine for an anthropological philosophy with the category 'man' at its heart. (It is interesting to note that in *The Poverty of Theory and Other Essays*, E.P. Thompson [1978], at points, actually makes *both* these mistakes.) A second response, one favoured by certain Marxists, is that social theory was never meant to be applied to the small-scale and the unique. An either/or situation is assumed to exist. The choice is either general theory or unique description. No doubt, this reaction is partly due to a reductionism that characterises some Marxist analyses, both of the concrete to the merely abstract and of social science to philosophy.[4] But perhaps it is also partly linked to a view of social theory that is still wedded to a conception of (social) science and scientific statements as merely being generalisations about social phenomena. (This chapter, therefore, is 'realist' in intent [cf. A. Sayer, 1981].) It is an unintended consequence of this view that 'consideration of the possibility of coming to terms with the unique aspects of situations (as against their common characteristics) within a generalising frame of reference is neglected because of the seeming refractoriness of the problem to the conventional canons of scientific analysis' (Layder, 1981, p. 49). The significance of small-scale human interaction is therefore bound to be minimised. A third view is that a major shift is required in the theoretical centre of gravity of social science that will lead towards a new 'structurationist' problematic based upon a theory *of* social action (or practice) that complements theories *about* social action (Dawe, 1979). This is a view that has gained considerable support in human geography (for example, see Carlstein, 1981; Gregory, 1981; Pred, 1981b) and is now being put forward as the touchstone of recent developments in other subjects, for instance in historical sociology (Abrams, 1980, 1982) and in administrative science (Ranson et al., 1980). A fourth view, the one to which I shall subscribe in this chapter, is that it is possible to produce general knowledge about unique events, but that this is best achieved through the intertwining of these structurationist concerns with existing, specifically Marxist, social theory, because Marxism, for all its very definitive sins and omissions, has a strong notion of *determination*. No doubt such an extension will prove anathema to many Marxists, but, to foreshadow the argument,

> it is unclear why a preoccupation with the material practices of everyday life – or for that matter the structure of popular belief – is either Utopian or undesirable from a Marxist point of view. Nor is there any reason to counterpose the personal and familial with global and overall views. (Samuel, 1981, p. xxi)

This does not mean, however, that I am in favour of the 'rambling impressionism' (Abrams, 1982, p. 328) which it is possible to find in certain texts that have been concerned with, for example, daily life in the past. Rather, I am looking for a theoretically structured approach to the 'real world of real human beings', which is not 'held at a safe distance by [the] extreme forms of idealist abstraction' (Selbourne, 1980, p. 158) that are so characteristic of a substantial proportion of the Marxist tradition.

This chapter is therefore arranged as follows. A general synoptic overview of modern social theory lends to a consideration of the four major concerns of what I shall call the structurationist 'school'. I will want to argue that these concerns are crucial to any non-functionalist Marxist social theory, which must take into account 'contextual' as well as 'compositional' determinations. I will then sketch, in the final section of the chapter, an outline of what such a social theory might begin to look like when extended to the smaller scale and to the consideration of unique events. A new kind of regional geography/sociology would be integral to this project.

The Two Responses to the Problem of Structure and Agency: Determinism and Voluntarism

Most social theory is not reflexive. It does not consider its own origin in the theoretical and practical thought of a period, as this is determined by the prevailing social and economic conditions. Thus it does not consider what there is to be thought and, in particular, what material is present that can provide the simple metaphorical equivalence on which human 'language-thought' is based (cf. Bourdieu, 1977; Lakoff and Johnson, 1980; Keesing, 1981; and see *1979f*). Yet no social theorist can, other than very partially, escape thinking in terms of the society she or he is socialised into. Why, otherwise, was Marxism, an admittedly determinist set of theories, born under the crushing economic imperatives of the nineteenth century (*and* the labour unrest that accompanied it). Similarly, it is quite impossible to believe that there is no connection between the pessimistic view of society of the Frankfurt School and the Weimar and National Socialist Germanies of the 1920s and 1930s. Theories as diverse in their content and aims as the various forms of Marxism or phenomenology are all bound both by the limits of the knowledge they can utilise and by the ways they can combine this knowledge in theories which are imposed upon them as a result of being children of the same society at a particular time. In particular, social theory born under capitalism must reflect many of the features of capitalism and, in particular, the basic contradictions of this system.

Since the Enlightenment, and the intellectual vacuum caused by the gradual dwindling away of notions of cosmic order, humankind has been beset by two tendencies, partly causes of and partly the result of capitalism. The first has been the tendency towards the seemingly ever-greater scale and extent at which the production and reproduction of society takes place; a tendency marked off by such indicators as the continuing concentration

and centralisation of capital (Marx), the dramatic increase in and concentration of population (Malthus), the growth of the State and the
penetration of its bureaucracy into every corner of our lives (Weber, the
Frankfurt School), rapid time-space convergence and the formation of all
those 'masses' – mass education, mass consumption, mass culture, and so
on (Arnold, Veblen, the Frankfurt School).[5] The experience of these
phenomena is now commonplace in our daily lives. But for the nineteenth-
century middle and upper classes, from which so many significant social
theorists were drawn, these were new experiences that were conceived as
real and immediate problems. To give but one example, domestic and
foreign visitors to Manchester in the early nineteenth century constantly
remarked upon the vast and noisy working-class crowds, whether these
crowds were celebrating at a fair or a wake, demonstrating at a Chartist
rally, shopping at night or even travelling to and from work. There was a
general sigh of relief as the workers filed into the factories and workshops
where they could be neatly closeted away for the day (Storch, 1977). It is
therefore not surprising that for the nineteenth-century middle class the
problem of scale was above all perceived as centring on words like 'order'
and 'control' and on the question of how social order could come about or
was possible in such rapidly changing circumstances.

To deal with the changing situation, new practical and theoretical
categories are formulated and old categories are revised. The idea of a
population to be counted out and analysed, the idea of a moral topography
and the whole semantic field of political economy (containing such
terminology as 'manufacture', 'industry', 'factory', 'class', 'capital', 'labour'
and finally 'industrial revolution') gradually all come into being (Bezanson,
1922; R. Williams, 1976; Foucault, 1977; Tribe, 1978, 1981; Briggs, 1979;
Jones and Williamson, 1979). Above all, the medical metaphor of the
anatomy of society leads to a concern with 'structural' explanation
(Ginzburg, 1979, 1980b).

This tendency was reinforced by the one that grew up beside it. The
conception of the individual had gradually and decisively changed – to its
precise antithesis. In medieval times 'individual' meant inseparable or
indivisible (R. Williams, 1961, 1976; Weintraub, 1978). A 'single individual'
would have had no meaning. The relatively closed and static medieval
community was one founded on a minimal division of labour and the
sharing of many tasks. The system was based on the control of social
interaction in order to limit interactions to members of the known social
world. Everyone therefore knew everyone else and there was no need for
a particularly developed system of control and surveillance. It could be local
(cf. Giddens, 1981). This system gradually gave way, for a variety of
interrelated reasons that eventually led to capitalism – the increasing
division of labour, the rise of wage labour, the rise of calculative rationality,
the increase in urban populations, and so on – to a strong individuality
based upon the concept of human rather than divine will, on the idea that a
human being had a choice over the form of self that might be sought, and

to self-control (Weintraub, 1978). The connection between individuality and the problem of social control is once more a strong one. The idea of the individual acquires its modern secularised meaning in relation to the state (rather than the church) (Foucault, 1977; Elias, 1978, 1982). Through all number of new institutions like the civil service and the police, the state gradually builds up a 'grid of intelligibility'. Everyday life is brought into scientific discourse (Smart, 1982).[6] Individuality is linked with identification; as a concept, individuality now pertains to specific social groups and to the idea of an individual as a set of developing attributes describing a 'career' over time (Ginzburg, 1979). The individual is made an operational concept, the object of scientific knowledge (Foucault, 1972). The underlying epistemology is again medical, but it is now based on the diagnosis of symptoms. It leads directly to the deciphering of signs, as in semiotics, and to Freud.

In capitalism these two tendencies come together as a major contradiction between socialised production and private appropriation. Capitalist societies are both collectivist and individualist. On the one hand, each individual lives in a highly socialised world; on the other hand, each individual lives in a privatised world (Brittan, 1977). The position is uneasy and ambiguous. This tension, I submit, is as obvious in social theory as it is in everyday life (Dawe, 1979).[7] These two contradictory tendencies, pulling either one way or the other, are therefore found in most nineteenth- and twentieth-century social theory. Thus each particular social theory tends to stray, in varying degrees, towards either the determinism of capitalist society or to the voluntarism of capitalist individuality. Thus there are 'two' sociologies (Dawe, 1970, 1979), 'two' anthropologies (Sahlins, 1976), 'two' Marxisms (Albrow, 1974; Veltmeyer, 1978; Gouldner, 1980; S. Hall, 1980), and so on and so forth. In reality, of course, such a distinction is a simplification of the highest order. Most social theories, and variants thereof, put forward by particular 'individuals', are an admixture of both dimensions, and are best represented as points of a continuum between the two polarities.

In a related and important way, social theory tends towards either the *compositional* or the *contextual* (Hägerstrand, 1974b). (Simpson [1963] and Kennedy [1979] make a similar distinction between *immanent* and *configurational* approaches.) In the compositional approach, which reaches its apogee in the 'structural-genetic' method of Marx (D. Sayer, 1979; Zeleny, 1980), human activity is split up into a set of broad structural categories founded on the property of 'alikeness' and derived via a formal-logical method based on the tool of abstraction.

The Structurationist School: Towards a Non-Functionalist Social Science

That Valéry is a petit-bourgeois intellectual is beyond doubt. But all petit-bourgeois intellectuals are not Valéry. The heuristic inadequacy of

Marxism – and, let us add, of the traditional biographical method – is contained in these two statements. To grasp the processes which produce the person and his [sic] production within a given class and society at a given historical moment, Marxism lacks – and so does sociology – a hierarchy of mediations. . . . [One must] find the mediations which can give birth to the concrete, singular life and the real historical struggle, out of the general contradictions of the productive forces and the relations of production.

(Sartre, 1960, pp. 44–5, my translation)[8]

In the preceding section, I tried to show, albeit briefly, that a basic duality, one that can partly be traced to capitalism, lies at the heart of modern social theory between determinist and voluntarist approaches and between their versions of human agency, respectively, 'plastic' and 'autonomous' man [sic] (M. Hollis, 1977). Can this duality be recast in such a way that it dialectically recombines social structure and human agency? Certainly this is the hypothesis of a number of authors who espouse, in one form or another, a theory of 'structuration', elements of which were first put forward by Berger and Luckmann (1966), but which has now reached maturity with the more sophisticated 'recursive' or 'transformational' model proposed by Giddens (1976, 1977, 1979a, 1981), Bhaskar (1979) and Bourdieu (1977).[9] It is important to emphasise that the theories put forward by these three individuals have strong differences, but the similarities are, I think, still sufficiently great for these authors to be described as belonging to a structurationist 'school'.

Four common concerns unite these authors. First, they are (explicitly or implicitly) anti-functionalist. That is, they recognise that functionalist 'explanation' is simply an evasion.[10] At one point, Giddens (1979a, p. 7) likens his project to *'show[ing] what a non-functionalist social science actually involves'* (my emphasis), and this might well be taken to be the motto of the structurationist school, for each of the other three shared concerns flow into and out of this node.

The second concern is a common message, that neither a structural-determinist (objectivist) nor a voluntarist (subjectivist) approach is satisfactory, joined to a common goal, to link these two approaches together in a dialectical synthesis. Structural-determinist approaches are criticised because they treat human practices as being mechanical and devoid of creativity, what Castoriadis (1987) and others have called 'alterity',[11] the quality of newness. Voluntarist approaches, on the other hand, are equally problematic because, in concentrating on interaction, they become blind to the fact that

interpersonal relations are never, except in appearance, individual-to-individual relationships . . . the truth of the interaction is never entirely contained in the interaction. This is what social psychology and interactionism or ethno-methodology forget when reducing the objective structure of the relationship between the individuals to the conjunctural structure of their interaction in a particular situation or group. (Bourdieu, 1977, p. 81)

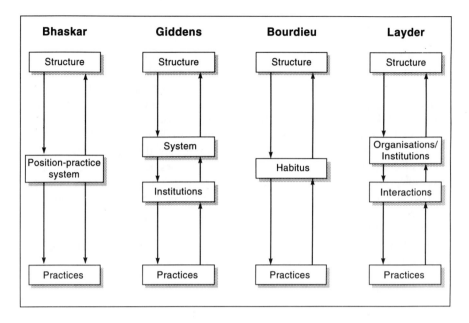

Figure 2.1   *Mediating concepts in the schemas of various members of the structurationist school*

No, social structures are characterised by their *duality*.[12] They are constituted by human practices, and yet at the same time they are the very medium of this constitution. Through the processes of socialisation, the extant physical environment, and so on, individuals draw upon social structure. But at each moment they do this they must also reconstitute that structure through the production or the reproduction of the conditions of production and reproduction. They therefore have the possibility, as, in some sense, capable and knowing agents, of reconstituting or even transforming that structure. Hence, the 'transformational' model (Bhaskar, 1979). Social life is therefore fundamentally recursive (Giddens, 1979a) and expresses the mutual dependence of structure and agency. Social structure cannot exist independently of motivated (but not necessarily reasoned) activity, but neither is it simply the product of such activity.

However, by far the more important problem is how to forge a non-functionalist link between structure and agency. Here individual members of the structurationist school differ in their approach (see Figure 2.1), but no doubt each would concur with Bhaskar (1979, p. 51) that

> we need a system of mediating concepts . . . designating the 'slots', as it were, in the social structure into which active subjects must slip in order to reproduce it; that is, a system of concepts designating the 'point contact' between human agency and social structures.

What these Sartrian *mediating concepts* are differs from author to author. Bourdieu's (1977) answer is to insert a third 'dialectical' level between social structure and human practices, a 'semi-structure' called 'habitus' consisting of cognitive, motivating ('reason-giving') structures that confer certain objective conditions and predefined dispositions on actors based on the objective life-changes which are incorporated into the strategies involved in particular interactions, these interactions being improvisations regulated by the habitus. Thus each class, for instance, has a particular habitus that results from a common set of material conditions and, therefore, expectations (Pinçon, 1978; Garnham and Williams, 1980; Acciaoli, 1981). Each mode of production has, so to speak, its own modes of perception. Giddens (1979a), by contrast, refines existing concepts. For example, structure is limited in its meaning to rules and resources, to particular structural properties. An essentially new concept of 'system' is then added as reproduced and regular social practices. Institutions are the basic building blocks of these social systems. Finally Bhaskar (1979, p. 51) offers the rather more general concept of a position-practice system; he argues that

> it is clear that the mediating system we need is that of *positions* (places, functions, rules, tasks, duties, rights, etc.) occupied (filled, assumed, enacted, etc.) by individuals, and of the *practices* (activities, etc.) in which in virtue of their occupancy of these positions (and vice versa) they engage.

A third major tenet of the structurationist position is the lack of an explicit theory of (practical) action (Giddens), of the acting subject, of a theory of practice (Bourdieu) in most of social theory. (Such a theory should not be confused with sociological theories of individual action [for a review of which see Lazarsfeld, 1972].) There is, therefore, a need for an explicit theory of practical reason and practical consciousness that can account for human intentionality and motivation. This project is vital for three reasons. First, as already pointed out, there is no direct connection between human actions and social structure in social theory. Indeed the properties possessed by social forms are often very different from those possessed by the individuals upon whose activity they depend. Thus motivation and intentionality may characterise human activity, but they do not have to characterise social structure or transformations in it. Second, it is also obvious that ordinary people do not spend their whole time reflecting upon their social situation and how to change it. Indeed much of their thinking is bent towards actually carrying out pre-assigned tasks with no definite goals in mind. And third, there is no reason to believe that when an actor does rationalise an act it will necessarily be the real reason why she or he is doing it (Mills, 1959). Thus,

> people in their conscious activity, for the most part unconsciously reproduce (and occasionally transform) the structures governing their substantive activities of production. Thus people do not marry to reproduce the nuclear family or work to sustain the capitalist economy. Yet it is nevertheless the unintended consequence (and inexorable result) of, as it is also a necessary condition for their

activity. Moreover, when social forms change, the explanation will not normally lie in the desires of agents to change them that way, though as a very important theoretical and political limit it *may* do so. (Bhaskar, 1979, p. 44)

It is therefore important to make a distinction between *practical* and *reflexive* (or discursive) consciousness and reason. Practical activity is not theorised reflexively. Practical consciousness is 'tacit knowledge that is skilfully applied in the enactment of courses of conduct, but which the actor is not able to formulate discursively' (Giddens, 1979a, p. 57). The reasons an actor gives for an action are not necessarily the real ones – which *may* operate outside the understanding of an agent. They are part of a set of 'reason-givings', which must, of course, relate to the real reasons, but which can be refracted or even reflected back as their inverse.[13]

The fourth major component of the structurationist case, one that is necessarily related to the third, is that time and space are central to the construction of all social interaction and, therefore, to the constitution of social theory. This does not just mean that social theory must be historically and geographically specific. More importantly, social theory must be about the time-space constitution of social structure *right from the start*. Thus, for Giddens (1979a, p. 54), 'social theory must acknowledge, as it has not done previously, time-space intersections as essentially involved in all social existence'. Such a viewpoint has a number of important consequences. Social structure, for example, cannot be divorced from spatial and temporal structure. The two have to be theorised conjointly (see Giddens, 1981; Gregory, 1982), not as the impact of one upon the other. Further, human agency must be seen for what it is: a continuous flow of conduct in time and space constantly interpolating social structure. Such a view of human agency is necessarily *contextual*. As Bourdieu (1977, p. 9) puts it: 'practices are defined by the fact that their temporal structure, direction and rhythm are constitutive of their meaning'. The point is that human action takes place in time as a continual time- (and space-)budgeting process and as an irreversible sequence of actions. There is no doubt that social theory, which has a time that is only partly that of practice, has tended to forget this. Yet it is the *ad hoc* improvisatory strategy imposed on people's practices by the fact that they have a limited time in which to carry out particular activities (and a limited time in which to decide to do them) that is a crucial part of practice, practical consciousness and practical meaning. Practice, therefore, is always situated in time and space. This is one link to structure for the structurationists, since the places at which activity is situated are the result of institutions which themselves reflect structure – home, work, school, and so on. These institutions form nodes in time and space around which human activity is concentrated. As Giddens (1979a) points out, this is an area that human geographers, through the study of 'time-geography', have been particularly involved in for the last few years (Hägerstrand, 1970, 1973, 1974a, 1982).

These, then, are the four common elements of the structurationist school. In the next section I will argue that they provide an important means of progressing towards a non-functionalist Marxism. However, in order to justify this claim it is important, at this juncture, to understand what I take to be at the core of Marx's work and what, in effect, I consider to be 'historical materialism'. For me, Marx's work has a threefold significance. First, it subscribes to the simple transhistorical fact that at the core of all human social structure is 'the production of material life itself'. Second, and at the next level of abstraction, social structure is constructed around particular organisations of production which characterise particular times and places. One aim of 'historical materialism' is to uncover the 'mechanisms'[14] which underlie these organisations. Third, 'historical materialism' tries to reconstruct the 'concrete in thought' (and not the empirical, which is inevitably contingent) as the result of the successive addition of determinations from different levels of abstraction. When placed together these determinations form a hierarchical set of dynamic or process categories (cf. D. Sayer, 1979; A. Sayer, 1981; Zeleny, 1980). I consider other intermittently important features of Marx's work to be more period- and place-specific. As Giddens (1979a, 1981) notes, some of these features must be seen as the excess baggage of nineteenth-century thought. They are therefore transitory. These features include functionalism, evolutionism and essentialism (see Keat and Urry, 1982). Yet other features can now be seen to exist at a different level of historical specificity to the level at which Marx considered them. Thus, in the light of recent research, the overarching transhistorical statement 'the history of all hitherto existing society is the history of class struggles' is more properly considered at the more historically specific mode-of-production level of abstraction (cf. Giddens, 1981).

The Implications of the Structurationist School for Marxist Social Theory

> It is easier to turn against the initiators than to take them further.
>
> (Lefebvre, 1976, p. 57)

The interpenetration of the insights of the structurationist school with Marxism to form a non-functionalist Marxism will be no easy task. The problem is well put by Giddens (1981, p. 16):

> In diverging from functionalism . . . we need to be able to recognise *both* what might be called the theorem of 'knowledgeability' – that we are all purposeful, knowledgeable agents who have reasons for what we do – *and* that social processes at the same time work 'behind our backs', affecting what we do in ways of which we are unaware. Marx summed this up in the famous aphorism, 'Men make history, but not in circumstances of their own choosing'. However, working out the implications of this unobjectionable statement is difficult.

What seems certain is that the structurationist approach cannot simply be laid alongside Marxism (see Wiener, 1981).[15] The implications of the approach are more far-reaching than this and demand a thorough reworking of Marxism. But neither is the approach so far removed from at least some interpretations of Marx as to make this an impossibility. For example, the second element in the structurationist approach, that social structure is both constituted by and the medium of human agency, can be interpreted as being consistent with Marx's model of society. Bhaskar (1979) approvingly quotes Marx (from Marx and Engels, 1965, p. 65) thus:

> History is nothing but the succession of the separate generations, each of which exploits the materials, the capital funds, the productive forces handed down to it by all preceding generations and thus, on the one hand, continues the traditional activity in completely changed circumstances and, on the other, modifies the old circumstances with a completely changed activity.

This is not to suggest, however, that the marriage will be an easy one. In particular, the writings of members of the structurationist school suffer from a number of failings. First, they provide no clear notion of *determination*. Marxism can be criticised for many things, but at least the forces and relations of production on which it has concentrated give it a strong notion and scheme of determination. Although the structurationist school acknowledges the strength of the forces and relations of production (see especially Giddens, 1981), the complexity of determination that is provided in their schemes is obviously much greater (Gregory, 1982). Partly, of course, this is the result of a concentration on other things; for example, the constitution and reproduction of individual subjectivities (Bhaskar), cultural capital (Bourdieu) or authoritative resources (Giddens). But partly it is also the result of an unresolved ambiguity about the relative importance of economic determination which sometimes allows structurationist models to appear far more individualist and voluntarist than is the intention (see Clegg, 1979, and Layder, 1981 for criticisms based on this misunderstanding). Second, *conflict* is dealt with only in the most axiomatic and general way in the writings of the structurationist school. Third, and closely related to the second point, although Giddens, for example, proclaims that history is indistinguishable from social science, his notion of history still tends to the systematic and general. The use by the structurationist school of history remains firmly compositional rather than contextual,[16] and this has important implications. For the structurationists, Perry Anderson's (1980, pp. 21–2) judgement on E.P. Thompson is no less valid:

> A *historical,* as opposed to an axiomatic, approach to the problem would seek to trace the curve of (deliberate) enterprises, which has risen sharply, in terms of mass-participation and scale of objective, in the last two centuries, from previously low levels. Even so, however, it is important to reveal that there are huge areas of existence which remain largely outside any form of concerted agency at all. . . . The area of self-determination has been widening in the past 150 years. But it is still very much less than its opposite. The whole purpose of historical materialism, after all, has precisely been to give men and women the means with which to exercise *a real popular self-determination for the first time in history.*

The point of historical materialism is to allow conscious, directed and reflexive human agency to become the social structure. It is ironic, then, that the whole point of Marx's work, to identify in an objective and rational fashion the bounds to human agency so that social structure might be refashioned, sometimes seems to be seen by the structurationist school as deterministic, although actually it is (or, at least, tries to be) a realistic assessment of the prevailing conditions under which agency must work or has had to work.

These reservations apart, the benefits that would flow from the interpenetration of Marxism and the structurationist school are many. Certainly, there is no all-embracing panacea to be found in Marx for the problems that beset Marxism now (Giddens, 1979b). Most obviously, the problem of functionalism has to be solved. This will require a change in the orientation of Marxism towards a number of new areas of study which are not just additions to the domain of Marxism but are integral to the revision of Marxist theory.

The Reproduction of Labour-Power

Nearly all the new areas of study are to be found grouped under the problem of an adequate account of the reproduction of labour-power within the realm of practices, of the constitution and reproduction of individual subjects, which Urry (1981a, p. 39) calls 'civil society':

> The problem is that labour-power, unlike all other commodities, is not produced by capitalists for profit. It is produced, or reproduced, in the sphere of civil society. So while all other commodities are produced within capitalist production, labour-power is produced elsewhere, outside capitalist relations of production.

In *Capital* labour-power is relevant only insofar as it enters, active and refreshed, into the sphere of production. The reproduction of this labour-power and the constitution of labour-power as a conscious subject are things Marx dealt with barely, if at all. Concrete individuals, worker and capitalist alike, are depicted only to the extent that they are 'personifications' or 'functionaries' of economic categories (Molina, 1979; Urry, 1981a); that is, as instances of the economic existences of men and women undifferentiated by other determinations. Of course, it can be argued, as Perry Anderson (1980) does, that the subjects that have to be dealt with when the reproduction of labour-power is acknowledged to be important, such as the different historical forms of everyday life or the formation of human individuality, were outside the substantive domain of Marx's interest, as was a theory of ethics or, at an even further remove, as were subjects in the natural sciences like biology or physics. Considering the period and place in which he lived, so Anderson's argument goes, it is not surprising that Marx's major concern was the economy and that the only tools available to him were French socialist thought, German idealist philosophy and English political economy. Sociology, psychology and a host of other modern areas of knowledge simply did not exist to be drawn upon. No doubt this argument is substantially correct, but it does not in any way excuse the necessity of revising Marx's social theory to take such concerns into account now, nor does it temper the urgency of the task.

Some Marxists, of course, regard all efforts to deal with individuals as somehow irredeemably humanist. There is, however, nothing in Marxist literature that leads to this conclusion; not even, indeed, in the work of that most anti-humanist of all Marxists, Althusser. As Molina (1979, p. 239) points out, Marx

> explicitly formulates a clear distinction between a theoretical treatment of individuals as *personifications* (as bearers of economic categories) and a treatment of individuals as individuals (according to individual differences which do not arise from the economic relation itself). The question and its answer correspond clearly to a difference between what is the problem of the states of the category of 'individual' in Marx's theory and what would be the problem of a theory of individuality as such, the latter problem not being present in Marx.

Thus the problem of individuals and individuality is not closed off in Marx; rather individuals appear shorn of every determination except those coming from economic relations. On this skeleton, however, can be hung the flesh of other, more contingent determinations. Marx, then, provides a set of theoretical principles with which to think both the problem of conceptualising the different historical laws of the existence of individuality and the most basic determinations of that individuality. Other Marxists, quite accurately as we have noted, see problems like everyday life and the formation of individuality as still lying outside the substantive domain of Marxism, and they then extrapolate from this current state of affairs to reach the conclusion that such subjects must forever remain beyond the pale. There is, however, little evidence to justify this stance. In particular, there are three objections. First, one of the consequences (and indeed one of the goals) of Marxist theory has been the continuing 'transformation of domains in which a Marxist theoretical practice does not yet really exist' (Althusser, 1969, p. 169). This transformation will surely continue. Second, it might well be argued that the continuation of such a myopic view only reproduces capitalism in the theoretical domain of Marxism. For, of course, one of the most significant features of capitalism is its indifference to the particularity and individuality of and between its elements[17]. And third, Marxism, unless it is assumed that it already encompasses all that it is significant to know about social practice, can gain from contacts with new material. There must surely be the possibility that certain lacunae in Marx's theory can be filled in, that Marxism can be developed by such contact just as it develops what it contacts. The reproduction of labour-power, then, is of crucial importance, in particular as it informs and makes concrete the study of three closely interrelated areas of Marxist analysis: class conflict, ideology and hegemony, and personality.

Human labour-power is unlike other commodities. Because it has creative capacities it is the source of expanded capital and profit. But it is also a source of resistance. Such labour-power has conscious will, it is possessed of *agency* (Willis, 1977). As Yeo and Yeo (1982, p. 147) put it:

> The act of selling labour-power is not the same in meaning whenever and however it is done. . . . What does the labour-power actually consist of? It is abstract only for the purpose of commensuration. How is it seen and valued by the sellers and buyers? What is its meaning in relation to the rest of life? What is obtained, denied, dreamed of in return for the sale? All these questions are historical and material, not abstract and transcendent and not to be answered by any single theorised version of a constant, still less a hierarchical relationship between work and leisure. The wage relation is more than an economic one: producing things entails relations: relations are *social*, between whole beings who exist, including capitalists, in many dimensions.

Labour-power, its scale, its purchase, its existence, this is the subject of conflict. And class conflict is meant to occupy a central place in the Marxian framework. Yet all too often, in Marx and in subsequent Marxist analyses, class conflict occupies an interstitial, functional position sandwiched between capital and labour and acting more like a coefficient of friction between the two warring blocs than as a central dynamic. Tribe's (1981, p. 32) criticism of the Brenner/Dobb position in the 'transition from feudalism to capitalism debate' is just as relevant elsewhere:

> The gap was, however, tentatively closed through the invocation of politics. The Marxist precept, 'the class struggle is the motor of history', is inserted between the shafts of the feudal wagon and is encouraged to drag the immobile economic order of feudalism into capitalism through periodic dialectical interventions. But this 'politics' on closer inspection turns out to be constituted by a projection of economic relations onto a space which they already occupy: politics is used to explain the contradictory progress of the economic order, but it is itself no more than an expression of this order. Notwithstanding such difficulties, 'politics' does the job: the gap between feudalism and capitalism is closed and an orderly genesis is re-established.

It is little wonder, then, that Marxism has no adequate theory of 'politics' and that there is still little idea either of how the process of class structuration (Giddens, 1973) in the realm of practices takes place (that is, as the formation of *social* classes within civil society [Urry, 1981a]) or of how class awareness and class consciousness are constituted, notwithstanding the explanations by E.P. Thompson (1963) and J. Foster (1974). Similar problems beset Marxist notions of how the dominant order is maintained, especially outside work. Categories like ideology and hegemony have been, of course, the subject of notoriously functionalist usage (see Abercrombie et al., 1980); further, they are often wielded in such a general and abstract fashion that it is difficult to use them to capture the diversity of practices in civil society (see Urry, 1981a). Finally, Marxism has no adequately developed theory of concrete human personality. Indeed, as presently constituted, it cannot have.

The filling out of each and every one of these three areas of analysis, with their emphasis on everyday life and the formation of individuality, demands the development of a contextual dimension to Marxist theory, a dimension which can be constructed only by building upon the major elements of structurationist writing: the importance of non-functionalist links between structure and agency, practical reason, and time and space intersections. The investigation of subjects like class conflict, ideology and hegemony, and the formation of personality all demand not only a measure of theoretical generality but also a theory that can deal with specificity as a *theoretical* as well as an empirical object. For example, part of the reason why some people do certain things at certain places in certain periods while other people at other places in other or the same periods do not, or why different forms of protest and patterns of organisation arise in apparently similar conditions (Bleitrach and Chenu, 1979; Groh, 1979; Lojkine, 1981), is quite specific to particular contexts, to particular *places*. In brief, there is a need to develop a *contextual science*, a sociology of detail or, as others have called it, 'sociopsychology' (Bhaskar, 1979), the 'science of the singular' (Sève, 1975) or the 'science of the specific' (Layder, 1981), in which determinations can be traced out as they occur in particular individuals and particular groups of individuals in a particular locality.

Some Problems

How, then, do we obtain a non-functionalist theory which 'neither reduces interaction to the exclusive and mechanical effects of structure nor reduces structure to the accomplishments of actors, or the outcome of their interactions' (Layder, 1981, p. 94)? How, in other words, do we cross from the compositional to the contextual? Certainly, the problem of moving between social structure and human agency cannot be as simply resolved as, for instance, a Marxist like Hobsbawm (1980, p. 7) attempts to make out in his discussion of the apparent movement of analysis in social history to smaller scales:

> There is nothing new in choosing to see the work in a microscope rather than a telescope. So long as we accept that we are studying the same cosmos, the choice between microcosm and macrocosm is a matter of selecting the appropriate technique.

There are, in fact, formidable problems in studying in a theoretically informed way from a Marxist viewpoint subjects such as class conflict, hegemony and ideology, and personality formation as they occur in everyday life. To name but two of the more immediate difficulties:

1   Participants in the processes of class formation, class awareness and class consciousness often perceive only the concrete events and experiences that impinge on their own collective lives in a particular area. To assess the impact of these events and experiences on participants' actions is a formidable task.

2   The lived *interrelationship* between various 'segments' of life is crucial to this process, yet it is nearly always studied in a *fragmented* way as 'the family', 'the factory', 'sexuality', 'housing', and so on. As Foster-Carter

(1978, p. 75) puts it, current Marxist analysis sometimes seems to resemble 'little rock pools increasingly unconnected to one another, in which narrowly circumscribed issues are discussed separately and without thought of their mutual implications'. The *generality of individual action* is lost. So, therefore, is its theoretical promise.

Layder (1981) provides one particularly interesting means of making a non-functionalist link between the compositional and contextual. He points, first of all, to objective social structure. This objective structure consists of two main types of structure, *formal and substantive*. Formal structure exists at a high level of abstraction and influences action in a diffuse way. It consists of a set of process categories like class, the tendencies of capital accumulation, and so on. Substantive structure refers to the actual sites of interaction, the level of institutions. Finally, and crucially, there is an *interaction* structure within which actual human interaction takes place. Each type of structure is relatively autonomous and there is no necessary connection between them. Rather this connection is historically contingent (Figure 2.1).

The crucial point is that agents produce, in the first instance, an interaction structure. This structure is situation-specific, and it is 'over-determined', that is, certain activities are simply reproductive (of the interaction structure), and can be unimportant from an analytic point of view. The reproduction or transformation of social structure is very rarely dependent upon *particular* instances of human interaction. The concept of interaction structure also points to the fact that human behaviour is never simply a function of the objective social structure (or structures) that constitute the conditions of existence. The connections can be direct, but equally they can be oblique or even *non-existent*. The task is to sort out what these connections are and their degree of importance.

A Non-Functionalist Theory of Social Action in Space and Time: A Research Agenda

> What a man [*sic*] makes of his life and what his life makes of him, that is what I want to understand.
>
> (Sève, 1975, p. 19)

In this final section, I want to sketch in some of the components of what an historically specific, non-fragmented, contextual theory of human action, which at the same time has clear lines of communication to a compositional theory about human action, might look like. I will want to be able to incorporate the four structurationist concerns into this outline without reducing it, however, to just them. Thus the outline stresses the integral importance, for example, of practical reason and action and of concrete interaction in time and space.

What follows at this juncture is, of necessity, programmatic and skeletal. And little of it is novel. Many parts of the outline are already being filled in by various workers, most especially in social history, historical sociology and historical anthropology, but also now in human geography and regional sociology. My aim here is to stress two things: first, the essential *unity* of the concerns of workers in many subject areas; and, second, the very great importance of *empirical* investigations as a necessary moment in any social theory. Along the way, I also hope to show that there is a place for a *reconstructed regional geography* (a regional geography that builds upon the strengths of traditional regional geography, for example the feel for context, but that is bent towards theoretical and emancipatory aims) (A.R.H. Baker, 1979; Gregory, 1981), not only as the focus of all these divers concerns, but also as the subject and object of a theory of social action. The 'region' (I expand upon this term below) can be seen, in this conception, as the 'actively passive' (I have borrowed this term from Sartre) meeting place of social structure and human agency, substantive enough to be the generator and conductor of structure, but still intimate enough to ensure that the 'creature-like aspects' (Heller, 1982, p. 21) of human beings are not lost.

It is important to note at the outset, however, the compartmentalised nature of this account. This is, at one level, an admission of failure; social activity in any region takes place as a continuous *discourse*, rooted in a staggered series of shared material situations that constantly arise out of one another in a dialectically linked distribution of opportunity and constraint, presence and absence. A region is lived *through*, not in. The term 'discourse' is intended to convey something more than the fact that human communities exist socially through the medium of language, important though this aspect is (Pred, 1981b). It is also intended to convey the wider sense of a lived world of material practices implicit in Raymond Williams's (1977, p. 110) notion, which is different from a number of the meanings used by Gramsci, of *hegemony* as a silent but deafening contextual field:

a wide body of practices and expectations, over the whole of living: our senses and assignments of energy, our shaping perceptions of ourselves and the world. It is a lived system of meanings – constitutive and constituting – which as they are experienced as practices appear reciprocally confirming. It thus constitutes a sense of reality beyond which it is difficult for most members of the society to move beyond in most areas of their lives. It is, that is to say, in the strongest sense a culture, but a culture which has also to be seen as the lived dominance and subordination of particular classes.

Further, 'discourse' must be seen as an *active* category. The inhabitants of the culture or cultures of a region must not be seen as simply the passive recipients of class or any other social relations, as cultural dupes for whom socialisation is simply conditioning. This would be to fall into the trap of the functionalism that underlies all social control explanations (Stedman Jones, 1978; Peet, 1982; Yeo and Yeo, 1982). Rather, each culture has *limitations* and an ability to *penetrate* the existing order, the one often being linked to the other (R. Williams, 1977). For example, Willis (1978, p. 6) has shown that even commodities, which are, after all, the hallmark of capitalism, have uses other than blind consumption:

> Though the whole commodity form provides powerful implications for the manner of its consumption, it by no means enforces them. Commodities can be taken out of context, clarified in a particular way, developed and repossessed to express something deeply and thereby to change somehow the feelings which are their product. And all this can happen under the very nose of the dominant class – and with their products. We might even say that the characteristic of a certain kind of creative cultural development is the exploitation of qualities, capacities and potentials in those profane things which the dominant society has thrown aside, produced as 'business' or left undeveloped for cultural meaning.

No doubt, any reconstituted regional geography can start conventionally enough with a compositional account of 'the regional setting'. This involves, first of all, all those geographical determinations that can be grouped under the general heading of topography: such things as geology, hydrology and climatic conditions, which have likely been changed already by the impacts of societies over the years. An account of the organisation of production in a region is then needed, which involves ascertaining the level of the productive forces and the form of the productive relations, concentrating on the labour process (Dunford, 1981).[18] This emphasis on production leads, under capitalism in particular, to an outline of the class structure of a region and to the history of class formation, themes which are inevitably cross-cut by other divides: the prevailing sexual division of labour, of course, but also ethnic, racial and religious divisions. Finally, the local form of the state must be taken into account. Already written into such a compositional analysis is the *possibility* of quite dramatic inter-actions along the boundaries of one or all these divides. Wilson (1981, p. 68), for example, demonstrates how feuding and the institution of the vendetta in Corsica were implicit in an extremely complex socio-economic system which

> included transitional pastoralism alongside horticulture and itinerant cereal culture on land away from centres of population, collective land use alongside private property, work in family units on land of both kinds alongside share cropping and wage labour, and dependence on mutual aid within and among families to carry out basic tasks.

A compositional account of a region is obviously a difficult enough task in itself, both theoretically and empirically. Perhaps it is for this reason that most analyses stop at this point. But, since the concern here is with developing a (contextual) theory of social action that can interpenetrate and ultimately change the conventional (compositional) theoretical account about social action, it is necessary to go one step further. The process of discourse in which human agency is produced and spun out cannot be reduced to a compositional account without jettisoning the very qualities that make it a discourse; the intricacies of interaction, the specificity of particular times and spaces, the sense of living as meeting, the context.

The Locale

To constitute a region as an interaction structure requires a notion of interaction that is mediated by institutional correlations with social structure. The region, initially at least, must not be seen as a *place*; that is, a matter for investigation. Rather, it must be seen as made up of a number of different but connected *settings for interaction.* Giddens (1979a, 1981) uses the word *locale* to carry this meaning. It is a useful term and I will adopt it here.

Any region provides the opportunity for action and the constraints upon action; that is, the base for what is known about the world and the material with which to do (or not to do) something about it. In any region the *life paths* of particular individuals *can* interact, simply because they are collateral, near to one another in time and space. Whether they *will* inter-act, however, depends on the particular pattern of production (and, in a related way, consumption), and that, in turn, results in (and stems from) a particular pattern of locales that punctuate the landscape. Each life path is, effectively, an *allocation of time* between these different locales. In any particular organisation of production, certain of these locales will be *dominant*; that is, time *must* be allocated to them. They are economic (and state) imperatives. Under capitalism, for example, home (reproduction), work (production) and, later, school (reproduction) are determinant. (Under other modes of production other nodes might be determinant. In Bali, for example, religion takes up more time than even work.) These dominant locales provide the most direct link between the interaction structure of a region and objective social structure, because they are the main sites of class production and reproduction. Such locales have five main effects. First, they structure people's life paths in space and time. They provide the main nodes through which a person's life path *must* flow and, since these locales are class-structured and/or class-differentiated, they will structure people's life paths in ways that are class-specific (Figure 2.2). As Therborn (1980, p. 23) puts it:

> being 'in the world' is both *inclusive* (being a member of a meaningful world) and *positional* (having a particular place in the world in relation to other members of it, having a particular gender and age, occupation, ethnicity, and so on).

Second, these institutions can have effects on *other* people's life paths through the constraints they place on a person's ability to interact with other people engaged in activities within them. Third, they provide the main arenas (in time terms) within which interaction with other people takes place; thus they are sites of class and other conflicts, the medium and the source of most practical and reflexive reason, and, generally, the major context in which knowledge-experience about the world is gathered and common awareness engendered. Fourth, they provide the activity structure of the day-to-day *routines* that characterise most parts of most people's lives. (The importance of routine as a 'second-order' or 'officialising' strategy [Bourdieu, 1977] cannot be overestimated, since routine can quickly

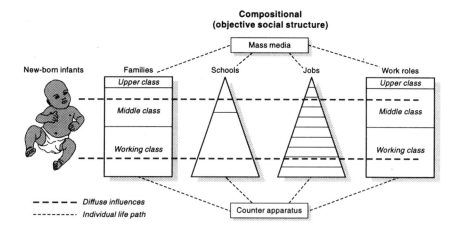

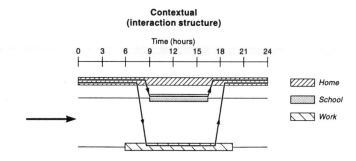

Figure 2.2 *The life path seen as a compositional ordering and a contextual field (adapted from Therborn, 1980, p. 87)*

make pieces of behaviour appear not only natural but also disinterested.) And fifth, they are the major site of the processes of *socialisation* (seen in the active sense) that take place from birth to death within which collective modes of behaviour are constantly being negotiated and renegotiated, and rules are learned but also created (Ricouer, 1981). It is also important to consider the particular internal *organisations* of time and space *within* each type of dominant locale (which Giddens [1981] calls 'regionalisation'); that is, to look both at the routines that characterise different homes, different workplaces, and so on, and at the content of each locale in terms of accumulation of knowledge-experience. In the workplace, for instance, the spatial and temporal organisation of the particular labour process, and how this varies from industry to industry, will be crucial (cf. Bleitrach and Chenu, 1979, 1981).

To these dominant locales must, of course, be appended the consideration of the position and internal organisation of interrelated institutional locales (in particular, locales at which consumption activities take place), which will, within a particular organisation of production, sometimes be of importance and sometimes not. To say that these institutions are dependent upon the dominant locales for their existence and importance is not to denigrate them, it is simply to situate them within a particular historical pattern of determination. For instance, under capitalism the allocation of time to 'leisure' (a specifically capitalist term) is determined, in the first instance, by hours of work. Thus, in many of the industrial areas of early nineteenth-century England, the pub was the only important extra-domestic leisure institution, because hours of work (combined with income) made any alternative problematic. Finally, it is important to consider the *counter-institutions* that challenge the ruling orthodoxy (Therborn, 1980). Such institutions often tend to be coincident with other sites, like those of work and school; indeed they often grow up in reaction to them. Their importance (especially as focuses of human agency) varies with history and location. The reasons for such variation are addressed below.

The study of the effects of changes in the functioning of such institutional locales on people's life paths is now becoming quite common. For instance, Hareven (1975, 1982) and Pred (1981a) have considered how changes in work hours and the organisation of work each rebounded on the organisation of family life and 'leisure' time in nineteenth-century United States. Similarly, Stedman Jones (1974) and Thrift (*1981e*) have documented how changes in work hours and the rise of compulsory primary education led to corresponding changes in the nature of the family, the social definition of home and the use of 'leisure' time in nineteenth-century England. Joyce (1980) has considered, in some detail and in specific regional settings, how the factory became the dominant focal point of lived experience and popular culture in nineteenth-century English factory towns, and, importantly, how the flow of factory life spilt over into the (few) hours outside work, into the form that home, school and leisure took.

It is important to point out that, increasingly, a locale does not have to be local. The phenomenon of time-space convergence has meant that the setting for interaction common to certain social groupings has become differentially more extensive. For example, the middle class typically acts out its presence in a more extensive spatial setting than the working class. Interaction is more often at a distance. Factors such as commuting and the increased mobility associated with many white-collar jobs have ensured that this is so. Further, as the locales of social groupings have become more differentiated by their spatial extent, so they have become more fragmented by a process of homogenisation that is the result of factors like the influence of a relatively free housing market and the housing estate, the advent of mass media and educational systems, and so on. Space is increasingly created as a series of commodified enclaves (mobility is crucial in differentiating these spaces), within which at least parts of everyday life can be carried on by one social group in isolation from other social groups (Lefebvre, 1971, 1976; Giddens, 1981; Soja, 1983). Giddens (1981) calls this a tendency to 'sequestration' and relates it to the rise of so-called 'total' or 'greedy' institutions like asylums and hospitals as well as to commodification in the strict sense.

But these tendencies do not mean that the *region*, seen as a particular intersection of these locales, has therefore lost its coherence or its distinctiveness. Common experiences engendered by the mass media, common school curricula or the homogenisation of residential space are still mediated by distinctively local references. Moreover, although the circumference of most parts of everyday life may have increased with practices like commuting, most individuals still follow well-worn paths during most parts of their daily existence. Even more importantly as a result of distinctive and cumulative historical patterns of class and other forms of social differentiation, the social complexity of regions has probably, on the whole, increased rather than decreased, bringing with it richer possibilities of interaction. This observation is enhanced by Urry's (1981b, p. 464) argument that variations in local class structures have not only been ignored but are also of increasing importance: 'Important changes in contemporary capitalism are at present heightening the economic, social and political significance of each locality.' And, of course, the complexity of locality can be appropriated as a resource. Crossick (1977), for example, has argued that in the late nineteenth and early twentieth centuries the English middle class seized upon local politics as a means of exerting influence, an observation that might be extended to much of the current literature on urban social movements.

Four Aspects of Social Action

To capture the sense of social action as discourse through and in a region is no easy task, and it is true to say that, as yet, this goal has not been achieved, although it is often enough hinted at. Programmes like those of the structurationalist school remain provisional and all too often are linked to rather general statements backed up by three or four references to particular cases. A concentrated programme of theoretically informed empirical research is needed if this theoretical elaboration is not to occur in a vacuum (see Appendix to this chapter). In this final subsection I will consider only four particular pre-theoretical aspects of this programme which seem to me to be amongst the most pressing. These may be considered as an affirmation of the importance of studying human agency and social structure as a duality, but more importantly as an historical and geographical inquiry into the respective variations in this duality, as they are fought through in conflict, in particular contexts.

Personality and Socialisation: The Historical Geography of Life-Path Development Personality can be seen as the total constellation of an individual's psychological characteristics and it therefore subsumes the different aspects of personality, such as conception of *self* (Rosenberg, 1979), *identity* (Robertson and Holzner, 1980; Abrams, 1982) and *individuality*.

Personality necessarily involves the three sets of relations that Giddens (1979a) considers necessary for a theory of the subject – the unconscious, practical consciousness and discursive or reflexive consciousness. Seen in the contextual sense, personality is a constant *process* of 'internalisation' or 'interiorisation' of social relations along the course of a life path set within civil society. 'Social relations penetrate the body, structure its psychic "central fire"; psychic structure is social structure alive in the heart of the body' (Bertaux and Bertaux-Wiaume, 1981a, p. 174). Personality, therefore, can never be universal. Rather it is a continuously negotiated and renegotiated expression of social and economic relations that vary, in other than their most basic form, according to locale and region.

Sève (1975, 1978) has provided the most complete interpretation of what a materialist and contextual theory of human personality might look like as a 'general theory of the concrete individual'. In this conception every adult personality appears as a series of sedimented activity-experiences carried forward in time at the tip of the life path. These activity-experiences have taught us 'how to do' and therefore 'how to be', messages which are constantly reaffirmed by the routine of everyday life, but which may also be reinterpreted in the light of new activity-experience – memory is an active not a passive process. Sève argues that at the core of personality is an historically (and, by implication, geographically) specific structure of allocation of time to particular activity-categories.[19] Personality, therefore, is an expression of the *objective social logic* of this variable set of activities into categories; in other words, you are what you do and you do what you are. (This representation, although now situated in the context of particular individuals, is not so very different from Bourdieu's [1977, 1980] notion of habitus).

Quite obviously, a conception of personality like this could, if taken to its logical conclusion, come dangerously close to the idea of individuals as cultural dupes and as merely an encapsulated microcosm of social relations. This makes it even more imperative to stress the transformative side of the individual, which, in turn, must be seen as an aspect of the penetrative possibilities of the society and region in which she or he is situated. An individual is a product of social interaction rather than of individual action. Therefore the study of personality involves, necessarily and integrally, the study of *socialisation* as a process of domination and resistance, the one dialectically linked to the other. Willis (1977), for example, shows how some working-class schoolchildren build up a resistance to mental work out of their resistance to the authority of school. Manual work is invested with seemingly opposite qualities to mental work – aggressiveness, solidarity, sharpness of wit, masculinity – and becomes a positive affirmation of freedom. Here resistance has the effect that working-class schoolchildren accept working-class jobs through 'free' choice. They willingly embrace their own repression (Abrams, 1982).

The historical study of personality and socialisation is a rapidly growing field, most particularly in terms of the literature on education and the reproduction of class (for example, Bettelheim, 1969; Holzner, 1972; P. McCann, 1977; Gerger and Hoppe, 1980; Schlumbohm, 1980), the family (for example, Hareven, 1975, 1982; L. Stone, 1977; Flandrin, 1979; Elder, 1980) and, of course, the *mentalités* tradition of French history (for a critical review of which see Darnton, 1978).[20] But it can also be found grouped around more particular themes: for instance, puritanism (for example, Bushman, 1967; Demos, 1970; Watkins, 1972; Delaney, 1976; Greven, 1977) or fascism (for example, Merkl, 1975, 1980). Even in literary theory and semiotics, the study of personality and socialisation is in evidence. For example, Bakhtin (1968), in an extraordinary study, has considered the socialisation effects of the experience of folk culture on the writing of Rabelais. Rabelais's life path was submerged in and washed by the stream of folk culture rather than by official 'high' culture. Each of these diverse perspectives is able to add to the concept of personality as a continuously socialised trajectory varying with time and space in time and space.

The beginnings of a contextual approach to personality and socialisation, which has been hinted at in these studies, brings to light an obvious complement to them, which is important enough to be separated out because, in particular, it gives some notion of the uneven flow, when seen in a life-path perspective, of highly differential processes of personality formation. Divisions in society do not occur just because of grand compositional relations such as class, sex or race. The more mundane but just as important forces of time and space are also at work. Perhaps one of the most important of these forces is the population cohort into which an individual is born,[21] since this influences an individual's life chances, subsequent history of socialisation and 'structure of feeling' (R. Williams, 1977, 1979, 1980).[22] Particular cohorts, sorted by social groups, have different collective experiences of period and place, and, compared with other cohorts, they experience the impact of particular events differentially. These factors mark out their personality from those of other cohorts. Studies abound of the collective experience of, for example, the First World War (for example, Wohl, 1980) or the Depression (for example, Elder, 1974). The context provided by a region is also sometimes studied. For example, Elder (1981) traced the life courses of two groups which had roughly similar socio-economic characteristics and whose members were born in 1928/9 in Oakland and Berkeley, California, through to 1950, a period covering the Depression and the post-war boom. The two cohorts had markedly different histories of personality formation, which were partially dependent on the context of the places themselves.

Penetration and the Availability of Knowledge   The study of ideology and hegemony is tainted, seemingly inevitably, by functionalism. In the three most extreme cases, ideology becomes a level or instance which acts as a receiver of the impulses of the economy, or ideology is passed down to the working class by capital and uncritically accepted, or everything is reduced to a constituent part of an overwhelming 'ideological state apparatus'.[23] In the contextual sense, neither ideology or hegemony can be seen in these ways. Rather, within the overall structure of discourse, certain social practices may have 'ideological' or 'hegemonic' effects, which are not, however, necessarily functional to the continuation of the existing dominant order and which may, indeed, not have had their origins in that order (Urry, 1981a). And what effect these practices have on particular individual subjects is highly contingent and depends on the balance of other social practices. Certainly, it is doubtful that a general notion of ideology or hegemony can contribute much to the actual analysis of particular societies. Rather, it is more appropriate to consider, as has been pointed out above, the degree of understanding of or penetration into the existing social order that particular social groupings (and, therefore, the individuals within them) can achieve. Such an understanding will always be contingent and will always be linked to various limitations on that understanding, so that no social grouping will ever achieve more than a partial penetration into the conditions of its existence. Seen in this way – as a creative process of limitation and a limiting process of creation – a number of factors can be considered. An important one is variability in the availability of knowledge, which will depend upon the particular setting of a region and will be mediated by class and other group memberships as they are present in that region. At least five types of interrelated *unknowing* can exist in a locale or region at any one time (*1979f*):[24]

1   *unknown*, and not possible to know, in terms of being totally unknown at a particular time, either to a society, a locale, or a region, or to members of them;
2   *not understood*, in terms of not being within the frame of meaning of a society, a locale or a region, or not being with the frame of meaning of certain members of a society, locale or region;
3   *hidden*, in terms of being hidden from certain members of a society, locale or region;
4   *undiscussed*, in terms of being taken for granted as 'true' or 'natural', either by a society, a locale or a region, or by certain members of them; and
5   *distorted*, in terms of being known only in a distorted fashion by a society, a locale or a region, or certain members of them.

Studies on the spatially variable acquisition of written[25] knowledge and ideas have become quite common in social history, although usually at the large scale (for example, Burke, 1978; H.J. Martin, 1978; Darnton, 1979; Eisenstein, 1979). However, studies are beginning to appear on the process of acquisition of reading material with application to more local areas (for example, Judt, 1979; Ginzburg, 1980a; Spufford, 1979, 1981; cf. R. Williams, 1980). These studies show the strong effects of isolation on what a person knows. Similarly, studies of the specific effects of mass media are becoming more common (see R. Williams, 1980). Such studies must combine the diffusion of knowledge with information about the institutions through which this knowledge has diffused. Such institutions usually have had particular degrees of class allegiance and bias, which structure the information that is disseminated. In nineteenth-century England, for example, one might consider the distribution of the Mechanics Institutes, but equally the Radical press, as well as the spatially differential impact of schools of various types (for example, see Laqueur, 1973; Stephens, 1973; P. McCann, 1977). An interesting but neglected part of this new field of study concerns the impact of certain kinds of knowledge on people's thought processes as they switch from practical to 'reflexive' or 'discursive' reason. Ginzburg (1980a) provides one particularly useful example of this impact in his study of a sixteenth-century Italian miller. Having catalogued the written knowledge available to the miller, Ginzburg shows how it was systematically misappropriated because the miller had been socialised into a predominantly oral culture. Abstract words like 'matter', 'nature', 'unity', 'elements' and 'substance' were all related quite literally to cues from the particular region in which the miller lived. Even metaphors were taken in a quite literal sense: '*like* cheese' becomes cheese, for instance. And God *is* a father. God *is* a lord. These processes of misappropriation are crucial because they are political. They have strong parallels now. Yet we know so very little about them. When do people pass from practical reason to reflexive reason? What makes them leave off from what they are doing to think reflexively about it? The fact that the evidence of these inner thought processes must be indirect (cf. Steiner, 1978, on 'inspeech') does not mean that such processes cannot be studied.

The example of Ginzburg's miller also points to the crucial importance of language as a creative element of discourse in terms of a particular group's penetration of social practice within a particular region, for language is still primarily a practical tool that gains its meaning from doing. Language is therefore always in a state of becoming (Pred, 1981b). It is a semantic field that shifts as the practices and projects of the material world alter, setting new limits as old ones are overtaken, inventing new meanings for old words or bringing new words and meanings into existence. The limitations of language are intimately related to social practices carried out within a regional context (see Le Roy Ladurie, 1978; Kirk et al., 1983). Hélias (1978, p. 334), for example, lists a whole web of words that have fallen out of use in the Breton language, their demise reflecting the shattering of one particular discourse:

Nothing is left of my early civilisation but wreckage. There are still some trees, but no more forests. To speak only of its objects, as soon as they were dispersed, they lost almost all their meaning. Museums have been built for them; and sometimes, with touching care, the larger room of some farmhouse has been reconstructed down to the last detail. But that room doesn't live anymore, doesn't work anymore.

Sociability and Community   The ability of any social grouping, set within a region, to penetrate the conditions of its existence must depend upon its social institutions and whether these are distinctive or are combined in a distinctive way. Yet we know very little, in any systematic fashion, about how particular *organisations* of social institutions allow, promote or inhibit understanding. Thus,

> not all complex and lively communities are politically radical . . . there are good grounds for supposing that above a certain size, towns develop political patterns owing little or nothing to the presence or absence of active political debate among the populace. Other factors intervene, notably the predominant local occupations and the way in which they are organised, and the ideas and identity they help impose upon those who work in them. Sociability, the tendency to active public life rather than an isolated private existence, appears to have been most significant in small communities where the population was, if not economically homogeneous, then at least economically interdependent. (Judt, 1979, p. 155)

There are some factors that are obviously local. For people living in certain areas of dispersed dwelling, the difficulty of meeting with one another is a very simple example. Factors like this have become less important over time, however. What is perhaps more important is the overall institutional context of sociability. Judt (1979), for instance, shows how in Provence, in the period from 1881 to 1914, communal festivals and church attendance declined in importance and were replaced or augmented by union meetings, political clubs and cafés based on the same sense of community but bent to more consciously political ends. Such studies of sociability have become quite common, especially in the literature on French and Spanish peasant societies in transition (for example, Agulhon, 1970; Martinez-Alier, 1971; Kaplan, 1977; Judt, 1979), but also, increasingly now, in the literature on other peasant societies (for example, Hunt, 1982) and in urban history (for example, J. White, 1979, 1980). The problem of sociability is obviously linked to the interrelated problems of *sense of community* and *sense of place*, yet even the scale at which such factors work is problematic. What areas actually have a self-sufficient character? The answer may be a town, a village, a neighbourhood, or even a single street (cf. Clark, 1973; Macfarlane, 1977; Calhoun, 1978; Joyce, 1980; Neale, 1981). Sense of community is assumed to have been greater in the classical European working-class communities prior to the Second World War than it is now (Joyce, 1980; MacIntyre, 1980; Therborn, 1980). And it is regarded as a stronger factor in multi-ethnic societies and in countries with certain communal institutions like the café, the street and the market. Such a sense is

> a matter of long term co-operation. Many of the results of this co-operation are not conscious goals in the minds of participants. More exactly, many actions may fit these 'goals' without being explicitly instrumental. At particular junctures people may decide to pursue one or another task of societal development; practices they may consider as instrumental are later taken for granted. At the

simplest level, we all need to limit the range of possibilities which we take into consideration when choosing an action. Habit is by no means the least important way in which this is done; cultural rules are another; social constraints on the availability of information add to the limitation. The efficiency of habit and culture clearly depends on the familiarity of situations and events. Community both depends on this familiarity and helps produce it. Being able to predict the behaviour of those with whom one must deal is one of the social advantages of community membership. This ability comes not only from long observation of particular persons but from the systematicity of the communal relationships. The former provides for collective definitions of relationships and the obligations they entail and expectations they justify. The latter increases people's investment in particular relationships, and causes them to be much more influenced by the wishes of others. (Calhoun, 1980, pp. 126–7)

But a sense of community and a sense of place can, of course, be a two-edged sword. Once again, it is a matter both of penetration *and* of limitation. Thus Joyce (1980, p. 116) links working-class deference in nineteenth-century factory towns precisely with sense of community and place:

> The *milieus* of ordinary life were impregnated with the authority and influence of an élite, so that the habit of neighbourhood community, expressed in the terminology of sociology as 'communal sociability', was the source of subordination as well as of class selfhood.

Conflict and Capacity   Each of the three foregoing aspects of social action come together as part of a closely interrelated inquiry into the nature of conflict and the *capacity* (Wright, 1978) of particular social groups living through particular regions to carry on class conflict and other forms of conflict. Capacity can be thought of here as the ability of different social groupings, themselves organised in particular historically and geographically specific ways, to organise and then to carry on various historically and geographically specific kinds of opposition to other social groupings. In particular, capacity can be measured by the ability of a group to penetrate the conditions of its existence and to express solidarity with that critique through the insertion of new social practices into its discourse. Marx's likening of the French peasantry to a 'sack of potatoes' is one (notoriously incorrect) example of a judgement on a social group's capacity. Capacity is clearly a function of the ability of a social grouping to produce transformative individuals (personality formation), particular forms of knowledge and particular forms of sociability, each of these being inseparable from the others (see Figure 2.3). None of these functions can be torn apart from the discourse of the region through which they are lived as social practices, which together constitute a particular 'structure of choice' (Przeworski, 1977) with a unique form of social logic (Offe and Wiesenthal, 1980). (The classic example of such a logic is, of course, the rationality of practices implicit in E.P. Thompson's [1971] idea of a moral economy [see also J. Scott, 1976; Popkin, 1980; Bechhofer and Elliott, 1981].) Transgressions of this logic may result in what seem to be 'spontaneous' protests,

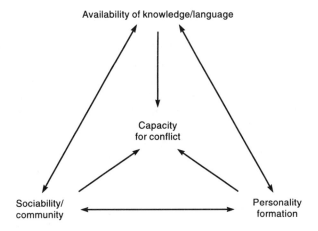

Figure 2.3 *Elements of conflict in context*

but these are really only the visible part of an offended organisation of practice in a region. As Groh (1979, p. 278) points out:

> in the case of strikes which broke out apparently without warning and, in traditional terms, 'spontaneously', we have been able to show that the stereo-typical formulation of a trade union or party press – that an industrial struggle had 'broken out with the elemental force of an act of nature' – was usually just a rationalisation of their own inability to identify the aims and causes of the action. This thesis is supported by the interesting fact that the police authorities observing labour conditions and organisations were often able to predict the location of strikes and their participants. The same applies to 'social protest' and 'collective violence'. Here, too, the outbreaks and development of the incidents were not spontaneous . . . to put it in extreme terms, in our field spontaneity is at worst a bourgeois myth and at best bad psychology. Until we have found a better word, we prefer to speak of non-organised rather than spontaneous actions, directing our attention to their specific logic.

Conclusions

> The human being is in the most literal sense a political animal, not merely a gregarious animal, but an animal which can individuate itself only in the midst of society.

> (K. Marx, 1973, p. 84)

In this chapter, I have tried to show, albeit briefly, that it is possible to conjoin a theory about social action, that of Marx, to the structurationist analysis of social action, utilising the richness and the importance of what Marx called the 'active life process' as it *must* take place in space and time, but retaining the crucial element of determination. I have no doubt that it is the lack of a theory of social action that has disabled Marxism, both practically and theoretically, and that has led to it becoming, in practice, a force for emancipation *and* a force for great oppression (Dawe, 1979; Giddens, 1981). A more *human* (not humanist) Marxism is needed, one that can give theoretical respectability to the practical '"problems" of motivating people to behave in altruistic and considerate, dignified and conscientious ways without transcendental goals. This is not a matter of "ideals" or "morals" but of a daily practical mechanism of conduct, keyed-in to practices and institutions' (Hirst and Woolley, 1982, p. 139).[26]

The position I have outlined in this chapter is very much a first approximation, open to revision as further work is carried out; comparatively little is yet known about so many of the issues that have been raised. But, whatever the problems, there is little doubt that it is becoming increasingly rare to find social action in space and time treated by social theorists as simply an afterthought, or as the mere imprint of social structure, or as belonging, in some way, to an autonomous realm of existence. Space and time are always and everywhere social. Society is always and everywhere spatial and temporal. Easy enough concepts, perhaps, but the implications are only now being thought through.

Appendix: A Note on Methods of Analysis

The outline of a reconstructed regional geography which I have given in this chapter gives a quite natural eminence to the 'life history approach' – oral history and the use of autobiographies and diaries – and to local history techniques as well as to the more conventional compositional approaches. Oral history is a rich source of contextual knowledge that is increasingly being tapped, especially in Britain and the United States (for a review, see P. Thompson, 1978), France (for a review, see P. Thompson, 1981), Germany (for example, Niehammer, 1980) and, of course, Australia and the Pacific (for example, Lowenstein, 1978). No doubt it has value as a means of commemorating and honouring the past and it can be very useful in an explanatory and sensitising role when there is no clear theoretical base upon which to build (Faraday and Plummer, 1979). But oral history is now increasingly being applied to the study of archetypal class-structured experiences such as migration (for example, Bertaux-Wiaume, 1977; Bertaux and Bertaux-Wiaume, 1981a, 1981b), to the working experiences of different fractions of the working class (for example, Sennett and Cobb, 1972; Hareven and Langenbach, 1978; Bleitrach and Chenu, 1979; Hareven, 1982) and to the life experiences of a society as a whole (for example, P. Thompson, 1975; T. Thompson, 1980). It also provides a useful adjunct to give 'depth' to conventional compositional accounts in, for instance, social history and sociology (for example, Fraser, 1979). However, as presently constituted, oral history has no coherent theoretical organising principle and is rarely systematic except in terms of broad population types. The account in this chapter suggests that some theoretical background might be given to history by adding a new set of tasks, specifically by recording how personality grows up in a particular region, by trying to find the exact content of sociability and sense of community, by investigating practical reason, and so on. Against such a programme, of course, must be set the practical limitations of oral history – data collection, interview time, the problems of analysis, and so on and so forth.

Autobiographies and diaries can also be used effectively in exploring contextual issues (for example, Macfarlane, 1970; Burnett, 1974; Delaney, 1976; Vincent, 1977, 1980, 1981). The relative sparseness of these sources (especially diaries) means that there are considerable problems, which are difficult to overcome, in using them representatively in specific contexts. However, even one diary can provide a multitude of information on personality formation, sociability, and so forth (see Abrams, 1982, for an excellent discussion).

Finally, extant local histories provide a rich vein to be tapped and to be reworked. Although initially rather bucolic in character, many rural local histories have become increasingly systematic (for example, Hey, 1974; Spufford, 1974). Further, a new branch of urban local history has now grown up (for example, J. White, 1980). Often, these histories are very susceptible to reconstitution in a fully contextual sense and are a means of posing a series of contextual questions (cf. Thrift, *1980e*), although too much can be made of their value (see J. White, 1981; Worpole, 1981; Yeo, 1981).

As a postscript to this Appendix, I want to suggest one method that, so far as I am aware, has not been used in the literature. That is 'reconstruction' of individuals. This method consists of deducing the characteristics of the life paths of a set of specified individuals within a locale and thereby suggesting what would be the main features to be found in an interview, diary (the source I have used) or autobiography (cf. Thrift, *1979f*).

Notes

This chapter was originally published in *Environment & Planning D. Society and Space*, 1983, 1: 23–57. Reprinted by permission of Pion Ltd, London.

1. I had considered using the mechanistic metaphor of 'transmission' here, but the linguistic metaphor provided by the word 'translation' seems to convey more exactly the meaning intended.

2. 'Humanistic' geography is a difficult term: it covers a confusion of approaches from phenomenology through symbolic interactionism to what is, in effect, behaviourism.

3. There is a strong distinction, not usually appreciated, between structuralism and the structural-genetic approach of Marx (cf. S. Hall, 1980; Zeleny, 1980). Marx was *not* a structuralist.

4. Marx (in Marx and Engels, 1956, p. 236) once jibed that 'philosophy and the study of the actual world have the same relation to one another as onanism and sexual love.' Philosophy is as much something to be explained by social science as social science is something to be explained by philosophy. Philosophy can provide no guarantees, by itself or in advance, of the actual work of social science.

5. This emphasis does *not* mean that I am trying to downplay the shifts in economic and social relations that were taking place. Rather, it is to argue that these changes in the scale of human operations made such shifts plainer for all to see.

6. Smart's (1982) criticism of Giddens assumes that Giddens identifies human agency with everyday life, with the individual and with individuality. This is not necessarily the case, as will be shown in this chapter. Further, even Smart's mentor, Foucault, has a notion of 'resistance'.

7. Dawe (1979) sees a contradiction here between Marx's ideas of a determinant social structure and of a creative individual, yet this is what history teaches us has happened.

8. This translation comes from Ferrarotti (1981, p. 23). It is a far better rendering than that to be found in Sartre (1964, p. 56).

9. I have chosen to concentrate on these three authors only. A number of other authors have what may at first appear as partially overlapping concerns, for instance with the problem of non-functionalist theories of structure and agency (for example, Sartre, 1964, 1976; Castoriadis, 1975; Kosik, 1976; Touraine, 1977, 1981; Harré, 1978, 1979; Dawe, 1979; Urry, 1981a) or with the history of ego development (for example, Elias, 1978, 1982; Habermas, 1979). But these authors usually take an overwhelmingly compositional approach to these problems, generally, but not always, ignoring the way that they are embedded in space and time.

10. 'Functionalism' can be considered here as a general term covering structural and Marxist functionalism. It is a term that can be applied to a number of first-order mistakes that characterise too much of current social science. These include: (i) the attributing of 'needs' to social systems; (ii) the assumption that social systems are functionally ordered and cohesive; (iii) the imputing of a teleology to social systems; (iv) the characterisation of effects and causes; and (v) the setting up of empirically unverifiable propositions via tautological statements. Parts of Marx's work were undeniably functionalist. If nothing else, G.A. Cohen (1978) makes this clear. Excellent critiques of functionalism (and its partner, reductionism) in Marxism can be found in Giddens (1979a, 1981) and Urry (1981a).

11. The French word *alterité* has been borrowed from nineteenth-century French hermeneutics and the even older form of the word in poetics. The first problem with using it here to describe a quality of newness is that it can be used only in the sense of the newness that results from intrinsically *social* action (interaction) which produces new forms of social action. The second problem is that Sartre (1976) has already bought the term into English in a somewhat different usage. 'Alterity' is still therefore, in part, a translator's device, an uncritical transposition into English which works only because English does not have such a word.

12. Bhaskar (1979) has a slightly different usage from Giddens, in that he limits the duality of structure to production and calls reproduction of the conditions of reproduction the duality of praxis.

13. Sartre (1976) makes a useful distinction here between *comprehension*, the understanding of human activity in terms of the purposes of its agents, and *intellection*, the understanding of human activity which is not necessarily in terms of the purposes of its agents. In a similar vein, Bourdieu (1977) points out that we need not only a theory of practice but also a theory of theory and a theory of the relation of theory to practice (and vice versa).

14. Conventionally, the word 'mechanism' has become the outward sign of a realist approach (cf. Bhaskar, 1975, 1979; Keat and Urry, 1975; D. Sayer, 1979; A. Sayer, 1981). Although there is much to commend this conception of science, there are still a number of unresolved problems. It is interesting to note, for example, that Keat and Urry (1975), who have probably done more to popularise the idea of realism than anyone else, have now, individually and collectively, expressed doubts about certain aspects of the realist conception of science (cf. Keat, 1981; Urry, 1981a; Keat and Urry, 1982). In particular, there are the problems of how distinct mechanisms are related to one another, how such mechanisms can be verified, and whether taking a realist approach does not automatically justify reductionism (see also Benton, 1981; Collier, 1981; McLennan, 1981). Another chapter would be required even to begin to exhaust these topics. However, it is possible to see the work of the structurationist school (which, of course, includes Bhaskar) as exactly an inquiry into realist tenets, and especially, I think, into the problem of contingency.

15. Wiener's (1981) analysis of Giddens's work is based on a number of misunderstandings. In particular, by ignoring Giddens's work on the time-space constitution of societies, Wiener is able to convert Giddens into a compositional thinker similar to Habermas. The force of Giddens's critique is then neutralised, since Wiener makes his work complementary to that of structural Marxism, when in actual fact his work challenges the legitimacy of the latter.

16. With the possible exception of Bourdieu (1977), who tries to apply his very abstract model to the situation of the Kabyle tribe. But Bourdieu's work on cultural capital still lacks historical specificity; indeed, Garnham and Williams (1980) effectively have to construct cultural capital as a shifting historical category.

17. In capitalism, specific individuality is irrelevant to economic relations. Thus the wage labourer is the 'carrier of labour as such', of abstract labour. The capitalist is similarly capital-personified, the agent of capital. The same negation of individuality occurs with other categories as well: for example, money and exchange relations.

18. The labour process is probably the main link between the compositional and the contextual. First, it is the site of an important series of mediating concepts to do with the management of time. Second, 'the labour process (properly conceived) is the very locus of structuration since, in Marx's words, "labour is, first of all, a process between man and nature" through which "he acts upon external nature and changes it, and in this way he simultaneously changes his own nature"' (Gregory, 1982, p. 214). Of course, a lot of weight in this sentence is borne by 'properly conceived'. Third, although the labour process is a pivotal concept, it remains true that we have yet to learn how to handle it contextually when more than one labour process is found in a region. Most successful regional studies (for example, Martinez-Alier, 1971; Kaplan, 1977; Judt, 1979) are based in agricultural districts or tight-knit industrial and mining communities where one labour process is dominant. Bleitrach and Chenu's (1979, 1981) work is important in this regard because it tries to take into account a number of labour processes as they affect life paths.

19. I disagree with the crude analogies and the humanist emphasis in Sève's work. See Julkunen (1977) and Shames (1981) for English summaries.

20. Such objects are often studied in history through the method known as 'prosopography', the 'investigation of the common background characteristics of a group of actors in history by means of a collective study of their lives' (L. Stone, 1974, p. 46). See also Billinge (1982) for the geographical possibilities of this method.

21. Obviously, the interaction of the various models of the development of ego-identity with this factor are important here, although I will not go into them in this chapter (for example, see Erikson, 1959, 1963, 1975; Piaget, 1965; Kohlberg, 1971; Habermas, 1979).

22. Raymond Williams (1977, 1979) is trying to capture with the concept of 'structure of feeling' the quality of *presence* of a particular society, social group or region; that is, how the society, social group or region appears to those who live through it at the point that they live it. This has obvious connections with other phenomena, for example the commodification of memory currently taking place (see F. Davis, 1979).

23. It is ironic that Althusser, who was able to see ideology as a matrix of social practices, displaced nearly all such practices into state apparatuses. Clearly, many of the 'apparatuses' that Althusser considered to be in the domain of the state, for example the family, exist in civil society (see Larrain, 1979; Therborn, 1980: Urry, 1981a).

24. This schema bears some resemblance to that proposed by Habermas (1982, p. 264) in a different (compositional) context.

25. There are, of course, many other forms of knowledge than just the written. I take the written as one example of what is needed.

26. This is not to be seen as an argument for unalloyed rationalism. As Perry Anderson (1980, p. 61) points out: 'there is a real and complete silence in Marx himself – who never had a proper sense of the force of morality and affectivity, as opposed to interest and ideology, in history. Even at his best, he was too rationalist.' Rather, it is an argument for the working out of morality as practices, something which necessarily requires an investigation of the constitution of subjectivity.

3
Flies and Germs:
A Geography of Knowledge

Mother: We have to keep the screen door closed, honey, so the flies won't come in. Flies bring germs into the house with them.
Child: [*when asked later what the germs were*] Something the flies play with.[1]

Introduction

This little vignette in which the child uses what knowledge is available to her to interpret her mother's interdiction, illustrates the central theme of this chapter, namely that what we know is an important constraint on what we can think and do. It also illustrates two other important themes which grow out of and into this central theme. The first is that knowledge is historically specific. Thus, before 1871, knowledge of 'germs' did not exist.[2] The mother could not have known of their presence and the child would not have had to answer her interrogator. Second, knowledge is geographically specific. Even now, the knowledge of germs does not stretch everywhere in the world and in these nescient places mothers do not have to tell their children something they cannot know.

This chapter thus forms part of a continuing attempt to develop a theory of *situated* social action. Such theory must continually intersect both with the presences and absences of social structure (Giddens, 1976, 1981) and with the continual turmoil of social groups in conflict in a complex process of 'structuring',[3] but I would argue that it still forms a relatively separate focus of attention.[4] Elsewhere, I have outlined the three most important elements of this project, which are the study of the process of personality formation, the study of the organisation of sociability and the study of the availability of knowledge (where knowledge is defined in its broadest sense as information about the world) (Chapter 2, *1983d*). Since the availability of knowledge forms only *one part* of this project, and is inevitably linked to the others, its explanation necessarily involves some consideration of questions of personality formation and sociability, but in what follows my primary focus is the 'geography of knowledge'.

The chapter is divided into four sections. The first considers, in very general terms, how 'stocks of knowledge' are continually being built up, and the second describes the types of knowledge from which such stocks have been constructed historically. A third section considers three case studies of the spatial availability of knowledge, and the final section traces some of the links between availability of knowledge and social action through a case study of political knowledge. Most of the illustrations are taken from Europe between the sixteenth and nineteenth centuries and are limited to knowledge disseminated through the medium of print. There are obvious disadvantages in such a restricted scope but they are, I hope, outweighed by a greater coherence. It follows of course that any illustration is evocative rather than exhaustive.

Two other qualifications are necessary. First, my emphasis on a situated theory of social action means that I will have rather less to say on the production, distribution and circulation of knowledge than on its availability.[5] This is not a derogation of these other elements but merely an effect of the emphasis I have chosen: *I am primarily interested here in what knowledge actors have at their disposal.* Second, and closely connected to this, the fact that knowledge is physically available does not mean that it has to be acted upon nor that it is unquestioned or undisputed. This entails important issues of 'ideology' and of 'hegemony', but again I will hardly touch upon them here.

Social Knowing and Social Unknowing

'Social knowing' is the term I will use to denote the continual process of the creation of the *stocks of knowledge*[6] within a society upon which actors, who are always members of various social groups, can draw in the production of their life and the reproduction or transformation of the forms of life of social groups (their own and other) and ultimately of society.[7] I see this process as being an essentially recursive one, the result of *practices* that both provide the medium for and the outcome of social structure (Giddens, 1976, 1979a, 1981; Elias, 1978, 1982; Bhaskar, 1979, 1980; Abrams, 1982).

From the Perspective of the Actor

All groups of actors have some degree of 'penetration'[8] of what is going on within the reciprocal flow of action and structure in which they are both constituted and constituting. But their ability to draw on and generate knowledge, whether this knowledge is discursively constructed or an unacknowledged reapplication of practical schemas, is simultaneously *limited* by the very experience of the production of practices and the continual monitoring and reinterpretation of this experience in the light of subsequent events. At least four closely interwoven limits are involved. First, all actors' knowledge is grounded in their biographically unique *experience* of practising a particular social system, and the power to reason can exist only relatively autonomously from this grounding in experience. The structures of domination, signification and legitimation that are woven into the patterning of this system resist the discovery of certain kinds of knowledge and can form unacknowledged conditions for action in the knowledge that

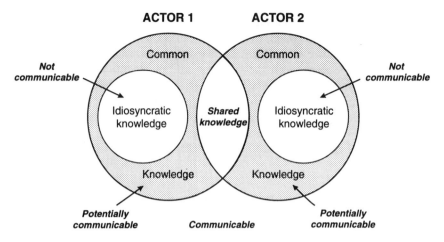

Figure 3.1 *Knowledge and communication (adapted from Kreckel, 1982, Figure 2, p. 277)*

is available. Second, all knowledge is the result of the particular *habitus*[9] used to generate practices and monitor, interpret, reconstruct and ultimately confirm them. Once again, the effect is to provide a particular horizon on upcoming experience and the conception of experience, and in this way to set a limit. Third, there is the basic fact that all practices are situated in *time and space*. The constraints of the human body and the extant physical infrastructure of society are such that knowledge must be generated from a finite series of practices (and experiences of these practices) that form part of an irreversible and repetitive form of conduct, one that usually sets quite severe limits on what can be thought – and on the amount of time available to think it – within each actor's allotted span of history. Finally, and as a result of these three limits, no two actors can *communicate* knowledge perfectly, and this in turn sets a fourth limit. If the actors' experience (for example, of being a member of the same family), habitus (for example, being a member of the same social class) and position in time and space (for example, being an inhabitant of the same region) are the same, then communication will be easier and knowledge more likely to be disseminated than if any one of these factors is different (Figure 3.1).[10] To summarise, actors usually have only very partial knowledge of or access to knowledge that is available within a particular social group or society, let alone the time to produce the finished conceptual goods.

From the Perspective of Society

Every society has an overall stock of knowledge, and although some of this will be available to all its members, some will be differentially distributed amongst various social groups; there is thus a *social distribution of knowledge*. This distribution will be dependent upon all the numerous

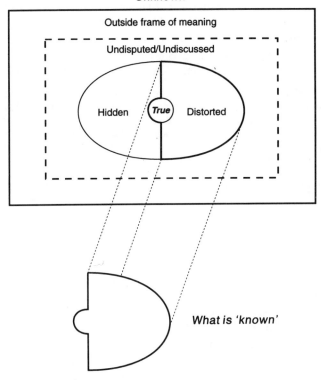

Figure 3.2 *The five kinds of unknowing*

dimensions of social group structuration (Urry, 1981a, p. 70), such as biological differentiation (gender, age, race, etc.), class (the capital–labour relation), the state, the region and all their cross-correlations.

Each society, and each social group within it, will have its own degree of penetration of the conditions of its existence dependent upon the stock of knowledge that is available to it. We can codify this penetration as five types of 'unknowing' (Figure 3.2) (Thrift, *1979f*; Chapter 2, *1981c*). First, there is 'knowledge' that is *unknown*. This is a knowledge that it is simply not possible for members of society to have because of its position in history and space.[11] As Castoriadis (1971, p. 217) puts it:

> To have an experience of history as a historical being is to be *in* and *part of* more history, as well as *in* and *part of* society. It necessarily means thinking of history in terms of categories of one's own epoch and one's own society (these categories being themselves the products of historical evolution). It also means thinking history in relation to some objective or purpose, which purpose is history itself.

Second, there is knowledge that is *not understood*. That is, it is not within the frame of meaning of a society, a social group within that society, or members of a social group living in a particular region. This lack of understanding can come about for a number of reasons. For example, a group whose form of life is essentially practical will have difficulties in grasping the form of life of a group based, at least in part, in discursive practices. This type of unknowing is well summarised in a passage from H.G. Wells's *Men Like Gods* (cited in Bourdieu and Passeron, 1977, p. 71):

> *Serpentine*: When I think of you, the thought, so far as it finds corresponding ideas and suitable words in your mind is reflected in your mind. My thought clothes itself in words in your mind, which words you seem to hear – and naturally enough in your own language and habitual phrases . . .
> *Barnstaple*: And that is why . . . when you soar into ideas of which we haven't a shadow in our minds, we just hear nothing at all.

Third, and intimately related to the second type of unknowing, there is knowledge that is *undiscussed*. This is knowledge that is taken-for-granted either by a society, or a social group or the members of a social group living in a social region. This form of unknowing is a prime characteristic of many systems of practical knowledge but it should not be seen as their exclusive prerogative. The acceptance by many scientists of 'the scientific method' as a model illustrates the use of a system of concepts that effectively conceals the nature, causes and consequences of a set of practices that is just that – a set of practices. Fourth, there is the type of unknowing that results from knowledge being actively and consciously *hidden* from a society, certain groups within that society or groups within a particular region. Fifth, there is the type of unknowing that results from *distortion*, in terms of being known in a distorted fashion by a society, social groups within a society or social groups within a particular region. Here, care must be taken to separate, *insofar as this is possible*, the distortion that arises from the history of the particular forms of life of social groups, with their 'traditional' systems of belief and knowledge, from the distortion that is part of an active process of manipulation by other social groups.[12]

The first type of unknowing can be seen as an historical constant. The other types come together in different combinations in different societies and social groups to produce a social distribution of knowledge (and non-knowledge).[13]

Types of Knowledge

I want to claim that four main types of knowledge go to make up the stocks of knowledge that are available to social groups and to individual actors in modern society. These are: (i) the unconscious; (ii) practical knowledge; (iii) empirical knowledge; and (iv) 'natural philosophy'. These types of knowledge form loose clusters of information around particular *practices* ordered in particular ways, and this emphasis on practice has two important consequences. First, these types of knowledge are not meant to be seen as arising from distinctive forms of rationality,[14] nor are they meant to be depicted as the product of long-term changes in metaphysics or beliefs. The decline of witch-hunting in seventeenth-century Europe, for example, has been explained as a function of the rise of capitalism or of the new 'mechanical philosophy'. But:

> Two explanations seem more compelling. One is the loss of confidence in the ability of the courts to decide who the witches were, an increasing recognition of the weakness in the procedures of forensic demonology. . . . The other is the stabilisation and territorialisation of religious authority which permits other and more regular and systematic means of disciplining flocks and the control of heresy. The success of the Counter-Reformation and the mutual exhaustion and stabilisation following the Wars of Religion bring heresy within the manageable limits of religious 'police'. (Hirst, 1982, pp. 444–5; see also Hirst and Woolley, 1982, Chapter 14)

Second, these types of knowledge do not form separate discourses or categories of belief. Human beings are *bricoleurs* and conventionally conjoin what may seem to be quite different types of knowledge. The very nature of human conduct as a compartmentalised stream of action and thought in space and time means that very few actors have a completely and consistently developed world view (while even fewer apply it to their actions). Thus, for example, the diary of Ralph Josselin (1617–83), an Essex clergyman, shows that he could quite confidently combine commercial capitalist calculation with Calvinistic religious practices and a degree of belief in witchcraft.[15] As Spufford (1981, p. 155) puts it, it is 'extremely easy for academics to over-emphasize the degree to which the majority of ordinary people are either aware of, or bothered by, different categories of belief'.

Unconscious Knowledge

Unconscious knowledge is based upon forgotten practices still remembered in the limning of action. As Bourdieu (1977, p. 79) puts it, 'the unconscious is never anything other than the forgetting of history which history itself produces by incorporating the objective structures it produces in the second natures of habitus'. Interpreting the unconscious as an historically changing and geographically variable phenomenon, let alone the variations in the type of knowledge it provides, is the domain of an historical and geographical psychology that as yet hardly exists.[16]

Practical Knowledge

Practical knowledge can be defined as that informal (but not therefore unstructured) type of knowledge that is learnt from the experience of watching and doing in highly particular contexts in direct mutual interaction. It still forms 'the massive central core of human thinking' that goes unrecorded in so many histories of social thought.[17]

Practical knowledge has four major components. First, it is *unarticulated*; that is, it is based upon practices that have, over the course of history, become naturalised so that much of its content now inhabits the realm of the undiscussed and, certainly, the uncodified. To have to ask about practical knowledge is to miss the point of practical knowledge (Bourdieu, 1977). Second, practical knowledge is part of a *continuous* and *repetitive* flow of conduct which takes place in finite time and which is oriented towards doing. This is a world in which 'I think' (*cogito*) is inseparable from 'I can' (*practico*) and in which long-term goals are submerged by immediate objectives. Third, practical knowledge is *local*, that is, it is knowledge produced and reproduced in *mutual interaction* that relies on the *presence* of other human beings on a direct, face-to-face basis (Giddens, 1979a, 1981). Such knowledge is deeply imbued with both historical and geographical specificity, taking its cues from local contexts each with their own particular ensemble of practices and associated linguistic usages. Nowhere is this made clearer than in historical accounts of local communities which include glossaries of terms that describe practices (and the experience of those practices) now long past. These are words which not only capture the attributes of a particular practice but also begin to conjure up the ghost of the whole language of practice and practice of language associated with living a set of social relations in a specific physical setting. Finally, practical knowledge tends to be based upon *organic analogy* or *metaphor* and, following from the third component, these analogies or metaphors are usually based upon proximity.

The importance of analogy and metaphor in systems of practical knowledge should not be understated for they function as the correlates of patterns of bodily action and interaction which instantiate social relations. In the following passage, for example, it is possible to see how metaphors are used to fix the patterns of economic co-operation and exchange in an African village which form the material base of that community's life.

> The Kuranko of Sierra Leone use the word *kile* ('path' or 'road') as a metaphor for social relationship. For instance, the adage *nyendan bin to kile a wa ta an segi* describes the way a particular species of grass (used for thatching) bends back one way as you go along a path through it, and then bends back the other way as you return along the path. This movement to and fro of grass along the pathway is used as a metaphor for the movement of people and of goods and of services within a community; it is a metaphor for reciprocity. Thus, in Kuranko one often explains the reason for giving a gift, especially to an in-law, with the phrase *kile ka na faga*, 'so that the path does not die'. However, if relations between affines or neighbours are strained, it is often said that 'the path is not good between them' (*kile nyuma san tema*), and if a person disappoints a friend then people may comment *a ma kile nyuma tama a boma* ('he did not walk on the good path with his friend'). (Jackson, 1982, p. 16)

Systems of practical knowledge are often sophisticated (de Schlippe, 1965; IDS Bulletin, 1979; Brokensha et al., 1980). But the connections made between various phenomena in these systems have to be based upon the known world, so that, once again, the limits to knowledge operate. G.P. Chapman (1985, p. 83) provides the following example:

> Dutt lists a few of the beliefs[18] or the omens of Bihar with respect of insect and pest attacks on their crops. In particular, he notes that there are many farmers

who believe that certain caterpillars fall from the sky with the rain, and their cure for the attack is accordingly usually religious. The reason for the belief is that the caterpillars emerged from their eggs in cloudy, rainy conditions, and their life-cycle is not understood. That man is born of woman, and a calf of a cow is well known, but that a moth or butterfly produces eggs which produce larvae which produce pupae which produce moths, going through great changes of shape and form, is not understood. It is intelligent to associate the pest with the weather conditions, and only someone in possession of a 'parity framework' which would reject this interpretation would be unsatisfied by it.

Empirical Knowledge

The stock of empirical knowledge is built up as a result of the general process of *rationalisation* of knowledge,[19] which has a double interpretation as the proffering of a rational explanation and the organisation of knowledge in a systematic fashion. Empirical knowledge, like practical knowledge (with which it continues to share many similarities), is bent towards the mastery of the conditions of existence, but it is exercised within a learning process which is not only cumulative but systematised and co-ordinated over large tracts of space and over longer time-horizons, particularly by modern state and economic institutions. The modern state is based upon the various practices associated with *surveillance* (that is, the accumulation of information on the population, the supervision of the population and the characterisation of the population in such a way that it can be supervised) and proceeds from the institution of regular armies and the systematic registration of births and deaths via the census and fingerprinting to modern computer data-banks. Similarly, the capitalist economy is based upon the co-ordination of the labour process and the complex exchange of commodities, both of which require the extensive collection of systematic knowledge, and proceeds from double-entry bookkeeping via modern accounting practices to – again – the computer. In both bases, the institutions engendered by these practices produce a network of space-time locations at which knowledge is stored, received and transmitted. The schooling system forms a particularly crucial set of nodes within this network (Foucault, 1977; Giddens, 1981).

What, then, are the major characteristics of empirical knowledge? Above all, it is *heterodynamic* (Kreckel, 1982), that is, it is acquired by virtue of an actor's membership of class and other social groups, and it is *distanciated*,[20] that is, it is removed in both time and space from the experiences and events it describes. Empirical knowledge does not depend for its acquisition upon the direct presence of people, but is transmitted through institutions and technologies which allow personal contact to be either by-passed or made specific to particular 'packets' of information. These two characteristics account for much of the *homogeneous* and *objectified* character of empirical knowledge.

The chief components of the stock of empirical knowledge are, I believe, crucially dependent upon the written word (Goody and Watt, 1963; Goody, 1968a, 1968b, 1977; Ginzburg; 1980b; Giddens, 1981), but also and more particularly, upon the practices engendered by the invention of printing (and the modern book). Since most commentators have underestimated the importance of this medium, I want to discuss it in some detail. The difference that the invention of printing made both to the stock of available knowledge *and* to the type of knowledge can be seen by considering what, historically, has been a transitory form between systems of practical knowledge and systems of empirical knowledge (and between oral and literate cultures), namely systems of *practical literacy* (Goody, 1986b; Tambiah, 1968; Clanchy, 1993).[21] Before the invention of printing, these systems – usually associated with the collection of statistics and the transmission of orders by the emerging bureaucracy of an expanding state – were necessarily restricted by the strict limits imposed by the use of scribes.[22] 'Just as geographic space stopped short of the Pillars of Hercules, so too did knowledge itself appear to stop short at fixed limits set by scribal data pools' (Eisenstein, 1979, p. 518).

The invention of printing changed all this.[23] First, and most obviously, the stock of available knowledge expanded rapidly, in terms of both absolute quantity and the amount of knowledge available in any one place. Second, the codification of knowledge became both possible and, with the expansion in knowledge, a necessity. Third, for many, consultation, comparison and choice between different items of knowledge became both possible and practicable for the first time. For example, a number of texts could be assembled in the same place and did not need to be transcribed. Fourth, knowledge became more accurate. Codification and comparison combined with the elimination of the errors that result from continual transcription ensured this. Finally, stocks of literature began to be built up which opened up the possibility of learning by reading, that is, of learning skills at a distance instead of in mutual interaction. These are all key features of empirical knowledge.

Empirical knowledge can, of course, be divided further and I will now identify three main subsets in terms of their propinquity to practical knowledge. First, there is the empirical knowledge that now infuses a whole series of practices that were carried on before the advent of empirical knowledge (and which could, in principle, still be carried on without it). These practices have been systematised by the application of empirical knowledge and by learning about these practices via empirical knowledge. This knowledge stretches all the way from that found in gardening and cookery books to much of the knowledge disseminated via the media about politics and current events. Second, there is empirical knowledge that is oriented to the whole set of practices that are directly bent toward reproducing the state and the economy and whose existence is closely tied to the existence of empirical knowledge. This subset would include the aggregation and codification of knowledge and forms the basis of most of the 'professions', which is hardly surprising since the profession is, historically, one of the first devices used to differentiate a body of knowledge from practical knowledge, so bestowing on its practitioners a margin of respectability and economic and social recognition.[24] Third, there is knowledge generated by the restricted empirical model of the natural sciences (which is, effectively, a set of instructions on ways of proceeding *in practice*). This knowledge, which is generated by many of the social sciences (and especially economics and demography) as well as the bulk of the natural sciences, comes from practices whose conduct is resolutely oriented to the practical. It is the knowledge that arises from the practice of 'normal science'.[25]

> Normal science is the linchpin of the scientific enterprise; it is how knowledge is developed and accumulated nearly all the time. Yet it is in no way a radically innovative activity. On the contrary, it is very much a routine carrying on of a given form of scientific life, employing accepted procedures along the lines indicated by accepted standards, and largely assuming the correctness of existing knowledge. (Barnes, 1982, p. 10)

Natural Philosophy

The third type of knowledge (empirical knowledge) overlaps with knowledge gleaned from 'natural philosophy'. I use 'natural philosophy' in the most catholic of senses, to denote knowledge that attempts to unify a number of bodies of knowledge into one whole, as knowledge about knowledge.[26] It has at least three interrelated characteristics. First, it requires much time both to absorb a number of bodies of knowledge and to synthesise them.[27] As Kierkegaard put it, 'Life can only be understood backwards but it has to be lived forwards.' Second, although it may be part of a practice, it is only indirectly related to immediate practical needs. Third, its content is related to what knowledge is available to be thought with, whether of the practical, empirical or natural philosophy types. For example, the types of analogy or metaphor upon which systems of knowledge can be built become more sophisticated as the objects that can be thought with become more sophisticated. Thus 'it is said that Aristotle thought of causal effects in terms of a horse drawing a cart and that Galileo thought of heavenly bodies as something like ships moving in an ocean without friction' (Lane, 1966, p. 654). But now the analogies of the steam engine (machinery), the microscope (the infinitely small), the telescope (the infinitely large) and a host of others are all available for use (Lakoff and Johnson, 1980; Hill, 1982). There has been, quite literally, a mechanisation of our world picture.

Types of Knowledge and the Availability of Knowledge

That the availability of knowledge has a crucial effect on the form and content of natural philosophy and, indeed, on the other types of knowledge is worth establishing in some detail. I will do this by considering the case of magic, which, since it was evolved 'to fill in the gaps left by the limitation of techniques' (Bernal, 1965, p. 40), can be seen as an attempt to control the conditions of existence like any other.[28] The practice is the word and the word is the practice. This kind of magic still existed in England in the seventeenth century:

> Almost every English village had its 'cunning man', its white magician who told those who had been robbed how to recover their property, advised on propitious times and seasons for journeys and foretold the future. Nor were such beliefs limited to ignorant villagers. (Hill, 1982, p. 176)

But, at the same time as this, there existed another magic in England, one enjoying a 'renaissance' in the universities and at court thanks to the discovery in the fifteenth century of texts attributed to Hermes Trismegistus (Yates, 1964, 1972, 1979). The Hermetic tradition, meant to be based on the magical religion of the Egyptians, had spread rapidly (at least in part through the new medium of print). Alongside it the bodies of knowledge known as astrology and alchemy also still flourished (Rattansi, 1973; Righini Bonelli and Shea, 1975; Webster, 1982). The dividing line between these three bodies of knowledge and 'science' was problematic. On one side were the mages who incorporated scientific discoveries into their work: Giordano Bruno, who hailed the discoveries of Copernicus as proof of Hermetism; Tommaso Campanella, who was willing to allow a category of 'real artificial magic' (such as mechanical statues) (Yates, 1964); the astrologer and herbalist Nicholas Culpeper, who made use of the recent invention of logarithms to aid his calculations; and the inventor of logarithms, John Napier, who 'was said to value them most because they speeded up his calculations of the mystic figure 666, the number of the Beast in *Revelations*' (Hill, 1982, p. 177). On the other side was Isaac Newton, who has been described as 'not the first of the age of reason' but 'the last of the magicians' and who left hundreds of pages of unpublished manuscripts on alchemy and turned to mathematics in order to understand astrology (Webster, 1982). Tycho Brahe made the vast collection of observations which enabled him to redraw the map of the night sky, primarily for astrological purposes; and John Locke and Robert Boyle used astrological reckoning to find a time 'favourable for planting peonies' (Hill, 1982, p. 191). The connections are great enough for it now to be said that 'practical science can be seen to have developed, at least in part, out of the renewed interest in magic' (French, 1972, p. 109).

The reason why magic, astrology and alchemy died out are complex. One was that they were opposed in England by a religion which had its own competing world system, and which had always been associated with a different kind of 'rationality'. A second reason was that it became obvious that, when *compared* with other systems (*which had not existed before*), magic did not work. A third reason is that systems of practical and empirical knowledge based upon 'science' were gradually slotted into place, which began to confirm this view of the world, rather than one based upon 'magic'. But we can legitimately wonder if

> the circumstances of the acceptance of the mechanical philosophy allowed ideological elements to be incorporated into it from the start, which today have

become hindrances to its further advance; total rejection of the ways of the *magi* may have closed some doors which might with advantage to science have been left open. Science, in Bernal's striking phrase, is not only 'ordered technique', it is also 'rationalised mythology'. (Hill, 1982, p. 191)

The example of the rise and fall of magic illustrates two major themes. First, the connections between practical knowledge, natural philosophy and, later, empirical knowledge are by no means one-way: from natural philosophy to empirical knowledge and so on down to the person in the street. For example, practical knowledge can intervene in the building of empirical knowledge or natural philosophy, and this can happen in the most unexpected ways. Thus,

> In Bengal, as well as in China, there was a custom of imprinting letters and documents with a fingerprint tipped in ink or tar: this was probably a consequence of knowledge derived from divinatory practice. . . . In 1860 Sir William Herschel, District Commissioner of Hooghly in Bengal, came across this usage, common among local people, saw its usefulness, and thought to profit by it to improve the functioning of the British administration. . . . But really . . . there was a great need for some such means of identification: in India as in other British colonies the natives were illiterate, disputatious, wily, deceitful, and to the eyes of a European all looked the same. In 1880 Herschel announced in *Nature* that after 17 years of tests, fingerprints had been officially introduced in the district of Hooghly and since then had been used for three years with the best possible results. The imperial administrators had taken over the Bengalis' . . . knowledge and used it against them. (Ginzburg, 1980b, pp. 26–7)

Francis Galton saw Herschel's article in *Nature*, combined it with the theoretical work of Purkyné, and introduced fingerprinting to England and thence to the rest of the world. Second, the example of magic shows that all actors, including 'scientists' and natural philosophers, can only work with the knowledge they have and that knowledge shapes what they can perceive as and fashion into 'rationality'. As Thomas (1971, p. 799) puts it:

> If magical acts are ineffective rituals employed as an alternative to sheer helplessness in the face of events, then how are we to classify the status of 'scientific' remedies, in which we place faith, but which are subsequently exposed as useless? This was the fate of Galenic medicine, which in the sixteenth century was the main rival to folk-healing. But it will also be that of much of the medicine today. Sociologists have observed that contemporary doctors and surgeons engage in many ritual practices of a non-operative kind.

Further:

> all the evidence of the sixteenth and seventeenth centuries suggests that the common people never formulated a distinction between magic and medicine. . . . The modern working-class woman who remarks that she doesn't 'believe' in doctors is acknowledging the fact that the patient still brings with him [*sic*] an essentially unformed allegiance. Usually she knows no more of the underlying rationale for his treatment than did the client of a cunning man. In such circumstances it is hard to say where 'science' stops and 'magic' begins. . . . If magic is to be defined as the employment of ineffective techniques to allay anxiety when effective ones are not available, then we must recognise that no society will ever be free from it. (Thomas, 1971, p. 800)

In everyday life these types of knowledge are, more often than not, unproblematically fitted together by each actor in an ongoing bricolage, closeted away in the stream of each person's daily conduct. This is not to say there are *no* problems, however; and these are compounded by variations in the availability of printed knowledge over space and by social group.

The Geography of Social Knowing and Unknowing

The purpose of this section is to establish, first, that spatial variations in types of knowledge (particularly the empirical) exist and, second, that within the constraints set by those broader patterns the different social groups present in each location have different degrees of access to the types of knowledge which go to make up their stock of knowledge: in short, that types of knowledge are socially distributed over space. I will begin with two illustrations from the seventeenth and eighteenth centuries, when the distribution of knowledge was not complicated by the noise of media other than print or the rise of mass state schooling systems. I will then try to show how in the nineteenth and twentieth centuries there has been an increase in the spatial variation of knowledge, which reflects changes in the spatial organisation of society and in the social distribution of knowledge.

In the mid-sixteenth century empirical knowledge began to become widely available in the form of printed books. This new medium transformed the technique and character of reading, writing and learning as well as what could be read, written and learnt. The rise of the printed book was rapid. It has been estimated that even *before* 1550, 20 million copies of books had been printed in Europe: a further 150 to 200 million books were published in the century after (Febvre and Martin, 1976). It is evident that these were not for the exclusive consumption of the upper classes, although consumption was just as evidently bent this way if only because of constraints of cost and literacy. The books themselves covered a vast range of subjects from prayer books and devotional literature through scholarly texts and textbooks to books of hours and rewritten medieval romances. But by the 1490s cheap books or 'chapbooks' had made their appearance in France. They gained a wider audience in the early seventeenth century in the form of little blue paper-covered books sold at two *sous* a time by a vast network of vendors, pedlars, hawkers and packmen. Known as the *bibliothèque bleue*, these books are the subject of numerous historical studies in France (for example, Mandrou, 1964; Bollème, 1971; Burke, 1978; H.J. Martin, 1978). Recently a comparable English literature has begun to grow up around twopenny chapbooks of the sixteenth, seventeenth and eighteenth centuries, which makes it possible to say something about the spatial distribution of the various types of knowledge in England during this period (for example, Neuberg, 1977; Burke, 1978; Spufford, 1981).

Caxton set up the first printing press in England in 1476. By the sixteenth century chapbooks were in circulation and by the seventeenth century there was 'a steady hail of printed pamphlets of news, political and religious propaganda, astrological prediction and advice, songs, sensation, sex and fantasy' (Spufford, 1981, p. xviii). The increase in circulation was spurred on, in particular, by the rapid rise in elementary schooling for the masses (at least until the Restoration), so that by the end of the seventeenth century English society had become one in which

> a boy even from a relatively poor family might have a year or two's education to the age of six or eight. His almost invisible sister, historically speaking, sometimes was taught to read. If a boy was at school until seven, he could read; if he was at school until eight, or at the latest nine, he could write. Either way he would be able to make sense of whatever cheap print the pedlars brought within his reach. Either way his mental environment had undergone an enormous and very important change. (Spufford, 1981, pp. 36–7)[29]

The impact of this literature was twofold. First, it signified the beginning of a gradual transition from a predominantly oral to a print culture and from practical learning and reckoning to a more rationalised, systematic and distanciated view of the world. But the transition was very gradual; it must be remembered that many chapbooks were meant for reading aloud and many were not much more than transcriptions into print of an oral tradition (Goody, 1977). Second, chapbooks were a means of disseminating the new type of empirical knowledge. The example of the almanac is important here. It is estimated that by the 1660s some 400,000 almanacs were being produced in England annually; one family in three were buying an almanac (Capp, 1979). Such almanacs were not simply sources of astrological predictions and agricultural calendars. They provided information upon society and religion and, more particularly, they 'played an important role, especially in the seventeenth century, in the popularisation of the new science' (Capp, 1979, p. 180), especially by offering up information on astronomy (including advice on building instruments and dials), mathematics and medicine. The almanacs also provided almost the only systematic source of generally available information on politics, history (usually a single-page history of the world) and geography. Thus 'in the second half of the seventeenth century *White* provided its readers each year with a crude map of England showing the county boundaries' (Capp, 1979, p. 203).

But, as Figure 3.3 shows, the spatial distribution of this knowledge was variable.[30] In general, those in the outlying districts outside the major metropolises were more likely to suffer, not only from a lack of schooling but also from a relative paucity of reading matter. Their ability to compare and contrast, to break out of the limits of the practical world, was therefore severely constrained, although via the chapmen 'chapbooks were available to the reader who wanted them, even in very remote areas' (Spufford, 1981, p. 126).

Class considerations intrude more forcefully when we come to consider

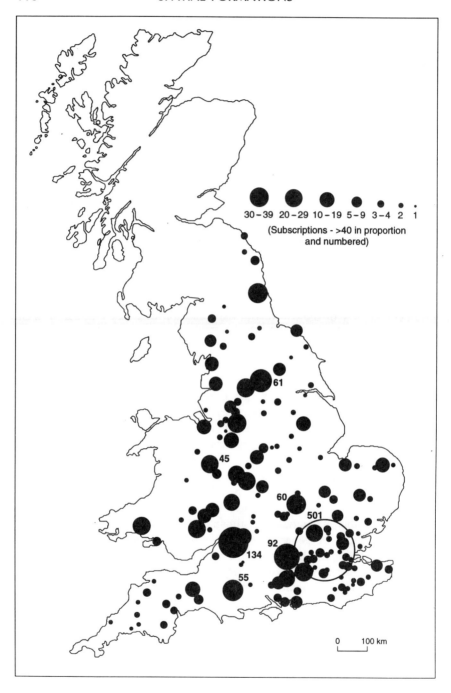

Figure 3.3 *The spatial distribution of chapmen licensed in England and Wales, 1697–8 (Spufford, 1981, Map 2, p. 119)*

empirical knowledge of a more systematic and less generally available character than that offered by the almanacs. To illustrate this point we must come forward in time to the eighteenth century and to that remarkable enlightenment publishing venture, Diderot's *Encyclopédie* (Lough, 1971; Darnton, 1979), which from the appearance of the first volume in 1751 was an attempt to:

> map the world of knowledge according to new boundaries, determined by reason and reason alone. As its title page proclaimed, it pretended to be a *'dictionnaire raisonné des sciences, des arts et des métiers'* – that is, to measure all human activity by rational standards and so to provide a basis for rethinking the world. (Darnton, 1979, p. 9)

The *Encyclopédie* is crucial in the history of the stock of empirical knowledge because it represents a *de facto* attack on traditional learning, which, it was implied,

> amounted to nothing but prejudice and superstition. So beneath the bulk of the *Encyclopédie*'s twenty-eight folio volumes and the enormous variety of its 71,818 articles and 2,885 plates lay an epistemological shift that transformed the topography of everything known to man [*sic*]. (Darnton, 1979, p. 7)[31]

The first four editions were luxurious folio publications that only a few could have afforded and, when taken together, account for only 40 per cent of the *Encyclopédies* in existence prior to 1789. The great mass of the *Encyclopédies* sold came from the cut-rate quarto and octavo editions printed between 1777 and 1782. Of those produced in France some 50 to 65 per cent were quartos and all these subscriptions can be traced, at least to the booksellers, so allowing Figures 3.4 and 3.5 to be drawn.[32]

The class-specific nature of these patterns can be elicited by the example of the town of Besançon.[33] In some respects Besançon does not seem the most fertile ground for the *Encyclopédie* – it was a provincial capital based upon religion and administration, a veritable bastion of Bourbon bureaucracy; but it also had a public library, *cabinet littéraire* and four booksellers. Literacy rates were high (95 per cent for men, 60 per cent for women). In the event, the *Encyclopédie* sold well – to noblemen, to the military, to parliamentarians, to doctors and to lawyers. In contrast, the artisans, shopkeepers, day-labourers and servants who made up the other three quarters of Besançon's population do not appear at all amongst the subscribers, nor do the peasants and shopkeepers of the surrounding province of Franche-Comté. Certainly some of these may have consulted the *Encyclopédie* in the reading clubs of the area, but for the vast majority access to its knowledge was severely limited – by a whole host of closely interwoven factors such as distance, class, time and ability to read. Indeed, in France as a whole,

> Although one cannot exclude the possibility that the *Encyclopédie* reached a great many readers in the lower classes, its main appeal was to the traditional élite – the men who dominated the administrative and cultural life of the provincial capital and small towns. (Darnton, 1979, p. 299)

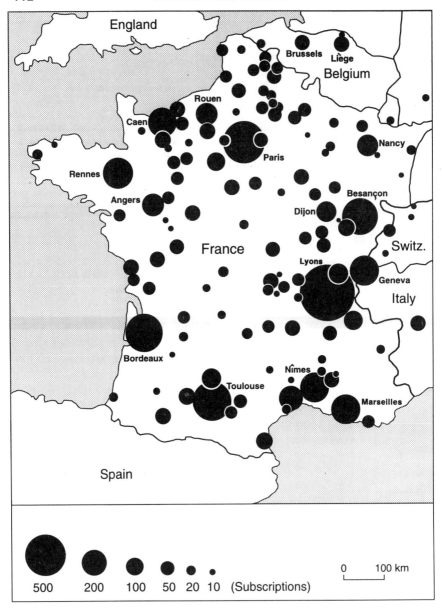

Figure 3.4   *The diffusion of the quarto edition of the Encyclopédie in France, 1777–82 (Darnton, 1979, Figure 5, p. 27)*

Thus, the diffusion of the *Encyclopédie* is a record of the spatial differentiation of knowledge, one that is explicitly based, at least in France, in the class composition of the urban system. The *Encyclopédie*'s store of empirical knowledge was, from its inception, marked as 'reserved'.

In the seventeenth and eighteenth centuries the acquisition of knowledge

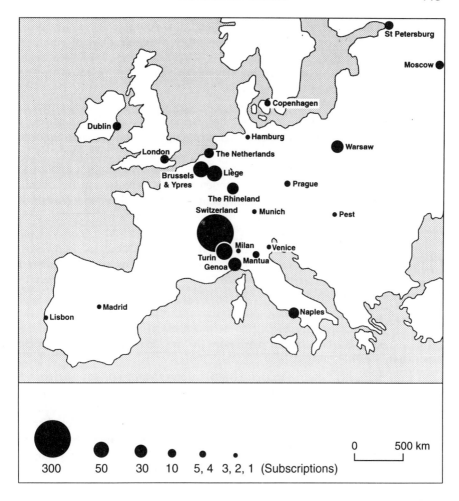

Figure 3.5   *The diffusion of the quarto edition of the Encyclopédie outside France, 1777–82 (Darnton, 1979, Figure 8, p. 301)*

(of all but *some* members of the upper and middle class) was still dependent upon where a person was born (and subsequently lived out her/his life) and upon the corresponding local availability of schools, booksellers and other means of dissemination of empirical knowledge. The nineteenth and twentieth centuries, in contrast, can be interpreted as a period of rapid homogenisation in the degree of spatial variation of availability of empirical knowledge. At least three trends support such a stance. First, the coming of mass schooling systems and compulsory education means that a common level of knowledge was brought into existence. Second, improvements in the speed and efficiency of transport communications, the phenomenon of 'time-space convergence' (Abler et al., 1975), mean that more institutions which disseminate knowledge become potentially available. Third, mass

circulation newspapers, radio, television and now computerised home information systems provide a large and generally available fund of common
empirical knowledge.

But there are two countervailing tendencies, which can be traced before
the nineteenth century but which now become different facets of the same
process of mobilisation of social groups around various specialised stores of
knowledge. The 'constituency' of the various mass media is strongly
differentiated by class and other social groupings to such a degree that the
actual fund of knowledge common to all social groups (and likely to be
spatially homogeneous) may well be quite small; the same point applies to
mass schooling systems.[34] The first tendency is the explosion in the overall
stock of knowledge in the nineteenth century as a result of the growth of
the state, the capitalist economy and the various sciences which brings with
it specialists in particular stocks of knowledge. The second tendency is the
seizure by various social groups upon this growing body of knowledge
(over and above that knowledge which becomes common to all or most of
the population) as a fertile source of 'cultural capital'[35] with which to
differentiate themselves from other social groups and thereby gain economic and social advantages. (Thus the education system provides the
grounds of heterogeneity as well as homogeneity.)

The result is that spatial variation in the distribution of empirical
knowledge still exists and may even be relatively stronger than in the past,
but is increasingly tied to the *social* distribution of empirical knowledge in a
pattern of sequestered life-spaces (Foucault, 1977; Giddens, 1981). Thus,
the social distribution of empirical (and practical) knowledge is associated
with institutional nodes like home, school, university or office which form a
set of points that selectively channel the life-paths of actors according to
their membership of a particular social group (Chapter 2, this volume).
This channelling results in the acquisition of particular common kinds of
knowledge (and the limits on that knowledge) that ultimately ensure the
reproduction of that group as a socio-spatial entity. Furthermore, the
organisation of these nodes into distinctively sequestered life-spaces occurs
at different scales. Working-class life-spaces are even now predominantly
local: a local school is followed by a local job. Middle class life-spaces are
most spatially extensive: a local school may be followed by a university in a
different location and then a job somewhere else again.

These claims can be made more concrete by another example from the
eighteenth century, a study of two particular doctors, James Clegg (1679–
1756) and Richard Kay (1716–51).[36] They were members of the same
social group, solidly Presbyterian and middle class, and although they lived
out their lives some kilometres apart they shared common interests, had
friends in common[37] and had heard sermons preached by the same people.
Indeed, they may even have met. Their respective life paths and the daily
paths they rode and trod for a week in July 1745 are depicted in time-
geographic fashion in Figure 3.6. Immediately the common nodes of this
particular social group's form of life stand out – home, school, chapel.

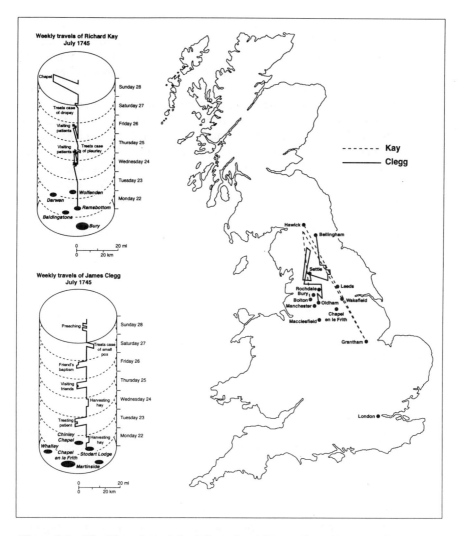

Figure 3.6   *The life paths and the daily paths of James Clegg (1679–1756) and Richard Kay (1716–51) during one week in July 1745*

What can we say about the stocks of knowledge upon which Clegg and Kay drew? First, they would have had a common pool of natural philosophy. Their upbringing was, in both cases, based upon a number of religious schools and dissenting academics. Second, they would both have had a common store of practical knowledge, a closed homodynamic code founded in and naturalised by the localised routines of family, farm and chapel. Third, they would both have had access to much the same supply of empirical knowledge – from school, from meetings of the Book Society and philosophical lectures and from various books and journals.[38] In particular, of course, they would have shared much of the same medical knowledge, which was primitive but becoming more systematic as physiology and anatomy slowly developed.[39] Their diaries show they were well-versed in drawing blood, applying leeches and glysters, setting broken limbs and removing tumours. But there is one important change between Clegg's life path and that of Kay. Clegg was essentially an ordained Presbyterian minister with a small farm who practised medicine to make ends meet, a practice common in remote rural areas of England but one that was already dying out in his lifetime. His medical knowledge was picked up by some reading, of course, but also through apprenticing himself to another doctor in Macclesfield. His right to practise without a licence was guaranteed by a medical degree obtained *in absentia* from Aberdeen on the recommendation of other (Presbyterian) doctors. In some respects Clegg was an 'amateur' doctor and the localised life-space of his life-path reflects this fact. In contrast, Kay had a year's formal training at Guy's Hospital in London, and his diary makes it clear that medicine was his first priority and that his living came from the practice of it. Here we see the beginnings of the formation of the medical profession as we now understand it, of a segment of a new professional middle class and of a new social distribution of empirical knowledge with the attendant qualifications serving as its cultural capital. We can also observe the corresponding change in Kay's life-space, when compared with that of Clegg – only a year in London perhaps, but soon to burgeon into a much longer period of formal training.

The Politics of Knowing and Unknowing

Finally, I want to turn to a more detailed discussion of the *links* between availability of knowledge and action by considering the implications that the availability of *printed* 'political' knowledge has for political organisation and action.[40] In order to anchor the discussion, I will limit my attention to how the 'working class' was able to gain access to 'radical' literature in England in the early to mid-nineteenth century. But four more general themes underlie this particular experience: first, the physical availability of political knowledge; second, the relation of political knowledge to literacy and education; third, the organisational framework for dissemination of political knowledge; and, finally, the cognitive framework within which political knowledge is interpreted.

The Physical Availability of Political Knowledge

There is little doubt that the spatial distribution of knowledge has its effects. In particular, isolation takes its toll on what can be known. One particularly doleful example of this is the Pentridge 'rebellion' of 1817 during which 200 or at most 300 men gathered in Pentridge and other villages at the foot of the Derby Peak, expecting their fellows in other centres to rise in revolt with them (E.P. Thompson, 1963, pp. 711–34; Calhoun, 1982). Their actions were, in part, predicated upon misinformation from the notorious *agent provocateur* 'Oliver', whose success depended upon the isolation of these villages from news which in turn had much to do with their lack of contact with and access to the political organisations of London and the regional centres. But we should not make too much of the factor of isolation. It can also have the threefold counter-effects of fostering community cohesion, nurturing political traditions and making communities opaque to the surveillance of the authorities. Further, the evidence from early to mid-nineteenth century England is that political knowledge does reach what might seem to be isolated rural communities surprisingly often. For example, in the early nineteenth century many of the dying breed of chapmen hawked not only the ordinary run of dying speeches and chapbooks but also political pamphlets and almanacs (Capp, 1979). The latter had their accounts of political events, which were often spiced with quite salty political commentaries. Other 'link men'[41] provided political news and comment too, particularly the carriers and coachmen, who not only brought deliveries of newspapers, journals and radical books but also acted as conveyors of political opinion and as witnesses of actual events.[42] Of course, the spread of the Radical press and of newspapers in general, as well as the unprecedented success of publications like Paine's *Rights of Man*, increased the level of available political knowledge in England dramatically. E.P. Thompson (1963, pp. 789–90) summarises the early to mid-nineteenth-century scene as well as anyone:

> Cobbett's 2nd *Register* at its meridian, between October 1816 and February 1817, was running at something between 40 000 and 60 000 each week, a figure many times in excess of any competitor of any sort. The *Black Dwarf* ran at about 12 000 in 1819, although this figure was probably exceeded after Peterloo. Thereafter the stamp tax (and the recession of the movement) severely curtailed circulation, although Carlile's periodicals ran in the thousands through much of the Twenties. With the Reform Bill agitation, the Radical press broke through to a larger circulation once more: Doherty's *Voice of the People*, and *The Pioneer* all had circulations above ten thousand . . . while a dozen smaller periodicals, like the *Destructive*, ran to some thousands. The slump in the sale of costly weekly periodicals (at anything from 7d to 1s.) during the stamp tax decade was to a great degree made up by the growth in the sales of cheap books and individual pamphlets. . . . In the same period, in most of the great centres there were one or more (and in London a dozen) dailies or weeklies which, while not being avowedly 'Radical', nevertheless catered for this large Radical public.[43]

Nineteenth-century developments in communication also played their part in the availability of political knowledge, but it was a part that, initially at least, was by no means entirely positive. Thus, in the rural areas:

> One factor in the relative quiescence of the period from 1830 to 1870 may have been the disintegration of the network of long-distance carriers and coaches after the coming of the railway. The railway may have united the urban proletariat but in rural areas it could not perform the role the link men of the road had. Its network was much less integrated, sparse, and its stopping places much rarer. Indeed, initially, it isolated the rural labourer and artisans from regular and direct contact with the urban centres of political radicalism and with labourers in other areas. No wonder Chartism barely touched the countryside. It is even

possible that the village world of the 1840s and 1850s had a more restricted horizon than had the village in 1830. By the 1860s however, this horizon was beginning to widen again. Cheap daily newspapers, national networks of benefit societies, the penny post . . . all of which depended to some extent on a national railway network, gradually helped to restore the contacts between the village and the outside world that the railway had originally destroyed. The development of agricultural trade unionism on a national scale then became a possibility. (Charlesworth, 1979, p. 46)[44]

The Relations of Political Knowledge to Literacy and Education

Some degree of literacy is needed in a community that is to receive printed political knowledge and indeed by the early nineteenth century literacy had become widespread in England as the possibility of at least some education had become a probability. It has been estimated that, even at the beginning of the century, in the two most illiterate groups (agricultural labourers and servants) one in three possessed sufficient literacy to sign a marriage register and the proportion of tradesmen and artisans capable of signing on the register was about double the proportion of these two groups (L. Stone, 1969; Schofield, 1973). This degree of literacy was obviously spatially variable and, in general, literacy was greatest in the cities and towns and lowest in the agricultural villages and hamlets. Yet even in the rural areas most homes had a few books, albeit mainly religious.[45] And of course literacy was not a necessary prerequisite for acquiring political knowledge. Those amongst the working class who were literate (particularly the artisans) could act as scribes for their non-literate fellows and were often nominated to read out newspapers in public houses and other associative locations. James Dawson Burn (1978, p. 94; see also Vincent, 1981) provides one out of many similar autobiographical reminiscences:

> There was a young man in Bellingham, named George Seaton, who had served his apprenticeship with a Mr Gibson, a saddler. Seaton was a person of studious habits, and an inquiring turn of mind: he was also a very good public reader. For some time after the *Black Dwarf* made its appearance in the village, Seaton was in the habit of reading it to a few of the more intelligent working people, at the old fashioned cross which stood in the centre of the village.

The Organisational Framework for the Dissemination of Political Knowledge

The institutional framework in which political knowledge is transmitted is clearly crucial, and just as clearly there is a sea-change in this organisation that begins in the early nineteenth century. In England, a whole network of new or adapted knowledge-disseminating nodes springs up at which newspapers, journals and books could be obtained. For example, newspapers were stocked in the new type of coffee shop, which sometimes even had a small library,[46] or could be heard being read aloud in the public houses and beershops. Artisans' libraries became common. Market stalls sold radical literature. Even the members of some workshops clubbed together to buy a journal or a newspaper. For those who were committed, these nodes now formed an integral part of the routinised channel through which their life path ran; they acted as the founts of a new popular sociability.[47] Thomas Carter (b. 1792), a Colchester tailor, was one of these committed men:

> The workshop employed a shopman, two apprentices, a foreman, and six journeymen, a sufficient number of individuals to combat the then high price of radical literature and to introduce Carter to contemporary politics . . . 'they clubbed their pence to pay for a newspaper, and selected the "Weekly Political Register" of that clever man the late William Cobbett.' Later he moved to London and was able to avail himself of two more methods of extending the scope of his reading matter. He made a habit of taking his breakfast at one of the coffee shops, 'which were just then becoming general', on his way to work where he would read the previous day's newspapers, the contents of which he would relay to his fellow workmen. And in his spare time he found an opportunity for supplementing his own small library: 'At home I acquired increased facilities for reading, by means of a small book club, consisting of my landlord and a few of his friends. Of this I became a member; and thus had the means of becoming a little acquainted with works which I had not seen before'. (Vincent, 1981, p. 118)

The Interpretation of Political Knowledge

It seems clear that the working classes in England in the early nineteenth century were, in many respects, still in the transition from an oral to a print culture, with print still only 'one of' rather than 'the major' means of disseminating and receiving political knowledge. Interpretation of print is concrete and literal. This is not so surprising. In England,

> the ability to read was only the elementary technique. The ability to handle abstract and consecutive argument was by no means inborn; it had to be discovered against almost overwhelming difficulties – the lack of leisure, the cost of candles (or spectacles), as well as educational deprivation. Ideas and terms were sometimes employed in the early Radical movement which, it is evident, had for some ardent followers a fetishistic rather than rational value. Some of the Pentridge rebels thought that a 'Provisional Government' would ensure a more plentiful supply of 'provisions'; while, in one account of the pitmen of the north-east in 1819, 'Universal Suffrage is understood by many of them to mean universal suffering . . . if one member suffers, all must suffer'. (E.P. Thompson, 1963, p. 783)

The relationship between political action (and inaction) by members of a particular social group and the availability of political knowledge must be related to the internal organisation of the institutions of that social group, the organisation of the (often intersecting) institutions of other social groups and the objective structural conditions which form the grounds of possibility (Calhoun, 1982, Chapter 8). The connections are often oblique and are continually changing over space and in time. But the fact remains that in many places in England during the early to mid-nineteenth century access to political knowledge not only sensitised actors to current events but also helped to inspire them to action, however limited. For example, in 'radical Oldham' in the 1830s the cultural field sees

The biggest and most undeniable development of all – a mass readership of the radical press. While this cannot be precisely measured, the descriptive evidence indicates that the London and Lancashire working-class newspapers achieved something near a monopoly in Oldham. (J. Foster, 1974, p. 147)

And such a process of getting knowledge is often cumulative, for one part of a political tradition is to know how to know about politics.

The problems of making the connections between political action and the availability of political knowledge become even greater in the twentieth century, when, for example, other media than print come into play (each with their own distinctive ways of disseminating, rationing and biasing knowledge),[48] when mass schooling systems guarantee a print culture's existence and when organised political parties hold sway. These changes are not within the scope of this chapter. But at the most general level, the difference between the nineteenth and twentieth centuries are probably not as great as might at first be assumed. In most social groups political commitment remains diffuse, those who read political books remain in a minority, those who know about politics and political institutions are relatively few (Dennis et al., 1971). It can be safely assumed that political knowing and unknowing remain differentially distributed amongst social groups, over space and in time (Mann and Burgoyne, 1969; Mann, 1970).

Conclusions

Four main threads can be teased out from this chapter. First, the availability of knowledge must be seen as an important component in the construction of a theory of situated social action. It is not the only component; it is probably not the most important component, but neither is it a component that can any longer be passed over. Ignorance may be no excuse in the eyes of the law, but it is a fact of social life that can no longer be overlooked. Second, the sociology of knowledge can be given a more coherent base, since it is now generally agreed that

> an excessive interest in intellectual and intellectualised belief is a weakness of the conventional sociology of knowledge. Of much greater importance is the way that ideologies are represented and diffused in the relatively untheoretical 'ways of life' of whole social groups. It is notably difficult to provide a way of identifying these 'ways of life' or common-sense beliefs, and providing substantive studies of them . . . is a major task of a sociology of knowledge. (Abercrombie, 1980, p. 176)

I hope that this chapter goes some way towards beginning to overcome this difficulty. Third, epistemology must be seen for what it is. Thus, it

> is not an emanation of 'reason' but is made up of doctrines and standards which themselves demand evaluation. One does not gain exemption from evaluation by claiming to be rational, any more than by claiming to be scientific. In the last analysis a community evaluates all its cognitive authorities in relation to its overall way of life, not by reference to a specific set of standards. (Barnes, 1982, p. 93)

This is not an argument for an unalloyed historicism or a recalcitrant

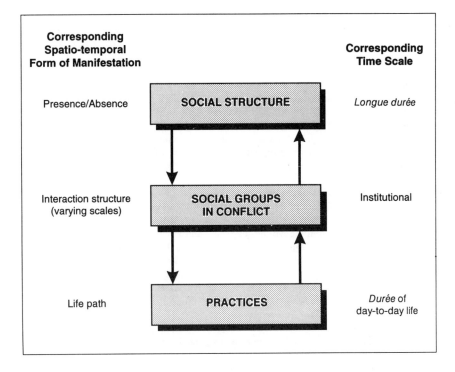

Figure 3.7   *The major components of the process of structuring*

relativism.[49] But it is an argument for a situated or contextual epistemology, which acknowledges that people are historical, geographical and
social beings (Thrift, *1979f*).[50] Finally, a conclusion tinged with a certain
amount of irony. We know very little about what people know and do not
know. From the many indirect studies, we can expect there to be systematic
variations in the knowledge available to and taken up by various social
groups set in particular regions and times. Yet what is systematically
known about these variations is restricted to a few desultory studies. This
chapter is therefore at best a prelude to a pressing empirical task. It is the
germ of an idea.

Notes

This chapter was originally published in D. Gregory and J. Urry (eds) *Social Relations and
Spatial Structures*, 1985. Reprinted with permission from Macmillan Press Ltd.

   1. Cited in Kreckel (1982, p. 270).
   2. According to the *Oxford English Dictionary* 'germ' in its modern meaning as a micro-
organism did not come into existence until this date (although germ meaning a seed of disease
as in 'germ of the smallpox' was current in 1803).
   3. Social groups (which include classes) can be seen as the intermediate point in the process
of 'structuring' between social structure and individual and between individual and social
structure (Figure 3.7). The formation and reformation of social structure cannot be understood

without considering this continual process of social group formation and reformation and neither can the formation and reformation of individuals. Thus a situated theory of human action must be built upon and necessarily intersect with an understanding of factors such as how such groups are continually organised and reorganised *in conflict* (and coalition) with other groups, how their distinctive spatial and temporal interaction structures (Layder, 1981) produce, at a variety of scales, distinctive strengths and weaknesses, and how these social groups are produced, reproduced or transformed by the actions of the individuals that are both constituted by and partially constitutive of them. This formulation makes it possible to reconcile 'way of conflict' with 'way of life' (E.P. Thompson, 1963) and 'economy' with what some Marxists continue to insist is a ragbag of superstructures but which is, in reality, an integral part of the production and reproduction of society, namely 'civil society' (see Urry, 1981a), a term which, of course, goes under many other names such as 'culture', 'civilisation' or *'mentalités'*.

4. See the remarks by Bhaskar (1980, p. 18).

5. For a systematic account of the production, distribution and circulation system, albeit a rather abstract and partial one, see Raymond Williams (1980).

6. This term, derived from the writings of Schutz and Luckman (see, for example, Schutz, 1962; Berger and Luckman, 1967; Schutz and Luckman, 1973; Luckman, 1982), is useful almost in spite of their work. Schutz, in particular, has an unfortunate tendency to reduce the social world to stocks of knowledge. See Hindess (1977, Chapter 2) for a particularly hostile view of Schutz, and Abercrombie (1980) for a more sympathetic appraisal.

7. I want to use this term without its implications of a series of completely self-contained universes or of relativism. See Giddens (1976, p. 18).

8. See Chapter 2; my subsequent presentation is overwhelmingly biased to the negative side of knowing because we know so little about human creativity.

9. The term 'habitus' is taken from Bourdieu (1977) and refers to the cognitive structure of any social group which is the sedimented history of practices improvised to meet particular objective conditions which then tends to reproduce these conditions.

10. In modern societies media like books or television may complicate this picture but they do not fundamentally change the situation. Indeed we might think of these media as having some of the same qualities as human actors, in terms of communicability of knowledge.

11. Until quite recently in human history, of course, human societies were often still isolated from one another. Countries like China, for example, all but formed their own universes, devoid of outside influence or knowledge.

12. And which we might call 'ideology'. Habermas (1982, p. 264) makes some similar observations in a rather different context.

13. It is important to guard against reductionism here, of course. Marxists have been particularly guilty, in that they too often *assume* direct connections between the capitalist economy and, for example, the division of the labour force into skilled and unskilled or into those with qualifications and those without. Abercrombie and Urry (1983) provide an excellent critique of this kind of tendency which is *still* apparent in many works (for example, Carchedi, 1977). However, there have been works which have avoided this tendency, for example Zilsel and de Santillana (1941).

14. Such as those offered, most notably, by Habermas, but also by Willer and Willer (1973).

15. See Macfarlane (1970, Chapter 12). The diary is available. See Macfarlane (1976).

16. Thus Freud's work is restricted to a particular class operating in a particular place and time. See Fromm (1981). But historical psychology is now receiving increasing attention with the impetus provided by Elias's work (1978, 1982).

17. Neisser's definition of practical knowledge is as good as any. Practical knowledge is

the human knowledge that is not based on a systematic knowledge of the laws governing nature or society but, though obtained pragmatically, possesses a high degree of certainty: for example, how to till the soil, how to make simple tools, how to care for a herd, how to hunt. (Neisser, 1965, p. 24)

But I would want to add to this definition, 'knowledge of social interaction', especially that gained in close-knit groups, such as the family. See Kreckel (1982).

18. Note how the word 'beliefs' automatically denies that there is any truth in what is thought.

19. I mean 'rationalisation' to be taken here in the Weberian sense. For an excellent reconstruction of Weber's theory of rationalisation see Habermas (1982).

20. I have taken this term from Giddens, who uses it to refer to distance in space and time.

21. The form and extent of these systems should not be underestimated. For example, in England:

> By Edward I's reign serfs possessed seals to sign their names and they recorded their property transactions in writing. Thus the *nativi* – the natives, villeins and serfs – who had thought the Domesday Book to be the Last Judgement (according to FitzNeal in the twelfth century) had charters of their own (the *Cartae Nativorum*) by the 1300s. (Clanchy, 1979, p. 518)

22. These were particularly limits imposed by *time*. Thus in twelfth- and thirteenth-century England cursive script came into extensive use as pressure of business built up on scribes (Clanchy, 1979).

23. The discussion which follows draws on Chaytor (1945); Febvre and Martin (1976); Hirst and Woolley (1982); and, in particular, Eisenstein (1979, Chapter 2). (There are, of course, many other effects of printing than those catalogued there. For example, the idea of the author dates from this invention.) It is a worthwhile exercise to compare the four characteristics listed here with those characteristics of a 'knowledgeable society' listed in Lane (1966, pp. 653–7).

24. See the remarks on professions in Lane (1966) and in Ginzburg (1980b).

25. Thomas S. Kuhn (1970, p. 5) likens normal science to 'a strenuous and devoted attempt to force nature into the conceptual boxes supplied by professional education'.

26. Sohn-Rethel (1978) considers that abstract thought comes from the practice of commodity exchange. Whilst this may be a part of the picture, I remain to be convinced that it is anything like the whole explanation.

27. It is therefore debarred from many people. See Steiner (1978) on the death of the book.

28. It should not be thought that magic is now the exclusive prerogative of the developing countries: see, for example, Favret-Saada (1980) on the Bocage of Western France. Hirst (1982) makes the point that the form of magic is intimately related to the spatial layout of a community. The Bocage area's form of magic, for example, relies on small family enterprises, settled residence and familial-patriarchal relations. It would not work in a factory.

29. This conclusion is, of course, open to debate since it is based upon partial knowledge, but I am sure it is correct. See also Schofield (1968, 1973); Spufford (1979); Cressy (1980).

30. There are obvious problems in using a surrogate variable like number of licensed chapmen to represent the patterns of distribution of cheap books. First, chapmen certainly did not sell only books. These were usually just one of their wares, although some were specialists in bookselling. Second, many chapmen, although resident in one town, worked a periodic market system. Third, there were many other retailers of cheap books, most notably specialist booksellers, but also some shopkeepers. The map is therefore indicative at best.

31. In fact, much of the *Encyclopédie* represented not much more than a codification of practical knowledge. Ginzburg (1980b, p. 22), talks of 'a massive process of culture invasion . . . the symbol and crucial instrument of this offensive was the French *Encyclopédie*.'

32. There are also problems in mapping distribution of books sold. First, salesmen were unevenly effective in selling *Encyclopédies*. Second, the density of booksellers varies. Third, the density of primary and secondary schools varies. However:

> In general, it seems clear that the quarto reached every corner of the country, including the remote areas of the *Pays Basque* and the *Massif Central*. Its diffusion corresponded fairly well to the density of population on a national scale, despite important discrepancies from city to city. (Darnton, 1979, p. 281)

33. This account follows that of Darnton (1979, pp. 287–94).

34. I know of no research which has considered systematically the common funds of knowledge learnt from the various media or at school, or what the differences are, although these can of course be inferred from the many studies on the media and schooling.

35. See Bourdieu and Passeron (1977, 1980) and Garnham and Williams (1980). Cultural capital does not come just from the knowledge engendered and protected by professions of course, but also from the investment of time in and exercise of various cultural practices which legitimise class and other divisions. The acquisition of this kind of knowledge can be seen in a life-path perspective as a continuous process of the acquisition of various cultural competences at home, in school and elsewhere.

36. The information on Clegg and Kay comes from their diaries edited by Doe (1978) and Brockbank and Kenworthy (1968) respectively.

37. For example, the Reverend John Bent, Dr Samuel Kay and James Day.

38. The exact size of their libraries remains in doubt. Friends of Clegg's whose books he valued on their death had libraries of at least 1,500 books, however.

39. See the account of seventeenth-century medical knowledge in Thomas (1971). 'Germs' were not known!

40. I am taking 'political' knowledge here to mean information about political events *and* ways of organising this information of the kind to be found in pamphlets, newspapers, journals and books. I am not including the political messages to be found in literature like the popular novel, however potent these may sometimes be.

41. A phrase originally used by Richard Cobb.

42. However, the carriers and coachmen were mainly restricted to major highways (see Charlesworth, 1979).

43. For details of the press and, in particular, the Radical press at this time see, for example, Hollis (1977); Koss (1981). For details of Radical books available see Webb (1950, 1955); Altick (1957); Vincent (1981). See also the set of maps in Lee (1976) which show the diffusion of newspapers in England and their political affiliation.

44. Thus, in the nineteenth century in particular, different social organisations were effective at different scales, at different 'levels of integration'.

45. Further, literacy does not guarantee the habit of reading. See Vincent (1981, p. 110).

46. The first of these opened in 1811. By 1849 there were some 2,000 in London alone.

47. Other libraries and other sources of political knowledge also grew up at the time, of course, although usually a non-radical nature; for example, those of the Mechanics Institutes, the Society for the Diffusion of Useful Knowledge, chapel libraries, even a few school libraries.

48. See the reviews in Swingewood (1977); Barnett et al. (1979); Corrigan and Willis (1980).

49. One seeming gap in this chapter is the work of Foucault, but this is a result of his relative lack of emphasis on practices, even as he proclaims their importance.

50. See Bhaskar's (1979, 1980) comments on the activity, concept and space-time dependence of theories.

4

Little Games and Big Stories: Accounting for the Practices of Personality and Politics in the 1945 General Election

> Children, only animals live entirely in the Here and Now. Only nature knows neither meaning nor history. But man [*sic*] – let me offer you a definition – is the story-telling animal. Wherever he goes he wants to leave behind him not a chaotic wake and an empty space, but the comforting marker-buoys and trail-signs of stories. He has to go on telling stories. As long as there's a story, it's all right. Even in his last moments, it's said, in the split second of a fatal fall – or when he's about to drown – he sees, passing quickly before him, the story of his whole life.
>
> (Swift, 1983, pp. 53–4)

Introduction

This chapter represents the third of a series of essays inquiring into the nature of social action. Chapter 2 was concerned with providing a general theory of social action, conceived as a situated and never-ending discourse driven by conflict. Chapter 3 took up one necessary component of any theory of social action, the geography of knowing and unknowing within which social action must be developed. This chapter is concerned with another such component, the human agent. For as Giddens (1982, p. 535) puts it, 'formulating a theory of social action in the social sciences demands theorising the human agent.' Understanding the agent is not a modest aim. Clearly, in a short chapter like this one, I cannot and will not present any finished or even half-finished theory of the human agent (see *1987p*). Like the other two chapters, this chapter is 'pre-theoretical'.

Still there are important issues to be addressed.[1] On the theoretical front there is the problem of how it is possible to interpret a whole constellation of terms which are routinely used in social science but whose routine usage conceals very considerable problems – terms like 'experience', 'consciousness', 'ideology', 'action', 'belief', 'self', 'attitude', and so on. On the practical front, there is a problem of what is being talked about when political consciousness (and beliefs and attitudes) is considered, and under what conditions political consciousness can be changed.[2]

The chapter is in two main parts. The first part sketches an outline of how human agents might legitimately be theorised through a discursive model of how people build themselves through others and what it is that they build. The second part narrows the terms of the discussion a little by concentrating on the problem of how 'political' attitudes towards the left changed in England in the Second World War.

Telling It Like It Is: A Discursive Model of Human Agents

What is a human agent? This is a short enough question but it requires a long answer. What I want to suggest is that in many contemporary theories of social action, the conception of the human agent is deficient.

Human Agent/Negative Ascriptions

Theories of social action must include within them a more or less explicit conception of the human agent. In many current theories of social action, the conception is deficient, usually because the human agent appears in the theory by default, very much as the ill-considered trifle (Geras, 1983). Three deficiencies are particularly common.

The first of these deficiencies is one that is now less common than it was, but it is by no means laid to rest. This is that the human agent can be reduced to a cognitive drone, to a string of internal programmes responding to an external environment. People's action is governed by some 'inner', on-board computer which assimilates all the available knowledge, works out the angles and decides on an appropriate course of action. It has surely been argued often enough by now that human beings are not rational beings, at least in this sense of rationality. People live in a social world and they cannot therefore be reduced to episodes of theoretical reasoning, followed by appropriate action. This is an incorrigibly contemplative view of the world which flies in the face of the evidence; evidence which suggests that people act to reason to act. Such a reduction is only possible because the 'intellectual fallacy' is still so pervasive in social science; a fallacy which enables middle-class academics to pass off 'their curious customs and those of their students as the psychology of all mankind [*sic*]' (Harré, 1983, p. 260).

The second deficiency found in certain theories of social action is that the human agent can be reduced to a moral incompetent. Human agents are partly knowledgeable, creative (rule-making as well as rule-following) and responsible beings who – under pressure from their peers – make judgements, evaluate and give accounts of themselves. To say that there are limits on the kind of judgements, evaluations and accounts people can make is not to absolve them of the responsibility for their actions (see Parfit, 1984).

The third deficiency, found especially but not exclusively in Marxist and neo-Marxist theories of social action, is that the human agent can be reduced to the outcome of whatever is the current positive. Conventionally this is achieved through a category like 'ideology'. In the most rigorous case there is the Althusserian notion that ideology interpellates individuals as subjects. Less rigorously, the category of 'ideology' can be used simply to indicate that a certain set of beliefs or preoccupations can be linked to the material situation of a particular social group. Both cases generate problems. In the most rigorous case the major problem is that no room is left for human beings as creative agents. Ideology functions 'as the secret police of the social structure, arresting the suspects and shoving them into the correct cells' (Connell, 1983, p. 227). In the least rigorous case, the problem is that there is no guarantee that particular beliefs and preoccupations are tied to particular material situations, so that the need for the category disappears. Further, the whole question of what 'beliefs' and 'preoccupations' actually are is left unanswered. Thus even used in the least rigorous way the category 'ideology' 'proves inert and unilluminatingly reductive' (Stedman Jones, 1983a, p. 18).

> In the case of a set of political beliefs and preoccupations like Chartism, for example, a preoccupation with ideology simply missed what was most urgent to explain about Chartism – its political character, the specific reasons for its rise and fall, its focus upon representation and its lack of interest in the demarcation of socio-economic status within the unrepresented. 'The difficulty of an explanation in terms of the limitations of an artisanal consciousness or ideology . . . was that it did not identify with any precision what it was that declined'. (Stedman Jones, 1983a, p. 19)

One alternative to ideology has been the category 'hegemony', but it is difficult to see how, in many of its usages, a category like 'hegemony' escapes the problems posed by a category like 'ideology'. It 'may register some moral distance from the apologetic complacency of functionalist theory' (Stedman Jones, 1983a, p. 86), but it makes no real break from the whole theoretical bloodline.

One answer to these problems has been to redefine ideology and hegemony in such a way that these categories become broad enough to escape the charges of reductionism. Thus Stuart Hall (1983, p. 59) defines ideology as

> mental frameworks – the languages, the concepts, categories, imagery of thought, and the systems of representation – which different classes and social groups deploy in order to make sense of, define, figure and render intelligible the way society works.

Similarly, Raymond Williams (1977, pp. 112–13) defines hegemony as

> a realised complex of experiences, relationships and activities, with specific and changing pressures and limits. In practice, that is, hegemony can never be singular. Its internal structures are highly complex as can readily be seen in concrete analysis. Moreover . . . it does not just possibly exist as a form of dominance. It has continually to be renewed, recreated, defended and modified. It is also continually resisted, limited, altered, challenged by pressures not all its own.

The problem with definitions like these, of course, is that in order to avoid a charge of reductionism they are so broad that few would disagree with them. Further each definition is made up of the undefined. All the work is left to do.[3]

These, then, are three of the most common deficiencies to be found in conceptions of the human agent. If nothing else, they show that rationalism still holds much of social science in a terrible stranglehold. Human agents are rational beings, living in a theoretical world. But what of the real social world, as opposed to this academic world? What beings dwell there?

Human Agent/Positive Prescriptions

Luckily, there is a developing consensus in much of philosophy and social science (insofar as they can be separated) concerning what a human agent is; a conception which theories of social action must begin to take into account.

At the epistemological level, this consensus invokes a rejection of the old concepts of rationality; 'science' is a problem not a solution. In particular, there is a desire to recover a sense of practical rationality (summarised in Bernstein, 1983, p. 270). Old scientific modes of inquiry are faulty:

> We must appreciate the extent to which our sense of community is threatened not only by material conditions but by the faulty epistemological doctrines that fill our heads. The moral task of the philosopher or the cultural critic is to defend the openness of human conversation against all those temptations and real threats that seek closure. (Bernstein, 1992, pp. 204–5)

At the ontological level, the consensus involves a new account of what a human being is (though one with a very long bloodline),[4] which is, essentially, the discovery that hermeneutics is what people are and that psychology is not a science but a humanity.

The depiction of the human agent built in this new consensus is founded on a number of prescriptions, three of which are particularly important. The first is that any depiction of a human agent must be contextual, must accept that agents live in pockets of space and time and are not universals. There are a number of consequences of this prescription.

Human agents live a context which is predicated upon action in time, not contemplation. This is a fact of life: 'no psychological explanation of why a human being does one thing after another is required. We assume that human psychology is such that a person is continuously busy. It is a matter of energy exchange and biochemistry to explain why a human being is always in action' (Harré, 1979, p. 246). Upon action everything else is predicated. It follows that:

1 'Sometimes I don't know anything at all for large spaces: sometimes I know many things all in the same place. My perceptions are uneven, my understanding patchy but I have action; I go' (Hoban, 1983, p. 38).
2. Human agents are developing systems that grow from simple individuals into richly structured ones. They are never complete. They are always growing. Human agents are 'dynamic structures' (Prigogine,

1980; Prigogine and Stengers, 1984), producing and reproducing themselves and others through a continuous flow of conduct and varying in how they are made up according to the vagaries of history, geography and the prevailing systems of social stratification that shape the contexts they live.

3. 'Human agents must live contexts that at any one time can only be partially determined, for in acting we do something; we make something take on a form other than that which it would have had if we had not acted; thus we determine the world. For this to be possible the world must be capable of being given a form which it did not already possess, that is, the world must be essentially indeterminate' (Shotter, 1984, p. 45).

4. Contexts are active networks of people and things gathered in particular social situations, not passive 'environments'. Action-in-context is therefore always joint action.

The second prescription is that language must be taken seriously as an operator, and not just as a parameter, as an action and not just as a representation – language is not just a passive, static framework through which 'experience' finds expression. It is a complex, context-dependent and therefore continually shifting rhetoric, that is, a way of telling others what is being done in that context, 'binding together, in a systematic way, shared premises, analytical routines, strategic options and pragmatic demands' (Stedman Jones, 1983b, p. 107). It is not a logic, but a way of making oneself understood to others:

> remember that, in general, we don't use language according to strict rules – it hasn't been taught us by means of strict rules, either. We are unable to circumscribe the concepts we use clearly; not because we don't know their real definitions, but because there is no real 'definition' to them. To suppose there must be would be like supposing that whenever children play with a ball they play a game according to strict rules. (Wittgenstein, 1964, p. 25)

In this conception of language as a way of co-ordinating action,

> linguistic activities can be seen as working materially to structure social relations by 'in-forming', or instructing the participants in them in various ontological skills, in how to be parameters of this or that kind of activity, so that as persons they come to see and hear and act and do appropriate things in the appropriate contexts, 'routinely', 'naturally', one might say, as if without a moment's thought. (Shotter, 1985a, p. 11)

The third and final prescription is that human agents must be seen as socially constructing, not socially constructed. There is a world of difference between the '-ing' and the '-ed'. People are not just passively socialised into various social institutions. They are continually constructing these institutions and themselves and others anew – the three are difficult to separate – according to the particular context.

Some examples of how social relations are continually constructed are in order. Let us start, appropriately enough, with childhood, with the process of constructing of 'how to be' being encountered by a child for the first few times.

A mother looks at her young baby:

> 'Oh look', she says after having got her infant to look at her by cooing and smiling at her, having placed her face in her line of regard, 'she's looking at me'. So she replies to 'her'[?] look with a 'Hello, hello, you cheeky thing'. The point here being that whatever mothers do to motivate their babies' activity, when they respond, mothers still interpret their response as something which their babies themselves do, not merely as something which they have succeeded in eliciting from them; it is thus treated as activity worthy of being an expression in a dialogue, an expression requiring a meaningful reply . . . in this situation babies can learn what they bring about by their own actions. (Shotter, 1984, pp. 82–3)

Another example; a mother showing her 11-month-old child, Samantha, how to place shaped pieces on a form-board.

> Having just physically helped her little girl to place one of the pieces, Samantha's mother says 'Oh clever girl!' But Samantha had not paused in her activity and signalled by eye-contact that she knew she had done something socially significant; she just went straight on to manipulating something else. So her mother leant forward, caught her eye, and repeated her 'marker' with emphasis: 'AREN'T YOU CLEVER?'. Samantha then stopped and smiled.
>
> Mothers are not just satisfied with their children doing the tasks that they require of them. They must also give indications in their actions that they did what they did as a result of trying to do it, that 'they' knew what was required of them, that their actions were based in some socially defined requirement of the situation. Thus children must come to show in their actions, not just awareness of their physical circumstances, but *self*-awareness; an awareness of the nature of their relations to others. (Shotter, 1984, pp. 86–7; my emphasis)

Later on in life the mode of constructing particular negotiated contents can become a powerful resource. A particular social group's 'how to be' can be more confident, more manipulative. Take the example of a tightly knit group of the most powerful Philadelphia families. These are 'old' families bonded together by interlocking directorships and their membership of their exclusive Philadelphia Club.

> These are families with a keen sense that their primary resources derive from their own past: the powerful mixture of historical distinction . . . and accumulated wealth. Because the very kernels of the families' conception of their social environment lies within themselves, not the outer world, we could call these families 'solipsistic'. . . . But these are also powerful, accomplished families who understand the underlying business structures of their city and know how to control those structures for their own ends. In an important sense, the families' ties to corporate directorships and their ties to the exclusive clubs provide complementary support to the families' conceptions of themselves in the world. The corporate directorships reinforce the families' sense of power and control; the social clubs reinforce the importance of their historical roots. (Reiss, 1981, pp. 299–302)[5]

The conception of the human agent that springs from these prescriptions is very different from that found in most theories of social action. Human agents are not rounded theoretical beings, receiving information, contemplating it, translating it. This kind of depiction has only come about because those who have studied social action have increasingly transferred features of their idea of discourse on social action to social action. Rather, human agents are contextual beings, negotiating each given context in joint action with other agents with the aid of a particular store of practical knowledge of whose meaning they are often unaware. Thus the isolated individual ceases to exist:

> In other words, in many actions in daily life, we are ignorant as to what it is exactly we are doing, not because the 'ideas' or whatever is supposedly informing our conduct are too deeply buried in us somewhere to be brought out into the light of day, but because formative influences shaping our conduct are not wholly there in our individual heads to be brought out. Our actions occur interlaced in with those of others, and their actions are just as much a formative influence determining what we do as anything within ourselves. (Shotter, 1985a, p. 15)

Storytime

Clearly the conception of the human agent outlined above has connotations for what we can regard as 'consciousness', 'belief', 'self', 'attitude', and all the other terms that are routinely applied to human agents, yet alone for how these terms can be stitched together into elements of a theory of social action like 'class consciousness', or 'ideology', or 'hegemony'. Just as clearly, as yet no strong theory of the human agent has come out of this conception of the human agent. Luckily, there is a model that is becoming generally accepted in disciplines as diverse as anthropology, sociology and social psychology, which begins the task of building such a theory, the so-called 'discursive', or 'constructionist' or 'constructivist' model,[6] with its five main elements – 'person', 'self', 'account', 'folk model' and 'intention'. These models are based upon the existence of human agents as contextual beings, structured out of joint action in joint action, and irredeemably social. Out of joint action human agents produce institutions which provide 'stocks of knowledge (of various kinds but most especially the 'practical', 'tacit' or intuitive knowledge[7] that enables them to 'understand' what it is they are doing/saying/thinking). And these stocks of knowledge define their commonsense view of the world. Since at any point in time institutions will be structured in various ways, by social group and in space, so the knowledge institutions can impart will be differentially available to make persons.

So far, so good. But human beings (or, rather, 'becomings') do not simply draw upon these stocks of knowledge, as if they were books on a shelf; for stocks of knowledge are not neutral: they come invested with the meaning of the interactions that obtained them and these interactions also teach the human agent how to be a person at the same time that the knowledge is imparted. (Indeed that is what much of the knowledge is about.) So one learns to be a person over a long period of time in a process of progressive self-specification, the lessons of which are continually relearnt, even modified, in interaction with other people in specific contexts. The person emerges; she or he is not there to begin with. Take the three examples cited above. In the first example the mother imparts her notion of 'baby' to the baby while in the second example the mother imparts her notion of being a competent 'girl' to Samantha. In the last example the Philadelphia family creates persons competent to exercise power. And in each case, the activities that constitute these reasons are going on 'out in the open, between people, rather than inside their heads, hidden from being directly perceived by others' (Shotter, 1984, p. 23).[8] This is social being.

Two things follow from this depiction of person-making. First, it becomes clear that persons are differentially constituted within society. The opportunities for development of persons are differentially distributed through society – at home, at school, at work – so some human agents can grow into particular kinds of persons with particular kinds of resources while others cannot. There is a political economy of 'development opportunities'.[9] Second, where the boundaries of the 'self', the 'inner core' of a person, are drawn will vary too. There is persuasive evidence that ideas of self vary from society to society.[10] There seems little reason, then, why there should not be a varying conception of self within societies. Thus, there is also a 'political economy of selfhood'.

How, given this radically social depiction of human agents and how it is that they grow into persons, is it possible to characterise the inner workings of individual human agents? In part, it is not. As the examples of the socialisation of young human agents as 'babies' and 'children' show, what we take to be 'ourselves' is to be a great extent defined for us by other persons. But there is still a core of personal being in 'self' (even if what is regarded as this core varies from social group to social group), which arises precisely because human agents are social beings, forged in action. For social beings must continually attempt to grasp what other persons mean (what they have 'in mind', so to speak). And to do this, they must also develop a facility for self-monitoring – one needs to recognise what one is doing oneself in order to make sense of and to others. But this is not action oriented towards explaining its own causal antecedents via theories (as in a 'science'), nor is it action motivated by some grand internal plan (as in cognitive theories). Rather persons are concerned to give narrations or accounts of what they are doing to themselves/to others (the two cannot be separated)[11] motivated by intentions.

There is crucial difference between a theory and an account (Table 4.1). A theory is concerned with taking a set of events that already existed prior to it and made one kind of sense and reshaping them to make quite another kind of sense. It is a cognitive operation. In contrast, an account is a perceptual operation, a more explicit description of what an action taking place with a particular everyday context actually *is*:

Table 4.1 *Some characteristics of theories and accounts*

Theories	Accounts
retrospective	prospective
cognitive	perceptual
universal	contextual
logical	rhetorical
abstract	metaphorical/examples
reasons	causes
reporting	telling
believing	knowing

The rhetorical essence of an account is that in its telling it serves a formative function, it works practically, to instruct or inform others as to how, in a sense, to be; it works to influence how they understand and experience things practically, i.e., in a direct and unmediated way; in other words, immediately and routinely. In its telling it is self-specifying in the sense of constructing or organising a setting or context within which its telling makes sense. (Shotter, 1985a, p. 40)

Of course, persons cannot account for all their conduct, and nor do they need to. For it is often quite obvious to others what they are doing. It is only normal to request an account when it is not immediately obvious what a person is up to (for example, by reference to future aims, or by outlining what criteria they were trying to apply). But crucially, in making these accounts, persons do not only explain themselves to themselves. Thus a person's account is also a process of self-monitoring through the medium of these accounts, a kind of internalised accounting, a working out of what one is doing. And as the ways of accounting for oneself change, so the person and the self can change.

Through their accounts, fashioned out of joint action, persons also construct the world beyond their immediate context. They learn progressively to specify regions of the world beyond themselves – school, the state, work, the economy.[12] Often these accounts are loosely interlinked. When such linkages take place, the resulting assemblage forms a 'folk model' (Holy and Stuchlik, 1981, 1983), an account-based notion of what some piece of the world is like. Such folk models can be conjured up to justify particular actions of other persons and social institutions. Thus, 'I always vote Labour. But when they get into power they always let us down,' or 'I shall vote Conservative again. With the Tories the small man has a chance to improve,' or 'I'm not sure there is a God. If there is one, why should He allow all the terrible things that are happening,' or 'Nothing much ordinary people can do' (Mass-Observation, 1947, 1950). According to how well these folk models allow people to account for the world and for themselves, they invest people with a capacity for action. They are, therefore, the chief source of agency, the explicit formulation by a person of what she or he is capable of doing and of what powers that person has.

Finally, intentions (see Gauld and Shotter, 1977; Harré, 1979, 1983; Shotter, 1984). Just as accounts are not the same as theories, so intentions are not the same as plans. Rather, they are more like signposts. Intentions are usually vague and indeterminate, and by no means always directed to well-specified ends. Rather they consist of the progressive self-specification of projects already vaguely formulated, projects which change as they are more completely specified.

These, then, are the bare bones of the constructivist model of the human agent, at the core of which, it should now have become clear, is the notion that humans are story-telling animals. It should also have become clear that the content of persons, selves, accounts and folk models must vary according to the contexts which have to be negotiated, contexts whose form will in turn depend upon the presence or absence of particular social institutions and the stocks of knowledge these institutions hold. Clearly, the exact extent of such variation is contingent on the precise nature of these institutions in particular places and times and must be empirically specified.

This is all well and good, but how is it possible to get at persons' accounts and folk models, at how persons tell the world to themselves and themselves to the world? In the next section, I want to outline, in a preliminary way, how I am attempting to set about this task through a study I am carrying out of the well-documented 'leftwards' shift in political 'attitudes' or 'consciousness', that is, in persons' accounts and folk models of politics, in England during the Second World War. Clearly, such an account must also involve the consideration of other elements of a theory of social action, most especially the stocks of knowledge and 'the social' institutions from which the construction of persons, selves, accounts and folk models are inseparable (see Chapters 2 and 3).

A Better World? The Shift to the Left in English Political Accounts During the Second World War

> I feel quite exhausted after seeing and hearing so much sadness, sorrow, heroism and magnificent spirit. The destruction is so awful and the people so wonderful – they deserve a better world.

> (Queen Elizabeth to Queen Mary in a letter,
> 19.10.1940, cited in Calder, 1969, p. 605)

> Promises of a New World won't help us.

> (Mass-Observation, 1947, p. 322)

It is important to avoid exaggerating the extent of the shift to the left[13] in England during the Second World War leading to the Labour victory in the 1945 General Election, especially since the whole episode has taken on something of the status of a latter-day myth amongst the left – the build-up

Table 4.2 *The General Elections of 1935 and 1945*

	Per cent electorate voting	Per cent Conservative, National Liberal, Independent Conservative, National	Per cent Liberal	Per cent Labour, ILP, Commonwealth, Communist	Others
England					
1935	71	55	21	41	14
1945	73	40	17	50	9
Great Britain and Northern Ireland					
1935	71	55	24	41	20
1945	73	40	18	50	11

Source: McCallum and Readman, 1947

of working-class aspirations, the great victory and then the betrayal (see Stedman Jones, 1983a; Pimlott, 1985). Politics occupies very little of the accounting of most persons' lives and even the extreme circumstances of the Second World War did not lead everyone to reconsider their accounts and revise them (indeed, for many it simply confirmed what they already 'knew'). Thus the emphasis in this section is on the fairly large minority whose accounts did change in some way during the Second World War.[14] Even this minority constituted a quite remarkable shift – at least in the context of British politics – more particularly because it came about in the absence of much in the way of party organisation (on left or right) and was therefore relatively spontaneous. In what follows, in order to restrict the example to a manageable length, I have concentrated on changes on the Home Front. Although it has become something of a truism that it was the Forces vote that accounted for the 1945 Labour victory, 'in point of fact although in June 1945 there were 4,531,000 men and women in the Forces over 21 years of age, only 1,701,000 were able to cast votes' (Calder, 1969, p. 671). 'In total it did not amount to the number of votes separating the two major parties, let alone account for the strong swing of the pendulum' (Harrington and Young, 1978, p. 202). Rather, a considerable number on the Home Front had also changed their accounts, so that the Home Front is a valid focus of interest.

The 1945 Election provides a very rough guide to who these people were and where they lived. Table 4.2 outlines the 1945 General Election results (Butler and Stokes, 1969; Eatwell, 1979). Between the 1935 and 1945 elections there was a 12 per cent swing (in both England and the United Kingdom as a whole) to Labour and the associated parties on the left (Commonwealth, Independent Labour Party [ILP], Communists) from the Conservatives and their associates on the right (the National Liberals, the National Party and various Independent Conservatives) (McCallum and

Readman, 1947). Labour won 393 seats, up from 154 in 1935.[15] The Labour vote increased from 8,325,491 in 1935 to 11,992,292 in 1945; so more than three and a half million more people voted Labour.

Studies of the social composition of the Labour vote showed that this increase depended upon three interrelated groups. First, there was considerable support from the young; Labour won 61 per cent of the new votes in 1945 (Eatwell, 1979). (This support continued on; according to Butler and Stokes [1969], people who were young in the 1940s were of all age groups most prone to vote Labour in the 1960s.) Second, there was evidence of a limited swing to Labour amongst the middle classes. 'Polls showed that Labour received 21 per cent of the middle class vote, almost certainly more than ever before, though well below the Conservatives' 54 per cent' (Eatwell, 1979, p. 42). Some of this vote came from reforming idealists, but much of it could be accounted for by the growth of 'white-collar' office workers (Bonham, 1954). Butler and Stokes (1969), for example, found that the 1935–50 cohort of electors contained 7 per cent more middle-class voters, most of whom were white collar office workers. Third, and most important of all, Labour gained the working-class vote, probably as much as 70 per cent of it (Calder, 1969). Indeed, more than ever before, the Labour vote was a class vote. Mass-Observation found that by far the main reason given for voting Labour was 'class identity'; 43 per cent gave this as their reason, compared with 6 per cent for nationalisation, the next specific reason.

The electoral geography of Britain changed in line with the social composition of the vote (Figures 4.1 and 4.2).[16] The strongest Labour gains were in three places. First, there were the London suburbs where Labour won many 'white-collar' constituencies. Second, there was the West Midlands; before 1945 the traditional home of the working-class Conservative. Finally, there were the agricultural counties of East Anglia, where many agricultural labourers voted Labour. To summarise, in the 1945 Election, 'the working class of the declining areas of heavy industry joined forces through the ballot box with much of the more prosperous working class in the Midlands and South East, and a substantial section of the urban middle classes' (Addison, 1975, p. 268).

But how did changes in political accounts and folk models come about in the Second World War that laid the foundations for the Labour victory? Conventionally, a number of reasons are put forward. The first, and the most often cited, is the amount of left-wing 'propaganda' that was being disseminated, compared with right-wing material. Certainly, the need for the creation of a new Britain was strongly pressed in newspapers like the *Daily Herald*, the *Daily Mirror*, even *The Times* and in magazines like *Picture Post*. Pamphlets, periodicals and most particularly the Penguin Specials helped the process along. Some programmes on the radio had a pronounced left-wing bias or, as in the case of J.B. Priestley's *Postscripts*, gave voice to a general feeling of discontent. Films were made that scored left-wing political points. The Church of England, in contrast to its loyal

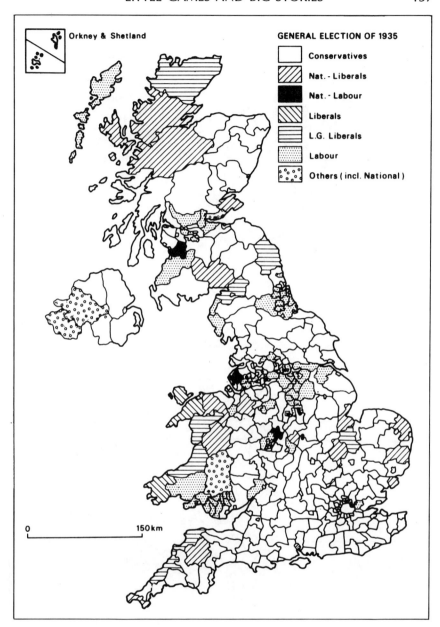

Figure 4.1 *The geography of the 1935 General Election*

jingoism in the First World War, showed distinct signs of independence, embodied in the person of Archbishop Temple of Canterbury. Even the government, to some extent, pushed the process along through praise for the Soviet Union at particular junctures in the war.[17] But, as has been pointed out by a number of writers (for example, Calder, 1969; Harrington

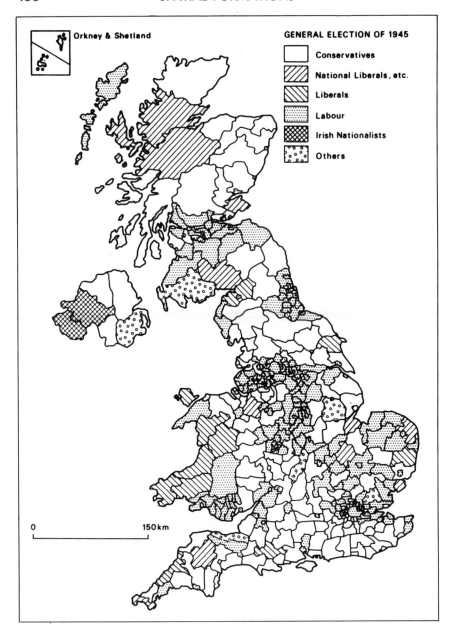

Figure 4.2 *The geography of the 1945 General Election*

and Young, 1978; Pelling, 1984), just because such 'propaganda' was about does not mean that people were automatically receptive to it; indeed, the evidence is that outright propaganda aroused antagonism. More likely is it that the availability of left-wing material tended to reinforce existing views and tendencies, so that it is reasonable to doubt the extent to which it produced socialists in any serious sense of the word, especially as much of the propaganda was compatible with moderate reformism. If anything, the propaganda served more to reinforce Labour's attack on the record of the inter-war Conservatives. Reformist and socialist propaganda also had to be seen against a counter-cultural background, and one in this case which stressed strong traditional values. For example, the majority of literature produced during the war, let alone read, had far from socialist implications or values. (Eatwell, 1979, p. 39)

A second and probably more salient reason for the shift to the left in accounts and folk models – because it was firmly grounded in people's lives – was that genuine economic changes came about during the Second World War, most especially the creation of full employment[18] and significant wage rises amongst the working class so that, even given considerable increases in the cost of living, earnings were substantial (although much of the increase in working-class prosperity could be accounted for by the massive amount of overtime that was worked rather than dramatic rises in the hourly earnings paid). 'There is no doubt that large sections of the working class were better off as a result of the war, and that there was levelling up, as well as levelling down, towards a skilled artisan's standards' (Calder, 1969, p. 63). Clearly, there was concern amongst the working class that full employment and economic gains should not be eroded after the war (when so many in the Armed Forces would be demobilised) and the party which had secured the credit for making a stand in favour of the Beveridge Report was clearly the one most likely to protect them.

A third reason, one that clearly had influence on the formulation of some people's accounts and folk models, was the practical demonstration brought about by the massive state intervention in the direction of industry during the war (see Ministry of Labour and National Service, 1947) that nationalisation was a feasible course to take. This reason combined, to some extent, with the general popularity of Russia.

A fourth reason for left-wing changes in accounts and folk models was the general desire for better housing and welfare. The Gallup Polls show housing, not surprisingly given bomb damage relocation and cessation of building, to be a continual preoccupation through the course of the war. 'Housing was for the most electors the most important social issue. . . . Labour candidates stressed the importance of this issue and many of them had served on the housing committees of their local Councils which dealt directly with the problem' (Pelling, 1984, p. 32).

Finally, there was the 'swing of the pendulum'. There had been a parliament with a Conservative majority since November 1931 and discontent had accumulated against it.

But the problem is that people's accounts and folk models are not constructed as a disembodied set of 'reasons', all neatly ordered. They are situated in, and adjusted to, particular contexts. They are active talk, not passive contemplations. They are set 'within the socially organised worlds in which they participate as constituting and constitutive elements'

(Heritage, 1984, p. 178). People's accounts and folk models are contextual and what is certain about the Second World War is that a number of these contexts changed very dramatically indeed.

The Contexts of Talk

Perhaps the main reason why the shift to the left was so marked was the substantial number of changes that took place in the intricate mosaic of contexts that went to make up English society. Those changes were sufficient to force some people to re-account for their world, either by virtue of changes to the contexts that they knew or by catapulting them into contexts to which they had never previously been exposed (and to which they had to try to adjust). In this joint talk, people were therefore able to reach different conclusions from those that they had come to before the war. There were many changes to the mosaic of contexts; here I will concentrate on just two. The first was the enormous amount of movement that took place in the Second World War. The second was the growth of new institutions of sociability and the transformation of a number of the old institutions.

The amount of movement that took place in the Second World War, and with it new patterns of social interaction, was considerable. There were three main sources of movement. The first of these was evacuation from the urban areas most vulnerable to bombing to rural 'reception' areas. By 1939, some two million people (mostly those with some means) had evacuated independently and another million-and-a-half (mainly poorer) people had been evacuated in the government scheme (see Mass-Observation, 1940; Padley and Cole, 1940; Titmuss, 1950) (Figure 4.3). There was a great difference in response (Table 4.3) – under half of London's schoolchildren went but over 70 per cent of Newcastle and Gateshead's. The 1939 evacuation was often chaotic and suffered from a strong drift back to the cities when the expected bombing did not immediately materialise, but this and the subsequent evacuations (particularly at the height of the bombing in 1941 and during the V1 attacks in 1944) had important social effects, intimately exposing people from quite different classes to one another for the first time.

The second source of movement, and probably the one with the greatest effects, stemmed from employment policy. The composition of the labour force changed dramatically during the Second World War (Table 4.4) (see Fogarty, 1945; Ministry of Labour and National Service, 1947; *Planning*, 1948). From June 1939 to June 1944 some four-and-a-half million people were added to the Armed Forces, two million to the munitions industries and between a quarter and a half-a-million to Civil Defence and the essential industries.

Of this total, 3.25 million were found by transference from less essential industries and services, the largest single contribution coming from the distributive trades (almost a million) and building. A million-and-a-quarter

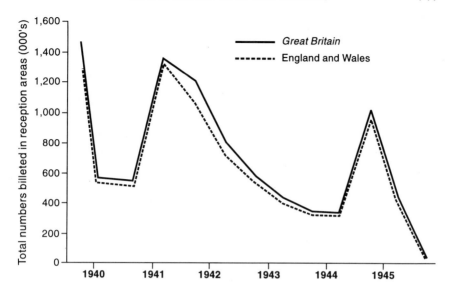

Figure 4.3 *Total numbers billeted in reception areas under the official scheme, 1940–5*

unemployed were brought back to work and the balance was made up with nearly 2.5 million people not normally engaged in paid work other than domestic service, including two million women. In all, the number of workers in the less essential (Group III) industries was reduced by 35 per cent between 1939 and 1944, and 20 per cent of the 'rest of the population' were transferred into war work of one kind or another. If each part-time worker were counted separately the latter proportion would be around 23 per cent. (Fogarty, 1945, p. 48)

The result of this reorganisation was a much longer journey to work for many workers and, more particularly, numbers of workers were directed to move to new areas where they were then billeted in hostels, lodging houses and private homes. Some smaller towns received large influxes of population (Table 4.5) and suffered from severe overcrowding as a result.[19]

A special effect of the wartime employment policy was the enormous number of women who went to work. Many went voluntarily but from 1942 'conscription' operated (Mass-Observation, 1942; Minns, 1980). Some 80,000 women joined the Land Army over the course of the war; 100,000 women worked on the railways; 300,000 women joined the chemical industries; and another one-and-a-half million women went to the engineering and metal industries (Table 4.4). Most women worked relatively near their homes, but those unmarried and over 19 years of age and less than about 50 years were declared 'mobile' and likely to be moved considerable distances (Ministry of Labour and National Service, 1947).

The final source of movement stemmed from the direct effects of the war itself, especially the bombing. In particular, many people were made homeless (Table 4.6). At least one in six London households (or 1,400,000

Table 4.3 *Proportion of unaccompanied schoolchildren and mothers and children evacuated from some of the major urban areas of England at the outbreak of war*

County borough	Percentage of children evacuated	Percentage of mothers and children evacuated
Newcastle	71	57
Gateshead	71	49
South Shields	31	26
Tynemouth	32	29
Sunderland	33	20
West Hartlepool	36	24
Middlesbrough	31	18
Leeds	33	26
Bradford	25	17
Bootle	68	66
Liverpool	61	44
Wallasey	76	–
Birkenhead	62	44
Manchester	69	44
Salford	76	56
Rotherham	8	6
Sheffield	15	13
Derby	27	14
Nottingham	22	12
Walsall	18 ⎫	11
West Bromwich	26 ⎭	
Smethwick	24	15
Birmingham	25	21
Coventry	20	14
Portsmouth	30	20
Southampton	37	28
London Administrative County	49	–
County Boroughs and London Administrative County	46	37

Source: Titmuss, 1950, pp. 550–2

people) faced homelessness at some time during the war. In Plymouth the figure was one in four (Calder, 1969).

The magnitude of these three movements can be seen, in net terms, from the redistribution of population during the war. In particular, there was a net shift of between one-and-a-half and one-and-three-quarter million people from London, the South-east and the East Coast regions towards the North and West between 1938 and 1942. The full pattern of inter-regional shifts is shown in Table 4.7. This table does not, of course, take into account intra-regional population movements, but

> the most striking changes took place for the most part within regions, without affecting the inter-regional balance. In the towns and districts which have been most heavily hit by evacuation, or in areas such as the belt of counties to the

Table 4.4 Employment in Great Britain, 1938 and 1944 (thousands)

| | Males aged 14–64 | | | | Females aged 14–59[1] | | | | Total | | | |
| | Number | | Per cent | | Number | | Per cent | | Number | | Per cent | |
Category of employment	June 1939	June 1944	June 1939	June 1944	June 1939	June 1944	June 1939	June 1944	June 1939	June 1944	June 1939	June 1944
Armed Forces and Women's												
Auxiliary Services	477	4,502	3.0	28.3	–	467	–	2.9	477	4,969	1.5	15.6
Civil Defence	80	225	0.5	1.4	–	56	–	0.3	80	281	0.2	0.9
Group I (munitions)												
Metal and Chemical Industries[2]	2,600	3,210	16.2	20.2	506	1,851	3.1	11.6	3,106	5,061	9.7	15.9
Group II (essential services)												
Agriculture, horticulture	1,046	948	6.5	6.0	67	184	0.4	1.1	1,113	1,132	3.5	3.5
Mining	868	802	5.4	5.0	5	13	–	0.1	873	815	2.7	2.5
National Government Service	416	520	2.6	3.3	123	495	0.8	3.1	539	1,015	1.7	3.2
Local Government Service	520	322	3.2	2.0	326	468	2.0	2.9	846	790	2.6	2.5
Gas, Water and Electricity Supply	225	160	1.4	1.0	17	32	0.1	0.2	242	192	0.8	0.6
Transport, Shipping and Fishing	1,222	1,038	7.6	6.5	51	212	0.3	1.3	1,273	1,250	4.0	3.9
Food, Drink and Tobacco	391	269	2.5	1.7	263	240	1.7	1.5	654	509	2.0	1.6
Total, Group II	4,688	4,059	29.2	25.5	852	1,644	5.3	10.2	5,540	5,703	17.3	17.8
Group III (less essential services)												
Building and Civil Engineering	1,294	600	8.1	3.8	16	23	0.1	0.1	1,310	623	4.1	2.0
Textiles	401	221	2.5	1.4	601	405	3.8	2.5	1,002	626	3.1	2.0
Clothing/Boots	138	65	0.9	0.4	449	284	2.8	1.8	587	349	1.8	1.1
Boots and shoes	108	64	0.7	0.4	57	43	0.4	0.3	165	107	0.5	0.3
Other Manufactures[3]	1,004	542	6.2	3.4	440	414	2.7	2.6	1,444	956	4.5	3.0

continued overleaf

Table 4.4 *continued*

Category of employment	Males aged 14–64				Females aged 14–59[1]				Total			
	Number		Per cent		Number		Per cent		Number		Per cent	
	June 1939	June 1944	June 1939	June 1944	June 1939	June 1944	June 1939	June 1944	June 1939	June 1944	June 1939	June 1944
Distributive Trades	1,888	972	11.8	6.1	999	956	6.2	6.0	2,887	1,928	9.0	9.0
Other Services[4]	965	436	6.0	2.7	917	977	5.7	6.1	1,882	1,413	5.9	4.4
Total, Group III	5,798	2,900	36.2	18.2	3,479	3,102	21.7	19.4	9,277	6,002	28.9	21.8
Total of Armed Forces, Auxiliary Services, Civil Defence and Industry	13,643	14,896	85.1	93.6	4,837	7,120	30.1	44.4	18,480	22,016	57.7	69.0
Unemployed	1,043	71	6.5	0.4	302	31	1.9	0.2	1,345	102	4.2	0.3
Rest of population	1,324	943	8.4	6.0	10,901*	8,869*	68.0	55.4	12,225	9,812	38.1	30.7
Total	16,010	15,910	100.0	100.0	16,040	16,020	100.0	100.0	32,050	31,930	100.0	100.0

Notes

1 Women working part-time are included throughout, two being counted as one unit. At the middle of 1944 about 900,000 women were doing part-time work.
2 Metal manufacture, engineering, motors, aircraft and other vehicles, shipbuilding and ship-repairing, metal goods manufacture, chemicals, explosives, oil, etc., industries.
3 Leather, wood, paper, bricks, tiles, pottery, glass and miscellaneous manufactures.
4 Commerce, banking, insurance, finance; professional services; entertainment; hotels, restaurants, etc.; laundries and cleaning.
* Mainly housewives. Domestic servants are also included.

Source: Fogarty, 1945, pp. 46–7

Table 4.5   *Population increases in selected towns whose population increased by 4 per cent or more, 1938–42*

Town	Population in October 1942	Percentage increase in population	
		Mid-1938 to October 1942	Mid-1938 to June 1942
Reading	115,193	19.7	28.6
Slough	63,712	25.9	21.1
Cheltenham	60,488	16.5	15.4
Swindon	67,862	12.0	9.6
Blackpool	152,128	20.9	15.3
Southport	88,708	12.9	4.9
Luton	100,480	10.6	9.6
Romford	60,487	10.8	9.8
Watford	68,789	4.7	1.9
Northampton	100,502	4.1	1.9
Enfield	95,579	4.0	2.9
Harrow	193,745	5.6	3.4

Source: Combined Production and Resources Board, 1945, p. 103

Table 4.6   *Housing out of civilian use in the United Kingdom, 1944*

	Mid-1944	End 1944
Houses destroyed or damaged beyond repair by enemy action	175,000	205,000
Houses damaged, uninhabitable and awaiting repair	80,000	100,000
Houses requisitioned for military use or otherwise withdrawn	70,000	–
Houses evacuated in south-eastern coastal areas	125,000	–

Source: Combined Production and Resources Board, 1945, p. 42

North and West of London, or the counties of North Wales, or the parts of Western Scotland which are not yet industrialised, there have been changes very much greater than any recorded [inter-regional changes]. (Fogarty, 1945)[20]

The second change that made some people reassess their world and themselves was the enormous growth of institutions of sociability. These institutions can be divided into two types, those promoted by the state (and other compulsory) and voluntary organisations.

Amongst the new state institutions of sociability the most notable were the Home Guard, the Royal Observer Corps and Civil Defence (that is, air-raid parties, report and control centre staff and messengers). The Home Guard, originally formed as the Local Defence Volunteers (LDVs) in 1939, employed the talents of one-and-a-half million people during most of the War (see Figure 4.4), mainly part-time. The Royal Observer Corps, founded

Table 4.7   *The distribution of population of Great Britain by region, 1938 and 1942*[1]

Region	Percentage of population living in each region		Actual estimated population	Estimated increase or decrease in the civilian population, 1938–42, allowing for the change in the civil population in the country as whole[2]	
	June 1938 total population	April 1942 civilian population	June 1938 Number 000's	Number 000's	Per cent of 1938
London (LCC and Middlesex)	13.3	10.3	6,121	−1,308	−21.4
Eastern (Hertford, Bedford, Essex, Cambridge, Ely, Huntingdon, Norfolk, Suffolk)	8.4	8.1	3,858	−95	−2.5
South-eastern (Kent, Surrey, Sussex)	7.9	7.6	3,670	−153	−4.2
Southern (Oxford, Berkshire, Buckingham, Hampshire, Isle of Wight, Dorset)	4.9	5.3	2,286	+170	+7.4
South-western (Wiltshire, Gloucester, Somerset, Devon, Cornwall)	5.7	6.7	2,646	+406	+15.3
West Midlands (Warwick, Stafford, Shropshire, Worcester, Hereford)	8.5	9.1	3,935	+269	+6.8
North Midlands (Northampton, Peterborough, Rutland, Leicester, Lincoln, Nottingham, Derby)	6.6	7.2	3,050	+280	+9.2
North-western, (Cheshire, Lancashire, Cumberland, Westmorland)	14.2	14.4	6,541	+91	+1.4
North-eastern (East and West Ridings: York)	8.6	8.4	3,964	−77	−1.9
Northern (Durham, Northumberland, North Riding)	5.8	5.9	2,677	+63	+2.4
Wales	5.3	5.9	2,466	+226	+9.2
Scotland	10.8	11.1	4,993	+128	+2.6
Total	100.0	100.0	46,207	+1,633-−1,633	

[1]   The population figures are estimates only.
[2]   Calculated given that the total civilian population was 5.7 per cent smaller in 1942 than in 1938.

Source: Fogarty, 1945, p. 42

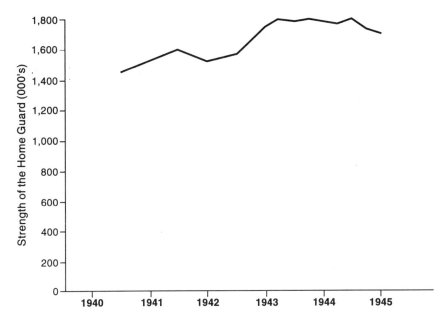

Figure 4.4   *Strength of the Home Guard, 1940–5*

in the 1920s, also had a large complement of part-timers and set to work over 30,000 in its ranks during the rest of the war (Figure 4.5). Finally, there was the whole group of Civil Defence occupations (Figure 4.6). Prominent amongst these were the air-raid wardens. There were some 200,000 to 250,000 of these in London alone (Calder, 1969).

There is little systematic information about the social composition of the Home Guard, the Royal Observer Corps and Civil Defence. In the Home Guard there were few women; in the Royal Observer Corps the proportion was one in eight; in Civil Defence the proportion was one in six. Social composition varied strongly with the social composition of the neighbourhood. For example, in many boroughs of London, as might be expected, two-thirds of air-raid wardens were working class, but in areas outside London the proportion was usually less (Calder, 1969). Certainly, however, the three new institutions were not, given the pronounced class nature of British society at the time, as strongly class-divided as might have been thought. For example, the Home Guard

was not just a regrouping of the British Legion. In the villages, poachers and game-keepers, farmers and farm hands, marched together. In the mining districts, the colliery L.D.V.'s would parade 'in their dirt' soon after coming off a shift. Southern Railways set a lead for public utility companies by organising its own L.D.V. (Calder, 1969, p. 193)

Further, the three institutions were not just semi-military organisations. They performed numbers of social functions (which further promoted the

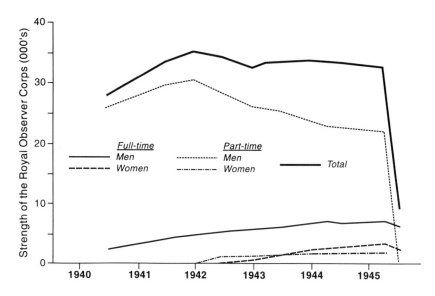

Figure 4.5   *Strength of the Royal Observer Corps, 1940–5*

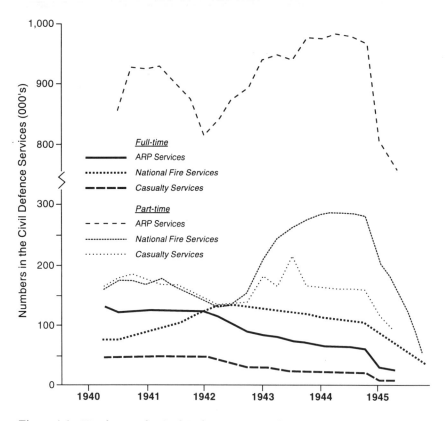

Figure 4.6   *Numbers in the Civil Defence Services of Great Britain, 1940–5*

mixing of their members), from dances to darts matches, from football leagues to whist drives.

Many new voluntary organisations also grew up. Amongst the most important was the Women's Voluntary Service (WVS), founded in 1938. The exact numbers in the Service are unknown but certainly numbered in the 'hundreds of thousands' (Calder, 1969; Minns, 1980). Most of the women involved were older – over the 'mobile' age limit – and middle class (most working-class women did not have the time to belong), yet

> such was the onslaught of the . . . War that the W.V.S., in certain times and places, transcended its apparently basic middle classness. A post-war observer has revealed that before 1939 it 'would have been inconceivable that in a philanthropic organisation the relatives of e.g. committee members and clients could be interchangeable or that members of particular trades or industries or even residents in a "poor" locality could take part in voluntary services.' But war disrupted the lives of middle-class and working-class women indiscriminately. (Calder, 1969, p. 224)

Apart from new organisations, many existing institutions also grew during the war. In particular, trade unionism became a much more important force. Overall union membership in Britain increased from 6,053,000 at the end of 1938 to 7,805,000 by the end of 1945 (Ministry of Labour and National Service, 1947). The unions involved in the expanding war effort obviously registered the largest increases. The Amalgamated Engineering Union, for example, had 413,000 members in 1939. But by 1943 membership had more than doubled to 909,000 (Calder, 1969). The boost in union membership was, of course, helped along by full employment, and, in many cases, severe labour shortages. Government intervention also contributed. By 1943, 4,500 joint production committees had been set up which all required the presence of unions in factories.[21] However, the unions were not the only existing institutions to receive a boost from the war. For example, existing voluntary organisations like the Women's Institutes and the Red Cross also grew.[22]

These changes in spatial and social organisation meant that the contexts within which new information, economic prosperity and the other likely determinants of change in people's accounts had an impact were radically different from before the war. Thus, England in the Second World War had become a society over which a new 'developmental matrix' (Shotter, 1984), which included elements of many new contexts, had been laid, a matrix in which spaces were opened up in which some persons could live and develop in ways that previously would have been unavailable to them. These persons could account for the world in different ways and create new folk models of politics. They might even become different persons.

The New Accounts

In this final section of the chapter I want to consider the changed accounts and folk models of the Second World War which led to the Labour victory

in the 1945 Election. It is natural in these circumstances to turn to the work
of Mass-Observation, that unique organisation founded in 1937 which –
amongst other things – collected accounts throughout the course of the war
and billed itself as creating 'the science of ourselves'. I am currently
involved in a study aimed at reconstructing the multiple contexts of two of
Mass-Observation's key locations – 'Worktown' (Bolton) and 'Metrop'
(Fulham) – with a view to eliciting how working-class accounts and folk
models could and did change during the Second World War. In what
follows I provide, in lieu of this specific study, a very general illustrative
survey stretching across different contexts drawn from all classes, with a
short election postscript from Fulham. I will illustrate the survey with
snippets of accountings but it is vitally important to stress that these
snippets are but fragments of an ongoing process of talk developing out of
particular contexts. These snippets are not (although, out of context, they
may appear to be) 'reasons', finished contemplative conclusions. They
might well have changed in another context. The ebb and flow and the kind
of talk from which these accounts are drawn, and from which they are
separated at such peril, is well illustrated by the following report on the
aftermath of the 1945 Election:

> We got a real shock when we heard our Conservative member had been beaten
> by 12,000 – we simply could not believe it. Then, more women came in to sew, it
> was like a jam session, everyone talked at once, and I gave up trying to sew or
> give out work, and sat round talking – or, more correctly, listening. The general
> opinion was that the 'soldiers' vote had swung the election. Some thought that
> England would go down in the world's opinion, and that no one would believe in
> her stability, and that Russia would rejoice since it would suit Stalin. Someone
> wondered if we could get the road across Morecambe Bay now, as Labour
> 'doesn't care about spending money or consider whether it is practical': 'Now the
> coal mines will be nationalised – see what they make of that.' I heard remarks
> about soldiers 'going solidly for Labour', – of 'agents' in the Army who had
> plugged Labour views. The Tories, the big business-men, had always made the
> war in the first place – it was the big men who put Hitler into power, who sold
> armaments to any nation whether they were going to use them against our
> friendly nations or not, that it was the Tory plan to send girls away from home
> to work, send boys into the mines, dole out rations barely enough to keep people
> alive. Any stick seemed good or bad enough to beat the 'Tory dog'. Some
> soldiers seemed to think the Government had fallen down on the housing plan.
> One woman told of a lad who voted Labour because he knew he would get out
> quicker to his father's butcher business. (Broad and Fleming, 1981, p. 296)

Out of the very many ways in which the 'developmental matrix' of
contexts within which people lived shifted during the Second World War,
three are of particular importance. The first of these was the generally
increased level of sociability, promoted by both movement and the new
institutions of sociability. A much greater degree of interaction was forced
upon people, often for the first time in their lives, and this interaction was
not just within classes but between classes. Two examples of the impacts of
this interaction on accounts will suffice. One example, the first wave of
government-sponsored evacuations, springs to mind as a particularly

graphic example of this phenomenon. 'Social mismatching was inherent in the scheme' (Calder, 1969, p. 46). For the first time many working-class parents and children who were billeted with middle-class families got to see how the other half lived, while the middle class got to see how the working-class parents and children lived.[23] The shock was great on both sides (although it has been exaggerated since). Here were children who never wore pyjamas,[24] who had few clothes, who suffered from lice, scabies and impetigo, and who, worst of all, in 5 to 10 per cent of cases lacked proper toilet training. On both sides prejudices were confirmed. Indeed, rather interestingly, on both sides the accounts are nearly all made in class terms. For example, from the working class:

'Think it was bloody Buckingham Palace the way she goes on.' (Mass-Observation, 1940, p. 319)

'It's too posh for me.' (ibid., p. 314)

'We'd rather have our meals in the kitchen.' (ibid., p. 330)

'Two children from a very poor house were taken care of by very nice people who were teaching them to use table napkins and such like things that the children had never seen before. The mother came to see them and complained that they were being brought up 'narky' and that she wasn't going to have it.' (ibid., p. 314)

or most to the point:

'You can't be yourself here.' (ibid., p. 314)

And from the middle class, the reaction was not much different:

'The butler has been disgruntled ever since I told him we were having a number of children, and consequently would start living more simply ourselves – stopping entertaining and so forth.' (ibid., p. 329)

Mass-Observation reported of the middle class, with some degree of hyperbole:

A minority, mainly represented in the women's organisations, have turned horror into pity, and have determined that the appalling conditions which the evacuee children reflect shall be swept away, and very soon; the majority have turned their horror into fear and even hatred, seeing in this level of humanity an animal threat, that vague and horrid revolution which lurks in the dreams of so many supertax payers. (ibid., pp. 336–7)

Another example of the generally heightened level of interaction was, of course, the number of people – particularly women – who went to work for the first time or went to work in quite different locations. In the factories and workshops there was considerable forced mixing of people from quite different backgrounds which showed up in accounts of the time. Take the case of women in production (Mass-Observation, 1942). Not only working-class women were mobilised. One young teacher who helped make anti-tank mines in her summer holiday noted in her diary:

Chief topic of conversation the Dizzy Blonde. She arrived last Monday and has caused quite a sensation, partly by her appearance – wonderful peroxide curls, exquisite make-up, etc. – but much more by her conversation. Has told everyone that she has never worked before as she has an allowance and is going to frame the first pound she gets. Another tale runs that she lost a wallet with £100 in but 'just didn't bother'; she's saving up for a fur coat, a really good one; 'I had 5 but I've given 3 away.' Mrs. Barratt's comment, 'Now we know what she did before the war.' (Mass-Observation Diary, cited in Calder, 1969, p. 385)

Many women tasted independence for the first time:

When you get up in the morning you feel you go out with something in your bag, and something coming in at the end of the week, and it's nice. It's a taste of independence, and you feel a lot happier for it. (File Report No. 2059, cited in Calder and Sheridan, 1984, p. 179)

But only the young seemed willing to continue their independent lifestyle after the war was over:

I'd like a real change after the war, but I'll have to see what jobs are going. I think a lot will leave this country after the war – those that have married Americans and Canadians, and those that have heard what it's like over there – I know a lot would like to get right out of this country, they think there'll be more freedom over in America and Canada. I should think a lot more will want to go than can get. I'd like to myself. (ibid., p. 180)

Most worries for the future seemed to centre on employment after the war.

We shall be kicked out. . . . There won't be jobs for people like myself. . . . There won't be jobs for women. (Mass-Observation, 1942, p. 328)

I think there'll really be a lot of unemployment – look at all the girls in the services coming back and wanting jobs, to say nothing of the men. They can stay in the army for a time but the girls can't. I think we're in for a very difficult time. (File Report No. 2059, cited in Calder and Sheridan, 1984, p. 182)

It's not so much what's going to happen to us, as what's going to happen to the men who come home. Will there be jobs for them? (ibid.)

I think there ought to be plenty of work for everybody after the war, if they manage it properly. (ibid.)

The second, closely interrelated, way in which changes in contexts came about was through an increase in the stocks of knowledge that were available and through changes in what constituted these stocks of knowledge. Stocks of knowledge were greatly increased. Ways of doing things that had been considered inadmissible before the war became acceptable behaviour. Availability of printed knowledge was probably much greater than before the war and was likely to be taken advantage of (certain jobs like fire-watching promoted a reading habit – there was little else to do). Book sales went up by 50 per cent. Newspaper sales increased. Only magazine sales decreased, and this because numerous magazines were no longer printed (Table 4.8). Much of the increase in book sales can be accounted for by mundane facts – over a million volumes were lost from public libraries in

Table 4.8 *Consumer purchases of newspapers, magazines and books in the United Kingdom, 1938–44*

	1938	1939	1940	1941	1942	1943	1944
Total value of current prices (£ million)	62	61	62	70	73	77	78
Total value at 1938 prices (£ million)	62	61	57	58	60	63	64
Per capita value at 1938 prices (£)							
(a) Total	1.31	1.28	1.19	1.22	1.26	1.33	1.33
(b) Newspapers and magazines	1.10	–	–	–	–	1.00	1.01
(c) Books	0.21	–	–	–	–	0.33	0.32
Physical quantities per capita							
(a) Newspapers (copies per week)	2.8	–	–	–	–	2.9	3.0
(b) Newsprint (lbs per week)	59.0	–	–	–	–	12.0	13.0
(c) Magazine purchases (copies per month)	2.5	–	–	–	–	2.0	2.1

Source: Combined Production and Resources Board, 1945, p. 120

bombing and had to be replaced (Calder, 1969) – but still even this evidence suggests that the reading habit had spread to new sections of the population. And, of course, such evidence says nothing of the greatly increased incidence of multiple readership of single volumes in the Second World War – books were passed around.[25] The increased awareness of the world brought about by wartime experience and increased reading seems to have had a cumulative effect on some people's accounts and it was these people that were more likely to be gripped by left-wing material. Here is a young Clive Jenkins, later a leading figure in the Trades Union Movement:

> There were lots of private libraries in Wales and the manager of our local Co-op Insurance lent me books. He gave me an *Introduction to Marx*. The full-time secretary of the Band of Hope and Temperance Union was a social democrat and lent me [Left] Book Club choices like Attlee's *The Labour Party in Perspective*, which was really a pretty boring old book. And then I got introduced to things like *Guilty Men* and *The Trial of Mussolini*. I remember you had to put your name down on the waiting list for your copy of *Guilty Men*. (quoted in Harrington and Young, 1978, p. 66)

Certainly, the demand for 'serious' books (and radio programmes like the *Brains Trust*) concerned with current affairs seems to have increased. For example, Penguin Specials had an average sale of 80,000 copies each and books like *Guilty Men* sold many more. When the Beveridge Report (Cmnd 6404) on social security was published in December 1942, it sold 635,000 copies in full or summary form.[26] People queued outside the HMSO bookshops for it and, within two weeks of publication, a Gallup Poll found that nineteen out of twenty people had heard of the report (Calder, 1969).

By the time of the 1945 Election, Richard Crossman, later a Labour minister, could write that there had been

> a serious and absurd underestimate of the Print Order from Transport House for reading material. Every twopenny or threepenny pamphlet at open air meetings is immediately snapped up and usually paid for with silver, for which no change is asked. I believe if we had in stock 40,000 Penguins we could have sold them easily. What we sell is taken home and thrown back at us at the next open air meeting in the form of precise and thoughtful questions. (quoted in Harrington and Young, 1978, p. 66)

The third and final way in which changes in accounts came about, and the most difficult to pin down, was through the responsibility that men and women were forced to take for their lives. The pressures of this responsibility forced them to learn more about themselves and the world.

> I don't expect many changes in practical form – but I do think the war has already shaken many people, once apathetic because they felt secure and did not know other people's lives, into at least an interest in securing healthier and less degrading conditions for the country. (quoted in Calder and Sheridan, 1984, p. 210)

Some working-class people lost the habit of 'deference' and again this must have had an effect on political accounts.

A Postscript: Fulham in 1945

In 1945 the two Fulham constituencies (East and West) were predominantly artisanal working class but with a substantial lower-middle-class presence made up of shopkeepers, clerks and so on (Pelling, 1967). The constituencies had a solid record of voting Conservative until 1938, when, in a by-election caused by the death of the sitting MP, Fulham West returned a Labour candidate. In the 1945 Election both constituencies recorded a large swing to Labour and substantial Labour majorities (Table 4.9). What were the accounts being offered in the months up to the Election? For many in the two constituencies, which had been much transformed by the war and its damage, their accounts had rarely changed. Class solidarity was all.

> Well, I think that its out to help the working class. . . . Well, Labour's for the workers and its no good being a worker and voting for the bosses. . . . Well, its supposed to be for the working man and not against him. . . . Well, I'm a working man myself. I think a working man that votes Conservative is barmy. (File Report 2270A)

Most of these voters had always voted Labour:

> Well, I've always voted Labour. I've been a Labour man all my life. . . . I wouldn't think of voting any other way. My family would never forgive me. (ibid., p. 111)

Table 4.9 *Fulham Election results, 1935 and 1945*

	Date	Electors	Turnout (per cent)	Candidates	Votes cast	Per cent
Fulham East	1935	50,682	71.9	W.W. Astor (Con.)	18,743	51.4
				J.C. Wilmot (Lab.)	17,689	48.6
	1945	38,311	73.8	R.M.M. Stewart (Lab.)	15,662	55.4
				W.W. Astor (Con.)	10,309	36.4
				P.M. Synett (Lib.)	2,315	8.2
Fulham West	1935	49,480	69.9	C.S. Cobb (Con.)	18,461	53.4
				M. Follick (Lab.)	14,998	43.3
				W.J. Johnia (Lib.)	1,138	3.3
	1938	48,469	65.5	E. Summerskill (Lab.)	16,583	52.2
				C. Busby (Con.)	15,162	47.8
	1945	41,329	76.3	E. Summerskill (Lab.)	19,537	61.9
				P. Lucas (Con.)	12,016	38.1

Source: Craig, 1969

The chief issue that had attracted previously non-Labour voters as well as reinforcing the accounts of previously Labour voters was housing, of which there was a critical shortage in the constituencies.

> Oh, I'm voting for the Labour women, and I'll tell you why. I think there'll be a proper bloody revolution when the boys come home, if something isn't done about the housing and by all I've read it's only Labour that's got a policy about the housing. (ibid., p. 109)

> Housing, most of all. I was browned off of Churchill's last speech, nagging about the birth rate again. Give people houses and the jobs and they'll have the kids. Have you seen the boxes they're putting up for people to live in? (ibid., pp. 109–10)

> I think all the parties will have to do something about the rehousing – they'll have to make some attempt. The mood of the people won't be trifled with! (ibid., p. 109)

Nationalisation also sparked off some pro-Labour accounts:

> Well, I'm going to vote Labour because I believe it's the only party likely to get things done and I believe that in the country's interest it would be best to nationalise the mines and public utilities. Speaking quite plainly, I think these measures are very much overdue. (ibid., p. 89)

Finally, the swing of the pendulum effect was evident, especially amongst middle-class voters:

> From a business point of view I ought to vote Conservative, but somehow I feel that the Conservative party has had its run; we want something wider, and despite the fact that Labour doesn't represent the views of the people 100% it is more likely to benefit the country as a whole. (ibid., p. 89)

These voters, who were previously non-Labour, had spent considerable time talking about which way to vote and in addition had read more: 'Well

I think I'm right in saying I've reached this decision by simply reading and thinking about it' (ibid., p. 89).

All in all, this section has tried to show in the most preliminary way – in principle rather than in practice – how contexts and accounts and folk models changed in the circumstances of the Second World War, leading to a particular political outcome. Three final points are in order. First, more work needs to be done before it is possible to be certain how and in what ways people's accounts and folk models did change. Second, it is vital to re-emphasise the extent of this change. It was limited to a minority – a large minority, but still a minority. Third, it is important to stress that 'political' accounting is not some sacred activity to be divorced from the secular flow of other kinds of talk:

> We sat on the slope of the Head to watch the circus, and I saw a group sitting near in very earnest conversation, with their heads together. I'd have loved to go and butt in. I love being in an argument, and thought, 'Perhaps they are talking about the atomic bomb – or the result of the Election'. I've very good hearing, and when I'd got used to the different sounds around, I could hear what they were discussing – the new 'cold perm'! (Broad and Fleming, 1981, p. 303)

Conclusion

An elaborated conception of the human agent is an important part of any theory of social action and this is something that has now increasingly come to be realised in many areas of social science. Geras (1983, p. 107) states the case for historical materialism but his strictures apply as well to any other social theory:

> There are features of the [social] relations in question . . . that are due precisely to the nature of the entities they relate, that is to say, to the general make-up of human beings, to human nature. The latter is therefore a constitutive element in any concept of the ensemble of social relations, a view of it either explicit or implicit, absolutely necessary to any social theory, and discounting its theoretical role while simultaneously talking, under whatever name, about human society, a logical absurdity. The supposed replacement of the idea of human nature by the central concepts of historical materialism . . . is merely bombast.
>
> It is true certainly that one can overstate how much it is possible to explain by reference to human nature . . . it is also true, however, that one can understate it and, in the context of historical materialism, the temptation to do so has become endemic.

In this chapter I have tried to take note of these strictures. I have outlined how the human agent can be satisfactorily rendered as a creative discursive and social being and, in the subsequent empirical example, I have considered a period of history in which some persons were, more than is usually the case, forced to face up to the world with the result that their accounts and folk models of themselves and the world were changed. The challenge is to extend this work to how these persons' constructions of themselves as persons and selves changes as the telling of these accounts and models proceeded.

I want to conclude by making two more points, both about class. First, it seems important that, if 'class consciousness' is to be located anywhere, rather than being characterised as a generalised amorphous sentiment emanating out of a population like some kind of ectoplasm or as imagery distilled from dead questionnaires,[27] then it must be seen as part of the discursive process of persons' accounts and folk models. This is, I believe, a conclusion quite similar to that reached by other writers recently (for example, Stedman Jones, 1983a; Joyce, 1984; Langton, 1984).[28]

> Language disrupts any simple notion of the deformation of consciousness by social being because it is itself part of social being. We cannot therefore decode political language to reach a primal and material expression of interest since it is the discursive structure of political language which conceives and defines interest in the first place. What we must therefore do is to study the production of interest, identification, grievance and aspiration within political languages themselves. (Stedman Jones, 1983a, pp. 21–2)

This task is particularly crucial in English society because 'one of the peculiarities of England has been the pervasiveness of the employment of diverse forms of class vocabulary' (Stedman Jones, 1983a, p. 2). Second, a discursive concept of class consciousness gives a more concrete expression to notions of community 'bonding' (R. Williams, 1983). It shows that this bonding is created in a very complex and diffuse way which can only rarely be reduced to a set of simple solitary links. One of the problems with so many studies in recent years on the origins of class consciousness has been that they have concentrated on a small, tightly knit set of contexts – from weavers to miners – where such links are readily and too easily apparent (Calhoun, 1982). But the problem with modern societies is that they consist of sets of contexts which are more diffuse and less localised within which common elements of perception are developed in more diffuse and less localised ways (*1987f, 1987g*).

Notes

This chapter was originally published in K. Hoggart and E. Kofman (eds) *Politics, Geography and Social Stratification*, 1986, Croom Helm.

1. For example, current political debates on the futures of the left nearly all assume a fearsomely academic view of agents. These debates are therefore too often irrelevant.

2. As I hope to show, the definition of the 'political' is problematic in an account-based conception of the human agent.

3. None of this means that a category like 'ideology' or 'hegemony' might not prove useful, but only given a clearly prescribed theory of social action which as yet does not exist within the Marxist tradition. There have of course been Marxist attempts to account for the individual but these tend to veer between extreme reductionism (for example, Sève, 1978) and extreme generality (for example, Leonard, 1984). A similar kind of reduction to those imposed by categories like 'ideology' or 'hegemony' is that of classes having 'interests', a viewpoint nicely demolished by Hindess (1982).

4. A bloodline that starts with Vico and works on through luminaries such as Heidegger and the later Wittgenstein to sociologists like Garfinkel, Mills and, latterly, Giddens.

5. Further examples of power 'games' can be found in Henriques et al. (1984).

6. The constructivist model is usually associated with the work of Harré and Shotter in social psychology but elements of it can be found in many other disciplines, for example in the work of Garfinkel and Giddens in sociology, or Bourdieu and Geertz in anthropology.

7. That is, knowledge learnt from within a social system, like that gained from walking the streets of a city, rather than knowledge learnt from without, as from a city map (*1985a*).

8. The intention is both to abolish the distinction between an inner and outer characteristic of Cartesian thinking and to lessen the emphasis on an 'unconscious'.

9. I have taken the terms 'a political economy of development opportunities' and 'a political economy of selfhood' from Shotter (1984).

10. See, for example, Elias (1978); Harré (1979, 1983), Tuan (1983). I mark myself as myself according to cultural norms.

11. The crucial elements of these narrations are the metaphor and the metonym (*1985a*).

12. See, for example, the work on political and other forms of socialisation such as that of Stevens (1982) and the volumes edited by Tajfel (1984) and Doise and Palmonari (1984). It is in these institutions that story-telling begins to take on some 'theoretical' characteristics. This is not a subject which I have space to explore here but it is clearly important (see Luria, 1979; Ong, 1982, Chapter 3).

13. 'Left' is a term I have purposely kept fuzzy in this chapter for reasons that will become clear.

14. These accounts had already begun to change early on in the war. In 1943, for example, a Gallup Poll conducted entirely among the civilian population already showed a marked left-wing lead (Pelling, 1984).

15. In addition the Parliamentary Party could count on three ILP Members of Parliament and one Commonwealth Member of Parliament to vote with it.

16. Clearly geographical comparison of the 1935 and 1945 Election results is complicated by the presence of the National Government in 1935. But the 1935 Election is generally recognised as inaugurating the period of Labour–Conservative dominance in British politics. The National Labour Party won only 339,811 votes and gained only eight seats compared with the Labour Party's 8,325,491 votes and 154 seats (see Kinnear, 1968).

17. For example, a Gallup Poll of June 1942 found that 62 per cent of those questioned thought that Russia was more popular with the British than the United States.

18. Unemployment had decreased from 1,270,000 in mid-1939 to 103,000 by mid-1945. Of course, some districts had already been doing well before the war (see Richardson, 1967).

19. In terms of labour supply, regions were designated as 'importing', 'exporting' or 'self-sufficient' in 1943, whilst local offices of the Ministry of Labour had been designated from 1941 as 'green', 'amber', 'red' or 'scarlet', according to the intensity of their mainly female labour requirements (Ministry of Labour and National Service, 1947).

20. Short-term migration, like evacuation, was not easily monitored by official statistics during the war.

21. There was a general increase in union militancy over the course of the war.

22. Although the Women's Institute retained its basic class character, the Red Cross was much less class-divided because of the stringencies of examinations. For a number of interesting studies of voluntary organisation during the war, see Bottomore (1954); Ferguson and Fitzgerald (1954); R.C. Chambers (1954).

23. The official evacuees came disproportionately from the poorest strata of society. Of course, some better off working-class people were billeted with poorer working-class people as well. This caused friction too.

24. Few could afford them.

25. This increase in readership should not be exaggerated. See Mass-Observation File Reports 47, 48, 227oc.

26. This has been described as a political portent.

27. The questionnaire tendency has been well criticised by Emmison (1985).

28. However, these writers go too far at times in making language the font of all action.

Later . . .

Hulton Deutsch Collection

Independent/Brian Harris

Later . . .

These three later chapters are attempts to relate the kind of theoretical background I outlined in Chapter 1 to the ontic realm. This work of relation has mainly concentrated on three different socio-historical arenas: time, money and machine technology.

Chapter 5 continues to elaborate my very longstanding interest in time-space (for example, *1975a, 1977b, 1977c, 1978a, 1980a, 1981e*). In this chapter, I attempt to turn the theories of Shotter and the nascent actor-network theory of Law to good account as a means of explaining the development of time consciousness in England from 1100 to 1300. In a sense, this chapter is transitional: in the 1981 paper that prefigured this one I clung to E.P. Thompson's (1967) Marxian-cum-Whig history of time, work discipline and industrial capitalism; in this chapter Thompson's account still figures large, although it is identified as flawed; in more recent work, Thompson's account has finally been all but jettisoned (*1995i, 1995j*).

Thompson's account can be criticised on a number of grounds. First, it is founded in a single overarching narrative. But nowadays time is rarely conceived as

> a single medium of consciousness, as a unified moment in history. It is intrinsically manifold. Numerous chronotypes intertwine to make up the fabric of time. The social and historical processes of temporal construction rely on and also re-elaborate antecedent rhythms and articulations. These multiple ties can become objects of construction because individuals experience them differently and because they have ideological implications. Time asserts itself in contemporary enquiry less as a given than as a range of problems the solutions to which are constantly open to renegotiation. (Bender and Wellbery, 1991, p. 15)

Second, Thompson's account constantly confuses lack of clock time with lack of temporal exactitude and therefore assumes that pre-industrial time had an inherently more leisurely character, a point of view which is, to say the least, suspect. There is nothing implicitly leisurely about pre-industrial life; that the senses of what time *was* often came from natural cues, like the passage of the sun and the seasons, cannot be denied, but this does not mean that these senses of time were somehow free of standardisation, regularity or co-ordination. Third, Thompson's views on the availability of means of time-reckoning are empirically suspect. He chronically under-estimates access to clock time and he minimises the importance of other ways of time-reckoning which, as the medieval case shows, were able to be used to sustain what were often extremely demanding time schedules. In other words, and to summarise, where Thompson sees pre-industrial cultures as lacking in time sense I prefer to see them as offering examples of time senses which are often just as acute but in different ways, conditioned by different cultural understandings of time (*1995i, 1995j*).

Chapter 6 is also part of a longstanding project which dates from the early 1980s describing the spaces of money (for example, *1982d, 1983a, 1986e, 1987c, 1988c, 1988e, 1989d, 1989f, 1992b, 1992c, 1993m, 1994g, 1994l, 1995d*). My concern here was initially to describe the *social* character of economic (and especially financial) systems and thus to move away from a favourite academic myth of an impersonal economic other operating on either an ethereal *or* a base level; as Boden (1994, p. 201) pointedly writes: 'society does not happen at different levels, research does.' But, as this research has proceeded so I have become particularly involved in considering the different interactional orders that make up the international financial system (*1994e*), and especially the constitutive properties of face-to-face meetings, telephone calls, and the like, for the very good reason that 'caught in a meeting and connected through a series of interactions are the people, ideas, and actions that make the organisation' (Boden, 1994, p. 106). Paralleling this emphasis on interactional orders I have tried to make an inquiry into the different social meanings of international money (see also Zelizer, 1993, 1994) and how they circulate as particular metaphors and narratives around the globe in specific (and powerful) practical communities of talk, sometimes with extensive 'economic' effects. After all, as Grant (1992, p. 8) points out,

> people in markets are more suggestible than a layman might imagine. Try as they might, they can never know the one thing they really want to know, the future. Not knowing, they compare notes with others. They work in units, not alone. They are brave together at the tops of markets and meek together at the bottoms.

In turn, this interest in the communities of international money has led to a more general concern with the social practices of these markets, in line with the general resurgence of interest in the social and cultural determinants of the economic (see, for example, C.W. Smith, 1983, 1989; Dodd, 1994; Mizruchi and Stearns, 1994). 'As such, markets can be seen as the effects of certain cultural configurations and the causes of others' (Haskell and Teichgraber, 1993, p. 2). Put in another way, I want to put 'the economic' into play as a diachronic rather than a synchronic category, especially since many of the social practices we connect to the trope of 'the economic' have died away whilst many other 'out of category' (Douglas, 1966) practices that we do not associate with 'the economic' have become vital to sustaining it (Lash and Urry, 1993). Fictionality becomes facticity and facticity becomes fictionality.

The final chapter reiterates my concern with processes of knowing and specifically with how what we can know is consequent on how we frame (or attend to) what we know, and connects to a general concern with the changing nature of time-space produced by different modes of transport and communication (see *1990b*). In particular, I have become intrigued by the prospect of the re-metaphorisation of and the consequent redrawing of the lines between the human subject and the machine now that the sheer density of machines has become apparent; thus, in just one laboratory, Law (1994, p. 141) can note that:

> Everywhere you go there are machines. Computer terminals, Macintoshes, Sun stations, cameras, photocopiers, telephones, printers, lathes, drills, milling machines, pumps of all sizes and descriptions, cranes, bending magnets, trolleys, vacuum cleaners, coffee-dispensers, centrifuges, ovens, refrigerators, calculators, shredding machines, faxes, transistors, current breakers, TV-monitors, public address systems, water de-ionising plants, compressors.

In the eighteenth lecture of his *Introductory Lectures to Psychoanalysis* (originally delivered at the University of Vienna between 1915 and 1917), Freud (1974, pp. 284–5) suggested that through western history three great shocks had been administered to human pride. The first of these was cosmological. According to Freud, Copernicus thought that the earth 'was not the centre of the universe, but only a tiny fragment of a cosmic system of scarcely imaginable vastness'. The second was biological. Darwin 'destroyed man's [sic] supposedly privileged place in creation and proved his descent from the animal kingdom'. The third was psychological. Freud claimed that 'the ego . . . is not even master [sic] in its own house, but must content itself with scanty information of what is going on unconsciously in the mind.' Mazlish (1993, p. 3) suggests that a fourth shock is now being administered: 'humans are not as privileged in regard to machines as has been unthinkingly assumed.' The last chapter considers the nature of this fourth shock and how the changing boundaries between human subject and machines can be interpreted as a part of a gradual rewriting of the 'parliament of things' (Latour, 1993) which is gradually seeping into our ways of going on, providing new affordances and resources for thinking which I argue are most apparent currently in poststructuralist thought. At the same time, this fourth shock allows us to stare over into the abyss of alterity, into an unknowable otherness that already exists:

> I've talked of ordering modes, and I've named a few of them. But what about the others, those of which we do not tell? Now, for ever? Did you ever read *The Ship Who Sang*? Who can tell what songs machines sing to themselves?
> You accuse me of romanticism? Perhaps you are right, though I would prefer to say that I am a mystic. I believe there are songs which are sung and which we have not heard. But my romanticism is also a method. I prefer to be cautious, to find ways of telling stories of ordering [rather] than blaspheming with stories of pure order, even sociological pure order. (Law, 1994, p. 142)

The Magic Has Not Gone Away

What, then, do these three later chapters have in common? Most of all, they are part of a developing critique of the notion of 'modernity' (and, by implication at least, of the doubly absurd notions of 'post-modernity', 'late modernity', 'hyper-modernity' or 'super-modernity'). 'Modernity' is, of course, a word with a long and chequered history, signifying many things –

from the birth of Man to the death of God. But I take it to mean, above all, the identification of a period of acceleration which marks a decisive break with a slower, more stable past, a period of remorselessly constant renewal in which the experience of 'the ephemeral, the fugitive, the contingent' (Baudelaire, 1964, p. 13) becomes increasingly and jarringly apparent. This 'principle of western society' (Kumar, 1988) has, in turn, allowed writers – from Hegel onwards – to write the West as 'the stuff of saga, a vast saga of radical rupture, fatal destiny, irreversible good or bad fortune' (Latour, 1993, p. 48), a stirring saga, of fleeting times, fleeting spaces and fleeting identities.

My criticisms of the notion of modernity are fourfold. The first is theoretical. I have been concerned to show that much of what we regard as modernity is generated by intellectual forms of life which, because of their allegiance to a textualist model of the world (and a corresponding fear of the papistry of the image [Stafford, 1994]), systematically exaggerate transience, fragmentation and loss of meaning, consistently over-emphasise systematicity (and in any case are blind to the many creative acts which keep systematic orders as systematic as they are) and downgrade the 'lifeworld' to residual Rabelaisian pockets of resistance in an ever more programmed *and* ever more frantic world. My only theoretical truck with the idea of modernity is its allegiance to the provisionality of all existing economic social, cultural and political structures, but this is hardly a striking insight. Otherwise, I cleave to a model of the world which interprets social change as the result of – less dramatic but still remarkable – 'small extensions of practices, slight accelerations in the circulation of knowledge, a tiny extension of societies, minimal increases in the number of actors, small modifications of old beliefs' (Latour, 1993, p. 48).

My second criticism of the notion of modernity consists of a challenge to the supposed chronologies that undergird it. Thus, with Paul Glennie (*1992g, 1993i, 1993j, 1995g, 1995h*), I have pushed back the onset of so-called 'modern' consumption practices to at least the early eighteenth century. With Paul Glennie again (*1995i, 1995j*), I have been concerned to show that what we fondly regard as a 'modern' time sense dates from much earlier than is commonly supposed and that the sophistication of historical cultures with regard to temporal co-ordination, standardisation and regularity is much greater than is usually allowed for. In turn, these findings suggest that a linear history of progressively increasing temporal sophistication is unsustainable. In other words, in large part, 'modernity' simply seems to be a way for current cultures to establish dominion over their historical forebears through a process of economic, social and cultural cleansing.

My third criticism of the notion of modernity is one that identifies it with both orientalism (Said, 1978) and its silent partner, occidentalism (Carrier, 1992, 1995), in that the modern is nearly always assumed to be a property of a western 'core' which depends upon stylised images of what is both inside and outside this core. The notion of modernity works to sanctify the modern West by propelling it away from the mundane history and geography of the rest of the world, usually by constructing decisive breaks in a univocal historical time, and by emphasising the qualities – be they good or bad – of certain spaces over others. In both cases, the aim is separation from any potential space of co-activity.

Then, there is a fourth criticism of the notion of modernity which is the one I want to dwell on at slightly greater length. This is the idea that modernity involves the gradual triumph of ordered and secularised systems which, in turn, make the experience of everyday life into a sterile and antiseptic one. Put brutally, I think that the evidence is against this proposition. For a start, any glance at the headlines in a daily newspaper shows the sheer ordinariness of quite extraordinary events. Then again, it seems almost impossible to argue that we live in a secular age. We still have our Cathars. As many commentators in theology and in the sociology of religion have pointed out, myths and miracles and rituals, covens and cults and sects, blessings and festivals and pilgrimages (Reader and Walter, 1993) all still persist. We live in an age which has seen, for example, a rebirth of evangelical Christianity *and* paganism (Olivier de Sardan, 1993), in an age in which many people still take astrology seriously and many others at least take note of it, in an age in which many people believe in UFOs and others at least follow *Star Trek* (Jenkins, 1992), in an age in which near-death experience has its own academic journals and death still has its very definite rituals, in an age in which older religious traditions like New Thought, Theosophy, Spiritualism, stirred and shaken by the psychological and eastern religious imaginings of the 1950s and 1960s counter-cultures, have seen a rebirth as 'New Age' (Alexander, 1992; Heelas, 1990, 1991, 1993), and in an age in which the study of 'implicit religion', which recognises the implicit religiosity of the structure of everyday life, has rightly become an important area of research (Bailey, 1983, 1990; Nesti, 1990a, 1990b). The whole fabric of everyday life, in other words, is shot through with dreams, fantasies, superstitions, religious yearnings and millenarian movements. *The magic has not gone away.* Take but one example. Roberts (1995, pp. 179–80) documents just one of the ways in which the City of London currency dealers we meet in Chapter 6 weave superstitions into their practices: 'we had one very good dealer and we had a building site just outside with a crane. . . . And he'd say "The crane's moving to the left, that's sterling going down, going to the right it is going up."'

Again, it is arguable that the bodily experience of everyday life has become increasingly sterile and antiseptic: it is just as likely that the shocks to what Prendergast (1992, pp. 18–19) calls our 'epidermal sensibility' are registered in different areas of the senses:

For example, is the late-twentieth century city smellier or noisier than, say, the mid-nineteenth century city? It is probably noisier (as a result of developments in urban transport), and probably not smellier (owing to the extraordinary, and often anthropologically exotic investment in what Corbin has described as the strategy of progressive urban 'deodorization'). But, even if quantitative measurement of a comparative sort were possible, this would not of itself yield a phenomenology of the *vécu*! Corbin's work on the sense of smell and the olfactory environment tells us, for example, that Paris in the middle of the nineteenth century was almost certainly no smellier than Paris in the middle of the eighteenth century; that what had changed were not the 'facts', but forms of social perception and levels of human tolerance. Perhaps our urban world is in fact noisier than that of the nineteenth century, but this does not tell us much about relative responses to different auditory environments.

Let me summarise: 'No one has ever been modern. Modernity has never begun. There has never been a modern world' (Latour, 1993, p. 47). But this does not have to be a cause for ontological weeping and epistemological wailing. Rather, it suggests much greater attention is needed to what Latour (1993) calls the 'anthropological matrix' and to a refigured anthropology/ethnology. The chapters that follow are cast in this spirit.

Now, of course, none of this is to suggest that nothing ever changes. Precisely the opposite – everyday life is always changing, powered by myriad creative responses to myriad constrained situations. And I want to end this introduction to these later chapters by suggesting just where one of the decisive shifts is currently taking place in western societies, a shift which connects back to earlier interests of mine in the shift from orality to literacy.

Each of these three chapters is about the way in which the largely invisible processes of information production and circulation upon which our world increasingly depends have produced a problem of imagining what cannot be seen – time, many newer forms of money, machines that depend on non-present sources of power. That problem – how to make what is prismatic, indistinct or simply unseen into something seen and expressible – has been solved in two dialectically related ways: by the deployment of numerous 'lived concepts' of sensing and by the invention of various technologies of spatialisation which have acted to stabilise and 'realise' these concepts (Stafford, 1991). In turn, these two processes have worked to produce all manner of changes in our concepts of embodiment, personification, space, time and other beings.

One mode of spatialising and stabilising the unseen, working in tandem with numerous lived concepts of sensing, is the technology of writing. Now, it seems to me, this technology is being displaced (not replaced) by the rise of technologies of image production based in the new information technologies. But our ability to understand this new *oral-visual culture* has been made difficult by the reactions of a number of different sets of actors. There are, first of all, the manufacturers of the new digital electronic devices whose sales pitch is bound up with techno-hyperbole. Then there are all manner of enthusiastic cultural commentators who, especially in their writings on 'cyberspace', seem to do little more than reproduce the techno-hyperbole of earlier ages, but with Deleuzian as well as Nietzschean flourishes (for example, Land, 1995). Finally, there are the other sceptical rather than enthusiastic cultural commentators who have simply continued to purvey a suspicion of non-textualisable phenomena which dates from at least the Enlightenment, and who have therefore 'reproduced, without realising it, the Enlightenment critique of merely beautiful appearances. Like the early moderns, they too deride the charlatanism of a bewitching optical technology and a cunning manual skill without compelling content performed to trick the masses' (Stafford, 1994, p. lxviii). But, as Stafford points out, there is another way. That is to critically embrace this new oral-visual culture and to do so for a positive political reason.

Stafford argues that, while reading gradually over time became a silent and, to an extent, isolated and isolating activity, the advent of an electronic oral-visual culture bears the possibility of promoting a more open social universe criss-crossed by 'extra-linguistic messages, interactive speech acts, gestured conversations, and vivid pantomime' (Stafford, 1994, p. 3), a universe in which the exchange of information is both creative *and* playful. Most particularly, it is to recognise the possibility of entrenching 'a culture of high-level visual education to accompany the advances in visualisation', and to dispel the idea of a dichotomy between higher cognitive functions, represented by serious textual methods, and the physical manufacture of 'pretty pictures', which are merely hedonistic entertainment. In other words, Stafford is working towards the idea of reinstating the mobile thought of colloquial discussion in new ways as an oral-visual drama in which image-concepts are variably generated and played with as tangible objects. In turn, argues Stafford, this kind of pleasurable 'learning' will require a new 'culture of politeness' (of the kind already found on e-mail) which can cope with this kind of discussion. To summarise, Stafford (1994, p. 286) argues that

> we are returning to the oral-visual culture of early modernism. To be sure, our world is more heterogeneous, fragmented, indeterminate and speeded up, because of computers and robotic systems. Indeed, it is difficult to imagine students in the manipulative and 'movieola' period of video or of electronic texts returning to scribal techniques. It is all the more important, then, to understand the role of visual analysis for abstract concepts such as human development, cognition, memory, intelligence. No longer pre-literate, we are post-literate. Yet, ironically, even within 'postcolonial critical discourses' emphasising the global importance of 'hybridity' and the value of 'alterity' the temporal linearity of texts serves as a model for a transnational countermodernity. Might the patterns and shape of cultures, their transformation, and shifting relations, not be explored more effectively through randomisation, animation, computer modelling and morphing?

Interestingly, such a view is echoed by Sherry Turkle, who argues that the iconic style of modern computerised telecommunications can support a move towards a much greater emphasis on 'concrete' thinking based on the rise of computational 'objects', and towards greater 'epistemological pluralism' which is more inclusive:

> The development of a new computer culture would require more than environments where there is permission to work with highly personal approaches. It would require a new social construction of the computer, with a new set of intellectual and emotional values more like those applied to harpsichord than

hammer. Since, increasingly computers are the tools people use to write, to design, to play with ideas and shapes and images, they should be addressed with a language that reflects the full range of human experiences and abilities. Changes in this direction would necessitate the reconstruction of our cultural assumptions about formal logic as the 'law of thought'. (Turkle and Papert, 1990, p. 153)

Stafford and Turkle may exaggerate (much of the new information space will remain resolutely based on text, as the example of e-mail makes clear), but they also seem to me to have produced a relatively optimistic point of view which navigates between the acolytes and the doomsayers, the spirit of which I like to believe also informs these three chapters.

5

Vivos voco[1]: Ringing the Changes in the Historical Geography of Time Consciousness

Nearly forty years ago, when teaching in South Wales, I often spent the summer half-holidays between noon and midnight, in tracking some small tributary of the Towy to its source in the mountains; and this led me by devious ways through many solitary fields. Over and over again, when the slanting shadows were beginning to show that beautiful countryside in its most beautiful aspect – when those words of Browning's Pompilia came most inevitably home: 'for never, to my mind, was evening yet but was far beautifuller than its day' – over and over again, at these moments, I found myself hailed by some lonely labourer, or by one of some small group, leaning on his hoe and crying to me across the field. It was always the same question: 'What's the time of day?' – the question implicit in that verse of Job: 'As a servant earnestly desireth the shadow, and as an hireling looketh for the reward of his work.' The sunlight was not long enough for me on my half-holiday; it was too long for these labouring men; and the memory of those moments has often given a deeper reality to that other biblical word:

Behold, the hire of the labourers who have reaped down your fields, which is of you kept back by fraud, crieth: and the cries of them which have reaped are entered into the ears of the Lord of the Sabaoth. . . . Behold, the husbandman waiteth for the precious fruit of the earth, and hath long patience for it, until he receive the early and later rain. Be ye also patient; stablish your hearts: for the coming of the Lord draweth nigh.

(Coulton, 1926, p. 1)

Introduction

Some years ago, I set myself the task of writing a book on the historical geography of time consciousness in England. But the task proved more taxing than I first envisaged; the shadows have lengthened, night is drawing in. There are many reasons why I have encountered difficulties but the one I want to concentrate upon in this chapter is the actual object of the study – time consciousness itself. For time consciousness has proved to be a far from innocent concept.

Accordingly, the chapter is in three sections. The first section outlines three of the main 'approaches' that I have attempted to draw upon in drawing up a historical geography of time consciousness.[2] These are, first of all, an 'ecological' approach. Then, second, there is a Marxist approach. Finally, there is an approach that understands time consciousness as an 'ideology of everyday time practice' which, in particular, stresses the importance of language. The second section of the chapter is concerned with applying the insights gained in this first section to the study of time consciousness in England in a part of the medieval period. This historical sketch of the development of new forms of time consciousness in the twelfth and thirteenth centuries forms the main part of the chapter. Some brief conclusions are offered in the third and last section.

Three Approaches to the Historical Geography of Time Consciousness

Human Ecology

The human ecological approach to the geography of time consciousness was the first to attract me. Human ecology has a long tradition in human geography, dating back to Barrows' (1922) seminal paper in which he asserted that 'geography is the science of human ecology' (p. 3). Briefly, human ecology is concerned with 'the development and organisation of the [human] community' (Hawley, 1950, p. 73), seen as 'an organisation of organisms adjusted or in process of adjustment to a given unit of territory' (p. 68), or as 'the human interdependencies that develop in the action and reaction of population to its habitat' (p. 72). Whilst human geographers have denied that human geography is identical to human ecology and human ecologists have denied that human ecology is identical to human geography, still human ecology has exerted a powerful influence on human geography, especially filtered through the work of some of the Chicago School sociologists (see Park and Burgess, 1924). If its influence has now lessened, it still retains a residual presence in certain ways of thinking such as organicism, naturalism and evolutionism.

One of the most recent applications of a kind of ecological thinking in human geography is the time-space demography (or time-geography) of the Swedish human geographer Torsten Hägerstrand. Time-geography has a number of aims that might be described as ecological in character. Specifically, it is an attempt, first of all, to describe the interpenetrated actions of communities and then, second, to make possible an analysis of the degree and type of interpenetration in these communities, understood as a function of the amount of time and space available to them (see *1977a, 1980a*). In the first instance, these two tasks are achieved via simple time-space diagrams which allow the paths of people to be traced out over a given period of time and assess the opportunity costs associated with choosing certain paths over others. Thus, a 'typical' medieval English peasant might have described a time-space path which demonstrated a very limited degree of latitude in the choice of activities. A path must be traced out which follows a particular activity sequence, dictated by the necessity to carry out tasks that reproduce life, give cultural sustenance, satisfy the labour demands of the lord of the manor and conform to the actual spatial layout of the territory involved. A further constraint is placed on this sequence of activities by the need to carry out some tasks in co-operation with other people who can only be present at particular times and in particular places. In more general terms, time-geography can also be used to describe how the physical conditions of existence have been changed by new modes of travel (like the automobile) and new media of communication (like the telephone) which afford opportunities for enhanced access and free time for new combinations of activities, and the way in which these new physical conditions of existence reverberate through the schedules of everyday life.

The links to practical consciousness (and, implicitly, to time consciousness) are obvious enough. A lot of what is denoted as practical consciousness must be formed by the repetitive inter-actions of everyday life encapsulated in time-geographic diagrams (Zerubavel, 1981). Routine is crucial to the maintenance of communities as communities and many of the modern developments in timing can be interpreted as ways of making routines (and communities) more exact, more predictable (and more able to be controlled). For Giddens (1984), in particular, drawing upon time-geography, routinisation is the lodestone of practical consciousness – not only by our schedules shall you know us but by our schedules shall we know what we know, even apprehend what 'we' are.

Evans-Pritchard's (1940) classic work on the Nuer is still a paradigm for this kind of approach. Evans-Pritchard interweaves the schedules of the Nuer, the way that these schedules can be timed (via, for example, the movements of the sun and the moon) and Nuer practical consciousness, especially the consciousness of time. Many authors before and after Evans-Pritchard have followed this kind of approach and it does not take much imagination to link it with time-geography and other ecological approaches. Quite clearly this way of approaching time consciousness has some considerable validity (see Gell, 1992) but it is a validity that is still limited. First of all, it tends to convey a partial vision of society as most now know it. It is most effective in small, relatively isolated communities in which the interweavings of the paths of residents are easy to apprehend and clearly spatially delimited, in which, in other words, 'outside' influences are controlled. It is rather less effective in modern societies, locked together by new transport and telecommunications technologies which have 'shrunk' space and time, and in which, as a consequence, communities are no longer discrete bubbles of time-space. Second, the approach is cautious about introducing struggle between different people and social groups into its analyses. The emphasis is on small organic groups; on communities as communities. Third, although this is not a criticism that could ever be levelled at Evans-Pritchard, the approach tends to neglect the importance of the symbolic dimension (Gregory, 1985, 1989). This is in line with the tradition of human ecology which has been to try to separate out moral

and psychological aspects of the human conditions from the human ecological task. Thus, Hägerstrand (1982, p. 323) can write that 'people are
not paths but they cannot avoid drawing them in space-time' without
noticing the explicit symbolism of his own attempts to draw these paths (G.
Rose, 1993). Hawley (1950, pp. 73–4) is even more explicit:

> Man's [sic] collective life involves, in greater or lesser degree, a psychological and
> a moral as well as a functional integration. But these, so far as they are
> distinguishable, should be regarded as complementary aspects of the same thing
> rather than as separate phases or segments of the community. Sustenance
> activities are inextricably interwoven with sentiments, value systems, and other
> constructs. Human ecology is restricted in scope, then, not by any real or
> assumed qualitative differences in behaviour but simply by the manner in which
> its problem is stated. The question of how men relate themselves to one another
> in order to live in their habitat yields a description of community structure in
> terms of overt and measureable features.

Marxism

One solution to at least some of the problems with the human ecological
approach is postulated by Marxism. Here the conflicts inherent in a
particular system of economic relations (or mode of production) result in
the formation of different classes, and the struggle between these classes is
the chief catalyst of social change, leading in turn to new systems of
economic relations. The Marxist depiction of society is thus of a vast
battlefield in which the rules of combat constantly change. Communities
can form but they can also be torn apart as the battle progresses and the
battlefield changes shape. Marxism has, of course, been very influential in
human geography, especially through the development of a theory of
uneven development encapsulated in notions like the spatial division of
labour. In such notions, the world becomes a mosaic with each piece
(whether it is a country, a region or a community), corresponding to a
different moment in the process of production and consumption.

Time is an integral part of the Marxist approach. 'Economy of time, to
this all economy ultimately reduces itself.' So goes Marx's (1973, p. 173)
dictum. There are many versions of Marxism but still the principle behind
this dictum can be spun out into a single, synthetic Marxist account of the
increasing importance of time in the development of western economy and
society. This account goes something like this: the rise of money allows
time to be economised in new and striking ways. Money is a token which
allows people to see that profit and the more exact use of time are linked
together. In particular, in Europe from the thirteenth century onwards, the
relationship between money, profit and use of work time became very clear
for a variety of reasons, including, for example, the growing scale of
business made manifest in the organisation of more and more extensive
commercial networks requiring careful spatial and temporal co-ordination.
More particularly labourers are socialised into more exact (and more
exacting) work schedules as 'productivity' becomes something able to be

measured by the spread of new timekeeping devices like bells and clocks. Temporal exactitude was clearly a precondition of the massive 'proto-industrial' outwork systems that reached their peak in Europe in the seventeenth and eighteenth centuries, but it was not until the industrial revolution that temporal exactitude became pervasive in the process of production and distribution. The labour force had to be entrained to the new factory time discipline based upon the factory hooter, the time sheet, fines, and so on:

> The battle over minutes and seconds, over the pace and intensity of work schedules, over the working life (and rights of retirement), over the working week and day (with rights to 'free time'), over the working year (and rights to paid vacations) has been, and continues to be, royally fought. (D.W. Harvey, 1985, p. 8)

But this new capitalist time discipline hardly extended everywhere in Europe all at once. It was the spread of the railway, the tram, the newspaper, the telegraph, the telephone and the radio signal that forced matters. These new transport and communications innovations acted to tighten the chronological net within which modern societies function and so extend temporal exactitude into the life of workers outside work and production, especially by increasing the spatial separation of modern societies through the phenomenon of suburbanisation and longer journeys to work. The lengthening of the journey to work had 'all manner of secondary effects . . . upon customary meal times, household labour (and its sexual division), family interactions, leisure activities, and the like' (D.W. Harvey, 1985, p. 9). The new temporal exactitude brought on by these transport and communications innovations also had striking effects on the economic system as a whole. In particular, the process of production became even more exact and the circulation of money was able to be speeded up, presaging today's 24-hour international money and stock markets.

The effects of these changes in the temporal infrastructure of western society had inevitable effects on time consciousness (Hearn, 1978). In the Marxist account the new time consciousness is primarily learnt through the internalisation of the time discipline inculcated at work, as in this passage from E.P. Thompson's (1967, p. 90) classic paper:

> The first generation of factory workers were taught by their masters the import-ance of time; the second generation formed their short-time work committees in the ten hour movement; the third generation struck for overtime or time-and-a-half. They had accepted the categories of their employers and learned to fight back within them. They had learned their lesson, that time is money, only too well.

Of course, this new internalised sense of time discipline does not come just from the workplace. Other institutions, like the school, also take their share of the responsibility. But just as clearly it is through the world of work that the world becomes like work.

The geography of time consciousness follows easily enough from this depiction. In effect, the uneven development of capitalism produces an uneven development of time consciousness. Thus, in depictions based upon E.P. Thompson's (1967) paper, the new time discipline forays out from the factory towns, moving gradually through society as the economic relations typified by the factory extend their range and influence (see, for example, *1981e*). There are problems with such simplistic accounts, however, as writers like D.W. Harvey (1985) and Whipp (1986) have pointed out, for the simplicity is both alluring and dangerous. The process by which a new time discipline was inculcated was contested and it was hardly so monocausal, so a Thompsonian geography of time consciousness will, at best, be an idealised one.

Although the Marxist approach to the problem of changes in time consciousness balances out some of the failings of the ecological approach, it is not without its own shortcomings, of which two are particularly important. First, there is the emphasis given to time consciousness as a by-product of the discipline of labour-power. Whilst this is clearly an important determinant of time consciousness it is by no means the only one. Other institutions, like the state, intervene. Thompson in his classic (1967) paper concedes this fact in his discussion of 'preachings and school-ings'. But, peculiarly enough, given his emphasis on agency, Thompson ultimately reduces this moral-psychological dimension to a mere hand-maiden of the task at hand – getting workers to work hard. Thompson's workers are made single-minded.

This kind of reductionist account works well enough in certain places at certain times. It is very effective in what David Harvey (1985, p. 6) calls 'the Manchesters, Mulhouses and Lowells of the early industrial revolution', the towns bent to factory production. But it says little about changes in time consciousness which occurred in other places earlier and later in history, of the kind to be found in the (non-Marxist) accounts of time consciousness proffered by authors like Lowe (1982) or Kern (1983). These accounts only tangentially discuss time discipline but they are still able to point to important components of modern time consciousness. Kern (1983, pp. 317–18) provides both a warning and an illustration:

> The historian ought not to try to make the thought of an individual, let alone that of an age, cohere 'all-of-apiece' but must try to identify the fluctuations between opposing ideas. . . . If, in the interests of literary unity . . ., I were to suggest a drawstring for the multiplicity of development (in the period from 1880 to 1918) it would be (and here technology supplies the metaphor) the miles of telephone wire that criss-crossed the Western world. They carried signals for World Standard Time and first public broadcasts; revolutionised newspaper reporting, business transactions, crime detection, farming, and courting; made it possible for callers to control the immediate future of anyone they wished and intrude upon the peace and privacy of homes; accelerated the pace of life and multiplied contact points for varieties of lived space; levelled hierarchical social structures; facilitated the expansion of suburbs and the upward thrust of skyscrapers; complicated the conduct of diplomacy; forced generals to leave their lofty promontories and retire behind the front lines to follow battles from telephone headquarters; brought the voices of millions of people across regional and national boundaries; and worked to create the vast extended present of simultaneity.

A second, interrelated, shortcoming is that doubts have been cast upon the historical accuracy of certain elements of the Marxist account of the formation of time consciousness. In particular, it now seems likely that systems of timing and time discipline of considerable complexity and rigour already ruled the labourer's day long before the industrial revolution, with all the implications that this fact has for the treatment of the industrial revolution as an important cusp. This is a point I will want to take up again below.

The Ideology of Everyday Time Practice

Both the ecological and the Marxist approaches to time consciousness have their own specific failings. But they also share some common tendencies which make their accounts of time consciousness unsatisfactory. In the account that follows I want to concentrate upon correcting three of these tendencies whilst, at the same time, *retaining the good features of the two approaches*. First of all, both approaches share a propensity for totalising, 'all-of-a-piece' explanations. Foucault (1970, p. 23) notes how certain researchers have often

> supposed that between all the events of a well-defined spatio-temporal area, between all the phenomena of which traces have been found, it must be possible to establish a system of homogeneous relations: a network of causality that makes it possible to derive each of them, relations of analogy that show how they symbolise one another, or how they all express one and the same central core; it is also supposed that one and the same form of historicity operates upon economic structures, social institutions and customs, the invention of mental attitudes, technological practice, political behaviour, and subjects them all to the same type of transformation; lastly, it is supposed that history itself may be articulated into great units – stages or phases – which contain within themselves their own principles of cohesion.

In this view of history, time consciousness emanates out, like a beacon in a lighthouse, from one well-defined source. In the case of Marxism, the tendencies against which Foucault warns have already been noted. But, in the case of the ecological approach, there are similar problems. As already pointed out, communities are too often assumed to be island worlds in which conflict is minimised. In a sense, the Marxian approach too often envisages one totalised society, while the ecological approach too often envisages a network of totalised societies. Surely neither depiction is correct. A more accurate view of society might be that of Giddens (1979a, 1984). In Giddens's 'structurationist' depiction, societies are fragmented in time and space, achieving more and more cohesion over the course of history but, precisely because they are historical and geographical objects, never able to reach the stage where they become an unproblematical functioning whole.

Thus a more subtle, *contextual* approach to the geography of time consciousness is called for. Such an approach must recognise that societies are made up of institutions with different fields of effectivity (which are not spatially discrete), of people who have multiple membership of these institutions (so that their influence can often be hard to determine), and of particular contexts (in which institutions and people make each other in differentially effective ways).

The second tendency common to both approaches is that they rarely specify what precisely the phrase 'time consciousness' might actually describe. The ecological approach has often tried to avoid moral-psychological issues. Hägerstrand (1974b, p. 53), for example, professes to feeling 'safer at a somewhat greater distance from the minds of others'. Similarly, the Marxian approach too has often denigrated the idea of investigating subjectivity as 'humanist' or has assumed that if social being determines consciousness then knowing the one means knowing the other. Thus the introduction of a moral-psychological dimension is a pressing need for any account of time consciousness. As Castoriadis (1991a, p. 50) has it:

> There is and always has to be identitary . . . time, the backbone of which is calendar time, establishing common, public benchmarks and durations, roughly measurable and characterised essentially by repetition, recurrence, equivalence.
> But social time is and always has to be also, and more importantly, imaginary time. Time is never instituted as a purely neutral medium of or receptacle for external coordination of activities. Time is always endowed with meaning. Imaginary time is significant time and the time of signification. This manifests itself in the significance of the scansions imposed on calendar time (recurrence of privileged points: feast, rituals, anniversaries, etc.), in the instauration of essentially imaginary bounds or limit-points for time as whole, and in the imaginary significance with which time as a whole is invested by each society.

The tendency to downgrade the moral-psychological dimension in the ecological and the Marxian approaches leads directly to a third tendency and I want to link the one with the other. Little or no account is taken by either approach of the chief component of consciousness and, it might well be argued, *the* central human activity, namely 'language'. In what follows, I will therefore want to take language seriously.

But I shall take the term 'language' to signify an extended notion of language-*in-use* that is not a formal linguistic one. In particular, by 'language' I mean to signify the hermeneutic *process* by which people make *accounts* of the *practical actions* of themselves and others.[3] These accounts must constitute a considerable part of what constitutes human consciousness; people talk to others and become people through that talk. In Harré's (1984, p. 127) terms, 'interpersonal conversation is the fundamental psychological reality.'

Clearly this linguistic conception of consciousness is radically social. It makes it possible to operationalise the Marxist dictum that social being determines consciousness by asking 'where do accounts come from?' To answer this question I want to conjure up the idea of an 'ideology of everyday practice' (Law, 1986), the mediated imposition of a particular set of practices upon a population which in turn affects the way a population makes accounts of practice. Such an ideology comes about through three interrelated channels (Lave, 1986). First of all, there is the discourse of *documents* or *texts* – books, papers, government reports, and so on – which both provide evidence of changing interpretations and, more importantly, act, either implicitly or explicitly, to confirm or change interpretations, that is, as prescriptive tools. Obviously the power of texts is not routinely effective. In part this is because there are many different kinds of reading practice (Chartier, 1989, 1994). In part it is also because texts have a geography; not all texts are available everywhere (Chapter 3).

The second channel for an ideology of everyday practice will be *devices* or *instruments*. These might vary in form from a ruler to an astrolabe to a micrometer to a computer, but all such devices can be powerful elements of a system of meaning. Their usage can enforce a particular conception of the world. Again, such devices have a geography which gives them only a differential power to influence practices.

Finally, there is the matter of *disciplining* or *drilling* people, so as to *routinise* a set of practices. Here is more familiar territory. Systems of disciplining people are an object of commonplace study in the social sciences, especially since the work of Foucault. And, as Foucault amongst others has shown, their geography is a powerful determinant of their effectiveness. It is a powerful determinant because nearly all systems of discipline require the setting up of specific spatio-temporal arenas in which discipline can be effective, able to draw people, texts and devices together in routine ways. It is also a powerful determinant because these arenas constitute the nodes of more or less spatially distributed networks of power, which require people, texts and devices to maintain (Law, 1994).

These three channels of an ideology of everday practice come together in all manner of ways, enabling particular accounts to be both communicated *at a distance* and continually maintained *at a distance* in a whole set of different contexts. Law (1986), for example, notes the example of late medieval navigation. The ideology of practice underlying the ability of sailors to find their way about the oceans of the world depended upon tables of declination, a calendar and books of sailing instructions (texts), the astrolabe and the quadrant (devices), and a set of routines incorporating the use of these texts and devices which were systematically drilled into mariners (systems of discipline). The point here is that most sailors were untutored. Certainly few would have known the principles of astronomy. But with these texts, devices and systems of discipline they could offer practical accounts of the world that worked.

However, it is important to note, at the same time, that systems of documents, devices and drills that go to make up an ideology of everyday practice can never be fully effective. There is too much indeterminacy in the contexts in which people actually make up their accounts for outcomes to be easily anticipated. In particular, people can resist one or more of the elements of such an ideology, so undermining its purpose and effectiveness or changing it into something quite different.

One part of the consciousness formed by ideologies of everyday practice is a consciousness of time and quite clearly accounts of time have changed over the course of history. To the normal ecological determinants of the passing of time – the rumble of the belly, the beat of the heart, the death of a relative – have been added over the course of history a set of *accounts* of what time is that determine how time is practised. For example:

> in our culture TIME IS MONEY in many ways: telephone message units, hourly wages, hotel room rates, yearly budgets, interest on loans, and paying your debt to society by 'serving time'. They have arisen in modern industrialised societies and structure our basic everyday activities in a very profound way, corresponding to the fact that we *act* as if time is a valuable commodity – a limited resource, even money – we *conceive* of time that way. Thus we understand and experience time as the kind of thing that can be spent, wasted, budgeted, invested wisely or poorly, saved or squandered. (Lakoff and Johnson, 1980, p. 8)

This metaphor of time as money is now imbricated in all our accounts. Lakoff and Johnson (1980, pp. 8–9) proffer just a few examples:

> You're *wasting* my time.
> This gadget will *save* you hours.
> I don't *have* the time to *give* you.
> How do you *spend* your time these days?
> The flat tyre *cost* me an hour.
> I've *invested* a lot of time in her.
> I don't *have enough* time to *spare* for that.
> You're *running out* of time.
> You need to *budget* your time.
> *Put aside* some time for ping-pong.
> Is that *worth your while*?
> Do you have *much* time *left*?
> He's living on *borrowed* time.
> You don't use your time *profitably*.
> I *lost* a lot of time when I was sick.
> *Thank you for* your time.

And so on.

Clearly accounts like these encapsulate a whole *ideology of everyday time practice*, which consists of a set of everyday interpretations of time which may appear quite simple and prosaic now but which have a complex and sedimented history, constructed from a succession of different texts, devices and systems of discipline. How has such an ideology come into existence? Drawing upon the framework outlined above, the range of what has to be examined and explained becomes much clearer. There will be documents to be scanned, including those exhorting new forms of time consciousness and those that form part of a new time consciousness. There will be numerous timekeeping devices to be considered, from clepsydra to clocks, as well as other devices like the telephone which have had impacts on the use and perception of time. There will be systems of work discipline, and discipline in state institutions and civil society to be explored, each with their particular routines, set in particular arenas, moulding the direction of accounts. With these thoughts in mind, the next section of the chapter turns to a brief examination of the dawning of modern accounts of time consciousness in the period from 1100 to 1300 in England.

It is important to note three caveats at this point. First, I do not want to claim that the period from 1100 to 1300 is *the* period in which certain aspects of time consciousness in England start to take on a recognisably modern form; even as early as the Anglo-Saxon period the growth of social institutions and a corresponding increase in the sophistication of territorial organisation (typified by hides, renders, etc.) required a practical organisation of time which must have led to a more acute temporal consciousness (Borst, 1993). Rather, I want to suggest that recognisably modern accounts of time can already be found between 1100 and 1300 which, at the very least, give pause to the idea that certain aspects of modern time consciousness are phenomena rooted in the eighteenth and nineteenth centuries. This rather arbitrary form of bracketing will be alien to many historians, who tend to start a project with a significant date. Whilst there are clearly many significant dates in the history of time consciousness in and around the period from 1100 to 1300 – for example, the creation of Chancery by the early Plantagenet (Angevin) Kings – I am more concerned here with establishing how in an arbitrarily chosen part of the medieval period changing customs and practices were already tending to produce 'modern' forms of time consciousness.

Second, in making this examination of changing customs and practices, I will want to move away from those works that posit a single medieval world view of time, often culled from the literary, historical and religious sources of the period. Such studies are quite common, but they are also suspect, not only because of their attempt to create a unified, unitary and non-contextual time consciousness but also because, given the sources they use, they nearly always constitute 'the view from the top'. This distancing means that I will also have little to say about issues like 'cyclical' versus 'linear' time, or medieval theology and eschatology or the development of 'historical' thought, important though these may be (see, for example, Borst, 1993; Wilcox, 1987). Instead I will be concerned here with how more prosaic changes in the material culture of the period led to changes in the ideology of everyday time practice (and so time consciousness) and how these changes were sieved through the grills of social rank (who) and location (where).

Third, I am well aware that the historical account given below may lean towards a technological determinism. This is, partly at least, a function of the evidence that still survives – books and bells leave their trace longer than the 'forgotten gestures and habits' (Chartier, 1994, p. 8) of the past. But it is also a part of an attempt to understand culture as material.

> The things that people make embody the sets of relations that went into their making: material culture represents in congealed form both subject and object relations. Material culture can seem to us like a series of stable entities, but tables

and chairs are the results of moving sets of relations, a moment in the ongoing process of production and consumption. The mutually creative relations between people and the world help break down the distinction between passive objects and active subjects. (Gosden, 1994, p. 76)

An Exploration of New Forms of Time Consciousness in Medieval England

It would be possible to draw a picture of England in the period from 1100 to 1300 as inhabited by a people of great temporal innocence, and this is a common strategy in the literature. Natural rhythms dictate the pace of life and work and the content of language. Memory of the past is scanty or non-existent – for example, few people have any idea of their calendrical birth date but instead refer to genealogy and important events to locate themselves in time past. Expectation of the future centres on a short life-span and the imminence of the Day of Judgement. Above all, 'in high technology cultures today, everyone lives in a frame of abstract computed time enforced by millions of printed calendars, clocks and watches. In twelfth-century England there were no clocks or watches or wall or desk calendars' (Ong, 1982, p. 97). All this is true – to an extent. But that extent is more limited than was once imagined. For the twelfth and thirteenth centuries are being revealed as a time when time consciousness was somewhat more developed than was originally thought. In particular, it is important to stress that just because people have no access to sophisticated time-reckoning instruments this does not mean that they are unsophisticated about time.

Thus, even in the deepest countryside, the rhythm of the year was never simply the twelve lunar months and the four seasons, for there was always the rich temporal patchwork of the ecclesiastical round (Philip, 1921; Homans, 1941), the key system of time discipline. In the context of the countryside the ecclesiastical calendar (a merging of a calendar of Christ's life with a calendar of saints) had become the centre of a sophisticated ideology of everyday time practice, a storehouse of different but interrelated practices and traditions (Homans, 1941) in which the basic routines of life revolved around the four great pivots of Christmas, Easter, Lammas and Michaelmas. It was a religious calendar, certainly. It was, as well, a secular calendar (insofar as the division had meaning in medieval times) referring to days of work, days on which no work was done, feast days, market days, days for paying rent, and so on. It was also a ritual calendar complete with, for example, lucky and unlucky days for holding baptisms and seasons when marriage was forbidden. And, finally, it was an almanac of arable agriculture. The peasant *knew*, with the kind of certainty that we now reserve for principles of natural science, that 'lambs conceived at Michaelmas would be born before Candlemas; that the ploughing should be over by Andrewmas; that ewes should go to tup at St Luke; that servants were hired at Martinmas; and that hay fields should not be grazed for more than a fortnight after Lady Day' (K. Thomas, 1971, p. 738). Homans (1941, p. 379) summarises the calendar as well as any:

> By the thirteenth century the sequence of the husbandman's feast days had become well adapted to the sequence of the weeks of the year. The greater feasts fell in the interstices between the farming seasons, when one kind of work had been finished and another not yet begun. Thus Christmas came after a Season dominated by the sowing of the winter cornfield had ended and before the sowing of the spring field had begun, Easter at the end of spring sowing, and the wake commonly between harvest and the (autumn) ploughing. This arrangement is the natural one, if only for the reason that men must have leisure for sport and ceremony. As for the lesser feasts, many of them had become linked with a particular kind of farm work. Thus Martinmas was the traditional time for slaughtering, and Candlemas the traditional time for putting meadows in defence. The working of the year and its festivals intermeshed to make a single and stable cycle.

For a much later period, Pierre-Jakez Hélias (1978, p. 10) gives some notion of what it was like to live this calendar:

> The whole year was punctuated, divided and rhythmically measured out by religious feasts, some of which were dazzling, whereas others came and went without my even noticing. There were even certain old people who paid little mind to dates as such and who figured out what day it was depending on its relation to Sundays and Feast Days. 'I'll come to your house the day after Michaelmas' or 'on the Thursday before the "Seven Weeks" (Septuagesima) Sunday' or 'on the eve of Trinity Sunday'. They knew which days were favourable and which were not. They had a certain number of proverbs that fit those Feast Days so that they could plan the work that had to be done in the countryside – sowing, weeding, the care of animals, harvesting. Their religious calendars were absolutely precise and accurate. As for me, I used to get awfully confused, especially when it came to celebrating the Virgin: 'Mary in December' (the Immaculate Conception), 'Mary full of light' (Candlemas), 'Mary in March' (the Annunciation), 'Mary in July' (the Visitation), 'Mary in mid-August' (the Assumption), 'Mary in the black month' (the Presentation), and so on. But all that my mother managed to make out perfectly well.

Into this calendar were set the other units of time. There was the month, ruled by the waxing and waning of the moon. There was the week, marked out by the sacred and secular significance of Sunday (Colson, 1926). And, if there was no bell in earshot to mark the passage of the day, there might be the hayward's horn or just a simple stick searched out to stand in the ground to act as a primitive sundial.

As if the sophistication of this basic system of time discipline is not evidence enough, there are other indicators. Certainly, the sense of the past and future imbricated in the accounts of the inhabitants of medieval England would have been much attenuated, but it is important to remember that here were people who built cathedrals which required quite exact temporal planning and an idea of a project lasting well into the future (Fentress and Wickham, 1992).

Thus England in the twelfth and thirteenth centuries was never a bucolic dreamtime. Certainly awareness of the passage of time was still in many places what Gurevich (1985, p. 143) calls a 'slow-moving, leisurely and protracted affair', but it was not unsophisticated. Coulton's (1926) nineteenth-century rural South Wales would not have seemed too different. Further, amongst certain social ranks living in certain places awareness of the passage of time and what this passage signified was being changed by the advent of new texts, devices and systems of discipline that went to make up a new ideology of everday time practice. The new forms of time consciousness thus engendered had a very definite social geography.

Texts

'When the voice has perished with the man, writing still enlightens posterity'. Thus runs a twelfth-century Winchcombe Abbey cartulary (cited in Clanchy, 1979, p. 202). It points out that texts enable memory to be organised in a way different from that found in oral cultures and, in doing so, they promote a different kind of time consciousness. But, of course, in medieval England texts were only fitfully available, even to those who could read. Ong (1982, pp. 97–8) provides one account of the resultant culture:

> Before writing was deeply interiorised by print, people did not feel themselves situated every moment of their lives in abstract computed time of any sort. It appears unlikely that most persons in medieval . . . western Europe would have been aware of the number of the current calendar year – from the birth of Christ or any other point in the past. Why should they be? Indecision concerning what point to compute from attested the trivialities of the issue. In a culture with no newspapers or other currently dated material to impinge on consciousness, what would be the point for most people in knowing the current calendar year? The abstract calendar number would relate to nothing in real life. Most persons did not know and never even tried to discover in what calendar year they had been born. . . . Persons whose world view has been formed by high literacy need to remind themselves that in functionally oral cultures the past is not felt as an itemised terrain, peppered with verifiable and disjointed 'facts' or bits of information. It is the domain of the ancestors, a resonant source for renewing awareness of present existence, which itself is not an itemised terrain either. Orality knows no lists or charts or figures.

But Ong's account is overdone. The predominantly oral culture of twelfth- and thirteenth-century England was by no means unsophisticated in the arts of remembrance and calculation. The oral tradition had ensured the survival of King lists from Anglo-Saxon times. The minor courts and folk-moots all functioned with unwritten precedents handed down from generation to generation. Certain monetary transactions (such as payments made and received) could be recorded with tally sticks. Dates could be marked out via 'clog almanacs'.[4] Further up the social scale, the multiple arts of memory were cultivated (Yates, 1966; Fentress and Wickham, 1992; Clanchy, 1993).[5]

Thus, many of the earliest texts described customs and practices *already in position*. These customs and practices were not immediately transformed by the fact of being written down. The process was gradual. But as the technology of reading, writing and producing texts spread, so the consciousness of time past could be extended (and manipulated) and new ways of organising time present (which enabled time to be equated with monetary values) became embedded in everyday practices.

In the twelfth and thirteenth centuries texts can be divided into three types (Clanchy, 1993), as long as it is realised that the delineation of each type is bound to be catholic in the extreme. First, there are books; second, 'letters'; and third, 'records'. What seems clear, taking care to avoid equating the currency of these texts with their survival in the historical record, is that all three kinds increased in number over the period, and, by its end, use of certain of these texts had even percolated down to village level.

Books remained rare throughout the twelfth and thirteenth centuries, which, given the manuscript form of production, is no surprise. Perhaps most books were to be found in the sacred realm. Thus Durham Cathedral had 490 volumes in the twelfth century; Christ Church, Canterbury, had 1,300 volumes over the same period; Rochester Cathedral had 241 volumes in 1202. It seems likely that some of the monasteries had even larger libraries, especially those of the Dominican order. In the secular realm, King Henry I had a limited library, arguably as large as that of a monastery.[6] But many other kings did without the benefit of books (Clanchy, 1979, 1993). A few individuals also possessed books, mainly the nobility and professionals.

> Robert Grosseteste, the greatest English scholar and bishop of the thirteenth century, perhaps had about 90; Master John of Foxton, who sold his books on Scripture to Lincoln Cathedral in c. 1235, possessed about 34 volumes on that subject; Master Peter of Peckham, a lawyer, had 18 works in a coffer when he died in 1293; Guy de Beauchamp, Earl of Warwick, gave away about 40 books in 1306. (Clanchy, 1979, p. 82)

The books in institutional and personal libraries would have covered a range of subjects but they were primarily divided into works of reference, religious books and tables, and Latin classics. Each of these kinds of book promoted a particular attitude to time. Thus, religious works and the classics provided at least some notion of long periods of historical time, although their function as exemplars of events in the Bible and antiquity clouded this perception. But the period also saw the production of books that were specifically concerned with the marking of time becoming more common. Of these, the most important were the books of hours (*horae*) (Harthan, 1977; Backhouse, 1985; K.E. Harvey, 1986; Wieck, 1988; Donovan, 1991). 'Books of hours were portable prayer books' (Wieck, 1988, p. 27). The books usually consisted of a series of eight services, which included the eight services (or 'hours') of the canonical day, a 365-day calendar and sundry other additions. The calendar often noted lesser feasts in black and major feasts in red, and was sometimes illustrated with the typical agricultural tasks pertaining to each month. The earliest surviving English example of a book of hours was produced by William de Brailes in Oxford in 1240 for a rich woman named Susanna (Donovan, 1991). What limited evidence there is of patterns of use suggests that these books were chiefly used at home in the morning or in church at Mass, rather than on the regular seven- or eight-times-a-day basis that their form might imply.

In addition to the *horae*, other books which marked time became more common. For example, a few almanacs circulated (K. Thomas, 1971; Capp, 1979). These contained information on the days of the week, the months, the fixed church festivals, moveable feasts, astronomical events and astrological changes. There were also the *horologia*, tables giving the length of night and day for every day in the year (Landes, 1983), and in some cases divisions by hours and even smaller units.

The next type of text consisted of letters. Letters can be found in Anglo-Saxon times between kings. By the twelfth and thirteenth centuries their use had become much broader. Letters were mainly used to record financial transactions, such as charters recording titles to property, chirographs, usually noting money debts, and *brevia* and writs, usually emanating from the Court (which by Henry I's time was issuing 4,500 letters a year). Letters as we now understand them probably only became (relatively) common in the thirteenth century, as people became familiar with the new medium. Until that time the spoken word had sufficed.

Systematically compiled records, archives and lists, the third type of text, are a comparatively late arrival on the medieval scene. The exceptions to this observation are the monastic chronicles and cartularies and the records of the King's Court. The chronicle, which 'had its origins in the Benedictine preoccupation with the careful regulation of time' (Clanchy, 1979, p. 78), was an historical record of a monastic house, usually meant both to inform and to edify by producing role models for new generations of monks.[7] In *c.* 1188 Gervase of Canterbury described its function:

> The chronicler computes years *Anno Domini* and months and Kalends and briefly describes the actions of kings and princes which occurred at those times; he also communicates events, portents and wonders. (cited in Clanchy, 1979, p. 78)

The cartulary recorded the title deeds of the monastery in a book for convenience and as a security against fire. The practice spread from the monasteries to other institutions in England during the twelfth century. At the King's Court (where the chief justiciar and Chancellor was as often as not a notable cleric) financial records can be found through the twelfth century, but cumulative non-financial records (especially legal records) date mainly from the 1193–1205 period, for most of which time the innovative Archbishop Hubert Walter was Chancellor, the person who also created central government archives. It seems, then, that the practice of both financial and non-financial record-making and -keeping, with all its implications for the consciousness of the past and a calculation of the value of time present, spread out from the Court and so onwards to the bishops and other magnates.

Thus, financial accounts may now seem the most obvious way of stating time as money, but outside the Exchequer there was no conception of the keeping of a continuous series of financial records to guide the management of an estate throughout most of the twelfth century. If, for example, a landlord wanted to summarise the circumstances of his estate he undertook a *descriptio* or *kalendarium*, a general description of its workings. However, by the end of the twelfth century such a description could be quite astute, showing all the signs of a management very near to the stage of record-keeping. For example, Abbot Samson ordered a general description to be made:

> in each hundred of leets and suits, hidages and corn dues, renders of hens, and of other customs, rents and issues, which had always been largely concealed by the farmers: and he had all these reduced to writing, so that within four years of his election [in 1182] there was no one who could deceive him concerning the revenues of his abbey to a single pennyworth, and this although he had not received anything in writing from his predecessors concerning the administration of the abbey, save for one small sheet containing the names of the knights of St Edmund, the names of the manors and the rent due from each farm. Now this book, in which were also recorded the debts which he had paid off, Samson called his *kalendarium*, and he consulted it almost every day, as though he could see therein the image of his own efficiency as in a mirror. (The Chronicle of Jocelin Brakelond, cited in Clanchy, 1979, p. 72)

Then in the thirteenth century a whole series of milestones are passed. In 1208 the earliest extant accounts of a bishopric are found. The earliest records calculating the profits of actual manors date from the Christ Church, Canterbury, accounts of 1224–5, but such records remain rare until the latter half of the thirteenth century. It is during this same period that financial accounts can be found spreading to the great religious houses (from the 1260s), the Oxford colleges (from 1277) and the towns (from 1256). And 'by the middle of the thirteenth century many magnates' households, both clerical and lay, were keeping daily accounts of expenditure in writing on parchment' (Clanchy, 1979, p. 72).

Non-financial records follow a similar pattern of diffusion to financial records. Legal records are the most important. Custumnals detailing common laws and rules are found early on in the medieval period but the writing down and storing of the details of individual cases does not come in until the late twelfth century. The practice spreads from the King's Court to the ecclesiastical courts to the county courts and so finally to the local courts; the general impression left by the evidence 'is that the habit of making and keeping records of proceedings in continuous series stemmed from the King's Court at the end of the twelfth century and took another century to spread across the country' (Clanchy, 1979, p. 77).[8] Lists appear in the same sequence. By the end of the thirteenth century listing had become a commonplace activity. For example, lists of men over the age of 12 were compiled for the view of frankpledge by seignorial bailiffs, and stewards and bailiffs were expected to make lists of everything on the manor.

These developments (and many others) show time consciousness developing over the course of the twelfth and thirteenth centuries in the matter of texts. In particular, a sense of time as ordered and as stretching into the past becomes more obvious as 'the business of government, whether ecclesiastical or secular, . . . gradually becomes associated with both learning and written precedents' (Clanchy, 1979, p. 132). Nowhere is this clearer than in the practice of dating documents. Thus, most twelfth-century charters do not record dates. If they do, then these dates are clumsily put and related to significant events. It is not until the last decade of the twelfth century that royal letters are uniformly dated (by place of issue, day of the month and regnal year). From the Court the practice spread to the bishops, but it is not until well into the thirteenth century that the practice of dating letters and other texts (such as books) becomes routine (although remaining far from consistent in form).

> Why not always give the date on a document in a precise and uniform way, if only as a routine precaution? Various explanations can be suggested for not doing so. One sometimes mentioned is that charters were seen as mere confirmation of transactions which had already taken place, and there was no point in dating them. . . . Another possible explanation is that they were difficult to compute without printed diaries. . . . Other reasons for not putting dates on documents are more profound. Until putting the date on a document became a mindless routine, dating required the scribe to express an opinion about his place in time. . . . Paradoxically monks may have so rarely dated documents in the twelfth century or earlier because they were too conscious of the significance of time and of their place in posterity.
>   The non-religious, by contrast, had such a personal and short view of time that they too found it difficult to specify a numerical year on a document. Everyone knew which year was meant, the present one, and if there were doubt, some notable event could be referred to. (Clanchy, 1979, p. 238)[9]

It is tempting to look for some symbolic final seal on the matter of dating texts. The year 1290 suggests itself, when legal memory was set at the accession of Richard I in 1189, where it was to remain throughout the rest of the Middle Ages. (Up until the reign of Edward I the assumption of the legal system seems to have been that time extended only to the memory of the oldest living person. From 1290 time was set fast in the artificial memory of royal bureaucratic records and archives.) But history is never so neat. The creation of legal memory was a fiction designed to suit royal bureaucrats and only royal courts functioned in that way. For some time to come, manorial and other folk courts continued to operate with a mixture of written and unwritten precedents which were often little more than a codification of oral memory.

In all this, little mention has been made of the towns and the developing merchant class within them. The period from 1100 to 1300 is certainly a period of the growth of industry (although much of this industry was located in rural areas) and of the growth of trade (signified by, for example, the increase in the number of market towns). But, perhaps surprisingly, the growth of industry and commerce in the towns did not lead to rapid increases in the use of documents. The management of boroughs led to the need for documentation, for example summarising municipal bye-laws. The guilds, many formed in the twelfth century, needed lists of guildsmen and summaries of rules. But the practice of trade was still often at a non-textual stage. Contracts were often oral, especially in the twelfth century. Not until 1285, with the statute of merchants, was every important town in England obliged to have a clerk to enrol debts (although written contracts were certainly quite extensively used before this time). The great merchant dynasties (most of which were knightly) were as educated as the knights over the period and no doubt used documents towards its end, but the lesser merchants (who made up the bulk of trade) were a different prospect altogether:

> It is doubtful whether literacy in Latin was yet an essential skill, as they worked from memory and tally sticks. Book learning and book keeping became crucial to lesser merchants only when they ceased to travel with their wares and sat in offices instead. On the whole, that is a development of the fourteenth century rather than the twelfth, as far as England is concerned. (Clanchy, 1979, p. 188)

Beginning from the Court and the church in the twelfth century, the rising tide of documents washes up on the shores of local courts by the end of the thirteenth century, bringing with it new forms of awareness of time. Further, there is evidence to suggest that those who could read and therefore be influenced by the time sense purveyed by the documents were, by the end of the thirteenth century, a fairly sizeable group (J.W. Thompson, 1963). The extent of medieval English literacy is a notoriously difficult area of research, complicated by such factors as the existence of three languages, the differences between reading and writing literacy, and so on. But, of familiarity with documents as a prerogative of a large proportion of the population there is, by the end of the period, no doubt. One index of this familiarity is ownership of a seal (to authenticate documents). On this index, whereas in 1100 only rulers and bishops possessed seals, by 1300 all freemen and even some serfs owned them (Clanchy, 1979). Of minimal literacy (comprising reading literacy in a little Latin, and perhaps French), a similar distribution seems at least possible.

In summary, the historical geography of the new forms of time consciousness engendered by texts in the twelfth and thirteenth centuries is the geography, above all, of the presence or absence of particular social ranks. In the twelfth century only the Court and the monastic orders are strongly under the spell of reading and writing. Then gradually through the course of the thirteenth century, the spell's sphere of influence gradually reaches out to touch the bishops and the clerics, then the lay barons, then the gentry and knights, and finally the humble peasant, even down to some serfs. The progress of the spell down through the social ranks is uneven, according to the type of document in use, but it is remorseless.

Devices

In the period from 1100 to 1300 there was not only a change in time consciousness emanating from the increase in textual usage associated with the new ideology of everyday practice. As or more important was the increase in devices that marked out the time. Of these devices, bells and associated timekeeping devices are by far the most important (Downman, 1898; Raven, 1906; Walters, 1912; Coleman, 1928; Ingram, 1954; E. Morris, 1955; P. Price, 1983).

Bells were the major markers of time through the period under discussion, nearly all located in churches. 'It was mainly by the ear that medieval people knew the time, not by eye' (Gurevich, 1985, p. 106). The growth in the power of bells as markers of time can be noted in three ways.[10] First of all, there was the sheer number and size of some bells in the chief locations. Thus at Exeter Cathedral by 1050 there were seven bells, to which Bishop Leofric added six more in the twelfth century (J.G.M. Scott, n.d.). By the twelfth century Canterbury Cathedral was reported to have five large bells which reputedly needed 10, 10, 11, 8 and 24 men to ring them, respectively. Later a larger bell was added which required the services of no less than 32 men![11] In the same century enormous bells could be found at the cathedrals at Winchester, Lincoln, York and St Albans, as well as at the abbeys of Westminster and Bury St Edmunds (the latter probably destroyed in 1210 when the abbey towers fell in). Second, the number and size of bells to be found can be indexed through the diversity of church architecture in the period (Walters, 1912; E. Morris, 1955; Rodwell, 1981). Bells were housed in three ways. There was the bell-tower, already common in late Anglo-Saxon and early Norman England. Then there was the separate bell-tower (campanile), able to take large bells without threatening the structure of the main church building (and found even in major cathedrals like Salisbury and Chester). There was also the bell turret (bell cote), often at first made of wood. This construction was ideal for smaller bells. A final index of the number and size of bells in the twelfth and thirteenth centuries is the presence of bell-foundries, found first in England in the tenth and eleventh centuries. Many bells were made by itinerant bell-founders on site. Other bells were made by monks. There is evidence of their activity at Bury St Edmunds, York and Canterbury. Still other bells were made at professional bell-foundries and then transported, possibly along the waterways, to their destinations. The distances involved could be great. For example, bells made at Gloucester ended up in Northampton. The major professional foundries were in London, where the founders congregated in the district between St Andrew Undershaft and St Botolph Aldgate.[12]

In the period from 1100 to 1300 the main source of time-marking was therefore the church bell. In the humble life of a small rural community this might only be one bell hung over the roof of the choir. But larger churches would, as has been noted, have many bells. The bells were used to decorate and intersperse services but they also had distinct functions, the most important of which was undoubtedly to call the celebration of Mass. The service had been held daily from the sixth century in England and bells called for it at noon or afternoon on workdays and on the mornings of

Sundays and holy days. At cathedrals and other important churches the bells also summoned people to early morning matins and later afternoon vespers (P. Price, 1983). Indeed, by the end of the period some bells were being used to ring out the full set of canonical hours (see below).[13] Thus,

> As cities grew additional masses were celebrated, particularly on Sundays, to service the increased population of the parish. The ringing for these, along with a growing number of religious activities in the church – special sermons, rosaries, novenas, catechisms, public instructions to adults and children – so increased the sounding of bells that in time the air over the housetops was seldom void of the sound of a bell calling to some church. (Price, 1983, p. 107)

To the basic religious ringing were added sets of secular signals. In many places these could be very mundane, for example to indicate that the parish oven was ready. But the most important secular signal was undoubtedly the curfew bell which indicated that all fires must be out and all lights extinguished at a certain time of night. Curfew was imposed by William I and, except for a brief repeal by Henry I initiated in 1100, it was rung throughout the twelfth and thirteenth centuries, except on festival days. The curfew bell sounded at different times in different places. At St Albans in the thirteenth century it was rung at 9 o'clock. This was the hour in London as well and in most large towns. But in the countryside the hour was more flexible (partly because of the lack of time devices). In summer it was at sundown, in winter at a convenient time after dark (Price, 1983).

The dividing line between secular and sacred was a thin one, however. For example the curfew bell became associated with the saying of three 'Ave Marias', a practice formalised in a decree issued by Pope Gregory IX in 1230. (Gradually, however, this practice became separated from curfew and later became the Angelus, with its own bell, with the frequency of the observances increased to three times a day.)

If in the churches the ringing of bells was an important part of life, in the monasteries it was an obsession. In the monasteries the day was, in principle, divided into eight 'canonical hours':

> An office every three hours except for one at midnight made seven offices of 'hours' every day. Some monasteries also held one at midnight. . . . The twenty four hour day started at 6 am . . ., or at sunrise, at which the office known as prima (*hora prima*) was held. Three hours later (9 am) came the office of tierce (*hora tertia*); at noon, sext (*hora sexta*); at 3 pm, none (*hora nona*); and at 6 pm, or at sunset, vespers (*hora vespera*). Around 9 pm compline (*hora completarum*) completed the day before retiring (in some monasteries, before supper and retiring). Where an office was celebrated at midnight it was known as nocturns (*hora nocturna*) or matins (*hora matunita*). (Price, 1983, p. 116)

However, the canonical hours were only very rarely equal in length because the exact times of day at which offices were held often varied. This was so because certain orders were stricter than others. More particularly it was because the daily round of the monastery was, in the 1100 to 1300 period, still often regulated by hours of daylight. The canonical hours therefore often still changed with the seasons (unless a *horologia* was available). For example, the Benedictines rose at 1.30 a.m. and retired at 8.30 p.m. in summer and at 2.30 a.m. and 6.30 p.m. in winter (Dickinson, 1961).[14] Thus there was tremendous variation in the times at which bells were rung:

> Some of the divine offices were taken into the secular churches, and particularly into cathedrals, schools and hospitals. To hold them at convenient times in these places, two or three would be grouped after a Mass, and others shifted in time or omitted. Not so the monasteries, which held them all at fairly regular intervals. Some orders even held additional prayers for laymen and women working in their institutions, known as 'little offices'. Thanks to the monastery bell, the devout within hearing could also share the hours where they were. (Price, 1983, pp. 116–17)

Daily life in the twelfth and thirteenth centuries was therefore conducted by and to the sound of church bells. Le Goff (1980) and others have talked of a change, in the period from 1100 to 1300, in the hours at least, from the time of the church to the time of the merchant, from the sacred to the secular. But it is important not to overstate this tendency. To begin with, medieval English society had no clear idea of a distinction between sacred and secular. Ecclesiastical and lay interests were often integrated. Further, as the number of church bells increased in what were larger and larger towns, surrounding themselves with walls, the attachment to the church bells became, if anything, greater, since they were now needed to regulate the new internal threats of fire and disturbance of the peace.

> It was therefore necessary to pass civil enactments in relation to certain church-bell signals, and as these internal changes were greatest at night, the first concerned curfew. We see the religious and secular authorities working together to carry out a law passed by the Common Council of London in 1282 which was that 'at each parish church curfew shall be rung at the same hour as St Martin's (Le Grand) beginning and ending at the same time, and then all the gates, as well as taverns, whether of wine or ale, shall be closed and no one shall walk the streets or places'. (Price, 1983, p. 135)

In certain places, however, secular signals were given via special bells belonging to the town but installed in the church, or even installed in a separate tower set off from the main church building. In addition, by the thirteenth century, bells were starting to be installed outside churches to signal time. They could be found in institutions with fixed timetables like hospitals, on watch and gate towers (where they were rung to signal the opening and closing of the town gates) and on civic and mercantile buildings. Thus, some guild halls had bells. Some of the bells on these buildings were rung at different times from the church bells; for example, to signal transactions. In addition, markets, which had been opened and closed via church bells, were gradually switched to civic bells, although the time when market halls were built with bells atop them is still in the future.
To summarise:

> As commerce developed and industry expanded, the complexity of life and work required an ever larger array of time signals. These were given, as in the monasteries, by bells; the urban commune in this sense was the heir and imitator

of the religious community. Bells sounded for start of work, meal breaks, end of work, closing of gates, start of market, close of market, assembly emergencies, council meetings, end of drink service, time for street cleaning, curfew, and so on through an extraordinary variety of special peals in individual towns and cities. (Landes, 1983, p. 72)

It is important to stress that in medieval times these bells were not just time signals. There was a moral-psychological dimension to their existence. For example, bells were thought to be able to drive away evil and disease, and able to help boost the prayers of the faithful towards heaven. Thus, bells were often baptised, named and given personal attributes:

> in the Middle Ages the church tower bell was not held to be mere metal. With its reception into Christianity through baptism, with its possession of a nave, with its mantle of iconography and holy symbols exposed to the powers of the air, with its voice which spoke to heaven and earth in a distinctive tone known to the whole community (for no bell sounded quite like any other), with the translation of this sound into words on its surface, and above all with the trust that the whole community had in the effectiveness of these attributes, the bell was regarded as a half-divine being with a personality. It was therefore natural that any inscribed statements of the bell's purpose or power which were cast on it when it was made should be made in the first person.
>
> These statements give us a glimpse of life in former times from a little known vantage point. They were called virtutes, literally (strengths), but they ranged from the common functions of a bell to stupendous miracles. . . .
>
> It did not matter if they were in a speech not understood by (some of) the people. They were not there to be viewed by men, but to be spoken to angels and demons contending for men's souls. (Price, 1983, p. 127)

Bells had to be rung at particular times, but during the period from 1100 to 1300 these times were difficult to determine. Thus a London-based common law judge, Roger of Seaton, acknowledged receipt of one letter from the Chancery in 1279 at 'about the ninth hour' and another 'just a little after dark' (Clanchy, 1979, p. 236). The passage of the day – sunrise, noon and sunset (in clear weather) – was still, bells or no, a powerful timekeeper. But other timekeepers existed to help keep the bells accurate. The sundial (which included a portable variant) was ubiquitous and was used with full knowledge that days became longer as the year approached the solstice and shorter as it left it; on some sundials lines pointed out the differences. A very few persons had access to *horologia* and even astrolabes (L. White, 1962). Of course, days were not always clear and sundials were of no use at night, so there was also the candle marked with equidistant lines and, later in the period, the hourglass (Borst, 1993). Both of these devices had to be carefully watched; it was even possible to fit primitive alarm mechanisms signalling the night offices to be celebrated to keep the watcher alert. This was especially important in monasteries, where prayers chanted at a fixed speed and rhythm covered a fixed period of time and were therefore a useful supplementary timing device.

Nearer to the apex of sophistication was the water clock (clepsydra). There was one such clock at the abbey at Bury St Edmunds in 1198, for example. It is recorded because its water helped to extinguish a fire but

there were certainly others at the same time, records for which have not
survived, especially in cathedrals and monasteries. By the thirteenth century
these water clocks were of a considerable sophistication (L. White, 1962).
Finally, right at the end of the thirteenth century, mechanised clocks begin
to appear. These early clocks could be major engineering projects so it is no
surprise that records of their construction or other mention of their
existence have survived. Beeson (1971) argues that the earliest known
mechanical clock in England was located at Dunstable Priory. It is first
mentioned in records in 1283. Other such clocks are first mentioned at
Exeter Cathedral (1284); Old St Pauls, London (1286); Merton College,
Oxford (1288?); Norwich Cathedral Priory (1290); Ely Abbey, a
Benedictine house, in 1291; and Christ Church Cathedral, Canterbury, in
1292 (North, 1975). Mechanical clocks then appear regularly through the
fourteenth century, starting out at Salisbury Cathedral (1306), Norwich
Cathedral (1322), Lincoln Cathedral (1324) and St Albans Abbey (1327)
(Figure 5.1). At this early stage, most of the clocks proper had no dials and
only counted hours. Further, they were not always linked directly to
outside bells. Sometimes, they acted as alarms to get the bell-ringer to the
bell (see Graham, 1956; Beeson, 1971; North, 1975; Watson, 1976;
Backinsell, 1977; Duley, 1977). But by the early fourteenth century directly
linked clocks had appeared, at least to judge from a 1306 regulation from
Sarum (Salisbury) which states that 'before the clock of the Cathedral had
struck one no person was to purchase or cause to be purchased flesh, fish or
victuals' (Beeson, 1971, p. 16). The new mechanical clocks also announced
the prestige of their owners in no uncertain manner. As Landes (1983)
points out, this totemic function was sometimes as important as the
timekeeping function.

Clearly, the use of water clocks and mechanical clocks from the thirteenth century onwards had important consequences for time consciousness. In particular, it meant that, for the first time, the passage of time
could be followed independently of the passage of night and day through
an organisation of the day into strictly equal periods of time. Thus, a
wholly artificial system of time-reckoning was possible for the first time in
daily life. This had certain consequences and, most particularly, it helped
people to measure and calculate durations of time and allocate this time in
new, more exact ways.

In summary, the historical geography of the new forms of time
consciousness engendered by devices in the twelfth and thirteenth centuries
is, in the main, the geography of the church. The church and the associated
monastic orders (see below) were more likely to have need of bells and
timekeeping devices. Because so many of these devices were publicly in
earshot or on display, sacred time was also increasingly secular time and
nowhere more so than in the towns. But, in general, it was not until the
fourteenth century that certain bells and clocks became totally secular
devices as bells and clocks began to be found on, for instance, market or
guild buildings or at the King's Court.

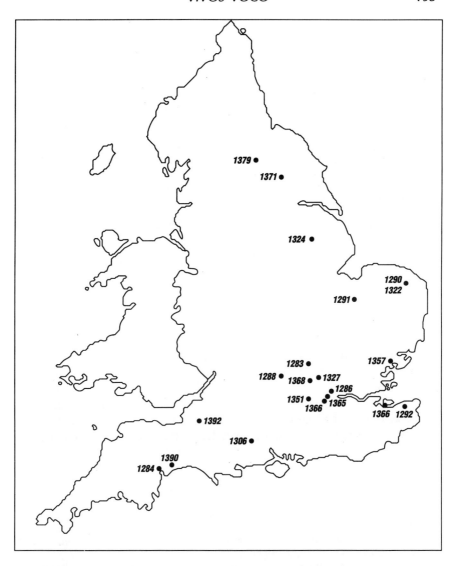

Figure 5.1   *Date of first report of mechanical clock (Beeson, 1971)*

Systems of Discipline

The third element of the newly developing ideology of everyday time practice consists of systems of time discipline. There were two main exemplars of time discipline in the twelfth and thirteenth centuries, one sacred and one secular.

The sacred exemplar was the monastic system with its offices set at canonical hours. As pointed out above, the strictness of the monastic system of time discipline varied from order to order according to the rigour with which each order applied *The Rules of Saint Benedict*, which had been extant in English monasteries from the seventh century. The monastic attitude to time is summed up in Rule XLVIII of *The Rule of Saint Benedict*, 'Idleness is the enemy of every soul.'

The timetables (*horaria*) of the monastery run along the lines of *The Rule of Saint Benedict* were therefore carefully planned out to make sure that the brothers were never idle. First of all, there was an annual timetable:

> There was a separate *horaria* for the summer and for the winter, and even three separate ones with respect to mealtimes ... there were also various routine activities such as bathing, bloodletting, head shaving, and mattress refilling, which were performed on a regular basis a fixed number of times during the year. (Zerubavel, 1981, p. 33)

Second, there was also a weekly timetable. Certain psalms were said only on certain days of the week:

> Further, mealtimes and wake-up time also varied in accordance with the day of the week, and even feet and beer jugs were to be washed on a weekly basis. To appreciate the weekly 'beat' of monastic life, note also that the reading of the full cycle of 150 psalms began on Sunday, as did the rotations of kitchen service and of reading to the community during meals. (Zerubavel, 1981, p. 34)

Finally, there was the daily round (Table 5.1). The offices associated with the canonical hours (for which there were careful rules of sequence) were the framework around which a whole set of activities were spun. The daily order of prayer was only a part of the ordering of all daily life. Indeed for monks there was no distinction between the religious and the worldly – work was not an end in itself, rather *laborare est orare*, to work is to pray. So there were rules setting aside times for work, study, eating, sleeping, as *The Rule of Saint Benedict* makes clear in almost neurotic detail:

> The brethren ... must be occupied at stated hours in manual labour, and again at other hours in sacred reading. To this end we think that the times for each may be determined in the following manner ... the brethren shall start work in the morning and from the first hour until almost the fourth do the tasks that have to be done. From the fourth hour until about the sixth let them apply themselves to reading. At the sixth hour, having left the table, let them rest on their beds in perfect silence. (J. McCann, 1970, p. 16)

At night:

> the brethren shall rise at the eighth hour ..., so that their sleep may extend for a moderate space beyond midnight ... let the hour of rising be so arranged that there may be a short interval after Matins, in which the brethren may go out for the necessities of nature. (J. McCann, 1970, p. 20)

The rules for lateness were strict with penalties in the form of penances for latecomers (see Zerubavel, 1981):

> Why was punctuality so important? One reason was that lateness – 'God forbid!' – might make it necessary to abridge an office, in particular matins: 'let great care be taken that this shall not happen.' Another, I think, was that simultaneity was thought to enhance the power of prayer. (Landes, 1983, pp. 62–3)

Table 5.1 *Reconstruction of the monastic day at the beginning of the period*

Winter		Summer	
		1.30 a.m.	Preparation for night office; trina oratio and gradual psalms
		2.00 a.m.	*Nocturns* (night office) (later known as matins) including prayers for the royal family and for the dead.
2.30 a.m.	Preparation for night office; trina oratio and gradual psalms.		
3.00 a.m.	*Nocturns* (night office) (later known as matins) including prayers for the royal family and for the dead.		
		3.30/ 4.00 a.m.	*Matins* (*lauds*) at daybreak; wash and change
5.00 a.m.	Reading	5.00 a.m.	Trina oratio Reading
6.00 a.m.	*Matins* (*lauds*) at daybreak *Prime*	6.00 a.m.	*Prime* Morrow Mass; Chapter
7.30 a.m.	Reading	7.30 a.m.	Work
8.00 a.m.	Wash and change *Terce* Morrow Mass; Chapter	8.00 a.m.	*Terce* Sung Mass
9.45 a.m.	Work	9.30 a.m.	Reading
		11.30 a.m.	*Sext*
12.00 p.m.	*Sext* Sung Mass	12.00 p.m.	Dinner
		c. 1.00 p.m.	Siesta
1.30 p.m.	*None*		
2.00 p.m.	Dinner		
		2.30 p.m.	*None* Drink
2.45 p.m.	Work	3.00 p.m.	Work
4.15 p.m.	*Vespers*		
5.30 p.m.	Change into night shoes Drink	5.30 p.m.	Supper
6.00 p.m.	Collatio	6.00 p.m.	*Vespers*
6.15 p.m.	*Compline*		
6.30 p.m.	Bed		
		7.30 p.m.	Change into night shoes Collatio
		8.00 p.m.	*Compline*
		c. 8.15 p.m.	Bed

Source: Burton, 1994, pp. 160–1

Twelfth- and thirteenth-century England was subject to successive inva-
sions by various time-conscious monastic orders establishing themselves in
the wake of the Norman Conquest (Figure 5.2) and, by the end of the
period, the population had reached some 18,000–20,000 monks, canons
and nuns and members of the military orders (Dickinson, 1979; Burton,
1994) or, on one calculation, *one in every 150 of the population*. Thus after
the Benedictines (who were present in England before the Conquest) came
a number of other orders whose common feature was their willingness to
adhere strictly to, and even build upon, *The Rule of Saint Benedict* as other
orders gained wealth and lost their enthusiasm for rigour. In the Cluniac
monasteries:

> The now traditional Benedictine insistence that nothing was to be given pre-
> cedence to the maintenance of an elaborate round of worship was much amplified
> by the adoption of an immensely complex music and various expansions in the
> texts of the offices which led to communal worship completely dwarfing all other
> aspects of the Cluniac monastic life. (Dickinson, 1979, p. 102)

After the Cluniacs came the Cistercians, an austere order keeping to remote
places and following *The Rule of Saint Benedict ad apicem litterae*, to the
last letter. The list goes on.[15]

Importantly, the importance of the system of time discipline in the
monasteries spilt over into the estates in their care, which were run on the
same precise temporal lines. Later in the period lay brethren extended
monastic concern for proper timekeeping even into non-monastic estates.
Thus the Cistercians divided their communities into monks (*monachi*) and
lay brethren (*conversi*). The lay brethren acted as a bridge over the
religious/secular divide, carrying time discipline into the countryside. It also
seems likely that the vision of time of orders like the Benedictines, Cluniacs
and Cistercians would have made its way into the running of ecclesiastical
and royal estates, if nowhere else.

Not only monks, canons, nuns and lay brethen came under the influence
of monastic time discipline. Every monastery or nunnery also contained a
large number of laypeople who would also have been at least touched by
the rhythms and routines of monastic life.

> Indeed, there were probably twice as many sewarts as monks, canons, or nuns,
> except in Cistercian houses, where some manual work would have been
> undertaken by lay brethren, and Gilbertine houses, where there were lay sisters to
> undertake the preparations of food, cleaning, and other domestic duties as well as
> to serve formal guests. (Burton, 1994, p. 178)

The second major exemplar of time discipline was secular, insofar as the
word had meaning in twelfth- and thirteenth-century England, and consisted of a set of interconnected changes in the functioning of the medieval
economy. Of these changes, by far the most important was the change in
the calculation of time economy allowing for the intensification of work
practices.

In the countryside, work hours tended to be from sunrise to sunset, but

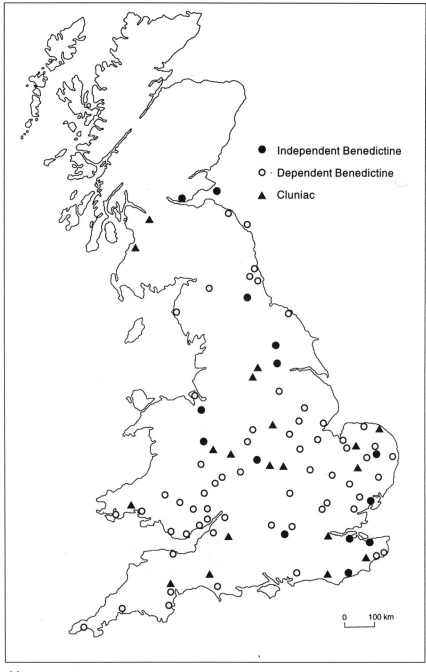

(a)

Figure 5.2 *Distribution of monasteries and other religious houses (Burton, 1994): (a) Benedictine and Cluniac houses founded before 1150; (b) regular canons, c. 1300; (c) the new orders; (d) religious houses for women, c. 1300; (e) priories, c. 1300*

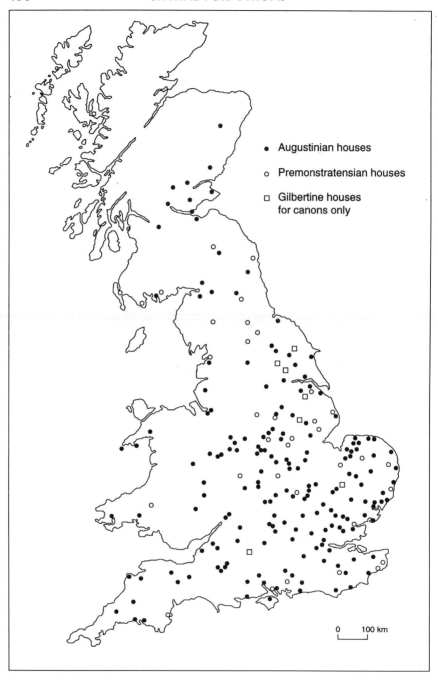

● Augustinian houses

○ Premonstratensian houses

□ Gilbertine houses
  for canons only

0   100 km

Figure 5.2   (b)

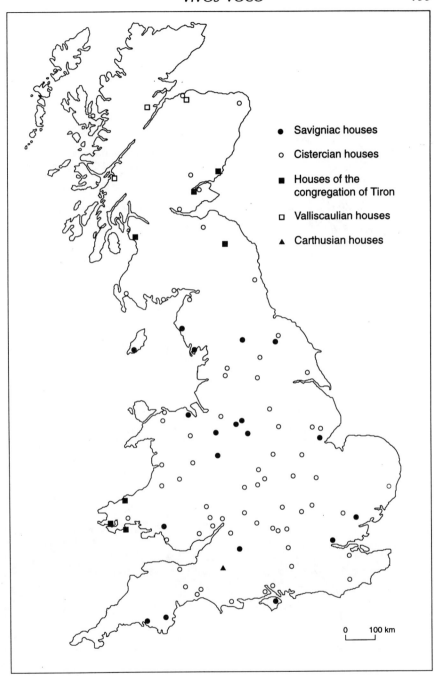

Figure 5.2 (c)

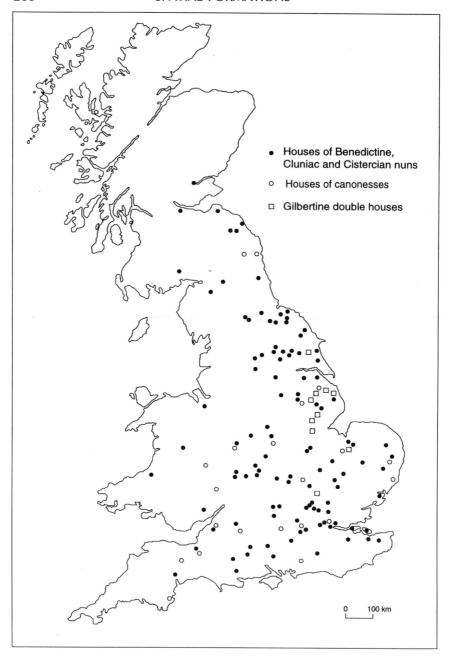

Figure 5.2   (d)

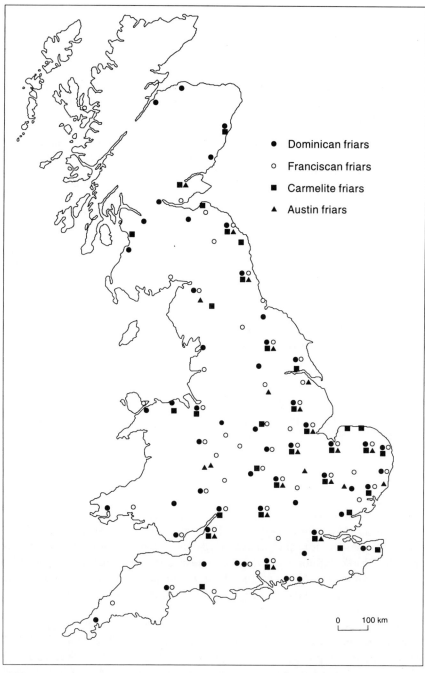

Figure 5.2 (e)

the more important event here, so far as work practices were concerned, was the attempt to calculate work hours as units of labour time with a set value. (For more detail, see Coulton, 1926; Homans, 1941; Bennett, 1956; Hallam, 1981). Obviously, before the thirteenth century the fact that the serf (and in some regions the free at set times of the year) had to render labour services meant that measurement of the value of time was needed to some degree, as Coulton (1938, p. 73) makes clear:

> For those unfree there was one general rule . . . that principle was, that the serf possessed nothing of his own; yet he might enjoy his land so long as he rendered three days work in the week to his lord. Before those days of the thirteenth century, when the multiplication of records enables us to get a far clearer view of the details, it is evident that a so-called 'day's work' had been reduced to a half-day of real honest labour. At Great Chesterford in 1270, each villein owed 714 week-works, (the main unit of labour services, rendered week by week through the year) each of which occupied a quarter of his day. In addition, at ploughing time he had to plough 16¼ acres. This totals at nearly three days a week. Some of these customary burdens are very complicated indeed; here, for instance, are the requirements on a Glastonbury manor. Between Michaelmas and November 11th the serf had to plough one acre; another half acre when called upon. He must harrow every Monday in the year; three times a year he must carry a load for my lord; he must mow three days, and go to the vineyard. All this he must do anyhow; then comes a rather more complicated list of works for which he may compound, if he chooses, by a payment of 3s.4d. a year.

In such a system, money-value measures of output per unit of time were still comparatively crude (as indeed were the measures themselves; see Coulton, 1926, Chapter 5; Kula, 1986). But such measures became more sophisticated through the thirteenth century, for two main reasons. The first was the increasing commutation of labour services for money and especially the payment of money rents. The second was the increasing use of surveys and the keeping of records. By the end of the century calculations were routinely recognising time as money. For example, by 1303 the records of the Cuxham manor demesne note 1323 customary labour service 'dayworks' (a measure of area, probably the amount of land customarily delved in a day) carried out at a value of £7.2.10½ as well as 2,060 dayworks for the *famuli* (full-time workers) and payments to unskilled hired labour made partly in cash and partly in corn. Tasks like ditching, muckspreading and threshing were charged at one daywork rate, while tasks like reaping or carrying were charged at another rate (P.D.A. Harvey, 1965).

But the system of time discipline and valuation was undoubtedly more rigorous in the towns, where, by the end of the thirteenth century, probably one-tenth of the population of England could be found (Treharne, 1971) (Figure 5.3). In the towns work hours were generally accepted in the guild statutes of the time as from dawn until 9 p.m. in winter (Michaelmas to Easter) or from sunrise until 30 minutes before sunset in summer (Bienefeld, 1972), with a break in both cases at midday. But, within these bands, there were great variations according to type of work and the skill

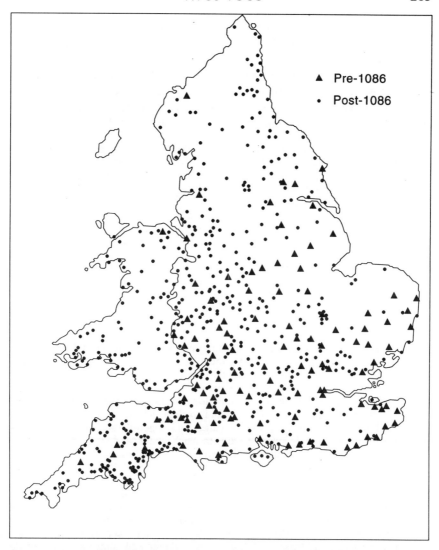

▲ Pre-1086

• Post-1086

Figure 5.3   *Distribution of medieval boroughs (Dodgshon, 1978, p. 107)*

of the worker. For example, some workers might work less time, while other workers – if the project was urgent – might work on by artificial light. Work days were usually from Monday to Saturday, with some workers taking Monday off as well, the beginning of the practice of 'Saint Monday' (Reid, 1976). But, of course, there were feast days and saints' days to be taken as well. Some of these days, like Christmas and Easter, were nationally taken, but others were local in character. For example, the dedication saint's day of the local church was usually a local holiday. Thus in 1297 the workmen at Windsor did not work on Monday 7 October, which was 'the feast of dedication of the church in the township' (cited in

Salzman, 1967, p. 59). There was also a general custom that when two or more feast days coincided the workmen received wages for one day in every two holidays.[16]

Regulations about length and value of work hours became remarkably exact as writing became more common. Not so far outside the period, in 1352 for example, the craftsmen employed at York Minster were enjoined to follow these elaborate regulations, worth quoting in full:

> That the masons, carpenters and other workmen ought to begin work, on all working days in the summer, from Easter to Michaelmas, at sunrise and ought to work from that time until the ringing of the bell of the Blessed Virgin Mary, and then they should sit down to breakfast in the lodge of the works, if they have not breakfasted, for the space [of the time that it takes to walk] half a league; and then the masters, or one of them, shall knock upon the door of the lodge, and all shall at once go to their work; and so they shall diligently carry out their duties until noon, and then they shall go to their dinner (*prandia*). Also, in winter, from Michaelmas to Easter, they shall come to their work at dawn and everyone when he comes shall immediately start work, and so continue in the said way until noon. From the feast of the Invention of the Holy Cross (3 May) to the feast of St Peter's Chains (1 August), they ought to sleep in the lodge after dinner; and when the vicars come out from the canon's hall (*mensa*) the master mason, or his deputy, shall cause them to rise from slumber and get to work; and so they ought to work until the first bell for vespers, and then they shall sit and drink in the lodge, from the said first bell to the third bell, both in summer and winter. Also from the (1 August) to the (3 May), they shall return to their work immediately after their dinner, for which reasonable time shall be taken, without waiting for the return of the vicars from the canon's hall; and so they shall work until the first bell for vespers and then they shall drink in the lodge until the third bell has rung, and shall return to their work, and so they shall work until the ringing of the bell of St Mary's Abbey, which is called Le Langebell, namely, every working day from the feast of St Peter's Chains to Michaelmas, and from Michaelmas to the said feast of St Peter, they shall continue to work as long as they can see by daylight. Also each mason shall take less for the week in winter, that is from Michaelmas to Easter, than in summer by one day's wage. Also when two feasts happen in one week, each loses one day's pay (*dietam*) and when three occur, half that week. Also on vigils and on Saturdays, when they rest after noon, out of respect for the next day, then shall they work until noon strikes. Also the said two master masons and the carpenter of the works shall be present at every pay-day (*pacacione*), and these shall inform the workmen and controller of the works of any defaults and absence of masons, carpenters, and other workmen, and according to his lateness (*moram*) or absence deductions shall be made from each man's wages, both for a whole day and a half day, as is reasonable. Also the said two master masons and carpenter, for the time being, ought faithfully to observe the said regulations, in virtue of the oath which they take, and they shall see that they are kept by the other masons and workmen working here, on pain of dismissal. And if anyone refuses to work in the said manner, let him be dismissed at once and not taken back again on to the works until he is willing to keep the rules in every detail. (cited in Salzman, 1967, pp. 56–7)

Rates of pay in the towns show a general appreciation of the value of labour time. As the passage shows, greater rates of pay were awarded: in summer than for the shorter days of winter time (Table 5.2); for different types of skill; for foremen (who all received paid holidays); for overtime

Table 5.2 *Rates of pay at two of the King's works in the thirteenth century*

	Vale Royal, 1278		Carnary	
	Summer	Winter	Summer	Winter
Masons				
Master	14s.	14s.	14s.	14s.
Under-Master	3s.	3s.	–	–
Others	30d.–15d.	25d.–12d.	2s.9d.–2s.3d.	2s.3d.–15d.
Layers	–	–	2s.4d.–14d.	2s.3d.–15d.
Quarriers	12d.	–	17d.–10d.	14d.–9d.
Quarriers, Master	18d.	–	–	–
Carpenters	18d.	–	18d.	–
Sawyers	12d.	–	–	–
Smiths	–	–	2s.4d.–12d.	2s.–12d.
Plasterers	–	9d.	–	–
Labourers	10d.	–	–	–
'Vintenars'	12d.	–	18d.	16d.
Barrowmen	–	–	12d.	10d.–9d.
Hodmen	–	–	12d.	–
Faukionaris	–	–	6d.	5d.

Source: Salzman, 1967, p. 70

(called 'respite hours'); and at harvest time (when many were liable to work in the countryside and had to be attracted back).[17] It was also quite traditional to give gifts (usually of drink, but also of money and clothing) to encourage industry, although it is important to point out that these gifts were no innovation but rather relics of the *corrodium* (food and drink) given to boon workers as subsistence when in the fields on the lord's work.

Other changes in the medieval economy also had repercussions for time consciousness. On the subject of the towns, it is important to remember the impact that the expansion of trade, finance and industry was making upon the boroughs and market towns, especially in the thirteenth century. The expansion of trade (especially in wool) brought with it periodic market systems and trade networks of considerable intricacy and correspondingly more exact and more exacting timetables.[18] For merchants, for example:

> Once commercial networks were organised ... time became an object of measurement. The duration of a sea voyage or a journey by land from one place to another, the problem of prices which rose or fell in the course of a commercial transaction (the more so as the circuit became increasingly complex, affecting profits), the character of the labor of craftsmen and workers (since the merchant was almost always an employer of labor), all made increasing claims on [the merchant's] attention and became the object of ever more explicit regulation. (Le Goff, 1980, p. 35)

New monetary instruments and forms of credit (overcoming the medieval distrust of usury) were also introduced which required more adequate measurement of time.[19]

The expansion of urban industry was another notable feature of the thirteenth century (although a corresponding increase in rural industry also took place) and the new processes of production also needed exact time measurement. These new demands for more exact time measurement could have reciprocal effects. For example, they could be called into service in measuring the output of workmen and women. Time therefore became thought of independently of what was happening in time. Finally, the expansion of the medieval state over the period from 1100 to 1300 deserves mention, bringing with it new and more complex judicial and other time-tables which intermeshed with and regulated those of the economy.

In summary, the historical geography of the new forms of time consciousness born of the development of system of discipline had its roots in the exact and exacting regimen of the monasteries and the calculative demands of the towns. From these two 'lighthouse' sites the idea of time discipline makes its way outward into a whole set of different contexts. Most obviously, the monastic idea of time discipline makes its way into associated institutions: the monastic estates, hospitals, and so on. But, more indirectly, it also makes its way into the royal bureaucracy (still run by the church) and, through lay brethren, into other estates. The idea of such discipline would also have lain heavy over the towns, characterised by the ringing of the canonical hours. But, as Foucault (1977, p. 154) points out, the idea of time discipline in the monastery was essentially *negative*: 'it was the principle of non-idleness: it was forbidden to waste time, which was counted by God and paid for by men; the timetable was to eliminate the danger of wasting it – a moral offence and economic dishonesty.' The system of time discipline adopted in the towns (although clearly influenced by the monastic regimen) was rather different in focus. It was becoming oriented towards a more modern, *positive* use of time, based upon the intensification of work, 'as if time, in its very fragmentation, were in-exhaustible or as if, at least by an ever more detailed internal arrangement, one could tend towards an ideal point at which one maintained maximum speed and efficiency' (Foucault, 1977, p. 154). Clearly, in the twelfth and thirteenth centuries, this process still has a long way to go, but certain elements of such a system are already in place; for example the ability to value use of time and, consequently, to begin to measure productivity (see Tribe, 1981). As Gurevich (1985, p. 150) puts it: 'Time was recognised as a commodity of great value and as a source of material gain.'

Conclusions

The period from 1100 to 1300 is a period when the ideology of everyday time practice is changing and, with it, the consciousness of time. There are several indexes of this change. First, there are the practices associated with the writing and reading of texts, as in the cases of the dating of documents and the keeping of records. As a result, for those exposed to texts, the past was able to be extended further backwards while the present became more predictable and more open to manipulation. Timekeeping devices not only became more accurate but inspired a new idea of time as an artificial reckoning grid, encapsulated in the advent of mechanical clocks and equal hours. As a result, the passage of time could be more exactly measured with consequences for the calculation of labour time and the spawning of attempts to make time more productive. Finally, there are the routinised practices associated with new systems of time discipline and valuation. These become more rigorous over the twelfth and thirteenth centuries. As a result, the planning of the position of people and objects over periods of time, an activity that had started with hidation and carucation in the seventh and eighth centuries, becomes more and more sophisticated. In a sense, time-geography became possible.

These changes were all, of course, interrelated in complex ways. To take one example only, effective systems of time discipline need some form of timekeeping. The more ambitious these systems become, the more a need for exact timekeeping will be felt. Mumford's (1934) classic statement that the invention of the clock is linked to the rigour of the monastic system of time discipline therefore still rings true (see the discussion of this point in Landes, 1983, pp. 53–7). But the relationship between systems of time discipline and timekeeping devices was reciprocal. The invention of time-keeping devices gradually opened up possibilities of new interpretations of time leading to new systems of time discipline. Landes (1983, pp. 77–8) puts this well:

Medieval man [*sic*], it has been observed, was innumerate as well as illiterate. How much reckoning could he do in a world that knew no uniformity of measurement? Units of distance were linked to physical characteristics that vary as people do (the English *foot*, for instance, and the French inch, called a *pouce*, which means thumb); while weights typically were converted to volume standards (a *bushel* of grain) that inevitably varied from place to place and mill to mill. Even the learned were not accustomed to using numbers. The calculation of the calendar, for example – a crucial aspect of liturgical discipline – was confined to specialist computists. The schools offered little if any training in arithmetic, and persistence of roman numerals was both symptom and cause of calculational paralysis.

All of this began to change in the twelfth and thirteenth centuries. . . . This was a period of growing trade and he who trades must reckon. So must clerks and functionaries who count taxes and expenditures, and these were years of rapid development of royal power and government apparatus.

It was the urban, commercial population that seems to have been quickest to learn the new language and teachings. Arithmetic was the province above all of the intellectual speakers of the vernacular (as opposed to Latin). Many of these learned arithmetic in the shop or on the road, but even before they entered trade, they learned to count by the bells or the clock. Not by the old church bells ringing the canonical hours; these did not mark equal units and hence did not lend themselves to addition or subtraction. But the new bells and the calculations they made possible (how long until? how long since?) were a school for all who listened and began to organise their lives around them. Meanwhile the church clung to old ways and, so doing, yielded the rhythm of life and work to the lay authorities and the bourgeoisie. Equal hours announced the victory of a new cultural and economic order. Here indeed was an unintended consequence: the monks had wrought too well.

Above all, the new time consciousness wrought by the complex interplay between new expressions and new mediums of expression was formulated as accounts, accounts pregnant with new possibilities (how long until? how long since?), accounts containing new metaphors (time as a clock, time as money), accounts presaging greater use of past- and future-oriented tenses. Such evidence as we have of these changes in interpretation is largely indirect; we cannot capture shifts in the conversations of the past easily at this distance in time from them. More than now, 'the written record does not give us the whole of medieval man's [sic] way of perceiving and representing his world which has been irretrievably lost' (Gurevich, 1985, p. 37). Thus documents can only give, at best, tantalising glimpses. For example:

> The drafting rule became general that the past tense should be used in charters for the act of giving: 'know that I, A of B, *have* given', not simply 'I give'. This emphasised that the ceremonial conveyance was the crucial transaction, whereas the charter was merely a subsequent confirmation of it. This rule only became general in the thirteenth century. Numerous charters of the twelfth century depart from it, presumably because their amateur draftsmen did not appreciate the relationship between written record and the passage of time. (Clanchy, 1979, p. 208)[20]

As has been shown, the new forms of time consciousness, seen, in this chapter, as new accounts of time, have a geography, or rather a set of interconnected geographies. First of all, there is a geography of time consciousness born of social rank. New accounts of time were more likely to be exact amongst the Court and the Church. The lay nobility, the knights and the merchants were next in line. Finally there was the peasantry. Where these different groups are found, the new time consciousness is more or less likely to flourish. Second, there is a geography of time consciousness born of the church. The church and the monasteries had a need for precise timekeeping which often spilt over into the secular medium. Finally, there is a geography born of the growth of the towns. In the period from 1100 to 1300 the urban population of England and Wales grew significantly (if only in line with general population growth). By 1300 London had a population of 50,000; Bristol had a population of 17,000 and York's population was 8,000. By 1300, again, the number of boroughs had increased to 480 from 111 in 1086. Most of these were rural market centres but in the few centres of population like London or Bristol large enough to be relatively insulated from rural rhythms, the new accounts of time took root amongst the populace.[21]

It would not do to exaggerate these points. By the end of the thirteenth century, most of England was still rural and still in train to the rhythms of sowing and harvesting and the bells tolling out the time of Mass. These natural and sacred rhythms still cast a powerful spell over the English social formation. Nor should it be thought that Le Goff's (1980) 'time of the merchant' had yet taken over from 'the time of the church'. At this stage in English history it was more the case that the time of the church was being taken over by the merchant. The schism between sacred and secular time was still some way off.[22] The sacred calendars, the bells calling to Mass, the eschatology of the Day of Judgement – these still exerted a powerful hold on the medieval imagination.

Three final points are in order, two procedural and one substantive. First, this sketch of a historical geography of medieval time consciousness stresses that the ecological approach and the Marxist approach must be reconsidered in the light of an approach that recognises the importance of the 'linguistic' formation of consciousness. In Harré's (1984, p. 127) terms, 'not only is language the central human activity that thinkers themselves produce: it is the central process by which thinkers are produced.' Such an approach will concentrate on outlining the similar accounts that are engendered in many different contexts by texts, devices and systems of discipline acting at a distance. But it will also recognise that these accounts, whether they are welcomed or imposed, are likely to be interpreted differently in these different contexts and can therefore, in turn, be used as the basis of actions that change their form and content.

As a second related point, time consciousness can clearly never be seen as a unitary phenomenon. Different accounts of time develop at different times in people according to the vagaries of history, membership of particular social groups and geography. In the twelfth and thirteenth century certain texts containing certain interpretations of time reach out only to certain people and places; certain devices are the preserve of only certain people and places; certain systems of discipline are only to be found touching certain social groups and places. The accounts people can give of 'time' must depend on the practices they can be involved with in a particular context and the way these practices are influenced by a peculiar mix of local social relations.

Third, some doubt must be cast on the standard Marxist account of the genesis of modern time discipline and consciousness in England, as first formulated by E.P. Thompson in 1967, with its emphasis on industrial-isation as the pivotal event. For what the account of the medieval ideology of time practice laid out above shows is that significant portions (if by no means the majority) of the population of England were already changing their accounts of time towards fairly modern interpretations quite early on in history. Texts were becoming more time-aware. Timekeeping devices were becoming more sophisticated. Rigorous systems of time discipline were already regulating work habits, and not only in the towns; think only of the example of the Benedictine and Cistercian estates. Time was valued, in however primitive a fashion. There is even evidence of conflict over the ownership of time – why otherwise the need for work hour regulation? Harrison has already come to similar conclusions for the eighteenth and early nineteenth centuries. He notes, for example, that 'work habits were, in fact, far from irregular and haphazard' (M. Harrison, 1986, p. 174), as the Thompson account implies. Similarly, T.C. Smith (1986) provides evidence from pre-industrial Japan of sophisticated attitudes to time at variance with Thompson's thesis. It becomes possible to suggest that Thompson made a number of major errors of interpretation in his 1967 paper. First, he underestimated the rigour of pre-industrial work patterns. Even in the medieval period, the evidence is that work patterns were rarely sporadic or wilful, given the need to conform to the pattern of the seasons: 'time derived from nature, supposedly the heart and soul of task orientation, [can] be just as rigid, just as controlling, just as conducive to discipline as the clock time that replaced it' (O'Malley, 1992, p. 353). Second, Thompson too easily assumed that clock time and temporal exactitude were isomorphic. Yet the medieval evidence suggests that exacting, even rigorous, timing systems could be constituted without resource to clocks. Third, he conflated lack of ability to measure time precisely with lack of perception that time can be measured precisely. But the evidence from the medieval period suggests that many people were quite aware that time could be measured more accurately. They were simply unable to do so. Thus the Thompson thesis that modern (or, in Foucault's term, positive) time discipline finally appeared in its full form with capitalist industrialisation is questionable, to say the least.

Harrison (1986) has suggested that it is urbanisation, and, in particular, the strictly timed contexts of the larger towns, that holds the key to the advent of modern time discipline, rather than industrialisation, and, on the available evidence, this conclusion certainly seems more realistic. As this chapter has shown, it can be extended back, in embryo form at least, even to the towns of the medieval period. It is in these towns that the institutions of government, church, trade and industry were most likely to come together, increasingly acting to impose artificial schedules on a population which then began to talk about these schedules as a natural occurrence.

Notes

This chapter was originally published in T. Schuller and M. Young (eds) *The Rhythms of Society*, 1988, Routledge, London.

1. 'I call the living'. One of the most popular inscriptions on medieval church bells.

2. Clearly each of these accounts is much simplified.

3. The idea of accounting is complex, as are its antecedents. See Chapter 1 and Chapter 4 for more detailed exposition.

4. Clog almanacs were carved sticks or rods on which notches and symbols provided a calendar showing the lunar cycle and the Christian feasts. Some were small enough to fit in the pocket. Most were larger versions which hung on the wall (Capp, 1979).

5. The production of texts had definite impacts on these acts of memory, a case of the power of oral devices being enhanced by writing.

6. All estimates of numbers are subject to qualification. In particular what was called a 'book' could vary radically from a bound volume through an unbound quire to a table containing but a few pages.

7. Borst (1993) has pointed to the importance of monks as more general chroniclers as well, and especially to their importance in producing general dated histories. Indeed Burton (1994, p. 198) claims that 'the emergence of chronicles was the main feature of historical writing in the early thirteenth century.' Further, the works of writers like William of Malmesbury, William of Newburgh and Matthew Paris showed what 'could be achieved by those who received their education without the cloister and relied on books in the monastic library' (Burton, 1994, p. 200).

8. Even so, proclamations of laws by the town crier would continue for some time yet.

9. To these reasons might be added others. First, writing only slowly became a trusted medium. Second, exactitude of temporal reckoning was not necessary as long as the temporal infrastructure of documents stayed loose. It was only with the advent of exact administration that exact reckoning became necessary. It is important to remember that by the end of the thirteenth century births were still not recorded and if the age of a person had to be proved in courts (for example, in the matter of wardships) then the normal practice was to ask acquaintances to date births by significant events. Of course, the importance of the spread of texts is paralleled by the importance of the spread of new reading practices. See especially Goody (1991).

10. A major problem in considering the spread of bells is that, at this time, significantly, bells were rarely dated. The earliest dated bell in England is for the year 1255 (Downman, 1898).

11. These bells were worked by treadle planks. Hence the number of men needed to ring them.

12. Billiter Street in London EC3 remains to remind us of their location, a corruption of 'bellytere'.

13. Handbells were probably widely used by clergymen to signal the daily canonical hours during most of the period, with church tower bells often only being used to signal Mass (Borst, 1993). It seems likely that, as a result, the clergy were often expected to be the experts in the calculation of calendrical and daily time in their localities. Note that the German word for bell, *glocke*, still survives as o'clock in the English language.

14. *The Rule of Saint Benedict* (J. McCann, 1970, p. 23) specifies:

From the feast of Easter until Pentecost let the brethren dine at the sixth hour and sup in the evening. From Pentecost throughout the summer . . . let them fast on Wednesdays and Fridays until the ninth hour; on the other days let them dine at the sixth hour.

A major complicating factor in all this was the migration of *hora nona* during the period to become noon, midday. Le Goff (1980, pp. 44–5) offers an explanation that the change emanated from the towns, where the pressure for a marker at midday, half the whole day, was great. Alternative explanations by Landes (1983, pp. 404–5) and Gurevich (1985, p. 106) seem just as plausible. This is clearly an area in which debate will be fierce for years to come because there is so little evidence of the reasons for the change.

15. Not forgetting the nunneries, of course. See Dickinson (1979); Rowley (1983); Burton (1994).

16. If Sundays, feast days and saints' days are added together, then up to a third of the year was apparently taken off from work. As Gurevich (1985) points out, this demonstrates that the work ethic was still subordinate, in many ways, to the demands of religion. However, I admit to being sceptical about the degree to which all these days were taken off work, and this scepticism is reinforced by Hutton's (1994) study of the ritual year in the later Middle Ages, which suggests a large amount of local latitude in which days were taken and which not.

17. Thus the guilds were still as much concerned with quality of work as quantity: 'Work in a guild had not yet degenerated into a total indifference towards its objective content' (Gurevich, 1985, p. 267). Use value and exchange value were not coincident.

18. It is worth noting that the Cistercians, with their rigorous notions of time discipline, were important agents in the wool trade. It is also worth noting the difficulties of international trade, since calendars were often unsynchronised from country to country (for example, the year began at Christmas in Germany, at Easter in France and at the Annunciation in England

and Italy until the late twelfth century, when common reckoning systems began to spread based on 1 January as the beginning of the year) (Borst, 1993).

19. For the financial world, exactitude of time was very important, but there is remarkably little in the literature on this aspect of the history of time-reckoning and time consciousness (see Borst, 1993).

20. A glance at the *Oxford English Dictionary* seems to provide some evidence that the vocabulary of time changed quite markedly from the thirteenth century onwards. 'Clock' (from the German *glocke* and also *cloche*, French for bell) begins to take on its modern meaning. Particular phrases start to circulate such as 'times to come' (first found in 1340) and 'what is the time?' (1200). But, unfortunately (though understandably), these dates only record the first written occurrence of a particular word or phrase. Here the whole problem that new classes of documentation could record older words or phrases for the first time becomes a hideous complication.

21. The importance of gender should not be overlooked. But apart from the case of nunneries it is difficult to find good information on the different time consciousness of men and women in this period (but see Davies, 1990).

22. The symbolic turning point is probably the dissolution of the monasteries.

6

A Phantom State? International Money, Electronic Networks and Global Cities

An Empire is partly a fiction.

(Richards, 1993, p. 1)

My concern with the limits of the modern political imagination is informed both by a sense of the need for alternative forms of political practice under contemporary conditions and a sense that fairly profound transformations are currently in progress. But it is also informed by a sense that our understanding of these transformations, and of the contours of alternative political practices, remains caught within discursive horizons that express the spatiotemporal configurations of another era.

(Walker, 1993, pp. ix–x)

The City no longer trades in money: it trades in know-how.

(Rajan and Van Eupen, 1994, p. 4)

In London you've got to create a relationship so you get information. Like for instance Deutsche Bank called up and said they think the Banque de France is in the DM: Paris. They've given me information hoping I give them information. I'll take a position and hopefully we'll make some money. Its important to see the business, to see the flows, to make money and the only way to do that is to get out and meet people.

(trader, quoted in Roberts, 1995, p. 206)

Question: why is a fundamental analyst like a black box? Answer: because he tells you what went wrong when it is too late to do anything about it.

(City saying)

Introduction

There is an account of the modern international financial system which has become dominant, an account which is believed not only by many academic commentators but also by many of its practitioners. Amongst the main elements of this account might be found the following: the international financial system pushes unimaginable sums of money around the world; the international financial system has become hegemonic over the nation state; the international financial system has achieved a 'degree of autonomy from real production unprecedented in capitalism's history'

(D.W. Harvey, 1989, p. 194); the international financial system is built on 'imaginary properties of imaginary things' (Denzin, 1991, p. 91); the international financial system relies on ever more rapid reaction times; the international financial system is becoming disembedded from actual places; and the international financial system is peopled by greedy young men and women parading their libidos across the computer screens.

A good part of this account clearly depends upon an appeal to the apparently magical powers of modern information technologies. Electronic networks provide a 'space of flows' (Castells, 1989, 1993), through which money can pass swiftly and effortlessly. Money becomes a free-floating signifier circulating in an economic stratosphere and 'space is no longer in geography – it's in electronics. Clarity is in the terminals' (Virilio, 1983, p. 115).

The net effect of this account is to construct money as the new sublime (Eagleton, 1993) and the international financial system, which, until recently, still had a 'well-nigh dickensian flavour of title and appropriation, coupon-clipping, mergers, investment banking, and other such transactions, [as]*sexy*' (Jameson, 1991, p. 274).

Now I do not want to dispute this account head-on. Clearly its individual elements, though often exaggerated, are founded in the actual situation. Rather, my concern is that when these elements are pieced together, as they often are, they are woven into a story of an abstract and inhuman force, a financial leviathan which it is increasingly impossible to withstand. The result is that our ability to fight to change a system which can clearly have monstrous effects is diminished.

But, it is possible to write the account in another way, one based on a more human vision of what the international financial system is like, one in which hegemony is essentially contested, outcomes are always open to interpretation and geography matters. In this chapter, I want to fashion such an account by concentrating on the social and cultural determinants of money and the international financial system, determinants which, I will argue, are not incidental, or additional, to a pure and hermetic economic sphere, but are central. Most particularly, I want to argue that the power of the international financial system rests on the link between money power and communicative power and that the business of money is therefore, as Boden (1994) puts it, 'the business of talk'.

The chapter therefore proceeds in three parts. In the first part, I want to examine the nature of modern international credit money, by concentrating on the way in which money is constructed out of time, space and infor- mation. In particular, I will stress that money cannot be divorced from representational practices, and that it cannot be quarantined within an imagery of quality-less and rationalising universalism (Shapiro, 1992).

In the second part of the chapter, I want to suggest that, in contradiction to the story of an abstract and inhuman international financial system, there is another story to tell, of an international financial system that has actually become *more* social, *more* reflexive and *more* interpretive since the breakdown of Bretton Woods. I argue that the current international financial system can be interpreted as an outcome of four types of 'actor-network' which are continually attempting to construct powers of governance. These networks – nation states, the media, money capitalists and machines – sometimes act in coalition with one another, and at other times act against each other. I then ask whether these networks can be understood as a government. I draw on four different bodies of theory in an attempt to answer this question – regulation theory, the theory of international regimes, autopoietic systems theory and poststructuralist theory.

Much of the power of money capitalists in the post-Bretton Woods international monetary system is often, as I have noted, ascribed to the speed of electronic telecommunications. In this chapter I argue that the impact of telecommunications is more subtle than this. In particular, the use of electronic telecommunications has generated more and more information which, in turn, produces a requirement for more and more interpretive work, leading to the formation of a variety of interpretive communities. This increasing interpretive load has had other effects. For example, I argue that it has fuelled the need for face-to-face communication, producing a renewed need for 'embedded' meeting places in what is often considered to be an increasingly 'disembedded' electronic 'space of flows'.

The third part of the chapter illustrates some of these arguments via a study of the City of London pre- and post-Bretton Woods. The success of the pre-Bretton Woods City was based on particular sources of social power which I outline. I argue that the success of the post-Bretton Woods City is increasingly based on the social power to launch and validate discourses within electronic networks, which in turn forces face-to-face communications in its space. In other words, I argue that authors like O'Brien (1992) who have pronounced that the rise of electronic telecommunications will produce an 'end to geography' need to think again.

International Credit Money

Money is conventionally described through four functions: as a medium of exchange; as a store of value; as a unit of account; and, latterly, as a standard for deferred payment. As history has proceeded, so the latter function, in which money increasingly becomes distributed over time and space as part of a burgeoning system of credit, has become the most important: credit money has displaced commodity money (Altvater, 1993). In one sense, there is now only international credit money, ceaselessly 'circulating' bits of information, ceaselessly regenerating obligations as old obligations shrivel and die: 'modern money is everywhere debt' (Peebles, 1991, p. 131) – or credit. In turn, the existence of this network of international credit money poses a challenge to conventional economic accounts of money.

How, then, can modern international credit money be characterised? It is possible to argue that international credit money is a set of transacting networks that both constitute and are constituted by time, space and information. In turn, such an argument implicitly questions orthodox accounts of money based on functions since it focuses on the *social relationships* that are involved in monetary transaction, rather than the *objects* which mediate these relationships.

International credit money constitutes and is constituted by *time*. Time figures in a number of ways. First of all, time is a vital part of monetary transaction. Ease of transaction is an important element of a monetary instrument or a financial asset and this ease of transaction tends to be measured in terms of time periods which, in the transacting networks of international credit money, become ever more exact and exacting. Second, international credit money 'brackets' time, since a period of the future is reserved or 'colonised' as a stream of obligations (Giddens, 1991). The time structure of credit money is clearly important and it has become increasingly complex (Shackle, 1972; Cencini, 1984). Further, the time horizon over which enterprises and other agents must calculate

> turns out to be an endogenous aspect of these credit relations: when expectations concerning future system-wide developments are stable and widely shared, then a wide spectrum of private liabilities will be regarded as liquid and will find a place in the portfolios of those units whose current operations generate a surplus of revenues over expenditures. (Grahl, 1991, pp. 172–3)

International credit money also constitutes and is constituted by *space*. At the most basic level, credit money brackets space since 'standardised value allows transactions between a multiplicity of individuals who never physically meet one another' (Giddens, 1991, p. 18). However, space plays a more important role than simply as a medium to be overcome. In recent times this role has tended to be connected with the territorial limits imposed by nation states, within which only particular monetary forms can be used. First, the territorial boundaries of the state have had a constitutive effect on modern monetary networks. Many monetary practices depend upon their existence, whether these practices involve the negotiation of monetary forms across these boundaries, or simple arbitage (Ingham, 1984). But, second, many monetary practices are concerned with avoiding territorial controls. In the seventeenth century the bill of exchange was hailed in part because it enabled merchants to move their money out of the hands of absolutist states. In the eighteenth century, the 'circular note' (an early form of the traveller's cheque) was invented to overcome the problems travellers met in moving from country to country (Booker, 1994). In the same way, one of the main purposes of many modern monetary instruments is to evade state controls – over interest rates, currencies, and the regulation of money.

Of course, no clear distinction can be made between the articulation of money, time and space. From the use of the share as a means of financing long-distance exploration, by extending monetary obligations over the period of time needed to complete a voyage, to the use of the swap as a means of providing the best probable interest rate structure on a loan in the best possible currencies, money has been about the complex articulation of time and space.

An important indicator of the temporality and spatiality of modern international credit money is usually considered to be its increasingly chimerical character (a contention usually illustrated by reference to the stomach-churning world of foreign exchange). Money, so the saying goes, has become disembedded. Through the medium of electronic communications and expert systems international credit money can flow efficiently without barriers. It has become simply a set of accounts; credits and debits constantly notching up like the tally sticks of old, a single quality-less and rationalising market money (Cencini, 1984). Now, in a sense, this is precisely what has happened, or is happening. But, at the same time, precisely in order to achieve this kind of universalism, international monetary instruments have often had to become *more* complex and specific. In order to attain exactly the right articulation of time and space, new and often very particular monetary instruments have been invented at a break-neck pace. Nowhere is this clearer than in the sphere of derivatives, complex financial instruments (like options, futures and swaps) whose values derive from other assets, and indices of these asset values, and whose function, at least to begin with, was simply to transfer price risks associated with fluctuations in these assets' values.

International credit money constitutes and is constituted by *information* as well. In a number of different ways, information is crucial to the constitution of international credit money (Goodhart, 1989). It cannot be reduced to the function of a 'lubricant' within a pre-existing monetary order. Thus,

> the role of information in the transactions of money is not confined merely to observation about an external and independent economic environment. Information is on the contrary the defining feature of monetary networks, for they are networks of, not just containers of information. (Dodd, 1994, pp. 156–7)

Further, this information is not neutral. It is continually open to interpretation, and the interpretation becomes a part of the information:

> the notion that information is simply 'transmitted' and 'received', as if meaning remains constant and unimpaired throughout, is unsustainable. Both the meaning and effectiveness of the information transmitted by transactors, and thereby its entire character in the first place, is chronically dependent on the process by which it is interpreted. To transmit and receive information in this context is not simply to project an independent body of facts through space and time, but to bring these facts into being as facts. (Dodd, 1994, p. 113)

In turn, the interpretation of information depends upon ideas, expectations and symbolic associations which must therefore play an integral role in how money is constituted, and what is regarded as money in the first place. As Simmel put it, 'money is influenced by the broad cultural trends and is, at the same time, an independent cause of these trends' (cited in Frisby, 1992, p. 93).

Money certainly has a broad range of meanings associated with it which influence how it is used, but comparatively little is known about the range of these meanings, because money is still too often regarded as 'not socio-logical enough' (R. Collins, 1979, p. 190). Yet what research there is has shown that socio-cultural meanings are integral to what is regarded as money and thereby to the practices of money. There are multiple monies, with qualitatively different characteristics generated by their situations and meanings (Zelizer, 1989, 1994) which are, in turn, influenced by much larger and longer-term shifts in the meaning of money which work to open up cultural spaces in which new meanings and practices of money can flourish. Some of these longer-term shifts in the meaning of money have been rather better documented. For example, there is the gradual redefinition of usury documented by Le Goff (1988), Kerridge (1988) and others involving in particular a general concept of purgatory, which opened up a cultural space for new practices of money in the thirteenth century: 'the hope of escaping hell, thanks to purgatory, permitted the usurer to propel the economy and society of the thirteenth century ahead toward capitalism' (Le Goff, 1988, p. 93). Again, there is the social and intellectual history of 'the money question' in the later nineteenth century and especially the spread of bimetallism, with its potent arguments about what constituted the 'intrinsic value' of money in an increasingly international monetary system (for example, Unger, 1964; Nugent, 1967).

At much the same time Zelizer (1979, p. 26) shows that there was a general revaluation of what counted as rational speculation which can be seen as part of a more general reassessment of money, time and human life which opened up a cultural space for life assurance and thereby solved 'the cultural and structural dilemma of putting death on the market'. Finally, we can note the struggle in the twentieth century between socialist notions of a 'passive' money, serving the interests of the state and often taken to be simply an expression of labour, and modern western economic rhetorics with their ideas of money as an excessive force (Goux, 1990b). (Indeed, not the least interesting of observations is the way in which many 'postmodern' accounts of money as a free-floating signifier often simply simulate these rhetorics [Goux, 1990b]).

This consideration of the importance of ideas, expectations and symbolic associations is nowhere better illustrated than by turning to a consideration of what much of the information produced in monetary networks is actually concerned with, the assessment of 'risk'. What constitutes risk is, itself, a constantly changing, morally and politically charged notion (Barty-King, 1991; Knights and Verdubakis, 1993). Since its invention in the thirteenth century, 'risk' has been a shifting ensemble of meanings about the timing and spacing of credit and debt which depict whether a credit/debt relation is viable. Early notions of risk were akin to wagers, encapsulated in devices like tontines and lotteries. Although banks began to understand and articulate risk early on – even as early as the seventeenth century the Bank of Amsterdam understood the difference between liquidity and credit risk – it was not until the late eighteenth century that calculation of risk became possible and not until the late nineteenth century that risk became an integral part of the monetary system as speculation came to be seen as a wholly legitimate activity: 'As risk became an integral part of the . . . economic system, certain forms of risk-taking and speculation assumed new respectability. Rational speculation that dealt with already existent risks was differentiated from pure gambling which created artificial risk' (Zelizer, 1979, p. 86).

However, risk in modern monetary systems has presented something of a paradox, especially since the death of the Bretton Woods system of fixed exchange rates and capital controls and extensive national systems of regulation has produced new and higher levels of volatility in the money and capital markets. More is now known about risk, and that knowledge is often formalised in the credit ratings of firms like Moody's or Standard and Poor as well as in expert systems dependent upon mathematics and computing power (OECD, 1992). But this knowledge can, in turn, be used to produce new substitute forms of money (which have often started out as instruments to control risk) whose exact risk profile is unknown and may even lead to systemic risk. Again, the case of derivatives shows this paradox only too clearly. Originally instruments for hedging, derivatives have often become simply tools of speculation. As a result they may as often have increased volatility as they have damped it down (Bank for International Settlements, 1992). In other words, the systematic assessment of risk allows new forms of risk to be generated and promotes volatility in time and space, which is now both necessary in order to make money and itself creates more risks. No clearer illustration can be found of Giddens's (1991, p. 118) assertion that the international monetary system is an institutionally structured risk environment which is constituted through risk, rather than risk being an incidental factor.

To summarise, international credit money has a number of properties which mean that although it is often thought of as abstracted, it can never become an entirely abstract system, because it must remain a complex articulation of time, space and information which, to some extent, defines how time, space and information are conceived. In other words, at root, international credit money must depend upon conventions – relatively stable inter-subjective representations – of what economic life is all about. These conventions will be forced by one final property of international credit money which is that its value is critically dependent upon credibility, upon *trust* that money assets will not lose their value (de Grauwe, 1989).

Trust in money assets operates on two levels (Dodd, 1994).[1] First, there is trust in money as a social institution, as money in general. Second, there is trust in specific monetary forms. The existence of this trust clearly depends to a degree on the prior conditions in which a monetary network has been established (for example, the political means employed to validate money, or the institutional mechanisms for operating a payment system). But, such prior conditions need constant recharging through various confidence-building devices. The material and symbolic costs of building up the fiduciary dimension of international credit money, of sustaining what Shackle (1972, p. 447) called the 'morale of expectation', are great. Since the decline of Bretton Woods they have clearly become greater. It is to this upheaval that I now turn.

The New International Financial System: Governing without Government?

From the middle of the nineteenth century until the decline of Bretton Woods, the international financial system was, in effect, run by nation states, latterly under US hegemony. National banks, government departments and civil servants held power over much of the business of international finance. Money capitalists were a critical and vibrant part of this international financial system, often operating with a considerable degree of independence, but they were held in check by state regulation of credit and state power to define what counted as money (Helleiner, 1993).

However, the decline of Bretton Woods has once again demonstrated that the links between money and the nation state are contingent rather than necessary (Dodd, 1994). Much of the power over the international financial system, and especially power over how credit is created, bought and sold, has transferred back to money capitalists, for at least three reasons. First, money capitalists have been increasingly able to 'define money through their collective acts', that is, to legislate on what is money and how money is used (W.E. Baker, 1987, p. 110), especially through the development of 'substitute monies' (Dodd, 1994) like derivatives. Second, processes like the rise of the Eurodollar markets and, latterly, disintermediation and securitisation, although often involving transferring power between money capitalists (for example, between banks and markets), have produced new sources of profit for money capitalists which are outside state controls (*Economist*, 1994a). Third, with the growth of electronic telecommunications, these money capitalists are able to operate on a global scale and with a speed of reaction which states find very difficult to emulate. In the new international financial system, then, 'the balance has shifted from a financial structure which was predominantly state-based with some transnational links, to a predominantly global system in which some residual local differences in markets, institutions and regulations persist' (Stopford and Strange, 1991, p. 41).

In other words, the old state-centric international financial system has been replaced by a system that is more obviously the preserve of both state and non-state actors (Cerny, 1993a, 1993b; Gill, 1993; Rosenau, 1993; Ruggie, 1993; Walker, 1993; Agnew, 1994). In this new multicentric international financial system, there are clearly structures of governance, understood as sources of rule (Miller and Rose, 1990), which function effectively even though they are not necessarily endowed with formal authority. The interaction between these sources of rule constitutes what Rosenau and Czempiel (1992) call 'governance without government'.

Perhaps the best way to conceive of the status of this untidy but decidedly influential system is through an appeal to actor-network theory (Callon, 1986, 1991; Latour, 1986, 1993; Law, 1994). Actor-network theory suits my purposes well because it echoes a number of themes which are integral to this chapter:

> it is symbolic interaction with an added dash of machiavellian political theory, a portion of (suitably diluted) discourse analysis, and a commitment to the project of understanding the material character of the networks of the social. (Law, 1994, p. 100)

Actor-networks are associations of actors *and* resources (intermediaries like texts, human and non-human beings and money) which are put into circulation in a continual effort to construct and maintain power relations. They are performative definitions of what society is about. In this view, 'power is clearly not something you can hold and possess, it is something that has to be made' (Latour, 1986, p. 27). It is equally clear that, on this view, actor-networks can never be completely stable entities. They are constantly redefined *in interaction* through resources which cannot themselves be considered as passive. The extent that these networks are maintained will depend upon the degree to which actor-networks are able to 'translate' situations, that is, bring together and define the bits and pieces needed to assemble a large and powerful network and delete the efforts of other actor-networks (Law, 1994). In turn, this process of translation demands the utilisation of materials of association which are able to act *at a distance*, thus constructing time and space *within* these networks. These materials, which depend upon a particular combination of actors and resources, are socio-technical innovations like 'writing, paper, a postal system, cartography, navigation, ocean-going vessels, cannons, gunpowder [and] telephony' (Law, 1991, p. 103), techniques which can generate required effects and definitions that will last over varying periods of time and cover varying distances. Thus, in actor-network theory, agency, power and size are always uncertain capillary effects which have to be constantly worked on by an actor-network. They are achieved, they are not a right.

In the current international financial system it is possible to posit four overlapping but relatively stable types of actor-network. These actor-networks have been able to assemble the agency, power and size needed to develop, produce and distribute money. We might see them as the chief structures of governance in the international financial system which together constitute the fragmenting 'post-politics' of international money.

The first of these types of actor-network is the nation state. It would be foolish to contend that the nation state has lost all its powers to order the international financial system. State financial regulation still imposes important limits (and creates its own problems of interpretation, as the large number of compliance officers in many financial services firms only too readily attest to). States can still, to some extent, rein in parts of the financial services industry through concerted action, as the impact of the Bank for International Settlements' capital adequacy ratios on banks shows only too clearly. State monetary policy still makes a difference, as the effects of German monetary policy on other European countries makes clear. Further, nation states continually struggle to extend their powers over the international financial system, both through new modes of regulation (for example, international contract law, international accounting standards or the current struggle by states to extend control to derivatives) and through new international organisations of nation states (for example, G7 or the EU; see Held, 1991). But state networks are not as extensive or as concerted as they once were. To a large extent, the international financial system has been privatised, and this privatisation has involved not just the circulation of money but increasingly also its production, as new forms of substitute money are constantly invented which are outside state control (see W.E. Baker, 1987).

The result is a more complex, sprawling, volatile and reflexive international financial system, with many different networks of players dealing in many different types of financial market, with associated risks which are very difficult to calculate. Further, it is a system which is now, in effect, designed to continually outrun prevailing state norms and rules.

The second type of actor-network is the media. The press and television have become powerful ordering forces in the modern international financial system, not only through their increasing ability to transmit the information integral to the use of money but also through their ability to give that information shape and meaning (Dodd, 1994). The inception of a modern financial press in the nineteenth century has been followed by the increasing ability of the media to give definition to money for four main reasons. First, there has been the extension of the media into new arenas concerned with the supply of commodified information, and most particularly electronic information like market quotation systems and cd-rom databases. According to one estimate, the market for such electronic information grew at 35 per cent a year in the 1980s (Parsons, 1989). Second, there has been an increase in specialised financial publishing tied to particular segments of the market. Some commentators have even talked of the disaggregation of economic news and commentary. Third, there has been the growth of global media outlets, newspapers like *The Financial Times* (Kynaston, 1989) and television stations like CNN.

Fourth, there has been the demise of grand interpretive schemes like Keynesianism or monetarism, and the growth of a multiplicity of different explanations of financial events, leading some commentators to talk of 'the relativism of the electronic age' (C.W. Smith, 1983, p. 325). In other words,

the powerful macro-frameworks of the past are no longer adequate as contexts of reporting modern transnational capitalism. The continued privatisation of economic discourse has not helped to provide any new popular paradigm. But another reason for this splintering process is the sheer expansion in the availability of greater qualities of information itself. (Parsons, 1989, p. 218)

That the media now constitute a powerful source of governance is nowhere better illustrated than by the growth of bond credit-rating agencies (Sinclair, 1994). As disintermediation has proceeded, so these agencies have become *the* major sources of information on creditworthiness, not only for corporations but also for financial institutions, local governments and nation states. Two agencies – Moody's (owned by Dun and Bradstreet) and Standard and Poor (a subsidiary of McGraw-Hill) – dominate the business. They clearly act as regulators, as sources of financial discipline, even though they have no formal statutory position. Just as clearly, part of their power comes from their privileged interpretive position, which renders the financial realm knowable through a simple and easily understood letter symbol.

The third type of actor-network, and the one to which I want to devote considerable attention, consists of the organisations of the money capitalists themselves, which go to make up the modern global financial services industry. It is debatable whether this group of money capitalists actually cohere as a class. Some argue that they do (see Van der Pijl, 1989), others that they do not. Whatever the actual case, it is clear that there are certain processes in common that do bind these actors together and that allow them to exert a degree of control over the international financial system, over and above their ability to own or manipulate large sums of money. Four of these processes now seem particularly important, each of them closely interrelated with the others.

The first of these is the construction of trust and reciprocity. Enough has been written now of the need for trust and reciprocity in monetary systems to forestall further expansion here. Suffice it to say that building and maintaining co-operative relationships of trust and reciprocity in the monetary system has always been a high priority because of the need to retain the credibility of the value of money and monetary instruments. It is now probably greater than ever, because of the overwhelming importance of credit money, because the international monetary system has become a system of structured risk, because disintermediation has produced an 'increasingly deinstitutionalised context, where traditional forms of authority and organisation are less evident' (Sinclair, 1994, p. 144), and because the overall level of trust has declined. This overall decline in trust can be traced, in particular, to the decline in one-to-one relationships between firms and clients as price competition has become more important. Thus, clients have become more and more likely to want to do business on a competitive, 'transactional', deal-by-deal basis. Four chief strategies have been instituted to cope with this decline in trust. One has simply been the institution of more formal controls on employees (including strategies of surveillance such as the video-taping and tape-recording of the deals made in dealing rooms). Second, there has been increased use of formal legal contracts. Third, recourse is more often made to credit-rating agencies. But fourth, and finally, the construction of trust has become more active. Money capitalists are a particularly good example of what Giddens (in Beck et al., 1994, p. 186) calls 'active trust', 'trust that has to be energetically treated and sustained'.

Thus, so-called 'relation managers' and 'relationship management' (Eccles and Crane, 1988, 1993) have become crucial: money capitalists have to try harder to get to know more people and to get to know them better in order to both earn their trust and assess who is trustworthy. In turn, the interactional frenzy that has resulted from relationship management has made work on presenting the self a central project of the international financial system (*1994f*). Work on the self is of crucial importance since it is often only through such work that money capitalists can now build up trust and reciprocity. In many of the situations of monetary negotiation, especially those involving a high degree of uncertainty, it is presentation of knowledge[2] and self (the two being related) which is the main resource brought to the situation by participants. Self-identity can therefore become a crucial determinant of economic success.[3]

The second process is the increasing requirement for interpretation. The international financial system now generates a massive load of information and the power goes, to an extent, to those able to offer the most convincing interpretations. The problem is no longer necessarily a shortage of information but how to make sense of the masses of information that exist. As a *Wall Street Journal* journalist explains in a Robert Erdman novel, 'Well I'm plugged in and, true, I've got information coming out of my ears. But what that information *means* I haven't got a clue about' (cited in Parsons, 1989, p. 227). Thus the generation of interpretive schemes is now crucial.

This uncertainty is perhaps most obvious in the markets where participants often have to produce interpretations very rapidly. As one stock dealer put it, 'the one obvious problem is that you're only as good as your last bargain. Each day starts a new, complete sheet' (Lazar, 1990, p. 58).

As the markets have grown larger, more volatile and uncertain and correspondingly less easy to interpret, so sociologists like W.E. Baker (1984b) have demonstrated their tendency to break up into social cliques. These cliques tend to be based around discursive schemes, interpretations of what the markets are like (Mayer, 1988; C.W. Smith, 1983). C.W. Smith (1983), Roberts (1995) and others have suggested that there are a number of these discursive schemes in circulation. The first of these is a fundamentalist one. Fundamentalists look at the fundamental values which lie behind currencies – firms, profits, interest rates, and so on, or, in the commodity markets, crop reports, mining reports, changing patterns of consumer demand and the like. The second discursive scheme is one which is based on price, regardless of value. It relies on the belief that 'the market has a life of its own' (C.W. Smith, 1983, p. 48) and is best studied technically via charts of various kinds. For example, one study of the City of London (Taylor and Allen, 1989) found that for short-term time horizons, 90 per cent of dealing institutions used some charting and for two-thirds charts were at least as important as economic fundamentals. So-called 'chartists' have formulated their own well-formed vocabulary and methods of analysis over time: 'you work very hard at your charts. You look at them twice a day on a consistent basis across a variety of currencies. And you try to work out what's going on' (trader, cited in Roberts, 1995, p. 120). The third discursive scheme is one which conceives of market events in strictly interpersonal terms with the result that important individuals ('who really know what's going on') and powerful institutions who can move markets are taken as benchmarks (Soros, 1993). The fourth and final discursive scheme is one which is based on market psychology, on a 'feel' for the market: 'I think that it really comes down to psychology. The markets are all about psychology. It's not about how intelligent you are. It's about how lucky you are and how well you can read what the next guy's trying to do' (trader, cited in Roberts, 1995, p. 120). This scheme is becoming more and more influential as a result of economic work on fads and bubbles and more generally on behavioural finance (see *Economist*, 1994b).

Clearly the power of each of these schemes waxes and wanes. Currently, a new discursive scheme seems to be forming around 'rocket science'; mathematical market analysis using chaos theory, fractals, Fibonacci series, neural networks and the like to predict market changes. This new scheme can be interpreted as a consequence of the growth of more formally knowledgeable money capitalists.[4] But, on the other hand, old habits die hard: 'early in the morning, as the dealers arrived at their desks, several of the tabloid papers they discarded were open at the astrology pages' (Roberts, 1995, p. 180).

A third process is the growth of formalised 'knowledge structures' or 'expert systems' which modify and constantly revise knowledge about the international financial system (Strange, 1988; Giddens, 1991). International finance has gone from being something approaching a craft industry, learnt on the job, to an industry in which workshops, seminars, videos and round tables teach an endless round of not only vital textual knowledge (such as the importance of credit-rating agencies) but also interpersonal skills to 'knowledge workers'.

The fourth and most important process has been the growth of the resource of information technology and, most especially, the advent of 'intelligent networks' that integrate information and communication services (Mansell, 1993; Mansell and Jenkins, 1993). The growth of this technology has proved to be a particularly complex process because of the multiplicity of effects such technology has had. Four of these have marked the development of money capitalist organisations. First, information technology has, as Zuboff (1988) puts it, 'informated' these organisations. That is, information technology generates information that was previously unavailable, which both provides the possibility of more control but also provides a more complex and uncertain information environment of 'electronic texts'.

Second, this new information is used to generate new products, thus adding further to complexity and uncertainty. Third, information technology allows less hierarchical, more open, 'networked' organisations to develop. But, again, this is a two-edged sword. Such organisations allow 'positional' control strategies to be developed which can more easily accommodate complexity and uncertainty, but such organisations (which, in any case, have a long tradition in the financial services industry [Eccles and Crane, 1988]) also tend to have their own problems. Thus, the spread of these communication and control systems 'is as much a response to increasing uncertainty as a clear strategy to enhance control [and] the proliferation of industry response systems creating more interconnections and more transactions tends to undermine predictability rather than enhance it' (Mulgan, 1991, p. 242). Fourth, the importance of interpretation has become even more pressing. The turn to information technology solves few interpretive problems. Indeed it may even increase them. To begin with, information technology produces output which still has to be read, and read *in action*. As Wynne (1991, p. 37) puts it: 'of one thing . . . I am sure, even if there were no longer any printed texts to read, only screens, . . . there will still be the question of reading and the limits and effects of reading that-which-is-read upon its readable meaning.' Thus, increasingly, money capitalists are becoming

> a group of people gathered around a central core that is the electronic text. Individuals take up their relationship toward that text according to their responsibilities and their information needs. In such a scenario, work is, in large measure, the creation of meaning, and the methods of work involve the application of intellective skill to data. (Zuboff, 1988, p. 394)

Then again, the rhetorics and narrative possibilities of the software involved in electronic texts are very complex and demand new communicable forms which involve innovative and constantly developing combinations of actors, messages and stories (Dunlop and Kling, 1991; Sproull and Kiesler, 1991; Lea, 1992; see also Heath et al., 1993, and Jirotka et al., 1993, on the way in which share traders came to a collaborative view of the market in the City of London, especially through bodily comportment). As if this were not enough, it also has to be remembered that the total load of interpretation has become more rather than less pressing because all organisations tend to be acting in the light of improved information, with the effect that knowledge and certainty may actually be reduced, not enhanced.

The mention of information technology points to the final type of actor-network. This is the set of networks that is the most shadowy and the least understood. It is, quite simply, machine 'intelligence'. Until recently, intelligent machines could be subsumed under the general rubric of information technology as intermediaries without much harm. They had not been able to construct agency or power. That may now be changing, both practically and also theoretically as the networks of the social are seen to come in a variety of material forms of which people are only one (Haraway, 1991; Latour, 1993; Law, 1994; Chapter 7). Increasingly, the international financial system provides examples of networks of machine intelligence, usually in the form of artificial intelligence systems, usually deploying neural network techniques. These networks, which first came to general awareness because of the furore over the role of programme trading in the October 1987 stock-market crash, have become more and more sophisticated.

> last year Citibank, which handles at least 15 per cent of the currency dealings in London, gave a neural network system $10 million to play with for a few months. It made an 18 per cent annual return, compared with the 12 per cent typically achieved by traders using more conventional forecasting methods. A large pension fund in the United States is believed to be using the technique with larger sums of money. (Holderness, 1993, p. 23)

These four types of actor-network clearly interact with each other in myriad ways. In particular, Moran (1991) has pointed to the importance in the new international financial system of transient but still potent 'issue coalitions', made up of groupings of states, media, money capitalists, machines and other interested parties. Such coalitions focus on only one particular issue (usually a crisis or a financial scandal) and come together only around that issue to force through change.

It is clearly possible to describe these four types of actor-network as overlapping sources of governance of a new, privatised international financial system. But is it possible to describe this system as in any sense governed? The international financial system may have structures of governance, made up of the diverse and overlapping actor-networks of nation states, the media private money capitalists and machines. But do they add up to anything like a government? Is there, in other words, a phantom state?

There are a number of different theoretical schemas that can be drawn on to answer this question. I will concentrate on just four. The first of these is regulation theory (Jessop, 1990; Boyer, 1990; Leyshon, 1992). One of the most notable aspects of recent intellectual history has been the degree to which the original attempts by Aglietta and others to integrate monetary phenomena into the general framework of a regime of accumulation have been lost in subsequent discussions (Aglietta, 1979; Aglietta and Orléan, 1982). Yet, the regulationist scheme of things, with its synthesis of Marxian and Keynesian monetary concepts, allows the greater importance of credit in the modern world to be recognised, as well as the constantly shifting balance of power between creditors and debtors (Grahl, 1991). Under optimal conditions, stability of the regime of accumulation can be achieved because of a general match between supply and demand and the confidence of economic agents that this match will continue on. However, when . . . the coherence of the regime is disturbed, and when this disturbance is seen as undermining commercial asset values, the monetary authorities are forced to make critical strategic choices. On the one hand, the widespread refinance of illiquid deficit units can be encouraged in order to prevent the fragmentation of the networks of exchange relations, but this will provoke inflation to the extent that restructuring by debtors does not succeed in eliminating imbalances between cost and demand. This is a centralising strategy which carries the risk that initial imbalances may persist and even widen. On the other hand, a decentralising deflationary strategy – refusing or strictly curtailing refinance – although it will compel rapid adjustment of deficit positions, may prove too difficult for industrial agents, and then the elimination of loss-making units will threaten a cumulative breakdown of existing relations. (Grahl, 1991, p. 173)

But creditors and debtors will want to have their say. Thus,

Given the successful reproduction of an established regime of accumulation, creditors and debtors will be bound together by a solidarity that rests on an agreed valuation of financial investments. But when the regime can no longer orient investment activity towards a commercially accepted future for the system, this solidarity is disturbed. Nevertheless a collapse is not inevitable – debtors will pressure banks and monetary authorities to shield them from creditors; but the latter, although now anxious for rapid repayment or transfers of ownership, may hold back from foreclosure through the fear of failures that will devalorise their assets. The structures of intermediation, which determine the possibility of aggregating debtor or creditor interests, clearly play a key role in the development of these relations. Essentially the Central Bank now has to choose between antagonistic and incompatible restructuring projects, formulated by groups of agents who no longer share a common vision of the broad trends in the system as a whole, nor agree to the time horizon appropriate for individual investments and reconstructions. (Grahl, 1991, pp. 173–4)

Regulation theory has a clear advantage in describing certain situations. However, it also has very real disadvantages as an account of the international financial system post-Bretton Woods, even in its 'third wave' forms. Most particularly, there are three disadvantages. The first is that it is state-centred. Regulation theory still tends to speak the language of Bretton Woods. It can therefore only poorly account for situations, such as the current one, in which states are weaker sources of governance, having lost some of their power to order the financial system because of the growth in the power of private money capitalists and the media, because of their inability to react as rapidly to events as private money capitalists and the media, and because of the difficulty that states have faced engaging in monetary co-operation, as a result of a general lack of political and institutional integration (de Grauwe, 1989). In other words, regulation theory finds it difficult to conceive of the international financial system as autocentric. The second disadvantage is that the international financial system is reduced to an effect of capitalism or is allowed only the most limited differentiation from it, usually as part of a mode of social regulation. In other words, regulation theory denies the performative capacity of the international financial system. The third disadvantage is that regulation theory has real difficulties in describing the fluid nature of the international financial system, especially its speed of reaction, adaptability and speculative spirals. It finds it difficult to take into account the fact that 'time and space in the bankers' world [are] pliable, moveable, profitable constructions which might or might not correspond with the mundane geography of national territories' (Daly and Logan, 1989, p. 103).

Are there any theoretical approaches which might be more flexible and more sinuous? I will briefly note three. The first of these is the theory of international regimes (Krasner, 1983; O. Young, 1989; Murphy, 1994). Regimes are the 'principles, norms, rules and decision-making procedures around which actor expectations converge in a given issue area' (Krasner, 1983, p. 1). In effect, they are arrangements for governing or regulating specific activities that have resulted from the expanding domains of international life, domains which have arisen from the growing dependence of states and societies on global flows and connections. Thus, in O. Young's (1989, pp. 12–13) view, they represent 'social institutions governing the activities of those involved in specific activities or sets of activities . . . like other social institutions, regimes may be more or less formally articulated, and they may or may not be accompanied by explicit organisations.' International regimes can reflect the internationalisation of nation states, in their attempts to regulate or govern transnational activities and flows, trans-border externalities or global crises. But, equally, there are non-governmental international regimes which regulate specific private activities. Significantly, McGrew (1995) cites the example of SWIFT, the worldwide interbank payments system, as one such regime. More typically, international regimes embrace a wide range of different political actors, including government departments, sub-national governing authorities, multinational corporations, financial institutions, transnational pressure groups, even social movements.

Such a theoretical approach would envisage the new international financial system as comprising a number of different international regimes which are, in effect, a set of mechanisms of compromise which allow the system to work at a global scale.

The second theoretical approach is Luhmann's (1982, 1989) theory of autopoietic systems. Such a theory might envisage the current international financial system as having been built up from the interaction of varying social forces until it has reached the point where it has achieved a good deal of autonomy, and has become something close to an independently functioning system, differentiated from others:

> autopoiesis . . . is a property of a certain type of system and can be defined, in a nutshell, as a condition of radical autonomy. It emerges when the system in question defines its own boundaries relative to its environment, developing its own unifying operational code, implements its own programmes, reproduces its own elements in a closed system, obeys its own laws of motion. When a system achieves what we might call 'autopoietic take-off', its operations can no longer be

controlled from outside. Autopoieticist social theorists agree that modern
societies have seen many such systems develop along functional lines and have
therefore become so highly differentiated and polycentric that no centre could
coordinate all diverse interactions, organisations and institutions. Nor is there a
single functionally dominant system which could, *pace* marxists, determine
societal development 'in the last instance'. (Jessop, 1990, p. 320)

In other words, to translate Luhmann's insights into realist parlance, the
new international financial system is demonstrating 'emergent powers'.

The third approach might be to call on poststructuralism. In this
approach, the international financial system might be seen as an open and
constantly moving field of increasingly electronic discourses with the power
to define events and to force their pace: 'there is a movement from geo- to
chronopolitics: the distribution of territory becomes the distribution of
time. The distribution of territory is outmoded, minimal' (Virilio, 1986, p.
115). The discursive field is a massive structure of communication in which
the subject's relation to the world has been reconfigured and in which time
and space have been retooled so that the absent is as important as the
present (Poster, 1990; Deleuze, 1992). Following Poster (1990), we might
see new and partly unrecognisable modes of community coming into being,
imagined communities in which electronically mediated communication
both supplements and substitutes for existing forms of communication. To
put it another way, we might conceive of the international financial system
as an electronically networked, constantly circulating, nomadic 'state',
operating 24 hours a day around the world.

These four theoretical schemas therefore provide different answers to the
question of whether the international financial system constitutes a government. In regulation theory, the international financial system remains, in its
essentials, an adjunct of capitalism.

In contrast, in regime, autopoietic and poststructuralist theory, the
international financial system can take on a life of its own, become
something like a self-governing (although not sovereign) entity. Certainly
the switch in theoretical emphasis from regulation theory to regime or
autopoietic or poststructuralist theory makes it somewhat easier to envisage
what international financial centres are becoming as *electronic* flows of
information begin to predominate.

Global Cities

On the one hand, the international financial system has become increasingly 'disembedded' from place. It now consists of multiple discourse
networks (Kittler, 1990), networks of evaluation which are possible because
of the new information technology. In turn, these networks generate new
forms of discourse that would not be possible without them (Lea, 1992) and
which involve new forms of 'actant' (Haraway, 1991), subjects based on
new combinations of the body, self and machines producing new financial
products (Poster, 1990). In other words, a new space of communicative
materiality has been constituted over time (Beninger, 1986).

On the other hand, although this '"virtual" world of information hubs, data bases and networks' (Mulgan, 1991, p. 3) may appear as a kind of universal, its very universalism forces a new set of particulars. The pressures of the interpretive load of multiple networks of electronic texts and the 'fictive sociality' (Gergen, 1991) that it produces are so great that they force embodied, interpersonal, face-to-face interaction as the only way to come to fully finished mutual understandings. Helped by the fact that so many new financial instruments are more rather than less specific, this means that people have to make physical contact to argue their position: there is still a 'compulsion of proximity' (Boden and Molotch, 1994) – but only in very specific locations. In other words, greater universalism forces new kinds of particularism.

Thus the space of this new informated international financial system bends both ways. There is both waveform and point. There is an invisible and a visible hand. There is a disembedded electronic space. But there is also a re-embedded set of meeting places (from restaurants to trading floors) where many of the *practices* of this first space still have to be negotiated because 'there are now teeming images from which to draw, often fleeting in duration, and the options for action are enormous. The audience for such actions is also complex; what plays with ease in one context may seem superficial in another' (Gergen, 1991, p. 223). In other words the second, re-embedded space is increasingly an outcome of the first; it is an integral part of disembedded electronic space rather than a relict feature (see Heath et al., 1993; Jirotka et al., 1993; Kahn and Cooper, 1993).

In turn, this electronic world, with its emphasis on meaning and in-creased social connectedness (Gergen, 1991), forces an even greater reflexivity into the conduct of many meeting places. This increase in reflexivity is partly a result of the need to negotiate a wider spectrum of relationships as a result of an increase in the cosmopolitanism of the international financial system, partly the result of the need to cement relationships formed in the fragile and symbolic communities of electronic space, and, no doubt, partly a result of the general increase in reflexivity in societies as a whole (Giddens, 1991; Beck, 1992; Lash, 1993; Lash and Urry, 1993). Thus these meeting places become nodes of reflexivity, where people work hard to make contacts and to present themselves.

Further, the relationship between this new electronic world and meeting places is not all one-way. There is a dynamic and reciprocal relationship between telecommunication and context (Lea, 1992). Thus, social activity in these meeting places can resonate back through the electronic world of computer-mediated social interactions (Lancaster CSCW Centre, 1993).

Conventionally, the meeting places of the international financial system have been international financial centres. What seems to have happened post-Bretton Woods is that the number of these international financial centres that count – as meeting places, as generators of news and new meanings and, in general, as significant nodes of reflexivity in electronic discourse networks – has decreased but, in turn, those places that are left in contention have become more important. In other words, the interdependent connectedness of disembedded electronic networks promotes dependence on just a few places like London, New York and Tokyo where representations can be mutually constructed, negotiated, accepted and acted upon (*1992h*). In effect, these are the places that make the non-place electronic realm conceivable. They are what Law (1994, p. 104) calls 'ordering centres', constantly 'straining towards reflexivity and self-reflexivity'. Such centres are 'constituted by gathering, simplifying, representing, making calculations about, and acting upon the flow of [information]'.

In the next section, I want to turn to one of these ordering centres – the City of London – to exemplify some of the points made in this and the first part of the chapter (Figure 6.1). In describing the City of London, it is important to note that it is not a static object of study. In particular, the character of the City has varied over the course of its history in four significant ways. First, it has consisted of a differing mix of industries over time, which, to an extent, have had different social and cultural structures.

For example, Michie (1992) distinguishes over time between a commercial or trading City, a credit or banking City, a capital market City and a client or financial services City, each of which has shown some degree of dominance over the course of the City's history. Second, the size of firms in the City has varied over time. Until quite recently, the size distribution of firms in the City was overwhelmingly biased towards small firms, although this has now changed quite markedly. Third, it has varied over space. Until after the Second World War, the financial city of banking, capital markets and financial services occupied only a small part of the 'square mile' and it is only in comparatively recent times that the City has outgrown this boundary (Figure 6.2). Fourth, the numbers working in the City have fluctuated from 170,000 in 1866, to a peak of 500,000 in 1935, to about 307,000 in 1993 (even these numbers are difficult to rely on, since they depend upon what industries are counted as city industries [see Rajan and Van Eupen, 1994; St Quintin, 1994]) (Figure 6.3).

All these comments made, it is still possible, and indeed conventional, to study the City as a relatively coherent whole and, in turn, to make a break between the 'traditional' City which existed before the death of Bretton Woods and the 'de-traditionalising' City that existed thereafter. The break therefore takes in the point at which the City casts off the gloom of a moribund wartime and post-war trough and becomes a dynamic international financial centre again, partly because of the progressive collapse of the Bretton Woods system, which the City, as the major centre of the growing Eurodollar market, had a hand in.

The break also captures the point at which many social and cultural aspects of the City change quite decisively in ways which are intimately linked to its transformation into an outpost of an electronic 'phantom state' in which distinctions between 'inside' and 'outside' become increasingly difficult to make (Walker, 1993).

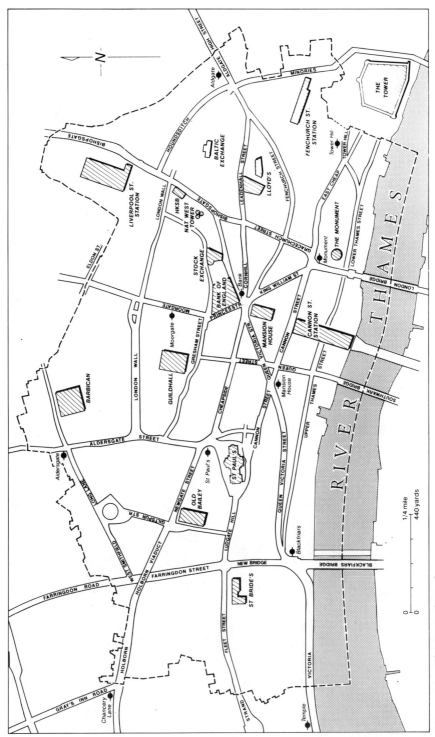

Figure 6.1 *The City of London*

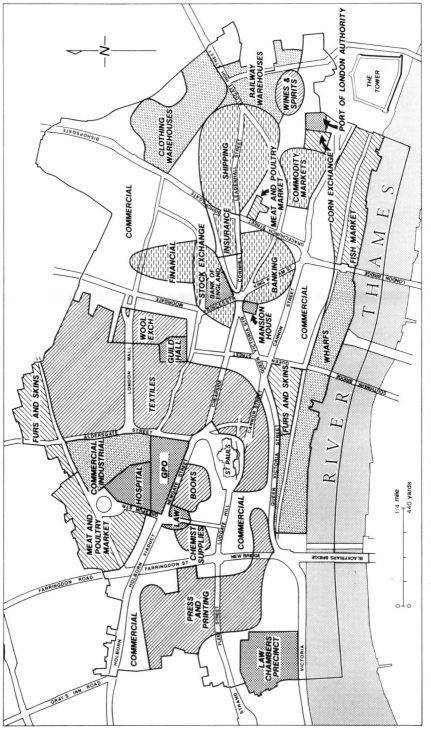

Figure 6.2 Business areas within the City of London, 1938/9 (Holden and Holford, 1951, p. 32)

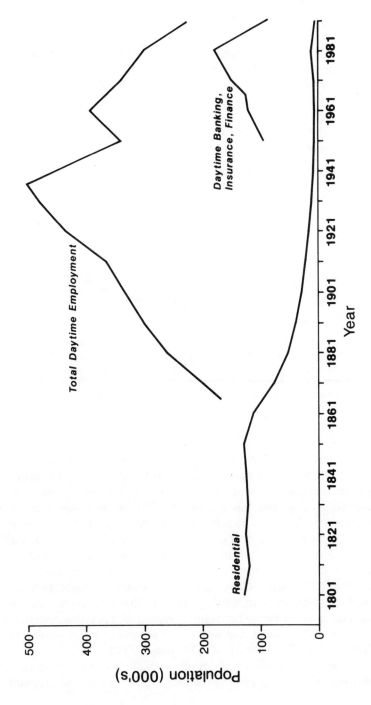

Figure 6.3 *Employment in the City of London, 1801–1991 (Dunning and Morgan, 1971, p. 34; Census)*

The City of London

The 'Traditional' City: The City of London pre-Bretton Woods

Before the death of the Bretton Woods system, the City's power to reproduce itself rested on four main foundation stones. The first of these was the City's compact with the British state. This relationship took two forms. One was the City's role in the British Empire, conventionally symbolised by Niels Lund's picture *The Heart of Empire*. Cain and Hopkins (1993a) have convincingly argued that the City was inexorably caught up in British imperial expansion, which created new export economies in many parts of the world where City finance, transport and allied commercial services were much in evidence (King, 1989, 1990). Thus,

> after 1815, and especially after 1850, City finance and associated services performed a vital, indeed historic, function of integrating countries that lacked adequate capital markets of their own. By funding export development overseas, the City enabled newly incorporated regions to raise and service an increasing volume of foreign loans; by generating a massive invisible income from these activities, the City made a crucial contribution to Britain's balance of payments. In this way, the City and sterling acquired a world role, and London became the centre of a system of global payments that continued to expand right down to the outbreak of war in 1914. (Cain and Hopkins, 1993a, p. 468)

Indeed, Cain and Hopkins (1993b, pp. 308–9) argue (rather less convincingly) that this relationship effectively continued after 1914:

> what changed after World War I was that Britain was no longer in a position to supply sufficient capital to fuel the international economy. Although successive governments struggled to create conditions which would encourage new overseas borrowing they became increasingly preoccupied with the problem of securing repayments on existing loans. The gentlemanly order marched on; but the adverse circumstances which affected the performance of overseas investment and other invisible earnings had a profound effect on the difficulties Britain faced and the means she [*sic*] adopted to meet her traditional priorities.

The other form of the City's relationship with the British state, a form directly related to the first, concerned the City's ability to retain its independence, combined with its ability to imprint its priorities on British economic policy. For this reason, the City is often described as a 'state within a state'. This is clearly an exaggerated description since at various times the British state intervened very effectively in the City in ways which were undoubtedly to its detriment (Ingham, 1984; Michie, 1992). It is more accurate to describe the City as having a 'meso-corporatist' relationship with the British state (Cawson, 1986) in which 'representation and regulation were fused' (Moran, 1991, p. 61). In other words, the City was able to maintain a relatively self-contained system of collective governance, with the Bank of England acting as a buffer against pluralist regulatory systems (Sayers, 1976; Chapman, 1992; Hennessy, 1992).

The second foundation stone of the City's power to reproduce itself consisted of a tightly knit 'gentlemanly order' (Cain and Hopkins, 1993a) based upon highly visible class, gender and ethnic divisions which in turn generated strong senses of self-identity. These divisions provided the means with which it was possible to recognise the insider and the outsider, the trustworthy and the non-trustworthy. Transgression of these divisions was therefore a potentially serious social and/or cultural offence.

In essence, until the 1960s, the City was composed of three relatively distinct *class* strata. At the top of the pile were the directors and partners of the numerous city firms (see, for example, Cassis, 1987). In the past, these directors and partners have often been seen as being drawn into the landed gentry over the course of the nineteenth century, their collective identity becoming increasingly bound up in aristocratic mores and practices. Such a depiction of a kind of mimetic aristocracy is now regarded with increasing suspicion. Current opinion on the class status of the directors and partners of the City is probably best summarised by Harris and Thane (1984, p. 83), who describe them as 'a distinct stratum, combining elements of bourgeois and aristocratic cultures but reducible to neither. It was a culture that (despite the trappings of landownership) was urban rather than rural, functionally progressive rather than reactionary, and combined grand dynastic aspiration with an unpretentious devotion to the ethic of work.' This description became, if anything, increasingly accurate after the professionalisation of British society in the late nineteenth century (Perkin, 1989) with its systems of public schools and universities, which offered the potential for City partners and directors to construct their own common background and world view. Thus, through the nineteenth and into the twentieth century the proportion of partners and directors going through the mill of public schools and Oxbridge gradually increased.

Of course, the directors and partners were not the only class stratum in the City. Increasingly, over time, they were joined by a professional and managerial middle class as a result of four linked processes. The first of these was the expanding system of professional institutions described above, and the credentials that resulted from them. The second process was the increasing demand for managers as firms increased in size. There were managers in the City in the 1830s but the chief influx was after the middle of the nineteenth century, as the retail banks and insurance companies increased markedly in size. The third process was an increasing demand for professionals, especially from the late nineteenth century. Indeed, some parts of the City suffered skill shortages because of lack of appropriate professionals (for example, actuaries). The fourth process was simply the expanding division of labour, which, by the end of the ninetenth century, led to the presence of 'hordes of specialists each making their own particular contribution to an increasingly complex process' of monetary creation and circulation (Michie, 1988, p. 196).

There was one final class stratum which also needs to be noted. This was the clerical labour force. By 1866, commercial clerks in the City numbered 17,225 (20 per cent of all commercial clerks in Britain). At first, clerks tended to come from relatively elevated backgrounds, but after the 1860s, as the number of clerks grew, so working-class clerks became more common. Even so, clerical wages were relatively high compared with the rest of the country, but reduced over time, probably reaching their lowest point in the 1950s. Clerks worked in diverse conditions. In the private banks, conditions were often paternalist. By contrast, in the developing joint stock banks and insurance companies, they tended to be more regimented (Kynaston, 1994).

The social atmosphere of the City was not just based on class, of course. It was characterised by other divides as well. Of these, the most important was *gender*. The City was a classically 'homosocial' (Kanter, 1976) environment, based on the interaction of class and a severe form of masculinity that produced what, in retrospect, seem like stifling forms of masculine identity based on quaint uniforms, exact dress codes, various boyish market rituals and japes, heavy drinking, and the like. Of course, to a degree such forms of identity were only exaggerations of upper- and upper-middle-class British society at large, but it is difficult not to come to the conclusion that their weight was sufficient to have produced a distinctive City patina. Certainly, in the early 1960s, Sampson (1965, p. 63) still found the atmosphere stuffy and uninspiring:

> Nearly everyone wears a dark suit and carries an umbrella, and discount brokers and gilt-edged stockbrokers still wear top hats. The restaurants are crowded with rows of pale faced, blackcoated men.

The closed effect of this environment was considerably reinforced by a network of men-only social institutions that functioned inside and outside work and which were both mechanisms of social regulation and ways of extending contact networks and, by implication, trust. These social institutions were diverse. They included institutions with formal membership requirements like the City Corporation, the livery companies, the London clubs, freemasons' lodges, and so on. They also included more general social arenas, of which the pubs and chophouses were perhaps the most important. All these institutions helped to dim the distinction between work and leisure: indeed, in a sense, for many a 'City man', work and leisure both involved mixing with the same round of people, cultivating the connections which were, at the same time, a vital source of business success.

The effect of this homosocial environment was to exclude women from the City's labour force.[5] Women first made an appearance as City workers in this forbidding environment only in 1872, as clerks at the Prudential insurance company (only daughters of 'professional men' were allowed to apply). By 1890, there were 200 female clerks at the Prudential. Then, in 1894, the Bank of England hired 25 female clerks, but, again, the conditions were strict: the women had to be nominated by directors of the bank and they had to pass entrance examinations (in other words they had to be 'gentlewomen' of good family) (Sayers, 1976).

The First and Second World Wars both saw large but temporary increases in female clerical labour in the City – for example, the Bank of England employed between 400 and 500 women in the First World War, whilst in the Second World War women were allowed to become settling room clerks in that male bastion, the Stock Exchange (a 'privilege' promptly withdrawn in 1946) – but it was not until sometime after the Second World War that women appeared in the City in large numbers. By 1961, the proportion of women office workers was actually greater than the average for England and Wales and even central London (Pryke, 1991), chiefly as a result of three labour force factors: the advent of the typewriter and shorthand, which produced both a system of credentials and an occupational niche for women; the fact that women could be paid less than men; and the possibility of excluding women from any real career structure.

Another important social schism in the city was based on *ethnicity*. The city was often seen, precisely because of its social structure, as a very 'English' place. But this sense of Englishness was necessarily ambivalent, since the history of the City's success was in part based upon a constant infusion of foreign immigrants, often as a result of persecution elsewhere in Europe (for example, the Huguenots). There were three main 'foreign' presences in the City, often interconnected (Chapman, 1992). The first of these was the Anglo-Jewish group that had built up in the City. This group was seen as insiders (for example, the Rothschilds and other Anglo-Jewish gentry) but also as outsiders. Indeed many of the group actively resisted assimilation into the City. Second, there was a constant stream of foreign immigrants, often Armenian or German–Jewish, who set up in the City throughout the period and who were often very successful. Finally, note must be taken of the foreigners connected with the growth of foreign bank branches – which date from a surprisingly early point in the City's history. From the 1860s onwards, foreign banks had been established in the City. By 1910 there were 28 such banks in the City, by 1913 there were 30, including German, Japanese and Russian branches. These figures ignore the large number of colonial bank branches of the time. By 1938 there were 85 foreign bank branches in the City, 'which was more than ever before despite the disappearance of German banks during the First World War and American banks in the wake of the 1929 crash' (Michie, 1992, p. 82).[6]

The ambiguous relationship with foreigners only rarely seems to have given way to outright hostility; usually as a result of warfare. For example, both world wars led to discrimination against particular groups, especially the Germans, who were excluded from membership of such bodies as the Baltic Exchange (Michie, 1992, p. 44). But a more generalised scepticism about foreigners does seem to have been general. In particular, foreign firms were often looked down upon by City partners and directors, who routinely only worked from 10.00 a.m. to 4.00 p.m., for starting work early and finishing work late (which, it is now generally acknowledged, gave these firms a major competitive edge).

The third foundation stone of the City's power to reproduce itself was the scarce resource that Cain and Hopkins (1993a, p. 261) describe as 'a form of capital in itself': information. This resource consisted of extensive networks of interconnected contacts, an expanding archive of knowledge and more and more particular kinds of expertise. The network of contacts was focused by the City's small spatial extent, and was further concentrated by the common social backgrounds of City men. It was a network whose force was most clearly felt when it was threatened. Thus Michie (1992, p. 45) argues that 'the Second World War represented a disaster for the City's trading interests, not so much from the physical damage but from the loss of contacts and expertise. During the war, valuable contacts were lost, while key staff left with many not returning.'

Another crucial element of the information base was the discourses that structured it, which in turn produced particular evaluations of the worth of people and business practices. The most obvious of these was the narrative of the 'gentleman' [sic], a widespread discourse based on values of honour, integrity and courtesy, manifested in ideas of how to act, ways of talk, suitable clothing, and the like, which enabled the City man to judge when and when not to extend trust and reciprocity, when contacts did 'fit' and when something 'smelt wrong'. This gentlemanly discourse, in part imported from the aristocracy and in part from the new professionalism, was sustained by close personal relationships, 'in which direct family ties were an important element but not outstandingly so for to have been at the same college at Oxford or Cambridge frequently forms a far closer bond between two men than the fact that they may be cousins' (Truptil, 1936, p. 174), by the City's high level of face-to-face contacts, and by a social round of sufficient leisure to allow relationships to be cultivated at length. Hence, the famous City motto 'the first thing is character', by which was meant character of a gentlemanly type. However, this gentlemanly discourse was hardly the only one circulating through the City. Many others did too, increasingly through the expanding medium of texts. In particular, through the nineteenth century the power of the financial press became much greater, as did the press's ability to distribute information, monitor actions, and so on. In other words, increasingly texts constituted 'the City'. They 'kept the City informed about itself' (Michie, 1992, p. 184). Starting with Lloyd's List in 1734, the financial press became increasingly important (Parsons, 1989). Thus in 1825 The Times started a regular City feature. In 1843 The Economist began to publish. In 1888 The Financial Times started up (from a merger with the Financial News). In 1893 The Investor's Chronicle began life. Finally, the information base of the city was also becoming increasingly specialised. This process was enshrined in a set of epistemic communities, each with their own particular vocabularies.

The fourth foundation stone of the City's power to reproduce itself came from spatial concentration. The City's activities were concentrated into a very small area with a number of recognisably monumental buildings that declared that the City was a centre of financial power.[7] Further, this concentration was strongly policed. From the micro-spaces of the partners' rooms in the merchant banks to the larger spaces of streets and squares the City was spatially regulated. In particular, a multitude of rules and rounds kept the City in the City. There were, first of all, the rules about spatial location. For example, all Stock Exchange members had to maintain an office within 700 yards of the Exchange to meet settlement deadlines. There was an (unwritten) accepting houses rule that all members had to locate within the City. The Bank of England insisted that all foreign bank offices were in close proximity to it. Second, there were rules that were the result of the need to intermesh time and space in various settlement systems. There were the daily discount house rounds. There were the 'walks' of the banks, trodden each hour to pick up cheques and other paper to pay into the Bank of England. There were the various clearing systems.

Most especially there was the cheque clearing system, used by the banks routinely but then extended to cover the Stock Exchange, insurance companies, and so on. 'General' clearing took place from 8.00 a.m. to 11.15 a.m. A later 'town' clearing took place at 3.50 p.m. Institutions had to be within half a mile radius of the clearing house to be included in this system. Third, there were the numerous prohibited spaces that could only be gained entry to by insiders, from market floors to clubs.

The City was not just reproduced by these intricate intermeshings of time and space, important though they were in producing a coherent City space and confirming the identity of place and person. The spatial concentration of the workforce that resulted from these rules and rounds was mirrored by residential concentration. Until the early nineteenth century, this was the result of the isomorphism between city workplaces and residences. Then, over time, as commuting into the City grew and residence in the City declined, so specific City residential areas sprang up. For example, by the end of the nineteenth century, a specific 'stockbroker belt' had formed in the Home Counties which persisted into the 1950s (Cassis, 1984, 1987; Kynaston, 1994).

However, this emphasis on spatial concentration can be misleading. Even in the nineteenth century there was no walled City. The world economy impinged in numerous ways. The thriving Port of London brought in a constant stream of visitors (and information) from overseas. There was a vast flow of bills and documents into and out of the City.[8]

Most importantly, the electronic space of flows so beloved of modern commentators had actually been a part of the City's operation over many years, the result of the invention and early application of the telegraph and telephone. The telegraph was first used in the City by Reuters in 1851 to transmit Stock Exchange prices between Paris and London.[9] In 1866, the first telegraph connection was made between London and New York, with immediate effect on the rapidity of market adjustment between the two cities (Kynaston, 1994). The telegraph and the attendant 'cable boys'[10] made it possible for the first time to trade systematically, and with a fair degree of confidence, in future delivery, rather than taking a gamble on a very risky speculation since it was possible to anticipate expected supply and demand with reasonable certainty . . . the telegraph, and later the telephone, and their use by intermediaries meant a qualitative change in the degree of risk. (Michie, 1992, pp. 53–5)

Again, the City had the first telephone exchanges in Britain, in 1879, and had large numbers of telephone users early on – by 1910 the number of telephone subscribers had reached more than 10,000. In 1937 a telephone link between London and New York was installed. By 1939 there were three City telephone exchanges, serving some 46,000 subscribers. By 1940 it was already possible for one commentator to describe a foreign exchange dealing room of the 1930s in terms redolent of those used today:

to describe exactly what goes on in the foreign exchange room of any of the big banks or foreign exchange brokers who compose the London foreign exchange market is beyond me. It is the nearest thing to bedlam that I know – half a dozen men in a little room, shouting in incomprehensible jargon into telephones, pushing switches up and down all the time in response to the flashing indicator lights. (Hobson, 1940, p. 71)

The innovations of the telegraph and telephone certainly reduced the need for physical proximity in certain cases but this was not as strong a phenomenon as might have been expected. Rather, what seems to have happened is that to existing levels of contact was added the supplement of the electronic realm and the new markets it made possible. Thus, at certain times before the 1950s, the City, through this realm, was able to become the centre of both a *global* foreign exchange market and an integrated *global* securities market. For example, Michie (1992, p. 62) points out that, even before the First World War,

with international communications transformed with the coming of the telegraph, and later the telephone, and the need to mobilise funds on a world scale for the finance of infrastructure developments, there appeared the possibility of creating global trading in securities. Information and orders could be quickly transmitted between exchanges and there existed a substantial pool of commonly-held securities, ownership of which could easily be changed between the nationals of different countries, especially in the absence of exchange controls. By 1913, securities with a paid-up value of $2bn were common to both the London and New York stock exchanges, and it took less than a minute to communicate between the two.

The 'De-traditionalising' City: The City of London post-Bretton Woods

Since the decline of Bretton Woods in the 1960s the City of London has changed its nature. To a degree, this shift has been prompted by a number of related changes in the nature and extent of international financial systems. These have included: the rise of a privatised credit system on a global scale (and especially the Euromarkets); the dramatic increase in the number, size, speed of response, volatility and interaction of markets, with a consequent increase in the general indeterminacy of the markets;

the increase in risk and the consequent need for sophisticated risk management; the rise of intermediation and securitisation; the increase in rates of product/market innovations; the development of large oligopolistic financial service firms; the rise of large institutional investors, pension funds, insurance companies and block trades; large amounts of technological change, especially in the field of telecommunications, leading to greater computing power, the decline of fixed open outcry markets and the rise of paperless settlement systems; and the spread of American-style regulatory systems.

Changes like these may have contributed to the success of the post-Bretton Woods City but there have also been actual or potential threats to the City's ability to reproduce itself, which it has had to contend with in a number of ways. Two chief threats are usually perceived. The first of these is technological change, which, in principle at least, allows financial markets to operate from anywhere, bypassing accepted geographic centres. However, this threat may be exaggerated. To begin with, there are still some formidable technological obstacles to this decentred vision. For example, paperless settlement and clearing systems have proved extremely difficult to implement and, even now, the financial system's appetite for paper and paper transactions is voracious. But, more to the point, this may be to misrecognise the problem. Not only is the City the hub of many electronic networks (Khan and Ireland, 1993; Ireland, 1994), but its frenzy of face-to-face interaction may be seen, as has been argued above, as increasingly the result of the vast penumbra of electronic networks that surround the City and the associated pressures of interpretation they exert. The second threat to the City is usually seen as arising from its changed relationship with the British state. The old meso-corporatist structure has faced unrelenting pressures – from technological change, from scandals and crises, and from the changing character of the British state (and, in particular, a new fair trading ideology and a greater inclination by those in government to intervene in City affairs). In turn, these pressures have led to the death of the monopoly powers of many of its institutions, typified by the desertion of one of the bastions of old-style regulation, the Stock Exchange, by the Bank of England in 1983 (Moran, 1991).

Thus, the old meso-corporatist structure has been replaced by new North American-style regulatory structures. However, to an extent, one might again argue that the perception of this threat is again overdone. The British state's ability to intervene in the City is limited by its ability to target the City, in that much of what the City is has moved on to electronic networks which are outside formal state (or even parastatal) jurisdiction. In other words there is less 'there' to regulate.

But, given that the City's power to reproduce itself has been under threat, how has it managed to stay at least relatively successful post-Bretton Woods? I believe that there are four chief answers to this question: answers which hold up mirrors to the foundation stones underlying the City's reproduction pre-Bretton Woods. I will address each of these answers in turn.

The first such answer is the City's relationship with the British state. As already pointed out, this relationship has transmuted, yet it has uncanny echoes of a previous time. The City can still be seen as at the heart of an empire, but now it is an empire of financial information that stretches around the globe. As Richards (1993, p. 3) has noted, the British Empire was always partly a fiction, a collective improvisation on the theme of control at a distance united by a fantasy of complete information made simultaneously available:

> from all over the globe the British collected information about the countries they were adding to their map. They surveyed and they mapped. They took censuses, produced statistics. They made vast lists of birds. Then they shoved the data into a shifting series of classifications. In fact, they often could do little other than collect and collate information, for any exact civil control, of the kind possible in England, was out of the question. The Empire was too far away, and the bureaucrats of Empire had to be content to shuffle papers.

There is an irony here. At the heart of the current international financial system, which now has some of the powers of an empire, whether these are described through regulation theory, the theory of international regimes, autopoietic systems theory or poststructuralist theory, are centres like the City which do produce a vast array of information, all but simultaneously. Yet the proliferation of databases, files, memoranda, documents and messages has not produced total control. Information still has to be interpreted and there are multiple interpretations of many of the pieces of information. In other words, the City survives by producing a problem of more and more information, and then by producing interpretations which in turn demand more information which in turn. . . . This, then, is 'less a form of control than a disposition to control' (Richards, 1993, p. 146).

The City is still at the heart of an empire in another way as well. The need for continual interpretation has produced serious problems in the construction of trust which cannot all be solved by now privatised systems of trust like credit rating agencies. Scepticism is inevitably widespread. Yet interpretations still have to be got from somewhere, and the workers in the City are meant to be 'in the know'.[11]

The second answer to the question of the City's continuing success is concerned with the City's 'de-traditionalising' social structure. The traditional social structures on which the City's collective self-definition in large part relied have quite clearly weakened and, in some cases, even faded away. Certainly, transgression of the identities forged by these social structures is a much less serious offence than before. So far as class is concerned, it is still possible to find a core of old-style white upper-middle-class homosocial merchant banks in which the directors and partners are recruited from only certain public schools and Oxbridge, as one 1986 survey found (*Business*, 1986).[12] Such results are echoed by one of Pahl's (1989) respondents in the late 1980s who noted that 'during most of those two years [in such a merchant bank], I was the only non-Etonian in the room and felt quite a social outcast'. But even these firms are nowhere near as closed as they were; especially if generational shifts are taken into account. Nor are they as influential: many of them are now relatively small firms in a larger complex of multinational financial services firms. Thus, *pace* Cain and Hopkins (1993b), I do not believe that the old gentlemanly order has survived into the present.

Increasingly, expertise and influence in the City resides in a reflexive group of managers and professionals: the 'knowledge workers'. These managers and professionals have a more heterogeneous social background, partly because during the 1970s and 1980s the City was forced to recruit from a wider pool of people to satisfy its demand for more and more skilled labour, partly because, even though many managers and professionals are still recruited from independent schools and from Oxford, Cambridge and a 'milk run' of other élite universities like Bristol, Durham and Exeter,[13] the social class constitution of these institutions has still become more heterogeneous (*1992b*), and partly because many of the new managers and professionals were, in fact, foreigners.

The influx of managers and professionals in such large numbers is relatively new. 'As late as 1965, few university careers advisers would mention finance as a possible choice for a first class honours student; it would be regarded as having rather low social status, and was seen to be unsuccessful and out of political fashion' (Fay, 1970, p. 76). In 1961, for example, the proportion of managers in the City was lower than in the rest of central London and England and Wales. By the 1980s it was much higher. The influx was the result of a number of processes (*1992b*), including a more complex division of labour, an increasing foreign (and especially North American) presence which encouraged more meritocratic selection procedures (and more foreign managers and professionals), an increase in the requirements for credentials, greater financial rewards and earlier career responsibility.

The primacy of professionals and managers was underlined by a considerable decline in the number of clerical workers, especially as a result of the general decentralisation of low-skill jobs out of London (although many low-skilled jobs do still remain in the City, from security guards to bicycle messengers to cleaners [see Allen and Pryke, 1994]). Many of the disappearing clerical jobs were held by women, and this brings me conveniently on to the question of gender.

The homosocial environment of the City has also weakened as the gender composition of the city has changed. After the Second World War, there was a rapid increase in the number of women working in the City, but nearly all these women were clerical workers who were socially and spatially segregated from the City's homogeneity by prevailing codes of sexuality, by the gendered nature of the labour process, and by these women's class position – many were working-class women from the East End. Even in the early 1970s, Sampson (1972, p. 123) could still write of these female clerical workers as almost a separate race which was automatically segregated in sandwich bars or canteens. The austere masculinity frightens away the more sophisticated secretaries who prefer the brightness and shops of the west end. The City remains the stronghold of male domination, whether social or financial, and women are kept out of nearly all the centres of its power.

But, since the 1970s, the social composition of women in the City has changed. Thus, even as clerical jobs have been declining, women have been able to keep and, in some cases, increase their proportional presence in the City because of the influx of professional and managerial women, especially into jobs which require skills and credentials, because they have increasingly been able to take up jobs which require high-level social interaction.[14]

The result is that women have to be admitted into what were once segregated male-only spaces. In turn, this change has required a renegotiation of modes of identification by both men and women. As one woman put it: 'I was not sure what my universe of men expected from me, but often neither were they' (cited in L. Davies, 1993, p. 33). Most research has been into the problems faced by women in the City (for example, McDowell, 1994). For example, professional and managerial women have had to take care in how they are identified in matters like dress: 'if you dressed casually it would be quite difficult for people to distinguish between you and a secretary' (cited in Dix, 1990, p. 171).

Ethnic divisions within the City have also been declining as a result of its increasing cosmopolitanism (Hannerz, 1992). There are now a large number of foreign workers in the City. There are also more British workers working for the large number of foreign financial service firms and more British workers also have considerable overseas experience, especially as a result of secondments. Indeed, for many professionals and managers overseas experience is a vital part of their career (Beaverstock, 1991).

In turn, this new cosmopolitanism has had other important effects. Thus, US banks and securities houses are more likely to hire women, and more likely to promote them to positions of responsibility. (However, it is worth noting that lower down the hierarchy, the City's record in hiring British people who belong to ethnic minorities has not been outstanding – see Rajan, 1988, 1990; Rajan and Van Eupen, 1994). Again, the new cosmopolitan has added to the City's competitive advantage by providing a diverse pool of foreign workers in one place. For example, the new European Bank for Reconstruction and Development employs 34 different nationalities. Three-quarters of these workers were able to be hired within the City itself.

The weakening of the social structures on which the old City's integrity was based has gone hand in hand with a heightening of the City's reflexivity. In the past, the City's business was chiefly based on face-to-face contacts that were made in order to stabilise relations of trust and reciprocity. However, much of the content of these transactions was foreordained, since they involved reading 'badges of office' which were readily recognisable signs of class, gender and ethnicity. This was what was meant by the famous phrase 'the first thing is character'. But, in current circumstances, the need for reflexivity has been much enhanced: because of the pressures for interpretation and negotiation arising out of electronic texts; because of the need to be able to gather information in a hurry so as to make appropriate market responses (which requires carefully garnered social networks); because of the general tendency in society towards greater reflexivity, leading to a greater emphasis on presentation of self, face-work, negotiating skills, and so on; because of the increasing requirement to be able to read people because the signs of their social positions are no longer necessarily foreordained; because of the increasingly uncertain 'transactional' nature of business relationships between firms and clients; and, as always, the need to be present to make unexpected contacts and business. Thus trust now has to be actively *constituted* through *work on relationships*, not *read off* from *signs of trustworthiness*. The formal gavottes of the old City have therefore become much more complicated dances: 'the first thing is presentation of self', and most especially a self which is able to manifest 'an instinctive, unforced clubbability' (Parton, 1994, p. 140) across a wide social spectrum.

This increased emphasis on reflexivity in the City has another consequence. The City's thick network of social institutions not only still exists but is actually thriving. In the past, such institutions were the continuation of the social structures of work by other means: places where the extant social structures of the City were confirmed and reinforced. Now they have become places to do face-work much more actively; to make contacts, to check people out, to tap into and to transmit discourses. There is certainly an enormous web of such social institutions, including the City Corporation (with 18,000 on the electoral roll in 1990), the livery companies (there are 100 guilds in the City with new ones still coming into existence, such as the Company of Information Technologists), the London clubs (which were very successful in the 1980s) and the freemasons' lodges (of which there are hundreds, including special lodges for the Bank of England, Lloyd's, and so on).

To these institutions must be added all manner of other social practices which have gained in prevalence in the City since the 1960s. Thus there is the growth of the business card, an amalgam of the old calling cards and trade cards of the nineteenth century. Exchanging business cards is now a part of the ritual of meetings in the City in a way that it never was before. There is the growth of the business lunch. There was always a lunching culture in the City, dating from the chophouses of the nineteenth century (see Kynaston, 1994). But, after a period in the 1980s when it looked as though this culture would disappear into in-house private dining rooms, it has now reappeared:

> laughing in the face of doomsters who forecasted the arrival of the desk sandwich lunch and the demise of the traditional City lunch, many restaurants claim they have never been busier. Evidence of restaurants full to the rafters at lunch periods

provides ample testimony of the continual popularity of lunch as an important part of the business tool [*sic*]. (*Square Meal*, 1995, p. 10)

There is the growth of the corporate hospitality industry. First coming to prominence in the 1970s, corporate hospitality has become one of the mainstays of City sociability. Covering the full range of 'hallmark' sporting and artistic events, as well as more mundane corporate golf and other 'getting-to-know-clients' days ('few will disagree that as a way of building a relationship golf has few equals'), corporate hospitality is now estimated to be a £1 billion industry by itself.

There is the growth of conferences and conventions. As McRae (1994, p. 16) has pointed out:

the world economy is developing in such a way that people need to communicate far more widely in order to do their jobs well. Professional jobs are becoming very complex, and anyone doing them needs to find ways of meeting other people in a similar field to improve performance . . . their peers in other corporations or countries. A conference is often the only way people can meet.

There is the growth of the limited-term secondment, as a means of allowing members of a City firm to make contact with their peers in other countries, thereby instituting relationships on a global scale (Beaverstock, 1991). Finally, there is the growth of the business qualification, especially the prestigious MBA, as a means of not only imparting knowledge but also producing contact networks, as Marceau (1989) has documented in the case of INSEAD MBAs.

Of course, none of the aforegoing is meant to suggest that social divisions no longer exist in the City. They clearly do. Thus, the influx of professionals and managers (especially foreign professionals and managers) has been resisted by the old-style white upper-middle-class core, as the recent example of the Swiss Bank Corporation (SBC) illustrates.[15] SBC has been publicly rebuked for 'fast' banking practices, leading its corporate finance director to argue that

the old school tie still owns the City. They take rumps out of rights issues and share out the proceeds through underwriting and subunderwriting. It's a scandal . . . we have not set out to put noses out of joint but we have probably not been very diplomatic. Maybe we have not been buying people lunch for long enough. (cited in Kay, 1994, p. 3)

Again, women are still excluded from many City social networks because so many of the City's social institutions are still men-only (although it is also the case that women have set up their own networks such as Women in Banking and the City Women's Network). However, these social divisions have weakened (Beck, 1992) and, as a consequence, the need for reflexivity has become greater.

In this, the City has now become much closer to the rest of British society (for example, the managerial and professional women in the City that McDowell [1994] describes have the same problems of identification in every other sector of British industry). If the City's social structure is still able to claim any uniqueness, then, it is probably on the basis of its very high degree of reflexivity: the City is, even more than in the past, a 'communicative commotion' (Shotter, 1989a) that enables money capitalists – from corporate financiers to stock-market traders – to interpret and construct their world.

To summarise, collective self-definition has widened and weakened in the City. People come from more diverse backgrounds. As a result, the networks that run the City are increasingly constructed out of the demands of reflexivity and not just social structure. Personal relationships are still vital in the City but they now have to be as often worked at, not through, constructed for their own sakes rather than for the sake of maintaining social structures. Indeed, this tireless working on relationships – whether face-to-face or at a distance – is now, more than ever, the primary focus of the City. The City no longer just looks for the signs of trust; it actively constructs them.[16]

The third answer to the City's continuing success is, quite simply, its role as an information base at the heart of numerous discourse networks. Clearly the City has seen an explosion of information on the financial services industry, and expertise in interpreting and disseminating that information, which has manifested itself in four very closely related ways. First, and as already pointed out, the City is a nexus of *face-to-face* communication through which information is interpreted – and gathered. Second, the City is a centre for *electronic* information gathering and transmission (Read, 1992). For example, by 1989 Reuters 'maintained 184,300 screens worldwide, providing groups of customers not only with instant access to information, but also allowing groups of them to communicate with each other, and so provide an international electronic market-place' (Michie, 1992, p. 185).

Third, the City is a centre of *textual* interpretation, whether the texts are printed or read from screens. The text can be a quotation system, a credit rating, a research analyst's report or even a humble tipsheet. But, most particularly, the City is now a centre of the *global financial media* – including *Euromoney, The Banker, The Economist* and *The Financial Times. The Financial Times* started a continental European edition in 1979, with a New York edition following in 1985. By 1993 40 per cent of the paper's circulation was abroad (Kynaston, 1989; *Financial Times,* 1993). The newspaper has now extended into television programmes, as well as numerous reports and conferences. Fourth and finally, the City is increasingly home to many different global 'epistemic communities', occupational communities each with their own specialised vocabularies, rhetorics, knowledges, practices and texts. From economists to foreign exchange dealers to Euro-bond traders each of these communities tends to live in increasingly specialised narrative worlds. In turn, these four different processes may begin to explain the City's high levels of financial innovation. It is worth remembering that the City now markets over 900 well-defined financial products, compared with about 70 in the early 1970s (Rajan and Van Eupen, 1994).

The emphasis on discursivity extends in other ways. Increasingly, the City markets itself as a centre of 'cultural authority' for global financial services. It is a place where people meet from around the world because of its associations with finance (and the knowledge, expertise and contracts concentrated there). In turn, the City has consciously begun to play to this role. The old gentlemanly discourse may have dissolved but the 'trappings of trust' still remain: quiet, wood-panelled dining rooms, crested china, discount round top hats, City police uniforms, and so on, are all used to 'brand' the City, to boost its image of solidity and trustworthiness. 'The rediscovery of tradition is the key to city trendsetting' (Pugh, 1988, p. 126). Indeed, so prominent has this 'very English' heritage style become that it might be argued that it has spilt over even into City 'fashion' for men. In the 1960s, the City seemed to begin to reflect broader trends in British society. There were distinct signs of a loosening of the sartorial bonds: one author of the time noted the presence of 'bright ties', 'soft collars', 'bright blue silky suits with a transatlantic feel', even 'ties with horizontal stripes in the continental fashion'. But by the 1980s a strict dress code had reasserted itself to an even greater extent than in Britain as a whole, one based on the dark suit: 'if you're not in a suit, you're invisible'; 'if you're not in a suit you must be a bike boy delivering sandwiches' (Pugh, 1988, p. 128). The dress code varied with age, with younger people tending to dress more sharply in bright shirts and ties and partners and directors clothed in tailored suits, but few signs of life outside the suit. Even the much vaunted (and rather rare) working-class 'barrow boy' traders conformed (Kahn and Cooper, 1993). Only the bright trading floor jackets of the London International Financial Futures Exchange (LIFFE) showed any measure of sartorial difference.[17]

The final answer to the City's continuing success may well be its tight spatial orbit. Convential accounts often argue that the City will gradually melt away. Three indicators are usually brought into pay to indicate this dissolution. First, the controls on the bounds of the City are much less strong than before. For example, in 1985 the Bank of England decided to take a less directive role in where foreign bank offices could locate (Pryke, 1991). Further, many of the walks and rounds which acted as a kind of socio-spatial glue are also dying out as electronic settlement systems come on line. Second, and as this example shows, the City's space is itself increasingly electronic. 'The City' is no longer fixed in the same way. Its space includes a massive shadow world of electronic networks. Third, the City's workers are now increasingly mobile. Many of them have lived abroad. Many of them spend much of their time travelling.

Yet, the City shows surprisingly few signs of deconstructing in the face of these tendencies. Since the 1960s it has become larger in extent, gradually extending its boundaries north and across the river. A few foreign bank offices have moved to the West End. Back-office operations tend to be dotted around London. Yet few foreign bank offices have moved very far away (Figure 6.4). London Docklands has never taken off as an extension

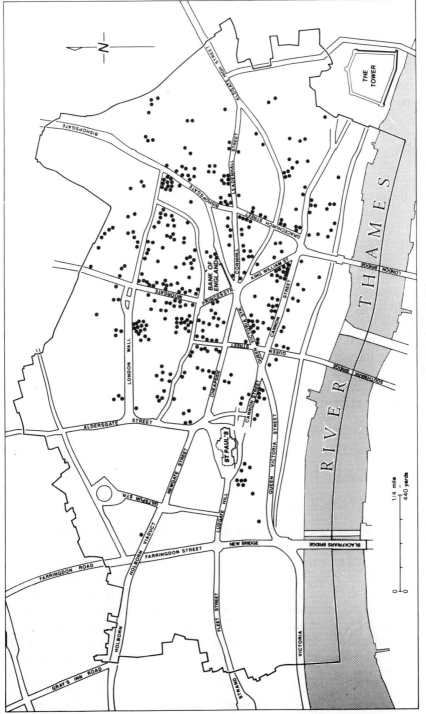

Figure 6.4 Location of City of London overseas banks, 1993 (The Banker, 1993)

of the City: probably only about 5,000 City jobs have been relocated there since the early 1980s. The spatial matrix of the City has enlarged comparatively little. Why? There are three main reasons, reasons which go to the heart of this chapter.

First, the need for face-to-face contact has not diminished. Indeed it has been argued above that it has, if anything, become greater as the need for reflexivity has increased. Second, there is little evidence to suggest that the growth of electronic space necessarily threatens the spatial integrity of the City. As has also been argued above, it may even help it to cohere. Further, it is worth pointing out again that the history of the City has been tied into this space of flows for over a hundred years now. For example, in 1956, the foreign exchange market reopened as an all-telephone market and has operated in such a mode ever since. Even in 1967 3 million telephone calls into and out of the City were being made daily (excluding inter-office calls) (Dunning and Morgan, 1971). This figure has clearly increased since then as a result of expanding business, satellite communications, computing demands, faxes, and so on. In other words, electronic communication seems to have fuelled the connectedness of the City by acting as a supplement to face-to-face communication, rather than an alternative, increasing the overall amount of communication between the City and the rest of the world (and this is to ignore the corresponding increase in paper communication, indexed by the rise in postal items delivered in, into and out of the City and by the rise of the cycle and motorbike messenger). Third, the increase in mobility actually seems to have helped the City to continue to cohere. The City is now an important transient space for international financiers, a place to do business. It has become a global node for circulating stories, sizing up people and doing deals. Thus, at any one time, much of the City's population will consist of visitors, but they are not incidental. They are part of why the City continues to exist. They are part of the communicative commotion that places the City in the electronic spaces of global finance.

Conclusions: A Phantom State?

I want to conclude by drawing on a distinction that Habermas (1992) makes between money power, administrative power and communicative power to add a certain nuance to the preceding parts of this chapter. In the preceding sections, I have very tentatively outlined the rise of a new 'phantom state', both constituting and representing money power, that is based on the communicative power of electronic networks and a few, selected (g)localities. It consists of actor-networks which increasingly rely on money power and communicative power without having to call on the degree of bureaucratic administrative power usually associated with the state form.

One reason for the success of this new kind of state has been the continuing evolution of a 'public sphere' for money capitalists. As Habermas

(1989) points out, an extended public sphere was originally able to develop, at least in part, because of the ability of early merchants (many of whom were the precursors of money capitalists), combined with the discovery of new communicative techniques associated with print, to extend market economies beyond local arenas, leading to long-distance trafficking in commodities, financial instruments, news and opinion: 'the flow of international news attendant on the growth of trading networks generated a new category of public knowledge and information' (Eley, 1992, p. 291). This archetypal public sphere was the prototype of a more general bourgeois public sphere that grew up in the eighteenth and nineteenth centuries between the state and the market.

But now, it might be argued, two changes have come about. First, the public sphere has split into a number of interlocking but increasingly self-contained 'public' spheres (see also Negt and Kluge, 1993; Robbins, 1993). One of these spheres belongs to money capitalists. In this phantom public sphere they are able to use money power to operate at very high levels of discursivity. Thus money power, especially through the construction of electronic networks and (g)localities, drives communicative power. But the presence of this particular public sphere also shows how communicative power increasingly drives money power. In this sense, the discourses of money have become money. Second, none of this could have happened to the same degree if it were not for the decline in the administrative power deployed by the nation state.

To an extent at least, the old nation state form has been outfoxed by a combination of money power and communicative power. In one sense, the power of the new 'phantom state' is still based in institutions, but in another sense it is based in the flow of communication itself. To this extent, Habermas (1992, p. 452) may be wrong to write that

> the responsibility for practically consequential decisions must be based in an institution. Discourses do not govern. They generate a communicative power that cannot take the place of administration but can only influence it. This influence is linked to the procurement and withdrawal of legitimation. Communicative power cannot supply a substitute for the systematic inner logic of public bureaucracies.

More and more, it might be argued that, in the modern world, money power and communicative power have been able to replace state authority based on administrative power with a discursive authority which is based in electronic networks and particular 'world cities'. This discursive authority is the stuff of a phantom state whose resonances are increasingly felt by all.

Notes

This chapter was originally published (with A. Leyshon) as 'A Phantom State? The Detraditionalisation of Money, the International Financial System and International Financial Centres' in *Political Geography*, 1994, 13: 299–327. Reprinted by permission of the publishers, Butterworth-Heinemann Ltd © 1994.

1. For reasons of space, I have not considered in this chapter systems of accountancy or legal systems, both of which are clearly important in articulating time, space and information and securing trust. These are clearly important basic properties of even minimal monetary networks which would need to be taken into account in any further exposition (see Dodd, 1994).

2. Knowledge will clearly include knowledge in the form of social contacts. An important part of the knowledge base (and the worth) of many practitioners in international finance is a contact network. Again, building up such a network involves presentation of the self.

3. In the world of money capitalists an important allied factor is reputation, especially for those who have already made large amounts of money. In their case, the concern is not so much losing money as the cost to their reputation of losing money. Hence the saying that another chance will always come along.

4. One of the most interesting geographies of international finance would be a geography of ignorance. For example very few money capitalists fully understand derivatives, or chaos theory (though they may well have bought books on these subjects which they ostentatiously display on their bookshelves or namedrop at job interviews). Parton (1994, p. 137) puts it cynically: 'a trustee really feels he is getting value for money if he doesn't understand how the money in his trust is being invested.' More accurately, one rule of thumb I have often heard is that most investors with under £10m will not fully understand what they are being told.

5. And from the City's numerous social activities. Of Garraway's Coffee House, one nineteenth-century commentator (cited in Kynaston, 1994, p. 144) remarked, 'I do not suppose a woman ever entered the place during the present century.'

6. The élite corresponding clerks were often of foreign extraction until the middle of the nineteenth century (see Kynaston, 1994).

7. However, the City's style of power has always been relatively muted. Power in the City is exerted behind closed doors, in buildings which are often low-key.

8. Mention should also be made of the foreign post nights on Tuesdays and Fridays.

9. Although telegraphic communication was not by any means instantaneous: the telegraphic transmission of news even from Paris to London still took half an hour in 1852.

10. 'Visitors to the City who are not familiar with its ways must observe a good many scenes which puzzle them. If they chance to be loitering about Bartholomew Lane or Throgmorton Street between three and four o'clock in the afternoon they may see telegraph boys racing along at a breakneck pace' (the *Statist*, 1886, cited in Kynaston, 1994, p. 348). This was the effect of the New York market coming 'on-line' at 3.15 p.m.

11. Although one of the widespread problems in the City is often identified as the propensity of its workers to ask each other, rather than acknowledged experts.

12. Typified by Lord Poole's reply to the question of how he had survived the 1974 banking crash. 'It was quite simple, really. I only lent money to people who had been at Eton.'

13. This point should not be overstated. The 1995 edition of *Who's Who in the City of London* found that, out of 15,000 professionals listed, 35 per cent went to Oxford or Cambridge compared with 28 per cent in 1988, perhaps illustrating Hirsch's (1977, p. 48) prescient point that,

> expansion of new universities has not weakened the hold Oxford and Cambridge graduates have on particular professions and instead may have increased the value set by employers on the Oxbridge degree. Not only does it convey information the employers can trust but, in addition, it enables them to buy the elite contacts of the employee. The importance of such contacts is systematically understated in the simple model of the economy in which firms respond to information and opportunities equally known and available to all.

14. Thus the 1995 edition of *Who's Who in the City of London* found that out of 15,000 City professionals, 7 per cent were women, compared with 2 per cent in 1988 (*Sunday Times*, 1995).

15. This is a process not so very different from the one Brenner (1993) describes in which the new colonial merchants gradually displaced the old merchant élite.

16. Typified by the use of computer programs to flag who to ring to make lunch appointments for a particular day of the month.

17. Significantly, the Swiss Banking Corporation approach 'extends to casual clothing at its Thames-side base rather than the formal suits that are still obligatory elsewhere in the City' (Kay, 1994, p. 3).

Inhuman Geographies: Landscapes of Speed, Light and Power

An authentically migrant perspective would, perhaps, be based on an intuition that the opposition between here and there is itself a cultural construction, a consequence of thinking in terms of fixed entities and defining them oppositionally. It might begin by regarding movement not as an awkward interval between fixed points of departure and arrival, but as a mode of being in the world. The question would be, then, not how to arrive, but how to move, how to identify convergent and divergent movements; and the challenge would be how to notate such events, how to give them a historical and social value.

(Carter, 1992, p. 101)

Between things does not designate a localisable relation going from one to the other and reciprocally, but a perpendicular direction, a transversal movement carrying away the one and the other, a stream without beginning or end, gnawing away at its two banks and picking up speed in the middle.

(Deleuze and Guattari, 1983, p. 58)

Now objects perceive me.

(Paul Klee, cited in Virilio, 1994, p. 59)

We no longer have origins, we have terminals.

(Wark, 1994, p. 126)

We have come or . . . reverted to dynamic contexts of performance (which may attract or disappoint) and to meaning effects (which may be fascinating or misleading. but hardly right or wrong). Where do we find conceptual powers for an explanation of the shift that, as always, is not confined to the present but must expand retroactively, too? 'Materialities of communication' is a name . . . for a scene of multidirectionality. It gains cohesion, a negative one certainly, by distancing itself from habits whose importance we have come to overestimate, that is, from habits of overestimation themselves. The main culprit, in that galle(r)y of habits . . . was, and to some extent is, the privileging of the semantic dimension. Cosmologies, philosophies of history, of ethnic, period, or national spirits, and finally, of communication, hermeneutic and otherwise, have been allies and successors in that privilege. Meanwhile some iconoclasts, including Jacques Derrida . . ., had become aware that centres of meaningfulness in philosophy had to be demoted to the rank of mere metaphors. But in that type of criticism, the driving powers behind conceptual interpretational metaphors remained hidden. Logocentrism, to be sure, like the Cartesian ghost in the machine, another skeleton in the

Western closet, was nailed to the cross. But the deconstructive move was of no . . . avail. The picture painted by that 'critique' (and it might have been better to leave the pathos of the term to the past) is historically misleading, perhaps downright wrong. Logocentrism, . . ., depth inter-relation . . ., and finally these interpretational hegemonies in (re)politicised versions of structuralism and poststructuralism are themselves *effects*: effects, among others, of situations, media, and technologies of 'communication'. Communication here is not supposed to connote understanding, coming to terms, mutuality, exchange. It unfolds as an open dynamic of means and effects.

(K.L. Pfeiffer, 1994, p. 3)

Introduction

This final chapter is another attempt to understand the changing 'nature' of contemporary western societies. My thoughts on 'modernity' – a word which, by the way, I thoroughly dislike[1] – have been crystallised by consideration of a commonplace, even banal, image; an urban landscape at night through which runs a river of headlight.[2] This frozen image of mobility summarises a number of the themes that I want to take up in this chapter – speed, light and power.[3] At the same time, it also signifies a shift in the realm of human experience, a shift in our affordances which we still find difficult to account for, towards what Haraway (1985, 1991a, 1991b, 1992a, 1992b, 1993) has called a 'cyborg culture', a culture of foregrounded codes and redundancies in which the boundaries between 'people' and 'machines' have started to break down.

What I want to suggest is that we have now reached a point where western cultures have become increasingly self-referential in the sense that, over a number of generations, sources and horizons of meaning have developed and become generalized, sedimented and then mutated, which are based in hybrid images of machine and organism, especially images based on speed, light and power. As a result, we now live in an almost/not quite world – a world of almost/not quite subjects; almost/not quite selves; almost/not quite spaces; and almost/not quite times – which has become one of the chief concerns of contemporary experience and social theory because it both poses the questions and provides the resources to answer them. This chapter, then, is an attempt to expand on and document a cultural hypothesis about a cultural hypothesis.

Accordingly, the chapter is in five main parts. In the first part I want to resurrect the concept of a structure of feeling. I will utilise this concept in the remainder of the chapter as a means of understanding the almost/not quite status of an intellectual 'project' which I have christened 'mobility'. This project is the attempt to describe new orders of experience constructed out of 'machinic'[4] sources and horizons of meaning (Kenner, 1987). In this part of the chapter I will also attempt to provide some notion of the contemporary social and cultural conditions of academe out of which this structure of feeling has arisen. However, much of this structure of feeling is clearly the result of much wider-ranging historical changes in discourse networks (Kittler, 1990; Gumbrecht and Pfeiffer, 1994). Therefore, in the second part of the chapter, I will document some of these changes, concentrating in particular on the machinic complexes of speed, light and power. This historical excursion provides the resources which allow me to go on in the third part of the chapter to try to identify some of the key elements of an almost/not quite ontology which is gradually gathering momentum around the key trope of 'mobility'; an ontology which arises, or so I argue, from the affordances made available by these new machinic complexes. In the fourth part of the chapter, I then try to show some of the ways in which this structure of feeling can be related to changing research agendas in the social sciences and humanities, concentrating on contemporary geographical work. Finally, I provide a brief set of conclusions.

An Emergent Structure of Feeling[5]

How is it possible to describe an almost/not quite intellectual project? That requires an almost/not quite concept. Such a concept is available in the form of Raymond Williams's (1954, 1977, 1979, 1980) notion of a 'structure of feeling'. Williams's conception is, of course, notoriously elusive. On one level, the term is simply intended to signify 'the culture of a period' (R. Williams, 1979, p. 48). But on another level it is an attempt to get at something more elusive: 'the *living* result of all the elements in the general organisation' (R. Williams, 1979, p. 48; my emphasis). Yet it is this very elusiveness which is particularly appropriate for my purposes, for at least five reasons. First of all, the idea of structure of feeling is intended to signal a *process* that is 'at the very edge of semantic availability' (R. Williams, 1977, p. 134), echoing a concern that nowadays is more likely to be addressed by terms like liminality and differend. Second, the notion fits well with the reading of current intellectual tendencies that I want to make. Williams wanted to stress the continual mobility of modern cultural processes; always 'present', 'moving', 'active', 'formative', 'in process', 'in solution'. Williams's interest was quite clearly to avoid reducing many aspects of the cultural to a fixed 'form'. Rather, there are traces, and traces of traces.[6] Third, Williams stresses over and over again that structures of feeling are never reducible to the institutional or formal. 'What really changes is something quite general, over a wide range, and the description that often fits the change best is the literary term "style"' (R. Williams, 1977, p. 131). Thus Williams envisaged structures of feeling as *cultural hypotheses* 'that do not have to await definition, classification, or rationalisation before they exact palpable pressures and set effective limits on experience and action' (R. Williams, 1977, p. 132). These cultural hypotheses will therefore include the recognition of new figurations of the self, new enunciative practices and new forms of 'livedness'. Fourth, the idea of structure of feeling is intended to signal a commitment to *experience*, to the fact that what experience is is something which is not reducible. It is what we live through. It is 'the movement of bone, of body, of breath, of imagination, of muscle, and the conviction of sheer stubborness that there are other possibilities' (Probyn, 1992, p. 172). It is that 'element for which there is no external counterpart' (R. Williams, 1954, p. 21). Thus, structure of feeling necessarily involves articulating emotions, bodily practices, the physical character of places, all of those differentiated and differentiating elements of comportment which are crucial to a culture, which may well be bound up with reading and writing it with a certain fidelity, yet which are so difficult to read and write from (J.W. Scott, 1992). In other words,

> Rather than dismissing experience out of hand, we can begin to see the potential that it carries both to designate the various levels of the social and to point to possible sites for critical intervention. Without being placed on a pedestal, experience can nevertheless give us something to speak from. (Probyn, 1992, p. 26)

Finally, the notion of structure of feeling can be seen, in some senses at least, as not merely methodological but as actually reflecting a specific historical period in which almost/not quite effects become more palpable. In other words, the notion of structure of feeling can also describe the practical penumbra of some current intellectual developments. It recognises a kind of shadow world which is now coming out into the light.

Where has this structure of feeling which I call mobility actually come from? What factors underlie such a redistribution of intellectual interest? To answer these questions requires a consideration of both the changing social field of academe and the nature of wider changes in the world with which this field must interact.

Certainly, over the last twenty years or so, there have been a number of important changes in what Bourdieu (1988, 1990a, 1991, 1993) calls the social field of academe, which have led to a greater emphasis on culture and cultural theory, and, in turn, have prepared the ground for the new structure of feeling. To follow Williams (1977) again, these changes have been a mixture of the institutional (most especially, major changes in higher education systems in a number of countries), the formal (in particular, the rise of poststructuralism and the associated transformation of academic heretics into establishment heresiarchs [Bourdieu, 1988; Lamont, 1987]) and the social (especially the gradual, uneven but still marked shift in the balance of intellectual power in academe based on the interests of new generations, new social groups, and new class fractions[7]). These different but cross-cutting changes in the social field have certainly all contributed to the new structure of feeling in various ways. The importance of institutions can be seen in the way that, in Britain, for example, it was the former polytechnics, with their clearer interests in the application of technology, that also took up cultural studies most keenly. The importance of forms can be seen in the way that many poststructuralist authors have used machinic means of metaphorisation. The importance of new generations and new social groups can be seen in the way that matters of gender, sexuality and race have been taken up and have led to much greater attention being given to borders, transgression, third cultures and other motifs of the new structure of feeling, while the importance of new class fractions can be seen in the role of academics in the rise of a new petit bourgeoisie (Bourdieu, 1984) with its base in the cultural industries and its stress on the construction and manipulation of images and related acts of consumer living.

Quite clearly the emergent structure of feeling has been influenced by these changes. However, equally clearly, it cannot 'without loss, be reduced to belief systems, institutions, or explicit general relationships' (R. Williams, 1977, p. 133). I want to claim that to get at the 'generative immediacy' of the new structure of feeling any analysis has to go much further, to consider how social changes can provide a set of imaginative resources, in this case a series of re-metaphorisations based in machinic complexes which I have termed speed, light and power, which go beyond the old organic and technological metaphors (Haraway, 1991a, p. 21). In other words, it is important to get at something we might loosely call 'a change of style', which also turns out to be a change in content.[8] That is the main purpose of this chapter.

By taking such a view, it will hopefully become apparent that the emergent structure of feeling is an attempt to articulate and be articulated by a cyborg culture (Haraway, 1985, 1991a). Following Haraway, such a culture can be described as a hybrid of machine and organism, 'a condensed image of both imagination and material reality, the two joined centres structuring any possibility of historical transformation' (Haraway, 1985, p. 191). In other words, it is a re-recognition of the difficulties associated with projects that divide the world into the human and the non-human, that insist that objects are 'shapeless receptacles of social categories' (Latour, 1993, p. 55) without agency, and that deny the multiplication of what Latour (1993) calls 'quasi-objects' and Haraway calls 'actants', collective ensembles 'which act, [have] will, meaning and even speech' (Latour, 1993, p. 136).[9] It is to point to the increasing difficulty of situating 'the human', to restore 'the share of things' (Latour, 1993, p. 136) and to recognise the increasing importance of 'in-between' life forms (Michaux, 1992).

That the structure of feeling I have called 'mobility' has emerged at this particular time I take to be no accident. In particular, I take it that it has been forced as a result of four closely connected imaginative adjustments. The first of these stems from the fact that we live in an increasingly artificial, or, more accurately, manufactured, environment. The transformation to this kind of environment has taken many hundreds of years and is of immense cultural significance. Raymond Williams (1990) compares it, in its scope and effect, to the transition from hunter-gatherer to agricultural civilisations, which also took many hundreds of years and which led to profound moral, political and spiritual upheavals as the one world was replaced by another.

> It is not only imaginable but probable that humanity's decision to unbind itself from the soil – not to return to a nomadic existence but to bind itself instead to a predominantly technological environment – has provoked a singularly profound spiritual crisis. We are now embarked upon another period of cultural mourning and upheaval, as we look back to a way of life that is ebbing away. (R. Williams, 1990, p. 2)

Or, as Jameson (1991, p. 35) puts it, 'the other of our society is in [a] sense no longer Nature at all, as it was in precapitalist societies, but something else which we must now identify.'

The second imaginative adjustment is to the scientific advances which have enabled this transition to take place. The structure of feeling called mobility emerges at a time of a kind of disillusionment with the science which has produced a manufactured environment. This disillusionment takes a number of forms. First, there are the various forms of 'life politics' (Giddens, 1991) which arise out of a greater level of reflexivity concerning scientific knowledge. Second, there is the anthropological importance of science:

> Threats from civilisation are bringing about a new kind of 'shadow kingdom', comparable to the realm of the gods and demons in antiquity, which is hidden behind the visible world and threatens human life on this Earth. People no longer correspond today with spirits residing in things, but find themselves exposed to 'radiation', ingest 'toxic levels' and are pursued into their very dreams by the anxieties of a nuclear holocaust. The place of the anthropomorphic interpretation of nature and the environment has been taken by the modern risk consciousness of civilisation with its imperceptible and yet omnipresent latent causality. (Beck, 1992, p. 72)

Third, there is a more general solidarity with other living things which is, at the same time, a renegotiation of the body and the self. Thus, awareness of the body increases: 'once thought to be the locus of the soul, then the centre of dark perverse needs, the body has become fully available to be "worked upon"' (Giddens, 1991, p. 218). Relatedly, the self becomes linked to 'nature'. 'Where trees are cut down and animal species destroyed, people feel victimised themselves in a certain sense. The threats to life in the development of civilisation touch commonalities of the experience of organic life that connect the human vital necessities to those of plants and animals' (Beck, 1992, p. 74). Finally, partly because much of what we regard as 'nature' can no longer survive without human intervention (Strathern, 1992a), society is no longer understood as separate from nature:

> the 'end of nature' means that the natural world has become in large part a 'created environment', consisting of humanly structured systems whose motive, power and dynamics derive from socially organised knowledge-claims rather than from influences exogenous to human activity. (Giddens, 1991, p. 144)

At the same time, the disillusionment with science also arises, in part, from an accommodation with it; science and its doings are no longer perceived as something 'new', 'modern' or 'progressive' but as simply a part of the fabric of everyday life, and as therefore subject to the same moral judgements (Beck, 1992).

The third imaginative adjustment stems from a re-view of machines and machinic complexes. Machines are no longer conceived of in the same way. They are no longer viewed as either a threat or a salvation but as troublesome companions (Bijker et al., 1989; Bijker and Law, 1991). The view, running from Babbage and Ure through to Fritz Lang's *Metropolis*, of a world of 'vast automatons' in which the machine is 'a creation destined to restore order amongst the industrious classes' (Ure, 1835, cited in Naylor, 1992, p. 228) has been replaced by a view of machinery that is more ambiguous. Increasingly, machines are no longer considered as a separate realm but, to use Haraway's term, they are seen as functioning parts of 'actants' – agencies in which the 'actors' are not all 'us': 'this is the barely admissible recognition of the odd sorts of agents and actors which/ whom we must now admit to the narrative of collective life' (Haraway, 1992b, p. 330). Such a recognition clearly requires a number of further imaginative compromises. First, there is the nature of what it is to be human. Thus machines can no longer be automatically regarded as without human characteristics. Indeed perhaps we now need to talk of a new category of people/machines – the inhuman (Lyotard, 1992). Second, there is the nature of the subject. Subjects can no longer be seen as bounded by human bodies. Or to put it another way, subjects can no longer be seen as fixed nodes. They are part of human–machine networks of social connectedness that change what it means to be human (Kittler, 1990) '*Ecce homo*: delegated, mediated, distributed, mandated, uttered' (Latour, 1993, p. 138). Third, there is the nature of action: 'action is not so much an ontological as a semiotic problem' (Haraway, 1992b, p. 331, fn. 11). In other words, what counts as an actor?[10]

The fourth and final imaginative adjustment is a political realignment, or, more precisely, a realignment of what counts as politics and the political. The questions posed by new political movements based around issues of gender, sexual preference, ethnicity, nature, and so on, are precisely questions of what it means to be human once claims to universality are put aside. Such movements are therefore faced with the prospect of making demands that they cannot always precisely articulate since the end-point of their struggles – new kinds of selves and persons – cannot be precisely known (Butler, 1992). In other words, such movements must forge an ongoing intentionality, rather than a finished political programme. They therefore need to imagine mobile, inclusive political configurations (or even transfigurations), rather than solid, exclusive, political figures:

> Feminist theory proceeds by figuration of just those moments when its own historical narratives are in crisis. Historical narratives are in crisis now, across the political spectrum, around the world. These are the moments when something powerful – and dangerous – is happening. Figuration is about resetting the stage

for possible pasts and futures. Figuration is the mode of theory where the more 'normal' rhetorics of systematic cultural analysis seem only to repeat and sustain our entrapment in the stories of established orders. Humanity is a modernist figure; and this humanity has a generic face, a universal shape. Humanity's face has been the face of man. Feminist humanity must have another shape, other gestures; but I believe we must have feminist figures of humanity. They cannot be man or woman; they cannot be the human as historical narrative has staged that generic universal. Feminist figures cannot, finally, have a name; they cannot be native. Feminist humanity must somehow resist representation, resist literal figurations, and still erupt in powerful new tropes, new figures of speech, new turns of historical possibility. (Haraway, 1992a, p. 86)

This, then, is something of what is meant by a change of style! In the next section of this chapter I will begin to articulate this structure of feeling by referring to the history of three of the main machinic complexes – speed, light and power – which, as we shall see, very soon begin to collapse into each other. Speed, light, power: mobility.

Speed, Light, Power: Mobility

A machinic complex is here taken to be a developing bundle of institutions and technologies, understood as non-exclusive and diverse organisations[11] of knowledge–discipline–perception circulating in a constantly shifting 'parliament of things': embodied subjects, machines, texts and metaphors, and the like (Haraway, 1992b), which undergo periodic modernisation, redirection and redefinition. In this section, I will provide a brief history of three of these machinic complexes: speed, light and power. The history of these complexes has been a highly uneven one, both between and within different western countries. To give some sense of this unevenness, I therefore make particular reference to the case of Britain, a country which has been less mobile than some (for example, the United States with its level of 1.3 people per automobile which Baudrillard [1988, p. 27], with, for once, a degree of understatement, has termed 'pure circulation') but more mobile than others. The section starts out by referring to the nineteenth century, when it is still possible to treat these machinic complexes as separate and separated. However, in the latter parts of the section, I will treat these three complexes as one, a simultaneous recognition of the way in which they have now come together in a kind of social-technological *jouissance*, and of the way in which these earlier technological developments have now soaked into the pre-discursive imaginary and become the ground on which we attend to later developments.

Of course, I am well aware of the dangers in this kind of account of a latent or explicit technological determinism in which 'an independent dynamic of mechanical invention, modification, and perfection imposes itself onto a social field transforming it from outside' (Crary, 1990, p. 8). However, at the same time, it is equally important not to produce a sociological or cultural determinism in which socio-cultural forces produce objects. Part of the point of this chapter is to achieve a balance; in Latour's (1987) terms, the 'technogram' is the other side of the 'sociogram' and 'every piece of information you obtain on one system is also information on the other' (Latour, 1987, p. 138). Or, as Deleuze and Guattari (1988, p. 90) put it: 'a society is defined by its amalgamations, not by its tools . . . tools exist only in relation to the intermingling they make possible or that make them possible.' In other words, we must see technologies as parts of networks, made up of actors (of whatever kind), and these 'constructed complexes of habits, beliefs and procedures' (Marvin, 1988, p. 8) are greater than the sum of their parts. But none of this is to suggest that these assemblages are neutral. They embody codes[12] (which might be seen as knowledge–power relations for connecting technograms and sociograms) which are institutionalised in various ways, and these institutions have margins of manoeuvre associated with them which can allow the institutions and even codes to be redefined (Feenberg, 1991).

The Nineteenth Century

Speed   I hardly need to reprise a history of the machinic complex of speed that results from the application of new technologies of transport and communication from the end of the eighteenth century onwards (see the very extensive review in *1990b*). I therefore provide here only the briefest sketch.

In the nineteenth century the technology of speed broke through the limits of walking and the horse into a period of progressively accelerating transport network technology – the stage coach and the horse-drawn tram, the railway and the electric train, and the bicycle. Thus in Britain by 1820 it was often quicker to travel by stage coach than on horseback. By 1830 movement between the major towns was some four or five times faster than in 1750. This increase in the speed of the stage coach was paralleled by an increase in both frequency of operation and in the number of destinations. The subsequent growth of the railway network made for even more dramatic leaps in speed, frequency and access. It is no surprise that 'the annihalation of space by time' was a favourite meditation for the Victorian writer.[13] The effects were all the more arresting because they came to be experienced by so many people. By 1870, 336.5 million journeys were made by rail, the vast bulk of them by third-class passengers. In the growing cities a parallel process of democratisation was taking place measured out by the advent of the horse-drawn tram, the underground and, latterly, electric tramways. But perhaps the most dramatic change in travel was the invention of the bicycle. By 1855 there were already 400,000 cyclists in Britain and the 1890s saw the peak of this simple machine's popularity. The bicycle, which started as a piece of fun for young swells, foreshadowed the automobile in providing immediate, democratic access to speed (Kern, 1983).

The nineteenth century also saw the beginnings of new networks of communication which began to displace face-to-face communication, especially a rapid and efficient mail service and, latterly, the telegraph and mass circulation newspapers. In Britain, the mail service expanded massively in the nineteenth century, as did new communication innovations like the postcard, Valentine cards, Christmas cards, and so on. By 1890, the Post Office was carrying 1,706 million letters a year. The telegraph was first used in 1839. By 1863 nearly 22,000 miles of line had been set up, transmitting over six million messages a year, from 3,381 points. However, it was not until the last quarter of the nineteenth century that the telegraph became an institution of communication genuinely used by the mass of the population. However, neither of these means of communication was instantaneous. The mail service still depended upon the velocity of a set of different means of transport while the telegraph service had to be actually reached (usually in a post office) before it could be used.

The exact social and cultural effects of this 'great acceleration' have certainly been disputed. But, amongst the changes attendant on a world of traffic flowing through multiple networks at least four might be counted as being significant. The first of these was a change in the consciousness of time and space. For example, so far as time consciousness was concerned, it seems clear that the population began to pay more attention to smaller distinctions in time (*1990b*; Zerubavel, 1981). Thus, in the last decade of the nineteenth century watches became more popular (Kern, 1983). Again, it seems clear that a sense of an enlarged, simultaneous presence became more common, especially as a result of the telegraph (Kern, 1983; Briggs, 1989). This was not just a temporal but also a spatial sense. In one sense space had been shrunk by the new simultaneity engendered by the shrinkage of travel and communication times, and by new social practices like travelling to work and tourism.[14] In another sense it was much enlarged. *The Times* of 1858 (quoted in Briggs, 1989, p. 29) wrote proudly of 'the vast enlargement . . . given to the sphere of human activity' by the telegraph and the press that now fed upon its pulses. It is also possible to identify, rather more tentatively, elements of a change in the perception of landscape. For example, following Sternberger (1977), Schivelsbuch (1986) has argued for the development of a 'panoramic perception' (see also Kern, 1983; Tichi, 1987) in which the world is presented as something seen from within a moving platform, as a passing, momentary spectacle to be glimpsed and consumed. A second change was the impact of this general speed-up on the texts of the period, whether in the form of enthusiastic paeans to machinery (see Naylor, 1992) or in the form of counter-laments for slower, less mechanical and decidedly more authentic times gone by (Sussman, 1967). For example, Wallace (1993) notes the way in which, over the course of the early nineteenth century, walking was repositioned as a practice in the texts of the period. Whereas it had been an activity chiefly associated with 'poverty, alienation from society whether for legal or non-legal reasons, possible moral turpitude, and probable danger to the individuals and communities touched by the act' (Wallace, 1993, p. 33), it gradually took on a more respectable tinge, especially under the impact of romanticism, as an activity defined against increasing speed, which took place in a natural landscape for its own sake, and without any particular destination in mind. Walking becomes 'true' or 'real' travel. Yet, ironically,

> the rise of the railroads actually fuelled the growing popularity of walking tours, presumably because one could now arrive relatively painlessly at the place where one did want to walk, without the gruelling task of walking all the way. (Wallace, 1993, p. 66)

A third change was in the nature of subjectivity. In particular, it is possible to note an increasing sense of the body as an anonymised parcel of flesh which is shunted from place to place, just like other goods. Each of these bodies passively avoided others, yet was still linked in to distant events, a situation typified by Victorian vignettes of the railway passenger in greater communion with the newspaper than companions (Schivelsbuch, 1986). 'Each individual paper, a replica of hundreds of thousands of others, served as a private opening to a world identical to that of one's companion on a street car, a companion likely to remain as distant, remote and strange as the day's news came to seem familiar, personal, real' (Trachtenberg, 1982, p. 125). A fourth and final change was in the metaphors that were becoming dominant, especially in bourgeois circles. Chief amongst these were metaphors of 'circulation' (usually via a semantic mixture of the bodily and the mechanical) and 'progress'. Thus speed: expansion: abundance (Buck-Morss, 1989) (connections usually made via a semantic operation in which spatial movement via a particular technology like the railway was wedded to historical movement). 'The formula is as simple as can be: whatever was part of circulation was regarded as healthy, progressive, constructive; all that was detached from circulation, on the other hand, appeared, diseased, medieval, subversive, threatening' (Schivelsbuch, 1986, p. 195). Schivelsbuch (1986, p. 197) is able to tie these metaphors of circulation and progress together through this formula:

> The notion that communication, exchange and motion bring to humanity enlightenment and progress, and that isolation and disconnection are the obstacles to be overcome on this course, is as old as the modern age. The bourgeois cultural development of the last three centuries can be seen as closely connected with the actual development of traffic. In retrospect, it is easy to see what significance the experience of space and time had for bourgeois education when one considers the Grand Tour, which was an essential part of that education before the industrialisation of travel. The world was experienced in its original spatio-temporality. The travelling subject experienced localities in their spatial individuality. His education consisted of his assimilation of the spatial individuality of the places visited, by means of an effort that was both physical and intellectual. The eighteenth century travel novel became the *Bildungsroman* (novel of education) of the early nineteenth century. The motion of travel, that physical and intellectual effort in space and time, dominated both.
>
> The railroad, the destroyer of experiential space and time, thus also destroyed the experience of the Grand Tour. Henceforth, the localities were no longer spatially individual or autonomous: they were points in the circulation of traffic that made them accessible. As we have seen, that traffic was the physical

manifestation of the circulation of goods. From that time on, the places visited by the traveller became increasingly similar to the commodities that were part of the same circulation system. For the twentieth century tourist, the world has become one huge department store of countrysides and cities.

In other words, increasingly 'travel' became a value in and for itself as speeds increased, another country with its own distinctive practices and culture.

Light Another important part of the history of the machinic complex of mobility has been the history of the machinic complex of artificial light. In effect, this history dates from the end of the eighteenth century, when, for the first time, a technology that had not significantly altered for several hundred years began to change. Before this time, artificial light had been in short supply. To an extent, the work day had been emancipated from dependence on daylight by candles and oil lamps, but most households still used artificial light only very sparingly (Schivelsbuch, 1988).

From the end of the eighteenth century through the early nineteenth centry a whole series of inventions began to change this situation. The Argand oil-burning light (1783) was the first such invention. It was soon followed by the gaslight which was made possible by the invention of systems to produce gas from coal *c.* 1800. These were first used in factories and then, with the setting up of central gas supplies in cities (the first gasworks was set up in Britain in London in 1814), they spread to the household (Barty-King, 1986). The networks of gas mains prefigured railway tracks and electrical networks. By 1822 there were already 200 miles of gas main in London, and 53 English cities in all had gas companies. By 1840 there was 'scarcely a town of any importance' that was not lit with gas (Clegg, 1841, cited in Robson, 1973, p. 178). The gas companies fuelled gas lamps in the household and in the street (although, as Robson [1973] shows, adoption was very uneven).

To some extent running in parallel with the development of gas lighting was the development of brighter and more spectacular electrical lighting. The arc light was invented in 1800 and was used in specific situations over long periods of time but was not put into general use in factories, shops and similar sites until the 1870s and 1880s. It was the invention of the electrical bulb in 1879 which heralded the widespread electrification of light and the decisive break between light and fire. The first central electricity-generating stations became operational in 1882 in New York and London. However, although London was amongst the first to have a fully functioning electric light system (around Holborn), subsequently, like Britain as a whole, it lagged in the adoption of electric light, partly because of economic conditions, partly because of legislation – which prevented the growth of electricity monopolies – and partly because of opposition from gas interests. Thus, it was not until the 1920s that electricity, and electrical light, was widely adopted in Britain (Hannah, 1979; Hughes, 1983). In contrast, by 1903 New York had 17,000 electric street lamps, 'while electric interior lighting and exterior displays had become "essential to competition" for downtown theatres, restaurants, hotels and department stores' (Nasaw, 1992, p. 274).

This history of an ever-expanding landscape of light which we now take so much for granted cannot be ignored. As a machinic complex it is particularly important because of five changes. The first of these is that it signifies the progressive colonisation of the night (Melbin, 1987; Alvarez, 1994). In the towns and cities, at least, night had never been regarded as a period of general inactivity. The early pleasure gardens, for example, were famous for their displays of nightly social bustle amidst much remarked upon artificial light. Similarly, Holmes (1993) documents the nocturnal wanderings of Dr Johnson and Mr Savage around the 'City of Dreadful Night', and the degree to which, in fact, eighteenth-century London was lit up at night. But, beginning in the late eighteenth century, the process of colonisation 'started to spread vigourously' (Melbin, 1987, p. 14). Communities started to become incessant with a consequent 'blurring of the division of day and night' (Kern, 1983, p. 29). However, as Schivelsbuch (1988) shows, even so there was a considerable period of adjustment away from more 'natural' rhythms. For example, it was only at the end of the nineteenth century that street lighting became independent of natural rhythms like moonlight: 'early in the twentieth century, public lighting in many cities was still regulated according to moonlight schedules. On clear moonlit nights lanterns were turned off earlier than usual, most shortly after midnight' (Schivelsbuch, 1988, p. 91).

A second change was that very gradually a separate set of human practices evolved which we now call 'night life'. In 1738 Hogarth had produced an engraving called *Night* as a part of a series, *The Four Times of Day*, which showed only lurching drunks and wandering vagrants inhabiting a night-time London street. But, it was an exaggeration. Lighted pleasure gardens and other places of entertainment had already started to produce a specific night social life, and through the eighteenth century this new kind of sociality was extended by the addition of theatres, shops (which used manufactured light to enhance their displays), cafés, and so on (M. Cohen, 1993). It is no surprise, then, that by the late Victorian period London at night was seen by many foreign visitors as almost another country:

Great city of the midnight sun
Whose day begins when day is done.
(Le Galliene, cited in Briggs, 1992, p. 24)

As the veil of night was lifted, so many effects were produced. Lighting removed some of the dangers that had once lurked in the dark.[15] Again, the advent of lighting in the household produced new timings and forms of social interaction (Schivelsbuch, 1988). Industrial production was also revolutionised as manufacturers began to work out shift systems which used light and night to enable continuous production.

A third change was that manufactured light was of central importance in the cultural construction of the 'dream spaces' of the nineteenth century (W. Benjamin, 1977; Buck-Morss, 1989; M. Cohen, 1993): the department stores (with their illuminated display windows), the hotels, the theatres, the cafés, the world fairs, and so on. These urban spaces, which transformed consumption into a mode of being, depended on visual consumption, which, in turn, depended upon artificial lighting. Such spaces rapidly became *the* urban experience and their 'spectacular lighting . . . quickly became a central cultural practice' (Nye, 1990, p. 383) providing the opportunity for a new nocturnal round.

A fourth change was that manufactured light produced major new opportunities for surveillance. Foucault (1977, p. 93) has stressed the importance of light to practices of surveillance. There is no hiding in the light. For example, in a prison 'the strong light and the stare of a guard are better captors than the dark, which formerly was protective. The visibility is a trap.' With a light source, a focusing cell and a directed looking all becomes visible (Batchen, 1991). (Similarly, Bachelard [1964, p. 63] notes the importance of light as a means of identification: 'Everything that casts a light sees'.) Manufactured light, then, extended the state and industry's powers of surveillance. The unease that was current in the nineteenth century about street lights that made the insides of houses visible, and the corresponding use of heavy curtains to block out this light (and the gaze of others), help to make this point (Schivelsbuch, 1988).

A final change produced by manufactured light was a re-metaphorisation of texts and bodies as a result of the new perceptions. There were, to begin with, new perceptions of landscape: the night under artificial light was a new world of different colours and sensations, modulated by artificial lighting, which painters like Joseph Wright of Derby had been amongst the first to explore (see R. Williams, 1990). Late Victorian London was often seen anew through the power of gaslight:[16]

London, London, our delight
Great flower that opens but at night.
(cited in Briggs, 1989, p. 25)

As importantly, manufactured light began to be used to produce new image technologies and new institutional forms. In particular, inspired by the camera obscura (which had, incidentally, been used as a model of subject and object by both Descartes and Locke), a new 'metaphysics of interiority' (Crary, 1990) was put into place, in which the camera obscura represented a 'sovereign, privatised subject who is enclosed and isolated in an observation space separate from the exterior world' (Lalvani, 1993, p. 445).

If the camera obscura functioned as one of the first models of ocularcentric knowing and transcendental subjectivity, 'the mechanically and chemically subtended camera legislated that model into everyday seeing' (Lalvani, 1993, p. 445). The camera and the photograph (literally 'light writing') in time produced serial images which could be industrialised.[17] This new 'scopic economy' (Jay, 1993) had a number of effects. On the one hand, the photograph signalled a kind of liberation. It produced a visual regime which permitted new types of image, novel forms of fantasy and desire and new forms of 'experience which [did not need] to be equated with presence' (Game, 1991, p. 147), as well as the opportunity for many of those who had previously been invisible to become visible as subjects of their own representations. On the other hand, a plurality of institutional and disciplinary means were found 'to recode the activity of the eye, to heighten its productivity and to prevent its distraction' (Crary, 1990, p. 24). No less than Foucault's panopticon, nineteenth-century image technologies were threaded through institutions and disciplining techniques (Sekula, 1986; Tagg, 1988; Lalvani, 1993) which, to an extent, determined not what was seen, but what was attended to, what was 'seeable'.[18] Thus, there were institutions, which

> invoked arrangements of bodies in space, regulation of activity, and the deployment of individual bodies, which codified and normalised the observer within rigidly defined systems of visual consumption. There were disciplinary techniques for the management of attention, for imposing homogeneity, anti-nomadic procedures that fixed and isolated the observer. (Crary, 1990, p. 18)[19]

Yet, at precisely the same time that the new institutions and technologies centred the empirical truth of vision 'in the density and materiality of the body' (Crary, 1994, p. 21) (rather than the stimulus of the environment) they also threw the essential objectivity of vision into doubt, precisely because they were so clearly open to, and intent on, an arbitrary order of normalisation, quantification and discipline. Thus, even in the 1820s and 1830s the observer already begins to be repositioned,

> outside of the fixed relations of interior/exterior presupposed by the camera obscura and into an undemarcated terrain in which the distinction between internal sensations and external signs is irrevocably blurred . . . there is a freeing up of vision, a falling away of the rigid structures that had shaped it and constituted its object. (Crary, 1990, p. 24)

But in all probability it was the beginning of the second half of the nineteenth century which proved to be the cultural threshold:

> Vision in a wide range of locations, was realigned as dynamic, temporal and synthetic – the demise of the punctual, anchored classical observer began in the early nineteenth century, increasingly displaced by the unstable attentive subject. . . . It is a subject competent both to be a consumer of and an agent of a proliferating diversity of 'reality effects' and a subject who will become the object of all the industries of image and spectacle in the twentieth century. (Crary, 1994, p. 44)

Power   A further important machinic complex is power. Electrical power is, of course, hardly a new invention. The invention of the Leyden jar sparked off the first electrical experiments in Germany and Switzerland in the 1740s. By the 1780s electricity had achieved some measure of recognition in medical circles, a popularity which it retained in the nineteenth century through devices like galvanic belts, electric baths, electric shock treatment and the like, for the treatment of physical and mental disorders (Nye, 1990; Armstrong, 1991). The telegraph reinforced this recognition by bringing about changes in 'the nature of language, of ordinary knowledge, of the very structures of awareness' (Carey, 1989, p. 202; see also Innis, 1951). It gave a particularly strong boost to a rapidly expanding 'rhetoric of the electrical sublime' (Carey, 1989). This rhetoric was particularly marked in the United States, where it tended to be couched in the language of either religious aspiration or secular millenarianism. Henry Adams, for example, saw the telegraph as a demonic device displacing the Virgin with the Dynamo. But for Samuel Morse, the telegraph was an electrical nervous system able 'to diffuse with the speed of thought a knowledge of all that is occuring through the land' (cited in Carey, 1989, p. 207). In Britain, the rhetoric of the telegraph tended to be less extreme but, even there, it fired a powerful flow of thought, most especially when connected with matters of Empire, for which the telegraph was a powerful integrative metaphor (Richards, 1993).

But it was the promise of infinite light and power that made electricity into a household term. In particular, it was the advent in the 1880s of power stations which distributed electricity along a network that allowed electricity to come into its own, rather as gas had some decades earlier. Indeed, at first, these power stations were often depicted as electrical gasworks. But as it became clear that high voltage could be transported over long distances, electricity power stations were located at long distances away from where the electricity was actually used, thus giving the impression that electricity was a sourceless source, an absent presence (Schivelsbuch, 1988). Further, unlike gas, electrical light was immediately accepted in drawing rooms as clean and odour-free. Electricity therefore reached more places more quickly and it quickly became a vast *collective* network of power.

Already in 1881 *Punch* was able to introduce into its pages a cartoon showing King Coal and King Steam watching the infant electricity grow and asking 'What will he grow in to?' Certainly, in the 1880s, it looked as though London might become an 'electropolis'. By 1891 London had 473,000 incandescent lamps, compared with Berlin's 75,000 and Paris's 67,600 (Hughes, 1983). But in the 1890s rates of electricity adoption in Britain slowed markedly – the result of a combination of recession, government legislation and opposition from gas interests – and never really recovered until the 1920s. By 1913 Berlin and Paris had more generating capacity than London, partly the result of having a few large generating stations compared with London's many local ones. Similarly, electricity seems to have failed to capture the British imagination in the same way that it did that of the United States or some countries of Europe, where popular absorption in the potentiality of electricity as a force for personal and social translation was much greater (Nye, 1990), and the mystery and magic of electricity was more appreciated (Briggs, 1992). In part, this seems to have been the result of the much greater purchase that romantic notions of an arcadian countryside and nature mysticism were able to get on the British imagination with an associated rejection of 'mechanisation' in all its forms (Naylor, 1992).

Like speed and light, electrical power produced a number of important changes. Three of these stand out. The first change was the boost electrical power gave to new conceptions of time and space. Through the telegraph and the instant power provided by the light switch came ideas of absent presence, of a geography of communication that no longer depended upon actual transport (Carey, 1989). A second change was the re-metaphorisation of the body into the body electric. From the time of *Frankenstein*, electricity, energy and life [had been] synonymous' (Schivelsbuch, 1988, p. 71). Now forces, engines, dynamos, discharges, currents and flow become a new linguistic currency of desire. More than even speed or light, electrical power:

> raised the possibility of an alteration in what Felix Guattari calls the 'social chemistry of desire', in the means through which physical desire, and motivation generally, could be represented, articulated and transmitted. If the social and the individual body are intimately related, then the massive programmes for the wiring of individual houses that went on throughout the late nineteenth century have a parallel in the wiring of individual bodies and in the way in which states of desire, animation, and incandescence are figured in literary and other texts. (Armstrong, 1991, p. 307)

Thus a whole vocabulary grew up (live wires, human dynamos, electric performances, and so on [Nye, 1990]) that depended upon electricity, conceived as 'shadowy, mysterious, impalpable. It lives in the skies and seems to connect the spiritual and the material' (Czitrom, cited in Carey, 1989, p. 206).

The third and final change was electricity's critical role in the transition to a new form of more integrated capitalism. Society was tied together and made subservient to the new networks of power.

> the transformation of free competition into corporate monopoly capitalism confirmed in economic terms what electrification had confirmed technically; the end of individual enterprise and an autonomous energy supply. It is well known that the electrical industry was a significant factor in bringing about these changes. An analogy between electrical power and finance capital springs to mind. The concentration and centralisation of energy in high capacity power stations corresponded to the concentration of economic power in the big banks. (Schivelsbuch, 1988, p. 74)

The Twentieth Century

Speed   In the twentieth century, the history of speed has been a continuation by other means of methods of transport and communication that started in the nineteenth century. The automobile has, perhaps, been the most important device. It is often viewed as the avatar of mobility. For Baudrillard (1988, pp. 52–3), for example, the Los Angeles freeways speak to a society built around the automobile and the 'only truly profound pleasure, that of keeping on the move':

> Gigantic, spontaneous spectacle of automobile traffic. A total collective act, staged by the entire population, twenty-four hours a day. By virtue of the sheer size of the layout and the kind of complicity that binds this network of thoroughfares together, traffic rises here to the level of a dramatic attraction, acquires the status of symbolic organisation. The machines themselves . . . have created a milieu in their own image.

But in Britain, in contrast to the United States, the automobile's status as the prime mover was hampered by the British class system. Private cars and vans on the road increased from 132,000 in 1914 to nearly two million in 1939 (*1990b*; Robson, 1990) but 'possession of a car still remained exclusive since those numbers represented only a very small proportion of the population' (Robson, 1990, p. 67). It was not until the late 1950s and early 1960s that car ownership started to become general as real car prices fell dramatically. Car ownership increased from under 4 million in 1956 to 6.5 million in 1962 and 10 million in 1967, but even so, there were dramatic spatial variations. By 1966 there were 3.8 people per car in Surrey but still only 11.2 in Glasgow Coatbridge (Plowden, 1971). The general increase in access to speed at this time was also underlined by the building of the motorway network which started with the opening of the 8-mile Preston bypass in 1958 (which was to become a part of the M6) and the first 72 miles of the M1 in 1959.[20] Britain can now lay claim to being a mobile society in the North American sense, but even in the 1990s car ownership levels have reached no more than 403 cars per 1,000 people, compared with 589 per 1,000 in the United States. (However, it is also worth remembering that in Britain the motor bus, which first came into operation in 1903, has had a compensating and largely unsung history as a mover of people.)

Again, unlike the United States, the aircraft did not come into general use as a mass passenger carrier until comparatively late on (Wohl, 1994). Although passenger services were instigated in the 1920s it was not until the 1970s and the advent of package tourism to Europe that the aircraft became a general means of travel. However, it is important to note that the aircraft had had a much more general impact on the popular imagination long before it came into general use both as a symbol of modernity and as a source of new perspectives.

New networks of instantaneous communication were also coming into being gradually replacing the telegraph. Bell's telephone was first exhibited in Britain in 1877. Although exchanges had opened in most major cities by 1882 (beginning in London in 1879) and an extensive network had developed by 1892, this did not signify any mass take-up of the telephone. Even in the 1880s, London had fewer subscribers than most major North American cities, or even Paris. By 1913 only 663,000 phones were in use in the whole of Britain (*1990b*). Indeed, usage of telephones was restricted to the middle and upper classes until well after the Second World War; it was not until the 1970s that telephone ownership began to become general and not until the 1980s that more than three quarters of British households had access to a telephone. Further, long-distance telephoning was relatively unusual for many decades, partly because of the local origins of the British telephone system. This slow diffusion of telephones was in marked contrast to the United States and was chiefly the result of different, more class-based perceptions of the telephone, the monopoly powers of the Post Office and the efficiency of the mail and telegraph systems (de Sola Pool, 1977; Fischer, 1992).

Light   In the United States electrical lighting was at first used chiefly in downtown shops and streets: 'the streets of the downtown entertainment districts . . . were by 1900 literally bathed in electric light' (Nasaw, 1992, p. 275). But residential areas were still usually lit by gas. It was not until after 1910 that electric lighting started to be used on a wide scale in urban areas and by 1930 'the majority of urban dwellers had electric lights' (Nye, 1990, p. 303) (although it was not until later still that rural electrification really began to bite). What is clear is that from an early date electric lighting had become a standard element of the North American urban experience, especially through street lighting and the use of electric lighting to create urban spectacles such as the Great White Way in New York (Nye, 1990). Thus, the novelty of electric lighting quietly faded (but see Marvin, 1986).

In Britain, by contrast, the progress of electric lighting was clearly slower, hampered by the lack of electrical power. For example, in Manchester in 1914 only one in 15 of the inhabitants of the administrative area supplied by the Manchester Electricity Department lived in houses which were either heated or lit by electricity. By the mid-1920s this figure had risen to one in seven and by the mid-1930s to one in two. These figures were probably good, compared with the nation as a whole. For example, as late as 1938, in many Welsh rural areas, wax candles and paraffin were still the main forms of lighting and in some remote Welsh rural areas rushlights and tallow-tip candles could still be encountered (Luckin, 1990).

Other new inventions based on electricity and light had a more dramatic impact, most particularly the cinema. In 1894 Edison unveiled the kineto-scope in Britain, and in 1896 a cinematograph was set up in London. By 1914 the cinema was already a major industry with somewhere between 4,000 and 4,500 picture houses and audiences counting in the millions. Cinema attendance reached a peak in 1939, a year in which 5,000 picture houses sold 20 million tickets a week (meaning that about 40 per cent of the population went to the cinema at least once a week, and about a quarter twice a week) (Robson, 1990). The invention of television took some of the characteristics of cinema into the home. Transmissions began in Britain in 1936 but it was not until television revived after the Second World War, in 1946, that it began to become popular as a cultural medium. In fact, at first the number of licences grew slowly, to 45,564 (in a population of approximately 50 million) by 1948. The catalyst that sparked mass ownership was clearly the Coronation of Elizabeth II in 1953. Over

20 million members of the population watched this event on television, nearly 8 million in their own homes and well over 10 million at the homes of friends (Briggs, 1985). By 1956, the year when commercial television first started broadcasting (Sendall, 1992) and broadcasting hours were significantly extended, 'the ownership or rental of a television set was passing through and out of the stage of being a matter of status' (Corner, 1991, p. 6). Certainly, by the late 1960s, when over 16 million licences were issued, television had become the principal instrument of public information and cultural identity.

Power   Finally, there is the history of power. In many parts of the world, electricity took on an almost mythical status (Carey, 1989). As a symbol of progress and modernity, 'electricity seemed to ensure a brilliant future for civilisation. Authors in the popular press referred to it as white magic that promised an electrical millenium' (Nye, 1990, p. 66). Cities like Berlin, New York and Chicago with their enormous power-generating capacity were thought of as 'electropolises'. Further, between 1880 and 1920 electrical power became increasingly important worldwide as the source of power for local traffic systems, the elevator, the radio and the cinema, and, increasingly, elaborate lighting displays.

However, in Britain the adoption of electricity as a routine source of power was actually quite slow:

> domestic use of electricity made no rapid advance in England, partly because only about two per cent of homes were connected to the mains in 1910 and partly because the cost remained high; a number of progressive power undertakings . . . were just beginning to cut charges from 8d to ½d a unit in 1914 when war intervened. (Burnett, 1986, p. 214)

Even in 1931, one article reported that 'of 10½ million houses in this country, less than 30 per cent are wired, and not 1 in 1000 is all-electric. There are nearly 8 million houses to go for, most of which are either within reach of distributing mains or in areas in which main-laying would prove profitable' (cited in Luckin, 1990, p. 52).

As a result electrical domestic appliances also spread slowly, especially compared to the United States (Hayden, 1981; Tichi, 1987). Thus Britain's 'grand domestic revolution' (Hayden, 1981) was, in effect, postponed until after the Second World War. Part of the reason for this slow domestic spread was that coal and gas remained cheap and easily accessible resources. Part of it was that domestic servants were still used to a much greater extent than in other countries like the United States, thus negating the need for many middle-class women to turn to 'time-saving' devices until the 1920s and 1930s. And part of it was the lack of constant, central power supplies. This latter problem began to be solved in 1926 by the enacting of a bill to establish a National Grid. Construction of the Grid ended in 1933 with fully 3,000 miles of high-voltage transmission lines and another 1,000 miles of lower-voltage lines connected up. By 1935 the Grid was in operation (although it was not until 1938 that it was fully integrated) (Hughes, 1983). The Grid both brought down the price of electricity and gave an enormous boost to British industry. But it was not until the period between 1945 and 1950, and nationalisation of the electricity industry, that 'electricity established itself in a growing number of urban areas and penetrated more deeply into hitherto poorly served county districts' (Luckin, 1990, p. 172).

None of this is to suggest that there were no advocates of the electrical sublime in Britain. There clearly were. Luckin (1990) has documented the rise of an 'electrical triumphalism' and the cult of electrical progress that sometimes seems every bit as pugnacious as its North American counterpart, although often with its own nuances (for example, a tendency to visions of a technological arcadia which would 'stimulate a second and cleaner industrial revolution, the decentralisation of mass production and a regeneration of a deeply depressed agrarian society' [Luckin, 1990, p. 11]). Further, this triumphalism was widely promoted, especially, in a domesticated form, to housewives through advertisements, journals and the Electrical Association for Women. But the opposition to the encroachment of electricity, especially in the form of pylons and power lines, was much greater, often predicated on romantic themes of neo-arcadianism and nature mysticism that had originated in the previous century, and before. The power of these discourses was sufficient to affect the enthusiasm for electricity in Britain.

Synthesis These changes in the machinic complexes of speed, light and power were, by themselves, remarkable. However, I think it would be possible to argue at rather greater length than I will here that their effects were essentially a continuation of tendencies set in train in the nineteenth century.

So far as the machinic complex of speed is concerned, there seems little reason to believe that consciousness of time and space altered radically from the later nineteenth century (Kern, 1983). Of course, the population did pay more attention to ever-finer durations of time, a necessary skill to deal with ever-finer timetables, but this was a quickening, not a qualitative change. Again it might be argued that panoramic perception was strengthened (especially by the invention of the cinema) rather than altered. The effects of the general speed-up on texts also continued apace (often taking on extreme forms as in Futurism), as did the modernisation of the subject. Metaphors of progress and circulation continued to abound.

So far as the machinic complex of light is concerned, a similar continuity between the late nineteenth and the twentieth century can be found. The spread of artificial lighting and the colonisation of the night continued apace.[21] In J.B.S. Haldane's (1925, cited in R. Williams, 1990, p. 36) words, 'the alternation of day and night is a check on the freedom of human activity which must go the way of other spatial and temporal checks'.[22] Perceptions of the new landscapes of night space – Virilio's

(1991a) 'false day' – created by artificial light also began to stabilise in at least three ways. First,

> electrification made possible a new kind of visual text, one that expressed an argument or view of the world without writing, solely through suppressing some features of a site and expressing others. The new rhetoric of night space edited the city down to a few idealised essentials. It underlined significant landmarks and literally highlighted important locations. By night, the spectators could grasp the city as a simplified pattern. The major streets stood out in white bands of light, the tall buildings shone against the sky, and other important structures such as bridges hung luminously in the air, outlined by a string of bulbs. The city centre blazed its importance . . . and the corporations erected electrical signs to proclaim their products and their importance. (Nye, 1990, p. 60)

Second, cultural workers like visual artists began to represent this new world in their work, often as a kind of 'electrical sublime'. As the work of artists like Hopper and O'Keefe attests, 'most of the important painters of the early twentieth century attempted to paint the city at night' (Nye, 1990, p. 76). Third, the city at night began to be perceived as just as real, or even more real, as the city in the daytime: lighting served to recover streets and buildings not only from dimness but also from banality (Nye, 1990, p. 61). Lighting became essential to glamorise the city; even poorer areas could take on a different kind of nuance (Nye, 1990). Thus night and light became intertwined. Not surprisingly Walter Benjamin's urban phantasmagoria of dream spaces was only strengthened by these kinds of developments. The intensity of surveillance resulting from the widespread use of artificial light had also grown.

However, perhaps, the most important developments in the effects of the machinic complex of light emanated from the development of cinema, and then television and video, the basis of the industries of the image and spectacle that now dominate our culture, whose industrialised images have, in effect, become the 'raw material of vision' (Virilio, 1989, p. 66).[23] The most notable of these developments was clearly the simple speed-up of the image: 'the very name of the new medium identified its effects – moving pictures' (Kern, 1983, p. 117). Early viewers were fascinated by any moving image, 'by the speed effects of light' (Virilio, 1989, p. 32), and subsequent advances in editing added to the breathlessness of many presentations. Another related effect was the new ways in which the passage of time could be conceived as a result of movement and editing:

> Chronological development gradually did away with the longeurs of the old photographic pose; the architecture of the set, with its spatial mass and partitions, supplanted free montage and created a new emphasis. Rather like my granddaughter, who, when she moved from one room of her flat to another, used to think that a different sun was shining into each one, so the cinema marked the advent of an independent and still unknown cycle of light. And if it was so hard for the photographs to move, this was above all because the operation of moving cinematic time – of preserving its original speed in an old, static and rigidly ordered environment – was as astonishing for these early pioneers as it was difficult to invent. (Virilio, 1989, p. 13)

Finally, cinema produced an 'aesthetics of astonishment' (Gunning, 1989) by making visible something which could not exist otherwise (Vasseleu, 1991; Virilio, 1994), through a process of re-cognising the familiar: 'opening up new possibilities for exploring reality and providing means for changing culture and society along with those possibilities. . . . All this is summed up in Benjamin's notion of the camera as the machine opening up the optical unconscious' (Taussig, 1993, pp. 23–4).

However, it is a moot point whether the advances in photography signalled by the cinema actually constituted a major shift in the machinic complex of light. Many of those who have investigated the prehistory of the cinema would want to insist that the subject had already been prepared for these developments over many decades and that, in a certain sense, the changing formation of the subject played a crucial role in the invention of cinematic technology by producing a new 'language' of spatio-temporal corporeality. In a previous section, we have already seen how that language was constructed – to begin with out of the bodily disciplines stemming from bio-political and anatomo-political imperatives, and then subsequently out of a problematising of these very impositions. In turn, this process of problematising led to a new, more mobile subject which was both more attentive and more distracted, and less concerned with the exact dividing lines between interiority and exteriority. Bruno (1993) insists that this new 'cinematic' subject actually developed in tandem with changing urban geographies which also emphasised circulation and spectacle:

> Thrown into the rhythm of the metropolis, a field of forces in motion, the body is affected. As a result of the flow of impressions, the optical montage, and the fluctuating nature of the metropolitan space, the unity of the body disintegrates. The subject becomes a fragmented body in space, a 'desiring machine'. When a nomadic dynamic prevails within a transitory space of traversing sites, one does not end where the body ends. . . .
>
> If we believe that 'whatever its particular function, the film produces a pleasure akin to that of the travelogue' (Doane, 1985, p. 42) we can go further and assert that cinematic pleasure is more than the unique product of a textuality produced in enclosed darkness of the apparatus – Plato's cave; it literally belongs to a wider territory. . . .
>
> Cinematic pleasure belongs to the range of erotic pleasures of the nomadic gaze first known to the traveller and the *flâneur* and then embodied, by way of panoramic spatio-visuality, in the modes of inhabiting space of transitorial architectures. . . .
>
> Embodying the dynamics of journey, cinema maps a heterotopic topography. Its heterotopic fascination is to be understood as the attraction to, and habitation of, a site without a geography, a space capable of juxtaposing in a single real place several possible incompatible sites as well as times, a site whose system of opening and closing both isolates it and makes it penetrable, as it forms a type of elsewhere/nowhere, where 'we calmly and adventurously go travelling' (Benjamin, 1970, p. 236). (Bruno, 1993, pp. 56–7)[24]

One might even question whether the advent of television, and subsequently video with its ability to 'time shift' (Cubitt, 1991) and its natural supplementarity, signify a new language of spatio-temporal corporeality. Each of these inventions seems to entrench (although they may elaborate) the language invented in the nineteenth century. Further, like the cinema, they are still essentially mimetic media that correspond to the optical wavelength of the spectrum (Crary, 1990).

So far as the machinic complex of power is concerned, a similar continuation of its effects can be found from the nineteenth century. Instantaneity was extended as electrical and communication networks continued to burgeon. The re-metaphorisation of the body as an electrical flow was continued (see Armstrong, 1991). Electricity continued to galvanise the practices of capitalism. By the middle of the twentieth century, the modern city was 'inconceivable without electricity' (Ward and Zunz, 1992, p. 11).

However, it has also been shown that the three machinic complexes of speed, light and power had quite different histories in different spaces. Using the example of Britain, it has been possible to show a quite different trajectory in a number of cases. Technocracy and Fordism never took on the extreme forms typical of North America and, in different guise, other parts of Europe (Ross, 1991). In North America, functionalist streamlining, prominent machinescapes and the work of novelists like Dreiser, Norris, London or Williams (Tichi, 1987) and artists like Sheeler (Lucic, 1991) gave shape to the values of speed and machine energy. In continental Europe, Bauhaus, Futurism (and especially Marinetti's celebration of the motor car), celebrations of 'Americanism' (Wollen, 1993) and the early Le Corbusier's vast utopian structures did the same. In Britain, in partial contrast, these values never came to a full flowering (but see Forty, 1986).

The Late Twentieth Century: Mobility

I want to argue that, beginning in the 1960s in most western countries, it becomes possible to begin to talk about a new synthesis of speed, light and power (which I have called mobility) resulting from the growth of what can be called 'active' machinery. No longer is it possible to see the human subject and the machine as aligned but separated entities, each with their own specific functions. No longer it is possible to conceive of the human subject as simply 'alive' and the machine as just so much 'dead labour', the two linked only by their capacity for movement.

This realisation is prompted by important changes in the machinic complexes of speed, light and power. First, the machinic complex of speed begins to transmute. In particular, there has been a massive increase in the volume of travel in and between western cultures. This is coincidental with the general democratisation of the automobile and the aircraft and is perhaps best illustrated by the case of mass tourism. By 1989 there were 400 million international arrivals a year, compared with 60 million in 1960. There were between three and four times this number of domestic tourists worldwide (Urry, 1990). Further, much of the population will travel somewhere to gaze upon it and stay there for reasons basically unconnected with work. Travel is now thought to occupy 40 per cent of available 'free time'. If people do not travel they lose status: travel is the maker of status. It is a crucial element of modern life to feel that travel and holidays are necessary. 'I need a holiday' is the surest reflection of a modern discourse based on the idea that people's physical and mental health will be restored if they can get away from time to time. (Urry, 1990, p. 5)

Communication technology has also been the subject of a surge with a consequent massive increase in the volume of indirect communication. Satellite communication (Jayaweera, 1983) and the fibre-optic cable, in conjunction with the computer, have revolutionised telephony, which has metamorphosed into 'telecommunications', involving not just voice messages but also high-speed data transfer, fax, and the like. The advent of the mobile telephone is likely to lead in time to direct person-to-person communication with no time lags.

It might just conceivably be argued that this transmutation is simply a continuation, by other means, of nineteenth-century themes. The same thought cannot be applied to the complexes of light and power (Hayward, 1991). Thus the machinic complex of light has seen a virtual trans-formation, which we might call, following Virilio (1994), the 'automation of perception'; an automation symbolised by the computer, the fibre-optic cable, the laser and the increasing use of the non-visible spectrum found in image technologies like computer-aided design and graphics, synthetic holography, flight simulators, computer animation, robotic image recognition, ray tracing, texture mapping, motion control, virtual reality helmets and gloves, magnetic resonance imaging, multispectral sensors, medical imaging and the like (Crary, 1990; Vasseleu, 1991; Mitchell, 1992). As Wollen (1993, p. 64) puts it:

the invention of the computer . . . has transformed the entire field of image production. We are now in the first phase of video-computer productions. In the 1920s Dziga Vertov described the camera as a mechanical eye; now it is the mechanical eye of an electronic brain. Indeed, the camera itself has been transformed. It is now simply one option within a whole range of sensors and information-recording devices, some visual, some non-visual. Images can be produced by means of x-rays, night vision, thermal, magnetic, electronic spin and a host of other kinds of sensors. The camera (film or video) is simply the one that still most closely appropriates 'natural vision'. Sensors are no longer hand-held or mounted on tripods with humans attached to them, looking down view finders. Their motion and action can be remote-controlled. They can circle the earth in satellites and transmit from within the human body.

These new image technologies have four consequences. First, they relocate vision to a plane severed from a human observer:

Most of the historically important functions of the eye are being supplemented by practices in which visual images no longer have any reference to the position of a observer in a 'real' optically perceived world. If these images can be said to refer to anything, it is to millions of bits of electronic mathematical data. Increasingly visuality will be situated on a cybernetic and electromagnetic terrain where abstract visual and linguistic elements coincide and are consumed, circulated and exchanged globally. (Crary, 1990, p. 2)

Second, they have produced, in conjunction with radar, radio and micro-wave technologies, new possibilities for surveillance. Delanda (1991) writes of the growth of new systems of 'panspectric' surveillance that are replacing panoptic systems, in which the visual is redefined to include more of the spectrum, both up and down, of a new non-optical (or rather extended optical) intelligence-acquisition machine based on 'dark light'.

Third, the relation of the subject to these new technologies is no longer the relation of the active to inactive. Increasingly the subject scans a real-time simulated field of action of which the body (or the observing body) is a component. Thereby, 'thereness' is redefined. This fusion of human and machine has gone farthest in the military sphere (Delanda, 1991):

the fusion is complete, the confusion perfect; nothing now distinguishes the functions of the weapon and the eye; the projectile's image and the image's projectile form a single composite. In its tasks of detection and acquisition, pursuit and destruction, the projectile is an image or signature on the screen, and the television picture is an ultrasonic projectile propagated at the speed of light. (Virilio, 1988, p. 83)

In turn,

the disintegration of the warrior's personality is at a very advanced stage – looking up s/he sees the digital display (opto-electronic or holographic) of the windscreen collimator; looking down, the radar screen, the onboard computer, the radio and the video screen, which enables him [sic] to follow the terrain with its four or five simultaneous targets and to monitor his self-navigating Sidewinder missiles, fitted with a camera or infra-red navigating system. (Virilio, 1988, p. 84)

Fourth, machines begin to 'see for themselves'. They achieve what Virilio (1994, p. 60) calls a 'sightless' or 'artificial' vision created 'by the machine for the machine . . .: having no graphic or video-graphic outputs, the automatic perception prosthesis will function like a kind of mechanised imaginary.' Or as Tagg (1992, p. 19) puts it: 'the images are neither visible nor viewed.'

Finally, there is the machinic complex of power. Here again enormous change has been generated, symbolised by the microchip and the computer. The history of the microchip and computer and cybernetics is now so well known that it hardly bears repeating. More important has been its recent history, and especially the increasing importance of software compared with hardware, and the consequent rise of 'artificial' intelligence. However, most importantly, as artificial intelligence has grown as an area of inquiry, so it has started to cast off the anthropocentrism of its earlier history, and has moved towards a view that artificial (or infra-human) intelligence is not a simulation of human intelligence but has to be understood as an 'other' order of intelligence (Dreyfus, 1992), as 'liveware':

it emphasises the commonality of human and infra-human intelligence on the one hand, and on the other hand it inspires a respect for infra-human aspects of intelligence by illuminating their immense sophistication and complexity as against the relative simplicity and mechanical reproductivity of the uniquely human aspects. (Preston, 1992, p. 19)

That these three different machinic complexes are now in the process of merging is nowhere better illustrated than by the case of the melding of the computer with old and new image-recording technologies (Wollen, 1993). The new integrated systems already include the following characteristics: access to a database of stored images in an electronic memory, with all the consequent possibility of combination with images from different sources; generation of images and text by computer; simulations of the 'real world'; hybrid imaging; and connection with new modes of transmission and reception. In turn the possibilities arising out of this melding open up new problems, especially the appropriate forms of logic and aesthetic:

> The first requirement is the development of a heterogeneous theory of meaning, open rather than closed, involving different types of sign, and bringing semantics together with hermeneutics, reference with metaphor. The second is a specific (formal) theory of intertextual meaning, the way in which re-contextualisation changes meaning, the double hybrid coding involved in quoting, plagarising, grafting and so on, the back and forth of meaning between texts. (Wollen, 1993, p. 67)

The changes in these three, once different, machinic complexes begin to offer us glimpses of a 'cyborg' culture of mobility in which machines constantly pose the problem, 'What counts as a unit?' (Haraway, 1991a, p. 212):

> Modern machines are quintessentially microelectronic devices. They are everywhere and they are invisible. Modern machinery is an irreverent upstart god, mocking the father's ubiquity and spirituality. Writing, power and technology are old partners in western stories of the origin of civilisation, but minaturisation has changed our experience of *mechanism* . . . our best machines are made of sunshine; they are all light and clean because they are nothing but signals, electromagnetic waves, a section of a spectrum, and these machines are eminently portable, mobile. . . . People are nowhere near so fluid, being both material and opaque. Cyborgs are ether, quintessence. (Haraway, 1991a, p. 153)

Cyborg culture is no longer concerned with mimetic, analog media (that constitute a point of view) but is establishing its own active actant reality (Poster, 1990). In the process the human subject is being modernised so that it is able to cope with this new order of reality in which machines are as active as human subjects, in which there is a very high degree of interactivity between machines and humans, and even in which, in certain cases, machines become parts of the human subject's body (as, for example, in the case of 'smart' materials like artificial pancreatic cells and 'menotic' implants that integrate with the host tissues [Coghlan, 1992]). There are, in other words, both new kinds of bodies and a technologising of the human body, events which are marked by a refiguring of human potential and an increasingly abstract awareness of the body as network and system (Armstrong, 1991). Thus it now becomes possible to consider a new contract between humans and machines and machinery and humans. This

contact has been described by many commentators in quasi-apocalyptic
tones in ways which even feminist writers like Haraway do not always
entirely avoid; as betokening the 'fourth discontinuity' between humans
and machines (Mazlish, 1993), as signifying the growth of a 'third nature'
of 'information flows, creating an information landscape which almost
entirely covers the old territories' (Wark, 1994, p. 120), or as heralding the
Third Machine Age (Mandel, 1978; Jameson, 1991):

> if motorised machines constituted the second age of the technical machine,
> cybernetic and informational machines form a third age that reconstructs a
> generalised regime of subjection; recurrent and reversible 'humans–machines'
> systems replace the old nonrecurrent and nonreversible relations of subjection
> between the two elements: the relation between human and machine is based on
> internal, mutual communication and no longer on usage or action. (Deleuze and
> Guattari, 1988, p. 3)

Now, this style of techno-writing is clearly open to abuse. It can and does
lead to 'Boys' Own' hyperbole of the worst kind:

> It is ceasing to be a matter of how we think about technics if only because
> technics is increasingly thinking about itself. It might still be a few decades before
> artificial intelligences surpass the horizons of biological ones, but it is utterly
> superstitious to imagine that the human dominion of terrestrial culture is still
> marked out in centuries, let alone in some metaphysical perpetuity. The high
> road to thinking no longer passes through a deepening of human cognition, but
> rather through a becoming inhuman of cognition, a migration of cognition out
> into the emerging planetary technosentience reservoir. (Land, 1992, p. 218)

But it is not necessary to go all the way towards all-seeing and clearly
masculinist fantasies of a world 'run without human interaction' (Strathern,
1992a, p. 161) in which the male body is disembodied, only to return as a
pure, de-spatialized, machinic gaze (Doane, 1993). It is possible to think
about the Third Machine Age in another, more prosaic and less
disembodied way (H.M. Collins, 1990). Then, it is possible to argue that
our relationship to machines has changed for three reasons (Sheehan and
Sosna, 1991). First, machines have got better at mimicking us through
more complex and rarefied behaviour. Second, we have become more
'charitable' (Gellner, 1974) to the strangeness of machines, both in the
sense that we are more likely to welcome 'mechanical strangers' (H.M.
Collins, 1990) and in the sense that we are more likely to behave like
machines ourselves. For example, we might adjust our writing style to the
new machines, as Innis (1951) and Carey (1989) document for the case of
the telegraph and press reporting in an earlier era. Third, our image of
ourselves becomes more like our image of machines. For example,

> Man's [sic] nature is indeed so malleable that it may be on the point of changing
> again. If the computer paradigm becomes so strong that people begin to think of
> themselves as digital devices on the model of work in artificial intelligence, then,
> since for the reasons we have been rehearsing, machines cannot be like human
> beings, human beings may become progressively like machines. During the past
> two thousand years the importance of objectivity, the belief that actions are
> governed by fixed values; the notion that skills can be formalised; and in general

that one can have a theory of practical activity, have gradually exerted their influence in psychology and in social science. People have begun to think of themselves as objects able to fit into the inflexible calculations of disembodied machines. (Dreyfus, 1979, cited in H.M. Collins, 1990, p. 189)

What seems clear is that our current ways of 'representing' a more mobile Third Machine Age, even in a form that is rather less dramatic and contains greater elements of continuity with the past than some authors might acknowledge, are not equal to the task. In part, this is a matter of the newness of much of the relevant machinery, which has not yet had time to become culturally 'bedded in'. In part, it is also because of the nature of the new machinery, which does not lend itself to conventional representations. Thus to a degree at least, it is possible to agree with Jameson (1991, p. 45) that one problem is that this new active, actant machinery, unlike older forms of machinery like the railway engine or the aircraft or even the electrical turbine, does not 'represent motion but can only be represented *in motion*'. Much the same problem occurs in the case of the depiction of new actant subjects which are *hybrids*, humans *and* machines in actant couplings.

This is why the notion of structure of feeling is so crucial. It is able to capture the importance *and* 'thisness' *and* liminality of much new experience and, at the same time, the difficulty of representing it in theory and in practice. The notion also suggests that in particular periods a general change of style is needed. It is this change of style which is the subject of the next two sections of this chapter.

The Unsettling: Travelling Between History and Geography

This brief history of the development of an emergent structure of feeling that I have called mobility is, I would claim, a necessary prologue to a consideration of current theoretical debates in the social sciences and humanities around poststructuralism, postmodernism and postcolonialism. In particular, I would claim that these debates are saturated by the 'landscapes' of the machinic world that I have attempted to outline in the previous section and that these landscapes provide both a means of asking new questions *and* a set of resources to answer them. For example, these landscapes provide a good deal of the basic vocabulary in which these debates are couched. Put at its crudest, this vocabulary describes the conditions of modern life as a mobile topology. From the tropic 'elements' of this topology new chronotopes can then be constructed. Six of these elements come to mind. The first element is *flow*, 'flows of energy that irradiate, condense, intersect, build, ripple' (Lingis, 1992, p. 3). The second element is *networks*. As Mulgan (1991, p. i) has pointed out:

The late twentieth century is covered by a lattice of networks. Public and private, civil and military, open and closed, the networks carry an unmanageable volume of messages, conversations, images and commands. By the early 1990s the world's population of 600 million telephones and 600 million television sets will have been joined by over 100 million computer workstations, tens of millions of home computers, fax machines, cellular phones and pagers. Costs of transmission and processing will continue their precipitate fall. (Mulgan, 1991, p. 6)

Social orders act by recording, channelling and regulating the flow of energies through these networks. The third element is *power*. The modern world is under the sway of powerful forces like capitalism and the state whose effectiveness depends on their ability to mobilise resources in war-like power struggles of deterritorialisation and reterritorialisation which reach down even to the capillary level. This power is both potential and determined (Massumi, 1992a). The fourth element is *boundaries*. The modern world is increasingly seen as decentralised and fragmented, whether the subject is states, capital, bodies, machines – or subjects. Space therefore takes on critical importance as both a territorialised battlefield and a zone of mixing, blending, blurring, hybridisations – both striated and smooth. The fifth element is *absence*. How is it possible to understand a world in which the event is always plural (A. Benjamin, 1993), can no longer exist independently because it is always filled with the echoes of other events pulsing through the network, in which every attempt to make a point is foiled by its own traces? In other words, presence, perspective and the whole visual metaphor on which so much knowledge is based become suspect (Jay, 1993). The final element is *time*, but now time becomes a complex and multiple phenomenon which respects no master narrative (Adam, 1990).[25]

What seems clear is that these and other tropic elements, drawn from the practical affordances which have been made available by the machinic complexes of speed, light and power which I outlined in the previous sections of this chapter, are being used in different combinations to produce new intellectual redescriptions of the world, descriptions that are concerned with redrawing the boundaries between what Marx (1956, p. 272) called 'the world of men' and 'the world of things', what Veblen called 'the animate and the inanimate' (cited in Seltzer, 1992, p. 3), and what Haraway (1985, p. 153) calls 'the physical and non-physical'. In what follows, I will simply list some of the chief moments in this developing 'ontology', as if the process of rediscription could be described as a composite whole, rather than as a set of more or less loosely connected parts.

(1) There is little sense to be had from making distinctions between time and space – there is only *time-space*. Attempts to privilege either time or space, suggesting that one or the other is the signature of an age, for example, make only limited sense (for example, Soja, 1990). First of all mobility takes up both space and time, one of the elementary insights of a time-geography now either forgotten or misunderstood (*1980a*).[26] Second, even if in some mystical past it had been possible to analytically separate space and time, in the contemporary world 'the notions of space as enclosure and time as duration are unsettled and redesigned as a field of

infinitely experimental configurations of space-time' (Emberley, 1989, p. 756). If there is a view of time and space that this corresponds most closely to, it is probably Bergson's (1950) view of time-space as a permanently moving continuity, a qualitative multiplicity (Deleuze, 1988; Game, 1991).

(2) In contemporary societies, *mobility* has become the primary activity of existence (Prato and Trivero, 1985). This is a perspective that has a long philosophical history, of course, one which is to a large extent consequent on the rise of machinic landscapes. For example, we can trace a direct line of descent back from modern poststructuralist authors to their precursors like Nietzsche, Heidegger, Bataille and Blanchot.[27] Running through these authors' work is the hum of mobility. Thus, in Nietzsche there is the conception of the world as a constant becoming of a multiplicity of interconnected forms. It is quite clear that, to an extent, Nietzsche took this idea from what he considered to be the world around him as well as the world of the text. 'Nietzsche speaks of the "haste and hurry now universal . . . the increasing velocity of life", of the "hurried and over-excited worldliness" of the modern age' (cited in Prendergast, 1992, p. 5). For him, the modern individual faces a crisis of assimilation because of the 'tropical tempo' of this modern world.

> Sensibility immensely more irritable; . . . the abundance of disparate impressions greater than ever; cosmopolitanism in foods, literatures, newspapers, forms, tastes, even landscapes. The tempo of this influx *prestissimo*, the impressions erase each other; one instinctively resists taking in anything, taking anything deeply, to digest anything; a weakening of the powers to digest results from this. A kind of adaptation to the flood of impressions takes place: men unlearn spontaneous actions, they merely react to stimuli from the outside. (Nietzsche, 1967, cited in Prendergast, 1992)

In other words, 'with the tremendous acceleration of life, mind and eye have become accustomed to seeing and judging partially or inaccurately, and everyone is like the traveller who gets to know a land and its people from a railway carriage' (Nietzsche, 1983, cited in Prendergast, 1992).

This same absorption into this new world can even be found in Heidegger's notion of encountering/letting it show up (Dreyfus, 1991). As Dreyfus (1992) has brilliantly shown, what in Heidegger is depicted as a primordial way of being actually reflects a profoundly modern experience of encountering equipment, the ground for which is prepared in *Being and Time* and elaborated on in Heidegger's later work on the 'total mobilisation' of all beings.[28]

Even in writers a little closer to the Parmenidean tradition, which reaches its acme in the inexorable working-out of Hegelian dialectic, there is the same concern with mobility.[29] Simmel, for example, takes up Marx's concerns with the general speed-up in the circulation of commodities and the consequent 'agitation' of modern life and Nietzsche's idea of modern anti-aesthetic distraction as a central feature of the modern world and links them together in his familiar critique of an 'impatient' modern urban life:

It is true that we now have acetylene and electrical light instead of oil lamps; but the enthusiasm for the progress achieved in lighting makes us sometimes forget that the essential thing is not the lighting itself but what becomes more visible. People's ecstasy concerning the triumph of the telegraph and the telephone often makes them overlook the fact that what really matters is the value of what one has to say, and that, compared with this, the speed or slowness of the means of communication is often a concern that could attain its present status only by usurpation. (Simmel, 1978, p. 482)

The same kind of concerns about this new 'mobile, swirling landscape' (Prendergast, 1992, p. 5) can be found in the work of Walter Benjamin (a writer for whom, of course, travel was fundamental [Kraniauskas, 1994]), especially in the by now overly familiar figure of the *flâneur* who becomes an extinct species but 'only by exploding into a myriad of forms, the phenomenological characteristics of which, no matter how new they may appear, continue to bear his traces, as ur-form. This is the "truth" of the Flaneur, more visible in his after-life than in his flourishing' (Buck-Morss, 1989, p. 346). Again the links with mobility are clear:

Around 1840 it was elegant to take turtles for a walk in the arcades (this gives a conception of the tempo of Flanerie). . . . By Benjamin's time taking turtles for urban strolls had become enormously dangerous for turtles, and only somewhat less so for Flaneurs. The speed-up principles of mass production had spilled over into the streets 'waging war on Flanerie'. *Le Temps* reported in 1936, 'Now it is a torrent where you are tossed, jolted, thrown back, carried right and left.' With motor transportation still at an elementary-stage of evolution, one risked being lost in the sea. . . . The utopian moment of Flaneurie was fleeting. But if the Flaneur has disappeared as a specific figure, the perceptive attitude that he embodied saturates modern existence, specifically, the society of mass consumption. In the Flaneur, we recognise our own commonest mode of being in the world.
  Benjamin wrote, 'the department store is [the Flaneur's] last haunt. But Flaneur as a form of perception is preserved in the characteristic fungibility of people and things in mass society, and in the merely originary sketch provided by advertising, illustrated journals, fashion and sex magazines, all of which go by the Flaneur principle of 'look, but don't touch'. If mass newspapers demanded an urban readership, more current forms of mass media loosen the Flaneur's essential connection to the city. It was Adorno who pointed to the station-switching behaviour of the radio listener as a kind of aural Flaneurie. In our time, television provides it in optical, non-ambulatory form. In the United States, particularly, the format of news programmes approaches the distracted, impressionistic, physiognomic viewing of the Flaneur, as the sights purveyed take one around the world. And, in connection with world travel, the mass tourist industry now sells Flaneurie in two- and four-week packets. (Buck-Morss, 1989, pp. 344–6)

But three more recent authors suffice to make the case about the apparent primacy of mobility. First, there is Virilio's work on speed, the 'dromocratic' revolution and the emptiness of the quick (Virilio, 1975, 1983, 1986, 1989, 1990, 1991a, 1991b, 1994). So far as Virilio is concerned we live in the 'age of the accelerator' in which 'power is invested in acceleration itself' (Virilio, 1983, p. 45). For Virilio speed has many effects. It consumes subjectivity, leading to 'the disappearance of consciousness as a direct perception of the phenomena that informs us about our existence'

(Virilio, 1991a, p. 23); it also alters the nature of time and narrative, making 'everyone a passer-by, an alien or a missing person' (Virilio, 1989, p. 28); it even drives place out of space so that 'speed is a non-place and the users of transit-spaces, transit-towns (like airports), are spectral–tenants for a few hours instead of years, their fleeting presence is in proportion to their unreality and to that of the speed of their voyage' (cited in M. Morris, 1988, p. 6). Second, there is Deleuze's work on nomadism, as something that happens between, only temporarily occupying a space and imposing no fixed and sedentary boundaries (Deleuze and Guattari, 1988; Bogue, 1989; Massumi, 1992a; Hardt, 1993). The nomadic subject traverses points of pure intensity in migratory fashion:

> Nomadic thought is a distribution of singular points of possible actualisation/ individuation/conductivity. 'Nomad thought' does not immure itself in the edifice of an ordered interiority; it moves freely in an element of exteriority. It does not suppose an identity; it notes difference. It does not respect the artificial division between the three domains of representation, subject, concept and being; it replaces restrictive analogy with a conductivity that knows no bounds. (Massumi, 1988, p. xii)

Finally, Sternberger (1977) and Schivelsbuch (1986) provide an account of an aesthetics of disappearance, of the landscape as a blur, a streak viewed from a moving platform, 'no longer experienced intensively, discretely, but evanescently, impressionistically – panoramically, in fact' (Schivelsbuch, 1986, p. 189).

(3) This emphasis on ceaseless mobility can be coupled with another related characteristic of the contemporary world, its im-mediation, its lack of presence, its *indirectness*. As Derrida (1987) and others have been concerned to show, indirect communication,[30] symbolised by the telephone, the postcard and various other ways of communicating at a distance, is a fundamental constant of contemporary everyday life. As Wood (1990) has pointed out, this view also has a long philosophical history in the work of Kierkegaard, Adorno and Heidegger (again), as a study of the relationship between subjectivity and linguistic expression. This emphasis on indirect, elliptical communication extends, of course, into the visual realm. Contemporary ways of seeing are indirect, formed via the television and the camera, thus providing an 'imposture of immediacy' (Virilio, 1989, 1994).

(4) The emphasis on ceaseless mobility and indirectness produces a quandary. How can categories, thought of as fixed in space and time with fixed qualities associated with them, be understood in a dynamic, de-territorialised world which admits of no stable entities and so can only be understood in terms of difference, not identity? Three categories cause particular problems: the subject, the body and place. Certainly in a world of mobility, the *subject* is a problematic category. If subjects are nomadic, fractured, heterogeneous and indirectly connected, then how can they be understood as agents at all? The answer would appear to be to refigure subjectivity as nomadic points, constantly shifting through strings of subject

positions/contexts, in some of which it is possible to speak, in others not, according to prevailing regimes of power (Grossberg, 1992).

> The nomadic subject exists within its nomadic wandering through the ever-changing places and spaces, vectors and apparatuses of everyday life . . . coherent subjectivity is always possible, even necessary, and always effective, even if it is also always fleeting. The subject's shape and effectivity are never guaranteed; its agency depends in part on where it is located, how it occupies its places within specific apparatuses, and how it moves within and between them. . . . The nomadic subject always moves along different vectors, always changing its shape. But it always has an effective shape as a result of its struggle to win a temporary space for itself within the places that have been prepared for it. Nomadic subjects are like 'commuters' moving between different sites of daily life, who are always mobile but for whom the particular mobilities or stabilities are never guaranteed. (Grossberg, 1988, p. 384)

(5) The problem of boundedness is also important in discussing the body. As Lyotard (1992, p. 50) puts it, 'what is a body . . . in tele-graphic culture?' The capacities of bodies have been extended in numerous ways by the new technologies. Equally, they have been intruded into and upon by developments like genetic engineering, new reproductive technologies, prosthetics and plastic surgery (Shilling, 1993; Synott, 1993). Parts of bodies can even be added or subtracted. Yet mobility is not just concerned with the extension of, or intrusion into, the body. It also concerns three other things. First, and most importantly, this history of speed, light and power calls on the human subject to abandon ideas of a Cartesian inner chamber and to enter into what Merleau-Ponty (1962) calls 'the flesh' of the world, a mutually tactile space in which the body and the world communicate with each other in a doubled and crossed situating through which both body and world are ramified. Second, this history leads to greater awareness of the mimetic qualities of the body, especially because of the ability of modern mimetic machines to make copies which in turn influence what is copied (W. Benjamin, 1979; Taussig, 1993).[31] This produces a new 'violence of perception' which operates directly on the body. Third, it is important to remember the sheer *joy* of bodies in movement. Movement is a sensuous pleasure in itself. It might even be possible to speculate that the general increase in mobility has highlighted and underlined this joy, as in the rise of walking and running as activities for and in themselves (Wallace, 1993). In other words human awareness of embodiment may have increased as technology has expanded.

(6) The same problem of understanding boundedness also crops up in the case of place. What is *place* in this new 'in-between' world? The short answer is – compromised: permanently in a state of enunciation, between addresses, always deferred. Places are 'stages of intensity', traces of movement, speed and circulation. One might read this depiction of 'almost places' (Kolb, 1990) in Baudrillardian terms as a world of third-order simulacra, where encroaching pseudo-places have finally advanced to eliminate places altogether. Or one might note the increase in 'hyper-modern' 'non-places' (Augé, 1995), where traffic circulates in perpetuity.

Or one might record places, Virilio-like, as strategic installations, fixed addresses that capture traffic. Or, finally, one might read them, as Meaghan Morris (1987) does, as frames for varying practices of space, time and speed. There is, in other words, 'no stability in the stopping place' (Game, 1991, p. 166). No configuration of time-space can be seen as bounded. Each is constantly compromised by the fact that what is outside can also be inside (Massey, 1992).

This problem of 'almost places' (Kolb, 1990) becomes particularly acute in the case of contemporary cities (Shapiro, 1992). It has become increasingly difficult to imagine cities as bounded space-times with definite surroundings, wheres and elsewheres. In Virilio's (1989) terms, they have 'exploded'. As Robins (1991, p. 4) puts it:

> We can now talk of process of globalisation or transnationalisation in the transformation of urban space or form. Manuel Castells describes the advent of the 'informational city', and identifies 'the historical emergence of the space of flows, superseding the meaning of places'. Others have described the same process in similar ways suggesting that 'things are not defined by their physical boundaries any more'. In the place of a discrete boundary in space, demarcating distinct space, one sees spaces co-joined by semi-permeable membranes, exposed to flows of information in particular.

Nowhere does this difficulty of imagining boundedness become clearer than in the increasing mobility and fluidity of the cultures of urban centres, an urban swirl of 'uprooted juxtapositions' (Gitlin, 1989, p. 104), sometimes expressed in totally inadequate phrases like 'multiculturalism' (Hannerz, 1992).

(7) This same problem of understanding the boundedness of place can be phrased in a more general way: 'all places have borders, even in their centres, and the deconstructive task is to find these borders and the ways in which our constructions cross them while denying that they do' (Kolb, 1990, p. 157). This problem of *borders* has been posed in a number of interrelated ways. It can be worked through as the interaction between the 'global' and the 'local' (whatever these words now mean) (*Theory, Culture & Society*, 1990; S. Hall, 1991a; King, 1991; Massey, 1991; Sklair, 1991; Hannerz, 1992). For example, in the realm of culture,

> new communications technologies are mobilised in the (re)creation and maintenance of traditions, cultural and ethnic identities which transcend any easy equation of geography, place and culture, creating symbolic networks throughout various . . . communities. (Morley, 1991, p. 14)

It can also be worked through as the increasing primacy of indirect communications and relationships, and the consequent blurring of the always questionable distinction between *Gemeinschaft* and *Gesellschaft* (B. Anderson, 1983; Poster, 1990; Wood, 1990; Calhoun, 1991). Again, it can be worked through as a questioning of the commonly constructed distinction between a world of intimate lived experience and large-scale social systems (Latour, 1993):

But *is* there really this distinction? Is it not more correct to say that people increasingly have their world of lived experience *within* corporate actors? Does not an expanding share of face-to-face relations arise, unfold and develop *within* organisations? (Hernes, 1991, p. 124)

Last, but not least, it can be worked through as a questioning of the distinction between the public and the private as separate spheres of existence (G. Rose, 1993; Squires, 1994).

(8) Perhaps this very indeterminacy of boundaries has led to a new form of institutionalising moment in which systems of domination are based on forms of dispersed power, rather than systematic and generalised forms of repression. This thought, prefigured in the work of the situationists, Foucault, Guattari and others (Plant, 1992), is crystallised by Deleuze (1992), who suggests that we can now see the advent of 'societies of control'. Deleuze distinguishes between three different kinds of societies. The first is societies of sovereignty whose goals and functions were to tax rather than organise production, and to rule on death rather than to administer life. Then came Foucault's disciplinary societies, which reached their height in the early twentieth century. They instituted vast spaces of enclosure – prisons, hospitals, schools, houses, asylums, factories – that moulded people. Now, new forces knock on the door, societies of control in which ultra-rapid forms of free-floating strategies of control modulate people:

> The numerical language of control is made of codes that mark access to information, or reject it. We no longer find ourselves dealing with the mass/ individual pair. Individuals have become 'dividuals', and masses, samples, data, markets or banks. Perhaps it is money that expresses the distinction best since discipline always referred back to minted money that uses gold as a numerical standard, while control related to floating rates of exchange, modulated according to a rate established by a set of standard currencies. The old monetary mole is the animal of the spaces of enclosure, but the serpent is that of societies of control. We have passed from one animal to the other, from the mole to the serpent, in the system in which we live, but also in our manner of living and in our relation with others. The disciplinary man was a discontinuous producer of energy, but the man of control is undulatory, in orbit, in a continuous network. [Thus,] what counts is not the barrier but the computer that tracks each person's position – licit or illicit – and effects a universal modulation. (Deleuze, 1992, pp. 5–7)

(9) The above musings might seem like another Deleuzean dark fantasy of acceleration,[32] moving ever faster both backwards and forwards between a Futurist or Vorticist manifesto and a cyberpunk novel (McCafferty, 1991). But the point is that all is not necessarily lost. In societies based on *strategies* of control the 'tactical' everyday practices of 'consumers' may take on a new potency. *Tactics* are, after all, *mobile* ways of using imposed systems: 'immersible and infinitesimal transformations'; 'swarming activity', 'jostlings for position'; 'errant trajectories' drawing partly unreadable paths across space (de Certeau, 1984, p. xviii). They are pure processes without textual form or realisation: 'doings' (*arts de faire*) like speaking, walking,

reading, poaching and tricking (de Certeau, 1984, 1986, 1988, 1991; Frow, 1991; Giard, 1991) which insinuate themselves 'into the other's place, fragmentarily, without taking it over in its entirety, without being able to keep it at a distance' (de Certeau, 1984, p. xix). They are 'challenging mobility that does not respect places', through a 'delinquent narrativity' made up of spatial stories/practices (de Certeau, 1984, p. 130).[33] 'In other words, they are practices through which people can escape without leaving' (Frow, 1991, p. 57). But de Certeau is no romantic: 'in our societies, as local stabilities break down, it is as if, no longer fixed by a civilised community, tactics wander out of orbit, making consumers into immigrants in a system too vast to be their own, too tightly woven for them to escape from it' (de Certeau, 1984, p. xx). In other words, mobility now has to challenge mobility.

There are some obvious objections to this developing ontology. I want to list four of them. The first and most important objection is that it is simply a means of carrying on the project of modernity, but under another name. For example, Crary's (1990, 1994) history of the reorganisation of the understanding of the observer during the nineteenth century can be read as simply a totalising account of the construction of a subject who is up to the 'new reality of fleeting images, exchangeability, flow. Modernity is here defined by the mobility of signs and commodities, the circulation of "vast" new amounts of visual imagery and information. Ultimately, for Crary, both modernity and modernism (as an aesthetic movement) are anti-referential' (Doane, 1993, p. 4). Certainly it cannot be denied that some of the writing which clings to the Parmenidean tradition of thinking does tend to reproduce simple modernist ideas in which the shock of a general speed-up threatens to disrupt (usually white, male) identity.[34] But this ontology can be used in another way, as the work of writers like Haraway shows. There, whilst the importance of current socio-technical changes as a new kind of metaphorical ground is acknowledged, the importance of situatedness is also never lost.

The second and related objection is that this ontology can easily be hijacked by being reduced to one theme. Thus Bataille might have reduced it to a carnival of ecstasy and loss. Baudrillard might want to drive to the astral extreme, to a new phase of excess and exorbitance. Harvey might want to write about the effects of the speed-up of circulation time. Jameson might want to write about the Kantian sublime. Derrida might want to write of distant voices and telegramaphones. Lyotard might want to write of telegraphy. And so on. The danger is real but the point is that these are all aspects of this developing ontology. They can never be a whole, single story. In the new elliptical ontology, there is no such be-all or end-all. There are only lines of flight.

A third objection is that this sketch of movement, displacement and rapidity, for all its commitment to the 'other', still bears too many traces of Eurocentrism, ethnocentrism and androcentrism. It is a rich, white, heterosexual man's ontology, more akin to tourism than travel; the 'suggestion of free and equal mobility is itself a deception, since we don't all have the same access to the road' (Woolf, 1993, p. 253; see also G.B. Pratt, 1992). What about the four-fifths of the world's population that live on one-quarter of its assimilative capacity (one-fifth of whom 'live in an unimaginable spiral of despair that the wealthy fifth would not tolerate for 10 seconds' [O'Riordan, 1992, p. 16]) who cannot get up to speed because of lack of income, immigration laws and so on? Or as Kolb (1990, p. 159) puts it, 'where will the septic system go?' Again, what about the ways in which mobility has been gendered? 'Western ideas about travel and the concomitant corpus of voyage literature have generally – if not charac- teristically – transmitted, inculcated, and reinforced patriarchal values and ideology' (Van den Abbeele, 1992, pp. xxv–xxvi). The objection is not that the dispossessed do not travel. They clearly do. It is rather that mobility is 'still the wrong language' to describe such activity because it implies that we are all 'on the road "together"' (Woolf, 1993, p. 235). 'The fantasy of escape from human locatedness' (Bordo, 1990, p. 142) is indulged, even cosseted. This is clearly a charge with some force. Certainly it is the case that the ceaseless migrations of contract workers, the waves of immigrants and refugees, and many of the multitude of women travel in different, more constrained ways, to a different purpose (Appadurai, 1990). But it is not immediately clear that the developing ontology of mobility has to be appropriated in a conservative way which would debar these kinds of experiences of what is still a rather mobile 'immobility' (Grossberg, 1988; Radway, 1988; Woolf, 1993). It should be possible to arrive at 'a less utopian, less arrogant, and less messianic theorisation of movement, a positive cosmopolitanism that remains meticulously aware of localities and differences, a more convincing ethic of flow' (Miller, 1993, p. 33). Further, it might also be argued that this ontology of mobility has provided some of the most useful ways of trying to decolonise western ways of thinking by showing that margins and centres, others and selves, exiles and metropoles, are always interconnected. Last, this kind of ontology simply does not lay claim to describing the world in quite the way of previous ontologies. It

> is not a description 'which reveals some hidden level of forces, waiting to be enlisted on our behalf. It can free us for more creative gestures and resistances, but it does not by itself take a stand on the issues of the day. To think it does is to change it into a haughty irony and hidden totality. (Godzich, 1986, p. xi)

A fourth, and perhaps most telling, objection is that this ontology is not as radical as it at first may appear. It simply substitutes one kind of additive infinity, that of the disciplinary society with its logocentric idea that things have finite characteristics and that the world is therefore full of individuated and countable things, for another kind of additive infinity, that of the society of control, where there is 'a grammatological under- standing of recurring operations: a constant substitution of functions such that terms simultaneously express and displace previous terms' (Strathern,

1992b, p. 8). Thus a Euro-American frame of meaning is still reproduced. It is this criticism that leaves me at something of a loss, most particularly because if the Euro-American frame of meaning is this pervasive, then it is difficult to know how we can ever move outside of it.

To summarise, it seems that the developing ontology of mobility that I have attempted to outline above can simply reproduce Eurocentrism, ethnocentrism and androcentrism. But the change of perspective it offers can also offer some gains by reformulating old questions and asking new ones. Five of these gains are apparent. The first is that we are forced to go beyond accounts which insist on regarding the importance of place and placement as self-evident in modern everyday life, as though somehow a mere statement of recognition is enough to provide an anchor, a certitude. Thus Meaghan Morris (1987, p. 23) can lay down the following challenge:

> The problem of feminism might be summed up by Prato and Trivero's claim in 'The spectacle of travel' that transport ceased to be a metaphor of Progress when mobility came to characterise everyday life more than the image of 'home and family'. Transport became 'the primary activity of everyday existence'. Feminism has no need whatsoever to claim the home and family as its special preserve, but it does imply a certain discretion about proclaiming its present marginalisation. . . . Yet the sort of claim made by Prato and Trivero does not seek its grounding in historical truth – even the truth of approximation – and this makes feminist criticism more difficult. It is meant, perhaps, to be a billboard, a marker in a certain landscape. It marks a recognisable trajectory along which it becomes possible not only for some to think their lives as a trip on a road to nowhere (etc.), but for others to think home-and-family as a comfortable, 'empowering' vehicle. . . . So rather than retreating to the invidious position of trying to contradict a billboard, feminist criticism might make it its own.

A second gain is that an ontology of mobility forces us to think about borders as productive, as, in Heidegger's (1977) terms, the places from which things unfold rather than stop, both away from and towards us. Borders therefore become processes, living pedagogies which force us to reconsider (Giroux, 1992; Tomas, 1992), here and there, margins and centres, convergences and overlaps, exiles and evicts (Hebdige, 1993; I. Chambers, 1994). It is no surprise, then, that we now pay more attention to the 'aesthetics of almost' (Stafford, 1991) to postcolonial, 'third' or 'contact' spaces, to the spaces in-between here and there, to margins and centres, to convergences and overlaps, to exiles and evicts which can all provide some kind of ground for meeting and dialogue – the creation of 'a speaking and signifying space large enough to accommodate difference, entertain rapprochement' (Carter, 1992, p. 147). For example, such an aesthetics can provide us with a way to escape from a growing 'ethnic absolutism' by concentrating on 'fractal patterns of cultural and political exchange that we try to specify through manifestly inadequate theoretical terms like creolisation and syncretism' (Gilroy, 1992, p. 193). The middle, the mediator and the hybrid are all OK.

A third gain is the way in which subjectivity necessarily has to be retheorised in terms of subject positions, strung out in time-space (Spivak,

1987, 1990). In place of a preoccupation with identity as a fortified or imploded monologue, we have to retheorise identity as a space-time distribution of hybrid and dialogical subject-contexts, constantly being copied, revised, enunciated; performed (Bhabha, 1986; S. Hall, 1991b; *1991b*; Wagner, 1991) in ways which constantly question the notions of interiority and exteriority and thereby constantly release fixed categories (like woman) from fixed referents (Butler, 1990, 1992; Grosz, 1994b). Thus, 'nomadism is therefore neither a rhetorical gesture nor a mere figure of speech but a political and epistemological necessity' (Braidotti, 1994, p. 182). Perhaps the best way to think of this kind of subject is in a Deleuzean way as a fold, an 'inside space' (where 'one becomes master [*sic*] of one's own speed' [Deleuze, 1993, p. 123]), which is always co-present with an outside space:

> To think means to be embedded in the present-time stratum that serves as a limit: what can I see and what can I say today? But this involves thinking of the past as it is condensed in the inside, in the relation to oneself (there is a Greek in me, or a Christian, and so on). We will then think the past against the present and resist the latter, not in favour of a return but 'in favour, I hope, of a time to come' (Nietzsche), that is, by making the past active and present to the outside so that something new will finally come about, so that thinking, always, may reach thought. (Deleuze, 1988, p. 119)

A fourth gain is the way in which time-space becomes a central component of the work of refiguration of the subject. The world of mobility which the new ontology is intended to dwell on/in is difficult to represent in older perspectivalist terms (Jay, 1992), due in part to the dislocation of absolute time and space. New figurations of the subject, like Haraway's 'cyborg' and other 'inappropriate(d) others', are meant to work through this problem of re-presentation of time-space whilst, at the same time, refiguring the subject and acting thereby as political interventions. They are all

> terms for that excessive critical position which I have attempted to tease out and rearticulate from various texts of contemporary feminism: a position attained through practices of political and personal displacement across boundaries between socio-sexual identities and communities, between boundaries of discourses by what I like to call the 'eccentric subject'. Such excessive and mobile figures can never guard what used to be called a 'fully human community'. That community turned out to belong only to the masters. However, these eccentric subjects can call us to account for our imagined humanity, whose pasts are always articulated through translation. History can have another shape, articulated through differences that matter. (Haraway, 1991a, p. 63)

A number of writers other than Haraway have tried to invent new chronotopes[35] based on re-presenting mobility as a positive process of meeting and encountering rather than as the circulation of sequestered and singular bodies. For example, Gilroy in *The Black Atlantic* (1993a) tries to make the shift from the chronotope of the road to the chronotope of the crossroads. Again, he settles on the image of ships in motion across the spaces between Europe, America, Africa and Asia as a central organising symbol for this enterprise and as my starting point. The image of the ship – a living, micro-cultural, micro-political system in motion – is empirically important. . . . Ships immediately focus attention on the middle passage, on the various projects for redemptive return to an African homeland, on the circulation of ideas and activists as well as the movement of key cultural and political artefacts: tracts, books, gramophone records and choirs. (Gilroy, 1993a, p. 6)

A final gain has been the way in which the difficulty of getting a perspective on a more mobile world has produced a questioning of orthodox modes of representation like science and narrative, at least as they have been conventionally understood. Science is in question because it is now revealed as a culture without any hard and fast protocols. Narrative is in question because it has too often been subsumed to the one true story, whether directly or by implication (Doel, 1993). The result is a move towards a new horizon of intelligibility which is perhaps best grasped in the work of de Certeau on what he calls 'science/fiction'.[36] This is a modest attempt to constitute a 'logic' (or heterology) which gives the Other a part and recognises that there is a constant tension between it and its overt representation in discourse. It is therefore a kind of journey (de Certeau talks constantly of voyages, journeys, travelling) in which the 'walk reveals the goddess' (Giard, 1991, p. 219). It is a kind of constant path-clearing. In using the metaphor of journeying/travelling so frequently, de Certeau is trying to point to three chief things. First, that there is a 'form of truth that is totally alien to me, that I do not discover within myself but that calls on me from beyond me, and . . . requires me to leave the realms of the human and of the sane in order to settle in a land that is under its rule' (Godzich, 1986, p. xvi). Second, he is trying to point to a sense of intellectual itinerary that comes with a recognition of the many forked paths and diversions reading and writing can take. Third, he is trying to point to a mobile sense of 'seeing': 'to travel is to see, but seeing is already travelling' (de Certeau, 1984, p. 26). Thus science/fiction is a third new space of reading/writing between science and fiction, involving elements of both: 'a mixture of narration and scientific practices' dependent upon the metaphor of travelling (Schirato, 1993).

This emphasis on new regimes of reading and writing based on journeying/travelling leads to new methods of writing based on journeys and travelling. These are hardly a new innovation, of course. Van den Abbeele (1992) provides a whole list of precursors, from Montaigne to Proust. Sieburth (1987), similarly, has pointed to the way in which Sterne consistently experimented with new modes of writing based in travel. What is most singular now is the attempt to write movement in a whole host of ways which involve, to adopt Marcus's (1992) list, both remaking the observed (through problematising the temporal and problematising perspective/voice) and revealing the observer (through making the text's conceptual apparatus explicit, through bifocality, and through critical juxtaposition). Each and every one of these devices involves the use of many different sites, both literally as specific places and metaphorically as different kinds of speaking position.

An Entire Future Geometry

In this section, I want to argue that the new structure of feeling that I have called 'mobility' is not just manifested in the higher intellectual realms of poststructuralist or postmodernist or postcolonialist theory, it is also to be found in intellectual work of a more practical, 'empirical' bent. I will therefore very briefly review some of the work which seems to me to have been influenced by this structure of feeling. This is not difficult to do. Research in the social sciences and humanities, especially but not only in cultural studies,[37] has become saturated with the vocabulary of mobility – from nomadic criticism and travelling theory through ideas of the ethnographer-as-tourist to the increasing use of metaphors based on maps, topography, billboards, networks, circuits, flows . . . the list goes on. But in particular, I will draw on work of an historical bent. This may seem a strange choice but I would suggest that it is historical work that is particularly likely to show the impact of the new structure of feeling. This is because I take it that, to a degree, history tends to project the concerns of the present on to the past, or, as W. Benjamin (1977, p. 128) puts it,

> for the materialist historian, every epoch with which he occupies himself [*sic*] is only a fore-history of that which really concerns him. And that is precisely why the appearance of repetition doesn't exist for him in history, because the moments in the course of history which matter most to him become moments of the present through their index as 'fore-history', and change their characteristics according to the catastrophic or triumphant determination of that project.

Thus, I think it is possible to see the past being rewritten, from the perspective of our cyborg culture, both in the terms of mobility and as a history of mobility. Indeed so great has been that rewriting that mobility is now coming to be seen as the normal historical state of affairs, and settlement as the problematic, 'other' category that needs to be explored.

Certainly, there is currently a massive outpouring of work concerned with the subject of mobility and the mobility of the subject and I cannot review it all. Rather I will simply make an indicative reference to certain areas of work under four main headings: speed, light, power and writing mobility.

Speed

The machinic complex of speed includes a number of different but interconnected forms of work. There is quite clearly a growing archive on the subject of travel and travellers stimulated in part by a general realisation that there have been few societies in which travel, contact and mobility have not been important (Helms, 1988) and many more societies, from colonial empires (Innis, 1950) to multinational corporations, in which travel, contact and mobility have been central. They have, in effect, drawn the diagrams of power. There is, first of all, work which considers travellers themselves down through history, in all their diversity. Clifford (1992) provides a bewildering list of missionaries, informants, mixed-bloods, translators, government officers, police, merchants, prospectors, tourists, ethnographers, pilgrims, servants, entertainers, migrant labourers and immigrants (to which, no doubt, could be added many other travelling figures: explorers, commuters, hobos and tramps, packmen, and so on). The underlying rationale behind this work is that these nomads can produce 'new spaces' which, although they are transient, can sometimes offer new possibilities. An important part of the study of travellers through history has concerned the study of women travellers. It is now realised that women were more mobile than has commonly been realised but mobile in quite different ways (M.L. Pratt, 1991; S. Mills, 1991; Blunt, 1994; Blunt and Rose, 1994).

Second, there is work on travel as a mode of being-in-the world. In particular, there is now more and more work using the *flâneur* as a basic category to interrogate the way in which a new ambulatory observer was formed in the nineteenth-century city through the 'convergence of new urban space, technologies and symbolic functions of images and products – forms of artificial lighting, new use of mirrors, glass and steel architecture, rail roads, museums, gardens, photographs, fashion crowds' (Crary, 1990, p. 20). Theoretical development and historical research, going hand in hand, have now shown that the category of *flâneur* is far too gender- and class-specific. Yet, at the same time, it contains some more general elements of a particular consumerist mode of being-in-the world (Buck-Morss, 1989; Corfield, 1990; Wilson, 1992) which have probably been most clearly developed in studies of the history (see Oasby, 1991; Buzard, 1993) and the current practices of tourists. This work which dates, in particular, from the influential book by MacCannell (1976) on the post-tourist is chiefly concerned with different kinds of traveller and travel experience. More generally it is concerned with different kinds of being in a mobile world and the different kinds of displaced self-understanding that result, chiefly in support of the argument that different kinds of tourist travel valorise the world in different ways (Urry, 1990, 1992; Game, 1991; Munt, 1994; Veijola and Jokinen, 1994). For example, MacCannell (1992, p. 5) argues that his work on tourism suggests that

> the current dialectic between the global versus local, or sedentary versus nomadic or any other dialectic that involves a contradiction between different levels of socio-cultural organisation, is about to be superseded. The emerging dialectic is between two ways of being out-of-place. One pole is a new synthetic arrangement of life which releases human creativity. The other is a new form of authority, containment of creativity, and control.

Third, there is work on the whole range of spatial practices that produce knowledge on and of mobility – maps, diaries, directories, guides, stories, poems, books, magazines, music, photographs, television programmes, videos and the like. In particular, the genre of travel writing – especially travel writing by women – is now coming under scrutiny as a moment in the construction of a particular kind of spatiality/narrativity (Domosh, 1991; S. Mills, 1991; M.L. Pratt, 1992; Blunt, 1994).

Fourth, there is a growing body of work (and especially ethnography) on the not quite/almost places of mobility – roads and railway lines, service stations and airports, hotels and motels, car parks and carports, shopping malls and heritage sites, as well as the media of mobility, like the automobile or the aircraft (for example, M. Morris, 1987; Augé, 1995). This is not to forget the extraordinary (and extraordinarily often forgotten) importance of the streets and street life (for example, Corfield, 1990; 1995h).

Fifth, there is now a yearly outpouring of work on the origins and meanings of electronic spaces. For example there is work on the communication spaces of the telephone, radio and fax (for example, Ronell, 1989). There is also work on the visual spaces of the cinema, television and video. More recently, a burgeoning amount of work has been appearing on the cyberspace of computers and computer networks and the new communicational techniques that have been made possible (for example, Poster, 1990; Benedikt, 1991; Wynne, 1991; Lea, 1992).

Sixth, there is the work on borders, frontiers, crossing points and crossroads to be found in the writings of Trinh T Minh-ha (1989), Rosaldo (1988), Flores and Yudice (1990), and others, from whence comes a realisation of the importance of the way in which spaces, which may well have been originally constructed as places of domination, in which difference and conflict were constructed and lived, also have the potential to become meeting places which promote different kinds of ethical spaces (perhaps this is part of what Derrida means when he writes of opening up new spaces of reading [Wood, 1990]), 'not quite, not white' spaces of 'hybridity and struggle, policing and transgression' (Clifford, 1992, p. 108). The importance of gender and race as transgressive categories becomes clear in these 'contact zones' (M.L. Pratt, 1991). More generally, the emphasis on such meeting spaces makes it possible to talk about the conditions under which communication can make space in-between (R. Price, 1990; Carter, 1992; Karras and McNeil, 1992; Gilroy, 1993a).

The current work on speed is perhaps best summarised by two papers. One is a study of the new nomads that traverse the United States (McHugh and Mings, 1991). Each year, hundreds of thousands of Americans and Canadians drive southward toward the sunshine in recreational vehicles, circulating around amongst a network of sites – campgrounds, national parks, resorts, and the like. These travellers are usually older, relatively well-off people. Opposed to the structured mobility of this group of nomads is Hebdige's witness to the travails of the homeless in New York City, seen through the lens of Wodickzo's Poliscar, a vehicle for the homeless which is 'a strategy for survival for urban nomads – evicts – in the existing economy' (Wodiczko and Luria, 1988, cited in Hebdige, 1993, p. 181). In one paper, the mobility of the centre, in the other the mobility of the margins, both acting to document and image the social structuring of mobility (Cresswell, 1993).

Finally, there is the extensive body of work on immigrant cultures. This last has, of course, existed for a long time. What is new are two things. To begin with, there is the almost/not quite normality of the migrant condition:

> This period of modernity has been characterised by the massive displacement of populations. We are almost all migrants; and even if we have tried to stay at home, the conditions of life have changed so utterly in this century that we find ourselves strangers in our own house. The true novelty is to live in an old country. But despite the normality of displacement, we find the migrant vilified. For alongside the fact of ethnic integration, we also witness a recrudescent nationalism, a yearning for the purification of racial roots and the extermination of alien elements. . . . In this situation it becomes more than ever urgent to develop a framework of thinking that makes the migrant central, not auxiliary to historical processes. We need to disarm the genealogical rhetoric of blood, property and frontiers and to substitute for it a lateral account of local relations, one that stresses the contingency of all definitions of self and the other, and the necessity always to tread lightly. Living in a new country is not an eccentricity; it is the contemporary condition. (Carter, 1992, p. 3)

Following on from this first point, migrant cultures are no longer seen as copies from an original, but as in constant interaction with 'home' cultures and, at the same time, evolving in their own ways, in part through contact with other cultures, often influencing the practices of their 'home' cultures as they do so (S. Hall, 1991a, 1991b; Ganguly, 1992; I. Chambers, 1994). These cultures are now seen as 'stratified' processes, their origins in question (Friedman, 1992), their destinations in suspension. They are crossroads at crossroads (James, 1992).

Light

Here I want to point chiefly to the growing literature on vision and visuality (H. Foster, 1988; Jay, 1993; Krauss, 1993). Much of this work has been stimulated by just the serial, reproducible image of still and cinema photography. In particular, there is now a large body of historical work on photography and the cinema and television. From this work, it is clear that these media have to be seen in at least three ways. First, they are an archive, albeit one that is open to many interpretations. As R. Porter (1991, p. 211) notes, in a discussion on the body and photography,

> we possess a photographic record now stretching back almost a century and a half of people's physical appearances. Once again, there is no need to belabour the misinterpretations which would result from a naive reliance on the veracity of visual images; of course, the camera lies or, more precisely, photographs are not snapshots of reality but, like, paintings, form cultural artefacts conveying complicated coded conventional signs to primed 'recorders'.
> But this caveat applies to some photographs more than to others. Posed portraits capture how people wish to be remembered, all scrubbed and dolled up

in their Sunday best. But Victorian photographers were also fond of taking 'documentary' street snapshots and these caught people in their everyday moments, gestures, and as a result recorded such aspects as body language and social space more informatively than any printed text. The photographic archive reveals and confirms a great deal about both the physical transformations of the human condition in modern times (ageing, deformities, malnutrition, etc.) and what Goffman has called 'the presentation of self' (body language, gestures, the appropriation of physical self). Photographs remain oddly underexploited as a historical resource.

The quotation is too innocent, of course, in that it neglects the power of the posed photograph to connote (Lalvani, 1993), or the way in which photographs were often a focus of urban expeditionary voyeurism. But the point is made.

Second, photographs are also a means of perception. They tell us about different regimes of visualisation according to which primary social processes and institutions function (Crary, 1990). For example, according to some commentators, we now live, or have lived until recently, in a society based on the semiotics of the spectacle (Debord, 1966). Whether this is the case or not, the idea has proved to have some currency in recent historical work as a model of the regime of the late nineteenth to mid-twentieth century, a model which makes it possible to locate certain other developments in the past, as in, for example, Richards' (1990) examination of late Victorian advertising or Crary's (1990) study of late eighteenth- and early nineteenth-century techniques of observation. In turn, the system of spectacle can be seen to be historically transient:

> Recently, Baudrillard has raised the possibility that capitalism has itself brought about 'the very abolition of the spectacular', by which he means that current technologies have far surpassed the spectacular system of representation. . . . Selling things has now become the domain of cybernetics, the modern science concerned with analysing the flow of information in electronic, mechanical pulses, blips on a television screen, and patented genetic structures count as quantifiable commodities; the days of spectacle may well be numbered. In the years to come it may turn out that the semiotics of spectacle played a transitional role in capitalist mythology. . . . For now it makes sense to render spectacle as one element among many in modern commodity culture, one manifestation of what Martin Jay has called the many 'scopic regimes of modernity'. (Richards, 1990, p. 258)

Third, photographs are a means of framing and constituting the body, and especially the body in motion. Thus Featherstone (1991, p. 178) has pointed to the way in which photography and film helped to create new standards of appearance and bodily presentation, at first chiefly for women but subsequently for men too, which would 'enable the body to pass muster under the camera'.

Power

Here I want to indicate the growing interest in electrical power, especially as a root metaphor in our societies, linked both to light (and the image) and to speed (and communication). This literature takes on three main forms. The first of these is quite straightforward. It is the growing literature on the social and cultural history of electrical power and the way in which

> in daily experience, adopting electricity changed the appearance and multiplied the meanings of the landscapes of life, making possible the street car suburb, the department store, the amusement park, the assembly-line factory, the electrified home, the modernised farm, and the utopian extension of all these, the world's fair. (Nye, 1990, p. x)

Such histories, which point to major differences in the ways in which electrical power was adopted and interpreted in different places, have now begun to burgeon (for example, Marvin, 1988; Luckin, 1990; Nye, 1990; Nasaw, 1992).

The second and third forms all concern the nexus between electricity and the concepts of the body, self and identity, and the subject. Thus the second form is the way in which work on the logistics and erotics of the body, self and identity and even the subject are described in terms of different forces and intensities. What was a psychoanalytic model (with interesting links to electricity) has become a general means of representing the social reproduction of desire and affect, and even, in the case of Deleuze and Guattari (1988), the 'body' of capital.

The third form concerns the articulation between the body, self and identity, and the subject and the information technologies of different eras. Thus Kittler (1990) suggests that the new information technologies of the turn of the century transformed the relationship between hand, eye and letter in such a way that the transition between the self that writes and the writing of the self was disputed, leading to new forms of writing and arche-writing of the kind that Derrida has tried to interrogate. More dramatically, Seltzer (1992) suggests that these new technologies put the anthropomorphism of writing to rest for all time and put in its place, through 'the violent immediacy promised by communication and control technologies operated by the electric signal or button . . . [a] pure performative that instantly connects conception, communication and execution'. This pure performative

> is legible, for instance in the rapid adoption of the electric chair and the 'deadly current' as the socially acceptable form of execution in the 1880s. . . . It is legible also in the communication technology of the telephone that could order or stay the execution. . . . And it is everywhere legible in the links between man-factories, death-factories, electric signals and body scents, and in the small marginal movement of the hand that, in effect, communicates execution. (Seltzer, 1992, pp. 11–12)

Poster takes this argument farther again, arguing that the new level of interconnectivity afforded by current electronic media and the success of electronically configured language have produced new forms of the body, self and subject in which 'the body . . . is no longer an effective limit of the subject's position' (Poster, 1990, p. 15) and 'new and unrecognisable forms of communicating are in formation' (Poster, 1990, p. 154). Possibly, possibly.

Writing Mobility

Finally, some note has to be taken of the problems of communicating mobility, of incorporating, to *précis* the intent of Walter Benjamin's significantly named *One Way Street* (1979), 'the outside world of gas stations, metros, traffic noises, and neon lights . . . into the text' (Buck-Morss, 1989, p. 17). These problems are, I think, extreme.

It is undoubtedly the case that communicating mobility demands a change in style of 'writing'. Indeed, as I have argued, that might be one of the ways in which this structure of feeling might be able to be described. Yet, on the whole, while declarations of intent have abounded, actual demonstrations have been rather thin on the ground. The reasons for this are not always clear. One may be that it is difficult to represent something that is not always meant to be open to representation. Ultimately, liminologies are, well, liminal. Another reason is that writing is not always the most appropriate form of representation of the elliptical world in which we now live, in part because it tends to be associated with relatively tight narrative structures (Goody, 1991). Communicating mobility may well demand the incorporations of other forms of expression than the written word, for example all kinds of visual and oral cues of the kind able to be used on laser discs, video, and so on – but we are not practised at these (Crawford and Turton, 1992).[38] A further reason is that by no means all of the possibilities of the new hybrid 'electric text' that melds texts and images in new software packages, hypertext, and so on, have been thought through. Finally, there is the problem of what metaphors to use to mark out a communicative scheme – journeys or roads, successions of places, billboards or landmarks, or even messages like postcards or electronic mail. We may still need narrative but it is clear, given this list of options, that traditional narrative is often ill-suited to communicating mobility.

This may, of course, be one of the reasons why some writers have turned to science for inspiration. This turn has taken two chief forms. There is, first of all, the emphasis on scientific metaphors as ways of thinking/writing mobility, as, for example, in the case of Derrida's use of cybernetic and, latterly, biogenetic themes (Johnson, 1993). Then, second, there is the enormous interest in science fiction, both because of its inherent motifs – technological sentience, hybridity, indeterminacy, transgression, and the like – and because of the examples found in the writings of authors like Delaney or Piercy of how to communicate these motifs (for example, A. Kuhn, 1990; Bukatman, 1993a, 1993b).[39]

The result of many of the writing experiments currently underway can, like much 'techno-art' (Pomeroy, 1991), be irredeemably awful, but given the plethora of worthy but dull academic publications it is difficult to criticise the impulse, if not the result, of these arguments. Further, they can work. I think of Meaghan Morris's 'At Henry Parkes motel' (1987), parts of Paul Carter's *The Road to Botany Bay* (1987) and *Living in a New Country* (1992), as well as more tangential works like Richard Price's *Alabi's World* (1990) or Susan Buck-Morss's *The Dialectics of Seeing* (1989), which have tried to write creatively, from many different positions, using a range of techniques to communicate the modern world's 'stereospecificity' (Johnson, 1993).

Conclusions

Clearly a chapter which is intending to describe a structure of feeling called mobility should not conclude. It should just keep on the move. But, just as clearly, academic convention suggests at least a few parting thoughts are in order.

I have tried to show the development of an emergent structure of feeling – a 'cultural hypothesis' – that I have termed 'mobility'. This almost/not quite intellectual 'project' is created from practices sedimented over many decades, even centuries, which therefore form a part of our pre-discursive imaginary as well as the symbolic realm. The structure of feeling therefore consists of both a series of 'questions' (a word that can only be used if questions are thought of as longings or desires) about the contemporary world and also the resources through which we must attend to this world. These questions are chiefly about the seemingly ever more permeable boundaries between humans and non-humans. In this chapter, I have concentrated on developing the image-concept of a mobile, 'cyborg culture' in which the boundaries between humans and machines have become ever more open to question, leading to an increasing emphasis on 'framing' the world in terms of actant subjects, machinic metaphors, and the like. But care needs to be taken with developing such an image-concept. Two caveats seem particularly important to register.

The first of these is that a cultural hypothesis like mobility can only be driven so far without breaking down. Some things are not as mobile as some writers like to claim: buses and trains are often late; the average speed of automobile traffic in London is less than 10 miles an hour; a large percentage of trips in Britain are on foot, and walking has probably never been a more popular recreation (Wallace, 1993). Again, many people in western societies are still hardly mobile at all; elderly people stuck in nursing homes, inner-city children who have never seen the sea though they live but a few miles from it; whilst, for all the population, waiting is an endemic fact of life (see Buck-Morss, 1989, p. 104, or Lash and Urry, 1993, on waiting). Then again, mobility requires paths, or roads, or airlines, or global digital highways. Mobility is not a free-for-all; it is guided by networks etched onto the ground, by air corridors, by frequencies, by maps, by itineraries, even by parking restrictions. Then, not least, every journey includes stops in places; continuity requires discontinuity (Game, 1991). In

turn, these stops may frame interaction at a more pedestrian pace: 'Loco-
motion. The slower the better. Stopping at question marks' (Sauer, 1956, p.
296). In other words, mobility is a cultural *hypothesis* which involves clear
and dangerous elements of exaggeration. On the other hand, it also has to
be asked whether the modern world can be understood (or even seen)
through a sedentary gaze.

But it is not just about exaggeration. The problem is more deep-seated
than that. It is a matter of gender. This is the second caveat. Feminist
writers like Woolf (1993) have argued that the idea of mobility is strongly
gendered and has to be appropriated in different ways before it can be used
effectively. Certainly, it is difficult not to come to the conclusion that many
of those who have written around mobility, like Deleuze and Guattari,
'have uncritically assimilated the modernist ethos of incessant self-
transformation, becoming, and psychic instability' (Best and Kellner,
1991, p. 107) and it is difficult not to come to the conclusion that part of
the reason for this is concerned with the gendered nature of their writing.
As Jardine (1984, p. 59) writes, 'when enacted, when performed [the
promises offered by Deleuze and Guattari's theory] are to be kept only
between bodies gendered male. There is no room for women's bodies and
their other desires in these creatively limited, mono-sexual, brotherly
machines.' Issues of intersubjectivity, and social connection more generally,
are simply not addressed[40] or are floated off into a cyberspace where, in the
latest version of the boys' adventure story:

> the earlier exploration of exterior space [is] now replaced by the full recognition
> of male narcissism in an interior journey, mirrored not merely in the face gazing
> into the monitor but, above all, in the interior oedipal language dialoguing in the
> circuitry of the mother board. (I. Chambers, 1994, p. 61; see also Springer, 1991,
> 1994; A.R. Stone, 1991)

This is why this chapter has relied so heavily on the work of writers like
Haraway, Latour and Strathern. Their writings add another dimension to
the structure of feeling I have called mobility for at least four reasons.
First, they are not caught up in the 'heady cartographic fantasy of the
powerful' (Ross, 1991, p. 148) in which some of the writing on mobility
tends to participate. For example, they do not play to the male fantasy of
the 'technobody' with its prosthetic add-ons, all meant to boost masculinity, which were such a prevalent theme of the 1980s, 'the enhancements
and retrofits . . . that boys always dreamed of having, but . . . were also
body-altering and castrating in ways that boys always had nightmares
about' (Ross, 1991, p. 153). In other words, these writings do not worship
'technology', either by celebrating it or by bewailing it. Insofar as
'technology' is seen as oppressive, it is as a part of the social organisation
of domination, as a part of new forms of regulatory authority.

Second, they do not write in ways which suggest an all-too-familiar
critical élitism. Thus, they do not tend to make the usual laments of the
western intellectual about the increasing pace of life, the spread of

homogeneity, fragmenting identities, fading attention spans or any of the other signs of incipient mental decomposition that apparently are companions to modernity. They are, in Haraway's phrase, 'ecstatic speakers' who are quite clear about the artifice of their ecstasy and the specificity of their speech. They are, in other words, trying to find the keys to connection, not to truth.

Third, notions like the 'cyborg', the hybrid or the mediator are all intended to take back some of the ground ceded to the technology as salvation, or doom, merchants. The ever more permeable boundaries between humans and machines are seen as not only a product of power relations but also as a site with the potential for contesting and reworking those relations. In other words, these writings believe in the power of transgression as well as regulatory authority, especially for women, who, stereotypically, are meant to be less technoliterate and more likely to be the victims of technology.

Fourth, these writings are important because they deny the opposition between a vaulting culture of technology and an untainted space of 'Edenic naturalism' (Ross, 1991). The opposition between technology, and society more generally, and nature, with human individuals at the hinge, is found to be groundless. Instead, what there is is a parliament of things which have different degrees and kinds of sentience. We can therefore move away from the question of humanism, with its species-centrism, and towards the question of new figurations of what it is to be 'the human in a post-humanist landscape' (Haraway, 1992a, p. 86) – or what Strathern (1992a) calls 'the aesthetics of personification'. In other words, entities become harder and harder to identify as identifiable entities. They are 'variable geometry' entities (Latour, 1993, p. 107). In turn, Latour argues that this state of affairs requires a new constitution which divides up beings, the properties ascribed to them, and their acceptable forms of mobilisation, in different ways. Or, as Strathern (1992a, p. 174) argues, we need to debate 'the kinds of things it is conceivable to think about in the late twentieth century'.

In turn, such a point of view quite clearly links to the growing 'leakiness of distinctions' (Haraway, 1985) in other domains as well; between not only the human and the technological world but also the human and the natural world (as well as 'within' the human world) (Sosna and Sheehan, 1991). Thus to 'boundary' debates on artificial intelligence, the extension of vision and prosethetics need to be added boundary debates on animal rights, *in vitro* fertilisation, transplants and genetic engineering. Debates like these have three functions. First, and most simply, they are the processes through which societies make culture explicit – through boundary-setting. Second, they bring into question standard modernist futures since they operate 'merographically' across divides which are normally considered to be connected, even analogous, but also different, not equal, which now do not appear to be as different, or as unequal, as they once did – just as the objects of attention (the technosphere, nature) no longer appear as different as they once did. Thus, 'facts' of the technosphere can become 'facts' of

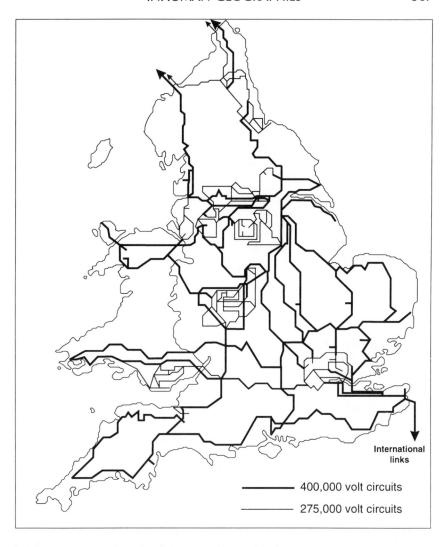

Figure 7.1 *The UK National Electricity Supply Grid, 1994*

culture and vice versa and 'facts' of nature can become 'facts' of culture
and vice versa. In turn, the kind of analogies and metaphors we can draw
on no longer perform well and others have to be created. Thus, conventional notions of 'the human' (but not necessarily humanity) are
gradually overturned because there is *no permanent representation*. Third,
the 'human' can no longer be seen as a hinge between the poles of the
technological and the natural. As Latour, (1993, p. 137) puts it:

> If the human does not possess a stable form, it is not formless for all that. If
> instead of attaching it to one constitutional pole or the other, we move it closer to
> the middle, it becomes the mediator and even the intersector of the two. The

human is not a constitutional pole to be opposed to that of the nonhuman. The two expressions 'humans' and 'nonhumans' are belated results that no longer suffice to designate the other dimension . . . we should be talking about morphism. Morphism is the place where technomorphisms, zoomorphisms, plausimorphisms, ideomorphisms, theomorphisms, sociomorphisms, psychomorphisms, all come together. Their alliances, and their exchanges, taken together, are what define the anthropos. A weaver of morphisms – Isn't that enough of a definition?

To summarise once more, the structure of feeling which I have attempted to outline is one which is an attempt to understand a world which is increasingly manufactured, increasingly far from a 'natural' environment (whatever that might be), a third rather than a second nature in which machines have their place. In the 1960s, Lewis Mumford used the word 'megatechnics' to describe this unprecedented stage of mechanisation:[41]

> In terms of the currently accepted picture of the relation of man [sic] to technics, our age is passing from the primeval state of man, marked by the invention of tools and weapons, to a radically different condition, in which he will not only have conquered nature but detached himself completely from the organic habitat. With this new megatechnics, he will create a uniform all-enveloping structure, designed for automatic operation. (Mumford, 1966, p. 303)

Nearly thirty years on, this kind of utterance seems to be both exaggerated (in the way in which it forecasts a phallocentric dominion over nature) and too cautious (in that it failed to foresee the birth of a new kind of hybrid nature). Yet the impulse to understand a manufactured 'microtechnic' world, and give voice to it, seems just as important. A change of style indeed.

Notes

This chapter was originally published in P.J. Cloke, M. Doel, D. Matless, M. Philips and N.J. Thrift, *Writing the Rural. Five Cultural Geographies*. Paul Chapman Publishing Ltd, London © 1994.

1. Because it perpetuates the idea that there are 'beginnings, enlightenments, and endings: the world has always been in the middle of things, in unruly and practical conversations, full of action and structured by a startling array of actants and of networking and unequal collectives' (Haraway, 1992b, p. 304). See also Latour (1993).

2. The point is that images like these are, are now *part* of the urban experience, not a 'reflection' of it. This is a point that Benjamin always wanted to make with his example of early twentieth-century photographs of signs reflected in water.

3. There are, of course, other machinic complexes (see below) that I could have drawn on, and most particularly sound (see Attali, 1991; I. Chambers, 1994, the rise of work on the history of radio, and the explosion of interest in popular music). The mechanical mediation of smell and touch are also still neglected (but see Claasen, 1993), but see recent work on the typewriter keyboard (for example, Bukatman, 1993b).

4. I use machinery and machinic in the widest possible sense here and in the rest of the chapter. The terms are not meant to imply a machinistic model of reality. Rather, they signify the existence of a set of machineries of desire (see Bogue, 1989, pp. 91–101) and they signal that nowadays 'our machines are disturbingly lively, and we ourselves frighteningly inert' (Haraway, 1991a, p. 144).

5. Raymond Williams (1977) makes a distinction between dominant, emergent and residual structures of feeling (see *1983b*).

6. It becomes clear, I think, that in his later work Williams may have had rather more in common with Derrida than is widely acknowledged.

7. One might also point to the increased national and international mobility of academics as another important factor.

8. The term 'style' is used here in the same sense as it is used by Wood (1990).

9. 'Non-humans are not "actors" in the human sense, but they are part of the functional collective that makes up an actant' (Haraway, 1992b, p. 331). I am aware that I am drawing the boundaries around what Latour calls 'quasi-objects' rather too tightly, if anything. This is for reasons of parsimony.

10. As will become clear, this viewpoint differs from that of many authors who believe that 'species' dividing lines are still clear-cut (for example, Benton, 1993).

11. I am trying here to signal an allegiance to Castoriadis's (1987) notion of magma.

12. Feenberg (1991) specifically links such codes to Foucault's notion of regimes of truth.

13. It is only a surprise that so many commentators seem to believe that Marx invented the term.

14. However, it is important to note that this expanded consciousness of space was not all one-way. The new large cities were often depicted as of endless extent, rather than as shrunken spaces.

15. At the same time, it is reasonable to suggest that the nature of darkness, and concepts and images of darkness, must have changed. See, for example, Baxandall's (1995) work on shadows. Later on, *film noir* specifically used light to create new forms of darkness, for example.

16. Note should be made here of Dickens' famous night walks (and especially his essay 'Night walks' in *The Uncommercial Traveller* [see Wallace, 1993]).

17. In following Crary's account here, I am, like Doane (1993), uneasy about his almost functionalist linking of changes in the subject with an accelerating modernity. In this account, I have tried to avoid Crary's excesses.

18. Foucault's notion of an 'optical unconscious' seems particularly useful here (see Jay, 1993; Krauss, 1993). So far as the sense of absent presence is concerned, other image technologies also heightened this sense, often through contrast between light and dark. Schivelsbuch (1988) shows how inventions of the early nineteenth century like the panorama (*c.* 1820) and the diorama (1822), and later the magic lantern and film, produced images that traded on the play between light and dark, day and night. 'The power of artificial light to create its own reality only reveals itself in darkness. In the dark, light is life' (Schivelsbuch, 1988, p. 221).

19. Foucault's notions of bio-politics and anatomo-politics fit well here (see Lalvani, 1993).

20. But Virilio (1991b) suggests that such a claim can be disputed. Whereas the freeway system can be regarded as a place of integration, doubling back on itself, the motorway system still chiefly consists of unique directional axes, intended to expel traffic. It is also important to remember, in this context, the role of the railway network in Britain.

21. Also, none of this is to suggest that night still does not hold its terrors, especially for women, as the numerous marches to regain the night attest.

22. In Britain, a large night-time labour force came into being, as did numerous incessant economic and social activities. By the 1970s 14 per cent of the UK workforce was doing shiftwork. In 1978 a 24-hour radio broadcasting service was set up and in the late 1980s all-night television broadcasting began. Again, in the late 1980s 24-hour shops on the American model became more and more common. (These figures cannot compare with those of the United States, where over 29 million people were active after 12 o'clock in 1980, where 24-hour radio broadcasting first started in the 1960s, where 24-hour television broadcasting started in the 1970s, and where there are now many 24-hour shops.)

23. There is no space here to note, in particular, the effect of advertising as a part of the developing technology of light (but see Taussig, 1993).

24. Bruno (1993, p. 37) makes much of the importance of cinema in expanding the space of

women, by allowing spatially constrained women spectators to 'go travelling', to reclaim 'forbidden pleasures' and to wander though 'erotic geographies'.

25. The old Newtonian linear time has, since Freud and Einstein, been replaced by a plurality of times (Balibar, 1972; Foucault, 1970; *1977b*, *1979d*, *1980a*; Major-Poetzl, 1979; Wilcox, 1987). Similarly, there has been a pluralisation of space (Lefebvre, 1991).

26. Time-geography has been chronically misunderstood in recent writings. It serves the purposes of this chapter well for two reasons. First, as an ecological approach, it makes no distinction between things. Hägerstrand was always clear that lifelines should apply equally to machines and animals as to human beings. Second, as an attempt to write mobility, Hägerstrand was always clear that he saw time-geography as an attempt to write a kind of musical score.

27. And, most especially, but running on a different track, Bergson.

28. This same modern experience of encountering passed off as a primordial way of being can, I think, be seen in other writers who have influenced debates on poststructuralism, postmodernism and postcolonialism. Most especially, there is Merleau-Ponty's idea of 'the flesh' and Bergson's ideas on matter and memory. In both cases being is profoundly im-mediated.

29. As well as other writers like Hobbes and Veblen (see Prendergast, 1992; Seltzer, 1992).

30. Derrida and Deleuze and Guattari are perhaps the chief contemporary exponents of this emphasis on indirect communication. For example, for Deleuze and Guattari, 'human language, rather than commencing with tropes of direct discourse, begins with indirect discourse, the repeating of someone else's words' (Bogue, 1989, p. 137). But again, the work of Bergson and Merleau-Ponty must be noted.

31. Through 'the unstoppable merging of the object of perception with the body of the perceiver and not just with the mind's eye' (Taussig, 1993, p. 25).

32. Interestingly, Deleuze writes approvingly of Hume: 'As in science fiction, one has the impression of a fictive, strange science-fiction world, seen by other creatures, but also the presentiment that this world is already ours, and these other creatures, ourselves' (cited in Bogue, 1989, p. 178, fn. 17).

33. Notice that de Certeau does not deny the importance of narrative. Like Carr (1986), he can see no alternative. Of course, for de Certeau every story is a travel story.

34. Most disappointing, of late, has been Brennan's (1993) use of this story. See also the story told by Frosh (1991).

35. A chronotope can be described as a time-space gate through which meaning must enter (Folch-Serra, 1990).

36. The idea of a science/fiction can be used in another way as well, to signify the construction of alternative theoretical worlds, rather in the manner of Deleuze:

he constructs imaginary worlds or alternative universes in the manner of a Borges or a le Guin, showing what reality would be like if it were made up of simulacra, virtual singularities and anonymous forces, or formless bodies and incorporeal surfaces. He invents paradoxical concepts . . . but rather than reinscribe these concepts within traditional texts, he uses them as the building blocks of an alternative world. (Bogue, 1989, p. 159)

37. Which, arguably, has been the subject area most influenced by poststructuralism, postmodernism and postcolonialism.

38. The increasing publication of graphic novels suggests another communicational idea.

39. I decided not to become involved in the debates on 'cyberspace' in this chapter (for example, Benedikt, 1991), but the notion clearly adds an extra dimension to debates on mobility.

40. Similar criticisms have been made from another angle, in work on science and nature. See, for example, Jordanova (1986, 1989); Driver and Rose (1992); G. Rose (1993).

41. By the 1960s Mumford had entered a more pessimistic phase. Perhaps his earlier more optimistic writings, especially *Technics and Civilisation* (1934), are in greater harmony with this chapter.

Selected Writings by
Nigel Thrift and Others

1975a. (with D.N. Parkes) 'Timing space and spacing time', *Environment and Planning A*, 7, 651–70.

1975b. (with J. Oakes) 'Spatial interpolation of missing data: an empirical comparison of some different methods', *Computer Applications*, 2, 335–55.

1977a. 'An Introduction to time-geography', *Concepts and Techniques in Modern Geography*, No. 12. Norwich: Geo-Abstracts.

1977b. 'Time and theory in human geography, Part 1', *Progress in Human Geography*, 1, 65–101.

1977c. 'Time and theory in human geography, Part 2', *Progress in Human Geography*, 1, 415–57.

1978a. (co-edited with T. Carlstein and D.N. Parkes) *Timing Space and Spacing Time* (3 vols). London: Edward Arnold.

1978b. (with D.N. Parkes) 'Putting time in its place', in T. Carlstein, D. Parkes and N.J. Thrift (eds) *Timing Space and Spacing Time. Volume 1*. London: Edward Arnold, pp. 119–29.

1978c. (with T. Carlstein) 'Afterword: towards a time-space structured approach to society and environment', in T. Carlstein, D. Parkes and N.J. Thrift (eds) *Timing Space and Spacing Time. Volume 2*. London: Edward Arnold, pp. 225–63.

1979a. (co-edited with R.L. Martin and R.J. Bennett) *Towards the Dynamic Analysis of Spatial Systems*. London: Pion.

1979b. (with R.L. Martin and R.J. Bennett) 'Future directions in dynamic modelling in geography', in R.L. Martin, R.J. Bennett and N.J. Thrift (eds) *Towards the Dynamic Analysis of Spatial Systems*. London: Pion, pp. 1–15.

1979c. 'Unemployment in the inner city: urban problem or structural imperative? A review of the British experience', in D.T. Herbert and R.J. Johnston (eds) *Geography and the Urban Environment. Volume 2*. Chichester: John Wiley, pp. 125–226.

1979d. (with D.N. Parkes) 'Time spacemakers and entrainment', *Transactions of the Institute of British Geographers*, NS4, 353–72.

1979e. (with K.P. Burnett) 'New approaches to travel behaviour', in P. Stopher and D.A. Hensher (eds) *Behavioural Travel Demand Modelling*. London: Croom Helm, pp. 116–34.

1979f. 'Limits to knowledge in social theory: towards a theory of human practice', *Australian National University, Department of Human Geography, Seminar Paper*.

1980a. (with D.N. Parkes) *Times, Spaces, Places. A Chronogeographic Perspective*. Chichester: John Wiley.

1980b. (with P. Keys) 'Industrial environments: a niche theoretic interpretation', *Urban Studies*, 14, 115–29.

1980c. 'Frobel and the new international division of labour', in J.R. Peet (ed.) *An Introduction to Marxist Theories of Underdevelopment*, Department of Human Geography Publication HG14, Canberra, pp. 181–9.

1980d. (with M.J. Taylor) 'Large corporations and concentrations of capital in Australia: a geographical analysis', *Economic Geography*, 56, 261–80.

1980e. 'Review of various books on local history', *Environment and Planning A*, 12, 855–62.

1981a. (with M.J. Taylor) 'Variations in enterprise: the case of firms headquartered in Melbourne and Sydney', *Environment and Planning A*, 13, 137–46.

1981b. (with M.J. Taylor) 'Flows of capital and the semiperipheral economy: some geographical implications', *Tidjschrift voor Economische en Sociale Geografie*, 58, 194–213.

1981c. (with A.R. Pred) 'Time-geography: a new beginning', *Progress in Human Geography*, 5, 277–86.

1981d. (with M.J. Taylor) 'British capital overseas: direct investment and firm development in Australia', *Regional Studies*, 15, 183–212.

1981e. 'Owners' time and own time: the making of a capitalist time consciousness, 1300–1880', in A.R. Pred (ed.) *Space and Time in Geography. Essays Dedicated to Torsten Hägerstrand.* Lund Studies in Geography, Series B, No. 48, Lund: C.W.K. Gleerup, pp. 56–84. (Reprinted in 1990 in J.S. Hassard (ed.) *The Sociology of Time.* London: Macmillan, pp. 105–29; and in 1996 in J. Agnew, D.N. Livingstone and A. Rogers (eds) *Human Geography. An Essential Anthology.* Oxford: Blackwell.)

1981f. (with M.J. Taylor) 'Variations in enterprise in Australia', *Australian Geographer*, 15, 98–105.

1982a. (co-edited with M.J. Taylor) *The Geography of Multinationals.* London: Croom Helm.

1982b. (with M.J. Taylor) 'Models of corporate development and the multinational corporation', in M.J. Taylor and N.J. Thrift (eds) *The Geography of Multinationals.* London: Croom Helm, pp. 14–32.

1982c. (with J. Hirst and M.J. Taylor) 'The geographical pattern of the Australian trading banks' overseas representation', in M.J. Taylor and N.J. Thrift (eds) *The Geography of Multinationals.* London: Croom Helm, pp. 117–35.

1982d. (with M.J. Taylor) 'Industrial linkage and the segmented economy 1: Theory', *Environment and Planning A*, 14, 1601–13.

1982e. (with M.J. Taylor) 'Industrial linkage and the segmented economy 2: An empirical reinterpretation', *Environment and Planning A*, 14, 1614–32.

1982f. 'Behavioural geography: paradigm in search of paradigm', in N. Wrigley and R.J. Bennett (eds) *Quantitative Geography. Retrospect and Prospect.* London: Routledge and Kegan Paul, pp. 352–65.

1983a. (with M.J. Taylor) 'The role of finance in the evolution and functioning of industrial systems', in F.E.I. Hamilton and G.J.R. Linge (eds) *Spatial Analysis, Industry and the Environment. Volume 3.* Chichester: John Wiley, pp. 359–85.

1983b. 'Literature, the production of culture and the politics of place', *Antipode*, 15, 12–24.

1983c. 'On the determination of social action in space and time', *Environment and Planning D. Society and Space*, 1, 23–57 (this volume).

1983d. (with D.K. Forbes) Review essay: 'A landscape with figures: political geography with human conflict', *Political Geography Quarterly*, 2, 247–63.

1983e. (with P. Williams and D.K. Forbes) 'The Institute of Australian Geographers', *Australian Geographical Studies*, 21, 3–8.

1983f. (with M.J. Taylor) 'Business organisation, segmentation and location', *Regional Studies*, 17, 445–65.

1984a. (co-edited with C. Adrian, C.C. Kissling and M.J. Taylor) *Regional Impacts of Resource Developments.* Sydney: Croom Helm.

1984b. (with D.K. Forbes) 'Town and city in Vietnam', *Vietnam Today*, 28, 3–7.

1984c. (with D.K. Forbes) 'Determination and abstraction in theories of the articulation of modes of production', in D.K. Forbes and P.J. Rimmer (eds) *Uneven Development and the Geographical Transfer of Value.* Department of Human Geography Publication HG16: Canberra, pp. 111–34.

1984d. (with M.J. Taylor) 'The regional consequences of a dualistic industrial structure: the case of Australia', *Australian Geographical Studies*, 22, 72–87.

1984e. (with D.K. Forbes) 'Urbanisation in non-capitalist developing countries: the case of Vietnam', in R.D. Bedford (ed.) *Urbanisation in Southeast Asia and the Pacific.* Proceedings of a Symposium of the Pacific Science Congress: Dunedin, pp. 1–27.

1985a. 'Taking the rest of the world seriously? British urban and regional research in a time of economic crisis', *Environment and Planning A*, 17, 7–24.

1985b. 'Flies and germs: a geography of knowledge', in D. Gregory and J. Urry (eds) *Social Relations and Spatial Structures*. London: Macmillan, pp. 330–73 (this volume).

1985c. (with D.K. Forbes) 'Cities, socialism and war: Hanoi and Saigon under socialist rule', *Environment and Planning D. Society and Space*, 3, 270–308.

1985d. Review essay: 'Bear and mouse or bear and tree? Anthony Giddens's reconstitution of social theory', *Sociology*, 19, 609–23. (To be reprinted in 1996 in C. Bryant and D. Jary (eds) *Anthony Giddens. Critical Assessments*. London: Routledge.)

1986a. (with D.K. Forbes) *The Price of War. Urbanisation in Vietnam 1954–1985*. London: George Allen and Unwin.

1986b. (co-edited with M.J. Taylor) *Multinationals and the Restructuring of the World Economy*. London: Croom Helm.

1986c. (with M.J. Taylor) 'New theories of the multinational corporation', in M.J. Taylor and N.J. Thrift (eds) *Multinationals and the Restructuring of the World Economy*. Beckenham: Croom Helm, pp. 1–20.

1986d. 'The internationalisation of producer services and the integration of the Pacific Basin property market', in M.J. Taylor and N.J. Thrift (eds) *Multinationals and the Restructuring of the World Economy*. Beckenham: Croom Helm, pp. 142–92.

1986e. 'The geography of international economic disorder', in R.J. Johnston and P.J. Taylor (eds) *A World in Crisis: Geographical Perspectives on Global Problems*. Oxford: Blackwell, pp. 12–67. (Reprinted in 1988 in D. Massey and J. Allen (eds) *Uneven Re-development. Cities and Regions in Transition*. London: Hodder and Stoughton, pp. 6–46.)

1986f. (with P. Daniels) 'The international context for producer services', in Producer Services Working Party, *Uneven Development in the Service Economy. Understanding the Location and Role of Producer Services*. London: Institute of British Geographers, pp. 98–130.

1986g. 'Little games and big stories: accounting for the practices of political personality in the 1945 General Election', in K. Hoggart and E. Kofman (eds) *Politics, Geography and Social Stratification*. Beckenham: Croom Helm, pp. 90–155 (this volume).

1987a. (co-edited with D.K. Forbes) *The Socialist Third World. Urban Development and Territorial Planning*. Oxford: Blackwell.

1987b. (with D.K. Forbes) 'Introduction', in D.K. Forbes and N.J. Thrift (eds) *The Socialist Third World. Urban Development and Territorial Planning*. Oxford: Blackwell, pp. 1–26.

1987c. (with D.K. Forbes) 'Territorial organisation, regional development and the city in Vietnam', in D.K. Forbes and N.J. Thrift (eds) *The Socialist Third World. Urban Development and Territorial Planning*. Oxford: Blackwell, pp. 98–128.

1987d. (co-edited with P. Williams) *Class and Space. The Making of Urban Society*. London: Routledge and Kegan Paul.

1987e. (with P. Williams) 'An introduction to the geography of class formation', in N.J. Thrift and P. Williams (eds) *Class and Space*. London: Routledge and Kegan Paul, pp. 1–22.

1987f. 'The geography of nineteenth-century class formation', in N.J. Thrift and P. Williams (eds) *Class and Space*. London: Routledge and Kegan Paul, pp. 25–50.

1987g. 'The geography of late twentieth-century class formation', in N.J. Thrift and P. Williams (eds) *Class and Space*. London: Routledge and Kegan Paul, pp. 207–53.

1987h. (with R. Harris) 'Internationalisation of demand', *World Property*, April, 65–7.

1987i. 'Manufacturing rural geography', *Journal of Rural Studies*, 3, 77–81.

1987j. (with D.K. Forbes) 'International impacts on the urban process in the Asian region: a review', in R.W. Fuchs, E. Pernia and G.W. Jones (eds) *Urbanisation and Urban Policies in Pacific Asia*. Boulder, CO: Westview, pp. 67–87.

1987k. 'The fixers: the urban geography of international commercial capital', in M. Castells and J. Henderson (eds) *Global Restructuring and Territorial Development*. London: Sage, pp. 219–47. (Reprinted in 1994 in R. Roberts (ed.) *International Financial Centres, Volume 1*. London: Edward Elgar, pp. 157–90.)

1987l. 'The growth of service class labour markets: the case of Britain', in M. Fischer and P. Nijkamp (eds) *Spatial Labour Markets*. Amsterdam: North Holland, pp. 313–44.

1987m. '"Difficult years": ideology and urbanisation in South Vietnam, 1975–1985', *Urban*

Geography, 8, 429–39. (Reprinted in 1993 in G. Demko and J. Regulska (eds) *Socialist Cities. A Comparative Perspective*, Durham, NC: Duke University Press.)

1987n. (with D. Drakakis-Smith and J. Doherty) 'Introduction: what is a socialist developing country?', *Geography*, 72, 333–5.

1987o. 'Vietnam: geography of a socialist siege economy', *Geography*, 72, 340–4.

1987p. 'No perfect symmetry: a response to David Harvey', *Environment and Planning D. Society and Space*, 5, 400–7.

1987q. (with P.J. Cloke) 'Intra-class conflict in rural areas', *Journal of Rural Studies*, 4, 321–33. (To be reprinted in 1996 in H. Newby (ed.) *Rural Studies*. London: Edward Elgar.)

1988a. (contribution to J.N. Marshall, P. Wood, P. Daniels, A. Mackinnon, J. Batchelor, P. Damesick, A. Gillespie, A. Leyshon and A. Green) *Services and Uneven Development*. Oxford: Oxford University Press.

1988b. '*Vivos voco*: ringing the changes in the historical geography of time consciousness', in T. Schuller and M. Young (eds) *The Rhythms of Society*. London: Routledge, pp. 53–94 (this volume).

1988c. (with A. Leyshon and P. Daniels) 'Large accountancy firms in the UK: operational adaptation and spatial development', *The Service Industries Journal*, 8, 315–44.

1988d. (with A. Leyshon and P. Daniels) 'Trends in the growth and location of professional producer services: UK property consultants', *Tijdschrift voor Economische en Sociale Geografie*, 79, 162–74.

1988e. (with A. Leyshon) 'The gambling propensity: banks, developing country debt exposures and the new international financial system', *Geoforum*, 19, 55–69.

1988f. (with A. Leyshon and P. Daniels) 'The internationalisation of professional producer services: accountancy conglomerates', in P. Enderwick (ed.) *Multinational Services Corporations*. Beckenham: Croom Helm, pp. 79–106.

1989a. (co-edited with R.J. Peet) *New Models in Geography. The Political Economy Perspective* (2 vols). London: Unwin Hyman.

1989b. (with R.J. Peet) 'Political economy and human geography', in R.J. Peet and N.J. Thrift (eds) *New Models in Geography. Volume 1*. London: Unwin Hyman, pp. 3–29.

1989c. (with A. Leyshon and C. Tommey) 'The rise of the British provincial financial centre', *Progress in Planning*, 31(3), 151–229.

1989d. (with M.J. Taylor) 'Battleships and cruisers: the new geography of multinational corporations', in D. Gregory and R. Walford (eds) *New Horizons in Human Geography*. London: Macmillan, pp. 279–97.

1989e. (with A. Leyshon) 'South goes north? The rise of the British provincial financial centre', in J. Lewis and A. Townsend (eds) *The North–South Divide. Regional Change in Britain in the 1980s*. London: Paul Chapman, pp. 114–56. (Reprinted in 1994 in R. Roberts (ed.) *International Financial Centres, Volume 3*. London: Edward Elgar, pp. 139–86.)

1989f. 'Images of social change', in L. McDowell, P. Sarre and C. Hamnett (eds) *The Changing Social Structure of Britain*. London: Sage, pp. 12–42.

1989g. (with P. Daniels and A. Leyshon) 'Internationalisation of producer services and metropolitan development', *Tijdschrift voor Economische en Sociale Geografie*, 80.

1989h. 'The geography of international economic disorder', in R.J. Johnston and P.J. Taylor (eds) *A World in Crisis: Geographical Perspectives on Global Problems* (2nd edn), pp. 15–77.

1990a. (with A. Leyshon) 'The chartered surveying industry', in P. Healey and R. Nabarro (eds) *Land and Property Development Processes in a Changing Context*. Farnborough: Gower.

1990b. 'Transport and communication, 1730–1914', in R.L. Dodgshon and R. Butlin (eds) *A New Historical Geography of England and Wales* (2nd edn). London: Academic Press, pp. 453–86.

1990c. 'Doing global regional geography: the City of London and the south-east of England', in R.J. Johnston, J. Hauer and G.A. Hoekveld (eds) *Regional Geography. Current Developments and Future Prospects*. London: Routledge, pp. 180–207.

1990d. (with P.J. Cloke) 'Rural change and intra-class conflict', in T.K. Marsden, S.

Whatmore and P. Lowe (eds) *Critical Perspectives on Rural Change: Volume 1. Rural Restructuring. Global Processes, Local Responses*. London: Fulton, pp. 165–81.

1990e. 'For a new regional geography 1', *Progress in Human Geography*, 14, 272–9.

1991a. 'Muddling through: world orders and globalisation', *Professional Geographer*, 44, 3–7.

1991b. 'For a new regional geography 2', *Progress in Human Geography*, 15, 456–65.

1991c. 'Over-wordy worlds? Thoughts and worries', in C. Philo (ed.) *New Words, New Worlds. Reconceptualising Social and Cultural Geography*. Lampeter: IBG Social and Cultural Study Group, pp. 144–8.

1992a. 'Light out of darkness? Social theory in Britain in the 1980s', in P.J. Cloke (ed.) *Policy and Change in Thatcher's Britain*. Oxford: Pergamon, pp. 1–32.

1992b. (with A. Leyshon) 'In the wake of money: the City of London and the accumulation of value', in L. Budd and S. Whimster (eds) *Global Finance and Urban Living*. London: Routledge, pp. 282–311.

1992c. (with J. Beaverstock, A. Leyshon, T. Rutherford and P. Williams) 'Moving houses: the geographical reorganisation of the estate agency industry in England and Wales in the 1980s', *Transactions of the Institute of British Geographers*, 17, 166–82.

1992d. (with P. Dicken) 'The organisation of production and the production of organisation', *Transactions of the Institute of British Geographers*, 17, 279–91.

1992e. (with A. Leyshon) 'Liberalisation and consolidation: the Single European Market and the remaking of European Financial Capital', *Environment and Planning A*, 24, 49–81.

1992f. 'Apocalypse soon, or, why human geography is worth doing', in A. Rogers, H. Viles and A. Goudie (eds) *The Student's Companion to Geography*. Oxford: Blackwell, pp. 8–12.

1992g. (with P. Glennie) 'Modernity, urbanism and modern consumption', *Environment and Planning D. Society and Space*, 10, 423–43.

1992h. (with A. Amin) 'Neo-Marshallian nodes in global networks', *International Journal of Urban and Regional Research*, 16, 571–87. (Reprinted in 1995 in W. Krumbein (ed.) *Ökonomische und Politische Netwerke in der Region*. Münster: LitVerlag, pp. 115–40; and in 1996 in S. Daniels and R. Lee (eds) *Modern Geography. A Reader*. London: Arnold.)

1993a. (with A. Leyshon and M. Justice) *Reversal of Fortune? Financial Services in the Southeast of England*. London: SEEDS.

1993b. Review essay: 'The arts of the living and the beauty of the dead: anxieties of being in the work of Anthony Giddens', *Progress in Human Geography*, 17, 111–21 (this volume). (To be reprinted in 1996 in C. Bryant and D. Jary (eds) *Anthony Giddens. Critical Assessments*. London: Routledge.)

1993c. 'For a new regional geography 3', *Progress in Human Geography*, 17, 92–100.

1993d. (with M. Dear) 'Unfinished business: ten years of Society and Space', *Environment and Planning D. Society and Space*, 10, 715–19.

1993e. Review essay: 'The urban impasse', *Theory, Culture & Society*, 10, 229–38.

1993f. (with J. Lovering) 'Bristol: a city which has reached the end of the old road', in B. Blanke and R. Smith (eds) *The Future of the Medium-Sized City in Britain and Germany*. London: Anglo-German Foundation, pp. 47–69.

1993g. (with J. Beaverstock, A. Leyshon, T. Rutherford and P. Williams) '"Agents of change": the restructuring of the estate agency industry in the East Midlands in the 1980s', *East Midland Geographer*, 16, 11–21.

1993h. 'Consumption', 'disorganised capitalism', 'money, geography of', 'producer services', 'services, geography of', 'tourism' – entries for R.J. Johnston, D. Gregory and D. Smith (eds) *The Dictionary of Human Geography* (3rd edn). Oxford: Blackwell.

1993i. (with P. Glennie) 'Historical geographies of urban life and modern consumption', in G. Kearns and C. Philo (eds) *Selling Places. The City as Cultural Capital, Past and Present*. Oxford: Pergamon, pp. 33–48.

1993j. (with P. Glennie) 'Modern consumption: theorising commodities and consumers', *Environment and Planning D. Society and Space*, 11, 606–9.

1993k. (with R.J. Johnston) 'Ringing the changes: the intellectual history of *Environment and Planning A*', *Environment and Planning A*, 25, 14–21.

1993l. (with R.J. Johnston) 'The futures of *Environment and Planning A*', *Environment and Planning A*, 25, 83–102.

1993m. (with A. Leyshon) 'The restructuring of the UK financial services industry in the 1990s: a reversal of fortune?', *Journal of Rural Studies*, 9, 223–41.

1993n. 'The light fantastic: culture, postmodernism and the image', in G.L. Clark, D.K. Forbes and R. Francis (eds) *Multiculturalism, Difference and Postmodernism*. Melbourne: Longman Cheshire, pp. 1–21.

1994a. (co-edited with A. Amin) *Globalisation, Institutions and Regional Development in Europe*. Oxford: Oxford University Press.

1994b. (with A. Amin) 'The local in the global', in A. Amin and N.J. Thrift (eds) *Globalisation, Institutions and Regional Development in Europe*. Oxford: Oxford University Press, pp. 1–22.

1994c. 'Holding down the global', in A. Amin and N.J. Thrift (eds) *Globalisation, Institutions and Regional Development in Europe*. Oxford: Oxford University Press, pp. 257–60.

1994d. (co-edited with S. Corbridge and R.L. Martin) *Money, Power and Space*. Oxford: Blackwell.

1994e. (with S. Corbridge) 'The geography of money', in S. Corbridge, N.J. Thrift and R.L. Martin (eds) *Money, Power and Space*. Oxford: Blackwell, pp. 1–25.

1994f. 'On the social and cultural determinants of international financial centres', in S. Corbridge, N.J. Thrift and R.L. Martin (eds) *Money, Power and Space*. Oxford: Blackwell, pp. 327–55.

1994g. 'Inhuman geographies: landscapes of speed, light and power', in P.J. Cloke, M. Doel, D. Matless, M. Phillips and N.J. Thrift *Writing the Rural. Five Cultural Geographies*. London: Paul Chapman, pp. 191–248 (this volume).

1994h. 'Globalisation, regulation, urbanisation: the case of the Netherlands', *Urban Studies*, 31, 365–80.

1994i. 'Taking aim at the heart of the region', in D. Gregory, R.L. Martin and G. Smith (eds) *Human Geography. Society, Space and Social Science*. London: Macmillan, pp. 200–31.

1994j. (with A. Leyshon) 'European financial capital: the global context', in L. Albrechts, S. Hardy, M. Hart and A. Katos (eds) *An Enlarged Europe. Regions in Competition?*. London: Jessica Kingsley, pp. 109–44.

1994k. (with A. Leyshon) 'A phantom state? The detraditionalisation of money, the international financial system and international financial centres', *Political Geography*, 13, 299–327 (this volume).

1994l. (with A. Leyshon) 'Access to financial services and financial infrastructure withdrawal: problems and policies', *Area*, 26, 268–75.

1994m. (with A. Amin) 'Globalisation, institutional thickness and local prospects', *Revenue d'Economie Régionale et Urbaine*, 3, 405–27.

1995a. (co-edited with A. Cliff, P. Gould and A.G. Hoare) *Diffusing Geography. Essays for Peter Haggett*. Oxford: Blackwell.

1995b. 'A life in geography', in A.D. Cliff, P.A. Gould, A.G. Hoare and N.J. Thrift (eds) *Diffusing Geography. Essays for Peter Haggett*. Oxford: Blackwell, pp. 375–95.

1995c. (co-edited with S. Pile) *Mapping the Subject. Geographies of Cultural Transformation*. London: Routledge.

1995d. 'Introduction', in S. Pile and N.J. Thrift (eds) *Mapping the Subject. Geographies of Cultural Transformation*. London: Routledge, pp. 1–12.

1995e. 'Mapping the subject', in S. Pile and N.J. Thrift (eds) *Mapping the Subject. Geographies of Cultural Transformation*. London: Routledge, pp. 13–51.

1995f. 'A hyperactive world', in R.J. Johnston, P.J. Taylor and M. Watts (eds) *Geographies of Global Change*. Oxford: Blackwell.

1995g. (with P. Glennie) 'Gender and consumption', in N. Wrigley and M. Lowe (eds) *Retailing, Consumption and Capital. Towards the New Retail Geography*. London: Longman, pp. 221–37.

1995h. (with P. Glennie) 'Consumers, identities, and consumption spaces in early modern England', *Environment and Planning A*, 28, 25–45.

1995i. (with P. Glennie) 'Time and work in historical perspective: three decades on', *Time and Society*, 4.

1995j. (with P. Glennie) 'Time standing still? Comments on a chapter absent from *Customs in Common*', *Social Science History*, 19.

1995k. (with A. Amin) 'Institutional issues for the European regions: from markets and plans to socioeconomics and powers of association', *Economy and Society*, 24, 41–66.

1995l. (with A. Amin) 'Territoriality in the global political economy', *Nordisk Samhalls-geografisk Tidskrift*, 20, 3–16.

1995m. (with A. Leyshon) 'Geographies of financial exclusion', *Transactions of the Institute of British Geographers*, 20, 312–43.

1995n. (with P.J. Cloke and M. Phillips) 'The new middle classes and the social constructs of rural living', in M. Savage (ed.) *New Theories of the Middle Class*. London: UCL Press, pp. 220–38.

1995o. (with P. Jackson) 'Geographies of consumption', in D. Miller (ed.) *Acknowledging Consumption. A Review of New Studies*. London: Routledge, pp. 204–37.

1995p. 'Classics in human geography revisited: on the determination of social action in space and time', *Progress in Human Geography*, 19, 528–30.

1996a. 'New urban eras and old technological fears. Reconfiguring the goodwill of electronic things', *Urban Studies*, 33.

1996b. (with K. Olds) 'Refiguring the economic in economic geography', *Progress in Human Geography*, 20.

1996c. (with A. Leyshon) *Money/Space*. London: Routledge.

Bibliography

Abercrombie, N. (1980). *Class, Structure and Knowledge*. Oxford: Blackwell.

Abercrombie, N. and Urry, J. (1983). *Capital, Labour and the Middle Classes*. London: Macmillan.

Abercrombie, N., Hill, S. and Turner, B.S. (1980). *The Dominant Ideology Thesis*. Hemel Hempstead: George Allen and Unwin.

Abler, R., Janelle, D., Philbrick, A. and Sommer, J. (1975). *Human Geography in a Shrinking World*. North Scituate, MA: Duxbury.

Abrams, P. (1972). 'The sense of the past and the origins of sociology', *Past and Present*, 55, 18–32.

Abrams, P. (1980). 'History, sociology and historical sociology', *Past and Present*, 87, 3–16.

Abrams, P. (1982). *Historical Sociology*. Shepton Mallet: Open Books.

Acciaoli, G.L. (1981). 'Knowing what you're doing: a review of Pierre Bourdieu's *Outline of a Theory of Practice*', *Canberra Anthropology*, 4, 23–51.

Adam, B. (1990). *Time and Social Theory*. Cambridge: Polity Press.

Adas, M. (1989). *Machines as the Measure of Men. Science, Technology and Ideas of Western Dominance*. Ithaca, NY: Cornell University Press.

Addison, P. (1975). *The Road to 1945. British Politics and the Second World War*. London: Jonathan Cape.

Adler, J. (1989). 'Travel as performed art', *American Journal of Sociology*, 94, 1366–91.

Aglietta, M. (1979). *A Theory of Capitalist Regulation*. London: New Left Books.

Aglietta, M. and Orléan, A. (1982). *La Violence de la monnaie*. Paris: Minuit.

Agnew, J.A. (1994). 'The territorial trap: the geographical assumptions of international relations theory', *Review of International Political Economy*, 1, 53–80.

Agulhon, M. (1970). *La République au village*. Paris: Librairie Plon.

Albrow, M. (1974). 'Dialectical and categorical paradigms of a science of society', *Sociological Review*, 22, 183–201.

Alexander, C. (1989). *Sociological Theory since 1945*. London: Hutchinson.

Alexander, K. (1992). 'Riots of the New Age', in J.R. Lewis and J.G. Melton (eds) *Perspectives on the New Age*. Albany: State University of New York Press, pp. 30–48.

Allen, J. and Pryke, M. (1994). 'The production of service space', *Environment and Planning D. Society and Space*, 12, 453–76.

Althusser, L. (1969). *For Marx*. Harmondsworth: Penguin Books.

Altick, R.D. (1957). *The English Common Reader*. Chicago: University of Chicago Press.

Altvater, E. (1993). *The Future of the Market. An Essay on the Regulation of Money and Nature after the Collapse of Actually Existing Socialism*. London: Verso.

Alvarez, A. (1994). *Night*. London: Allen Lane.

Anderson, B. (1983). *Imagined Communities. Reflections on the Origin and Spread of Nationalism*. London: Verso.

Anderson, P. (1980). *Arguments within English Marxism*. London: New Left Books.

Anscombe, G.E.M. (1981). *Collected Philosophical Papers*. Oxford: Clarendon Press.

Appadurai, A. (1990). 'Disjuncture and difference in the global cultural economy', *Theory, Culture & Society*, 7, 295–310.

Armstrong, T. (1991). 'The electrification of the body', *Textual Practice*, 8, 16–32.

Attali, J. (1982). *Histoires du temps*. Paris: Fayard.

Attali, J. (1991). *Noise*. Edinburgh: Marion Boyars.

Augé, M. (1986). *Un Ethnologue dans le métro*. Paris: Hachette.

Augé, M. (1995). *Non-places. Introduction to an Anthropology of Supermodernity*. London: Verso.

Bachelard, G. (1964). *The Poetics of Space*. Boston: Beacon Press.

Backhouse, J. (1985). *Books of Hours*. London: British Library.

Backinsell, W.G.C. (1977). *The Medieval Clock in Salisbury Cathedral*. Salisbury, South Wiltshire Industrial Archaeology Society Historical Monograph 2.

Bagley, J.J. (1960). *Life in Medieval England*. London: Batsford.

Bailey, E. (1983). 'The implicit religion of contemporary society', *Religion*, 13, 69–83.

Bailey, E. (1990). 'The implicit religion of contemporary society: some studies and reflections', *Social Compass*, 37, 483–97.

Baker, A.R.H. (1979). 'Historical geography: a new beginning?', *Progress in Historical Geography*, 3, 560–70.

Baker, W.E. (1984a). 'Floor trading and crowd dynamics', in P. Adler and P. Adler (eds) *The Social Dynamics of Financial Markets*. Greenwich, CT: JAI Press, pp. 107–28.

Baker, W.E. (1984b). 'The social structure of a securities market', *American Journal of Sociology*, 89, 775–821.

Baker, W.E. (1987). 'What is money? A social structural interpretation', in M. Mizruchi and M. Schwartz (eds) *Intercorporate Relations. The Structural Analysis of Business*. Cambridge: Cambridge University Press, pp. 109–44.

Baker, W.E. (1990). 'Market networks and corporate behaviour', *American Journal of Sociology*, 96, 589–625.

Bakhtin, M.M. (1968). *Rabelais and His World*. Cambridge, MA: MIT Press.

Bakhtin, M.M. (1984). *Problems of Dostoevsky's Poetics*. Minneapolis: University of Minnesota Press.

Bakhtin, M.M. (1986). *The Dialogical Imagination*. Austin: University of Texas Press.

Baldwin, J. (1955). *Notes of a Native Son*. Boston: Beacon Press.

Balibar, É. (1972). 'The basic concepts of historical materialism', in L. Althusser and E. Balibar, *Reading Capital*. London: Verso, pp. 199–308.

Bank for International Settlements (1992). *Recent Developments in International Interbank Relations*. Basle: Bank for International Settlements.

Barnes, B. (1982). *T.S. Kuhn and Social Science*. London: Macmillan.

Barnett, M., Corrigan, P., Kuhn, A. and Wolff, J. (eds) (1979). *Ideology and Cultural Production*. London: Macmillan.

Barrows, C. (1922). 'Geography as human ecology', *Annals of the Association of American Geographers*, 13.

Barthes, R. (1981). *Camera Lucida: Reflections on Photography*. New York: Noonday.

Barty-King, H. (1986). *New Flame. A Social History of Town Gas*. London: Alan Sutton.

Barty-King, H. (1991). *The Worst Poverty. A History of Debt and Debtors*. London: Alan Sutton.

Batchen, G. (1991). 'Desiring production itself: notes on the invention of photography', in R. Diprose and R. Ferrell (eds) *Cartographies*. Sydney: Allen and Unwin, pp. 13–26.

Baudelaire, C. (1964). *The Painter of Modern Life and Other Essays*. Oxford: Phaidon.

Baudrillard, J. (1988). *America*. New York: Verso.

Bauman, Z. (1989). 'Hermeneutics and modern social theory', in D. Held and J.B. Thompson (eds) *Social Theory of Modern Societies. Anthony Giddens and His Critics*. Cambridge: Cambridge University Press.

Baxandall, J. (1995). *Shadows and Enlightenment*. New Haven, CT: Yale University Press.

Beaverstock, J. (1991). 'Skilled international migration: an analysis of the geography of international secondments within large accountancy firms', *Environment and Planning A*, 23, 1133–46.

Bechhofer, F. and Elliott, B. (1981). 'Petty property: the survival of a moral economy', in F. Bechhofer and B. Elliott (eds) *The Petite Bourgeoisie. Comparative Studies of the Uneasy Stratum*. London: Macmillan, pp. 182–99.

Beck, U. (1992). *Risk Society: Towards a New Modernity*. London: Sage.

Beck, U., Giddens, A. and Lash, S. (1994). *Reflexive Modernisation. Politics, Tradition and Aesthetics in the Modern Social Order*. Cambridge: Polity Press.

Beeson, C.F.C. (1971). *English Church Clocks, 1280–1850. History and Classification*. London, Antiquarian Horological Society.

Bender, J. and Wellbery, D. (eds) (1991). *Chronotypes. The Construction of Time*. Stanford, CA: Stanford University Press.

Benedikt, R. (ed.) (1991). *Cyberspace. First Steps*. Cambridge, MA: MIT Press.

Beninger, J.R. (1986). *The Control Revolution. Technological and Economic Origins of the Information Society*. Cambridge, MA: Harvard University Press.

Benjamin, A. (1993). *The Plural Event. Descartes, Hegel, Heidegger*. London: Routledge.

Benjamin, J. (1988). *The Bonds of Love. Psychoanalysis, Feminism and the Problem of Domination*. London: Routledge.

Benjamin, W. (1970). *Illuminations*. London: Fontana.

Benjamin, W. (1977). *Charles Baudelaire*. London: Verso.

Benjamin, W. (1979). *One Way Street and Other Writings*. London: New Left Books.

Bennett, H.S. (1956). *Life on the English Manor. A Study of Peasant Conditions, 1150–1400*. Cambridge: Cambridge University Press.

Benton, T. (1981). 'Realism and social science: some comments on Roy Bhaskar's *The Possibility of Naturalism*', *Radical Philosophy*, Spring, 13–21.

Benton, T. (1993). *Natural Relations. Ecology, Animal Rights and Social Justice*. London: Verso.

Berger, P. and Luckmann, T. (1966). *The Social Construction of Reality. A Treatise on the Sociology of Knowledge*. Harmondsworth: Penguin Books.

Berger, P.L. and Luckmann, T. (1967). *The Social Construction of Reality. A Treatise on the Sociology of Knowledge*. Garden City.

Bergson, H. (1950). *Matter and Memory*. London: George Allen and Unwin.

Bernal, J.D. (1965). *Science in History*. London: Macmillan.

Bernstein, M.A. (1994). *Foregone Conclusions. Against Apocalyptic History*. Berkeley: University of California Press.

Bernstein, R.J. (1983). *Beyond Objectivism and Relativism. Science, Hermeneutics and Praxis*. Oxford: Blackwell.

Bernstein, R.J. (1992). *The New Constellation*. Cambridge: Polity Press.

Bertaux, D. (ed.) (1981). *Biography and Society. The Life History Approach in the Social Sciences*. Beverly Hills, CA: Sage.

Bertaux, D. and Bertaux-Wiaume, I. (1981a). 'Artisanal bakery in France: how it lives and why it survives', in F. Bechhofer and B. Elliott (eds) *The Petite Bourgeoisie. Comparative Studies of the Uneasy Stratum*. London: Macmillan, pp. 155–81.

Bertaux, D. and Bertaux-Wiaume, I. (1981b). 'Life stories in the baker's trade', in D. Bertaux (ed.) *Biography and Society*. Beverly Hills, CA: Sage, pp. 169–89.

Bertaux-Wiaume, I. (1977). 'The life-history approach to migration', *Oral History*, 7, 26–32.

Best, S. and Kellner, D. (1991). *Postmodern Theory. Critical Interrogations*. London: Macmillan.

Bettelheim, B. (1969). *The Children of the Dream*. New York: Macmillan.

Bezanson, A. (1922). 'The early use of the term "industrial revolution"', *Quarterly Journal of Economics*, 36, 343–9.

Bhabha, H. (1986). 'Signs taken for wonders: questions of ambivalence and authority under a tree outside Delhi, May, 1817', in H.L. Gates (ed.) *Race, Writing and Difference*. Chicago: University of Chicago Press.

Bhabha, H. (1994). *The Location of Culture*. London: Routledge.

Bhaskar, R. (1975). *A Realist Theory of Science*. Leeds: Leeds Books.

Bhaskar, R. (1979). *The Possibility of Naturalism. A Philosophical Critique of the Contemporary Human Sciences*. Hassocks: Harvester Press.

Bhaskar, R. (1980). 'Scientific explanation and human emancipation', *Radical Philosophy*, 26, 16–28.

Bhaskar, R. (1991). *Philosophy and the Idea of Freedom*. Oxford: Blackwell.

Bhaskar, R. (1993). *Dialectic: The Pulse of Freedom*. London: Verso.

Bienefeld, M.A. (1972). *Working Hours in British Industry. An Economic History.* London: Weidenfeld and Nicolson.

Bijker, W. and Law, J. (eds) (1991). *Shaping Technology/Building Society. Studies in Sociotechnical Change.* Cambridge, MA: MIT Press.

Bijker, W., Hughes, T.P. and Pinch, T. (eds) (1989). *The Social Construction of Technological Systems.* Cambridge, MA: MIT Press.

Billinge, M. (1982). 'Reconstructing societies in the past: the collective biography of local communities', in A.R.H. Baker and M. Billinge (eds) *Period and Place. Research Methods in Historical Geography.* Cambridge: Cambridge University Press, pp. 19–32.

Billinge, M. (1984). 'Hegemony, class and power in late Georgian and early Victorian England: towards a cultural geography', in A.R.H. Baker and D. Gregory (eds) *Explorations in Historical Geography. Interpretative Essays.* Cambridge: Cambridge University Press, pp. 28–67.

Birmingham, P. (1989). 'Local theory', in A. Dalley and C.E. Scott (eds) *The Question of the Other.* Albany: SUNY Press, pp. 205–12.

Bleitrach, D. and Chenu, A. (1979). *L'Usine et la vie. Luttes régionales: Marseilles et Fos.* Paris: Maspéro.

Bleitrach, D. and Chenu, A. (1981). 'Modes of domination and everyday life: some notes on recent research', in M. Harloe and E. Lebas (eds) *City, Class and Capital. New Developments in the Political Economy of Cities and Regions.* London: Edward Arnold, pp. 105–14.

Bloor, D. (1983). *Wittgenstein. A Social Theory of Knowledge.* London: Macmillan.

Blumer, H. (1969). *Symbolic Interactionism.* Englewood Cliffs, NJ: Prentice Hall.

Blunt, A. (1994). *Travel, Gender and Imperialism. Mary Kingsley and West Africa.* New York: Guilford Press.

Blunt, A. and Rose, G. (eds) (1994). *Writing Women and Space.* New York: Guilford Press.

Boddy, W. (1994). 'Archaeologies of electronic vision and the gendered spectator', *Screen*, 35, 105–22.

Boden, D. (1994). *The Business of Talk.* Cambridge: Polity Press.

Boden, D. and Molotch, H. (1994). 'The compulsion of proximity', in R. Friedland and D. Boden (eds) *Now/Here. Time, Space and Modernity.* Berkeley: University of California Press.

Bogue, R. (1989). *Deleuze and Guattari.* London: Routledge.

Bollas, C. (1987). *The Shadow of the Object. Psychoanalysis of the Unthought Unknown.* London: Free Association Books.

Bollème, G. (ed.) (1971). *La Bibliothèque Bleue.* Paris: Minuit.

Bonham, J. (1954). *The Middle-Class Vote.* London: Faber and Faber.

Booker, J. (1994). *Travellers' Money.* London: Alan Sutton.

Bordo, S. (1990). 'Feminism, postmodernism and gender – scepticism', in L. Nicholson (ed.) *Feminism/Postmodernism.* London: Routledge, pp. 133–56.

Bordo, S. and Moussa, S. (1993). 'Rehabilitating the "I"', in H. Silverman (ed.) *Questioning Foundations. Truth/Subjectivity/Culture.* London: Routledge, pp. 110–33.

Borst, A. (1993). *The Ordering of Time. From the Ancient Computus to the Modern Computer.* Cambridge: Polity Press.

Bottomley, G. (1992). *Out of Place.* Cambridge: Cambridge University Press.

Bottomore, T. (1954). 'Social stratification in voluntary organisations', in D.V. Glass (ed.) *Social Mobility in Britain.* London: Routledge and Kegan Paul, pp. 349–82.

Boundas, C.V. (ed.) (1993). *The Deleuze Reader.* New York: Columbia University Press.

Boundas, C.V. and Olkowski, D. (eds) (1994). *Gilles Deleuze and the Theater of Philosophy.* New York: Routledge.

Bourdieu, P. (1977). *Outline of a Theory of Practice.* Cambridge: Cambridge University Press.

Bourdieu, P. (1980). *Le Sens pratique.* Paris: Éditions de Minuit.

Bourdieu, P. (1981). 'Men and machines', in K. Knorr-Cetina and A.V. Cicourel (eds) *Advances in Social Theory and Methodology.* London: Routledge and Kegan Paul, pp. 364–320.

Bourdieu, P. (1984). *Distinction*. London: Routledge and Kegan Paul.

Bourdieu, P. (1988). *Homo Academicus*. Cambridge: Polity Press.

Bourdieu, P. (1990a). *In Other Words. Essays Towards a Reflexive Sociology*. Cambridge: Polity Press.

Bourdieu, P. (1990b). *The Logic of Practice*. Cambridge: Polity Press.

Bourdieu, P. (1991). 'Epilogue: on the possibility of a field of world sociology', in P. Bourdieu and J.S. Coleman (eds) *Social Theory for a Changing Society*. Boulder, CO: Westview Press, pp. 373–87.

Bourdieu, P. (1993). 'Concluding remarks', in C. Calhoun, E. Lipuma and M. Postone (eds) *Bourdieu. Critical Perspectives*. Oxford: Polity Press, pp. 263–75.

Bourdieu, P. and Passeron, J. (1977). *Reproduction in Education, Society and Culture*. London: Sage.

Bourdieu, P. and Passeron, J. (1980). *The Inheritors. French Students and their Relation to Culture*. Chicago: University of Chicago Press.

Bourdieu, P. and Wacquant, L. (1992). *An Invitation to Reflexive Sociology*. Cambridge: Polity Press.

Boyer, R. (1990). *The Regulation School. A Critical Introduction*. New York: Columbia University Press.

Boyne, R. (1991). 'Power-knowledge and social theory: the systematic misrepresentation of French social theory in the work of Anthony Giddens', in C. Bryant and D. Jary (eds) *Giddens' Theory of Structuration. A Critical Appreciation*. London: Routledge, pp. 52–73.

Bradley, D.J. (1988). 'The scope of travel medicine', in R. Steffen et al. (eds) *Travel Medicine*. Berlin: Springer Verlag, pp. 1–9.

Braidotti, R. (1994). 'Towards a new nomadism: feminist Deleuzian tracks; or metaphysics and metabolism', in C.V. Boundas and D. Olkowski (eds) *Gilles Deleuze and the Theater of Philosophy*. New York: Routledge, pp. 187–210.

Bremmer, J. and Rodenberg, H. (eds) (1991). *A Cultural History of Gesture*. Cambridge: Polity Press.

Brenner, R. (1993). *Merchants and Revolution. Commercial Change, Political Conflict and London's Overseas Traders, 1550–1653*. Cambridge: Cambridge University Press.

Brennan, T. (1993). *History after Lacan*. Cambridge: Polity Press.

Briggs, A. (1979). 'The language of mass and masses in nineteenth century England', in D. Martin and D. Rubinstein (eds) *Ideology and the Labour Movement*. Beckenham: Croom Helm, pp. 76–91.

Briggs, A. (1985). *The BBC. The First Fifty Years*. Oxford: Oxford University Press.

Briggs, A. (1989). *Victorian Things*. London: Batsford.

Briggs, A. (1992). 'The later Victorian age', in B. Ford (ed.) *Victorian Britain. The Cambridge Cultural History, Volume 7*. Cambridge: Cambridge University Press, pp. 2–38.

Brittan, A. (1977). *The Privatised World*. Henley-on-Thames: Routledge and Kegan Paul.

Broad, R. and Fleming, S. (1981). *Nella Last's War. A Mother's Diary 1939–45*. London: Sphere.

Broadhurst, J. (ed.) (1992). *Deleuze and the Transcendental Unconscious*. Warwick: PLI.

Brockbank, W. and Kenworthy, F. (eds) (1968). *The Diary of Richard Kay, 1716–51*. Manchester: Chetham Society/Manchester University Press.

Brokensha, D.W., Warren, D.M. and Werner, O. (eds) (1980). *Indigenous Knowledge Systems and Development*. Lanham, MD: IRS.

Bruno, G. (1993). *Streetwalking on a Ruined Map. Cultural Theory and the Films of Elvira Notari*. Princeton, NJ: Princeton University Press.

Bryant, C. and Jary, D. (eds) (1991). *Giddens' Theory of Structuration. A Critical Appreciation*. London: Routledge.

Buck-Morss, S. (1989). *The Dialectics of Seeing. Walter Benjamin and the Arcades Project*. Cambridge, MA: MIT Press.

Bukatman, S. (1993a). *Terminal Identity. The Virtual Subject in Postmodern Fiction*. Durham, NC: Duke University Press.

Bukatman, S. (1993b). 'Gibson's typewriter', *South Atlantic Quarterly*, 92, 627–45.

Burke, P. (1978). *Popular Culture in Early Modern Europe*. London: Maurice Temple Smith.

Burke, P. (1980). *Sociology and History*. Hemel Hempstead: George Allen and Unwin.

Burkitt, I. (1991). *Social Selves*. London: Sage.

Burkitt, I. (1994). 'The shifting concept of the self', *History of the Human Sciences*, 7, 7–28.

Burn, J.D. (1978). *The Autobiography of a Beggar Boy*. London: Europa.

Burnett, J. (1986). *A Social History of Housing*. London: Methuen.

Burnett, J. (ed.) (1974). *Useful Toil. Autobiographies of Working People from the 1820s to the 1920s*. London: Allen Lane.

Burns, T. (1992). *Erving Goffman*. London: Routledge.

Burton, J. (1994). *Monastic and Religious Orders in Britain, 1000–1300*. Cambridge, Cambridge University Press.

Bushman, R.L. (1967). *From Puritan to Yankee. Character and Social Order in Connecticut, 1690–1765*. Cambridge, MA: Harvard University Press.

Business (1986). 'Class and the City', *Business*, October, pp. 23–8.

Butler, D. and Stokes, D. (1969). *Political Change in Britain*. London: Macmillan.

Butler, J. (1990). *Gender Trouble. Feminism and the Subversion of Identity*. New York: Routledge.

Butler, J. (1992). 'Contingent foundations: feminism and the question of "postmodernism"', in J. Butler and J.W. Scott (eds) *Feminists Theorize the Political*. New York: Routledge, pp. 3–21.

Butler, J. (1993). *Bodies that Matter. The Discursive Limits of 'Sex'*. New York: Routledge.

Butler, J. (1994). 'Gender as performance', *Radical Philosophy*, Summer, 32–9.

Buzard, J. (1993). *The Beaten Track. European Tourism, Literature and the Ways to Culture, 1800–1918*. Oxford: Oxford University Press.

Cain, P.J. and Hopkins, A.G. (1993a). *British Imperialism. Innovation and Expansion, 1688–1914*. London: Longman.

Cain, P.J. and Hopkins, A.G. (1993b). *British Imperialism. Crisis and Deconstruction, 1914–1990*. London: Longman.

Calder, A. (1969). *The People's War. Britain 1939–1945*. London: Jonathan Cape.

Calder, A. and Sheridan, D. (1984). *Speak for Yourself. A Mass-Observation Anthology 1937–49*. London: Jonathan Cape.

Calhoun, C.J. (1978). 'History, anthropology and the study of communities', *Social History*, 3, 363–73.

Calhoun, C.J. (1980). 'Community: towards a variable conceptualisation for comparative research', *Social History*, 5, 105–29.

Calhoun, C.J. (1982). *The Question of Class Struggle*. Oxford: Blackwell.

Calhoun, C.J. (1991). 'Indirect relationships and imagined communities: large-scale social integration and the transformation of everyday life', in P. Bourdieu and J.S. Coleman (eds) *Social Theory for a Changing Society*. Boulder, CO: Westview, pp. 95–121.

Calhoun, C.J. (ed.) (1992). *Habermas and the Public Sphere*. Cambridge, MA: MIT Press.

Callon, M. (1986). 'Some elements of a sociology of translation', in J. Law (ed.) *Power, Action and Belief. A New Sociology of Knowledge*. London: Routledge and Kegan Paul, pp. 196–232.

Callon, M. (1991). 'Techno-economic networks and irreversibility', in J. Law (ed.) *A Sociology of Monsters?* London: Routledge, pp. 132–61.

Calvocoressi, P. (1978). *The British Experience 1945–75*. London: Bodley Head.

Camerer, C. (1989). 'Bubbles and fads in asset prices', *Journal of Economic Surveys*, 3, 3–41.

Capp, B. (1979). *Astrology and the Popular Press*. London: Faber.

Carchedi, G. (1977). *On the Economic Identification of Social Classes*. London: Macmillan.

Carey, J.W. (1989). *Communication as Culture. Essays on Media and Society*. London: Routledge.

Carlstein, T. (1981). 'The sociology of structuration in time and space: a time-geographic assessment of Giddens's theory', *Svensk Geografisk Arsbok*, 57, pp. 41–57.

Carlstein, T. (1982). *Time Resources, Society and Ecology*. London: George Allen and Unwin.

Carr, D. (1986). *Time, Narrative and History*. Bloomington: Indiana University Press.

Carrier, J.G. (1992). 'Occidentalism: the world turned upside-down', *American Ethnologist*, 19, 195–212.

Carrier, J.G. (ed.) (1995). *Occidentalism. Images of the West*. Oxford: Oxford University Press.

Carter, P. (1987). *The Road to Botany Bay*. London: Faber and Faber.

Carter, P. (1992). *Living in a New Country. History, Travelling and Language*. London: Faber and Faber.

Casey, E.W. (1993). *Getting Back into Place*. Bloomington: Indiana University Press.

Cassis, Y. (1984). *Les Banquiers de la City a l'Époque Edouardienne, 1890–1914*. Geneva: Droz.

Cassis, Y. (1987). *La City de Londres, 1870–1914*. Paris: Belin.

Castells, M. (1989). *The Informational City. Economic Restructuring and Urban Development*. Oxford: Blackwell.

Castells, M. (1993). 'The informational economy and the new international division of labour', in M. Carnoy, M. Castells, S. Cohen and F. Cardoso *The New Global Economy in the Information Age – Reflections on Our Changing World*. University Park: Pennsylvania State University Press, pp. 15–44.

Castoriadis, C. (1971). *History and Revolution*. London: Solidarity.

Castoriadis, C. (1975). *L'Institution imaginaire de la société* (3rd edn). Paris: Éditions du Seuil.

Castoriadis, C. (1984). *Crossroads in the Labyrinth*. Brighton: Harvester.

Castoriadis, C. (1987). *The Imaginary Institution of Society*. Cambridge: Polity Press.

Castoriadis, C. (1991a). 'Time and creation', in J. Bender and D.E. Wellbery (eds) *Chronotypes. The Construction of Time*. Stanford, CA: Stanford University Press, pp. 38–64.

Castoriadis, C. (1991b). *Philosophy, Politics, Autonomy. Essays in Political Philosophy*. Oxford: Oxford University Press.

Castoriadis, C. (1993). 'Merleau-Ponty and the weight of the ontological tradition', *Thesis Eleven*, 36, 1–36.

Castoriadis, C. (1994). 'The discovery of the imagination', *Constellations*, 1, 16–24.

Cawson, A. (ed.) (1986). *Organised Interests and the State*. London: Sage.

Cencini, A. (1984). *Money, Income, and Time*. Oxford: Blackwell.

Cerny, P.G. (ed.) (1993a). *Finance and World Politics. Markets, Regimes and States in a Post-Hegemonic Era*. Cheltenham: Edward Elgar.

Cerny, P.G. (1993b). 'Money and power: the American financial system from free banking to global competition', *PAIS Papers*, 116, University of Warwick.

Chambers, I. (1994). *Migrancy, Culture, Identity*. London: Routledge.

Chambers, R.C. (1954). 'A study of three voluntary organisations', in D.V. Glass (ed.) *Social Mobility in Britain*. London: Routledge and Kegan Paul, pp. 353–466.

Chapman, G.P. (1985). 'The folklore of the perceived environment in Bihar', *Environment and Planning A*, 15, 945–68.

Chapman, S. (1992). *Merchant Enterprise in Britain. From the Industrial Revolution to World War I*. Cambridge: Cambridge University Press.

Charlesworth, A. (1979). *Social Protest in a Rural Society*. Norwich: Geo-Abstracts.

Chartier, R. (1987). *The Cultural Uses of Print in Early Modern France*. Princeton, NJ: Princeton University Press.

Chartier, R. (1989). 'Texts, printings, readings', in L. Hunt (ed.) *The New Cultural History*. Berkeley: University of California Press, pp. 154–75.

Chartier, R. (1994). *The Order of the Book*. Cambridge: Polity Press.

Chaytor, H.J. (1945). *From Script to Print*. Cambridge: Cambridge University Press.

Cheal, P. (1988). *The Gift Economy*. London: Routledge.

Chesnaux, J. (1992). *Brave Modern World*. London: Thames and Hudson.

Childs, D. (1979). *Britain since 1945. A Political History*. London: Benn.

Christopherson, S. (1993). 'Market rules and territorial outcomes: the case of the United States', *International Journal of Urban and Regional Research*, 17, 274–88.

City of London Research Project (1992). *Intermediate Report*. London: City Corporation.

Claasen, C. (1993). *Worlds of Sense*. London: Routledge.

Clanchy, M.T. (1979). *From Memory to Written Record. England 1066–1307*. London: Edward Arnold.

Clanchy, M.T. (1993). *From Memory to Written Record. England 1066–1307* (2nd edn). London: Edward Arnold.

Clark, D.B. (1973). 'The concept of community: a re-examination', *Sociological Review*, 21, 63–82.

Clark, K. and Holquist, M. (1984). *Mikhail Bakhtin*. Cambridge, MA: Harvard University Press.

Classer, R. (1972). *Time in French Life and Thought*. Manchester: Manchester University Press.

Clegg, S. (1979). *The Theory of Power and Organisation*. Henley-on-Thames: Routledge and Kegan Paul.

Clifford, J. (1988). *The Predicament of Culture*. Cambridge, MA: Harvard University Press.

Clifford, J. (1992). 'Travelling cultures', in L. Grossberg, C. Nelson and P. Treichler (eds) *Cultural Studies*. London: Routledge, pp. 96–116.

Cobham, A. (ed.) (1992). *Markets and Dealers. The Economics of the London Financial Markets*. London: Longman.

Coghlan, A. (1992). *New Scientist*, 23 September.

Cohen, G.A. (1978). *Karl Marx's Theory of History. A Defence*. London: Oxford University Press.

Cohen, I. (1989). *Structuration Theory. Anthony Giddens and the Constitution of Social Life*. London: Macmillan.

Cohen, J.L. (1993). *Class and Civil Society. The Limits of Marxian Critical Theory*. Oxford: Martin Robertson.

Cohen, M. (1993). *Profane Illumination. Walter Benjamin and the Paris of Surrealist Revolution*. Berkeley: University of California Press.

Cohen, S. (1986). *Historical Culture. On the Recoding of an American Discipline*. Berkeley: University of California Press.

Coleman, S.N. (1928). *Bells. Their History, Legends, Making and Uses*. Chicago: Rand McNally.

Collier, A. (1981). 'Scientific realism and the human world: the case of psychoanalysis', *Radical Philosophy*, 16, 8–18.

Collins, H.M. (1990). *Artificial Experts. Social Knowledge and Intelligent Machines*. Cambridge, MA: MIT Press.

Collins, R. (1979). 'Review of Mayer', *American Journal of Sociology*, 85, 190.

Colson, F.H. (1926). *The Week*. Cambridge: Cambridge University Press.

Combined Production and Resources Board (1945). *The Impact of the War on Civilian Consumption*. London: HMSO.

Conley, T. (1993). 'A place for Leibniz', in G. Deleuze *The Fold. Leibniz and the Baroque*. Minneapolis: University of Minnesota Press, pp. i–xx.

Connell, R.W. (1983). *Which Way is Up? Essays on Class, Sex, and Culture*. Sydney: George Allen and Unwin.

Copjec, J. (ed.) (1994a). *Supposing the Subject*. London: Verso.

Copjec, J. (1994b). *Read My Desire. Lacan against the Historicists*. Cambridge, MA: MIT Press.

Corfield, P. (1990). 'Walking the city streets', *Journal of Urban History*, 16, 132–74.

Corner, J. (ed.) (1991). *Popular Television in Britain. Studies in Cultural History*. London: British Film Institute.

Corrigan, P. and Willis, P. (1980). 'Cultural forms and class mediations', *Media, Culture and Society*, 2, 297–312.

Coulter, J. (1989). *Mind in Action*. Cambridge: Polity Press.

Coulton, G.G. (1926). *The Medieval Village*. Cambridge: Cambridge University Press.

Coulton, G.G. (1938). *Medieval Panorama*. Cambridge: Cambridge University Press.

Courtney, J.E. (1926). *Recollected in Tranquility*. London: Heinemann.

Cowan, R.S. (1983). *More Work for Mother. The Ironies of Household Technology from the Open Hearth to the Microwave*. New York: Basic Books.

Craig, F.W.S. (1969). *British Parliamentary Results 1918–1949*. Chichester: Parliamentary Research Service.

Crary, J. (1990). *Techniques of the Observer. On Vision and Modernity in the Nineteenth Century*. Cambridge, MA: MIT Press.

Crary, J. (1994). 'Unbinding vision', *October*, 68, 22–44.

Crawford, D. and Turton, D. (eds) (1992). *Film as Ethnography*. Manchester: Manchester University Press.

Cresswell, T. (1993). 'Mobility as resistance: a geographical reading of Kerouac's *On the Road*', *Transactions of the Institute of British Geographers*, NS 18, 249–62.

Cressy, D. (1980). *Literacy and Social Order. Reading and Writing in Tudor and Stuart England*. Cambridge: Cambridge University Press.

Crossick, G. (1977). 'The emergence of the lower middle class in Britain: a discussion', in G. Crossick (ed.) *The Lower Middle Class in Britain, 1870–1914*. London: Croom Helm, pp. 11–60.

Crossley, N. (1994). *The Politics of Subjectivity*. Aldershot: Avebury.

Crump, T. (1990). *The Anthropology of Number*. Cambridge: Cambridge University Press.

Cubitt, S. (1991). *Timeshift. On Video Culture*. London: Routledge.

Curt, B. (1994). *Textuality and Tectonics. Troubling Social and Psychological Science*. Milton Keynes: Open University Press.

Daly, M.T. and Logan, M. (1989). *The Brittle Rim. Finance, Business and the Pacific Region*. Harmondsworth: Penguin Books.

Dancy, J. (1993). *Moral Reasons*. Oxford: Oxford University Press.

Darnton, R. (1978). 'The history of mentalities: recent writings on revolution, criminality and death in France', in R.H. Brown and S.M. Lyman (eds) *Structure, Consciousness, and History*. Cambridge: Cambridge University Press, pp. 106–36.

Darnton, R. (1979). *The Business of the Enlightenment. A Publishing History of the Encyclopédie, 1775–1800*. Cambridge, MA: Harvard University Press.

Davies, K. (1990). *Women and Time. The Weaving of the Strands of Everyday Life*. Aldershot: Avebury.

Davies, L. (1993). 'A raw deal', *The Sunday Times Magazine*, 4 July, 30–7.

Davis, E.P. (1990). *A Chance for the Top. The Lives of Women Business Graduates*. London: Bantam Press.

Davis, F. (1979). *Yearning for Yesterday. A Sociology of Nostalgia*. New York: Free Press.

Dawe, A. (1970). 'The two sociologies', *British Journal of Sociology*, 21, 207–18.

Dawe, A. (1979). 'Theories of social action', in T. Bottomore and R. Nisbet (eds) *A History of Sociological Analysis*. London: Heinemann Educational Books, pp. 362–417.

Debord, G. (1966). *The Society of the Spectacle*. Detroit: Black and Red.

de Certeau, M. (1984). *The Practice of Everyday Life*. Berkeley: University of California Press.

de Certeau, M. (1986). *Heterologies*. Manchester: Manchester University Press.

de Certeau, M. (1988). *The Writing of History*. New York: Columbia University Press.

de Certeau, M. (1991). 'Travel narratives of the French to Brazil: sixteenth to eighteenth centuries', *Representations*, 33, 221–6.

de Grauwe, P. (1989). *International Money. Post-war Trends and Theories*. Oxford: Oxford University Press.

Delanda, M. (1991). *War in the Age of Intelligent Machines*. New York: Zone Books.

Delaney, P. (1976). *The Puritan Experience*. Henley-on-Thames: Routledge and Kegan Paul.

Deleuze, G. (1988). *Foucault*. Minneapolis: University of Minnesota Press.

Deleuze, G. (1992). 'Postscript on the societies of control', *October*, 59, 3–7.

Deleuze, G. (1993). *The Fold. Leibniz and the Baroque*. Minneapolis: University of Minnesota Press.

Deleuze, G. and Guattari, F. (1983). *On the Line*. New York: Semiotext(e).

Deleuze, G. and Guattari, F. (1988). *A Thousand Plateaus. Capitalism and Schizophrenia*. London: Athlone Press.

Deleuze, G. and Guattari, F. (1994). *What is Philosophy?* London: Verso.

Deleuze, G. and Parnet, C. (1987). *Dialogues*. New York: Columbia University Press.

Demos, J. (1970). *A Little Commonwealth. Family Life in Plymouth Colony*. London: Oxford University Press.

Dennis, J., Lindberg, L. and McCrone, D. (1971). 'Support for nation and government among English children', *British Journal of Political Science*, 1, 25–48.

Denzin, N. (1991). *Images of Postmodern Society*. London: Sage.

Denzin, N. (1992). *Symbolic Interactionism and Cultural Studies. The Politics of Interpretation*. Oxford: Blackwell.

Der Derian, J. (1992). *Antidiplomacy. Spies, Terror, Speed and War*. Oxford: Blackwell.

Derrida, J. (1987). 'Heidegger's hand', in J. Sallis (ed.) *Deconstruction and Philosophy. The Texts of Jacques Derrida*. Chicago: Chicago University Press, pp. 161–96.

Derrida, J. (1988). *The Post Card. From Socrates to Freud and Beyond*. Chicago: University of Chicago Press.

de Schlippe, P. (1956). *Shifting Cultivation in Africa: the Zande System of Agriculture*. London: Macmillan.

De Sola Pool, I. (1977). *The Social History of the Telephone*. Cambridge, MA: MIT Press.

Diamond, C. (1991). *The Realistic Spirit. Wittgenstein, Philosophy and the Mind*. Cambridge, MA: MIT Press.

Dickinson, J.C. (1961). *Monastic Life in Medieval England*. London: Oxford University Press.

Dickinson, J.C. (1979). *An Ecclesiastical History of England. The Later Middle Ages from the Norman Conquest to the Reformation*. London: Black.

Dix, C. (1990). *A Chance for the Top*. London: Bantam.

Doane, M.A. (1993). 'Technology's body: cinematic vision in modernity', *Differences*, 5, 1–23.

Dodd, N. (1994). *The Sociology of Money: Economics, Reason and Contemporary Society*. Cambridge: Polity Press.

Dodgshon, R.A. (1978). 'The early Middle Ages, 1066–1350', in R.A. Dodgshon and R.A. Butlin (eds) *An Historical Geography of England and Wales*. London: Academic Press, pp. 81–117.

Doe, V.S. (ed.) (1978). *The Diary of James Clegg of Chapel-en-le-Frith 1708–1755* (2 vols). Matlock: Derbyshire Record Society.

Doel, M. (1993). 'Proverbs for paranoids: writing geography on hollowed ground', *Transactions of the Institute of British Geographers*. 18, 377–94.

Doise, W. and Palmonari, A. (eds) (1984). *Social Interaction in Individual Development*. Cambridge: Cambridge University Press.

Domosh, M. (1991). 'Towards a feminist historiography of geography', *Transactions of the Institute of British Geographers*, NS 16, 95–104.

Donovan, C. (1991). *The de Brailes Hours. Shaping the Book of Hours in Thirteenth Century Oxford*. London: British Library.

Dostal, R.J. (1993). 'Time and phenomenology in Husserl and Heidegger', in C. Guignon (ed.) *The Cambridge Companion to Heidegger*. Cambridge: Cambridge University Press, pp. 141–69.

Douglas, M. (1966). *Purity and Danger*. Oxford: Blackwell.

Dove, R.H. (1982). *A Bellringer's Guide to the Church Bells of Britain* (6th edn). Aldershot: Viggers.

Downman, E.A. (1898). *Ancient Church Bells in England*. Advance Edition issued privately.

Drainville, A.C. (1993). 'International political economy in an age of open Marxism'. *University of Amsterdam Department of International Relations Working Paper 27*.

Dreyfus, H. (1991). *Being-in-the-World. A Commentary on Heidegger's Being and Time, Division 1*. Cambridge, MA: MIT Press.

Dreyfus, H. (1992). 'Heidegger's history of the being of equipment', in H. Dreyfus and H. Hall (eds) *Heidegger. A Critical Reader*. Oxford: Blackwell, pp. 173–85.

Dreyfus, H. and Hall, H. (eds) (1992). *Heidegger. A Critical Reader*. Oxford: Blackwell.

Dreyfus, H. and Rabinow, P. (1993). 'Can there be a science of existential structure and social meaning?', in C. Calhoun, E. Lipuma and M. Postone (eds) *Bourdieu. Critical Perspectives*. Oxford: Blackwell, pp. 35–44.

Driver, F. and Rose, G. (eds) (1992). *Nature and Science. Essays in the History of Geographical*

Knowledge. Historical Geography Research Series No. 28. London: Institute of British Geographers.

Duley, A.J. (1977). *The Medieval Clock of Salisbury Cathedral.* Salisbury.

Dunford, M.F. (1981). 'Historical materialism and geography'. Research paper 4, Department of Geography, University of Sussex, Brighton, England.

Dunlop, C. and Kling, R. (eds) (1991). *Computerisation and Controversy. Value Conflicts and Social Choice.* New York: Academic Press.

Dunning, J.H. and Morgan, E.V. (1971). *An Economic Study of the City of London.* London: Allen and Unwin.

Eagleton, T. (1990). *The Ideology of the Aesthetic.* Oxford: Blackwell.

Eagleton, T. (1993). 'The new sublime', *London Review of Books,* pp. 6–7.

Eatwell, R. (1979). *The 1945–1951 Labour Governments.* London: Batsford.

Eccles, R.G. and Crane, D.B. (1988). *Doing Deals. Investment Banks at Work.* Boston: Harvard Business School Press.

Economist (1993). 'Putting the City together again', *The Economist,* 1 May, 15.

Economist (1994a). 'Recalled to life: a survey of international banking', *The Economist,* 30 April, 1–46.

Economist (1994b). 'Mind over matter', *The Economist,* 23 April, 105–6.

Eisenstein, E.L. (1979). *The Printing Press as an Agent of Change* (2 vols). Cambridge: Cambridge University Press.

Elder, G. (1974). *Children of the Great Depression.* Chicago: University of Chicago Press.

Elder, G. (1980). *Family Structure and Socialisation.* New York: Arno Press.

Elder, G. (1981). 'History and the life course', in D. Bertaux (ed.) *Biography and Society. The Life History Approach in the Social Sciences.* Beverly Hills, CA: Sage, pp. 77–115.

Eley, G. (1992). 'Nations, publics and political cultures: placing Habermas in the nineteenth century', in C.J. Calhoun (ed.) *Habermas and the Public Sphere.* Cambridge, MA: MIT Press.

Elias, N. (1978). *The Civilising Process 1. The History of Manners.* Oxford: Basil Blackwell.

Elias, N. (1982). *The Civilising Process 2. State Formation and Civilisation.* Oxford: Basil Blackwell.

Elias, N. (1992). *Time. An Essay.* Oxford: Blackwell.

Ellacombe, H.T. (1975). *The Church Bells of Somerset.* Exeter.

Elliott, A. (1992). *Social Theory and Psychoanalysis in Transition. Self and Society from Freud to Kristeva.* Oxford: Blackwell.

Emberley, D. (1989). 'Places and stories: the challenge of technology', *Social Research,* 56, 241–85.

Emmison, M. (1985). 'Class images of the economy: opposition and ideological incorporation within working-class consciousness', *Sociology,* 19, 19–38.

Eribon, D. (1991). *Michel Foucault.* Cambridge, MA: Harvard University Press.

Erikson, E.H. (1959). *Identity and the Life Cycle.* New York: W.W. Norton.

Erikson, E.H. (1963). *Childhood and Society* (2nd edn). New York: W.W. Norton.

Erikson, E.H. (1975). *Life History and the Historical Moment.* New York: W.W. Norton.

Evans-Pritchard, E.E. (1940). *The Nuer. A Description of the Modes of Livelihood and Political Institutions of a Nilotic People.* London: Oxford University Press.

Faraday, A. and Plummer, K. (1979). 'Doing life histories', *Sociological Review,* 27, 773–98.

Favret-Saada, J. (1980). *Deadly Words. Witchcraft in the Bocage.* Cambridge: Cambridge University Press.

Fay, B. (1970). *A Banker's World. The Revival of the City, 1957–70.* London: Collins.

Featherstone, M. (1991). 'The body in consumer culture', in M. Featherstone, M. Hepworth and B. Turner (eds) *The Body. Social Process and Cultural Theory.* London: Sage, pp. 170–96.

Febvre, L. and Martin, H.J. (1976). *The Coming of the Book. The Impact of Printing 1450–1800.* London: New Left Books.

Feenberg, A. (1991). *Critical Theory of Technology.* New York: Oxford University Press.

Fentress, J. and Wickham, C. (1992). *Social Memory.* Oxford: Blackwell.

Ferguson, S. and Fitzgerald, H. (1954). *Studies in the Social Sciences*. London: HMSO.

Ferrarotti, F. (1981). 'On the autonomy of the biographical method', in D. Bertaux (ed.) *Biography and Society. The Life History Approach in the Social Sciences*. Beverly Hills, CA: Sage, pp. 19–27.

Financial Times (1993). '100 years in the pink', *Financial Times*, 4 January, i–x.

Fischer, C.S. (1992). *America Calling. A Social History of the Telephone to 1940*. Berkeley: University of California Press.

Flandrin, J. (1979). *Families in Former Times. Kinship, Household and Sexuality*. Cambridge: Cambridge University Press.

Flores, J. and Yudice, G. (1990). 'Living borders/buscando America', *Social Text*, 24, 57–84.

Fogarty, M.P. (1945). *Prospects of the Industrial Areas of Great Britain*. London: Methuen.

Folch-Serra, M. (1990). 'Place, voice, space: Mikhail Bakhtin's dialogical landscape', *Environment and Planning D. Society and Space*, 8, 255–74.

Forty, A. (1986). *Objects of Desire*. London: Thames and Hudson.

Foster, H. (ed.) (1988). *Vision and Visuality*. London: Pluto Press.

Foster, J. (1974). *Class Struggle and the Industrial Revolution*. London: Weidenfeld and Nicolson.

Foster-Carter, A. (1978). 'The modes of production controversy', *New Left Review*, 107, 47–77.

Foucault, M. (1970). *The Order of Things. An Archaeology of the Human Sciences*. London: Tavistock.

Foucault, M. (1972). *The Archaeology of Knowledge*. Andover: Tavistock.

Foucault, M. (1977). *Discipline and Punish. The Birth of the Prison*. London: Allen Lane.

Foucault, M. (1985). *The Use of Pleasure. The History of Sexuality. Volume 2*. Harmondsworth: Penguin.

Fraser, R. (1979). *Blood of Spain. The Experience of Civil War, 1936–1939*. London: Allen Lane.

French, P.J. (1972). *John Dee: The World of an Elizabethan Magus*. London: Macmillan.

Freud, S. (1974). *The Standard Edition of the Complete Works of Sigmund Freud. Volume 16*. London: Hogarth Press.

Friedman, J. (1992). 'Narcissism, roots and postmodernity: the constitution of selfhood in the global crisis', in S. Lash and J. Friedman (eds) *Modernity and Identity*. Oxford: Blackwell, pp. 331–66.

Frisby, D. (1992). *Simmel and Since. Essays on Georg Simmel's Social Theory*. London: Routledge.

Fromm, E. (1981). *The Greatness and Limitations of Freud's Thought*. London: Picador.

Frosh, S. (1991). *Identity Crisis. Modernity, Psychoanalysis, and the Self*. London: Macmillan.

Frow, J. (1991). Michel de Certeau and the politics of representation, *Cultural Studies*, 5, 52–60.

Gallup, G.H. (1976). *The Gallup International Public Opinion Polls. Great Britain 1937–1975. Volume 1: 1937–1964*. New York: Random House.

Game, A. (1991). *Undoing the Social. Towards a Deconstructive Sociology*. Milton Keynes: Open University Press.

Ganguly, K. (1992). 'Migrant identities: personal memory and the constitution of selfhood', *Cultural Studies*, 6, 27–50.

Garfinkel, H. (1967). *Studies in Ethnomethodology*. Englewood Cliffs, NJ: Prentice Hall.

Garnham, N. and Williams, R. (1980). 'Pierre Bourdieu and the sociology of culture: an introduction', *Media, Culture and Society*, 2, 209–23.

Gauld, A. and Shotter, J. (1977). *Human Action and Its Psychological Investigation*. London: Routledge and Kegan Paul.

Geertz, C. (1983). *Local Knowledge. Further Essays in Interpretative Anthropology*. New York: Basic Books.

Geertz, C. (1989). *Works and Lives*. Cambridge: Polity Press.

Gell, A. (1992). *The Anthropology of Time*. Oxford: Berg.

Gellner, E. (1964). *Thought and Change*. London: Weidenfeld and Nicolson.

Gellner, E. (1974). 'The new idealism: cause and meaning in the social sciences', in A. Giddens (ed.) *Positivism and Sociology*. London: Heinemann.

Geras, N. (1983). *Marx and Human Nature. Refutation of a Legend*. London: Verso.

Gergen, K.J. (1991). *The Saturated Self. Dilemmas of Identity in Contemporary Life*. New York: Basic Books.

Gerger, T. and Hoppe, G. (1980). *Education and Society. The Geographer's View*. Stockholm: Almqvist and Wiksell.

Giard, L. (1991). 'Michel de Certeau's heterology and the New World', *Representations*, 33, 212–21.

Gibson, J.J. (1979). *The Ecological Approach to Visual Perception*. Boston: Houghton Mifflin.

Giddens, A. (1973). *The Class Structure of the Advanced Societies*. London: Hutchinson.

Giddens, A. (1976). *New Rules of Sociological Method*. London: Hutchinson.

Giddens, A. (1977). *Studies in Social and Political Theory*. London: Macmillan.

Giddens, A. (1979a). *Central Problems in Social Theory. Action, Structure and Contradiction in Social Analysis*. London: Macmillan.

Giddens, A. (1979b). 'Postscript 1979', in *The Class Structure of the Advanced Societies* (2nd edn). London: Hutchinson.

Giddens, A. (1981). *A Contemporary Critique of Historical Materialism*. London: Macmillan.

Giddens, A. (1982). 'Commentary on the debate', *Theory and Society*, 11, 527–39.

Giddens, A. (1984). *The Constitution of Society. Outline of the Theory of Structuration*. Cambridge: Polity Press.

Giddens, A. (1987). 'Structuralism, poststructuralism and the production of culture', in A. Giddens and J. Turner (eds) *Social Theory Today*. Cambridge: Polity Press.

Giddens, A. (1989). 'Comments', in D. Held and J.B. Thompson (eds) *Social Theory of Modern Societies. Anthony Giddens and His Cities*. Cambridge: Cambridge University Press.

Giddens, A. (1990). *Consequences of Modernity*. Cambridge: Polity Press.

Giddens, A. (1991). *Modernity and Self-Identity*. Cambridge: Polity Press.

Giddens, A. (1992). *The Transformation of Intimacy. Sexuality, Love and Eroticism in Modern Societies*. Cambridge: Polity Press.

Giddens, A. (1994). *Beyond Left and Right. The Future of Radical Politics*. Cambridge: Polity Press.

Gill, S. (1990). *American Hegemony and the Trilateral Commission*. Cambridge: Cambridge University Press.

Gill, S. (ed.) (1993). *Gramsci, Historical Materialism and International Relations*. Cambridge: Cambridge University Press.

Gilligan, C. (1982). *In a Different Voice*. Cambridge, MA: Harvard University Press.

Gilroy, P. (1992). 'Cultural studies and ethnic absolutisms', in L. Grossberg, C. Nelson and P. Treichler (eds) *Cultural Studies*. London: Routledge, pp. 187–98.

Gilroy, P. (1993a). *The Black Atlantic. Modernity and Double Consciousness*. London: Verso.

Gilroy, P. (1993b). *Small Acts. Thoughts on the Politics of Black Cultures*. London: Serpent's Tail.

Ginzburg, C. (1976). 'High and low: the theme of forbidden knowledge in the late 16th and 17th centuries', *Past and Present*, 73, 216–32.

Ginzburg, C. (1979). 'Clues: roots of a scientific paradigm', *Theory and Society*, 7, 273–88.

Ginzburg, C. (1980a). *The Cheese and the Worms. The Cosmos of a Sixteenth-Century Miller*. Henley-on-Thames: Routledge and Kegan Paul.

Ginzburg, C. (1980b). 'Morelli, Freud and Sherlock Holmes: clues and scientific method', *History Workshop*, 9, 5–36.

Giroux, H.A. (1992). 'Revisiting difference: cultural studies and the discourse of critical pedagogy', in L. Grossberg, C. Nelson and P. Treichler (eds) *Cultural Studies*. London: Routledge, pp. 199–212.

Gitlin, T. (1989). 'Postmodernism – roots and politics', *Dissent*, 16, 23–32.

Godzich, W. (1986). 'Foreword: the possibility of knowledge', in M. de Certeau *Heterologies. Discourse on the Other*. Manchester: Manchester University Press, pp. vii–xxi.

Goffman, E. (1974). *Frame Analysis*. New York: Harper and Row.

Goodhart, C. (1989). *Money, Information and Uncertainty*. London: Macmillan.

Goody, J. (ed.) (1968a). *Literacy in Traditional Societies*. Cambridge: Cambridge University Press.

Goody, J. (1968b) 'Restricted literacy in northern Ghana', in J. Goody (ed.) *Literacy in Traditional Societies*. Cambridge: Cambridge University Press, pp. 198–264.

Goody, J. (1977). *The Domestication of the Savage Mind*. Cambridge: Cambridge University Press.

Goody, J. (1991). 'The time of telling and the telling of time in written and oral cultures', in J. Bender and D.E. Wellbery (eds) *Chronotypes. The Construction of Time*. Stanford, CA: Stanford University Press, 77–96.

Goody, J. and Watt, I. (1963). 'The consequences of literacy', *Comparative Studies in History and Sociology*, 5, 304–45.

Gosden, C. (1994). *Social Being and Time*. Oxford: Blackwell.

Gouldner, A.W. (1980). *The Two Marxisms. Contradictions and Anomalies in the Development of Theory*. London: Macmillan.

Goux, J.J. (1990a). *Symbolic Economies. After Marx and Freud*. Ithaca, NY: Cornell University Press.

Goux, J.J. (1990b). 'General economics and postmodern capitalism', *Yale French Studies*, 78, 206–24.

Graham, R.P.H. (1956). 'Salisbury and the West Country Clocks', *Antiquarian Horology*, December, 2–7.

Grahl, J. (1991). 'Economies out of control', *New Left Review*, 185, 170–83.

Granovetter, M.S. (1985). 'Economic action and social structure: the problem of embeddedness', *American Journal of Sociology*, 91, 481–510.

Granovetter, M.S. and Swedberg, R. (eds) (1992). *The Sociology of Economic Life*. Boulder, CO: Westview Press.

Grant, J. (1992). *Money of the Mind. Borrowing and Lending in America from the Civil War to Michael Milken*. New York: Noonday Books.

Gregory, D. (1978). *Ideology, Science and Human Geography*. London: Hutchinson.

Gregory, D. (1981). 'Human agency and human geography', *Transactions of the Institute of British Geographers*, NS 6, 1–18.

Gregory, D. (1982). 'Solid geometry: notes on the recovery of spatial structure', in P. Gould and G. Olsson (eds) *A Search for Common Ground*. London: Pion, pp. 187–219.

Gregory, D. (1984a). 'Contours of crisis? Sketches for a geography of class struggle in the early industrial revolution in England', in A.R. Baker and D. Gregory (eds) *Explanations in Historical Geography. Interpretative Essays*. Cambridge: Cambridge University Press, pp. 68–117.

Gregory, D. (1984b). 'People, places and practices: the future of human geography' (mimeo).

Gregory, D. (1985). 'Suspended animation: the stasis of diffusion theory', in D. Gregory and J. Urry (eds) *Social Relations and Spatial Structures*. London: Macmillan, pp. 296–336.

Gregory, D. (1989). 'Presences and absences: time-space relations and structuration theory', in D. Held and J.B. Thompson (eds) *Social Theory of Modern Societies. Anthony Giddens and his Critics*. Cambridge: Cambridge University Press.

Greven, P. (1977). *The Protestant Temperament. Patterns of Child-Rearing, Religious Experience and the Self in Early America*. New York: Alfred Knopf.

Groh, D. (1979). 'Base-processes and the problem of organisation: outline of a social history research project', *Social History*, 4, 265–83.

Grossberg, L. (1988). 'Wandering audiences, nomadic critics', *Cultural Studies*, 2, 377–91.

Grossberg, L. (1992). *We Gotta Get Out of This Place. Pop, Politics and Postmodernity*. New York: Routledge.

Grosz, E. (1993). 'Merleau-Ponty and Irigaray in the flesh', *Thesis Eleven*, 36, 37–59.

Grosz, E. (1994a). 'A thousand tiny sexes: feminism and rhizomatics', in C.V. Boundas and D. Olkowski (eds) *Gilles Deleuze and the Theater of Philosophy*. New York: Routledge, pp. 187–210.

Grosz, E. (1994b). *Volatile Bodies. Towards a Corporeal Feminism.* Bloomington: Indiana University Press.

Grosz, E. (1994c). 'Experimental desire: rethinking queer subjectivity', in J. Copjec (ed.) *Supposing the Subject.* London: Verso, pp. 133–57.

Guignon, C. (ed.) (1993). *The Cambridge Companion to Heidegger.* Cambridge: Cambridge University Press.

Gumbrecht, H.U. and Pfeiffer, K.L. (eds) (1994). *Materialities of Communication.* Stanford, CA: Stanford University Press

Gurevich, A.J. (1985). *Categories of Medieval Culture.* London: Routledge and Kegan Paul.

Habermas, J. (1979). *Communication and the Evolution of Society.* London: Heinemann Educational Books.

Habermas, J. (1982). 'A reply to my critics', in J.B. Thompson and D. Held (eds) *Habermas. Critical Debates.* London: Macmillan, pp. 219–83.

Habermas, J. (1989). *The Structural Transformation of the Public Sphere.* Cambridge: Polity Press.

Habermas, J. (1992). 'Further reflections on the public sphere', in C. Calhoun (ed.) *Habermas and the Public Sphere.* Cambridge, MA: MIT Press.

Hägerstrand, T. (1970). 'What about people in regional science?', *Papers of the Regional Science Association,* 24, 7–21.

Hägerstrand, T. (1973). 'The domain of human geography', in R.J. Chorley (ed.) *Directions in Geography.* Andover: Methuen, pp. 67–87.

Hägerstrand, T. (1974a). 'Tidgeografisk beskrivning-syfte och postulat', *Svensk Geografisk Arsbok,* 50, 86–94.

Hägerstrand, T. (1974b). 'Commentary', in A. Buttimer (ed.) *Values in Geography.* Washington, DC: Association of American Geographers.

Hägerstrand, T. (1982). 'Diorama, path and project', *Tijdschrift voor Economische en Sociale Geografie,* 73, 323–39.

Hall, D. (1982). *Medieval Fields.* Princes Risborough: Shire Publications.

Hall, H. (1993). 'Intentionality and world', in C. Guignon (ed.) *The Cambridge Companion to Heidegger.* Cambridge: Cambridge University Press, pp. 122–40.

Hall, S. (1980). 'Cultural studies: two paradigms', *Media, Culture and Society,* 2, 57–72.

Hall, S. (1983). 'The problem of ideology', in E. Matthews (ed.) *Marx: A Hundred Years On.* London: Lawrence and Wishart, pp. 50–63.

Hall, S. (1991a). 'The local and the global: globalisation and ethnicity', in A.D. King (ed.) *Culture, Globalisation and the World-System.* London: Macmillan, pp. 19–40.

Hall, S. (1991b). 'Old and new identities, old and new ethnicities', in A.D. King (ed.) *Culture, Globalisation and the World-System.* London: Macmillan, pp. 41–68.

Hallam, H.E. (1981). *Rural England, 1066–1348.* London: Fontana.

Hannah, L. (1979). *Electricity before Nationalisation.* London: Methuen.

Hannah, M. (1992). 'Foucault on theorising specificity', *Environment and Planning D. Society and Space,* 11, 349–63.

Hannerz, U. (1992). *Cultural Complexity. Studies in the Social Organisation of Meaning.* New York: Columbia University Press.

Haraway, D.J. (1985). 'Manifesto for cyborgs: science, technology, and socialist feminism in the 1980s', *Socialist Review,* 80, 65–108.

Haraway, D.J. (1991a). *Simians, Cyborgs, and Women. The Reinvention of Nature.* London: Free Association Books.

Haraway, D.J. (1991b). 'The actors are cyborgs, nature is coyote, and the geography is elsewhere: postscript to "Cyborgs at large"', in C. Penley and A. Ross (eds) *Technoculture.* Minneapolis: University of Minnesota Press, pp. 21–6.

Haraway, D.J. (1992a). 'Ecce home, aint (arnt) I a woman, and inappropriate(d) others: the human in a post-humanist landscape', in J. Butler and J.W. Scott (eds) *Feminists Theorise the Political.* New York: Routledge, pp. 86–100.

Haraway, D.J. (1992b). 'The promises of monsters: a regenerative politics for inappropriate/d others', in L. Grossberg, C. Nelson and P. Treichler (eds) *Cultural Studies*. New York: Routledge, pp. 295–337.

Haraway, D.J. (1993). 'Modest witness @ second millenium: the female man meets oncomouse'. Paper given to British Association of Social Anthropologists, Oxford, July.

Hardt, M. (1993). *Gilles Deleuze. An Apprenticeship in Philosophy*. London: UCL Press.

Hareven, T.K. (1975). 'Family time and industrial time: family and work in a planned corporation town, 1900–1924', *Journal of Urban History*, 1, 365–89.

Hareven, T.K. (1982). *Family Time and Industrial Time. The Relationship between the Family and Work in a New England Industrial Community*. Cambridge: Cambridge University Press.

Hareven, T.K. and Langenbach, R. (1978). *Amoskeag. Life and Work in an American Factory-City*. New York: Pantheon Books.

Harré, R. (1974). 'Blueprint for a new science', in N. Armistead (ed.) *Reconstructuring Social Psychology*. Harmondsworth: Penguin, pp. 240–59.

Harré, R. (1978). 'Architectonic man: on the structuring of lived experience', in R.H. Brown and S.M. Lyman (eds) *Structure, Consciousness and History*. Cambridge: Cambridge University Press, pp. 139–72.

Harré, R. (1979). *Social Being. A Theory for Social Psychology*. Oxford: Blackwell.

Harré, R. (1983). *Personal Being*. Oxford: Blackwell.

Harré, R. (1984). 'Social elements as mind', *British Journal of Medical Psychology*, 57, 127–35.

Harré, R. (1991). *Physical Being*. Oxford: Blackwell.

Harrington, W. and Young, P. (1978). *The 1945 Revolution*. London: Davis Poynter.

Harris, J. and Thane, P. (1984). 'British and European bankers, 1880–1914: an aristocratic bourgeoisie?', in P. Thane, G. Crossick and R. Floud (eds) *The Power of the Past*. London: Methuen.

Harrison, M. (1986). 'The ordering of the urban environment: time, work and the occurrence of crowds 1790–1835', *Past and Present*, 110, 134–68.

Harrison, R. (1981). 'Marxism as nineteenth-century critique and twentieth-century ideology', *History*, 66, 208–20.

Harrison, T. (1942). 'Class consciousness and class unconsciousness', *Sociological Review*, 34, 16–23.

Hart, H.W. and Piersma, J. (1990). 'Direct representation in international financial markets: the case of foreign banks in Amsterdam', *Tijdschrift voor Economische en Sociale Geografie*, 81, 82–92.

Harthan, J.P. (1977). *Books of Hours and Their Owners*. London: Thames and Hudson.

Harvey, D.W. (1985). 'Money, time, space and the city', in D.W. Harvey *Consciousness and the Urban Experience*. Oxford: Blackwell, pp. 1–35.

Harvey, D.W. (1989). *The Condition of Postmodernity*. Oxford: Blackwell.

Harvey, K.E. (1986). *The Winchester Psalter. An Iconographic Study*. Leicester: Leicester University Press.

Harvey, P.D.A. (1965). *A Medieval Oxfordshire Village. Cuxham 1240–1400*. London: Oxford University Press.

Haskell, T.L. and Teichgraber, R.F. (eds) (1994). *The Culture of the Market*. Cambridge: Cambridge University Press.

Hawley, A.H. (1950). *Human Ecology. A Theory of Community Structure*. New York: Ronald Press.

Hawthorn, G. (1976). *Enlightenment and Despair. A History of Sociology*. Cambridge: Cambridge University Press.

Hayden, D. (1981). *The Grand Domestic Revolution. A History of Feminist Designs for American Homes, Neighborhoods and Cities*. Cambridge, MA: MIT Press.

Hayward, P. (ed.) (1991). *Culture, Technology and Creativity in the Late Twentieth Century*. London: John Libbey.

Hearn, F. (1978). *Domination, Legitimation and Resistance. The Incorporation of the Nineteenth-Century Working Class*. Westport, CT: Greenwood Press.

Heath, C., Jirotka, M., Luff, P. and Hindmarsh, J. (1993). 'Unpacking collaboration: the interactional organisation of trading in a City dealing room', *Proceedings of the European Conference on Computer Supported Cooperative Work (CSCW) '93*. Milan.

Hebdige, D. (1993). 'Redeeming witness: in the tracks of the homeless vehicle project', *Cultural Studies*, 7, 173–223.

Heelas, P. (1990). 'Review article: the economics of new religious life', *Religion*, 20, 297–302.

Heelas, P. (1991). 'Cults for capitalism: self religions, magic and the empowerment of business', in P. Gee and J. Fulton (eds) *Religion and Power. Decline and Growth*. London: British Sociology Association Study of Religion Group, pp. 27–41.

Heelas, P. (1993). 'The New Age in cultural context: the premodern, the modern and the postmodern', *Religion*, 23, 103–16.

Heidegger, M. (1962). *Being and Time*. New York: Harper and Row.

Heidegger, M. (1977). 'Building, dwelling, thinking', in M. Heidegger *Basic Writings*. New York: Harper and Row.

Heidegger, M. (1985). *History of the Concept of Time*. Bloomington: Indiana University Press.

Hekman, S. (1990). 'Structuration and time', in J. Clark, C. Modgil and S. Modgil (eds) *Anthony Giddens. Consensus and Controversy*. London: Falmer Press.

Held, D. (1991). 'Democracy, the nation-state and the global system', *Economy and Society*, 20, 138–72.

Held, D. and Thompson, J. (eds) (1989). *Social Theory of Modern Societies. Anthony Giddens and His Critics*. Cambridge: Cambridge University Press.

Hélias, P-J. (1978). *The Horse of Pride. Life in a Breton Village*. New Haven, CT: Yale University Press.

Helleiner, E. (1993). *The Resurgence of Global Finance*. Ithaca, NY: Cornell University Press.

Heller, A. (1982). 'Habermas and Marxism', in J.B. Thompson and D. Held (eds) *Habermas. Critical Debates*. London: Macmillan, pp. 21–41.

Helms, M.W. (1988). *Ulysses' Sail*. Princeton: Princeton University Press.

Hennessy, M. (1992). *A Domestic History of the Bank of England, 1930–1960*. Cambridge: Cambridge University Press.

Henriques, J., Holloway, W., Urwin, J., Couze, R. and Walkerdine, V. (1984). *Changing the Subject*. London: Methuen.

Heritage, J. (1984). *Garfinkel and Ethnomethodology*. Cambridge: Polity Press.

Hermes, J. (1993). 'Media, meaning and everyday life', *Cultural Studies*, 7, 493–506.

Hernes, G. (1991). 'Comments', in P. Bourdieu and J.S. Coleman (eds) *Social Theory for a Changing Society*. Boulder, CO: Westview, pp. 121–6.

Herzfeld, M. (1987). *Anthropology Through the Looking Glass*. Cambridge: Cambridge University Press.

Hey, D.G. (1974). *An English Rural Community: Myddle under the Tudors and Stuarts*. Leicester: Leicester University Press.

Hill, C. (1982). 'Science and magic in seventeenth century England', in R. Samuel and G. Stedman Jones (eds) *Culture, Ideology and Politics: Essays for Eric Hobsbawm*. London: Routledge and Kegan Paul, pp. 176–93.

Hindess, B. (1977). *Philosophy and Methodology in the Social Sciences*. Brighton: Harvester.

Hindess, B. (1982). 'Power, interests and the outcome of struggles', *Sociology*, 16, 498–511.

Hirsch, F. (1977). *Social Limits to Growth*. London: Routledge and Kegan Paul.

Hirst, P. (1982). 'Witchcraft today and yesterday', *Economy and Society*, 11, 428–48.

Hirst, P. and Woolley, P. (1982). *Social Relations and Human Attributes*. Andover: Tavistock.

History of the Human Sciences (1994). 'Symposium on social constructionism', *History of the Human Sciences*, 7(2), 81–123.

History Workshop (1979). 'Editorial: urban history and local history', *History Workshop*, 8, iv–vi.

Hoban, R. (1983). *Pilgermann*. London: Jonathan Cape.

Hobsbawm, E. (1980). 'The revival of narrative: some comments', *Past and Present*, 86, 3–8.

Hobson, O.R. (1940). *How the City Works*. London: Dickens Press.

Holden, C.H. and Holford, W.G. (1951). *The City of London. A Record of Destruction and Survival*. London: Architectural Press.

Holderness, M. (1993). 'It all adds up to money', *The Independent*, 13 December, 23.

Hollis, M. (1977). *Models of Man*. Cambridge: Cambridge University Press.

Hollis, P. (1970). *The Pauper Press*. Oxford: Oxford University Press.

Holmes, R. (1985). *Footsteps. Adventures of a Romantic Biographer*. London: Hodder and Stoughton.

Holmes, R. (1993). *Dr Johnson and Mr Savage*. London: Hodder and Stoughton.

Holy, L. and Stuchlik, M. (eds) (1981). *The Structure of Folk Models*. London: Academic Press.

Holy, L. and Stuchlik, M. (1983). *Actions, Norms and Representations. Foundations of Anthropological Inquiry*. Cambridge: Cambridge University Press.

Holzner, D. (1972). *Reality Construction in Society*. Cambridge, MA: Schenkman.

Homans, G.C. (1941). *English Villages of the Thirteenth Century*. Cambridge, MA: Harvard University Press.

Howard, A. (1963). 'We are the masters now', in M. Sissons and P. French (eds) *Age of Austerity 1945–1951*. London: Hodder and Stoughton.

Hughes, T.P. (1983). *Networks of Power. Electrification in Western Society 1880–1930*. Baltimore, MD: Johns Hopkins University Press.

Hull, J.M. (1990). *Touching the Rock*. London: SPCK.

Hunt, D. (1982). 'Village culture and the Vietnamese revolution', *Past and Present*, 94, 131–257.

Hurley, S. (1985). 'Objectivity and disagreement', in T. Honderich (ed.) *Morality and Objectivity*. London: Routledge, pp. 54–97.

Hutton, R. (1994). *The Rise and Fall of Merry England. The Ritual Year, 1400–1700*. Oxford: Oxford University Press.

IDS Bulletin (1979). 'Rural development: whose knowledge counts?', *Institute of Development Studies Bulletin*, 16(1).

Ingham, G. (1984). *Capitalism Divided? The City and Industry in British Social Development*. London: Macmillan.

Ingold, T. (1995). 'Work, time and industry', *Time and Society*, 4, 5–28.

Ingram, T. (1954). *Bells in England*. London: Frederick Muller.

Innis, H.A. (1950). *Empire and Communications*. Oxford: Oxford University Press.

Innis, H.A. (1951). *The Bias of Communication*. Toronto: University of Toronto Press.

Ireland, J. (1994). 'The importance of telecommunications to London as an international financial centre', *City Research Project Subject Report 6*.

Jackson, M. (1982). 'Thinking through the body: an essay on understanding metaphor', *mimeo*.

James, W. (1992). 'Migration, racism and identity: the Caribbean experience in Britain', *New Left Review*, 193, 15–55.

Jameson, F. (1991). *Postmodernism, or The Cultural Logic of Late Capitalism*. London: Verso.

Jardine, A. (1984). 'Women in limbo: Deleuze and his Br(others)', *Substance*, 13, 46–60.

Jay, M. (1992). 'Scopic regimes of modernity', in S. Lash and J. Friedman (eds) *Modernity and Identity*. Oxford: Blackwell, pp. 178–95.

Jay, M. (1993). *Downcast Eyes. The Negation of Vision in Twentieth-Century French Thought*. Berkeley: University of California Press.

Jayaweera, N.D. (1983). 'Communication satellites: a third world perspective', *Media Development*, 30, 12–31.

Jenkins, H. (1992). *Textual Poachers. Television and Participating Culture*. New York: Routledge.

Jessop, B. (1990). *State Theory. Putting Capitalist States in Their Place*. Cambridge: Polity Press.

Jirotka, M., Luff, P. and Heath, C. (1993). 'Requirements engineering and interactions in the workplace: a case study in City dealing rooms', *Proceedings of the Workshop on Social Science, Technical Systems and Cooperative Work*. Paris.

Joas, H. (1990). 'The moral stance of Giddens', in J. Clark, C. Modgil and S. Modgil (eds) *Anthony Giddens. Consensus and Controversy*. London: Falmer Press.

Johnson, C. (1993). *System and Writing in the Philosophy of Jacques Derrida*. Cambridge: Cambridge University Press.

Jones, K. and Williamson, K. (1979). 'The birth of the schoolroom: a study of the transformation in the discursive conditions of English popular education in the first half of the nineteenth century', *Ideology and Consciousness*, Autumn, 58–110.

Jordanova, L. (ed.) (1986). *Languages of Nature. Critical Essays on Science and Literature*. London: Free Association Books.

Jordanova, L. (1989). *Sexual Visions. Images of Gender in Science and Medicine in the Eighteenth and Twentieth Centuries*. Brighton: Harvester Wheatsheaf.

Joyce, P. (1980). *Work, Society and Politics. The Culture of the Factory in Later Victorian England*. Hassocks: Harvester Press.

Joyce, P. (1984). 'Languages of reciprocity and conflict: a response to Richard Price', *Social History*, 9, 225–31.

Judt, T. (1979). *Socialism in Provence, 1871–1914. A Study in the Origins of the Modern French Left*. Cambridge: Cambridge University Press.

Julkunen, R. (1977). 'A contribution to the categories of social time and the economy of time', *Acta Sociologia*, 20, 5–24.

Kahn, H. and Cooper, C.L. (1993). *Stress in the Dealing Room. High Performers under Pressure*. London: Routledge.

Kanter, R.M. (1976). *Men and Women of the Organisation*. New York: Basic Books.

Kaplan, T. (1977). *Anarchists of Andalusia, 1868–1903*. Princeton, NJ: Princeton University Press.

Karras, A. and McNeil, J.R. (eds) (1992). *Atlantic-American Societies*. London: Routledge.

Kay, W. (1994). 'Swiss grab for keys to City', *Independent on Sunday*, 10 April, 3.

Keat, R. (1981). *The Politics of Social Theory. Freud, Habermas and the Critique of Positivism*. Oxford: Blackwell.

Keat, R. and Urry, J. (1975). *Social Theory as Science*. Henley-on-Thames: Routledge and Kegan Paul.

Keat, R. and Urry, J. (1982). *Social Theory as Science* (2nd edn). Henley-on-Thames: Routledge and Kegan Paul.

Keesing, R.M. (1981). 'Literal metaphors and anthropological metaphysics: the problematic of cultural translation'. Available as a mimeograph from Department of Anthropology, Research School of Pacific Studies, Australian National University, Canberra, Australia.

Kennedy, B.A. (1979). 'A naughty world', *Transactions of the Institute of British Geographers*, 4, 550–8.

Kenner, H. (1987). *The Mechanic Muse*. New York: Oxford University Press.

Kern, S. (1983). *The Culture of Time and Space, 1880–1918*. Cambridge, MA: Harvard University Press.

Kerridge, E. (1988). *Trade and Banking in Early Modern England*. Manchester: Manchester University Press.

Khan, B. and Ireland, J. (1993). 'The use of technology for competitive advantage: a study of screen vs floor trading', *City Research Project Subject Report 4*.

Kilminster, R. (1991). 'Structuration theory as a world-view', in C.G.A. Bryant and D. Jary (eds) *Giddens's Theory of Structuration. A Critical Appreciation*. London: Routledge.

King, A.D. (1989). *Urbanism, Colonialism and the World Economy*. London: Routledge.

King, A.D. (1990). *Global Cities. Post-Imperialism and the Internationalisation of London*. London: Routledge.

King, A.D. (ed.) (1991). *Culture, Globalisation and the World-System*. London: Macmillan.

Kinnear, M. (1968). *The British Voter. An Atlas and Survey since 1885*. Ithaca, NY: Cornell University Press.

Kirby, A. (1985). 'Pseudo-random thoughts on space, scale and ideology in political geography', *Political Geography Quarterly*, 4, 5–18.

Kirk, J.M., Sanderson, S.F. and Widdowson, J.D.A. (eds) (1983). *Studies in Linguistic Geography*. London: Croom Helm.

Kittler, F.A. (1990). *Discourse Networks 1800/1900*. Stanford, CA: Stanford University Press.

Knights, D. and Verdubakis, T. (1993). 'Calculations of risk: towards an understanding of insurance as a moral and political technology', *Accounting, Organisation and Society*, 18, 729–64.

Knorr-Cetina, K. (1994). 'Primitive classification and postmodernity: towards a notion of fiction', *Theory, Culture & Society*, 11, 1–22.

Knowles, D. (1949). *The Monastic Order in England*. Cambridge: Cambridge University Press.

Kohlberg, L. (1971). 'From is to ought', in T. Mischel (ed.) *Cognitive Development and Epistemology*. New York: Academic Press, pp. 153–76.

Kolb, D. (1990). *Postmodern Sophistications. Philosophy, Architecture and Tradition*. Chicago: University of Chicago Press.

Kosik, K. (1976). *The Dialectics of the Concrete*. Dordrecht: D. Reidel.

Koss, S. (1981). *The Rise and Fall of the Political Press in Britain. Volume 1. The Nineteenth Century*. London: Collins.

Krais, B. (1993). 'Gender and symbolic violence: female oppression in the light of Bourdieu's theory of social practice', in C. Calhoun, E. Lipuma and M. Postone (eds) *Bourdieu. Critical Perspectives*. Cambridge: Polity Press, pp. 156–77.

Kraniauskas, J. (1994). 'Beware Mexican ruins! "One way street" and the colonial unconscious', in A. Benjamin and P. Osborne (eds) *Walter Benjamin's Philosophy. Destruction and Experience*. London: Routledge, pp. 139–54.

Krasner, (1983).

Krauss, R. (1993). *The Optical Unconscious*. Cambridge, MA: MIT Press.

Kreckel, M. (1982). 'Communicative acts and extralinguistic knowledge', in M. von Cranach and R. Harré (eds) *The Analysis of Action. Recent Theoretical and Empirical Analysis*. Cambridge: Cambridge University Press, pp. 267–308.

Kripke, S. (1982). *Wittgenstein on Rules and Private Language*. Oxford: Oxford University Press.

Kuhn, A. (ed.) (1990). *Alien Zone. Cultural Theory and Contemporary Science Fiction Cinema*. London: Verso.

Kuhn, T.S. (1970). *The Structure of Scientific Revolutions* (2nd edn). Chicago: University of Chicago Press.

Kula, W. (1986). *Measures and Men*. Princeton, NJ: Princeton University Press.

Kumar, K. (1988). *The Rise of Modern Society*. Oxford: Blackwell.

Kynaston, D. (1989). *The Financial Times. A Centenary History*. London: Viking.

Kynaston, D. (1994). *The City of London. Volume 1: A World of Its Own, 1815–1890*. London: Chatto and Windus.

Laing, R.D. (1971). *The Politics of the Family*. Harmondsworth: Penguin Books.

Lakoff, G. (1987). *Women, Fire and Dangerous Things*. Chicago: University of Chicago Press.

Lakoff, G. and Johnson, N. (1980). *Metaphors We Live By*. Chicago: University of Chicago Press.

Lalvani, S. (1993). 'Photography, epistemology and the body', *Cultural Studies*, 7, 442–65.

Lamont, M. (1987). 'How to become a dominant French philosopher: the case of Jacques Derrida', *American Journal of Sociology*, 9, 589–622.

Lancaster CSCW Centre (1993). *Interdisciplinarity in Cooperation Technology*. Lancaster: Lancaster CSCW Centre.

Land, N. (1992). 'Circuitries', in J. Broadhurst (ed.) *Deleuze and the Transcendental Unconscious*. Coventry: University of Warwick Press, pp. 217–36.

Land, N. (1995). 'Machines and technocultural complexity', *Theory, Culture and Society*, 12, 131–40.

Landes, D.S. (1983). *Revolution in Time. Clocks and the Making of the Modern World*. Cambridge, MA: Belknap Press.

Lane, R.A. (1966). 'The decline of politics and ideology in a knowledgeable society', *American Sociological Review*, 31, 649–62.

Langdon White, C. and Renner, G.T. (1936). *Geography. An Introduction to Human Ecology*. New York.

Langton, J. (1984). 'The industrial revolution and the regional geography of England', *Transactions of the Institute of British Geographers*, 9, 145–67.

Laqueur, T.W. (1973). *Religion and Respectability*. New Haven, CT: Yale University Press.

Larrain, J. (1979). *The Concept of Ideology*. London: Hutchinson.

Lash, S. (1993). 'Reflexive modernisation: the aesthetic dimension', *Theory, Culture & Society*, 10, 1–23.

Lash, S. and Urry, J. (1984). 'The new Marxism of collective action: a critical analysis', *Sociology*, 18, 33–50.

Lash, S. and Urry, J. (1993). *Economies of Signs and Spaces*. London: Sage.

Latour, B. (1986). 'The powers of association', in J. Law (ed.) *Power, Action and Belief. A New Sociology of Knowledge?* London: Routledge and Kegan Paul, pp. 264–80.

Latour, B. (1987). *Science in Action*. Milton Keynes: Open University Press.

Latour, B. (1988). 'The politics of explanation: an alternative', in S. Woolgar (ed.) *Knowledge and Reflexivity*. London: Sage, pp. 155–77.

Latour, B. (1991). 'Technology is society made durable', in J. Law (ed.) *A Sociology of Monsters*. London: Routledge, pp. 103–32.

Latour, B. (1993). *We Have Never Been Modern*. Hemel Hempstead: Harvester Wheatsheaf.

Lave, J. (1986). 'The values of quantification', in J. Law (ed.) *Power, Action and Belief. A New Sociology of Knowledge?* London: Routledge and Kegan Paul, pp. 88–111.

Lave, J. and Wenger, E. (1991). *Situated Learning. Legitimate Peripheral Participation*. Cambridge: Cambridge University Press.

Law, J. (1986). 'On the methods of long-distance control: vessels, navigation and the Portuguese route to India', in J. Law (ed.) *Power, Action and Belief. A New Sociology of Knowledge?* London: Routledge and Kegan Paul, pp. 234–63.

Law, J. (ed.) (1991). *A Sociology of Monsters*. London: Routledge.

Law, J. (1994). *Organising Modernity*. Oxford: Blackwell.

Law, J. and Whittaker, J. (1988). 'On the art of representation', in J. Law (ed.) *Picturing Power. Visual Depiction and Social Relations*. London: Routledge, pp. 160–83.

Layder, D. (1981). *Structure, Interaction and Social Theory*. Henley-on-Thames: Routledge and Kegan Paul.

Lazar, D. (1990). *Markets and Ideology in the City of London*. London: Macmillan.

Lazarsfeld, P. (1972). 'Historical anthropology and the study of action: an intellectual odyssey', in P. Lazarsfeld (ed.) *Qualitative Analysis. Historical and Critical Essays*. Boston: Allyn and Bacon, pp. 53–105.

Lea, M. (ed.) (1992). *Contexts of Computer-Mediated Communication*. Brighton: Harvester Wheatsheaf.

Lecercle, J.J. (1993). 'Review of Castoriadis', *Radical Philosophy*, Autumn, 58.

Leclercq, J. (1975). 'Experience and interpretation of time in the early Middle Ages', in J. Somerfeldt, L. Syndergaard and E.R. Elder (eds) *Studies in Medieval Culture. Volume 5*. Kalamazoo: Medieval Institute, Western Michigan University, pp. 9–19.

Lee, A.J. (1976). *The Origins of the Popular Press in England, 1855–1914*. London: Macmillan.

Leed, E.J. (1991). *The Mind of the Traveller. From Gilgamesh to Global Tourism*. New York: Basic Books.

Lefebvre, H. (1971). *Everyday Life in the Modern World*. London: Allen Lane.

Lefebvre, H. (1991b). *Critique of Everyday Life. Volume 1*. London: Verso.

Lefebvre, H. (1976). *The Survival of Capitalism*. London: Allison and Busby.

Lefebvre, H. (1991). *The Production of Space*. Oxford: Blackwell.

Le Goff, J. (1980). *Time, Work and Culture in the Middle Ages*. Chicago: University of Chicago Press.

Le Goff, J. (1988). *Your Money or Your Life. Economy and Religion in the Middle Ages*. New York: Zone Books.

Lenntorp, B. (1976). *Paths in Space-time Environments. A Time-geographic Study of Movement Possibilities of Individuals*. Lund Studies in Geography, Series B, no. 44.

Leonard, P. (1984). *Personality and Ideology. Towards a Materialist Understanding of the Individual*. London: Macmillan.

Le Roy Ladurie, E. (1978). *Montaillou. Cathars and Catholics in a French Village, 1299–1324.* London: Scolar Press.

Lévi-Strauss, C. (1973). *Tristes Tropiques.* London: Jonathan Cape.

Leyshon, A. (1992). 'The transformation of regulatory order: regulating the global economy and environment', *Geoforum*, 23, 249–67.

Lingis, A. (1992). 'The society of dismembered body parts', in J. Broadhurst (ed.) *Deleuze and the Transcendental Unconscious.* Coventry: University of Warwick Press, pp. 1–20.

Lingis, A. (1994). *Foreign Bodies.* London: Routledge.

Lipietz, A. (1978). *Le Monde Enchanté.* Paris: Maspero.

Livesay, J. (1989). 'Structuration theory and the unacknowledged conditions of action', *Theory, Culture & Society*, 6, 263–92.

Lodge, D. (1991). *Paradise News.* London: Secker and Warburg.

Lojkine, J. (1981). 'Urban policy and local power: some aspects of recent research in Lille', in M. Harloe and E. Lebas (eds) *City, Class and Capital. New Developments in the Political Economy of Cities and Regions.* London: Edward Arnold, pp. 89–104.

London Planning and Advisory Council (1990). *London: World City.* London: HMSO.

Lough, J. (1971). *The 'Encyclopédie'.* New York: Norton.

Lovibond, S. (1994a) 'Materialist ethics: a feminist perspective', *South Atlantic Quarterly*, 93, 779–802.

Lovibond, S. (1994b). 'Feminism and the crisis of rationality', *New Left Review*, 207, 72–86.

Lowe, D.M. (1982). *History of Bourgeois Perception.* Chicago: University of Chicago Press.

Lowenstein, W. (1978). *Weevils in the Flour. An Oral Record of the 1930s Depression in Australia.* Melbourne: Hyland House.

Lucic, S. (1991). *Charles Sheeler.* New York: Norton.

Luckin, B. (1990). *Questions of Power. Electricity and Environment in Inter-War Britain.* Manchester: Manchester University Press.

Luckman, T. (1982). 'Individual action and social knowledge', in M. von Cranach and R. Harré (eds) *The Analysis of Action. Recent Theoretical and Empirical Analysis.* Cambridge: Cambridge University Press, pp. 247–65.

Luhmann, N. (1982). *The Differentiation of Society.* New York: Columbia University Press.

Luhmann, N. (1989). *Ecological Communication.* Cambridge: Polity Press.

Luke, T. (1993). 'Space-time compression and de-traditionalisation: identity, meaning and globalisation'. Paper presented to the conference on De-traditionalisation, Lancaster University, 8–10 July.

Luria, A.R. (1979). *The Making of Mind.* Cambridge, MA: Havard University Press.

Lynch, K. (1972). *What Time Is This Place?* Cambridge, MA: MIT Press.

Lyotard, J.-F. (1992). *The Inhuman. Reflections on Time.* Stanford, CA: Stanford University Press.

McCafferty, L. (ed.) (1991). *Storming the Reality Studio.* Durham, NC: Duke University Press.

McCallum, R.B. and Readman, A. (1947). *The British General Election of 1945.* London: Oxford University Press.

McCann, J. (trans.) (1970). *The Rule of Saint Benedict.* London: Sheed and Ward.

McCann, P. (ed.) (1977). *Popular Education and Socialization in the Nineteenth Century.* Andover: Methuen.

MacCannell, D. (1976). *The Tourist. A New Theory of the Leisure Class.* New York: Schocken.

MacCannell, D. (1992). *Empty Meeting Grounds. The Tourist Papers.* London: Routledge.

McDowell, L. (1994). 'Social justice, organisational culture and workplace democracy: cultural imperialism in the City of London', *Urban Geography*, 17, 661–80.

Macey, D. (1991). 'Navigating by fixed stars', *Economy and Society*, 20, 328–37.

Macfarlane, A. (1970). *The Family Life of Ralph Josselin, a Seventeenth-Century Clergyman. An Essay in Historical Anthropology.* Cambridge: Cambridge University Press.

Macfarlane, A. (ed.) (1976). *The Diary of Ralph Josselin 1616–1683.* London: British Academy.

Macfarlane, A. (1977). 'Historical anthropology and the study of communities', *Social History*, 5, 631–52.

McGrew, A. (1995). 'World order and political space', in J. Anderson, C. Brook and A. Cochrane (eds) *A Global World*. Oxford: Oxford University Press, pp. 11–56.

McHugh, K.E. and Mings, R.C. (1991). 'On the road again: seasonal migration to a sunbelt metropolis', *Urban Geography*, 12, 1–18.

MacIntyre, S. (1980). *Little Moscows. Communism and Working-Class Militancy in Inter-War Britain*. London: Croom Helm.

Mack, P.A. (1990). *Viewing the Earth. The Social Constitution of the Landsat Satellite*. Cambridge, MA: MIT Press.

McLennan, G. (1981). *Marxism and the Methodologies of History*. London: New Left Books.

McNay, L. (1992). *Foucault and Feminism*. Cambridge: Polity.

McNay, L. (1994). *Foucault*. Cambridge: Polity.

McRae, H. (1994). 'Pack your skis, its conference time', *The Independent*, 16 March, 16.

Madell, G. (1981). *The Identity of the Self*. Edinburgh: Edinburgh University Press.

Major-Poetzl, P. (1979). *Michel Foucault's Archaeology of Western Culture*. Chapel Hill: University of North Carolina Press.

Mandel, E. (1978). *Late Capitalism*. London: Verso.

Mandrou, R. (1964). *De la culture Populaire aux 17e et 18e siècles*. Paris.

Mann, P.H. (1970). *Books, Borrowers and Buyers*. London: Methuen.

Mann, P.H. and Burgoyne, J.L. (1969). *Books and Reading*. London: Methuen.

Mansell, R. (1993). *The New Telecommunications. A Political Economy of Network Evolution*. London: Sage.

Mansell, R. and Jenkins, M. (1993). 'Electronic-trading networks: the emergence of new productive networks', *Commission of the European Communities. FAST Dossier. Continental Europe. Science, Technology and Community Cohesion*, Vols 23–4. Annex 5, pp. 127–72.

Marceau, J. (1989). *A Family Business? The Making of an International Business Elite*. Cambridge: Cambridge University Press.

Marcus, G. (1992). 'Past, present and emergent identities: requirements for ethnographies of late twentieth-century modernity worldwide', in S. Lash and J. Friedman (eds) *Modernity and Identity*. Oxford: Blackwell, pp. 309–30.

Marr, D. (1981). *Vietnamese Tradition on Trial, 1920–1995*. Berkeley: University of California Press.

Martensson, S. (1979). 'On the formation of biographies in space-time environments', *Lund Studies in Geography*, series B, no. 47.

Martin, E. (1990). 'The end of the body?', *American Ethnologist*, 19, 121–40.

Martin, H.J. (1978). 'The Bibliothèque Bleue: literature for the masses in the *Ancien Régime*', *Publishing History*, 3, 70–102.

Martinez-Alier, J. (1971). *Labourers and Landowners in Southern Spain*. Totowa, NJ: Rowman and Littlefield.

Marvin, C. (1986). 'Dazzling the multitude: imagining the electric light as a communications medium', in J. Corn (ed.) *Imagining Tomorrow. History, Technology and the American Future*. Cambridge, MA: MIT Press.

Marvin, C. (1988). *When Old Technologies Were New*. New York: Oxford University Press.

Marwick, A. (1982). *British Society since 1945*. Harmondsworth: Pelican.

Marx, K. (1956). *Economic and Philosophical Manuscripts of 1844. Collected Works. Volume III*. London: Lawrence and Wishart.

Marx, K. (1973). *Grundrisse*. Harmondsworth: Pelican.

Marx, K. and Engels, F. (1956). *The Holy Family*. London: Lawrence and Wishart.

Marx, K. and Engels, F. (1959). *Selected Correspondence*. London: Lawrence and Wishart.

Marx, K. and Engels, F. (1965). *The German Ideology*. London: Lawrence and Wishart.

Marx, L. (1964). *The Machine in the Garden. Technology and the Pastoral Ideal in America*. New York: Oxford University Press.

Massey, D. (1991). 'The political place of locality studies', *Environment and Planning A*, 23, 267–82.

Massey, D. (1992). 'Politics and space/time', *New Left Review*, 196, 65–84.

Mass-Observation (1939). *Britain*. Harmondsworth: Penguin Books.

Mass-Observation (1940). *War Begins at Home*. London: Chatto and Windus.

Mass-Observation (1942). *People in Production*. London: Advertising Service Guild.

Mass-Observation (1943a). *People's Homes*. London: Advertising Service Guild.

Mass-Observation (1943b). *War Factory*. London: Gollancz.

Mass-Observation (1947). *Puzzled People. A Study in Popular Attitudes to Religion, Ethics, Progress and Politics*. London: Gollancz.

Mass-Observation (1950). *The Voter's Choice*. London: Art and Technics.

Massumi, B. (1988). 'Translator's foreword' to G. Deleuze and F. Guattari *A Thousand Plateaus. Capitalism and Schizophrenia*. London: Athlone Press, pp. i–xv.

Massumi, B. (1992a). *A User's Guide to Capitalism and Schizophrenia. Deviations from Deleuze and Guattari*. Cambridge, MA: MIT Press.

Massumi, B. (1992b). '"Everywhere you want to be": introduction to fear', in J. Bradhurst (ed.) *Deleuze and the Transcendental Unconscious*. Coventry: University of Warwick Press, pp. 175–216.

Mathew, F. (1991). *The Ecological Self*. London: Routledge.

Matless, D. (1991). 'A modern stream: an essay in water, landscape, modernism and geography', *Environment and Planning D. Society and Space*, 9, 280–93.

Maturana, H.R. (1988). 'Reality: the seal for objectivity or the quest for a competing argument', *Irish Journal of Psychology*, 9, 25–82.

Maturana, H.R. and Varela, F.J. (1980). *Autopoesis and Cognition*. Dordrecht: D. Reidel.

Maturana, H.R. and Varela, F.J. (1987). *The Tree of Knowledge. The Biological Roots of Human Understanding*. New York: Shambhala.

Maturana, H.R., Cooldon, F. and Mendez, C.C. (1980). 'The bringing forth of psychology', *Irish Journal of Psychology*, 9, 144–72.

Matza, D. and Wellman, D. (1980). 'The ordeal of consciousness', *Theory and Society*, 9, 1–27.

Mayer, M. (1988). *Markets. Who Plays, Who Risks, Who Gains, Who Loses*. London: Simon and Schuster.

Mazlish, B. (1993). *The Fourth Discontinuity. The Co-evolution of Humans and Machines*. New Haven, CT: Yale University Press.

Melbin, M. (1987). *Night as Frontier. Colonising the World after Dark*. New York: Free Press.

Merchant, C. (1980). *The Death of Nature: Women, Ecology and the Scientific Revolution*. New York: Harper and Row.

Merkl, P.H. (1975). *Political Violence under the Swastika*. Princeton, NJ: Princeton University Press.

Merkl, P.H. (1980). *The Making of a Stormtrooper*. Princeton, NJ: Princeton University Press.

Merleau-Ponty, M. (1962). *The Phenomenology of Perception*. London: Routledge and Kegan Paul.

Merleau-Ponty, M. (1968). *The Visible and the Invisible*. Evanston, IL: Northwestern University Press.

Meyers, D.T. (1994). *Subjection and Subjectivity. Psychoanalytic Feminism and Moral Philosophy*. New York: Routledge.

Michaux, H. (1992). *Spaced, Displaced*. Newcastle upon Tyne: Bloodaxe Books.

Michie, R.C. (1988). 'Dunn, Fisher and Co. in the City of London', *Business History*, 30, 19–38.

Michie, R.C. (1992). *The City of London. Continuity and Change, 1850–1990*. London: Macmillan.

Miller, C. (1993). 'The postidentitarian predicament on the footnotes of A Thousand Plateaus', *Diacritics*, 23, 6–35.

Miller, P. and Rose, N. (1990). 'Governing the economy', *Economy and Society*, 19, 1–31.

Mills, C.W. (1940). 'Situated actions and vocabularies of motive', *American Sociological Review*, 5, 904–13.

Mills, C.W. (1959). *The Sociological Imagination*. London: Oxford University Press.

Mills, S. (1991). *Discourses of Difference. An Analysis of Women's Travel Writing and Colonialism*. London: Routledge.

Minh-ha, Trinh T. (1989). *Women, Nature, Other. Writing, Postcoloniality and Feminism.* Bloomington: Indiana University Press.

Ministry of Labour and National Service (1947). *Report for the Years 1939–1946.* London: HMSO, Command 7225.

Minns, R. (1980). *Bombers and Mash. The Domestic Front 1939–45.* London: Virago.

Mishra, V. and White, B. (1991). 'What is post(-)colonialism?', *Textual Practice*, 5, 399–414.

Mitchell, W.T.J. (1992). *The Reconfigured Eye.* Cambridge, MA: MIT Press.

Mizruchi, M.S. and Stearns, L.B. (1994). 'Money, banking, and financial markets', in N.J. Smelser and R. Swedberg (eds) *The Handbook of Economic Sociology.* Princeton, NJ: Princeton University Press, pp. 313–42.

Mol, A. and Law, J. (1994). 'Regions, networks and fluids: anaemia and social topology', *Social Studies of Science*, 24, 641–71.

Molina, V. (1979). 'Notes on Marx and the theory of individuality', in Centre for Contemporary Cultural Studies (ed.) *On Ideology.* London: Hutchinson, pp. 230–58.

Monk, R. (1990). *Ludwig Wittgenstein. The Duty of Genius.* London: Jonathan Cape.

Montrose, L. (1991). 'The work of gender in the discourse of discovery', *Representations*, 33, 1–36.

Moran, M. (1991). *The Politics of the Financial Services Revolution.* London: Macmillan.

Morley, D. (1991). 'Where the global meets the local: notes from the sitting room', *Screen*, 32, 1–15.

Morris, E. (1949/50). 'British bellfounders', in *Hinrichsen's Musical Year Book. Volume 6.* London: Hinrichsen, pp. 294–307.

Morris, E. (1955). *Tower and Bells of Britain.* London: Robert Hale.

Morris, M. (1987). 'At Henry Parkes motel', *Cultural Studies*, 3, 1–36.

Morris, M. (1988). 'Banality in cultural studies', *Discourse*, X(2), 3–29.

Morris, M. (1992a). 'The man in the mirror: David Harvey's "condition" of postmodernity', *Theory, Culture & Society*, 9, 253–79.

Morris, M. (1992b). 'On the beach', in L. Grossberg, C. Nelson and P. Treichler (eds) *Cultural Studies.* New York: Routledge, pp. 450–78.

Mulgan, G.J. (1991). *Communication and Control. Networks and the New Economics of Communication.* New York: Guilford Press.

Mumford, L. (1934). *Technics and Civilisation.* New York: Harcourt Brace.

Mumford, L. (1966). 'Technics and the nature of man', *Technology and Culture*, 7, 301–16.

Munt, I. (1994). 'The "other" postmodern tourism: culture, travel and the new middle classes', *Theory, Culture & Society*, 11, 101–23.

Murdoch, J. (1995). 'Actor-networks and the evolution of economic forms: combining description and explanation in theories of regulation, flexible specialisation, and networks', *Environment and Planning A*, 27, 731–58.

Murphy, C.N. (1994). *International Organisation and Industrial Change.* Cambridge: Polity Press.

Musselwhite, M. (1987). *Partings Welded Together. Politics and Desire in the Nineteenth-Century English Novel.* London: Methuen.

Nagel, T. (1979). *Mortal Questions.* Cambridge: Cambridge University Press.

Nasaw, D. (1992). 'Cities of light, landscapes of pleasure', in D. Ward and O. Zunz (eds) *The Landscape of Modernity.* New York: Russell Sage Press, pp. 273–86.

Naylor, G. (1992). 'Design, craft and identity', in B. Ford (ed.) *Victorian Britain. The Cambridge Cultural History. Volume 7.* Cambridge: Cambridge University Press.

Neale, R.S. (1981). *Bath. A Social History, 1680–1850.* Henley-on-Thames: Routledge and Kegan Paul.

Negt, O. and Kluge, A. (1993). *Public Sphere and Experience.* Minnesota: University of Minnesota Press.

Neisser, H. (1965). *On the Sociology of Knowledge.* New York: W.W. Norton.

Nesti, A. (1990a). 'Implicit religion: the issues and dynamics of a phenomenon', *Social Compass*, 37, 423–38.

Neuberg, V.E. (1977). *Popular Literature. A History and Guide.* Harmondsworth: Penguin.

Niehammer, L. (ed.) (1980). *Lebensfahrung und kollektives Gedächtnis die Praxis der 'Oral History'*. Frankfurt: Syndikat.

Noddings, N. (1984). *Caring*. Berkeley: University of California Press.

North, J.D. (1975). 'Monasticism and the first mechanical clocks', in J.T. Fraser and N. Lawrence (eds) *The Study of Time 2*. Berlin: Springer Verlag, pp. 381–98.

Nugent, W.T.K. (1967). *The Money Question During Reconstruction*. New Haven, CT: Yale University Press.

Nussbaum, M. (1990). *Love's Knowledge. Essays on Philosophy and Literature*. Oxford: Blackwell.

Nye, D. (1990). *Electrifying America. Social Meanings of New Technology*. Cambridge, MA: MIT Press.

Oakes, G. (ed.) (1984). *Georg Simmel: On Women, Sexuality, and Love*. New Haven, CT: Yale University Press.

Oasby, I. (1991). *The Englishman's England: Travel, Taste, and the Rise of Tourism*. Cambridge: Cambridge University Press.

O'Brien, R. (1992). *Global Financial Integration. The End of Geography*. London: Pinter.

OECD (1992). *Risk Management in Financial Services*. Paris: OECD.

Offe, C. and Wiesenthal, H. (1980). 'Two logics of collective action: theoretical notes on social class and organisation form', in M. Zeitlin (ed.) *Political Power and Social Theory. Volume 1*. Greenwich, CT: JAI Press, pp. 67–115.

Olivier de Sardan, P. (1993). 'Occultism and the ethnographic "I": exacting magic from Durkheim to postmodern anthropology', *Critique of Anthropology*, 12, 34–56.

O'Malley, M. (1992). 'Time, work and task orientation: a critique of American historiography', *Time and Society*, 1, 341–58.

Ong, W.J. (1982). *Orality and Literacy. The Technologising of the Word*. London: Methuen.

O'Riordan, T. (1992). 'Review', *The Higher*, 26 June, 16.

Padley, R. and Cole, M. (1940). *Evacuation Survey. A Report to the Fabian Society*. London: George Routledge.

Pahl, R.E. (1989). 'St. Matthews and the golden handcuffs' (mimeo).

Parfit, D. (1984). *Reasons and Persons*. Oxford: Clarendon Press.

Park, R.E. and Burgess, E.W. (1924). *Introduction to the Science of Sociology* (2nd edn). Chicago: University of Chicago Press.

Parsons, W. (1989). *The Power of the Financial Press*. London: Edward Elgar.

Parton, J. (1994). *The Bucks Stop Here*. London: Pocket Books.

Peebles, G. (1991). *A Short History of Socialist Money*. London: Allen and Unwin.

Peet, R.J. (1982). 'International capitalism, international culture', in M.J. Taylor and N.J. Thrift (eds) *The Geography of Multinationals*. London: Croom Helm, pp. 275–302.

Pelling, H. (1967). *Social Geography of British Elections*. London: Macmillan.

Pelling, H. (1984). *The Labour Governments, 1945–51*. London: Macmillan.

Penley, C. and Ross, A. (eds) (1991). *Technoculture*. Minneapolis: University of Minnesota Press.

Perez, R. (1990). *On Anarchy and Schizoanalysis*. New York: Automedia.

Perkin, H. (1989). *The Professionalisation of English Society, 1880–1980*. London: Routledge.

Pfeiffer, K.L. (1994). 'The materiality of communication', in H.U. Gumbrecht and K.L. Pfeiffer (eds) *Materialities of Communication*. Stanford, CA: Stanford University Press, pp. 1–12.

Philip, A. (1921). *The Calendar*. Cambridge: Cambridge University Press.

Philo, C. (1984). 'Reflections on Gunnar Olsson's contribution to the discourse on contemporary human geography', *Environment and Planning D. Society and Space*, 2, 119–248.

Philo, C. (1986). 'Geography, history and the mad-business'. Unpublished manuscript, Department of Geography, University of Cambridge.

Piaget, J. (1965). *The Moral Development of the Child*. New York: Free Press.

Pickering, A. (ed.) (1993). *Science as Practice and Culture*. Chicago: University of Chicago Press.

Piercy, M. (1991). *Body of Glass* [in the USA, *He, She and It*]. New York: Knopf.

Pimlott, B. (1985). 'The road from 1945', *The Guardian*, 27 July, 15.

Pinçon, M. (1978). *Besoins et habitus. Critique de la notion de besoin et théorie de la pratique.* Paris: Centre de Sociologie Urbaine.

Planning (1948). 'Manpower movements', *Planning*, 14, Pamphlet 276.

Plant, S. (1992). *The Most Radical Gesture. The Situationist International in a Postmodern Age.* London: Routledge.

Platt, C. (1969). *The Monastic Grange in Medieval England. A Reassessment.* London: Macmillan.

Platts, M. (1979). *Ways of Meaning. An Introduction to a Philosophy of Language.* London: Macmillan.

Plowden, W. (1971). *The Motor Car and Politics in Britain.* Harmondsworth: Penguin.

Plumwood, V. (1993). *Feminism and the Mastery of Nature.* London: Routledge.

Pollner, M. (1987). *Mundane Reason.* Cambridge: Cambridge University Press.

Pomeroy, J. (1991). 'Black box s-thetix: labour, research and survival in the he(art) of the beast', in C. Penley and A. Ross (eds) *Technoculture.* Minneapolis: University of Minnesota Press, pp. 271–94.

Popkin, S. (1980). 'The rational peasant: the political economy of peasant society', *Theory and Society*, 9, 411–71.

Popper, K. (1972). *The Poverty of Historicism.* London: Routledge and Kegan Paul.

Porter, D. (1991). *Haunted Journeys. Desire and Transgression in European Travel Writing.* Princeton, NJ: Princeton University Press.

Porter, R. (1991). 'The history of photography', in P. Burke (ed.) *New Approaches to Social History.* London: Methuen.

Porter, R. (1993). 'Baudrillard: hystory, hysteria and consumption', in C. Rojek and B. Turner (eds) *Forget Baudrillard.* London: Routledge, pp. 1–21.

Poster, M. (1990). *The Mode of Information. Poststructuralism and Social Context.* Cambridge: Polity Press.

Prato and Trivero, (1985). 'The spectacle of travel', *Australian Journal of Cultural Studies*, 5, 25–43.

Pratt, G.B. (1992). 'Spatial metaphors and speaking positions', *Environment and Planning D. Society and Space*, 10, 241–4.

Pratt, M.L. (1991). *Imperial Eyes. Travel Writing and Transculturation.* London: Routledge.

Pratten, C. (1993). *The Stock Market.* Cambridge: Cambridge University Press.

Pred, A. (1981a). 'Production, family and "free-time" projects: a time-geographic perspective on the individual and societal change in nineteenth-century US cities', *Journal of Historical Geography*, 7, 3–36.

Pred, A. (1981b). 'Social reproduction and the time-geography of everyday life', *Geografisker Annaler*, 63, series B, 5–22.

Prendergast, C. (1992). *Paris and the Nineteenth Century.* Oxford: Blackwell.

Preston, P. (1992). 'Life', *Times Higher Education Supplement*, 16 March, 11.

Price, P. (1983). *Bells and Man.* Oxford: Oxford University Press.

Price, R. (1990). *Alabi's World.* Cambridge, MA: Harvard University Press.

Prigogine, I. (1980). *From Being to Becoming. Time and Complexity in the Physical Sciences.* San Francisco: W.H. Freeman.

Prigogine, I. and Stengers, I. (1984). *Order out of Chaos.* New York: Bantam Books.

Probyn, E. (1990). 'Travels in the postmodern: making sense of the local', in L.J. Nicholson (ed.) *Feminism/Postmodernism.* London: Routledge, pp. 176–89.

Probyn, E. (1992). *Sexing the Self. Gendered Positions in Cultural Studies.* London: Routledge.

Pryke, M. (1991). 'An international city going global', *Environment and Planning D. Society and Space*, 9, 197–222.

Przeworski, A. (1977). 'Proletariat into a class: the process of class formation from Karl Kautsky's *The Class Struggle* to recent controversies', *Politics and Society*, 4, 342–401.

Pugh, P. (1988). *The City Slicker's Guide to the City.* London: Michael Joseph.

Radway, J. (1988). 'Reception study: ethnography and the problems of dispersed audiences and nomadic subjects', *Cultural Studies*, 2, 359–76.

Rajan, A. (1988). *Create or Abdicate. The City's Human Resource Choices for the 1990s.* London: Wetherby.

Rajan, A. (1990). *Capital People.* London: Industrial Society.

Rajan, A. and Van Eupen, P. (1994). *Winning People.* London Human Resource Group, Tunbridge Wells.

Rajchman, J. (1988). 'Foucault's art of seeing', *October,* 44, 89–119.

Ranson, S., Hinings, B. and Greenwood, R. (1980). 'The structuring of organisational structures', *Administrative Science Quarterly,* 25, 1–17.

Rattansi, P.M. (1973). 'Some evaluations of reason in sixteenth- and seventeenth-century natural philosophy', in R.M. Young and M. Teich (eds) *Changing Perspectives in the Historiography of Science.* London: Macmillan, pp. 146–66.

Raven, J.J. (1906). *The Bells of England.* London: Methuen.

Read, D. (1992). *The Power of News. The History of Reuters.* Oxford: Oxford University Press.

Reader, I. and Walter, J. (eds) (1993). *Pilgramage in Popular Culture.* London: Methuen.

Reed-Danahy, D. (1995). 'The Kabyle and the French: occidentalism in Bourdieu's theory of practice', in J.G. Carrier (ed.) *Occidentalism: Images of the West.* Oxford: Oxford University Press, pp. 85–108.

Reid, D.A. (1976). 'The decline of Saint Monday, 1766–1876', *Past and Present,* 71, 76–101.

Reiss, D. (1981). *The Family's Construction of Reality.* Cambridge, MA: Harvard University Press.

Rich, A. (1986). *Blood, Bread and Poetry.* New York: W.W. Norton.

Richards, T. (1990). *The Commodity Culture of Victorian Britain.* London: Verso.

Richards, T. (1993). *The Imperial Archive. Knowledge and the Fantasy of Empire.* London: Verso.

Richardson, H.W. (1967). *Economic Recovery in Britain, 1932–9.* London: Methuen.

Ricouer, P. (1981). *Hermeneutics and the Social Sciences. Essays on Language, Action and Interpretation.* Cambridge: Cambridge University Press.

Rigby, B. (1991). *Popular Culture in Modern France. A Study of Cultural Discourse.* London: Routledge.

Righini Bonelli, R.M. and Shea, W.R. (eds) (1975). *Reason, Experiment and Mysticism in the Scientific Revolution.* London: Methuen.

Robbins, B. (ed.) (1993). *The Phantom Public Sphere.* Minneapolis: University of Minnesota Press.

Roberts, J. (1995). *$1000 Billion A Day. Inside the Foreign Exchange Markets.* London: Harper Collins.

Robertson, R. and Holzner, B. (1980). *Identity and Authority. Explorations in the Theory of Society.* Oxford: Blackwell.

Robins, K.F. (1991). 'Prisoners of the City: whatever could a postmodern city be?', *New Formations,* 15, 1–22.

Robson, B.T. (1973). *Urban Systems.* London: Methuen.

Robson, B.T. (1990). 'The years between', in R. Dodgshon and R.A. Butlin (eds) *A New Historical Geography of England and Wales* (2nd edn). London: Academic Press, pp. 545–78.

Rodwell, W. (1981). *The Archaeology of the English Church. The Study of Historic Churches and Churchyards.* London: Batsford.

Rojek, C. (1993). *Ways of Escape. Modern Transformations in Leisure and Travel.* London: Macmillan.

Ronell, A. (1989). *The Telephone Book. Technology, Schizophrenia, Free Speech.* Lincoln: University of Nebraska Press.

Rosaldo, R. (1988). *Culture and Truth. The Remaking of Social Analysis.* Boston: Beacon Press.

Rose, D. (1981). 'Home-ownership and industrial change: the struggle for a "separate sphere"', WP-25, Department of Urban and Regional Studies, University of Sussex, Brighton, England.

Rose, G. (1993). *Feminism and Geography.* Cambridge: Polity Press.

Rosenau, J. (ed.) (1993). *Global Voices. Dialogues in International Relations.* Boulder, CO: Westview Press.

Rosenau, J.N. and Czempiel, E. (eds) (1992). *Governance without Government. Order and Change in World Politics.* Cambridge: Cambridge University Press.

Rosenberg, M. (1979). *Conceiving the Self.* New York: Basic Books.

Rosenberger, J. (1992). *Japanese Sense of Self.* Cambridge: Cambridge University Press.

Ross, A. (1991). *Strange Weather. Culture, Science and Technology in the Age of Limits.* London: Verso.

Rowley, T. (1983). *The Norman Heritage, 1066–1200.* London: Paladin.

Rubinstein, W. (1981). *Marx and Wittgenstein.* London: Routledge and Kegan Paul.

Ruddick, S. (1990). *Material Thinking. Towards a Politics of Peace.* London: Routledge.

Ruggie, J.G. (1993). 'Territoriality and beyond: problematising modernity in international relations', *International Organisations*, 47, 139–74.

Rustin, M. (1991). *The Good Society and the Inner World. Psychoanalysis, Politics and Culture.* London: Verso.

Sacks, O. (1989). *Seeing Voices.* Berkeley: University of California Press.

Sahlins, M. (1976). *Culture and Practical Reason.* Chicago: University of Chicago Press.

Said, E.W. (1978). *Orientalism.* Harmondsworth: Penguin Books.

Said, E.W. (1984). *The World, the Text and the Critic.* London: Faber and Faber.

St. Quintin (1994). *The City of London to the Year 2000 and Beyond.* London: St. Quintin.

Salzman, L.F. (1967). *Building in England Down to 1450.* London: Oxford University Press.

Sampson, A. (1965). *The Anatomy of Britain.* London: Hodder and Stoughton.

Sampson, A. (1972). *The Anatomy of Britain* (2nd edn). London: Hodder and Stoughton.

Samuel, R. (1981). 'People's history', in R. Samuel (ed.) *People's History and Socialist Theory.* Henley-on-Thames: Routledge and Kegan Paul, pp. xiv–xxxvii.

Sartre, J.-P. (1960). *Questions de méthode.* Paris: Gallimard.

Sartre, J.-P. (1964). *The Problem of Method.* Andover: Methuen.

Sartre, J.-P. (1976). *Critique of Dialectical Reason. I. Theory of Practical Ensembles.* London: New Left Books.

Sauer, C.O. (1956). 'The education of a geographer', *Annals of the Association of American Geographers*, 46, 287–99.

Saunders, I. (1995). 'The narrative construction of Australia', *Cultural Studies*, 9, 394–7.

Sayer, A. (1981). 'Abstraction: a realist interpretation', *Radical Philosophy*, 28, 6–16.

Sayer, A. (1984). *Method in Social Science. A Realist Approach.* London: Hutchinson.

Sayer, A. (1989). 'The new regional geography and the problem of narrative', *Environment and Planning D. Society and Space*, 7, 253–76.

Sayer, D. (1979). *Marx's Method. Ideology, Science and Critique in Capital.* Hassocks: Harvester Press.

Sayer, D. (1991). 'Comment', in C. Bryant and D. Jary (eds) *Giddens' Theory of Structuration. A Critical Appreciation.* London: Routledge.

Sayer, S. (1992). 'The City, power and economic policy in the UK', *International Review of Applied Economics*, 6, 125–51.

Sayers, R.S. (1976). *The Bank of England, 1891–1944* (3 vols). Cambridge: Cambridge University Press.

Schirato, T. (1993). 'My space or yours? De Certeau, Freud and the meanings of popular culture', *Cultural Studies*, 7, 282–91.

Schivelsbuch, W. (1986). *The Railway Journey. The Industrialisation of Time and Space in the Nineteenth Century.* Berkeley: University of California Press.

Schivelsbuch, W. (1988). *Disenchanted Night. The Industrialisation of Light in the Nineteenth Century.* Berkeley: University of California Press.

Schlumbohm, J. (1980). '"Traditional" collectivity and modern individuality: some questions and suggestions for the historical study of socialisation. The examples of the German lower and upper bourgeoisie around 1800', *Social History*, 5, 71–103.

Schmidt, J. (1985). *Maurice Merleau-Ponty. Between Phenomenology and Structuralism.* London: Macmillan.

Schofield, R.S. (1968). 'The measurement of literacy in pre-industrial England', in J. Goody (ed.) *Literacy in Traditional Societies*. Cambridge: Cambridge University Press, pp. 318–25.

Schofield, R.S. (1973). 'Dimensions of illiteracy 1750–1850', *Explorations in Economic History*, 10, 437–54.

Schutz, A. (1962). *Collected Papers: vol. 1: The Problems of Social Reality*. The Hague: D. Reidel.

Schutz, A. and Luckman, T. (1973). *The Structures of the Life-world*. Evanston, IL: Northwestern University Press.

Scott, J. (1976). *The Moral Economy of the Peasant*. New Haven, CT: Yale University Press.

Scott, J.G.M. (n.d.) *The Bells of Exeter Cathedral*. Exeter: Exeter Cathedral.

Scott, J.W. (1992). 'Experience', in J. Butler and J.W. Scott (eds) *Feminists Theorise the Political*. London: Routledge, pp. 22–40.

Searle, J. (1983). *Intentionality. An Essay in the Philosophy of Mind*. Cambridge: Cambridge University Press.

Secord, P.F. (ed.) (1982). *Explaining Human Behaviour. Consciousness, Human Action and Social Structure*. Beverly Hills, CA: Sage.

Sekula, A. (1986). 'The body and the archive', *October*, 36–9, 1–67.

Selbourne, D. (1980). 'On the methods of *History Workshop*', *History Workshop*, 9, 150–61.

Seltzer, M. (1992). *Bodies and Machines*. New York: Routledge.

Sendall, B. (1992). *Independent Television in Britain. Volume 1: Origin and Foundation, 1946–62*. London: Macmillan.

Sennett, R. and Cobb, J. (1972). *The Hidden Injuries of Class*. Cambridge: Cambridge University Press.

Serres, M. (1980). *Hermes V. Le passage du nord-ouest*. Paris: Minuit.

Serres, M. (1982). *Hermes. Science, Literature, Philosophy*. Baltimore, MD: John Hopkins University Press.

Serres, M. (1986). *Les Cinq Sens*. Paris: Seuil.

Serres, M. (1987). *Statues*. Paris: François Bourin.

Sève, L. (1975). *Marxism and the Theory of Human Personality*. London: Lawrence and Wishart.

Sève, L. (1978). *Man in Marxist Theory and the Psychology of Personality*. Hassocks: Harvester Press.

Shackle, G.L.S. (1972). *Epistemics and Economics. A Critique of Economic Doctrines*. Cambridge: Cambridge University Press.

Shames, C. (1981). 'The scientific humanism of Lucien Sève', *Science and Society*, 45, 1–23.

Shanon, B. (1993). *The Representational and the Presentational. An Essay on Cognition and the Study of Mind*. Hemel Hempstead: Harvester Wheatsheaf.

Shapin, S. (1988). 'The house of experiment in seventeenth century England', *Isis*, 79, 373–404.

Shapin, S. (1994). *A Social History of Truth. Civility and Science in Seventeenth-Century England*. Chicago: University of Chicago Press.

Shapin, S. and Schaffer, S. (1985). *Leviathan and the Air-pump*. Princeton, NJ: Princeton University Press.

Shapiro, M.J. (1992). *Reading the Postmodern Polity. Political Theory as Textual Practice*. Minneapolis: Minnesota University Press.

Sheehan, J. and Sosna, M. (eds) (1991). *The Boundaries of Humanity. Humans, Animals, Machines*. Berkeley: University of California Press.

Shilling, C. (1993). *The Body and Social Theory*. London: Sage.

Shotter, J. (1984). *Social Accountability and Selfhood*. Oxford: Blackwell.

Shotter, J. (1985a). 'Speaking practically: a contextualist account of psychology's context', in R. Rosnow and M. Georgodi (eds) *Contextualism and Understanding*. New York: Praeger, pp. 20–31.

Shotter, J. (1985b). 'Accounting for place and space', *Environment and Planning D. Society and Space*, 4, 447–60.

Shotter, J. (1989a). *Social Accountability and Selfhood*. Oxford: Blackwell.

Shotter, J. (1989b). 'Social accountability and the social construction of "you"', in J. Shotter and K. Gergen (eds) *Texts of Identity*. London: Sage, pp. 133–51.

Shotter, J. (1993a). *Cultural Politics of Everyday Life*. Milton Keynes: Open University Press.

Shotter, J. (1993b). *Conversational Realities. Constructing Life Through Language*. London: Sage.

Shotter, J. and Gergen, K. (1994). 'Social construction: knowledge, self, others, and continuous conversation', *Communication Yearbook*, 17, 3–33.

Sica, A. (1991). 'The California–Massachusetts strain in structuration theory', in C.G.A. Bryant and D. Jary (eds) *Giddens's Theory of Structuration. A Critical Appreciation*. London: Routledge, pp. 32–51.

Sieburth, W. (1987). 'Sentimental travelling: on the road (and off the wall) with Lawrence Sterne', *Scripsi*, 4, 196–211.

Silverstone, R. (1994). *Television and Everyday Life*. London: Routledge.

Silverstone, R. and Hirsch, E. (eds) (1992). *Consuming Technologies. Media and Information in Domestic Spaces*. London: Routledge.

Simmel, G. (1978). *The Philosophy of Money*. London: Routledge and Kegan Paul.

Simpson, G.G. (1963). 'Historical science', in C.C. Albritton (ed.) *The Fabric of Geology*. Stanford, CA: Stanford University Press, pp. 24–48.

Sinclair, T.J. (1994). 'Passing judgement: credit rating processes as regulatory mechanisms of governance in the emerging world order', *Review of International Political Economy*, 1, 133–60.

Sklair, L. (1991). *Global Sociology*. London: Macmillan.

Slagstad, R. (1980). 'On Norwegian Marxism', *Marxist Perspectives*, 2, 104–15.

Slater, D. (1992). 'On the borders of social theory: learning from other regions', *Environment and Planning D. Society and Space*, 10, 307–28.

Slusser, G. and Rabkin, E.S. (eds) (1992). *Styles of Creation. Aesthetic Technique and the Creation of Fictional Worlds*. Athens: Georgia University Press.

Slusser, G. and Shippey, T. (eds) (1992). *Fiction 2000. Cyberpunk and the Fiction of Narrative*. Athens: Georgia University Press.

Smart, B. (1982). 'Foucault, sociology and the problem of human agency', *Theory and Society*, 11, 121–41.

Smith, C.W. (1983). *The Mind of the Market*. New York: Harper Colophon.

Smith, C.W. (1989). *Auctions. The Social Construction of Value*. Hemel Hempstead: Harvester Wheatsheaf.

Smith, T.C. (1986). 'Peasant time and factory time in Japan', *Past and Present*, 111, 165–97.

Sohn-Rethel, A. (1978). *Intellectual and Manual Labour. A Critique of Epistemology*. London: Macmillan.

Soja, E. (1983). 'Redoubling the helix: space-time and the critical social theory of Anthony Giddens', *Environment and Planning A*, 15, 1267–72.

Soja, E. (1989). *Postmodern Geographies*. London: Verso.

Soros, G. (1993). *The Alchemy of Finance*. New York: John Wiley.

Sosna, M. and Sheehan, J. (eds) (1991). *The Boundaries of Humanity*. Stanford, CA: Stanford University Press.

Spivak, G.C. (1987). *In Other Worlds. Essays in Cultural Politics*. London: Methuen.

Spivak, G.C. (1990). *The Post-Colonial Critic. Interviews, Strategies, Dialogues*. New York: Routledge.

Springer, C. (1991). 'The pleasures of the interface', *Screen*, 32, 318–29.

Springer, C. (1994). 'Sex, memories and angry women', *South Atlantic Quarterly*, 92, 713–34.

Sproull, L. and Kiesler, S. (1991). *Connections. New Ways of Working in the Networked Organisation*. Cambridge, MA: MIT Press.

Spufford, M. (1974). *Contrasting Communities. English Villagers in the Sixteenth and Seventeenth Centuries*. Cambridge: Cambridge University Press.

Spufford, M. (1979). 'First steps in literacy: the reading and writing experiences of the humblest seventeenth-century autobiographers', *Social History*, 4, 407–35.

Spufford, M. (1981). *Small Books and Pleasant Histories. Popular Fiction and Its Readership in Seventeenth-Century England.* Andover: Methuen.

Square Meal (1995). *The Square Meal Guide to the City.* London: Monomax.

Squires, J. (1994). 'Private lives, secluded spaces: privacy as political possibility', *Environment and Planning D. Society and Space,* 12, 387–402.

Stafford, B.M. (1991). *Body Criticism. Imaging the Unseen in Enlightenment Art and Medicine.* Cambridge, MA: MIT Press.

Stafford, B.M. (1994). *Artful Science, Enlightenment, Entertainment and the Eclipse of Visual Education.* Cambridge, MA: MIT Press.

Steane, J.M. (1984). *The Archaeology of Medieval England and Wales.* London: Guild Publishing.

Stedman Jones, G. (1974). 'Working-class culture and working-class politics in London, 1870–1900: notes on the remaking of a working class', *Journal of Social History,* 4, 460–508.

Stedman Jones, G. (1978). 'Class expression vs social control', *History Workshop,* 4, 163–70.

Stedman Jones, G. (1983a). *Languages of Class: Studies in English Working-Class History, 1832–1982.* Cambridge: Cambridge University Press.

Stedman Jones, G. (1983b). 'Rethinking Chartism', in G. Stedman Jones *Languages of Class. Studies in English Working-Class History, 1832–1982.* Cambridge: Cambridge University Press, pp. 90–178.

Steiner, G. (1978). *On Difficulty and Other Essays.* London: Oxford University Press.

Stephens, W.B. (1973). 'Regional variations in education during the industrial revolution', *Educational Administration and History Monograph I.* Leeds: University of Leeds.

Sternberger, D. (1977). 'Panorama of the nineteenth century', *October,* 4, 3–20.

Stevens, O. (1982). *Children Talking Politics.* Oxford: Martin Robertson.

Stevenson, J. (1984). *British Society, 1914–45.* Harmondsworth: Pelican.

Stone, A.R. (1991). 'Will the real body please stand up?', in M. Benedikt (ed.) *Cyberspace. First Steps.* Cambridge, MA: MIT Press, pp. 81–118.

Stone, L. (1969). 'Literacy and education in England 1640–1900', *Past and Present,* 42, 69–139.

Stone, L. (1974). 'Prosopography', *Daedalus,* Winter, 46–79.

Stone, L. (1977). *The Family, Sex and Marriage in England, 1500–1800.* London: Weidenfeld and Nicholson.

Stone, L. (1979). 'The revival of narrative', *Past and Present,* 85, 3–24.

Stopford, J. and Strange, S. (1991). *Rival States, Rival Firms. Competition for World Market Shares.* Cambridge: Cambridge University Press.

Storch, R.D. (1977). 'The problem of working-class leisure: some roots of middle-class moral reform in the industrial north: 1825–1880', in A.P. Donajgrodski (ed.) *Social Control in Nineteenth-Century Britain.* London: Croom Helm, pp. 138–62.

Strange, S. (1988). *States and Markets.* London: Frances Pinter.

Strathern, M. (1992a). *After Nature. English Kinship in the Late Twentieth Century.* Cambridge: Cambridge University Press.

Strathern, M. (1992b). 'Writing societies, writing persons', *History of the Human Sciences,* 5, 5–16.

Strathern, M. (1992c). 'Reproducing anthropology', in S. Wallman (ed.) *Contemporary Futures.* London: Routledge, pp. 172–89.

Strohmayer, U. (1992). 'Beyond theory: the cumbersome materiality of shock', *Environment and Planning D. Society and Space,* 11, 323–97.

Sunday Times (1995). 'Oxbridge grip on top City jobs gets tighter', *The Sunday Times,* 26 March, Business, 2.

Sussman, O. (1967). *Victorians and the Machine.* Cambridge: Cambridge University Press.

Swingewood, A. (1977). *The Myth of Mass Culture.* London: Macmillan.

Swift, G. (1983). *Waterland.* London: Heinemann.

Synott, A. (1993). *The Body Social.* London: Routledge.

Tagg, J. (1988). *The Burden of Representation. Essays on Photographies and Histories.* Amherst: University of Massachusetts Press.

Tagg, J. (1992). *Grounds of Dispute. Art History, Cultural Politics and the Discourse Field.* London: Macmillan.

Tajfel, H. (ed.) (1984). *The Social Dimension* (2 vols). Cambridge: Cambridge University Press.

Tambiah, S. (1968). 'Literacy in a Buddhist village in N.E. Thailand', in J. Goody (ed.) *Literacy in Traditional Societies.* Cambridge: Cambridge University Press, pp. 85–131.

Taussig, M. (1993). *Mimesis and Alterity. A Particular History of the Senses.* New York: Routledge.

Taylor, C. (1989). *Sources of the Self. The Making of Modern Identity.* Cambridge: Cambridge University Press.

Taylor, C. (1988). *Sources of the Self.* Cambridge: Cambridge University Press.

Taylor, C. (1993a). 'To follow a rule', in C. Calhoun, E. Lipuma and M. Postone (eds) *Bourdieu: Critical Perspectives.* Cambridge: Polity Press, pp. 45–60.

Taylor, C. (1993b). 'Engaged agency and background in Heidegger', in C. Guignon (ed.) *The Cambridge Companion to Heidegger.* Cambridge: Cambridge University Press, pp. 317–36.

Taylor, M. and Allen, H. (1989). 'Chart analysis and the foreign exchange market', *Bank of England Quarterly Bulletin*, November, 12–31.

Theory, Culture & Society (1990). Special issue on global culture. *Theory, Culture & Society*, 7(2–3).

Theory, Culture & Society (1991). Special issue on Georg Simmel. *Theory, Culture & Society*, 8(3).

Therborn, G. (1980). *The Ideology of Power and the Power of Ideology.* London: New Left Books.

Theweleit, K. (1994). *Object-Choice (All You Need Is Love. . . .).* Verso: London.

Thomas, K. (1971). *Religion and the Decline of Magic.* London: Weidenfeld and Nicolson.

Thompson, E.P. (1961). 'The Long Revolution', *New Left Review*, no. 9, 24–33 and no. 10, 34–9.

Thompson, E.P. (1963). *The Making of the English Working Class.* London: Weidenfeld and Nicolson.

Thompson, E.P. (1967). 'Time, work-discipline and industrial capitalism', *Past and Present*, 38, 56–97.

Thompson, E.P. (1971). 'The moral-economy of the English crowd in the eighteenth century', *Past and Present*, 50, 76–136.

Thompson, E.P. (1978). *The Poverty of Theory and Other Essays.* London: Merlin Press.

Thompson, J.B. (1990). *Ideology and Modern Culture.* Cambridge: Polity Press.

Thompson, J.W. (1963). *The Literacy of the Laity in the Middle Ages.* New York: Burt Franklin.

Thompson, K. (1980). 'Folklore and sociology', *Sociological Review*, 28, 249–77.

Thompson, P. (1975). *The Edwardians. The Remaking of British Society.* London: Weidenfeld and Nicolson.

Thompson, P. (1978). *The Voice of the Past. Oral History.* London: Oxford University Press.

Thompson, P. (1981). 'The new oral history in France', in R. Samuel (ed.) *People's History and Socialist Theory.* Henley-on-Thames: Routledge and Kegan Paul, pp. 567–77.

Thompson, T. (1980). *Edwardian Childhoods.* Henley-on-Thames: Routledge and Kegan Paul, pp. 567–77.

Tichi, C. (1987). *Shifting Gears. Technology, Literature, and Culture in Modernist America.* Chapel Hill: University of North Carolina Press.

Titmuss, R. (1950). *Problems of Social Policy.* London: HMSO.

Tomas, D. (1992). 'From gesture to activity: dislocating the anthropological scriptorium', *Cultural Studies*, 6, 1–26.

Touraine, A. (1977). *The Self-Production of Society.* Chicago: Chicago University Press.

Touraine, A. (1981). *The Voice and the Eye. An Analysis of Social Movements.* Cambridge: Cambridge University Press.

Trachtenberg, A. (1982). *The Incorporation of America.* New York: Hill and Wang.

Trebitsch, M. (1991). 'Preface', in H. Lefebvre (ed.) *Critique of Everyday Life. Volume 1.* London: Verso, pp. ix–xxviii.

Treharne, R.F. (1971). *Essays on Thirteenth-Century England*. London: Historical Association.

Tribe, K. (1978). *Land, Labour and Economic Discourse*. Henley-on-Thames: Routledge and Kegan Paul.

Tribe, K. (1981). *Genealogies of Capitalism*. London: Macmillan.

Truptil, R.J. (1936). *British Banks and the London Money Market*. London: Jonathan Cape.

Tuan, Yi-Fu (1983). *Segmented Worlds and Self*. Minneapolis: University of Minneapolis Press.

Turkle, S. and Papert, S. (1990). 'Epistemological pluralism: styles and voices within the computer culture', *Signs*, 16, 128–57.

Turner, S. (1994). *The Social Theory of Practices. Tradition, Tacit Knowledge and Presuppositions*. Cambridge: Polity Press.

Unger, I. (1964). *The Greenback Era*. Princeton, NJ: Princeton University Press.

Urry, J. (1981a). *The Anatomy of Capitalist Societies. The Economy, Civil Society and the State*. London: Macmillan.

Urry, J. (1981b). 'Localities, regions and social class', *International Journal of Urban and Regional Research*, 5, 455–74.

Urry, J. (1989). 'Sociology and geography', in R.J. Peet and N.J. Thrift (eds) *New Models in Geography. Volume 2*. London: Unwin Hyman, pp. 295–317.

Urry, J. (1990). *The Tourist Gaze*. London: Sage.

Urry, J. (1992). 'The tourist gaze and the environment', *Theory, Culture & Society*, 9, 1–26.

Van den Abbeele, G. (1992). *Travel as Metaphor. From Montaigne to Rousseau*. Minneapolis: University of Minnesota Press.

Van der Pijl, K. (1989). 'Is there an Atlantic class?', *Capital and Class*, 25, 1–18.

Varela, F.J. (1989). 'Reflections on the circulation of concepts between a biology of cognition and systems of family therapy', *Family Process*, 28, 123–45.

Varela, F.J. and Anspach, M.R. (1994). 'The body thinks: the immune system and the process of somatic individualisation', in H.Y. Gombrecht and K.L. Pfeiffer (eds) *Materialities of Communication*. Stanford, CA: Stanford University Press, pp. 273–85.

Varela, F.J. and Dupuy, L. (eds) (1992) *Understanding Origins*. Dordrecht: Kluwer.

Varela, F.J., Thompson, E. and Rosch, E. (1991). *The Embodied Mind*. Cambridge, MA: MIT Press.

Vasseleu, C. (1991). 'Life itself', in R. Diprose and R. Ferrell (eds) *Cartographies*. Sydney: Allen and Unwin, pp. 63–78.

Vattimo, G. (1988). *The End of Modernity*. Cambridge: Polity Press.

Veesev, T. (ed.) (1989). *The New Historicists*. Cambridge, MA: MIT Press.

Veijola, S. and Jokinen, E. (1994). 'The body in tourism', *Theory, Culture & Society*, 11, 125–51.

Veltmeyer, H. (1978). 'Marx's two methods of sociological analysis', *Sociological Inquiry*, 48, 101–12.

Verdon, J. (1994). *La Nuit au Moyen Âge*. Paris: Librairie Perrin.

Vincent, D. (ed.) (1977). *Testaments of Radicalism*. London: Europa.

Vincent, D. (1980). 'Love and death and the nineteenth-century working class', *Social History*, 5, 223–47.

Vincent, D. (1981). *Bread, Knowledge and Freedom. A Study of Nineteenth-Century Working-Class Autobiography*. London: Europa.

Virilio, P. (1975). *Cause Commune, Nomades et Vagabondes*. Paris: UGE.

Virilio, P. (1983). *Pure War*. New York: Semiotext(e).

Virilio, P. (1986). *Speed and Politics*. New York: Semiotext(e).

Virilio, P. (1988). *La Machine de Vision*. Paris: Galilée.

Virilio, P. (1989). *War and Cinema. The Logistics of Perception*. London: Verso.

Virilio, P. (1990). *L'Inertie Polaire*. Paris.

Virilio, P. (1991a). *The Aesthetics of Disappearance*. New York: Semiotext(e).

Virilio, P. (1991b). *The Lost Dimension*. New York: Semiotext(e).

Virilio, P. (1994). *The Vision Machine*. London: British Film Institute.

von Cranach, M. and Harré, R. (eds) (1982). *The Analysis of Action. Recent Theoretical and Empirical Advances.* Cambridge: Cambridge University Press.

Vygotsky, L.S. (1962). *Thought and Language.* Cambridge, MA: MIT Press.

Vygotsky, L.S. (1978). *Mind in Society. The Development of Higher Psychological Processes.* Cambridge, MA: Harvard University Press.

Vygotsky, L.S. (1987). *The Collected Works of L.S. Vygotsky.* New York: Plenum Press.

Wagner, R. (1991). 'The fractal person', in M. Godelier and M. Strathern (eds) *Big Men and Great Men. Personifications of Power in Melanesia.* Cambridge: Cambridge University Press, pp. 201–23.

Walker, R.B.J. (1993). *Inside/Outside. International Relations as Political Theory.* Cambridge: Cambridge University Press.

Wallace, A.D. (1993). *Walking, Literature and English Culture. The Origins and Uses of Peripatetic in the Nineteenth Century.* Oxford: Clarendon Press.

Walters, H.B. (1912). *Church Bells of England.* London: Oxford University Press.

Ward, D. and Zunz, O. (eds) (1992). *The Landscape of Modernity.* New York: Russell Sage Press.

Ward, S.C. (1994). 'In the shadow of the deconstructed metanarratives: Baudrillard, Latour and the end of realist epistemology', *History of the Human Sciences*, 7, 73–104.

Wark, M. (1994). 'Third nature', *Cultural Studies*, 8, 115–32.

Watkins, O.C. (1972). *The Puritan Experience. Studies in Spiritual Experience.* New York: Schocken Books.

Watson, E.W. (1976). 'The St. Albans Clock', *Antiquarian Horology*, 11, 576–84.

Webb, R.K. (1950). 'Working class readers in early Victorian England', *Economic History Review*, 65, 333–57.

Webb, R.K. (1955). *The British Working-class Reader 1790–1848.* London: Oxford University Press.

Webster, C. (1982). *From Paracelsus to Newton. Magic and the Making of Modern Science.* Cambridge: Cambridge University Press.

Weintraub, K.J. (1978). *The Value of the Individual. Self and Circumstance in Autobiography.* Chicago: University of Chicago Press.

Wertsch, J.V. (1985a). *Culture, Communication and Cognition. Vygotskian Perspectives.* Cambridge: Cambridge University Press.

Wertsch, J.V. (1985b). *Vygotsky and the Social Formation of Mind.* Cambridge, MA: Harvard University Press.

Whipp, R. (1986). 'A "time to every purpose": an essay on time and work', in P. Joyce (ed.) *The Historical Meanings of Work.* Cambridge: Cambridge University Press, pp. 210–36.

White, J. (1979). 'Campbell Bunk: a community in London between the wars', *History Workshop*, 8, 1–49.

White, J. (1980). *Rothschild Buildings. Life in an East End Tenement Block, 1887–1920.* Henley-on-Thames: Routledge and Kegan Paul.

White, J. (1981). 'Beyond autobiography', in R. Samuel (ed.) *People's History and Socialist Theory.* Henley-on-Thames: Routledge and Kegan Paul, pp. 33–42.

White, L. (1962). *Medieval Technology and Social Change.* Oxford: Clarendon Press.

Whiteside, K. (1988). *Merleau-Ponty and the Foundations of an External Politics.* Princeton, NJ: Princeton University Press.

Wieck, R.S. (1988). *The Book of Hours in Medieval Art and Life.* London: Sotheby's.

Wiener, R.R. (1981). *Cultural Marxism and Political Sociology.* Beverly Hills, CA: Sage.

Wiggins, D. (1991). *Needs, Values, Truth.* Oxford: Oxford University Press.

Wilcox, D.J (1987). *The Measure of Times Past. Pre-Newtonian Chronologies and the Rhetoric of Relative Time.* Chicago: University of Chicago Press.

Wilkes, K.V. (1988). *Real People. Personal Identity without Thought Experiments.* Oxford: Oxford University Press.

Willer, D. and Willer, J. (1973). *Systematic Empiricism. Critique of a Pseudo-science.* Englewood Cliffs, NJ: Prentice-Hall.

Williams, B. (1973). *Problems of the Self.* Cambridge: Cambridge University Press.

Williams, B. (1985). *Ethics and the Limits of Philosophy*. London: Routledge.

Williams, J. (1992). 'Monitoring vs. metaphysical modelling', in J. Broadhurst (ed.) *Deleuze and the Transcendental Unconscious*. Warwick: PLI, pp. 41–66.

Williams, R. (1954). *Preface to Film*. London: Film Drama.

Williams, R. (1961). *The Long Revolution*. London: Chatto and Windus.

Williams, R. (1976). *Keywords*. London: Fontana.

Williams, R. (1977). *Marxism and Literature*. London: Oxford University Press.

Williams, R. (1979). *Politics and Letters*. London: New Left Books.

Williams, R. (1980). *Culture*. London: Fontana Books.

Williams, R. (1983). *Towards 2000*. London: Chatto and Windus.

Williams, R. (1990). *Notes on the Underground. An Essay on Technology, Society and the Imagination*. Cambridge, MA: MIT Press.

Willis, P.E. (1977). *Learning to Labour. How Working-Class Kids Get Working-Class Jobs*. Farnborough: Saxon House.

Willis, P.E. (1978). *Profane Culture*. Henley-on-Thames: Routledge and Kegan Paul.

Wilson, E. (1992). *The Sphinx in the City*. London: Virago.

Wilson, S. (1981). 'Conflict and its causes in Southern Corsica, 1800–1835', *Social History*, 6, 33–69.

Winnicott, D.W. (1974). *Playing and Reality*. Harmondsworth: Penguin.

Winnicott, D.W. (1975). *Through Paediatrics to Psychoanalysis*. London: Hogarth Press.

Wittgenstein, L. (1956). *Remarks on the Foundations of Mathematics*. Oxford: Blackwell.

Wittgenstein, L. (1958). *Philosophical Investigations*. Oxford: Blackwell.

Wittgenstein, L. (1964). *The Blue and Brown Books*. New York: Harper and Row.

Wittgenstein, L. (1967). *Zettel*. Oxford: Blackwell.

Wittgenstein, L. (1974). *Philosophical Grammar*. Oxford: Blackwell.

Wittgenstein, L. (1975). *Philosophical Remarks*. Oxford: Blackwell.

Wittgenstein, L. (1980). *Remarks on the Philosophy of Psychology. Volume 2*. Oxford: Blackwell.

Wohl, R. (1980). *The Generation of 1914*. London: Weidenfeld and Nicolson.

Wolin, R. (1990). *The Politics of Being. The Political Thought of Martin Heidegger*. New York: Columbia University Press.

Wolin, R. (1993). *The Heidegger Controversy. A Critical Reader*. Cambridge, MA: MIT Press.

Wollen, C. (1993). *Raiding the Ice Box. Reflections on Twentieth-Century Culture*. London: Verso.

Wood, D. (1987). 'Following Derrida', in J. Sallis (ed.) *Deconstruction and Philosophy. The Texts of Jacques Derrida*. Chicago: University of Chicago Press, pp. 143–60.

Wood, D. (1989). *The Deconstruction of Time*. Atlantic Highlands, NJ: Humanities Press.

Wood, D. (1990). *Philosophy at the Limit*. London: Unwin Hyman.

Woolf, J. (1993). 'On the road again: metaphors of travel in cultural criticism', *Cultural Studies*, 7, 224–39.

Worpole, K. (1981). 'A ghostly pavement: the political implications of local working-class history', in R. Samuel (ed.) *People's History and Socialist Theory*. Henley-on-Thames: Routledge and Kegan Paul, pp. 22–32.

Wright, E.O. (1978). *Class, Crisis and the State*. London: New Left Books.

Wynne, A. (1991). 'Electric writing: things, texts, people: agency and action' (mimeo).

Yates, F.A. (1964). *Giordano Bruno and the Hermetic Tradition*. London: Methuen.

Yates, F.A. (1966). *The Art of Memory*. Chicago: University of Chicago Press.

Yates, F.A. (1972). *The Rosicrucian Enlightenment*. London: Methuen.

Yates, F.A. (1979). *The Occult Philosophy in the Elizabethan Age*. London: Methuen.

Yeo, S. (1981). 'The politics of community publications', in R. Samuel (ed.) *People's History and Socialist Theory*. Henley-on-Thames: Routledge and Kegan Paul, pp. 42–8.

Yeo, E. and Yeo, S. (1982). 'Ways of seeing: control and leisure versus class and struggle', in E. Yeo and S. Yeo (eds) *Popular Culture and Class Conflict, 1590–1914. Explorations in the History of Labour and Leisure*. Hassocks: Harvester Press, pp. 128–54.

Young, I.M. (1990). *Throwing Like a Girl and Other Essays in Feminist Philosophy and Social Theory*. Bloomington: Indiana University Press.

Young, O. (1989). *International Regimes*. Ithaca, NY: Cornell University Press.

Young, R. (1990). *White Mythologies. Writing History and the West*. London: Routledge.

Young, R.M. and Teich, M. (eds) (1973). *Changing Perspectives in the Historiography of Science*. London: Macmillan.

Zajonc, A. (1993). *Catching the Light. The Entwined History of Light and Mind*. New York: Bantam.

Zaret, D. (1980). 'From Weber to Parsons and Schütz: the eclipse of history in modern social theory', *American Journal of Sociology*, 85, 1180–201.

Zeleny, J. (1980). *The Logic of Marx*. Oxford: Blackwell.

Zelizer, V. (1979). *Morals and Markets. The Development of Life Insurance in the United States*. New York: Columbia University Press.

Zelizer, V. (1989). 'The social meaning of money: special monies'. *American Journal of Sociology*, 95, 342–77.

Zelizer, V. (1993). 'Making multiple monies', in R. Swedberg (ed.) *Explorations in Economic Sociology*. New York: Russell Sage Foundation, pp. 193–212.

Zelizer, V. (1994). *The Social Meaning of Money*. New York: Basic Books.

Zerubavel, E. (1981). *Hidden Rhythms*. Chicago: University of Chicago Press.

Zilsel, E. and de Santillana, G. (1941). *The Development of Rationalism and Empiricism*. Chicago: University of Chicago Press.

Zimmerman, M.E. (1993). 'Heidegger, Buddhism and deep ecology', in C. Guignon (ed.) *The Cambridge Companion to Heidegger*. Cambridge: Cambridge University Press, pp. 240–69.

Zuboff, S. (1988). *In the Age of the Smart Machine. The Future of Work and Power*. London: Heinemann.

Zukin, S. and Dimaggio, P. (eds) (1990). *Structures of Capital*. Cambridge: Cambridge University Press.

Index

SPATIAL FORMATIONS

358

discursive schemes (markets), 224–5
disintermediation effect, 223*bis*
division of labour, 66, 172, 237, 245
  sexual, 80, 173
Doane, M.A., 278, 283, 292
documents (discourse of), 177
Dodd, N., 162, 217, 219–20, 222
Dodgshon, R.A., 203
Doel, M., 296
Domosh, M., 299
Donovan, C., 183
Dostal, R.J., 35
Douglas, M., 162
Downman, E.A., 188
dramaturgical models, 19
dream spaces, 269, 277
Dreyfus, H., 5, 10–11, 35, 37, 46,
  281, 286
Duley, A.J., 192
Dunford, M.F., 80
Dunlop, C., 226
Dunning, J.H., 252

Eagleton, T., 214
Eatwell, R., 135, 136, 139
Eccles, R.G., 224, 226
ecological approach, 170–2, 175, 209
ecological psychology, 6, 43
ecological self, 41
Economist, The, 220, 225, 240, 249
education, 83, 108–18
Eisenstein, E.L., 87, 104
Eley, G., 253
electric light, 267–9, 271, 274
electric power, 270–2, 275–6, 301–3
electronic networks, 214–15, 217, 220, 222–3,
  225–6, 230–6, 243, 249
electronic spaces, 215, 299
Elias, N., 59, 67, 97
Elliott, B., 21, 22, 90
Emberley, D., 286
empirical knowledge, 103–5, 107–9, 111–14
employment
  in City, 232, 235
  Marxist approach, 172–5
  wartime policy, 139–41, 143–5, 149
  women, 141, 143–4, 151–2, 238–9, 245–6,
  248
Encyclopédie, 111–13
Engels, F., 73
Enlightenment, 27, 32, 65, 167
epistemology, 32–5, 37, 40–1, 46, 120–1,
  167
Erdman, Robert, 224
ethics, 29–30, 35–7, 41, 58, 74

ethnicity (in City), 239, 246
ethnocentrism, 292, 294, 299
ethnomethodology, 18–19, 68
Eurocentrism, 28, 45, 292, 294
Eurodollar markets, 220, 232
European Bank for Reconstruction and
  Development, 246
evacuees/evacuation, 140, 142, 150–1
Evans-Pritchard, E.E., 171
everyday time practice, 165–6, 175–80
evolutionism, 72, 170
existence, 12–13, 34
experience, 35, 63, 81–2, 97, 259
expert systems, 58, 225

Faraday, A., 92
Fay, B., 245
feast days, 203–4
Featherstone, M., 301
Febvre, L., 108
feeling, *see* structure of feeling
Feenberg, A., 264
feminism, 36, 53, 56, 262–3, 294, 305
Fentress, J., 181, 182
field, *habitus* and, 14–15, 23
figuration theory, 262–3
Financial News, 240
financial system, 214–15, 220–30
Financial Times, The, 222, 240, 249
Fischer, C.S., 274
Flandrin, J., 86
flâneur, 278, 287, 298
Fleming, S., 150, 156
Fogarty, M.P., 140–1, 145–6
Folch-Serra, M., 6
folk culture, 86
folk models, 131–4, 139–40, 149–54, 156,
  157
Fordism, 279
foreshadowing, 4
formalism, 57, 78
Forty, A., 279
Foster, H., 300
Foster, J., 76, 120
Foster-Carter, A., 77–8
Foucault, M., 4, 7, 10, 23, 28–9, 55, 59, 66,
  67, 103, 114, 175, 177, 206, 210, 269–70,
  291
Frankfurt School, 65, 66
Fraser, R., 92
French, P.J., 106
Freud, S., 21, 56, 67, 163
Friedman, J., 300
Frisby, D., 218
Frow, J., 292